COLERIDGE

COLERIDGE

COLERIDGE

SELECT POETRY & PROSE

EDITED BY
STEPHEN POTTER

1962
LONDON
THE NONESUCH PRESS

First Published 1933
Second Impression 1942
Third Impression 1950
Fourth Impression 1962

CONTENTS

Each of the Poems is printed complete. In the other divisions, "complete" items (not including notes and scraps) are marked with an asterisk (*) in this Table of Contents.

I. POETRY *(continued)*

POEMS *(continued)*

I. POETRY *(continued)*

IV. LITERARY CRITICISM: p. 201

IV. LITERARY CRITICISM *(continued)*

BIOGRAPHIA LITERARIA *(continued)*

IV. LITERARY CRITICISM (continued)

IV. LITERARY CRITICISM *(continued)*

V. "THEOLOGICO-METAPHYSICAL" *(continued)*

VII. LETTERS: p. 523

VII. LETTERS *(continued)*

VII. LETTERS (continued)

VII. LETTERS (*continued*)

SUPPLEMENT

IV. LITERARY CRITICISM: p. 713

MISCELLANEOUS CRITICISM: p. 715

Chapman: p. 715
          [Homer translated]: p. 715

BIOGRAPHICAL INDEX

Note: (*q.v.*) refers to the Index at end of volume.

1796. Enthusiasm for the poems of Wordsworth, 230
Poems on Various Subjects published
Birth of son Hartley, 562
Poverty, 559, 560
Autumn. First (?) meeting with Wordsworth, 230

1797. At Nether Stowey. Intimacy with Poole (*cf.* 580); with the Wordsworths (*cf.* 577). Inception of *Lyrical Ballads*
Writes *Osorio, Ancient Mariner, Christabel* (part i)

1798. Hazlitt (*q.v.*) visits Stowey after hearing Coleridge preach
Coleridge accepts annuity from Wedgwoods, 574
Second productive poetical year (*Kubla Khan, Frost at Midnight,* etc.)
Lyrical Ballads published
Goes with Wordsworths to Germany, 305

1799. Tour of the Lakes
In London working for *Morning Post* and translating *Wallenstein,* 723

1800-04. Follows Wordsworths to Lakes. At Greta Hall, Keswick, 581 ff.
Health (*q.v.*) seriously affected by climate, and by dangerous over-indulgence in Opium (*q.v.*), 592
1801. "The Poet is dead in me," 591 (*cf.* 106)
Interest in Science (*q.v.*), *cf.* 587
First rift with wife, 601 (*cf.* 593)
Many Projected Works (*q.v.*)

1804-6. In Malta and the Mediterranean. Semi-official position at Malta, 615

1806. Return to London, no better in health. Prepares to separate from wife and children, 618

1808. First course of lectures on literature, at the Royal Institution

GENERAL
INTRODUCTION

In the planning of this book, which is an attempt to represent by selection different aspects of Coleridge's work, as many difficulties have arisen as there are principles of selection. For instance, it is often said that the best of Coleridge could be contained in fifty pages, but that these pages would be "pure gold." To name the few famous poems and a celebrated chapter which might come under the heading "golden" would not be difficult; but "I abhor Beauties," said Coleridge, and this remark ("Beauties" was of course the period word for anthologies) is a reminder that, where his work is concerned, the result of reading in bulk is always to leave the impression that isolated perfections are less important than the special contextual value which each section acquires when it is read with reference to the whole. Moreover, though the simplest method would be for an editor to retain only those passages which he likes best, or thinks most important, the result of this would be more representative of the taste of his own age than of Coleridge, whose work is valuable for such diverse reasons that each successive generation, in concentrating on a different aspect for praise, passes final judgement on itself rather than on the subject of its criticism.

There has been only one final judgement, that of his contemporaries; to whom Coleridge was above everything else a man with the gift of speech. Those who knew him read his printed words with their critical faculties silenced by the sound of his voice in their ears, a tone as fascinating to some as it was stupefying or maddening to others. It was only after his death that more detached judgement was possible and that his books and collected remains, making headway against a still doubtful and even antagonistic public, came separately into favour.

First there was the success of "Aids to Reflection," a book with the reputed powers of reconciling an exercise of the kind of knowledge which Coleridge called "Reason" with a belief in orthodox Christianity. Twenty years later, everything else was overshadowed by his reputation as a poet, as a pioneer of the new poetry, and as the friend and critic of Wordsworth. He became "great," and received his permanent order of merit as a classic. Then there were the editions of his lectures, of his Shakspere criticism; and the subtlety of his psychological comments was naturally re-discovered by an age well disposed to that kind of criticism. To a smaller number of readers, Coleridge's letters, with their half-unconscious self-analysis and continuous revelation of character from which almost nothing was withheld or disguised, presented yet another Coleridge, capable of a new kind of intensity of feeling. So his reputation has evolved, with the safe things, the permanent "Ancient Mariner," "Frost at Midnight" and the others, always in the background. For now or for the future it is more difficult to say where his chief value lies. Recently his words have been much quoted in what is perhaps a new context again. Much of Coleridge's life was not more than an existence, of dream and self-deception. He lived in moments, discontinuously, and in these moments he sometimes wrote sentences of that kind of profundity which loses its depth when it is historically related to official philosophy. They are Coleridge's attempt to construct his own metaphysic from his own experience, the necessity he felt of forming general principles and working from them—an attempt which in the history of English Neo-Platonism seems to be only a curious incident, but which is carried out with such integrity, such a knowledge of the real problems of philosophy, such a mixture of apparent vagueness and real clarity, that it seems to many that he had the kind of intuition which makes him a true modern, a true prophet. It is this sort of insight which relates him with Goethe, which places him in opposition to the scientific attitude, which explains how certain distinctions, such as that between "Reason" and "Understanding," were to him more than an academic commonplace. No "section" can be set aside for this, for it underlies most of his work and finds clear expression only in isolated paragraphs. Perhaps it is most obvious in "Anima Poetae," and those who prefer this book will incline to think that disconnected, notebook composition, with its freedom from all unpleasant compulsions, suited Coleridge best.

These are only some of the aspects which such a book as this must include. The leaving out has been sometimes less of a problem. For instance, the inability of Coleridge to write continuously on one set subject led him to insert irrelevancies which are occasionally better than the main theme but which are often not more than audacious padding—always badly written, because Coleridge had no well-formed prose style to fall back on in moments of apathy. Such makeweight chapters eliminate themselves, and so do the repetitions, the extent of which can only be explained by Coleridge's habit of borrowing from the *corpus* of past works in the belief, often well founded, that nobody had read them. He had favourite ideas, phrases, even quotations. Frequently it has been a question of choosing the best of numerous formulations of the same thought.

Less easy has been the question of the excision of all Coleridge's borrowings from other authors. During his lifetime he enjoyed amongst his enemies a certain fame as a plagiarist—of Schlegel in his lectures, of Kant and Schelling in the "Biographia Literaria." In the year of his death De Quincey made the charge definite, and drove it home by proving a certain "original" poem to be not much better than a translation (see p. 755). But the question is more complex than De Quincey makes it. Sometimes, when for a certain notorious reason he had omitted to make any preparation for an important public lecture, Coleridge would read out notes—private translations from Schlegel or Herder—without giving a hint that they were not his own: sometimes, he would with marvellous felicity incorporate into some verse a half-remembered, and by him transfigured, phrase from one of his favourite authors. In this last case the charge of plagiarism is obviously irrelevant, and in following the infinite gradations between the possibly culpable and the certainly innocent the whole question seems to lose its importance. When he repeats the words of others it generally represents a natural tendency on his part to discover authors who fundamentally agreed with and had given expression to ideas which were formulating in his own mind; authors who were subject, like him, to the new thought-processes and culture-tendencies of his time. For some of Coleridge's many references to this question see Index: *Plagiarism*. Perhaps his best remark on the subject is not the long defence in Letter LXXVII, but the note (quoted here on page 171) which ends: "I fear not him for a critic who can confound a fellow-thinker with a compiler."

PRINCIPLE OF ARRANGEMENT

"The chronological order is the best," Coleridge wrote: but his own lines of development are certainly too nebulous to be traced in a selection. This seemed

to be the perfect opportunity for a subject arrangement, with the pioneering ideal of an Ordered Coleridge. But no sooner was this tried than it became obvious that instead of clarification it would be a case merely of substituting unfamiliar chaos for familiar confusion. Coleridge, who was constitutionally, consciously, and even dogmatically parenthetic in his writing, employed discursiveness to the extent which makes titles only positionally related to the subject-matter appended, in itself so scattered that no one heading will serve to describe it. For this reason—and there are other considerations, such as the unequal authenticity of texts—each passage will be found in the usual context. An important exception is made in the case of the lecture reports, lecture notes and marginalia of the division "Miscellaneous Criticism," where consistency has been sacrificed for the sake of obvious convenience.

The seven divisions of the book are rough class divisions: Poems, Political Journalism, Notebooks, etc. Between "Poems" and "Letters," placed first and last respectively, divisions are arranged in a time-order corresponding to periods in Coleridge's life when he was most active in that kind of writing. Short introductions to each section explain this rough sequence of periods in more detail. When their dates are known, individual extracts are chronologically arranged within the section itself, with the year of composition printed at the end.

The index should be placed at the beginning of the book, as a symbolic reminder of the impossibility of imposing order on the works of Coleridge by any other means: but considerations of convenience have relegated it to the conventional position.

THE TEXT

Notes on individual texts will be found at the end of the book, where are also confined the inevitable accompaniments of reference, cross-reference and explanation. My general principle in the case of books published during Coleridge's lifetime has been to base the text on the latest edition published up to the time of his death in 1834. In the case of posthumous publication, I have made the earliest editions my authority, unless subsequent and more reliable editors have had renewed access to manuscripts. My basic text for the poems, for instance, is 1834. But for the Shakspere criticism it is Professor Raysor's edition of 1930, because this editor has been able to make a more complete review of existing MS. remains than has been hitherto attempted.

Coleridge was a careful corrector of his own proofs, so comparison with manuscripts in a selection such as this seems scarcely called for. The question of variant readings belongs chiefly to the poems, and I have only noted those having an importance or interest beyond that which they hold *qua* variant. With reference to my choice of the latest contemporary version it may be observed that on the whole when Coleridge corrected he improved. For comparison, I have printed the earliest and latest versions of the "Ancient Mariner" on opposite pages. With a few exceptions I have based my text on MSS. only when these have not previously been printed. Coleridge's unpublished remains are still extraordinarily plentiful, but very much shrunk in importance during the last forty years of intensive reclamation. I have confined my extracts from them to a few pages which represented some opinion or phase better than anything I could find in print.

In the case of spelling and punctuation I have followed the example of Shawcross, Griggs and other editors in keeping strictly to Coleridge's own habits in these matters, except in cases where exact imitation would lead to unnecessary obscurity. Coleridge's lavish capitalizations and underlinings are, I suppose, rightly considered "extremely characteristic"—the emphasis of a prophet without honour—though some of it is due to the practice of his own day. At first sight his punctuation seems much too heavy, but it is the inevitable result of his unperiodic structures and what he calls the *entortillage* of his style. He makes frequent use, for instance, of an indefensible double-stop redundancy [;—] which sometimes seemed to be used for the kind of pause certain modern writers represent by [. . .]. Sometimes in letters, as on p. 644, the punctuation reflects Coleridge's mood.

ACKNOWLEDGMENT

My chief indebtedness is to those Coleridge scholars whose editions are enumerated on p. 735. Of these Dykes Campbell, for his "Life" and notes to the Poems E. H. Coleridge, for his collation of the Poems and notes on the Letters, and Shawcross, have been most valuable. To Professor E. L. Griggs and Professor Raysor I am further indebted, to the first for help and suggestions in the selection of letters, to the second for valuable information on the text of the notebooks.

The Directors of the Nonesuch Press wish to join me in acknowledging the generosity of the Oxford University Press and of Messrs. William Heinemann Ltd. for giving permission for the use of their texts of "The Poems of S. T. Coleridge," and "Letters of S. T. Coleridge," "Anima Poetae" respectively. By arrangement with Messrs. Constable & Co., I have drawn on their editions of "Coleridge's Shakespearean Criticism" edited by T. M. Raysor and "Unpublished Letters of Samuel Taylor Coleridge" edited by E. L. Griggs.

Two commentaries not in my list which I have made much use of are the "Road to Xanadu" of Professor J. L. Lowes and the "Biographia Literaria Selections" of Mr. Sampson, especially the former.

I have also to acknowledge the great kindness of Mr. and Mrs. G. H. B. Coleridge in assisting me to explore the Coleridge MSS. at Leatherhead, and in allowing me to print an extract from one of them.

Of the many to whom thanks are due for information, I must mention in particular Mr. T. J. Wise, Mr. Lawrence Hyde (who has read, and is even familiar with, *The Friend*), Miss Hillyard, librarian of Birkbeck College, Mr. Harry Carter, of the Kynoch Press: also Mr. Lionel Millard and my father, for help in the preparation of the book. Finally I must thank Mary Potter, but for whose grudging help my work might never have been finished.

STEPHEN POTTER

INTRODUCTION TO THE PRESENT EDITION

I am grateful to The Nonesuch Press for allowing me to include in an Appendix to this edition some additional material. Most of it, by arrangement with Messrs. Constable & Co., is taken from T. M. Raysor's Collection of Coleridge's *Miscellaneous Criticism* and Marginalia, which was published too late for me to be able to incorporate extracts from it in 1933.

STEPHEN POTTER

POETRY

A chronological list of the poems shows that from 1787 Coleridge wrote verses in almost every year of his life. But a little analysis makes it clear that his poetical "period" is more isolated than any other. Over half his verses were written in the years 1794-9, and of these 1797 and 1798 were much the most prolific and far and away the most important. This time of fertility was scarcely foreshadowed by the merits of the juvenilia, and with the "Dejection" ode, written in April, 1802, soon after the move to Keswick, it seems to come to a definite conclusion. The two great years belong to the only time in Coleridge's life when he came near to being really happy, when his health was still good, his domestic life fairly calm, and when he was on terms of perfect understanding with his best friends, Poole and the Wordsworths. He knew, at Keswick, that the poetic faculty had deserted him, but he always believed it would return. Soon after 1820 he imagined it to be again stirring; but his constant wish, that he should be able to finish "Christabel," was never fulfilled.

Coleridge's verse drama "Osorio" was written between March and October, 1797, and belongs to the period of his admiration for Schiller, on an episode in whose "Der Geisterseher" the plot is based. This was one of his briefer enthusiasms, and Coleridge did not take his play seriously till the success of its production in a new form ("Remorse") fourteen years later. "Zapolya," which followed, is negligible.

Coleridge was a good translator, judging by his version of the two Schiller plays; but the six weeks' hard work it cost him (at the end of 1799) called for a kind of application which he found so detestable that later suggestions for translations from Goethe never seemed likely to mature.

POEMS

SONNET

TO THE AUTUMNAL MOON

MILD Splendour of the various-vested Night!
  Mother of wildly-working visions! hail!
I watch thy gliding, while with watery light
  Thy weak eye glimmers through a fleecy veil;
And when thou lovest thy pale orb to shroud
  Behind the gathered blackness lost on high;
And when thou dartest from the wind-rent cloud
  Thy placid lightning o'er the awakened sky.

Ah such is Hope! as changeful and as fair!
  Now dimly peering on the wistful sight;
Now hid behind the dragon-winged Despair:
  But soon emerging in her radiant might
She o'er the sorrow-clouded breast of Care
  Sails, like a meteor kindling in its flight.

1788

LIFE

AS late I journeyed o'er the extensive plain
  Where native Otter sports his scanty stream,
Musing in torpid woe a Sister's pain,
  The glorious prospect woke me from the dream.

At every step it widened to my sight—
  Wood, Meadow, verdant Hill, and dreary Steep,
Following in quick succession of delight,—
  Till all—at once—did my eye ravished sweep!

May this (I cried) my course through Life portray!
New scenes of Wisdom may each step display,
  And Knowledge open as my days advance!
Till what time Death shall pour the undarkened ray,
  My eye shall dart thro' infinite expanse,
And thought suspended lie in Rapture's blissful trance.

1789

ON IMITATION

ALL are not born to soar—and ah! how few
    In tracks where Wisdom leads their paths pursue!
Contagious when to wit or wealth allied,
Folly and Vice diffuse their venom wide.
On Folly every fool his talent tries;
It asks some toil to imitate the wise;
Tho' few like Fox can speak—like Pitt can think—
Yet all like Fox can game—like Pitt can drink.

?1791

SONNET

TO THE RIVER OTTER

DEAR native Brook! wild Streamlet of the West!
    How many various-fated years have past,
What happy and what mournful hours, since last
I skimmed the smooth thin stone along thy breast,
Numbering its light leaps! yet so deep imprest
Sink the sweet scenes of childhood, that mine eyes
    I never shut amid the sunny ray,
But straight with all their tints thy waters rise,
    Thy crossing plank, thy marge with willows grey,
And bedded sand that veined with various dyes
Gleamed through thy bright transparence! On my way,
    Visions of Childhood! oft have ye beguiled
Lone manhood's cares, yet waking fondest sighs:
    Ah! that once more I were a careless Child!

?1793

TO THE AUTHOR OF "THE ROBBERS"

SCHILLER! that hour I would have wished to die,
    If thro' the shuddering midnight I had sent
From the dark dungeon of the Tower time-rent
That fearful voice, a famished Father's cry—
Lest in some after moment aught more mean
Might stamp me mortal! A triumphant shout
Black Horror screamed, and all her goblin rout

Diminished shrunk from the more withering scene!
Ah! Bard tremendous in sublimity!
Could I behold thee in thy loftier mood
Wandering at eve with finely-frenzied eye
Beneath some vast old tempest-swinging wood!
Awhile with mute awe gazing I would brood:
Then weep aloud in a wild ecstasy!

?1794

TO A YOUNG ASS

ITS MOTHER BEING TETHERED NEAR IT

POOR little Foal of an oppressed race!
I love the languid patience of thy face:
And oft with gentle hand I give thee bread,
And clap thy ragged coat, and pat thy head.
But what thy dulled spirits hath dismayed,
That never thou dost sport along the glade?
And (most unlike the nature of things young)
That earthward still thy moveless head is hung?
Do thy prophetic fears anticipate,
Meek Child of Misery! thy future fate?
The starving meal, and all the thousand aches
"Which patient Merit of the Unworthy takes"?
Or is thy sad heart thrilled with filial pain
To see thy wretched mother's shortened chain?
And truly, very piteous is *her* lot—
Chained to a log within a narrow spot,
Where the close-eaten grass is scarcely seen,
While sweet around her waves the tempting green!

Poor Ass! thy master should have learnt to show
Pity—best taught by fellowship of Woe!
For much I fear me that *He* lives like thee,
Half famished in a land of Luxury!
How *askingly* its footsteps hither bend?
It seems to say, "And have I then *one* friend?"
Innocent foal! thou poor despised forlorn!
I hail thee *Brother*—spite of the fool's scorn!
And fain would take thee with me, in the Dell

Of Peace and mild Equality to dwell,
Where Toil shall call the charmer Health his bride,
And Laughter tickle Plenty's ribless side!
How thou wouldst toss thy heels in gamesome play,
And frisk about, as lamb or kitten gay!
Yea! and more musically sweet to me
Thy dissonant harsh bray of joy would be,
Than warbled melodies that soothe to rest
The aching of pale Fashion's vacant breast!

1794

TO THE NIGHTINGALE

SISTER of love-lorn Poets, Philomel!
How many Bards in city garret pent,
While at their window they with downward eye
Mark the faint lamp-beam on the kennelled mud,
And listen to the drowsy cry of Watchmen
(Those hoarse unfeathered Nightingales of Time!),
How many wretched Bards address *thy* name,
And hers, the full-orbed Queen that shines above.
But I *do* hear thee, and the high bough mark,
Within whose mild moon-mellowed foliage hid
Thou warblest sad thy pity-pleading strains.
O! I have listened, till my working soul,
Waked by those strains to thousand phantasies,
Absorbed hath ceased to listen! Therefore oft,
I hymn thy name: and with a proud delight
Oft will I tell thee, Minstrel of the Moon!
"Most musical, most melancholy" Bird!
That all thy soft diversities of tone,
Tho' sweeter far than the delicious airs
That vibrate from a white-armed Lady's harp,
What time the languishment of lonely love
Melts in her eye, and heaves her breast of snow,
Are not so sweet as is the voice of her,
My Sara—best beloved of human kind!
When breathing the pure soul of tenderness,
She thrills me with the Husband's promised name!

1795

THE EOLIAN HARP

COMPOSED AT CLEVEDON, SOMERSETSHIRE

MY pensive Sara! thy soft cheek reclined
　Thus on mine arm, most soothing sweet it is
To sit beside our Cot, our Cot o'ergrown
With white-flowered Jasmin, and the broad-leaved Myrtle,
(Meet emblems they of Innocence and Love!)
And watch the clouds, that late were rich with light,
Slow saddening round, and mark the star of eve
Serenely brilliant (such should Wisdom be)
Shine opposite! How exquisite the scents
Snatched from yon bean-field! and the world *so* hushed!
The stilly murmur of the distant Sea
Tells us of silence.
　　　　　　And that simplest Lute,
Placed length-ways in the clasping casement, hark!
How by the desultory breeze caressed,
Like some coy maid half yielding to her lover,
It pours such sweet upbraiding, as must needs
Tempt to repeat the wrong! And now, its strings
Boldlier swept, the long sequacious notes
Over delicious surges sink and rise,
Such a soft floating witchery of sound
As twilight Elfins make, when they at eve
Voyage on gentle gales from Fairy-Land,
Where Melodies round honey-dropping flowers,
Footless and wild, like birds of Paradise,
Nor pause, nor perch, hovering on untamed wing!
O! the one Life within us and abroad,
Which meets all motion and becomes its soul,
A light in sound, a sound-like power in light,
Rhythm in all thought, and joyance every where—
Methinks, it should have been impossible
Not to love all things in a world so filled;
Where the breeze warbles, and the mute still air
Is Music slumbering on her instrument.

And thus, my Love! as on the midway slope
Of yonder hill I stretch my limbs at noon,

Whilst through my half-closed eye-lids I behold
The sunbeams dance, like diamonds, on the main,
And tranquil muse upon tranquillity;
Full many a thought uncalled and undetained,
And many idle flitting phantasies,
Traverse my indolent and passive brain,
As wild and various as the random gales
That swell and flutter on this subject Lute!

And what if all of animated nature
Be but organic Harps diversely framed,
That tremble into thought, as o'er them sweeps
Plastic and vast, one intellectual breeze,
At once the Soul of each, and God of all?

But thy more serious eye a mild reproof
Darts, O beloved Woman! nor such thoughts
Dim and unhallowed dost thou not reject,
And biddest me walk humbly with my God.
Meek Daughter in the family of Christ!
Well hast thou said and holily dispraised
These shapings of the unregenerate mind;
Bubbles that glitter as they rise and break
On vain Philosophy's aye-babbling spring.
For never guiltless may I speak of him,
The Incomprehensible! save when with awe
I praise him, and with Faith that inly *feels;*
Who with his saving mercies healed me,
A sinful and most miserable man,
Wildered and dark, and gave me to possess
Peace, and this Cot, and thee, heart-honoured Maid!

1795

REFLECTIONS ON HAVING LEFT A PLACE OF RETIREMENT

Sermoni propriora.
Hor.

LOW was our pretty Cot: our tallest Rose
    Peeped at the chamber-window. We could hear
At silent noon, and eve, and early morn,
The Sea's faint murmur. In the open air
Our Myrtles blossomed; and across the porch
Thick Jasmins twined: the little landscape round
Was green and woody, and refreshed the eye.
It was a spot which you might aptly call
The Valley of Seclusion! Once I saw
(Hallowing his Sabbath-day by quietness)
A wealthy son of Commerce saunter by,
Bristowa's citizen: methought, it calmed
His thirst of idle gold, and made him muse
With wiser feelings: for he paused, and looked
With a pleased sadness, and gazed all around,
Then eyed our Cottage, and gazed round again,
And sighed, and said, it was a Blessed Place.
And we *were* blessed. Oft with patient ear
Long-listening to the viewless sky-lark's note
(Viewless, or haply for a moment seen
Gleaming on sunny wings) in whispered tones
I've said to my Beloved, "Such, sweet Girl!
The inobtrusive song of Happiness,
Unearthly minstrelsy! then only heard
When the Soul seeks to hear; when all is hushed,
And the Heart listens!"

But the time, when first
From that low Dell, steep up the stony Mount
I climbed with perilous toil and reached the top,
Oh! what a goodly scene! *Here* the bleak mount,
The bare bleak mountain speckled thin with sheep;
Grey clouds, that shadowing spot the sunny fields;
And river, now with bushy rocks o'er-browed,
Now winding bright and full, with naked banks;

And seats, and lawns, the Abbey and the wood,
And cots, and hamlets, and faint city-spire;
The Channel *there*, the Islands and white sails,
Dim coasts, and cloud-like hills, and shoreless Ocean—
It seemed like Omnipresence! God, methought,
Had built him there a Temple: the whole World
Seemed *imaged* in its vast circumference:
No *wish* profaned my overwhelmed heart.
Blest hour! It was a luxury,—to be!

Ah! quiet Dell! dear Cot, and Mount sublime!
I was constrained to quit you. Was it right,
While my unnumbered brethren toiled and bled,
That I should dream away the entrusted hours
On rose-leaf beds, pampering the coward heart
With feelings all too delicate for use?
Sweet is the tear that from some Howard's eye
Drops on the cheek of one he lifts from earth:
And he that works me good with unmoved face,
Does it but half: he chills me while he aids,
My benefactor, not my brother man!
Yet even this, this cold beneficence
Praise, praise it, O my Soul! oft as thou scannest
The sluggard Pity's vision-weaving tribe!
Who sigh for Wretchedness, yet shun the Wretched,
Nursing in some delicious solitude
Their slothful loves and dainty sympathies!
I therefore go, and join head, heart, and hand,
Active and firm, to fight the bloodless fight
Of Science, Freedom, and the Truth in Christ.

Yet oft when after honourable toil
Rests the tired mind, and waking loves to dream,
My spirit shall revisit thee, dear Cot!
Thy Jasmin and thy window-peeping Rose,
And Myrtles fearless of the mild sea-air.
And I shall sigh fond wishes—sweet Abode!
Ah!—had none greater! And that all had such!
It might be so—but the time is not yet.
Speed it, O Father! Let thy Kingdom come!

1795

TO A YOUNG FRIEND

ON HIS PROPOSING TO DOMESTICATE WITH
THE AUTHOR

Composed in 1796

A MOUNT, not wearisome and bare and steep,
But a green mountain variously up-piled,
Where o'er the jutting rocks soft mosses creep,
Or coloured lichens with slow oosing weep;
   Where cypress and the darker yew start wild;
And, 'mid the summer torrent's gentle dash
Dance brightened the red clusters of the ash;
   Beneath whose boughs, by those still sounds beguiled,
Calm Pensiveness might muse herself to sleep;
   Till haply startled by some fleecy dam,
That rustling on the bushy cliff above
With melancholy bleat of anxious love,
   Made meek enquiry for her wandering lamb:
   Such a green mountain 'twere most sweet to climb,
E'en while the bosom ached with loneliness—
How more than sweet, if some dear friend should bless
   The adventurous toil, and up the path sublime
Now lead, now follow: the glad landscape round,
Wide and more wide, increasing without bound!

O then 'twere loveliest sympathy, to mark
The berries of the half-uprooted ash
Dripping and bright; and list the torrent's dash,—
   Beneath the cypress, or the yew more dark,
Seated at ease, on some smooth mossy rock;
In social silence now, and now to unlock
The treasured heart; arm linked in friendly arm,
Save if the one, his muse's witching charm
Muttering brow-bent, at unwatched distance lag;
   Till high o'er head his beckoning friend appears,
And from the forehead of the topmost crag
   Shouts eagerly: for haply *there* uprears
That shadowing Pine its old romantic limbs,
   Which latest shall detain the enamoured sight

Seen from below, when eve the valley dims,
　Tinged yellow with the rich departing light;
　And haply, basoned in some unsunned cleft,
A beauteous spring, the rock's collected tears,
Sleeps sheltered there, scarce wrinkled by the gale!
　Together thus, the world's vain turmoil left,
Stretched on the crag, and shadowed by the pine,
　And bending o'er the clear delicious fount,
Ah! dearest youth! it were a lot divine
To cheat our noons in moralising mood,
While west-winds fanned our temples toil-bedewed:
　Then downwards slope, oft pausing, from the mount,
To some lone mansion, in some woody dale,
Where smiling with blue eye, Domestic Bliss
Gives *this* the Husband's, *that* the Brother's kiss!

　Thus rudely versed in allegoric lore,
The Hill of Knowledge I essayed to trace;
That verdurous hill with many a resting-place,
　And many a stream, whose warbling waters pour
　To glad, and fertilise the subject plains;
That hill with secret springs, and nooks untrod,
And many a fancy-blest and holy sod
　Where Inspiration, his diviner strains
Low-murmuring, lay; and starting from the rock's
Stiff evergreens, (whose spreading foliage mocks
Want's barren soil, and the bleak frosts of age,
And Bigotry's mad fire-invoking rage!)
O meek retiring spirit! we will climb,
Cheering and cheered, this lovely hill sublime;
　And from the stirring world up-lifted high
(Whose noises, faintly wafted on the wind,
To quiet musings shall attune the mind,
　And oft the melancholy *theme* supply),
　There, while the prospect through the gazing eye
　Pours all its healthful greenness on the soul,
We'll smile at wealth, and learn to smile at fame,
Our hopes, our knowledge, and our joys the same,
　As neighbouring fountains image each the whole:
Then when the mind hath drunk its fill of truth
　We'll discipline the heart to pure delight,

Rekindling sober joy's domestic flame.
They whom I love shall love thee, honoured youth!
Now may Heaven realise this vision bright!

1796

TO THE REV. GEORGE COLERIDGE

OF OTTERY ST. MARY, DEVON

With some Poems

Notus in fratres animi paterni.
HOR., *Carm., Lib.* II, ii

A BLESSED lot hath he, who having passed
His youth and early manhood in the stir
And turmoil of the world, retreats at length,
With cares that move, not agitate the heart,
To the same dwelling where his father dwelt;
And haply views his tottering little ones
Embrace those aged knees and climb that lap,
On which first kneeling his own infancy
Lisped its brief prayer. Such, O my earliest Friend!
Thy lot, and such thy brothers too enjoy.
At distance did ye climb Life's upland road,
Yet cheered and cheering: now fraternal love
Hath drawn you to one centre. Be your days
Holy, and blest and blessing may ye live!

To me the Eternal Wisdom hath dispensed
A different fortune and more different mind—
Me from the spot where first I sprang to light
Too soon transplanted, ere my soul had fixed
Its first domestic loves; and hence through life
Chasing chance-started friendships. A brief while
Some have preserved me from life's pelting ills;
But, like a tree with leaves of feeble stem,
If the clouds lasted, and a sudden breeze
Ruffled the boughs, they on my head at once
Dropped the collected shower; and some most false,
False and fair-foliaged as the Manchineel,
Have tempted me to slumber in their shade

E'en mid the storm; then breathing subtlest damps,
Mixed their own venom with the rain from Heaven,
That I woke poisoned! But, all praise to Him
Who gives us all things, more have yielded me
Permanent shelter; and beside one Friend,
Beneath the impervious covert of one oak,
I've raised a lowly shed, and know the names
Of Husband and of Father; not unhearing
Of that divine and nightly-whispering Voice,
Which from my childhood to maturer years
Spake to me of predestinated wreaths,
Bright with no fading colours!

     Yet at times
My soul is sad, that I have roamed through life
Still most a stranger, most with naked heart
At mine own home and birth-place: chiefly then,
When I remember thee, my earliest Friend!
Thee, who didst watch my boyhood and my youth;
Didst trace my wanderings with a father's eye;
And boding evil yet still hoping good,
Rebuked each fault, and over all my woes
Sorrowed in silence! He who counts alone
The beatings of the solitary heart,
That Being knows, how I have loved thee ever,
Loved as a brother, as a son revered thee!
Oh! 'tis to me an ever new delight,
To talk of thee and thine: or when the blast
Of the shrill winter, rattling our rude sash,
Endears the cleanly hearth and social bowl;
Or when, as now, on some delicious eve,
We in our sweet sequestered orchard-plot
Sit on the tree crooked earth-ward; whose old boughs,
That hang above us in an arborous roof,
Stirred by the faint gale of departing May,
Send their loose blossoms slanting o'er our heads!

Nor dost not thou sometimes recall those hours,
When with the joy of hope thou gavest thine ear
To my wild firstling-lays. Since then my song
Hath sounded deeper notes, such as beseem
Or that sad wisdom folly leaves behind,

Or such as, tuned to these tumultuous times,
Cope with the tempest's swell!

          These various strains,
Which I have framed in many a various mood,
Accept, my Brother! and (for some perchance
Will strike discordant on thy milder mind)
If aught of error or intemperate truth
Should meet thine ear, think thou that riper Age
Will calm it down, and let thy love forgive it!

NETHER STOWEY, SOMERSET, 26 *May*, 1797

THIS LIME-TREE BOWER MY PRISON

[ADDRESSED TO CHARLES LAMB, OF THE INDIA HOUSE, LONDON]

In the June of 1797 some long-expected friends paid a visit to
the author's cottage; and on the morning of their arrival, he met
with an accident, which disabled him from walking during the
whole time of their stay. One evening, when they had left him for
a few hours, he composed the following lines in the garden-bower.

WELL, they are gone, and here must I remain,
    This lime-tree bower my prison! I have lost
Beauties and feelings, such as would have been
Most sweet to my remembrance even when age
Had dimmed mine eyes to blindness! They, meanwhile,
Friends, whom I never more may meet again,
On springy heath, along the hill-top edge,
Wander in gladness, and wind down, perchance,
To that still roaring dell, of which I told;
The roaring dell, o'erwooded, narrow, deep,
And only speckled by the mid-day sun;
Where its slim trunk the ash from rock to rock
Flings arching like a bridge;—that branchless ash,
Unsunned and damp, whose few poor yellow leaves
Ne'er tremble in the gale, yet tremble still,
Fanned by the water-fall! and there my friends
Behold the dark green file of long lank weeds,
That all at once (a most fantastic sight!)
Still nod and drip beneath the dripping edge
Of the blue clay-stone.

Now, my friends emerge
Beneath the wide wide Heaven—and view again
The many-steepled tract magnificent
Of hilly fields and meadows, and the sea,
With some fair bark, perhaps, whose sails light up
The slip of smooth clear blue betwixt two Isles
Of purple shadow! Yes! they wander on
In gladness all; but thou, methinks, most glad,
My gentle-hearted Charles! for thou hast pined
And hungered after Nature, many a year,
In the great City pent, winning thy way
With sad yet patient soul, through evil and pain
And strange calamity! Ah! slowly sink
Behind the western ridge, thou glorious Sun!
Shine in the slant beams of the sinking orb,
Ye purple heath-flowers! richlier burn, ye clouds!
Live in the yellow light, ye distant groves!
And kindle, thou blue Ocean! So my friend
Struck with deep joy may stand, as I have stood,
Silent with swimming sense; yea, gazing round
On the wide landscape, gaze till all doth seem
Less gross than bodily; and of such hues
As veil the Almighty Spirit, when yet he makes
Spirits perceive his presence.

A delight
Comes sudden on my heart, and I am glad
As I myself were there! Nor in this bower,
This little lime-tree bower, have I not marked
Much that has soothed me. Pale beneath the blaze
Hung the transparent foliage; and I watched
Some broad and sunny leaf, and loved to see
The shadow of the leaf and stem above
Dappling its sunshine! And that walnut-tree
Was richly tinged, and a deep radiance lay
Full on the ancient ivy, which usurps
Those fronting elms, and now, with blackest mass
Makes their dark branches gleam a lighter hue
Through the late twilight: and though now the bat
Wheels silent by, and not a swallow twitters,
Yet still the solitary humble-bee

Sings in the bean-flower! Henceforth I shall know
That Nature ne'er deserts the wise and pure;
No plot so narrow, be but Nature there,
No waste so vacant, but may well employ
Each faculty of sense, and keep the heart
Awake to Love and Beauty! and sometimes
'Tis well to be bereft of promised good,
That we may lift the soul, and contemplate
With lively joy the joys we cannot share.
My gentle-hearted Charles! when the last rook
Beat its straight path along the dusky air
Homewards, I blest it! deeming its black wing
(Now a dim speck, now vanishing in light)
Had crossed the mighty Orb's dilated glory,
While thou stood'st gazing; or, when all was still,
Flew creeking o'er thy head, and had a charm*
For thee, my gentle-hearted Charles, to whom
No sound is dissonant which tells of Life.

1797

---

*Some months after I had written this line, it gave me pleasure to find that Bartram had observed the same circumstance of the Savanna Crane. "When these Birds move their wings in flight, their strokes are slow, moderate and regular; and even when at a considerable distance or high above us, we plainly hear the quill-feathers: their shafts and webs upon one another creek as the joints or working of a vessel in a tempestuous sea."

THE RIME OF THE ANCYENT MARINERE

[This, the first, version is printed on verso pages to p. 56, for comparison with the final version opposite]

IN SEVEN PARTS

ARGUMENT

How a Ship having passed the Line was driven by Storms to the cold Country towards the South Pole; and how from thence she made her course to the Tropical Latitude of the Great Pacific Ocean; and of the strange things that befell; and in what manner the Ancyent Marinere came back to his own Country.

I

*I*T is an ancyent Marinere,
  And he stoppeth one of three:
"By thy long grey beard and thy glittering eye
 "Now wherefore stoppest me?

"The Bridegroom's doors are open'd wide,
 "And I am next of kin;
"The Guests are met, the Feast is set,—
 "May'st hear the merry din."

But still he holds the wedding-guest—
  There was a Ship, quoth he—
"Nay, if thou'st got a laughsome tale,
 "Marinere! come with me."

He holds him with his skinny hand,
  Quoth he, there was a Ship—
"Now get thee hence, thou grey-beard Loon!
 "Or my Staff shall make thee skip."

He holds him with his glittering eye—
  The wedding-guest stood still
And listens like a three year's child;
  The Marinere hath his will.

The wedding-guest sate on a stone.
  He cannot chuse but hear:
And thus spake on that ancyent man,
  The bright-eyed Marinere.

THE RIME OF THE ANCIENT MARINER

[This, the final, version is printed on recto pages to p. 57]

IN SEVEN PARTS

Facile credo, plures esse Naturas invisibiles quam visibiles in rerum universitate. Sed horum omnium familiam quis nobis enarrabit? et gradus et cognationes et discrimina et singulorum munera? Quid agunt? quae loca habitant? Harum rerum notitiam semper ambivit ingenium humanum, nunquam attigit. Juvat, interea, non diffiteor, quandoque in animo, tanquam in tabula, majoris et melioris mundi imaginem contemplari: ne mens assuefacta hodiernae vitae minutiis se contrahat nimis, et tota subsidat in pusillas cogitationes. Sed veritati interea invigilandum est, modusque servandus, ut certa ab incertis, diem a nocte, distinguamus.
                                    T. BURNET, *Archaeol. Phil.*, *p.* 68

PART I

IT is an ancient Mariner,
    And he stoppeth one of three.
"By thy long grey beard and glittering eye,
Now wherefore stopp'st thou me?

An ancient Mariner meeteth three Gallants bidden to a wedding-feast, and detaineth one.

The Bridegroom's doors are opened wide,
And I am next of kin;
The guests are met, the feast is set:
May'st hear the merry din."

He holds him with his skinny hand,
"There was a ship," quoth he.
"Hold off! unhand me, grey-beard loon!"
Eftsoons his hand dropt he.

He holds him with his glittering eye—
The Wedding-Guest stood still,
And listens like a three years' child:
The Mariner hath his will.

The Wedding-Guest is spell-bound by the eye of the old seafaring man, and constrained to hear his tale.

The Wedding-Guest sat on a stone:
He cannot choose but hear;
And thus spake on that ancient man,
The bright-eyed Mariner.

The Ship was cheer'd, the Harbour clear'd—
Merrily did we drop
Below the Kirk, below the Hill,
Below the Light-house top.

The Sun came up upon the left,
Out of the Sea came he:
And he shone bright, and on the right
Went down into the Sea.

Higher and higher every day,
Till over the mast at noon—
The wedding-guest here beat his breast,
For he heard the loud bassoon.

The Bride hath pac'd into the Hall,
Red as a rose is she;
Nodding their heads before her goes
The merry Minstralsy.

The wedding-guest he beat his breast,
Yet he cannot chuse but hear:
And thus spake on that ancyent Man,
The bright-eyed Marinere.

Listen, Stranger! Storm and Wind,
A Wind and Tempest strong!
For days and weeks it play'd us freaks—
Like Chaff we drove along.

Listen, Stranger! Mist and Snow,
And it grew wond'rous cauld:
And Ice mast-high came floating by
As green as Emerauld.

And thro' the drifts the snowy clifts
Did send a dismal sheen;
Ne shapes of men ne beasts we ken—
The Ice was all between.

"The ship was cheered, the harbour cleared,
Merrily did we drop
Below the kirk, below the hill,
Below the lighthouse top.

The Sun came up upon the left,
Out of the sea came he!
And he shone bright, and on the right
Went down into the sea.

The Mariner tells how the ship sailed southward with a good wind and fair weather, till it reached the Line.

Higher and higher every day,
Till over the mast at noon—"
The Wedding-Guest here beat his breast,
For he heard the loud bassoon.

The bride hath paced into the hall,
Red as a rose is she;
Nodding their heads before her goes
The merry minstrelsy.

The Wedding-Guest heareth the bridal music; but the Mariner continueth his tale.

The Wedding-Guest he beat his breast,
Yet he cannot choose but hear;
And thus spake on that ancient man,
The bright-eyed Mariner.

"And now the STORM-BLAST came, and he
Was tyrannous and strong:
He struck with his o'ertaking wings,
And chased us south along.

The ship driven by a storm toward the south pole.

With sloping masts and dipping prow,
As who pursued with yell and blow
Still treads the shadow of his foe,
And forward bends his head,
The ship drove fast, loud roared the blast,
And southward aye we fled.

And now there came both mist and snow,
And it grew wondrous cold:
And ice, mast-high, came floating by,
As green as emerald.

The Ice was here, the Ice was there,
 The Ice was all around:
It crack'd and growl'd, and roar'd and howl'd—
 Like noises of a swound.

At length did cross an Albatross,
 Thorough the Fog it came;
And an it were a Christian Soul,
 We hail'd it in God's name.

The Marineres gave it biscuit-worms,
 And round and round it flew:
The Ice did split with a Thunder-fit,
 The Helmsman steer'd us thro'.

And a good south wind sprung up behind,
 The Albatross did follow;
And every day for food or play
 Came to the Marinere's hollo!

In mist or cloud on mast or shroud,
 It perch'd for vespers nine,
Whiles all the night thro' fog-smoke white,
 Glimmer'd the white moon-shine.

"God save thee, ancyent Marinere!
 "From the fiends that plague thee thus—
"Why look'st thou so?"—with my cross-bow
 I shot the Albatross.

II

The Sun came up upon the right,
 Out of the Sea came he;
And broad as a weft upon the left
 Went down into the Sea.

And the good south wind still blew behind,
 But no sweet Bird did follow
Ne any day for food or play
 Came to the Marinere's hollo!

And through the drifts the snowy clifts
Did send a dismal sheen:
Nor shapes of men nor beasts we ken—
The ice was all between.

The land of ice and of fearful sounds where no living thing was to be seen.

The ice was here, the ice was there,
The ice was all around:
It cracked and growled, and roared and howled,
Like noises in a swound!

At length did cross an Albatross,
Thorough the fog it came;
As if it had been a Christian soul,
We hailed it in God's name.

Till a great sea-bird, called the Albatross, came through the snow-fog, and was received with great joy and hospitality.

It ate the food it ne'er had eat,
And round and round it flew.
The ice did split with a thunder-fit;
The helmsman steered us through!

And a good south wind sprung up behind;
The Albatross did follow,
And every day, for food or play,
Came to the mariners' hollo!

And lo! the Albatross prov-eth a bird of good omen, and followeth the ship as it returned north-ward through fog and floating ice.

In mist or cloud, on mast or shroud,
It perched for vespers nine;
Whiles all the night, through fog-smoke white,
Glimmered the white moon-shine."

"God save thee, ancient Mariner!
From the fiends, that plague thee thus!—
Why look'st thou so?"—"With my cross-bow
I shot the ALBATROSS.

The ancient Mariner inhospitably killeth the pious bird of good omen.

PART II

The Sun now rose upon the right:
Out of the sea came he,
Still hid in mist, and on the left
Went down into the sea.

And I had done an hellish thing
And it would work 'em woe:
For all averr'd, I had kill'd the Bird
That made the Breeze to blow.

Ne dim ne red, like God's own head,
The glorious Sun uprist:
Then all averr'd, I had kill'd the Bird
That brought the fog and mist.
'Twas right, said they, such birds to slay
That bring the fog and mist.

The breezes blew, the white foam flew,
The furrow follow'd free:
We were the first that ever burst
Into that silent Sea.

Down dropt the breeze, the Sails dropt down,
'Twas sad as sad could be
And we did speak only to break
The silence of the Sea.

All in a hot and copper sky
The bloody sun at noon,
Right up above the mast did stand,
No bigger than the moon.

Day after day, day after day,
We stuck, ne breath ne motion,
As idle as a painted Ship
Upon a painted Ocean.

Water, water, everywhere,
And all the boards did shrink;
Water, water, everywhere,
Ne any drop to drink.

The very deeps did rot: O Christ!
That ever this should be!
Yea, slimy things did crawl with legs
Upon the slimy Sea.

And the good south wind still blew behind,
But no sweet bird did follow,
Nor any day for food or play
Come to the mariners' hollo!

And I had done a hellish thing,
And it would work 'em woe:
For all averred, I had killed the bird
That made the breeze to blow.
Ah wretch! said they, the bird to slay,
That made the breeze to blow!

His shipmates cry out against the ancient Mariner, for killing the bird of good luck.

Nor dim nor red, like God's own head,
The glorious Sun uprist:
Then all averred, I had killed the bird
That brought the fog and mist.
'Twas right, said they, such birds to slay,
That bring the fog and mist.

But when the fog cleared off, they justify the same, and thus make themselves accomplices in the crime.

The fair breeze blew, the white foam flew,
The furrow followed free;
We were the first that ever burst
Into that silent sea.

The fair breeze continues; the ship enters the Pacific Ocean, and sails northward, even till it reaches the Line.

Down dropt the breeze, the sails dropt down,
'Twas sad as sad could be;
And we did speak only to break
The silence of the sea!

The ship hath been suddenly becalmed.

All in a hot and copper sky,
The bloody Sun, at noon,
Right up above the mast did stand,
No bigger than the Moon.

Day after day, day after day,
We stuck, nor breath nor motion;
As idle as a painted ship
Upon a painted ocean.

Water, water, every where,
And all the boards did shrink;
Water, water, every where,
Nor any drop to drink.

And the Albatross begins to be avenged.

About, about, in reel and rout,
The Death-fires danc'd at night;
The water, like a witch's oils,
Burnt green and blue and white.

And some in dreams assured were
Of the Spirit that plagued us so:
Nine fathom deep he had follow'd us
From the Land of Mist and Snow.

And every tongue thro' utter drouth
Was wither'd at the root;
We could not speak no more than if
We had been choked with soot.

Ah wel-a-day! what evil looks
Had I from old and young;
Instead of the Cross the Albatross
About my neck was hung.

III

I saw a something in the Sky
No bigger than my fist;
At first it seem'd a little speck
And then it seem'd a mist:
It mov'd and mov'd, and took at last
A certain shape, I wist.

A speck, a mist, a shape, I wist!
And still it ner'd and ner'd;
And, an it dodg'd a water-sprite,
It plung'd and tack'd and veer'd.

With throat unslack'd, with black lips bak'd
Ne could we laugh, ne wail:
Then while thro' drouth all dumb they stood
I bit my arm and suck'd the blood
And cry'd, A sail! a sail!

The very deep did rot: O Christ!
That ever this should be!
Yea, slimy things did crawl with legs
Upon the slimy sea.

About, about, in reel and rout
The death-fires danced at night;
The water, like a witch's oils,
Burnt green, and blue and white.

And some in dreams assured were
Of the Spirit that plagued us so;
Nine fathom deep he had followed us
From the land of mist and snow.

A Spirit had followed them; one of the invisible inhabitants of this planet, neither departed souls nor angels; concerning whom the learned Jew, Josephus, and the Platonic Constantinopolitan, Michael Psellus, may be consulted. They are very numerous, and there is no climate or element without one or more.

And every tongue, through utter drought,
Was withered at the root;
We could not speak, no more than if
We had been choked with soot.

Ah! well a-day! what evil looks
Had I from old and young!
Instead of the cross, the Albatross
About my neck was hung.

The shipmates, in their sore distress, would fain throw the whole guilt on the ancient Mariner: in sign whereof they hang the dead sea-bird round his neck.

PART III

There passed a weary time. Each throat
Was parched, and glazed each eye.
A weary time! a weary time!
How glazed each weary eye,
When looking westward, I beheld
A something in the sky.

The ancient Mariner beholdeth a sign in the element afar off.

At first it seemed a little speck,
And then it seemed a mist;
It moved and moved, and took at last
A certain shape, I wist.

With throat unslack'd, with black lips bak'd
  Agape they hear'd me call:
Gramercy! they for joy did grin
And all at once their breath drew in
  As they were drinking all.

She doth not tack from side to side—
  Hither to work us weal
Withouten wind, withouten tide
  She steddies with upright keel.

The western wave was all a flame,
  The day was well nigh done!
Almost upon the western wave
  Rested the broad bright Sun;
When that strange shape drove suddenly
  Betwixt us and the Sun.

And strait the Sun was fleck'd with bars
  (Heaven's mother send us grace)
As if thro' a dungeon grate he peer'd
  With broad and burning face.

Alas! (thought I, and my heart beat loud)
  How fast she neres and neres!
Are those her Sails that glance in the Sun
  Like restless gossameres?

Are those her naked ribs, which fleck'd
  The sun that did behind them peer?
And are these two all, all the crew,
  That woman and her fleshless Pheere?

His bones were black with many a crack,
  All black and bare, I ween;
Jet-black and bare, save where with rust
Of mouldy damps and charnel crust
  They're patch'd with purple and green.

A speck, a mist, a shape, I wist!
And still it neared and neared:
As if it dodged a water-sprite,
It plunged and tacked and veered.

With throats unslaked, with black lips baked,
We could nor laugh nor wail;
Through utter drought all dumb we stood!
I bit my arm, I sucked the blood,
And cried, A sail! a sail!

At its nearer approach, it seemeth him to be a ship; and at a dear ransom he freeth his speech from the bonds of thirst.

With throats unslaked, with black lips baked,
Agape they heard me call:
Gramercy! they for joy did grin,
And all at once their breath drew in,
As they were drinking all.

A flash of joy;

See! see! (I cried) she tacks no more!
Hither to work us weal;
Without a breeze, without a tide,
She steadies with upright keel!

And horror follows. For can it be a ship that comes onward without wind or tide?

The western wave was all a-flame.
The day was well nigh done!
Almost upon the western wave
Rested the broad bright Sun;
When that strange shape drove suddenly
Betwixt us and the Sun.

And straight the Sun was flecked with bars,
(Heaven's Mother send us grace!)
As if through a dungeon-grate he peered
With broad and burning face.

It seemeth him but the skeleton of a ship.

Alas! (thought I, and my heart beat loud)
How fast she nears and nears!
Are those her sails that glance in the Sun,
Like restless gossameres?

Her *lips are red*, her *looks are free*,
   Her *locks are yellow as gold*:
Her skin is as white as leprosy,
And she is far liker Death than he;
   Her flesh makes the still air cold.

The naked Hulk alongside came
   And the Twain were playing dice;
"The Game is done! I've won, I've won!"
   Quoth she, and whistled thrice.

A gust of wind sterte up behind
   And whistled thro' his bones;
Thro' the holes of his eyes and the hole of his mouth
   Half-whistles and half-groans.

With never a whisper in the Sea
   Off darts the Spectre-ship;
While clombe above the Eastern bar
The horned Moon, with one bright Star
   Almost atween the tips.

One after one by the horned Moon
   (Listen, O Stranger! to me)
Each turn'd his face with a ghastly pang
   And curs'd me with his ee.

Four times fifty living men,
   With never a sigh or groan,
With heavy thump, a lifeless lump
   They dropp'd down one by one.

Their souls did from their bodies fly,—
   They fled to bliss or woe;
And every soul it pass'd me by,
   Like the whiz of my Cross-bow.

IV

"I fear thee, ancyent Marinere!
   "I fear thy skinny hand;
"And thou art long, and lank, and brown,
   "As is the ribb'd Sea-sand.

Are those her ribs through which the Sun
Did peer, as through a grate?
And is that Woman all her crew?
Is that a DEATH? and are there two?
Is DEATH that woman's mate?

And its ribs are seen as bars on the face of the setting Sun.

The Spectre-Woman and her Death-mate, and no other on board the skeleton ship.

Her lips were red, her looks were free,
Her locks were yellow as gold:
Her skin was as white as leprosy,
The Night-mare LIFE-IN-DEATH was she,
Who thicks man's blood with cold.

Like vessel, like crew!

The naked hulk alongside came,
And the twain were casting dice;
'The game is done! I've won! I've won,'
Quoth she, and whistles thrice.

Death and Life-in-Death have diced for the ship's crew, and she (the latter) winneth the ancient Mariner.

The Sun's rim dips; the stars rush out:
At one stride comes the dark;
With far-heard whisper, o'er the sea,
Off shot the spectre-bark.

No twilight within the courts of the Sun.

We listened and looked sideways up!
Fear at my heart, as at a cup,
My life-blood seemed to sip!
The stars were dim, and thick the night,
The steersman's face by his lamp gleamed white;
From the sails the dew did drip—
Till clomb above the eastern bar
The horned Moon, with one bright star
Within the nether tip.

At the rising of the Moon,

One after one, by the star-dogged Moon,
Too quick for groan or sigh,
Each turned his face with a ghastly pang,
And cursed me with his eye.

One after another,

Four times fifty living men,
(And I heard nor sigh nor groan)
With heavy thump, a lifeless lump,
They dropped down one by one.

His shipmates drop down dead.

"*I fear thee and thy glittering eye*
    "*And thy skinny hand so brown—*"
Fear not, fear not, thou wedding-guest!
    This body dropt not down.

Alone, alone, all all alone
    Alone on the wide wide Sea;
And Christ would take no pity on
    My soul in agony.

The many men so beautiful,
    And they all dead did lie!
And a million million slimy things
    Liv'd on—and so did I.

I look'd upon the rotting Sea,
    And drew my eyes away;
I look'd upon the eldritch deck,
    And there the dead men lay.

I look'd to Heav'n, and try'd to pray;
    But or ever a prayer had gusht,
A wicked whisper came and made
    My heart as dry as dust.

I clos'd my lids and kept them close,
    Till the balls like pulses beat;
For the sky and the sea, and the sea and the sky
Lay like a load on my weary eye,
    And the dead were at my feet.

The cold sweat melted from their limbs,
    Ne rot, ne reek did they;
The look with which they look'd on me,
    Had never pass'd away.

An orphan's curse would drag to Hell
    A spirit from on high:
But O! more horrible than that
    Is the curse in a dead man's eye!
Seven days, seven nights I saw that curse,
    And yet I could not die.

The souls did from their bodies fly,—
They fled to bliss or woe!
And every soul, it passed me by,
Like the whizz of my cross-bow!"

> But Life-in-Death begins her work on the ancient Mariner.

PART IV

"I fear thee, ancient Mariner!
I fear thy skinny hand!
And thou art long, and lank, and brown,
As is the ribbed sea-sand.*

> The Wedding-Guest feareth that a Spirit is talking to him;

I fear thee and thy glittering eye,
And thy skinny hand, so brown."—
"Fear not, fear not, thou Wedding-Guest!
This body dropt not down.

> But the ancient Mariner assureth him of his bodily life, and proceedeth to relate his horrible penance.

Alone, alone, all, all alone,
Alone on a wide wide sea!
And never a saint took pity on
My soul in agony.

The many men, so beautiful!
And they all dead did lie:
And a thousand thousand slimy things
Lived on; and so did I.

> He despiseth the creatures of the calm,

I looked upon the rotting sea,
And drew my eyes away;
I looked upon the rotting deck,
And there the dead men lay.

> And envieth that *they* should live and so many lie dead.

I looked to heaven, and tried to pray;
But or ever a prayer had gusht,
A wicked whisper came, and made
My heart as dry as dust.

---

*For the last two lines of this stanza, I am indebted to Mr.
WORDSWORTH. It was on a delightful walk from Nether Stowey
to Dulverton, with him and his sister, in the Autumn of 1797,
that this Poem was planned, and in part composed.

c

The moving Moon went up the sky,
  And no where did abide:
Softly she was going up
  And a star or two beside—

Her beams bemock'd the sultry main
  Like morning frosts yspread;
But where the ship's huge shadow lay,
The charmed water burnt alway
  A still and awful red.

Beyond the shadow of the ship
  I watch'd the water-snakes:
They mov'd in tracks of shining white;
And when they rear'd, the elfish light
  Fell off in hoary flakes.

Within the shadow of the ship
  I watch'd their rich attire:
Blue, glossy green, and velvet black
They coil'd and swam; and every track
  Was a flash of golden fire.

O happy living things! no tongue
  Their beauty might declare:
A spring of love gusht from my heart,
  And I bless'd them unaware!
Sure my kind saint took pity on me,
  And I bless'd them unaware.

The self-same moment I could pray;
  And from my neck so free
The Albatross fell off, and sank
  Like lead into the sea.

v

O sleep, it is a gentle thing,
  Belov'd from pole to pole!
To Mary-queen the praise be yeven
She sent the gentle sleep from heaven
  That slid into my soul.

I closed my lids, and kept them close,
And the balls like pulses beat;
For the sky and the sea, and the sea and the sky
Lay like a load on my weary eye,
And the dead were at my feet.

The cold sweat melted from their limbs,
Nor rot nor reek did they:
The look with which they looked on me
Had never passed away.

But the curse liveth for him in the eye of the dead men.

An orphan's curse would drag to hell
A spirit from on high;
But oh! more horrible than that
Is the curse in a dead man's eye!
Seven days, seven nights, I saw that curse,
And yet I could not die.

The moving Moon went up the sky,
And no where did abide:
Softly she was going up,
And a star or two beside—

In his loneliness and fixedness he yearneth towards the journeying Moon, and the stars that still sojourn, yet still move onward; and every where the blue sky belongs to them, and is their appointed rest, and their native country and their own

Her beams bemocked the sultry main,
Like April hoar-frost spread;
But where the ship's huge shadow lay,
The charmed water burnt alway
A still and awful red.

natural homes, which they enter unannounced, as lords that are certainly expected and yet there is a silent joy at their arrival.

Beyond the shadow of the ship,
I watched the water-snakes:
They moved in tracks of shining white,
And when they reared, the elfish light
Fell off in hoary flakes.

By the light of the Moon he beholdeth God's creatures of the great calm.

Within the shadow of the ship
I watched their rich attire:
Blue, glossy green, and velvet black,
They coiled and swam; and every track
Was a flash of golden fire.

The silly buckets on the deck
  That had so long remain'd,
I dreamt that they were fill'd with dew
  And when I awoke it rain'd.

My lips were wet, my throat was cold,
  My garments all were dank;
Sure I had drunken in my dreams
  And still my body drank.

I mov'd and could not feel my limbs,
  I was so light, almost
I thought that I had died in sleep,
  And was a blessed Ghost.

The roaring wind! it roar'd far off,
  It did not come anear;
But with its sound it shook the sails
  That were so thin and sere.

The upper air bursts into life,
  And a hundred fire-flags sheen
To and fro they are hurried about;
And to and fro, and in and out
  The stars dance on between.

The coming wind doth roar more loud;
  The sails do sigh, like sedge:
The rain pours down from one black cloud
  And the Moon is at its edge.

Hark! hark! the thick black cloud is cleft,
  And the Moon is at its side:
Like waters shot from some high crag,
The lightning falls with never a jag
  A river steep and wide.

The strong wind reach'd the ship: it roar'd
  And dropp'd down, like a stone!
Beneath the lightning and the moon
  The dead men gave a groan.

O happy living things! no tongue
Their beauty might declare:
A spring of love gushed from my heart,
And I blessed them unaware:
Sure my kind saint took pity on me,
And I blessed them unaware.

Their beauty and their happiness.

He blesseth them in his heart.

The self-same moment I could pray;
And from my neck so free
The Albatross fell off, and sank
Like lead into the sea.

The spell begins to break.

PART V

Oh sleep! it is a gentle thing,
Beloved from pole to pole!
To Mary Queen the praise be given!
She sent the gentle sleep from Heaven,
That slid into my soul.

The silly buckets on the deck,
That had so long remained,
I dreamt that they were filled with dew;
And when I awoke, it rained.

By grace of the holy Mother, the ancient Mariner is refreshed with rain.

My lips were wet, my throat was cold,
My garments all were dank;
Sure I had drunken in my dreams,
And still my body drank.

I moved, and could not feel my limbs:
I was so light—almost
I thought that I had died in sleep,
And was a blessed ghost.

And soon I heard a roaring wind:
It did not come anear;
But with its sound it shook the sails,
That were so thin and sere.

He heareth sounds and seeth strange sights and commotions in the sky and the element.

They groan'd, they stirr'd, they all uprose,
  Ne spake, ne mov'd their eyes:
It had been strange, even in a dream
  To have seen those dead men rise.

The helmsman steer'd, the ship mov'd on;
  Yet never a breeze up-blew;
The Marineres all 'gan work the ropes,
  Where they were wont to do:
They rais'd their limbs like lifeless tools—
  We were a ghastly crew.

The body of my brother's son
  Stood by me knee to knee:
The body and I pull'd at one rope,
  But he said nought to me—
And I quak'd to think of my own voice
  How frightful it would be!

The day-light dawn'd—they dropp'd their arms,
  And cluster'd round the mast:
Sweet sounds rose slowly thro' their mouths
  And from their bodies pass'd.

Around, around, flew each sweet sound,
  Then darted to the sun:
Slowly the sounds came back again
  Now mix'd, now one by one.

Sometimes a dropping from the sky
  I heard the Lavrock sing;
Sometimes all little birds that are
How they seem'd to fill the sea and air
  With their sweet jargoning.

And now 'twas like all instruments,
  Now like a lonely flute;
And now it is an angel's song
  That makes the heavens be mute.

The upper air burst into life!
And a hundred fire-flags sheen,
To and fro they were hurried about!
And to and fro, and in and out,
The wan stars danced between.

And the coming wind did roar more loud,
And the sails did sigh like sedge;
And the rain poured down from one black cloud;
The Moon was at its edge.

The thick black cloud was cleft, and still
The Moon was at its side:
Like waters shot from some high crag,
The lightning fell with never a jag,
A river steep and wide.

The loud wind never reached the ship,
Yet now the ship moved on!
Beneath the lightning and the Moon
The dead men gave a groan.

The bodies of the ship's crew are inspired and the ship moves on;

They groaned, they stirred, they all uprose,
Nor spake, nor moved their eyes:
It had been strange, even in a dream,
To have seen those dead men rise.

The helmsman steered, the ship moved on;
Yet never a breeze up-blew;
The mariners all 'gan work the ropes,
Where they were wont to do;
They raised their limbs like lifeless tools—
We were a ghastly crew.

The body of my brother's son
Stood by me, knee to knee:
The body and I pulled at one rope,
But he said nought to me."

It ceas'd: yet still the sails made on
  A pleasant noise till noon,
A noise like of a hidden brook
  In the leafy month of June,
That to the sleeping woods all night
  Singeth a quiet tune.

Listen, O listen, thou Wedding-guest!
  "Marinere! thou hast thy will:
"For that, which comes out of thine eye, doth make
  "My body and soul to be still."

Never sadder tale was told
  To a man of woman born:
Sadder and wiser thou wedding-guest!
  Thou'lt rise to-morrow morn.

Never sadder tale was heard
  By a man of woman born:
The Marineres all return'd to work
  As silent as beforne.

The Marineres all 'gan pull the ropes,
  But look at me they n'old:
Thought I, I am as thin as air—
  They cannot me behold.

Till noon we silently sail'd on
  Yet never a breeze did breathe:
Slowly and smoothly went the ship
  Mov'd onward from beneath.

Under the keel nine fathom deep
  From the land of mist and snow
The spirit slid: and it was He
  That made the Ship to go.
The sails at noon left off their tune
  And the Ship stood still also,

"I fear thee, ancient Mariner!"
"Be calm, thou Wedding-Guest!
'Twas not those souls that fled in pain,
Which to their corses came again,
But a troop of spirits blest:

For when it dawned—they dropped their arms,
And clustered round the mast;
Sweet sounds rose slowly through their mouths,
And from their bodies passed.

Around, around, flew each sweet sound,
Then darted to the Sun;
Slowly the sounds came back again,
Now mixed, now one by one.

Sometimes a-dropping from the sky
I heard the sky-lark sing;
Sometimes all little birds that are,
How they seemed to fill the sea and air
With their sweet jargoning!

And now 'twas like all instruments,
Now like a lonely flute;
And now it is an angel's song,
That makes the heavens be mute.

It ceased; yet still the sails made on
A pleasant noise till noon,
A noise like of a hidden brook
In the leafy month of June,
That to the sleeping woods all night
Singeth a quiet tune.

Till noon we quietly sailed on,
Yet never a breeze did breathe:
Slowly and smoothly went the ship,
Moved onward from beneath.

But not by th souls of the men, nor by daemons of earth or middle air, but by a blessed troop of angelic spirits, sent down by the invocation of the guardian saint.

The sun right up above the mast
  Had fix'd her to the ocean:
But in a minute she 'gan stir
  With a short uneasy motion—
Backwards and forwards half her length
  With a short uneasy motion.

Then, like a pawing horse let go,
  She made a sudden bound:
It flung the blood into my head,
  And I fell into a swound.

How long in that same fit I lay,
  I have not to declare;
But ere my living life return'd,
I heard and in my soul discern'd
  Two voices in the air,

"Is it he?" quoth one, "Is this the man?
  "By him who died on cross,
"With his cruel bow he lay'd full low
  "The harmless Albatross.

"The spirit who 'bideth by himself
  "In the land of mist and snow,
"He lov'd the bird that lov'd the man
  "Who shot him with his bow."

The other was a softer voice,
  As soft as honey-dew:
Quoth he "The man hath penance done,
  "And penance more will do."

VI

First Voice

"But tell me, tell me! speak again,
  "Thy soft response renewing—
"What makes that ship drive on so fast?
  "What is the Ocean doing?"

Under the keel nine fathom deep,
From the land of mist and snow,
The spirit slid: and it was he
That made the ship to go.
The sails at noon left off their tune,
And the ship stood still also.

The lonesome
Spirit from the
south pole
carries on the
ship as far as
the Line, in
obedience to
the angelic
troop, but still
requireth
vengeance.

The Sun, right up above the mast,
Had fixed her to the ocean:
But in a minute she 'gan stir,
With a short uneasy motion—
Backwards and forwards half her length
With a short uneasy motion.

Then like a pawing horse let go,
She made a sudden bound:
It flung the blood into my head,
And I fell down in a swound.

How long in that same fit I lay,
I have not to declare;
But ere my living life returned,
I heard and in my soul discerned
Two voices in the air.

The Polar
Spirit's fellow-
daemons, the
invisible in-
habitants of the
element, take
part in his
wrong; and two
of them relate,
one to the other,
that penance
long and heavy
for the ancient
Mariner hath
been accorded
to the Polar
Spirit, who
returneth
southward.

'Is it he?' quoth one, 'Is this the man?
By him who died on cross,
With his cruel bow he laid full low
The harmless Albatross.

The spirit who bideth by himself
In the land of mist and snow,
He loved the bird that loved the man
Who shot him with his bow.'

The other was a softer voice,
As soft as honey-dew:
Quoth he, 'The man hath penance done,
And penance more will do.'

Second Voice

"*Still as a Slave before his Lord,*
"*The Ocean hath no blast:*
"*His great bright eye most silently*
"*Up to the moon is cast—*

"*If he may know which way to go,*
"*For she guides him smooth or grim.*
"*See, brother, see! how graciously*
"*She looketh down on him.*"

First Voice

"*But why drives on that ship so fast*
"*Withouten wave or wind?*"

Second Voice

"*The air is cut away before,*
"*And closes from behind.*"

"*Fly, brother, fly! more high, more high,*
"*Or we shall be belated:*
"*For slow and slow that ship will go,*
"*When the Marinere's trance is abated.*"

I woke, and we were sailing on
As in a gentle weather:
'Twas night, calm night, the moon was high;
The dead men stood together.

All stood together on the deck,
For a charnel-dungeon fitter:
All fix'd on me their stony eyes
That in the moon did glitter.

The pang, the curse, with which they died,
Had never pass'd away:
I could not draw my een from theirs
Ne turn them up to pray.

And in its time the spell was snapt,
And I could move my een:
I look'd far-forth, but little saw
Of what might else be seen.

PART VI

First Voice

'But tell me, tell me! speak again,
Thy soft response renewing—
What makes that ship drive on so fast?
What is the ocean doing?'

Second Voice

'Still as a slave before his lord,
The ocean hath no blast;
His great bright eye most silently
Up to the Moon is cast—

If he may know which way to go;
For she guides him smooth or grim.
See, brother, see! how graciously
She looketh down on him.'

First Voice

'But why drives on that ship so fast,
Without or wave or wind?'

Second Voice

'The air is cut away before,
And closes from behind.

'Fly, brother, fly! more high, more high!
Or we shall be belated:
For slow and slow that ship will go,
When the Mariner's trance is abated.'

The Mariner hath been cast into a trance; for the angelic power causeth the vessel to drive northward faster than human life could endure.

I woke, and we were sailing on
As in a gentle weather:
'Twas night, calm night, the moon was high;
The dead men stood together.

All stood together on the deck,
For a charnel-dungeon fitter:
All fixed on me their stony eyes,
That in the Moon did glitter.

The super-natural motion is retarded; the Mariner awakes, and his penance begins anew.

Like one, that on a lonely road
  Doth walk in fear and dread,
And having once turn'd round, walks on
  And turns no more his head:
Because he knows, a frightful fiend
  Doth close behind him tread.

But soon there breath'd a wind on me,
  Ne sound ne motion made:
Its path was not upon the sea
  In ripple or in shade.

It rais'd my hair, it fann'd my cheek,
  Like a meadow-gale of spring—
It mingled strangely with my fears,
  Yet it felt like a welcoming.

Swiftly, swiftly flew the ship,
  Yet she sail'd softly too:
Sweetly, sweetly blew the breeze—
  On me alone it blew.

O dream of joy! is this indeed
  The light-house top I see?
Is this the Hill? Is this the Kirk?
  Is this mine own countrée?

We drifted o'er the Harbour-bar,
  And I with sobs did pray—
"O let me be awake, my God!
  "Or let me sleep alway!"

The harbour-bay was clear as glass,
  So smoothly it was strewn!
And on the bay the moon light lay,
  And the shadow of the moon.

The moonlight bay was white all o'er,
  Till rising from the same,
Full many shapes, that shadows were,
  Like as of torches came.

The pang, the curse, with which they died,
Had never passed away:
I could not draw my eyes from theirs,
Nor turn them up to pray.

And now this spell was snapt: once more
I viewed the ocean green,
And looked far forth, yet little saw
Of what had else been seen—

The curse is finally expiated.

Like one, that on a lonesome road
Doth walk in fear and dread,
And having once turned round walks on,
And turns no more his head;
Because he knows, a frightful fiend
Doth close behind him tread.

But soon there breathed a wind on me,
Nor sound nor motion made:
Its path was not upon the sea,
In ripple or in shade.

It raised my hair, it fanned my cheek
Like a meadow-gale of spring—
It mingled strangely with my fears,
Yet it felt like a welcoming.

Swiftly, swiftly flew the ship,
Yet she sailed softly too:
Sweetly, sweetly blew the breeze—
On me alone it blew.

Oh! dream of joy! is this indeed
The light-house top I see?
Is this the hill? is this the kirk?
Is this mine own countree?

And the ancient Mariner beholdeth his native country.

We drifted o'er the harbour-bar,
And I with sobs did pray—
O let me be awake, my God!
Or let me sleep alway.

A little distance from the prow
  Those dark-red shadows were;
But soon I saw that my own flesh
  Was red as in a glare.

I turn'd my head in fear and dread,
  And by the holy rood,
The bodies had advanc'd, and now
  Before the mast they stood.

They lifted up their stiff right arms,
  They held them strait and tight;
And each right-arm burnt like a torch,
  A torch that's borne upright.
Their stony eye-balls glitter'd on
  In the red and smoky light.

I pray'd and turn'd my head away
  Forth looking as before.
There was no breeze upon the bay,
  No wave against the shore.

The rock shone bright, the kirk no less
  That stands above the rock:
The moonlight steep'd in silentness
  The steady weathercock.

And the bay was white with silent light,
  Till rising from the same
Full many shapes, that shadows were,
  In crimson colours came.

A little distance from the prow
  Those crimson shadows were:
I turn'd my eyes upon the deck—
  O Christ! what saw I there?

Each corse lay flat, lifeless and flat;
  And by the Holy rood
A man all light, a seraph-man,
  On every corse there stood.

The harbour-bay was clear as glass,
So smoothly it was strewn!
And on the bay the moonlight lay,
And the shadow of the Moon.

The rock shone bright, the kirk no less,
That stands above the rock:
The moonlight steeped in silentness
The steady weathercock.

And the bay was white with silent light,
Till rising from the same,
Full many shapes, that shadows were,
In crimson colours came.

The angelic spirits leave the dead bodies,

A little distance from the prow
Those crimson shadows were:
I turned my eyes upon the deck—
Oh, Christ! what saw I there!

And appear in their own forms of light.

Each corse lay flat, lifeless and flat,
And, by the holy rood!
A man all light, a seraph-man,
On every corse there stood.

This seraph-band, each waved his hand:
It was a heavenly sight!
They stood as signals to the land,
Each one a lovely light;

This seraph-band, each waved his hand,
No voice did they impart—
No voice; but oh! the silence sank
Like music on my heart.

But soon I heard the dash of oars,
I heard the Pilot's cheer;
My head was turned perforce away
And I saw a boat appear.

This seraph-band, each wav'd his hand:
    It was a heavenly sight:
They stood as signals to the land,
    Each one a lovely light:

This seraph-band, each wav'd his hand,
    No voice did they impart—
No voice; but O! the silence sank,
    Like music on my heart.

Eftsones I heard the dash of oars,
    I heard the pilot's cheer:
My head was turn'd perforce away
    And I saw a boat appear.

Then vanish'd all the lovely lights;
    The bodies rose anew:
With silent pace, each to his place,
    Came back the ghastly crew.
The wind, that shade nor motion made,
    On me alone it blew.

The pilot, and the pilot's boy
    I heard them coming fast:
Dear Lord in Heaven! it was a joy,
    The dead men could not blast.

I saw a third—I heard his voice:
    It is the Hermit good!
He singeth loud his godly hymns
    That he makes in the wood.
He'll shrieve my soul, he'll wash away
    The Albatross's blood.

VII

This Hermit good lives in that wood
    Which slopes down to the Sea.
How loudly his sweet voice he rears!
He loves to talk with Marineres
    That come from a far Countrée.

The Pilot and the Pilot's boy,
I heard them coming fast:
Dear Lord in Heaven! it was a joy
The dead men could not blast.

I saw a third—I heard his voice:
It is the Hermit good!
He singeth loud his godly hymns
That he makes in the wood.
He'll shrieve my soul, he'll wash away
The Albatross's blood.

PART VII

This Hermit good lives in that wood   *The Hermit of*
Which slopes down to the sea.   *the Wood.*
How loudly his sweet voice he rears!
He loves to talk with marineres
That come from a far countree.

He kneels at morn, and noon, and eve—
He hath a cushion plump:
It is the moss that wholly hides
The rotted old oak-stump.

The skiff-boat neared: I heard them talk,
'Why, this is strange, I trow!
Where are those lights so many and fair,
That signal made but now?'

'Strange, by my faith!' the Hermit said—   *Approacheth*
'And they answered not our cheer!   *the ship with*
The planks looked warped! and see those sails,   *wonder.*
How thin they are and sere!
I never saw aught like to them,
Unless perchance it were

Brown skeletons of leaves that lag
My forest-brook along;
When the ivy-tod is heavy with snow,
And the owlet whoops to the wolf below,
That eats the she-wolf's young.'

He kneels at morn and noon and eve—
    He hath a cushion plump:
It is the moss, that wholly hides
    The rotted old Oak-stump.

The Skiff-boat ne'rd: I heard them talk,
    "Why, this is strange, I trow!
"Where are those lights so many and fair
    "That signal made but now?"

"Strange, by my faith!" the Hermit said—
    "And they answer'd not our cheer.
"The planks look warp'd, and see those sails
    "How thin they are and sere!
"I never saw aught like to them
    "Unless perchance it were

"The skeletons of leaves that lag
    "My forest-brook along:
"When the Ivy-tod is heavy with snow,
"And the Owlet whoops to the wolf below
    "That eats the she-wolf's young."

"Dear Lord! it has a fiendish look—"
    (The Pilot made reply)
"I am afear'd—" "Push on, push on!"
    Said the Hermit cheerily.

The Boat came closer to the Ship,
    But I ne spake ne stirr'd!
The Boat came close beneath the Ship.
    And strait a sound was heard!

Under the water it rumbled on,
    Still louder and more dread:
It reach'd the Ship, it split the bay;
    The Ship went down like lead.

Stunn'd by that loud and dreadful sound,
    Which sky and ocean smote:
Like one that had been seven days drown'd
    My body lay afloat:
But, swift as dreams, myself I found
    Within the Pilot's boat.

'Dear Lord! it hath a fiendish look'—
(The Pilot made reply)
'I am a-feared'—'Push on, push on!'
Said the Hermit cheerily.

The boat came closer to the ship,
But I nor spake nor stirred;
The boat came close beneath the ship,
And straight a sound was heard.

Under the water it rumbled on,   *The ship*
Still louder and more dread: *suddenly*
It reached the ship, it split the bay; *sinketh.*
The ship went down like lead.

Stunned by that loud and dreadful sound, *The ancient*
Which sky and ocean smote,   *Mariner is*
Like one that hath been seven days drowned *saved in the*
My body lay afloat;   *Pilot's boat.*
But swift as dreams, myself I found
Within the Pilot's boat.

Upon the whirl, where sank the ship,
The boat spun round and round;
And all was still, save that the hill
Was telling of the sound.

I moved my lips—the Pilot shrieked
And fell down in a fit;
The holy Hermit raised his eyes,
And prayed where he did sit.

I took the oars: the Pilot's boy,
Who now doth crazy go,
Laughed loud and long, and all the while
His eyes went to and fro.
'Ha! ha!' quoth he, 'full plain I see,
The Devil knows how to row.'

Upon the whirl, where sank the Ship,
　　The boat spun round and round:
And all was still, save that the hill
　　Was telling of the sound.

I mov'd my lips: the Pilot shriek'd
　　And fell down in a fit.
The Holy Hermit rais'd his eyes
　　And pray'd where he did sit.

I took the oars: the Pilot's boy,
　　Who now doth crazy go,
Laugh'd loud and long, and all the while
　　His eyes went to and fro,
"Ha! ha!" quoth he—"full plain I see,
　　"The devil knows how to row."

And now all in mine own Countrée
　　I stood on the firm land!
The Hermit stepp'd forth from the boat,
　　And scarcely he could stand.

"O shrieve me, shrieve me, holy Man!"
　　The Hermit cross'd his brow—
"Say quick," quoth he, "I bid thee say
　　"What manner man art thou?"

Forthwith this frame of mine was wrench'd
　　With a woeful agony,
Which forc'd me to begin my tale
　　And then it left me free.

Since then at an uncertain hour,
　　Now oftimes and now fewer,
That anguish comes and makes me tell
　　My ghastly aventure.

I pass, like night, from land to land;
　　I have strange power of speech;
The moment that his face I see
I know the man that must hear me;
　　To him my tale I teach.

And now, all in my own countree,
I stood on the firm land!
The Hermit stepped forth from the boat,
And scarcely he could stand.

'O shrieve me, shrieve me, holy man!'
The Hermit crossed his brow.
'Say quick,' quoth he, 'I bid thee say—
What manner of man art thou?'

The ancient Mariner earnestly entreateth the Hermit to shrieve him; and the penance of life falls on him.

Forthwith this frame of mine was wrenched
With a woful agony,
Which forced me to begin my tale;
And then it left me free.

Since then, at an uncertain hour,
That agony returns:
And till my ghastly tale is told,
This heart within me burns.

And ever and anon throughout his future life an agony constraineth him to travel from land to land;

I pass, like night, from land to land;
I have strange power of speech;
That moment that his face I see,
I know the man that must hear me:
To him my tale I teach.

What loud uproar bursts from that door!
The wedding-guests are there:
But in the garden-bower the bride
And bride-maids singing are:
And hark the little vesper bell,
Which biddeth me to prayer!

O Wedding-Guest! this soul hath been
Alone on a wide wide sea:
So lonely 'twas, that God himself
Scarce seemed there to be.

O sweeter than the marriage-feast,
'Tis sweeter far to me,
To walk together to the kirk
With a goodly company!—

What loud uproar bursts from that door!
  The Wedding-guests are there;
But in the Garden-bower the Bride
  And Bride-maids singing are:
And hark the little Vesper-bell
  Which biddeth me to prayer.

O Wedding-guest! this soul hath been
  Alone on a wide wide sea:
So lonely 'twas, that God himself
  Scarce seemed there to be.

O sweeter than the Marriage-feast,
  'Tis sweeter far to me
To walk together to the Kirk
  With a goodly company.

To walk together to the Kirk
  And all together pray,
While each to his great Father bends,
Old men, and babes, and loving friends,
  And Youths, and Maidens gay.

Farewell, farewell! but this I tell
  To thee, thou wedding-guest!
He prayeth well who loveth well,
  Both man and bird and beast.

He prayeth best who loveth best,
  All things both great and small:
For the dear God, who loveth us,
  He made and loveth all.

The Marinere, whose eye is bright,
  Whose beard with age is hoar,
Is gone; and now the wedding-guest
  Turn'd from the bridegroom's door.

He went, like one that hath been stunn'd
  And is of sense forlorn:
A sadder and a wiser man
  He rose the morrow morn.

1798

To walk together to the kirk,
And all together pray,
While each to his great Father bends,
Old men, and babes, and loving friends
And youths and maidens gay!

Farewell, farewell! but this I tell
To thee, thou Wedding-Guest!
He prayeth well, who loveth well
Both man and bird and beast.

And to teach,
by his own
example, love
and reverence
to all things
that God made
and loveth.

He prayeth best, who loveth best
All things both great and small;
For the dear God who loveth us,
He made and loveth all."

The Mariner, whose eye is bright,
Whose beard with age is hoar,
Is gone: and now the Wedding-Guest
Turned from the bridegroom's door.

He went like one that hath been stunned,
And is of sense forlorn:
A sadder and a wiser man,
He rose the morrow morn.

1798-1834

CHRISTABEL

PREFACE

THE first part of the following poem was written in the year 1797, at Stowey, in the county of Somerset. The second part, after my return from Germany, in the year 1800, at Keswick, Cumberland. It is probable that if the poem had been finished at either of the former periods, or if even the first and second part had been published in the year 1800, the impression of its originality would have been much greater than I dare at present expect. But for this I have only my own indolence to blame. The dates are mentioned for the exclusive purpose of precluding charges of plagiarism or servile imitation from myself. For there is amongst us a set of critics, who seem to hold, that every possible thought and image is traditional; who have no notion that there are such things as fountains in the world, small as well as great; and who would therefore charitably derive every rill they behold flowing, from a perforation made in some other man's tank. I am confident, however, that as far as the present poem is concerned, the celebrated poets whose writings I might be suspected of having imitated, either in particular passages, or in the tone and the spirit of the whole, would be among the first to vindicate me from the charge, and who, on any striking coincidence, would permit me to address them in this doggerel version of two monkish Latin hexameters.

> 'Tis mine and it is likewise yours;
> But an if this will not do;
> Let it be mine, good friend! for I
> Am the poorer of the two.

I have only to add that the metre of "Christabel" is not, properly speaking, irregular, though it may seem so from its being founded on a new principle: namely, that of counting in each line the accents, not the syllables. Though the latter may vary from seven to twelve, yet in each line the accents will be found to be only four. Nevertheless, this occasional variation in number of syllables is not introduced wantonly, or for the mere ends of convenience, but in correspondence with some transition in the nature of the imagery or passion.

PART I

'TIS the middle of night by the castle clock,
  And the owls have awakened the crowing cock;
Tu—whit !——Tu—whoo !
And hark, again! the crowing cock,
How drowsily it crew.

Sir Leoline, the Baron rich,
Hath a toothless mastiff bitch;
From her kennel beneath the rock
She maketh answer to the clock,
Four for the quarters, and twelve for the hour;
Ever and aye, by shine and shower,
Sixteen short howls, not over loud;
Some say, she sees my lady's shroud.

Is the night chilly and dark?
The night is chilly, but not dark.
The thin gray cloud is spread on high,
It covers but not hides the sky.
The moon is behind, and at the full;
And yet she looks both small and dull.
The night is chill, the cloud is gray:
'Tis a month before the month of May,
And the Spring comes slowly up this way.

The lovely lady, Christabel,
Whom her father loves so well,
What makes her in the wood so late,
A furlong from the castle gate?
She had dreams all yesternight
Of her own betrothed knight;
And she in the midnight wood will pray
For the weal of her lover that's far away.

She stole along, she nothing spoke,
The sighs she heaved were soft and low,
And naught was green upon the oak
But moss and rarest misletoe:
She kneels beneath the huge oak tree,
And in silence prayeth she.

The lady sprang up suddenly,
The lovely lady, Christabel!
It moaned as near, as near can be,
But what it is she cannot tell.—
On the other side it seems to be,
Of the huge, broad-breasted, old oak tree.

The night is chill; the forest bare;
Is it the wind that moaneth bleak?
There is not wind enough in the air
To move away the ringlet curl
From the lovely lady's cheek—
There is not wind enough to twirl
The one red leaf, the last of its clan,
That dances as often as dance it can,
Hanging so light, and hanging so high,
On the topmost twig that looks up at the sky.

Hush, beating heart of Christabel!
Jesu, Maria, shield her well!
She folded her arms beneath her cloak,
And stole to the other side of the oak.
　　What sees she there?

There she sees a damsel bright,
Drest in a silken robe of white,
That shadowy in the moonlight shone:
The neck that made that white robe wan,
Her stately neck, and arms were bare;
Her blue-veined feet unsandalled were,
And wildly glittered here and there
The gems entangled in her hair.
I guess, 'twas frightful there to see
A lady so richly clad as she—
Beautiful exceedingly!

Mary mother, save me now!
(Said Christabel,) And who art thou?

The lady strange made answer meet,
And her voice was faint and sweet:—
Have pity on my sore distress,
I scarce can speak for weariness:
Stretch forth thy hand, and have no fear!
Said Christabel, How camest thou here?
And the lady, whose voice was faint and sweet,
Did thus pursue her answer meet:—

My sire is of a noble line,
And my name is Geraldine:
Five warriors seized me yestermorn,
Me, even me, a maid forlorn:
They choked my cries with force and fright,
And tied me on a palfrey white.
The palfrey was as fleet as wind,
And they rode furiously behind.
They spurred amain, their steeds were white:
And once we crossed the shade of night.
As sure as Heaven shall rescue me,
I have no thought what men they be;
Nor do I know how long it is
(For I have lain entranced I wis)
Since one, the tallest of the five,
Took me from the palfrey's back,
A weary woman, scarce alive.
Some muttered words his comrades spoke:
He placed me underneath this oak;
He swore they would return with haste;
Whither they went I cannot tell—
I thought I heard, some minutes past,
Sounds as of a castle bell.
Stretch forth thy hand (thus ended she),
And help a wretched maid to flee.

Then Christabel stretched forth her hand,
And comforted fair Geraldine:
O well, bright dame! may you command

The service of Sir Leoline;
And gladly our stout chivalry
Will he send forth and friends withal
To guide and guard you safe and free
Home to your noble father's hall.

She rose: and forth with steps they passed
That strove to be, and were not, fast.
Her gracious stars the lady blest,
And thus spake on sweet Christabel:
All our household are at rest,
The hall as silent as the cell;
Sir Leoline is weak in health,
And may not well awakened be,
But we will move as if in stealth,
And I beseech your courtesy,
This night, to share your couch with me.

They crossed the moat, and Christabel
Took the key that fitted well;
A little door she opened straight,
All in the middle of the gate;
The gate that was ironed within and without,
Where an army in battle array had marched out.
The lady sank, belike through pain,
And Christabel with might and main
Lifted her up, a weary weight,
Over the threshold of the gate:
Then the lady rose again,
And moved, as she were not in pain.

So free from danger, free from fear,
They crossed the court: right glad they were.
And Christabel devoutly cried
To the lady by her side,
Praise we the Virgin all divine
Who hath rescued thee from thy distress!
Alas, alas! said Geraldine,
I cannot speak for weariness.
So free from danger, free from fear,
They crossed the court: right glad they were.

Outside her kennel, the mastiff old
Lay fast asleep, in moonshine cold.
The mastiff old did not awake,
Yet she an angry moan did make!
And what can ail the mastiff bitch?
Never till now she uttered yell
Beneath the eye of Christabel.
Perhaps it is the owlet's scritch:
For what can ail the mastiff bitch?

They passed the hall, that echoes still,
Pass as lightly as you will!
The brands were flat, the brands were dying,
Amid their own white ashes lying;
But when the lady passed, there came
A tongue of light, a fit of flame;
And Christabel saw the lady's eye,
And nothing else saw she thereby,
Save the boss of the shield of Sir Leoline tall,
Which hung in a murky old niche in the wall.
O softly tread, said Christabel,
My father seldom sleepeth well.

Sweet Christabel her feet doth bare,
And jealous of the listening air
They steal their way from stair to stair,
Now in glimmer, and now in gloom,
And now they pass the Baron's room,
As still as death, with stifled breath!
And now have reached her chamber door;
And now doth Geraldine press down
The rushes of the chamber floor.

The moon shines dim in the open air,
And not a moonbeam enters here.
But they without its light can see
The chamber carved so curiously,
Carved with figures strange and sweet,
All made out of the carver's brain,
For a lady's chamber meet:
The lamp with twofold silver chain
Is fastened to an angel's feet.

The silver lamp burns dead and dim;
But Christabel the lamp will trim.
She trimmed the lamp, and made it bright,
And left it swinging to and fro,
While Geraldine, in wretched plight,
Sank down upon the floor below.

O weary lady, Geraldine,
I pray you, drink this cordial wine!
It is a wine of virtuous powers;
My mother made it of wild flowers.

And will your mother pity me,
Who am a maiden most forlorn?
Christabel answered—Woe is me!
She died the hour that I was born.
I have heard the grey-haired friar tell
How on her death-bed she did say,
That she should hear the castle-bell
Strike twelve upon my wedding-day.
O mother dear! that thou wert here!
I would, said Geraldine, she were!
But soon with altered voice, said she—
"Off, wandering mother! Peak and pine!
I have power to bid thee flee."
Alas! what ails poor Geraldine?
Why stares she with unsettled eye?
Can she the bodiless dead espy?
And why with hollow voice cries she,
"Off, woman, off! this hour is mine—
Though thou her guardian spirit be,
Off, woman, off! 'tis given to me."

Then Christabel knelt by the lady's side,
And raised to heaven her eyes so blue—
Alas! said she, this ghastly ride—
Dear lady! it hath wildered you!
The lady wiped her moist cold brow,
And faintly said, "'tis over now!"

Again the wild-flower wine she drank:
Her fair large eyes 'gan glitter bright,

And from the floor whereon she sank,
The lofty lady stood upright:
She was most beautiful to see,
Like a lady of a far countree.

And thus the lofty lady spake—
"All they who live in the upper sky,
Do love you, holy Christabel!
And you love them, and for their sake
And for the good which me befel,
Even I in my degree will try,
Fair maiden, to requite you well.
But now unrobe yourself; for I
Must pray, ere yet in bed I lie."

Quoth Christabel, So let it be!
And as the lady bade, did she.
Her gentle limbs did she undress,
And lay down in her loveliness.

But through her brain of weal and woe
So many thoughts moved to and fro,
That vain it were her lids to close;
So half-way from the bed she rose,
And on her elbow did recline
To look at the lady Geraldine.

Beneath the lamp the lady bowed,
And slowly rolled her eyes around;
Then drawing in her breath aloud,
Like one that shuddered, she unbound
The cincture from beneath her breast:
Her silken robe, and inner vest,
Dropt to her feet, and full in view,
Behold! her bosom and half her side——
A sight to dream of, not to tell!
O shield her! shield sweet Christabel!

Yet Geraldine nor speaks nor stirs;
Ah! what a stricken look was hers!
Deep from within she seems half-way

To lift some weight with sick assay,
And eyes the maid and seeks delay;
Then suddenly, as one defied,
Collects herself in scorn and pride,
And lay down by the Maiden's side!—
And in her arms the maid she took,
　　　Ah well-a-day!
And with low voice and doleful look
These words did say:
"In the touch of this bosom there worketh a spell,
Which is lord of thy utterance, Christabel!
Thou knowest to-night, and wilt know to-morrow,
This mark of my shame, this seal of my sorrow;
　　　But vainly thou warrest,
　　　　For this is alone in
　　　Thy power to declare,
　　　　That in the dim forest
　　　Thou heard'st a low moaning,
And found'st a bright lady, surpassingly fair;
And didst bring her home with thee in love and
　　　in charity,
To shield her and shelter her from the damp air."

THE CONCLUSION TO PART I

It was a lovely sight to see
The lady Christabel, when she
Was praying at the old oak tree.
　　　Amid the jagged shadows
　　　Of mossy leafless boughs,
　　　Kneeling in the moonlight,
　　　To make her gentle vows;
Her slender palms together prest,
Heaving sometimes on her breast;
Her face resigned to bliss or bale—
Her face, oh call it fair not pale,
And both blue eyes more bright than clear,
Each about to have a tear.

With open eyes (ah woe is me!)
Asleep, and dreaming fearfully,
Fearfully dreaming, yet, I wis,

Dreaming that alone, which is—
O sorrow and shame! Can this be she,
The lady, who knelt at the old oak tree?
And lo! the worker of these harms,
That holds the maiden in her arms,
Seems to slumber still and mild,
As a mother with her child.

A star hath set, a star hath risen,
O Geraldine! since arms of thine
Have been the lovely lady's prison.
O Geraldine! one hour was thine—
Thou'st had thy will! By tairn and rill,
The night-birds all that hour were still.
But now they are jubilant anew,
From cliff and tower, tu—whoo! tu—whoo!
Tu—whoo! tu—whoo! from wood and fell!

And see! the lady Christabel
Gathers herself from out her trance;
Her limbs relax, her countenance
Grows sad and soft; the smooth thin lids
Close o'er her eyes; and tears she sheds—
Large tears that leave the lashes bright!
And oft the while she seems to smile
As infants at a sudden light!

Yea, she doth smile, and she doth weep,
Like a youthful hermitess,
Beauteous in a wilderness,
Who, praying always, prays in sleep.
And, if she move unquietly,
Perchance, 'tis but the blood so free
Comes back and tingles in her feet.
No doubt, she hath a vision sweet.
What if her guardian spirit 'twere,
What if she knew her mother near?
But this she knows, in joys and woes,
That saints will aid if men will call:
For the blue sky bends over all!

PART II

Each matin bell, the Baron saith,
Knells us back to a world of death.
These words Sir Leoline first said,
When he rose and found his lady dead:
These words Sir Leoline will say
Many a morn to his dying day!

And hence the custom and law began
That still at dawn the sacristan,
Who duly pulls the heavy bell,
Five and forty beads must tell
Between each stroke—a warning knell,
Which not a soul can choose but hear
From Bratha Head to Wyndermere.

Saith Bracy the bard, So let it knell!
And let the drowsy sacristan
Still count as slowly as he can!
There is no lack of such, I ween,
As well fill up the space between.
In Langdale Pike and Witch's Lair,
And Dungeon-ghyll so foully rent,
With ropes of rock and bells of air
Three sinful sextons' ghosts are pent,
Who all give back, one after t'other,
The death-note to their living brother;
And oft too, by the knell offended,
Just as their one! two! three! is ended,
The devil mocks the doleful tale
With a merry peal from Borodale.

The air is still! through mist and cloud
That merry peal comes ringing loud;
And Geraldine shakes off her dread,
And rises lightly from the bed;
Puts on her silken vestments white,
And tricks her hair in lovely plight,
And nothing doubting of her spell
Awakens the lady Christabel.
"Sleep you, sweet lady Christabel?
I trust that you have rested well."

And Christabel awoke and spied
The same who lay down by her side—
O rather say, the same whom she
Raised up beneath the old oak tree!
Nay, fairer yet! and yet more fair!
For she belike hath drunken deep
Of all the blessedness of sleep!
And while she spake, her looks, her air
Such gentle thankfulness declare,
That (so it seemed) her girded vests
Grew tight beneath her heaving breasts.
"Sure I have sinned!" said Christabel,
"Now heaven be praised if all be well!"
And in low faltering tones, yet sweet,
Did she the lofty lady greet
With such perplexity of mind
As dreams too lively leave behind.

So quickly she rose, and quickly arrayed
Her maiden limbs, and having prayed
That He, who on the cross did groan,
Might wash away her sins unknown,
She forthwith led fair Geraldine
To meet her sire, Sir Leoline.

The lovely maid and the lady tall
Are pacing both into the hall,
And pacing on through page and groom,
Enter the Baron's presence-room.

The Baron rose, and while he prest
His gentle daughter to his breast,
With cheerful wonder in his eyes
The lady Geraldine espies,
And gave such welcome to the same,
As might beseem so bright a dame!

But when he heard the lady's tale,
And when she told her father's name,
Why waxed Sir Leoline so pale,
Murmuring o'er the name again,
Lord Roland de Vaux of Tryermaine?

Alas! they had been friends in youth;
But whispering tongues can poison truth;
And constancy lives in realms above;
And life is thorny; and youth is vain;
And to be wroth with one we love
Doth work like madness in the brain.
And thus it chanced, as I divine,
With Roland and Sir Leoline.
Each spake words of high disdain
And insult to his heart's best brother:
They parted—ne'er to meet again!
But never either found another
To free the hollow heart from paining—
They stood aloof, the scars remaining,
Like cliffs which had been rent asunder;
A dreary sea now flows between;—
But neither heat, nor frost, nor thunder,
Shall wholly do away, I ween,
The marks of that which once hath been.

Sir Leoline, a moment's space,
Stood gazing on the damsel's face:
And the youthful Lord of Tryermaine
Came back upon his heart again.

O then the Baron forgot his age,
His noble heart swelled high with rage;
He swore by the wounds in Jesu's side
He would proclaim it far and wide,
With trump and solemn heraldry,
That they, who thus had wronged the dame,
Were base as spotted infamy!
"And if they dare deny the same,
My herald shall appoint a week,
And let the recreant traitors seek
My tourney court—that there and then
I may dislodge their reptile souls
From the bodies and forms of men!"
He spake: his eye in lightning rolls!
For the lady was ruthlessly seized; and he kenned
In the beautiful lady the child of his friend!

And now the tears were on his face,
And fondly in his arms he took
Fair Geraldine, who met the embrace,
Prolonging it with joyous look.
Which when she viewed, a vision fell
Upon the soul of Christabel,
The vision of fear, the touch and pain!
She shrunk and shuddered, and saw again--
(Ah, woe is me! Was it for thee,
Thou gentle maid! such sights to see?)
Again she saw that bosom old,
Again she felt that bosom cold,
And drew in her breath with a hissing sound:
Whereat the Knight turned wildly round,
And nothing saw, but his own sweet maid
With eyes upraised, as one that prayed.

The touch, the sight, had passed away,
And in its stead that vision blest,
Which comforted her after-rest
While in the lady's arms she lay,
Had put a rapture in her breast,
And on her lips and o'er her eyes
Spread smiles like light!
                    With new surprise,
"What ails then my beloved child?"
The Baron said—His daughter mild
Made answer, "All will yet be well!"
I ween, she had no power to tell
Aught else: so mighty was the spell.

Yet he, who saw this Geraldine,
Had deemed her sure a thing divine:
Such sorrow with such grace she blended,
As if she feared she had offended
Sweet Christabel, that gentle maid!
And with such lowly tones she prayed
She might be sent without delay
Home to her father's mansion.
                              "Nay!
Nay, by my soul!" said Leoline.
"Ho! Bracy the bard, the charge be thine!

Go thou, with music sweet and loud,
And take two steeds with trappings proud,
And take the youth whom thou lov'st best
To bear thy harp, and learn thy song,
And clothe you both in solemn vest,
And over the mountains haste along,
Lest wandering folk, that are abroad,
Detain you on the valley road.

"And when he has crossed the Irthing flood,
My merry bard! he hastes, he hastes
Up Knorren Moor, through Halegarth Wood,
And reaches soon that castle good
Which stands and threatens Scotland's wastes.

"Bard Bracy! bard Bracy! your horses are fleet,
Ye must ride up the hall, your music so sweet,
More loud than your horses' echoing feet!
And loud and loud to Lord Roland call,
Thy daughter is safe in Langdale hall!
Thy beautiful daughter is safe and free—
Sir Leoline greets thee thus through me.
He bids thee come without delay
With all thy numerous array
And take thy lovely daughter home:
And he will meet thee on the way
With all his numerous array
White with their panting palfreys' foam:
And, by mine honour! I will say,
That I repent me of the day
When I spake words of fierce disdain
To Roland de Vaux of Tryermaine!—
—For since that evil hour hath flown,
Many a summer's sun hath shone;
Yet ne'er found I a friend again
Like Roland de Vaux of Tryermaine."

The lady fell, and clasped his knees,
Her face upraised, her eyes o'erflowing;
And Bracy replied, with faltering voice,
His gracious Hail on all bestowing!—

"Thy words, thou sire of Christabel,
Are sweeter than my harp can tell;
Yet might I gain a boon of thee,
This day my journey should not be,
So strange a dream hath come to me,
That I had vowed with music loud
To clear yon wood from thing unblest,
Warned by a vision in my rest!
For in my sleep I saw that dove,
That gentle bird, whom thou dost love,
And call'st by thy own daughter's name—
Sir Leoline! I saw the same
Fluttering, and uttering fearful moan,
Among the green herbs in the forest alone.
Which when I saw and when I heard,
I wondered what might ail the bird;
For nothing near it could I see,
Save the grass and green herbs underneath the
    old tree.

"And in my dream methought I went
To search out what might there be found;
And what the sweet bird's trouble meant,
That thus lay fluttering on the ground.
I went and peered, and could descry
No cause for her distressful cry;
But yet for her dear lady's sake
I stooped, methought, the dove to take,
When lo! I saw a bright green snake
Coiled around its wings and neck.
Green as the herbs on which it couched,
Close by the dove's its head it crouched;
And with the dove it heaves and stirs,
Swelling its neck as she swelled hers!
I woke; it was the midnight hour,
The clock was echoing in the tower;
But though my slumber was gone by,
This dream it would not pass away—
It seems to live upon my eye!
And thence I vowed this self-same day
With music strong and saintly song

To wander through the forest bare,
Lest aught unholy loiter there."

Thus Bracy said: the Baron, the while,
Half-listening heard him with a smile;
Then turned to Lady Geraldine,
His eyes made up of wonder and love;
And said in courtly accents fine,
"Sweet maid, Lord Roland's beauteous dove,
With arms more strong than harp or song,
Thy sire and I will crush the snake!"
He kissed her forehead as he spake,
And Geraldine in maiden wise
Casting down her large bright eyes,
With blushing cheek and courtesy fine
She turned her from Sir Leoline;
Softly gathering up her train,
That o'er her right arm fell again;
And folded her arms across her chest,
And couched her head upon her breast,
And looked askance at Christabel——
Jesu, Maria, shield her well!

A snake's small eye blinks dull and shy;
And the lady's eyes they shrunk in her head,
Each shrunk up to a serpent's eye,
And with somewhat of malice, and more of dread,
At Christabel she looked askance!—
One moment—and the sight was fled!
But Christabel in dizzy trance
Stumbling on the unsteady ground
Shuddered aloud, with a hissing sound;
And Geraldine again turned round,
And like a thing, that sought relief,
Full of wonder and full of grief,
She rolled her large bright eyes divine
Wildly on Sir Leoline.

The maid, alas! her thoughts are gone,
She nothing sees—no sight but one!
The maid, devoid of guile and sin,
I know not how, in fearful wise,

So deeply had she drunken in
That look, those shrunken serpent eyes,
That all her features were resigned
To this sole image in her mind:
And passively did imitate
That look of dull and treacherous hate!
And thus she stood, in dizzy trance,
Still picturing that look askance
With forced unconscious sympathy
Full before her father's view——
As far as such a look could be
In eyes so innocent and blue!

And when the trance was o'er, the maid
Paused awhile, and inly prayed:
Then falling at the Baron's feet,
"By my mother's soul do I entreat
That thou this woman send away!"
She said: and more she could not say:
For what she knew she could not tell,
O'er-mastered by the mighty spell.

Why is thy cheek so wan and wild,
Sir Leoline? Thy only child
Lies at thy feet, thy joy, thy pride,
So fair, so innocent, so mild;
The same, for whom thy lady died!
O by the pangs of her dear mother
Think thou no evil of thy child!
For her, and thee, and for no other,
She prayed the moment ere she died:
Prayed that the babe for whom she died,
Might prove her dear lord's joy and pride!
 That prayer her deadly pangs beguiled,
  Sir Leoline!
 And wouldst thou wrong thy only child,
  Her child and thine?

Within the Baron's heart and brain
If thoughts, like these, had any share,
They only swelled his rage and pain,
And did but work confusion there.

His heart was cleft with pain and rage,
His cheeks they quivered, his eyes were wild,
Dishonoured thus in his old age;
Dishonoured by his only child,
And all his hospitality
To the wronged daughter of his friend
By more than woman's jealousy
Brought thus to a disgraceful end—
He rolled his eye with stern regard
Upon the gentle minstrel bard,
And said in tones abrupt, austere—
"Why, Bracy! dost thou loiter here?
I bade thee hence!" The bard obeyed;
And turning from his own sweet maid,
The aged knight, Sir Leoline,
Led forth the lady Geraldine!

1800

THE CONCLUSION TO PART II

A little child, a limber elf,
Singing, dancing to itself,
A fairy thing with red round cheeks,
That always finds, and never seeks,
Makes such a vision to the sight
As fills a father's eyes with light;
And pleasures flow in so thick and fast
Upon his heart, that he at last
Must needs express his love's excess
With words of unmeant bitterness.
Perhaps 'tis pretty to force together
Thoughts so all unlike each other;
To mutter and mock a broken charm,
To dally with wrong that does no harm.
Perhaps 'tis tender too and pretty
At each wild word to feel within
A sweet recoil of love and pity.
And what, if in a world of sin
(O sorrow and shame should this be true!)
Such giddiness of heart and brain
Comes seldom save from rage and pain,
So talks as it's most used to do.

1801

FIRE, FAMINE, AND SLAUGHTER

A WAR ECLOGUE

The Scene a desolated Tract in La Vendée. FAMINE *is discovered lying on the ground; to her enter* FIRE *and* SLAUGHTER.

  Fam. Sisters! sisters! who has sent you here?
  Slau. [*to Fire*]. I will whisper it in her ear.
  Fire. No! no! no!
Spirits hear what spirits tell:
'Twill make a holiday in Hell.
      No! no! no!
Myself, I named him once below,
And all the souls, that damned be,
Leaped up at once in anarchy,
Clapped their hands and danced for glee.
They no longer heeded me;
But laughed to hear Hell's burning rafters
Unwillingly re-echo laughters!
      No! no! no!
Spirits hear what spirits tell:
'Twill make a holiday in Hell!
  Fam. Whisper it, sister! so and so!
In a dark hint, soft and slow.
  Slau. Letters four do form his name—
And who sent you?
  Both.   The same! the same!
  Slau. He came by stealth, and unlocked my den,
And I have drunk the blood since then
Of thrice three hundred thousand men.
  Both. Who bade you do 't?
  Slau.   The same! the same!
Letters four do form his name.
He let me loose, and cried Halloo!
To him alone the praise is due.
  Fam. Thanks, sister, thanks! the men have bled,
Their wives and their children faint for bread.
I stood in a swampy field of battle;
With bones and skulls I made a rattle,

To frighten the wolf and carrion-crow
And the homeless dog—but they would not go.
So off I flew: for how could I bear
To see them gorge their dainty fare?
I heard a groan and a peevish squall,
And through the chink of a cottage-wall—
Can you guess what I saw there?

    Both. Whisper it, sister! in our ear.

    Fam. A baby beat its dying mother:
I had starved the one and was starving the other!

    Both. Who bade you do 't?

    Fam.   The same! the same!
Letters four do form his name.
He let me loose, and cried, Halloo!
To him alone the praise is due.

    Fire. Sisters! I from Ireland came!
Hedge and corn-fields all on flame,
I triumphed o'er the setting sun!
And all the while the work was done,
On as I strode with my huge strides,
I flung back my head and I held my sides,
It was so rare a piece of fun
To see the sweltered cattle run
With uncouth gallop through the night,
Scared by the red and noisy light!
By the light of his own blazing cot
Was many a naked Rebel shot:
The house-stream met the flame and hissed,
While crash! fell in the roof, I wist,
On some of those old bed-rid nurses,
That deal in discontent and curses.

    Both. Who bade you do 't?

    Fire.   The same! the same!
Letters four do form his name.
He let me loose, and cried Halloo!
To him alone the praise is due.

    All. He let us loose, and cried Halloo!
How shall we yield him honour due?

    Fam. Wisdom comes with lack of food.
I'll gnaw, I'll gnaw the multitude,
Till the cup of rage o'erbrim:

They shall seize him and his brood—
   Slau. They shall tear him limb from limb!
   Fire. O thankless beldames and untrue!
And is this all that you can do
For him, who did so much for you?
Ninety months he, by my troth!
Hath richly catered for you both;
And in an hour would you repay
An eight years' work?—Away! away!
I alone am faithful! I
Cling to him everlastingly.

1798

FROST AT MIDNIGHT

THE Frost performs its secret ministry,
  Unhelped by any wind. The owlet's cry
Came loud—and hark, again! loud as before.
The inmates of my cottage, all at rest,
Have left me to that solitude, which suits
Abstruser musings: save that at my side
My cradled infant slumbers peacefully.
'Tis calm indeed! so calm, that it disturbs
And vexes meditation with its strange
And extreme silentness. Sea, hill, and wood,
This populous village! Sea, and hill, and wood,
With all the numberless goings-on of life,
Inaudible as dreams! the thin blue flame
Lies on my low-burnt fire, and quivers not;
Only that film, which fluttered on the grate,
Still flutters there, the sole unquiet thing.
Methinks, its motion in this hush of nature
Gives it dim sympathies with me who live,
Making it a companionable form,
Whose puny flaps and freaks the idling Spirit
By its own moods interprets, every where
Echo or mirror seeking of itself,
And makes a toy of Thought.

                 But O! how oft,
How oft, at school, with most believing mind,

Presageful, have I gazed upon the bars,
To watch that fluttering *stranger!* and as oft
With unclosed lids, already had I dreamt
Of my sweet birth-place, and the old church-tower,
Whose bells, the poor man's only music, rang
From morn to evening, all the hot Fair-day,
So sweetly, that they stirred and haunted me
With a wild pleasure, falling on mine ear
Most like articulate sounds of things to come!
So gazed I, till the soothing things, I dreamt,
Lulled me to sleep, and sleep prolonged my dreams!
And so I brooded all the following morn,
Awed by the stern preceptor's face, mine eye
Fixed with mock study on my swimming book:
Save if the door half opened, and I snatched
A hasty glance, and still my heart leaped up,
For still I hoped to see the *stranger's* face,
Townsman, or aunt, or sister more beloved,
My play-mate when we both were clothed alike!

Dear Babe, that sleepest cradled by my side,
Whose gentle breathings, heard in this deep calm,
Fill up the interspersed vacancies
And momentary pauses of the thought!
My babe so beautiful! it thrills my heart
With tender gladness, thus to look at thee,
And think that thou shalt learn far other lore,
And in far other scenes! For I was reared
In the great city, pent 'mid cloisters dim,
And saw nought lovely but the sky and stars.
But *thou*, my babe! shalt wander like a breeze
By lakes and sandy shores, beneath the crags
Of ancient mountain, and beneath the clouds,
Which image in their bulk both lakes and shores
And mountain crags: so shalt thou see and hear
The lovely shapes and sounds intelligible
Of that eternal language, which thy God
Utters, who from eternity doth teach
Himself in all, and all things in himself.
Great universal Teacher! he shall mould
Thy spirit, and by giving make it ask.

Therefore all seasons shall be sweet to thee,
Whether the summer clothe the general earth
With greenness, or the redbreast sit and sing
Betwixt the tufts of snow on the bare branch
Of mossy apple-tree, while the nigh thatch
Smokes in the sun-thaw; whether the eave-drops fall
Heard only in the trances of the blast,
Or if the secret ministry of frost
Shall hang them up in silent icicles,
Quietly shining to the quiet Moon.

February, 1798

LEWTI

OR THE CIRCASSIAN LOVE-CHAUNT

AT midnight by the stream I roved,
  To forget the form I loved.
Image of Lewti! from my mind
Depart; for Lewti is not kind.
The Moon was high, the moonlight gleam
  And the shadow of a star
Heaved upon Tamaha's stream;
  But the rock shone brighter far,
The rock half sheltered from my view
By pendent boughs of tressy yew.—
So shines my Lewti's forehead fair,
Gleaming through her sable hair.
Image of Lewti! from my mind
Depart; for Lewti is not kind.

I saw a cloud of palest hue,
  Onward to the moon it passed;
Still brighter and more bright it grew,
With floating colours not a few,
  Till it reached the moon at last:
Then the cloud was wholly bright,
With a rich and amber light!
And so with many a hope I seek,
  And with such joy I find my Lewti;
And even so my pale wan cheek

Drinks in as deep a flush of beauty!
Nay, treacherous image! leave my mind,
If Lewti never will be kind.

The little cloud—it floats away,
    Away it goes; away so soon!
Alas! it has no power to stay:
Its hues are dim, its hues are grey—
    Away it passes from the moon!
How mournfully it seems to fly,
    Ever fading more and more,
To joyless regions of the sky—
    And now 'tis whiter than before!
As white as my poor cheek will be,
    When, Lewti! on my couch I lie,
A dying man for love of thee.
Nay, treacherous image! leave my mind—
And yet, thou didst not look unkind.

I saw a vapour in the sky,
Thin, and white, and very high;
I ne'er beheld so thin a cloud:
    Perhaps the breezes that can fly
    Now below and now above,
Have snatched aloft the lawny shroud
    Of Lady fair—that died for love.
For maids, as well as youths, have perished
From fruitless love too fondly cherished.
Nay, treacherous image! leave my mind—
For Lewti never will be kind.

Hush! my heedless feet from under
    Slip the crumbling banks for ever:
Like echoes to a distant thunder,
    They plunge into the gentle river.
The river-swans have heard my tread,
And startle from their reedy bed.
O beauteous birds! methinks ye measure
    Your movements to some heavenly tune!
O beauteous birds! 'tis such a pleasure
    To see you move beneath the moon,
I would it were your true delight

To sleep by day and wake all night.
I know the place where Lewti lies
When silent night has closed her eyes:
  It is a breezy jasmine-bower,
The nightingale sings o'er her head:
  Voice of the Night! had I the power
That leafy labyrinth to thread,
And creep, like thee, with soundless tread,
I then might view her bosom white
Heaving lovely to my sight,
As these two swans together heave
On the gently-swelling wave.

Oh! that she saw me in a dream,
  And dreamt that I had died for care;
All pale and wasted I would seem,
  Yet fair withal, as spirits are!
I'd die indeed, if I might see
Her bosom heave, and heave for me!
Soothe, gentle image! soothe my mind!
To-morrow Lewti may be kind.

1798

FEARS IN SOLITUDE

WRITTEN IN APRIL 1798, DURING THE ALARM OF AN INVASION

A GREEN and silent spot, amid the hills,
  A small and silent dell! O'er stiller place
No singing sky-lark ever poised himself.
The hills are heathy, save that swelling slope,
Which hath a gay and gorgeous covering on,
All golden with the never-bloomless furze,
Which now blooms most profusely: but the dell,
Bathed by the mist, is fresh and delicate
As vernal corn-field, or the unripe flax,
When, through its half-transparent stalks, at eve,
The level sunshine glimmers with green light.
Oh! 'tis a quiet spirit-healing nook!
Which all, methinks, would love; but chiefly he,

The humble man, who, in his youthful years,
Knew just so much of folly, as had made
His early manhood more securely wise!
Here he might lie on fern or withered heath,
While from the singing lark (that sings unseen
The minstrelsy that solitude loves best),
And from the sun, and from the breezy air,
Sweet influences trembled o'er his frame;
And he, with many feelings, many thoughts,
Made up a meditative joy, and found
Religious meanings in the forms of Nature!
And so, his senses gradually wrapt
In a half sleep, he dreams of better worlds,
And dreaming hears thee still, O singing lark,
That singest like an angel in the clouds!

My God! it is a melancholy thing
For such a man, who would full fain preserve
His soul in calmness, yet perforce must feel
For all his human brethren—O my God!
It weighs upon the heart, that he must think
What uproar and what strife may now be stirring
This way or that way o'er these silent hills—
Invasion, and the thunder and the shout,
And all the crash of onset; fear and rage,
And undetermined conflict—even now,
Even now, perchance, and in his native isle:
Carnage and groans beneath this blessed sun!
We have offended, Oh! my countrymen!
We have offended very grievously,
And been most tyrannous. From east to west
A groan of accusation pierces Heaven!
The wretched plead against us; multitudes
Countless and vehement, the sons of God,
Our brethren! Like a cloud that travels on,
Steamed up from Cairo's swamps of pestilence,
Even so, my countrymen! have we gone forth
And borne to distant tribes slavery and pangs,
And, deadlier far, our vices, whose deep taint
With slow perdition murders the whole man,
His body and his soul! Meanwhile, at home,

All individual dignity and power
Engulfed in Courts, Committees, Institutions,
Associations and Societies,
A vain, speech-mouthing, speech-reporting Guild,
One Benefit-Club for mutual flattery,
We have drunk up, demure as at a grace,
Pollutions from the brimming cup of wealth;
Contemptuous of all honourable rule,
Yet bartering freedom and the poor man's life
For gold, as at a market! The sweet words
Of Christian promise, words that even yet
Might stem destruction, were they wisely preached,
Are muttered o'er by men, whose tones proclaim
How flat and wearisome they feel their trade:
Rank scoffers some, but most too indolent
To deem them falsehoods or to know their truth.
Oh! blasphemous! the Book of Life is made
A superstitious instrument, on which
We gabble o'er the oaths we mean to break;
For all must swear—all and in every place,
College and wharf, council and justice-court;
All, all must swear, the briber and the bribed,
Merchant and lawyer, senator and priest,
The rich, the poor, the old man and the young;
All, all make up one scheme of perjury,
That faith doth reel; the very name of God
Sounds like a juggler's charm; and, bold with joy,
Forth from his dark and lonely hiding-place,
(Portentous sight!) the owlet Atheism,
Sailing on obscene wings athwart the noon,
Drops his blue-fringed lids, and holds them close,
And hooting at the glorious sun in Heaven,
Cries out, "Where is it?"

                Thankless too for peace,
(Peace long preserved by fleets and perilous seas)
Secure from actual warfare, we have loved
To swell the war-whoop, passionate for war!
Alas! for ages ignorant of all
Its ghastlier workings, (famine or blue plague,
Battle, or siege, or flight through wintry snows,)

We, this whole people, have been clamorous
For war and bloodshed; animating sports,
The which we pay for as a thing to talk of,
Spectators and not combatants! No guess
Anticipative of a wrong unfelt,
No speculation on contingency,
However dim and vague, too vague and dim
To yield a justifying cause; and forth,
(Stuffed out with big preamble, holy names,
And adjurations of the God in Heaven,)
We send our mandates for the certain death
Of thousands and ten thousands! Boys and girls,
And women, that would groan to see a child
Pull off an insect's leg, all read of war,
The best amusement for our morning meal!
The poor wretch, who has learnt his only prayers
From curses, who knows scarcely words enough
To ask a blessing from his Heavenly Father,
Becomes a fluent phraseman, absolute
And technical in victories and defeats,
And all our dainty terms for fratricide;
Terms which we trundle smoothly o'er our tongues
Like mere abstractions, empty sounds to which
We join no feeling and attach no form!
As if the soldier died without a wound;
As if the fibres of this godlike frame
Were gored without a pang; as if the wretch,
Who fell in battle, doing bloody deeds,
Passed off to Heaven, translated and not killed;
As though he had no wife to pine for him,
No God to judge him! Therefore, evil days
Are coming on us, O my countrymen!
And what if all-avenging Providence,
Strong and retributive, should make us know
The meaning of our words, force us to feel
The desolation and the agony
Of our fierce doings?

                    Spare us yet awhile,
Father and God! O! spare us yet awhile!
Oh! let not English women drag their flight

Fainting beneath the burthen of their babes,
Of the sweet infants, that but yesterday
Laughed at the breast! Sons, brothers, husbands, all
Who ever gazed with fondness on the forms
Which grew up with you round the same fire-side,
And all who ever heard the sabbath-bells
Without the infidel's scorn, make yourselves pure!
Stand forth! be men! repel an impious foe,
Impious and false, a light yet cruel race,
Who laugh away all virtue, mingling mirth
With deeds of murder; and still promising
Freedom, themselves too sensual to be free,
Poison life's amities, and cheat the heart
Of faith and quiet hope, and all that soothes,
And all that lifts the spirit! Stand we forth;
Render them back upon the insulted ocean,
And let them toss as idly on its waves
As the vile sea-weed, which some mountain-blast
Swept from our shores! And oh! may we return
Not with a drunken triumph, but with fear,
Repenting of the wrongs with which we stung
So fierce a foe to frenzy!

                        I have told,
O Britons! O my brethren! I have told
Most bitter truth, but without bitterness.
Nor deem my zeal or factious or mistimed;
For never can true courage dwell with them,
Who, playing tricks with conscience, dare not look
At their own vices. We have been too long
Dupes of a deep delusion! Some, belike,
Groaning with restless enmity, expect
All change from change of constituted power;
As if a Government had been a robe,
On which our vice and wretchedness were tagged
Like fancy-points and fringes, with the robe
Pulled off at pleasure. Fondly these attach
A radical causation to a few
Poor drudges of chastising Providence,
Who borrow all their hues and qualities
From our own folly and rank wickedness,

Which gave them birth and nursed them. Others,
    meanwhile,
Dote with a mad idolatry; and all
Who will not fall before their images,
And yield them worship, they are enemies
Even of their country!

           Such have I been deemed.—
But, O dear Britain! O my Mother Isle!
Needs must thou prove a name most dear and holy
To me, a son, a brother, and a friend,
A husband, and a father! who revere
All bonds of natural love, and find them all
Within the limits of thy rocky shores.
O native Britain! O my Mother Isle!
How shouldst thou prove aught else but dear and holy
To me, who from thy lakes and mountain-hills,
Thy clouds, thy quiet dales, thy rocks and seas,
Have drunk in all my intellectual life,
All sweet sensations, all ennobling thoughts,
All adoration of the God in nature,
All lovely and all honourable things,
Whatever makes this mortal spirit feel
The joy and greatness of its future being?
There lives nor form nor feeling in my soul
Unborrowed from my country! O divine
And beauteous island! thou hast been my sole
And most magnificent temple, in the which
I walk with awe, and sing my stately songs,
Loving the God that made me!—

           May my fears,
My filial fears, be vain! and may the vaunts
And menace of the vengeful enemy
Pass like the gust, that roared and died away
In the distant tree: which heard, and only heard
In this low dell, bowed not the delicate grass.

  But now the gentle dew-fall sends abroad
The fruit-like perfume of the golden furze:
The light has left the summit of the hill,

Though still a sunny gleam lies beautiful,
Aslant the ivied beacon. Now farewell,
Farewell, awhile, O soft and silent spot!
On the green sheep-track, up the heathy hill,
Homeward I wind my way; and lo! recalled
From bodings that have well-nigh wearied me,
I find myself upon the brow, and pause
Startled! And after lonely sojourning
In such a quiet and surrounded nook,
This burst of prospect, here the shadowy main,
Dim-tinted, there the mighty majesty
Of that huge amphitheatre of rich
And elmy fields, seems like society—
Conversing with the mind, and giving it
A livelier impulse and a dance of thought!
And now, beloved Stowey! I behold
Thy church-tower, and, methinks, the four huge elms
Clustering, which mark the mansion of my friend;
And close behind them, hidden from my view,
Is my own lowly cottage, where my babe
And my babe's mother dwell in peace! With light
And quickened footsteps thitherward I tend,
Remembering thee, O green and silent dell!
And grateful, that by nature's quietness
And solitary musings, all my heart
Is softened, and made worthy to indulge
Love, and the thoughts that yearn for human kind.

NETHER STOWEY, 20 *April*, 1798

THE NIGHTINGALE

A CONVERSATION POEM. APRIL, 1798

NO cloud, no relique of the sunken day
  Distinguishes the West, no long thin slip
Of sullen light, no obscure trembling hues.
Come, we will rest on this old mossy bridge!
You see the glimmer of the stream beneath,
But hear no murmuring: it flows silently,
O'er its soft bed of verdure. All is still,
A balmy night! and though the stars be dim,

Yet let us think upon the vernal showers
That gladden the green earth, and we shall find
A pleasure in the dimness of the stars.
And hark! the Nightingale begins its song,
"Most musical, most melancholy" bird!*
A melancholy bird? Oh! idle thought!
In Nature there is nothing melancholy.
But some night-wandering man whose heart was pierced
With the remembrance of a grievous wrong,
Or slow distemper, or neglected love,
(And so, poor wretch! filled all things with himself,
And made all gentle sounds tell back the tale
Of his own sorrow) he, and such as he,
First named these notes a melancholy strain.
And many a poet echoes the conceit;
Poet who hath been building up the rhyme
When he had better far have stretched his limbs
Beside a brook in mossy forest-dell,
By sun or moon-light, to the influxes
Of shapes and sounds and shifting elements
Surrendering his whole spirit, of his song
And of his fame forgetful! so his fame
Should share in Nature's immortality,
A venerable thing! and so his song
Should make all Nature lovelier, and itself
Be loved like Nature! But 'twill not be so;
And youths and maidens most poetical,
Who lose the deepening twilights of the spring
In ball-rooms and hot theatres, they still
Full of meek sympathy must heave their sighs
O'er Philomela's pity-pleading strains.

My Friend, and thou, our Sister! we have learnt
A different lore: we may not thus profane

---

*"*Most musical, most melancholy.*" This passage in Milton possesses
an excellence far superior to that of mere description; it is spoken
in the character of the melancholy Man, and has therefore a
dramatic propriety. The Author makes this remark, to rescue
himself from the charge of having alluded with levity to a line
in Milton; a charge than which none could be more painful to
him, except perhaps that of having ridiculed his Bible.

Nature's sweet voices, always full of love
And joyance! 'Tis the merry Nightingale
That crowds, and hurries, and precipitates
With fast thick warble his delicious notes,
As he were fearful that an April night
Would be too short for him to utter forth
His love-chant, and disburthen his full soul
Of all its music!

    And I know a grove
Of large extent, hard by a castle huge,
Which the great lord inhabits not; and so
This grove is wild with tangling underwood,
And the trim walks are broken up, and grass,
Thin grass and king-cups grow within the paths.
But never elsewhere in one place I knew
So many nightingales; and far and near,
In wood and thicket, over the wide grove,
They answer and provoke each other's song,
With skirmish and capricious passagings,
And murmurs musical and swift jug jug,
And one low piping sound more sweet than all—
Stirring the air with such a harmony,
That should you close your eyes, you might almost
Forget it was not day! On moon-lit bushes,
Whose dewy leaflets are but half disclosed,
You may perchance behold them on the twigs,
Their bright, bright eyes, their eyes both bright and full,
Glistening, while many a glow-worm in the shade
Lights up her love-torch.

    A most gentle Maid,
Who dwelleth in her hospitable home
Hard by the castle, and at latest eve
(Even like a Lady vowed and dedicate
To something more than Nature in the grove)
Glides through the pathways; she knows all their notes,
That gentle Maid! and oft, a moment's space,
What time the moon was lost behind a cloud,
Hath heard a pause of silence; till the moon
Emerging, hath awakened earth and sky

With one sensation, and those wakeful birds
Have all burst forth in choral minstrelsy,
As if some sudden gale had swept at once
A hundred airy harps! And she hath watched
Many a nightingale perch giddily
On blossomy twig still swinging from the breeze,
And to that motion tune his wanton song
Like tipsy Joy that reels with tossing head.

Farewell, O Warbler! till to-morrow eve,
And you, my friends! farewell, a short farewell!
We have been loitering long and pleasantly,
And now for our dear homes.—That strain again!
Full fain it would delay me! My dear babe,
Who, capable of no articulate sound,
Mars all things with his imitative lisp,
How he would place his hand beside his ear,
His little hand, the small forefinger up,
And bid us listen! And I deem it wise
To make him Nature's play-mate. He knows well
The evening-star; and once, when he awoke
In most distressful mood (some inward pain
Had made up that strange thing, an infant's dream—)
I hurried with him to our orchard-plot,
And he beheld the moon, and, hushed at once,
Suspends his sobs, and laughs most silently,
While his fair eyes, that swam with undropped tears,
Did glitter in the yellow moon-beam! Well!—
It is a father's tale: But if that Heaven
Should give me life, his childhood shall grow up
Familiar with these songs, that with the night
He may associate joy.—Once more, farewell,
Sweet Nightingale! once more, my friends! farewell.

1798

TO ——

I MIX in life, and labour to seem free,
   With common persons pleased and common things,
While every thought and action tends to thee,
   And every impulse from thy influence springs.

?1798

KUBLA KHAN:

OR, A VISION IN A DREAM

A FRAGMENT

THE following fragment is here published at the request of a poet of great and deserved celebrity [Lord Byron], and, as far as the Author's own opinions are concerned, rather as a psychological curiosity, than on the ground of any supposed *poetic* merits.

In the summer of the year 1797, the Author, then in ill health, had retired to a lonely farm-house between Porlock and Linton, on the Exmoor confines of Somerset and Devonshire. In consequence of a slight indisposition, an anodyne had been prescribed, from the effects of which he fell asleep in his chair at the moment that he was reading the following sentence, or words of the same substance, in "Purchas's Pilgrimage": "Here the Khan Kubla commanded a palace to be built, and a stately garden thereunto. And thus ten miles of fertile ground were inclosed with a wall." The Author continued for about three hours in a profound sleep, at least of the external senses, during which time he has the most vivid confidence, that he could not have composed less than from two to three hundred lines; if that indeed can be called composition in which all the images rose up before him as *things*, with a parallel production of the correspondent expressions, without any sensation or consciousness of effort. On awaking he appeared to himself to have a distinct recollection of the whole, and taking his pen, ink, and paper, instantly and eagerly wrote down the lines that are here preserved. At this moment he was unfortunately called out by a person on business from Porlock, and detained by him above an hour, and on his return to his room, found, to his no small surprise and mortification, that though he still retained some vague and dim recollection of the general purport of the vision, yet, with the exception of some eight or ten scattered lines and images, all the rest had passed away like the images on the surface of a stream into which a stone has been cast, but, alas! without the after restoration of the latter!

> Then all the charm
> Is broken—all that phantom-world so fair
> Vanishes, and a thousand circlets spread,
> And each mis-shapes the other. Stay awhile,
> Poor youth! who scarcely dar'st lift up thine eyes—
> The stream will soon renew its smoothness, soon
> The visions will return! And lo, he stays,
> And soon the fragments dim of lovely forms
> Come trembling back, unite, and now once more
> The pool becomes a mirror.

[From *The Picture; or, the Lover's Resolution*, ll. 91-100]

Yet from the still surviving recollections in his mind, the Author has frequently purposed to finish for himself what had been originally, as it were, given to him. Αὔριον ἄδιον ἄσω: but the to-morrow is yet to come.

As a contrast to this vision, I have annexed a fragment of a very different character ["The Pains of Sleep"], describing with equal fidelity the dream of pain and disease.

> IN Xanadu did Kubla Khan
>   A stately pleasure-dome decree:
> Where Alph, the sacred river, ran
> Through caverns measureless to man
>   Down to a sunless sea.
> So twice five miles of fertile ground
> With walls and towers were girdled round:
> And there were gardens bright with sinuous rills,
> Where blossomed many an incense-bearing tree;
> And here were forests ancient as the hills,
> Enfolding sunny spots of greenery.
>
> But oh! that deep romantic chasm which slanted
> Down the green hill athwart a cedarn cover!
> A savage place! as holy and enchanted
> As e'er beneath a waning moon was haunted

By woman wailing for her demon-lover!
And from this chasm, with ceaseless turmoil seething,
As if this earth in fast thick pants were breathing,
A mighty fountain momently was forced:
Amid whose swift half-intermitted burst
Huge fragments vaulted like rebounding hail,
Or chaffy grain beneath the thresher's flail:
And 'mid these dancing rocks at once and ever
It flung up momently the sacred river.
Five miles meandering with a mazy motion
Through wood and dale the sacred river ran,
Then reached the caverns measureless to man,
And sank in tumult to a lifeless ocean:
And 'mid this tumult Kubla heard from far
Ancestral voices prophesying war!

   The shadow of the dome of pleasure
   Floated midway on the waves;
   Where was heard the mingled measure
   From the fountain and the caves.
It was a miracle of rare device,
A sunny pleasure-dome with caves of ice!

   A damsel with a dulcimer
   In a vision once I saw:
   It was an Abyssinian maid,
   And on her dulcimer she played,
   Singing of Mount Abora.
   Could I revive within me
   Her symphony and song,
   To such a deep delight 'twould win me,
That with music loud and long,
I would build that dome in air,
That sunny dome! those caves of ice!
And all who heard should see them there,
And all should cry, Beware! Beware!
His flashing eyes, his floating hair!
Weave a circle round him thrice,
And close your eyes with holy dread,
For he on honey-dew hath fed,
And drunk the milk of Paradise.

1798

THE HOMERIC HEXAMETER

DESCRIBED AND EXEMPLIFIED

STRONGLY it bears us along in swelling and limitless
    billows,
Nothing before and nothing behind but the sky and the
    ocean.

?1799

THE OVIDIAN ELEGIAC METRE

DESCRIBED AND EXEMPLIFIED

IN the hexameter rises the fountain's silvery column;
  In the pentameter aye falling in melody back.

1799

LINES

WRITTEN IN THE ALBUM AT ELBINGERODE, IN THE HARTZ FOREST

I STOOD on Brocken's sovran height, and saw
  Woods crowding upon woods, hills over hills,
A surging scene, and only limited
By the blue distance. Heavily my way
Downward I dragged through fir groves evermore,
Where bright green moss heaves in sepulchral forms
Speckled with sunshine; and, but seldom heard,
The sweet bird's song became a hollow sound;
And the breeze, murmuring indivisibly,
Preserved its solemn murmur most distinct
From many a note of many a waterfall,
And the brook's chatter; 'mid whose islet-stones
The dingy kidling with its tinkling bell
Leaped frolicsome, or old romantic goat
Sat, his white beard slow waving. I moved on
In low and languid mood: for I had found
That outward forms, the loftiest, still receive

Their finer influence from the Life within;—
Fair cyphers else: fair, but of import vague
Or unconcerning, where the heart not finds
History or prophecy of friend, or child,
Or gentle maid, our first and early love,
Or father, or the venerable name
Of our adored country! O thou Queen,
Thou delegated Deity of Earth,
O dear, dear England! how my longing eye
Turned westward, shaping in the steady clouds
Thy sands and high white cliffs!

           My native Land!
Filled with the thought of thee this heart was proud,
Yea, mine eye swam with tears: that all the view
From sovran Brocken, woods and woody hills,
Floated away, like a departing dream,
Feeble and dim! Stranger, these impulses
Blame thou not lightly; nor will I profane,
With hasty judgment or injurious doubt,
That man's sublimer spirit, who can feel
That God is everywhere! the God who framed
Mankind to be one mighty family,
Himself our Father, and the World our Home.

                    17 *May*, 1799

THE DEVIL'S THOUGHTS

I

FROM his brimstone bed at break of day
  A walking the Devil is gone,
To visit his snug little farm the earth,
And see how his stock goes on.

II

Over the hill and over the dale,
  And he went over the plain,
And backward and forward he switched his long tail
As a gentleman switches his cane.

III

And how then was the Devil drest?
Oh! he was in his Sunday's best:
His jacket was red and his breeches were blue,
And there was a hole where the tail came through.

IV

He saw a Lawyer killing a Viper
On a dunghill hard by his own stable;
And the Devil smiled, for it put him in mind
Of Cain and his brother, Abel.

V

He saw an Apothecary on a white horse
    Ride by on his vocations,
And the Devil thought of his old Friend
    Death in the Revelations.

VI

He saw a cottage with a double coach-house,
    A cottage of gentility;
And the Devil did grin, for his darling sin
    Is pride that apes humility.

VII

He peeped into a rich bookseller's shop,
    Quoth he! we are both of one college!
For I sate myself, like a cormorant, once
    Hard by the tree of knowledge.*

---

*And all amid them stood the TREE OF LIFE
High, eminent, blooming ambrosial fruit
Of vegetable gold (query *paper-money*), and next to **Life**
Our Death, the TREE OF KNOWLEDGE, grew fast by.—

    *   *   *   *   *
    *   *   *   *

So clomb this first grand thief—
Thence up he flew, and on the tree of life
Sat like a cormorant.

Par. Lost, IV

The allegory here is so apt, that in a catalogue of *various readings* obtained from collating the MSS. one might expect to find it

VIII

Down the river did glide, with wind and tide,
  A pig with vast celerity;
And the Devil looked wise as he saw how the while,
It cut its own throat. "There!" quoth he with a smile,
  "Goes 'England's commercial prosperity.'"

IX

As he went through Cold-Bath Fields he saw
  A solitary cell;
And the Devil was pleased, for it gave him a hint
  For improving his prisons in Hell.

X

He saw a Turnkey in a trice
  Fetter a troublesome blade;
"Nimbly," quoth he, "do the fingers move
  If a man be but used to his trade."

XI

He saw the same Turnkey unfetter a man,
  With but little expedition,
Which put him in mind of the long debate
  On the Slave-trade abolition.

---

noted, that for "LIFE" *Cod. quid. habent*, "TRADE." Though indeed THE TRADE, *i.e.* the bibliopolic, so called κατ' ἐξοχήν, may be regarded as LIFE *sensu eminentiori;* a suggestion, which I owe to a young retailer in the hosiery line, who on hearing a description of the net profits, dinner parties, country houses, etc., of the trade, exclaimed, "Ay! that's what I call LIFE now!"—This "Life, *our* Death," is thus happily contrasted with the fruits of Authorship.—*Sic nos non nobis mellificamus Apes.*

Of this poem, which with the "Fire, Famine, and Slaughter" first appeared in the "Morning Post," the 1st, 2nd, 3rd, 9th, and 16th stanzas were dictated by Mr. Southey. See Apologetic Preface.

If any one should ask who General —— meant, the Author begs leave to inform him, that he did once see a red-faced person in a dream whom by the dress he took for a General; but he might have been mistaken, and most certainly he did not hear any names mentioned. In simple verity, the author never meant any one, or indeed any thing but to put a concluding stanza to his doggerel.

XII

He saw an old acquaintance
　　As he passed by a Methodist meeting;—
She holds a consecrated key,
　　And the devil nods her a greeting.

XIII

She turned up her nose, and said,
　　"Avaunt! my name's Religion,"
And she looked to Mr. ———
　　And leered like a love-sick pigeon.

XIV

He saw a certain minister
　　(A minister to his mind)
Go up into a certain House,
　　With a majority behind.

XV

The Devil quoted Genesis
　　Like a very learned clerk,
How "Noah and his creeping things
　　Went up into the Ark."

XVI

He took from the poor,
　　And he gave to the rich,
And he shook hands with a Scotchman,
　　For he was not afraid of the ——

XVII

General ——————— burning face
　　He saw with consternation,
And back to hell his way did he take,
For the Devil thought by a slight mistake
　　It was general conflagration.

1799

LOVE

ALL thoughts, all passions, all delights,
   Whatever stirs this mortal frame,
All are but ministers of Love,
   And feed his sacred flame.

Oft in my waking dreams do I
Live o'er again that happy hour,
When midway on the mount I lay,
   Beside the ruined tower.

The moonshine, stealing o'er the scene
Had blended with the lights of eve;
And she was there, my hope, my joy,
   My own dear Genevieve!

She leaned against the armed man,
The statue of the armed knight;
She stood and listened to my lay,
   Amid the lingering light.

Few sorrows hath she of her own,
My hope! my joy! my Genevieve!
She loves me best, whene'er I sing
   The songs that make her grieve.

I played a soft and doleful air,
I sang an old and moving story—
An old rude song, that suited well
   That ruin wild and hoary.

She listened with a flitting blush,
With downcast eyes and modest grace;
For well she knew, I could not choose
   But gaze upon her face.

I told her of the Knight that wore
Upon his shield a burning brand;
And that for ten long years he wooed
   The Lady of the Land.

I told her how he pined: and ah!
The deep, the low, the pleading tone
With which I sang another's love,
     Interpreted my own.

She listened with a flitting blush,
With downcast eyes, and modest grace;
And she forgave me, that I gazed
     Too fondly on her face!

But when I told the cruel scorn
That crazed that bold and lovely Knight,
And that he crossed the mountain-woods,
     Nor rested day nor night;

That sometimes from the savage den,
And sometimes from the darksome shade,
And sometimes starting up at once
     In green and sunny glade,—

There came and looked him in the face
An angel beautiful and bright;
And that he knew it was a Fiend,
     This miserable Knight!

And that unknowing what he did,
He leaped amid a murderous band,
And saved from outrage worse than death
     The Lady of the Land!

And how she wept, and clasped his knees;
And how she tended him in vain—
And ever strove to expiate
     The scorn that crazed his brain;—

And that she nursed him in a cave;
And how his madness went away,
When on the yellow forest-leaves
     A dying man he lay;—

His dying words—but when I reached
That tenderest strain of all the ditty,
My faultering voice and pausing harp
    Disturbed her soul with pity!

All impulses of soul and sense
Had thrilled my guileless Genevieve;
The music and the doleful tale,
    The rich and balmy eve;

And hopes, and fears that kindle hope,
An undistinguishable throng,
And gentle wishes long subdued,
    Subdued and cherished long!

She wept with pity and delight,
She blushed with love, and virgin-shame;
And like the murmur of a dream,
    I heard her breathe my name.

Her bosom heaved—she stepped aside,
As conscious of my look she stepped—
Then suddenly, with timorous eye
    She fled to me and wept.

She half enclosed me with her arms,
She pressed me with a meek embrace;
And bending back her head, looked up,
    And gazed upon my face.

'Twas partly love, and partly fear,
And partly 'twas a bashful art,
That I might rather feel, than see,
    The swelling of her heart.

I calmed her fears, and she was calm,
And told her love with virgin pride;
And so I won my Genevieve,
    My bright and beauteous Bride.

1799

APOLOGIA PRO VITA SUA

THE poet in his lone yet genial hour
  Gives to his eyes a magnifying power:
Or rather he emancipates his eyes
From the black shapeless accidents of size—
In unctuous cones of kindling coal,
Or smoke upwreathing from the pipe's trim bole,
    His gifted ken can see
    Phantoms of sublimity.

                                              1800

ODE TO TRANQUILLITY

TRANQUILLITY! thou better name
  Than all the family of Fame!
Thou ne'er wilt leave my riper age
To low intrigue, or factious rage;
For oh! dear child of thoughtful Truth,
To thee I gave my early youth,
And left the bark, and blest the steadfast shore,
Ere yet the tempest rose and scared me with its roar.

    Who late and lingering seeks thy shrine,
    On him but seldom, Power divine,
    Thy spirit rests! Satiety
    And Sloth, poor counterfeits of thee,
    Mock the tired worldling. Idle Hope
    And dire Remembrance interlope,
To vex the feverish slumbers of the mind:
The bubble floats before, the spectre stalks behind.

    But me thy gentle hand will lead
    At morning through the accustomed mead;
    And in the sultry summer's heat
    Will build me up a mossy seat;
    And when the gust of Autumn crowds,
    And breaks the busy moonlight clouds,
Thou best the thought canst raise, the heart attune,
Light as the busy clouds, calm as the gliding moon.

The feeling heart, the searching soul,
To thee I dedicate the whole!
And while within myself I trace
The greatness of some future race,
Aloof with hermit-eye I scan
The present works of present man—
A wild and dream-like trade of blood and guile,
Too foolish for a tear, too wicked for a smile!

1801

DEJECTION: AN ODE

WRITTEN 4 APRIL, 1802

Late, late yestreen I saw the new Moon,
With the old Moon in her arms;
And I fear, I fear, my Master dear!
We shall have a deadly storm.
Ballad of Sir Patrick Spence.

I

WELL! If the Bard was weather-wise, who made
The grand old ballad of Sir Patrick Spence,
This night, so tranquil now, will not go hence
Unroused by winds, that ply a busier trade
Than those which mould yon cloud in lazy flakes,
Or the dull sobbing draft, that moans and rakes
Upon the strings of this Aeolian lute,
    Which better far were mute.
  For lo! the New-moon winter-bright!
  And overspread with phantom light,
  (With swimming phantom light o'erspread
  But rimmed and circled by a silver thread)
I see the old Moon in her lap, foretelling
  The coming-on of rain and squally blast.
And oh! that even now the gust were swelling,
  And the slant night-shower driving loud and fast!
Those sounds which oft have raised me, whilst they awed,
    And sent my soul abroad,
Might now perhaps their wonted impulse give,
Might startle this dull pain, and make it move and live!

II

A grief without a pang, void, dark, and drear,
    A stifled, drowsy, unimpassioned grief,
    Which finds no natural outlet, no relief,
        In word, or sigh, or tear—
O Lady! in this wan and heartless mood,
To other thoughts by yonder throstle wooed,
    All this long eve, so balmy and serene,
Have I been gazing on the western sky,
    And its peculiar tint of yellow green:
And still I gaze—and with how blank an eye!
And those thin clouds above, in flakes and bars,
That give away their motion to the stars;
Those stars, that glide behind them or between,
Now sparkling, now bedimmed, but always seen:
Yon crescent Moon, as fixed as if it grew
In its own cloudless, starless lake of blue,
I see them all so excellently fair,
I see, not feel, how beautiful they are!

III

    My genial spirits fail;
    And what can these avail
To lift the smothering weight from off my breast?
    It were a vain endeavour,
    Though I should gaze for ever
On that green light that lingers in the west:
I may not hope from outward forms to win
The passion and the life, whose fountains are within.

IV

O Lady! we receive but what we give
And in our life alone does Nature live:
Ours is her wedding garment, ours her shroud!
    And would we aught behold, of higher worth,
Than that inanimate cold world allowed
To the poor loveless ever-anxious crowd,
    Ah! from the soul itself must issue forth
A light, a glory, a fair luminous cloud
        Enveloping the Earth—
And from the soul itself must there be sent

A sweet and potent voice, of its own birth,
Of all sweet sounds the life and element!

V

O pure of heart! thou need'st not ask of me
What this strong music in the soul may be!
What, and wherein it doth exist,
This light, this glory, this fair luminous mist,
This beautiful and beauty-making power.
    Joy, virtuous Lady! Joy that ne'er was given,
Save to the pure, and in their purest hour,
Life, and Life's effluence, cloud at once and shower,
Joy, Lady! is the spirit and the power,
Which wedding Nature to us gives in dower
    A new Earth and new Heaven,
Undreamt of by the sensual and the proud—
Joy is the sweet voice, Joy the luminous cloud—
        We in ourselves rejoice!
And thence flows all that charms or ear or sight,
    All melodies the echoes of that voice,
All colours a suffusion from that light.

VI

There was a time when, though my path was rough,
    This joy within me dallied with distress,
And all misfortunes were but as the stuff
    Whence Fancy made me dreams of happiness:
For hope grew round me, like the twining vine,
And fruits, and foliage, not my own, seemed mine.
But now afflictions bow me down to earth:
Nor care I that they rob me of my mirth;
        But oh! each visitation
Suspends what nature gave me at my birth,
    My shaping spirit of Imagination.
For not to think of what I needs must feel,
    But to be still and patient, all I can;
And haply by abstruse research to steal
    From my own nature all the natural man—
    This was my sole resource, my only plan:
Till that which suits a part infects the whole,
And now is almost grown the habit of my soul.

VII

Hence, viper thoughts, that coil around my mind,
 Reality's dark dream!
I turn from you, and listen to the wind,
 Which long has raved unnoticed. What a scream
Of agony by torture lengthened out
That lute sent forth! Thou Wind, that rav'st without,
 Bare crag, or mountain-tairn,* or blasted tree,
Or pine-grove whither woodman never clomb,
Or lonely house, long held the witches' home,
 Methinks were fitter instruments for thee,
Mad Lutanist! who in this month of showers,
Of dark-brown gardens, and of peeping flowers,
Mak'st Devils' yule, with worse than wintry song,
The blossoms, buds, and timorous leaves among.
 Thou Actor, perfect in all tragic sounds!
Thou mighty Poet, e'en to frenzy bold!
  What tell'st thou now about?
  'Tis of the rushing of an host in rout,
 With groans of trampled men, with smarting wounds—
At once they groan with pain, and shudder with the cold!
But hush! there is a pause of deepest silence!
 And all that noise, as of a rushing crowd,
With groans, and tremulous shudderings—all is over—
 It tells another tale, with sounds less deep and loud!
  A tale of less affright,
  And tempered with delight,
As Otway's self had framed the tender lay,—
  'Tis of a little child
  Upon a lonesome wild,
Not far from home, but she hath lost her way:
And now moans low in bitter grief and fear,
And now screams loud, and hopes to make her mother
 hear.

---

*Tairn is a small lake, generally if not always applied to the lakes up in the mountains and which are the feeders of those in the valleys. This address to the Storm-wind will not appear extravagant to those who have heard it at night and in a mountainous country.

VIII

'Tis midnight, but small thoughts have I of sleep:
Full seldom may my friend such vigils keep!
Visit her, gentle Sleep! with wings of healing,
   And may this storm be but a mountain-birth,
May all the stars hang bright above her dwelling,
     Silent as though they watched the sleeping Earth!
        With light heart may she rise,
         Gay fancy, cheerful eyes,
   Joy lift her spirit, joy attune her voice;
To her may all things live, from pole to pole,
Their life the eddying of her living soul!
   O simple spirit, guided from above,
Dear Lady! friend devoutest of my choice,
Thus mayest thou ever, evermore rejoice.

1802

HYMN BEFORE SUN-RISE, IN THE VALE OF CHAMOUNI

BESIDES the Rivers, Arve and Arveiron, which have their sources in the foot of Mont Blanc, five conspicuous torrents rush down its sides; and within a few paces of the Glaciers, the Gentiana Major grows in immense numbers, with its "flowers of loveliest blue."

HAST thou a charm to stay the morning-star
   In his steep course? So long he seems to pause
On thy bald awful head, O sovran BLANC,
The Arve and Arveiron at thy base
Rave ceaselessly; but thou, most awful Form!
Risest from forth thy silent sea of pines,
How silently! Around thee and above
Deep is the air and dark, substantial, black,
An ebon mass: methinks thou piercest it,
As with a wedge! But when I look again,
It is thine own calm home, thy crystal shrine,
Thy habitation from eternity!
O dread and silent Mount! I gazed upon thee,

Till thou, still present to the bodily sense,
Didst vanish from my thought: entranced in prayer
I worshipped the Invisible alone.

Yet, like some sweet beguiling melody,
So sweet, we know not we are listening to it,
Thou, the meanwhile, wast blending with my
    Thought,
Yea, with my Life and Life's own secret joy:
Till the dilating Soul, enrapt, transfused,
Into the mighty vision passing—there
As in her natural form, swelled vast to Heaven!

Awake, my soul! not only passive praise
Thou owest! not alone these swelling tears,
Mute thanks and secret ecstasy! Awake,
Voice of sweet song! Awake, my heart, awake!
Green vales and icy cliffs, all join my Hymn.

Thou first and chief, sole sovereign of the Vale!
O struggling with the darkness all the night,
And visited all night by troops of stars,
Or when they climb the sky or when they sink:
Companion of the morning-star at dawn,
Thyself Earth's rosy star, and of the dawn
Co-herald: wake, O wake, and utter praise!
Who sank thy sunless pillars deep in Earth?
Who filled thy countenance with rosy light?
Who made thee parent of perpetual streams?

And you, ye five wild torrents fiercely glad!
Who called you forth from night and utter death,
From dark and icy caverns called you forth,
Down those precipitous, black, jagged rocks,
For ever shattered and the same for ever?
Who gave you your invulnerable life,
Your strength, your speed, your fury, and your joy,
Unceasing thunder and eternal foam?
And who commanded (and the silence came),
Here let the billows stiffen, and have rest?

Ye Ice-falls! ye that from the mountain's brow
Adown enormous ravines slope amain—
Torrents, methinks, that heard a mighty voice,
And stopped at once amid their maddest plunge!
Motionless torrents! silent cataracts!
Who made you glorious as the Gates of Heaven
Beneath the keen full moon? Who bade the sun
Clothe you with rainbows? Who, with living flowers
Of loveliest blue, spread garlands at your feet?—
GOD! let the torrents, like a shout of nations,
Answer! and let the ice-plains echo, GOD!
GOD! sing ye meadow-streams with gladsome voice!
Ye pine-groves, with your soft and soul-like sounds!
And they too have a voice, yon piles of snow,
And in their perilous fall shall thunder, GOD!

Ye living flowers that skirt the eternal frost!
Ye wild goats sporting round the eagle's nest!
Ye eagles, play-mates of the mountain-storm!
Ye lightnings, the dread arrows of the clouds!
Ye signs and wonders of the element!
Utter forth GOD, and fill the hills with praise!

Thou too, hoar Mount! with thy sky-pointing peaks,
Oft from whose feet the avalanche, unheard,
Shoots downward, glittering through the pure serene
Into the depth of clouds, that veil thy breast—
Thou too again, stupendous Mountain! thou
That as I raise my head, awhile bowed low
In adoration, upward from thy base
Slow travelling with dim eyes suffused with tears,
Solemnly seemest, like a vapoury cloud,
To rise before me—Rise, O ever rise,
Rise like a cloud of incense from the Earth!
Thou kingly Spirit throned among the hills,
Thou dread ambassador from Earth to Heaven,
Great Hierarch! tell thou the silent sky,
And tell the stars, and tell yon rising sun
Earth, with her thousand voices, praises GOD.

1802

AN ODE TO THE RAIN

COMPOSED BEFORE DAYLIGHT, ON THE MORNING APPOINTED
FOR THE DEPARTURE OF A VERY WORTHY, BUT NOT VERY
PLEASANT VISITOR, WHOM IT WAS FEARED THE RAIN
MIGHT DETAIN

I

I KNOW it is dark; and though I have lain,
Awake, as I guess, an hour or twain,
I have not once opened the lids of my eyes,
But I lie in the dark, as a blind man lies.
O Rain! that I lie listening to,
You're but a doleful sound at best:
I owe you little thanks, 'tis true,
For breaking thus my needful rest!
Yet if, as soon as it is light,
O Rain! you will but take your flight,
I'll neither rail, nor malice keep,
Though sick and sore for want of sleep.
But only now, for this one day,
Do go, dear Rain! do go away!

II

O Rain! with your dull two-fold sound,
The clash hard by, and the murmur all round!
You know, if you know aught, that we,
Both night and day, but ill agree:
For days and months, and almost years,
Have limped on through this vale of tears,
Since body of mine, and rainy weather,
Have lived on easy terms together.
Yet if, as soon as it is light,
O Rain! you will but take your flight,
Though you should come again to-morrow,
And bring with you both pain and sorrow;
Though stomach should sicken and knees should
swell—
I'll nothing speak of you but well.

But only now for this one day,
Do go, dear Rain! do go away!

III

Dear Rain! I ne'er refused to say
You're a good creature in your way;
Nay, I could write a book myself,
Would fit a parson's lower shelf,
Showing how very good you are.—
What then? sometimes it must be fair
And if sometimes, why not to-day?
Do go, dear Rain! do go away!

IV

Dear Rain! if I've been cold and shy,
Take no offence! I'll tell you why.
A dear old Friend e'en now is here,
And with him came my sister dear;
After long absence now first met,
Long months by pain and grief beset—
We three dear friends! in truth, we groan
Impatiently to be alone.
We three, you mark! and not one more!
The strong wish makes my spirit sore.
We have so much to talk about,
So many sad things to let out;
So many tears in our eye-corners,
Sitting like little Jacky Horners—
In short, as soon as it is day,
Do go, dear Rain! do go away.

V

And this I'll swear to you, dear Rain!
Whenever you shall come again,
Be you as dull as e'er you could
(And by the bye 'tis understood,
You're not so pleasant as you're good),
Yet, knowing well your worth and place,
I'll welcome you with cheerful face;
And though you stayed a week or more,

Were ten times duller than before;
Yet with kind heart, and right good will,
I'll sit and listen to you still;
Nor should you go away, dear Rain!
Uninvited to remain.
But only now, for this one day,
Do go, dear Rain! do go away.

1802

ANSWER TO A CHILD'S QUESTION

DO you ask what the birds say? The Sparrow, the Dove,
The Linnet and Thrush say, "I love and I love!"
In the winter they're silent—the wind is so strong;
What it says, I don't know, but it sings a loud song.
But green leaves, and blossoms, and sunny warm weather,
And singing, and loving—all come back together.
But the Lark is so brimful of gladness and love,
The green fields below him, the blue sky above,
That he sings, and he sings; and for ever sings he—
"I love my Love, and my Love loves me!"

1802

THE PAINS OF SLEEP

ERE on my bed my limbs I lay,
It hath not been my use to pray
With moving lips or bended knees;
But silently, by slow degrees,
My spirit I to Love compose,
In humble trust mine eye-lids close,
With reverential resignation,
No wish conceived, no thought exprest,
Only a sense of supplication;
A sense o'er all my soul imprest
That I am weak, yet not unblest,
Since in me, round me, every where
Eternal Strength and Wisdom are.

But yester-night I prayed aloud
In anguish and in agony,
Up-starting from the fiendish crowd
Of shapes and thoughts that tortured me:
A lurid light, a trampling throng,
Sense of intolerable wrong,
And whom I scorned, those only strong!
Thirst of revenge, the powerless will
Still baffled, and yet burning still!
Desire with loathing strangely mixed
On wild or hateful objects fixed.
Fantastic passions! maddening brawl!
And shame and terror over all!
Deeds to be hid which were not hid,
Which all confused I could not know
Whether I suffered, or I did:
For all seemed guilt, remorse or woe,
My own or others still the same
Life-stifling fear, soul-stifling shame.

So two nights passed: the night's dismay
Saddened and stunned the coming day.
Sleep, the wide blessing, seemed to me
Distemper's worst calamity.
The third night, when my own loud scream
Had waked me from the fiendish dream,
O'ercome with sufferings strange and wild,
I wept as I had been a child;
And having thus by tears subdued
My anguish to a milder mood,
Such punishments, I said, were due
To natures deepliest stained with sin,—
For aye entempesting anew
The unfathomable hell within,
The horror of their deeds to view,
To know and loathe, yet wish and do!
Such griefs with such men well agree,
But wherefore, wherefore fall on me?
To be beloved is all I need,
And whom I love, I love indeed.

1803

A BECK IN WINTER

OVER the broad, the shallow, rapid stream,
The Alder, a vast hollow Trunk, and ribbed—
All mossy green with mosses manifold,
And ferns still waving in the river-breeze
Sent out, like fingers, five projecting trunks—
The shortest twice 6 (?) of a tall man's strides.—
One curving upward in its middle growth
Rose straight with grove of twigs—a pollard tree:—
The rest more backward, gradual in descent—
One in the brook and one befoamed its waters:
One ran along the bank in the elk-like head
And pomp of antlers—

January, 1804

[FRAGMENT]

THE silence of a City, how awful at Midnight!
Mute as the battlements and crags and towers
That Fancy makes in the clouds, yea, as mute
As the moonlight that sleeps on the steady vanes.

(or)

The cell of a departed anchoret,
His skeleton and flitting ghost are there,
Sole tenants—
And all the City silent as the Moon
That steeps in quiet light the steady vanes
Of her huge temples.

1804-5

[FRAGMENT]

WHOM should I choose for my Judge? the earnest,
impersonal reader,
Who, in the work, forgets me and the world and himself!
You who have eyes to detect, and Gall to Chastise the
imperfect,
Have you the heart, too, that loves,—feels and rewards the
Compleat?

1805

WHAT IS LIFE?

RESEMBLES life what once was deemed of light,
Too ample in itself for human sight?
An absolute self—an element ungrounded—
All that we see, all colours of all shade
    By encroach of darkness made?—
Is very life by consciousness unbounded?
And all the thoughts, pains, joys of mortal breath,
A war-embrace of wrestling life and death?

                      1805

[FRAGMENT]

LET Eagle bid the Tortoise sunward soar—
As vainly Strength speaks to a broken Mind.

                      1807

TO WILLIAM WORDSWORTH

COMPOSED ON THE NIGHT AFTER HIS RECITATION OF A POEM ON THE GROWTH OF AN INDIVIDUAL MIND

FRIEND of the wise! and Teacher of the Good!
Into my heart have I received that Lay
More than historic, that prophetic Lay
Wherein (high theme by thee first sung aright)
Of the foundations and the building up
Of a Human Spirit thou hast dared to tell
What may be told, to the understanding mind
Revealable; and what within the mind
By vital breathings secret as the soul
Of vernal growth, oft quickens in the heart
Thoughts all too deep for words!—

                   Theme hard as high!
Of smiles spontaneous, and mysterious fears
(The first-born they of Reason and twin-birth),

Of tides obedient to external force,
And currents self-determined, as might seem,
Or by some inner Power; of moments awful,
Now in thy inner life, and now abroad,
When power streamed from thee, and thy soul
   received
The light reflected, as a light bestowed—
Of fancies fair, and milder hours of youth,
Hyblean murmurs of poetic thought
Industrious in its joy, in vales and glens
Native or outland, lakes and famous hills!
Or on the lonely high-road, when the stars
Were rising; or by secret mountain-streams,
The guides and the companions of thy way!

Of more than Fancy, of the Social Sense
Distending wide, and man beloved as man,
Where France in all her towns lay vibrating
Like some becalmed bark beneath the burst
Of Heaven's immediate thunder, when no cloud
Is visible, or shadow on the main.
For thou wert there, thine own brows garlanded,
Amid the tremor of a realm aglow,
Amid a mighty nation jubilant,
When from the general heart of human kind
Hope sprang forth like a full-born Deity!
——Of that dear Hope afflicted and struck down,
So summoned homeward, thenceforth calm and sure
From the dread watch-tower of man's absolute self,
With light unwaning on her eyes, to look
Far on—herself a glory to behold,
The Angel of the vision! Then (last strain)
Of Duty, chosen Laws controlling choice,
Action and joy!—An Orphic song indeed,
A song divine of high and passionate thoughts
To their own music chaunted!

                  O great Bard!
Ere yet that last strain dying awed the air,
With stedfast eye I viewed thee in the choir
Of ever-enduring men. The truly great

Have all one age, and from one visible space
Shed influence! They, both in power and act,
Are permanent, and Time is not with them,
Save as it worketh for them, they in it.
Nor less a sacred Roll, than those of old,
And to be placed, as they, with gradual fame
Among the archives of mankind, thy work
Makes audible a linked lay of Truth,
Of Truth profound a sweet continuous lay,
Not learnt, but native, her own natural notes!
Ah! as I listened with a heart forlorn,
The pulses of my being beat anew:
And even as Life returns upon the drowned,
Life's joy rekindling roused a throng of pains—
Keen pangs of Love, awakening as a babe
Turbulent, with an outcry in the heart;
And fears self-willed, that shunned the eye of Hope;
And Hope that scarce would know itself from Fear;
Sense of past Youth, and Manhood come in vain,
And Genius given, and Knowledge won in vain;
And all which I had culled in wood-walks wild,
And all which patient toil had reared, and all,
Commune with thee had opened out—but flowers
Strewed on my corse, and borne upon my bier
In the same coffin, for the self-same grave!

That way no more! and ill beseems it me,
Who came a welcomer in herald's guise,
Singing of Glory, and Futurity,
To wander back on such unhealthful road,
Plucking the poisons of self-harm! And ill
Such intertwine beseems triumphal wreaths
Strewed before thy advancing!

                  Nor do thou,
Sage Bard! impair the memory of that hour
Of thy communion with my nobler mind
By pity or grief, already felt too long!
Nor let my words import more blame than needs.
The tumult rose and ceased: for Peace is nigh
Where Wisdom's voice has found a listening heart,

Amid the howl of more than wintry storms,
The Halcyon hears the voice of vernal hours
Already on the wing.

Eve following eve,
Dear tranquil time, when the sweet sense of Home
Is sweetest! moments for their own sake hailed
And more desired, more precious, for thy song,
In silence listening, like a devout child,
My soul lay passive, by thy various strain
Driven as in surges now beneath the stars,
With momentary stars of my own birth,
Fair constellated foam,* still darting off
Into the darkness; now a tranquil sea,
Outspread and bright, yet swelling to the moon.

And when—O Friend! my comforter and guide!
Strong in thyself, and powerful to give strength!—
Thy long sustained Song finally closed,
And thy deep voice had ceased—yet thou thyself
Wert still before my eyes, and round us both
That happy vision of beloved faces—
Scarce conscious, and yet conscious of its close
I sate, my being blended in one thought
(Thought was it? or aspiration? or resolve?)
Absorbed, yet hanging still upon the sound—
And when I rose, I found myself in prayer.

January, 1807

[FRAGMENT]

AS when the new or full Moon urges
The high, large, long, unbreaking surges
Of the Pacific main.

1811

---

*"A beautiful white cloud of Foam at momentary intervals coursed by the side of the Vessel with a Roar, and little stars of flame danced and sparkled and went out in it: and every now and then light detachments of this white cloud-like foam dashed off from the vessel's side, each with its own small constellation, over the Sea, and scoured out of sight like a Tartar Troop over a wilderness." "The Friend," p. 220. [No. 14, 23rd November, 1809.]

A PLAINTIVE MOVEMENT
(11′ 4` 11′ 4` | 10′ 6` 4′ 10`)

GO little Pipe! for ever I must leave thee,
   Ah, vainly true!
Never, ah never! must I more receive thee?
   Adieu! adieu!
Well, thou art gone! and what remains behind,
   Soothing the soul to Hope?
   The moaning Wind—
Hide with sere leaves my Grave's undaisied Slope.

        ?October, 1814

(It would be better to alter this metre—

 10′ 6` 6′ 10` | 11′ 4` 11′ 4`: and still more plaintive if the
1st and 4th were 11′ 11′ as well as the 5th and 7th.)

HUMAN LIFE

ON THE DENIAL OF IMMORTALITY

IF dead, we cease to be; if total gloom
 Swallow up life's brief flash for aye, we fare
As summer-gusts, of sudden birth and doom,
 Whose sound and motion not alone declare,
But are their whole of being! If the breath
 Be Life itself, and not its task and tent,
If even a soul like Milton's can know death;
 O Man! thou vessel purposeless, unmeant,
Yet drone-hive strange of phantom purposes!
 Surplus of Nature's dread activity,
Which, as she gazed on some nigh-finished vase,
Retreating slow, with meditative pause,
 She formed with restless hands unconsciously.
Blank accident! nothing's anomaly!

If rootless thus, thus substanceless thy state,
Go, weigh thy dreams, and be thy hopes, thy fears,
The counter-weights!—Thy laughter and thy tears
 Mean but themselves, each fittest to create
And to repay the other! Why rejoices
 Thy heart with hollow joy for hollow good?

Why cowl thy face beneath the mourner's hood?
Why waste thy sighs, and thy lamenting voices,
   Image of Image, Ghost of Ghostly Elf,
That such a thing as thou feel'st warm or cold?
Yet what and whence thy gain, if thou withhold
   These costless shadows of thy shadowy self?
Be sad! be glad! be neither! seek, or shun!
Thou hast no reason why! Thou canst have none;
Thy being's being is contradiction.

                              ?1815

TO NATURE

IT may indeed be phantasy, when I
   Essay to draw from all created things
  Deep, heartfelt, inward joy that closely clings;
And trace in leaves and flowers that round me lie
Lessons of love and earnest piety.
   So let it be; and if the wide world rings
   In mock of this belief, it brings
Nor fear, nor grief, nor vain perplexity.
So will I build my altar in the fields,
   And the blue sky my fretted dome shall be,
And the sweet fragrance that the wild flower yields
   Shall be the incense I will yield to Thee,
Thee only God! and thou shalt not despise
Even me, the priest of this poor sacrifice.

                                ?

THE KNIGHT'S TOMB

WHERE is the grave of Sir Arthur O'Kellyn?
   Where may the grave of that good man be?—
By the side of a spring, on the breast of Helvellyn,
Under the twigs of a young birch tree!
The oak that in summer was sweet to hear,
And rustled its leaves in the fall of the year,
And whistled and roared in the winter alone,
Is gone,—and the birch in its stead is grown.—
The Knight's bones are dust,
And his good sword rust;—
His soul is with the saints, I trust.

                              ?1817

ON DONNE'S POETRY

WITH Donne, whose muse on dromedary trots,
  Wreathe iron pokers into true-love knots;
Rhyme's sturdy cripple, fancy's maze and clue,
Wit's forge and fire-blast, meaning's press and screw.

?1818

YOUTH AND AGE

VERSE, a breeze mid blossoms straying,
  Where Hope clung feeding, like a bee—
Both were mine! Life went a-maying
      With Nature, Hope, and Poesy,
          When I was young!

When I was young?—Ah, woful When!
Ah! for the change 'twixt Now and Then!
This breathing house not built with hands,
This body that does me grievous wrong,
O'er aery cliffs and glittering sands,
How lightly then it flashed along:—
Like those trim skiffs, unknown of yore,
On winding lakes and rivers wide,
That ask no aid of sail or oar,
That fear no spite of wind or tide!
Nought cared this body for wind or weather
When Youth and I lived in't together.

Flowers are lovely; Love is flower-like;
Friendship is a sheltering tree;
O! the joys, that came down shower-like,
Of Friendship, Love, and Liberty,
          Ere I was old!

Ere I was old? Ah woful Ere,
Which tells me, Youth's no longer here!
O Youth! for years so many and sweet,

'Tis known, that Thou and I were one,
I'll think it but a fond conceit—
It cannot be that Thou art gone!
Thy vesper-bell hath not yet tolled:—
And thou wert aye a masker bold!
What strange disguise hast now put on,
To make believe, that thou art gone?
I see these locks in silvery slips,
This drooping gait, this altered size:
But Spring-tide blossoms on thy lips,
And tears take sunshine from thine eyes!
Life is but thought: so think I will
That Youth and I are house-mates still.

Dew-drops are the gems of morning,
But the tears of mournful eve!
Where no hope is, life's a warning
That only serves to make us grieve,
                              When we are old:

That only serves to make us grieve
With oft and tedious taking-leave,
Like some poor nigh-related guest,
That may not rudely be dismist;
Yet hath outstayed his welcome while,
And tells the jest without the smile.

1823-1832

WORK WITHOUT HOPE

LINES COMPOSED 21ST FEBRUARY, 1825

ALL Nature seems at work. Slugs leave their lair—
The bees are stirring—birds are on the wing—
And Winter slumbering in the open air,
Wears on his smiling face a dream of Spring!
And I the while, the sole unbusy thing,
Nor honey make, nor pair, nor build, nor sing.

Yet well I ken the banks where amaranths blow,
Have traced the fount whence streams of nectar flow.

Bloom, O ye amaranths! bloom for whom ye may,
For me ye bloom not! Glide, rich streams, away!
With lips unbrightened, wreathless brow, I stroll:
And would you learn the spells that drowse my soul?
Work without Hope draws nectar in a sieve,
And Hope without an object cannot live.

1825

SONG

THOUGH veiled in spires of myrtle-wreath,
Love is a sword which cuts its sheath,
And through the clefts itself has made,
We spy the flashes of the blade!

But through the clefts itself has made,
We likewise see Love's flashing blade
By rust consumed, or snapt in twain;
And only hilt and stump remain.

?1825

DUTY SURVIVING SELF-LOVE

THE ONLY SURE FRIEND OF DECLINING LIFE

A SOLILOQUY

UNCHANGED within, to see all changed without,
Is a blank lot and hard to bear, no doubt.
Yet why at others' wanings should'st thou fret?
Then only might'st thou feel a just regret,
Hadst thou withheld thy love or hid thy light
In selfish forethought of neglect and slight.
O wiselier then, from feeble yearnings freed,
While, and on whom, thou may'st—shine on! nor heed
Whether the object by reflected light
Return thy radiance or absorb it quite:
And though thou notest from thy safe recess
Old Friends burn dim, like lamps in noisome air,
Love them for what they are; nor love them less,
Because to thee they are not what they were.

1826

COLOGNE

IN Köhln, a town of monks and bones,
   And pavements fanged with murderous stones,
And rags, and hags, and hideous wenches;
I counted two and seventy stenches,
All well defined, and several stinks!
Ye Nymphs that reign o'er sewers and sinks,
The river Rhine, it is well known,
   Doth wash your city of Cologne;
But tell me, Nymphs, what power divine
Shall henceforth wash the river Rhine?

                                        1828

THE NETHERLANDS

WATER and windmills, greenness, Islets green;—
   Willows whose Trunks beside the shadows stood
Of their own higher half, and willowy swamp:—
Farmhouses that at anchor seemed—in the inland sky
The fog-transfixing Spires—
Water, wide water, greenness and green banks,
And water seen—

                                   June, 1828

FORBEARANCE

Beareth all things.
1 Cor. xiii, 7

GENTLY I took that which ungently came,
   And without scorn forgave:—Do thou the same.
A wrong done to thee think a cat's-eye spark
Thou wouldst not see, were not thine own heart dark.
Thine own keen sense of wrong that thirsts for sin,
Fear that—the spark self-kindled from within,
Which blown upon will blind thee with its glare,
Or smothered stifle thee with noisome air.
Clap on the extinguisher, pull up the blinds,
And soon the ventilated spirit finds
Its natural daylight. If a foe have kenned,

Or worse than foe, an alienated friend,
A rib of dry rot in thy ship's stout side,
Think it God's message, and in humble pride
With heart of oak replace it;—thine the gains—
Give him the rotten timber for his pains!

?1832

LOVE'S APPARITION AND EVANISHMENT

AN ALLEGORIC ROMANCE

LIKE a lone Arab, old and blind,
    Some caravan had left behind,
Who sits beside a ruined well,
    Where the shy sand-asps bask and swell;
And now he hangs his aged head aslant,
And listens for a human sound—in vain!
And now the aid, which Heaven alone can grant,
Upturns his eyeless face from Heaven to gain;—
Even thus, in vacant mood, one sultry hour,
Resting my eye upon a drooping plant,
With brow low-bent, within my garden-bower,
I sate upon the couch of camomile;
And—whether 'twas a transient sleep, perchance,
Flitted across the idle brain, the while
I watched the sickly calm with aimless scope,
In my own heart; or that, indeed a trance,
Turned my eye inward—thee, O genial Hope,
Love's elder sister! thee did I behold,
Drest as a bridesmaid, but all pale and cold,
With roseless cheek, all pale and cold and dim,
    Lie lifeless at my feet!
And then came Love, a sylph in bridal trim,
    And stood beside my seat;
She bent, and kissed her sister's lips,
    As she was wont to do;—
Alas! 'twas but a chilling breath
Woke just enough of life in death
    To make Hope die anew.

L'ENVOY

In vain we supplicate the Powers above;
There is no resurrection for the Love
That, nursed in tenderest care, yet fades away
In the chilled heart by gradual self-decay.

1824-1833

From

THE FALL OF ROBESPIERRE

SONG

TELL me, on what holy ground
  May Domestic Peace be found?
Halcyon daughter of the skies,
Far on fearful wings she flies,
From the pomp of Sceptered State,
From the Rebel's noisy hate.
In a cottaged vale She dwells,
Listening to the Sabbath bells!
Still around her steps are seen
Spotless Honour's meeker mien,
Love, the sire of pleasing fears,
Sorrow smiling through her tears,
And conscious of the past employ
Memory, bosom-spring of joy.

1794

REMORSE

ACT III, SCENE I

*A Hall of Armory, with an Altar at the back of the Stage. Soft
Music from an instrument of Glass or Steel.*

VALDEZ, ORDONIO, *and* ALVAR *in a Sorcerer's robe, are discovered.*

Ordonio. This was too melancholy, Father.
  Valdez.   Nay,
My Alvar loved sad music from a child.
Once he was lost; and after weary search
We found him in an open place in the wood,

F

To which spot he had followed a blind boy,
Who breathed into a pipe of sycamore
Some strangely moving notes: and these, he said,
Were taught him in a dream. Him we first saw
Stretched on the broad top of a sunny heath-bank:
And lower down poor Alvar, fast asleep,
His head upon the blind boy's dog. It pleased me
To mark how he had fastened round the pipe
A silver toy his grandam had late given him.
Methinks I see him now as he then looked—
Even so!—He had outgrown his infant dress,
Yet still he wore it.

    Alvar (*aside*).   My tears must not flow!
I must not clasp his knees, and cry, My father!

           Enter TERESA *and* Attendants.

    Teresa. Lord Valdez, you have asked my presence here,
And I submit; but (Heaven bear witness for me)
My heart approves it not! 'tis mockery.

    Ordonio. Believe you then no preternatural influence:
Believe you not that spirits throng around us?

    Teresa. Say rather that I have imagined it
A possible thing: and it has soothed my soul
As other fancies have; but ne'er seduced me
To traffic with the black and frenzied hope
That the dead hear the voice of witch or wizard.
[*To* ALVAR]. Stranger, I mourn and blush to see you here,
On such employment! With far other thoughts
I left you.

    Ordonio (*aside*). Ha! he has been tampering with her?

    Alvar. O high-souled Maiden! and more dear to me
Than suits the stranger's name!—

                  I swear to thee
I will uncover all concealed guilt.
Doubt, but decide not! Stand ye from the altar.

     [*Here a strain of music is heard from behind the scene.*

    Alvar. With no irreverent voice or uncouth charm
I call up the departed!

           Soul of Alvar!
Hear our soft suit, and heed my milder spell:
So may the gates of Paradise, unbarred,

Cease thy swift toils! Since haply thou art one
Of that innumerable company
Who in broad circle, lovelier than the rainbow,
Girdle this round earth in a dizzy motion,
With noise too vast and constant to be heard:
Fitliest unheard! For oh, ye numberless,
And rapid travellers! what ear unstunned,
What sense unmaddened, might bear up against
The rushing of your congregated wings?   [*Music.*
Even now your living wheel turns o'er my head!
Ye, as ye pass, toss high the desart sands,
That roar and whiten, like a burst of waters,
A sweet appearance, but a dread illusion
To the parched caravan that roams by night!
And ye upbuild on the becalmed waves
That whirling pillar, which from earth to heaven
Stands vast, and moves in blackness! Ye too split
The ice mount! and with fragments many and huge
Tempest the new-thawed sea, whose sudden gulfs
Suck in, perchance, some Lapland wizard's skiff!
Then round and round the whirlpool's marge ye dance,
Till from the blue swoln corse the soul toils out,
And joins your mighty army.

    [*Here behind the scenes a voice sings the three words,
       "Hear, Sweet Spirit."*

                    Soul of Alvar!
Hear the mild spell, and tempt no blacker charm!
By sighs unquiet, and the sickly pang
Of a half-dead, yet still undying hope,
Pass visible before our mortal sense!
So shall the Church's cleansing rites be thine,
Her knells and masses that redeem the dead!

SONG

Behind the Scenes, accompanied by the same Instrument as before.

       Hear, sweet spirit, hear the spell,
       Lest a blacker charm compel!
       So shall the midnight breezes swell
       With thy deep long-lingering knell.

And at evening evermore,
In a chapel on the shore,
Shall the chaunter, sad and saintly,
Yellow tapers burning faintly,
Doleful masses chaunt for thee,
Miserere Domine!

Hark! the cadence dies away
    On the quiet moonlight sea:
The boatmen rest their oars and say,
    Miserere Domine!   [*A long pause*

Ordonio. The innocent obey nor charm nor spell!
My brother is in heaven. Thou sainted spirit,
Burst on our sight, a passing visitant!
Once more to hear thy voice, once more to see thee,
O 'twere a joy to me!
    Alvar.   A joy to thee!
What if thou heard'st him now? What if his spirit
Re-entered its cold corse, and came upon thee
With many a stab from many a murderer's poniard?
What (if his stedfast eye still beaming pity
And brother's love) he turned his head aside,
Lest he should look at thee, and with one look
Hurl thee beyond all power of penitence?
    Valdez. These are unholy fancies!
    Ordonio.   Yes, my father,
He is in Heaven!
    Alvar (still to Ordonio). But what if he had a brother,
Who had lived even so, that at his dying hour,
The name of Heaven would have convulsed his face,
More than the death-pang?
    Valdez.   Idly prating man!
Thou hast guessed ill: Don Alvar's only brother
Stands here before thee—a father's blessing on him!
He is most virtuous.
    Alvar (still to Ordonio). What, if his very virtues
Had pampered his swoln heart and made him proud?
And what if pride had duped him into guilt?
Yet still he stalked a self-created god,
Not very bold, but exquisitely cunning;

And one that at his mother's looking-glass
Would force his features to a frowning sternness?
Young Lord! I tell thee, that there are such beings—
Yea, and it gives fierce merriment to the damned,
To see these most proud men, that loath mankind,
At every stir and buzz of coward conscience,
Trick, cant, and lie, most whining hypocrites!
Away, away! Now let me hear more music.   [*Music again.*

   Teresa. 'Tis strange, I tremble at my own conjectures!
But whatsoe'er it mean, I dare no longer
Be present at these lawless mysteries,
This dark provoking of the hidden Powers!
Already I affront—if not high Heaven—
Yet Alvar's memory!—Hark! I make appeal
Against the unholy rite, and hasten hence
To bend before a lawful shrine, and seek
That voice which whispers, when the still heart listens,
Comfort and faithful hope! Let us retire.

   Alvar (*to Teresa*). O full of faith and guileless love, thy Spirit
Still prompts thee wisely. Let the pangs of guilt
Surprise the guilty: thou art innocent!

       [*Exeunt* TERESA *and* Attendant. *Music as before.*

The spell is muttered—Come, thou wandering shape,
Who own'st no master in a human eye,
Whate'er be this man's doom, fair be it, or foul,
If he be dead, O come! and bring with thee
That which he grasped in death! But if he live,
Some token of his obscure perilous life.

       [*The whole Music clashes into a Chorus.*

CHORUS

   Wandering demons, hear the spell!
   Lest a blacker charm compel—

   [*The incense on the altar takes fire suddenly, and an
    illuminated picture of* ALVAR'S *assassination is dis-
    covered, and having remained a few seconds is then
    hidden by ascending flames.*

Ordonio (*starting*). Duped! duped! duped!—the traitor
Isidore!

> [*At this instant the doors are forced open*, MONVIEDRO
> *and the* Familiars of the Inquisition, Servants, &c.,
> *enter and fill the stage.*

Monviedro. First seize the sorcerer! suffer him not to speak!
The holy judges of the Inquisition
Shall hear his first words.—Look you pale, Lord Valdez?
Plain evidence have we here of most foul sorcery.
There is a dungeon underneath this castle,
And as you hope for mild interpretation,
Surrender instantly the keys and charge of it.

Ordonio (*recovering himself as from stupor, to Servants*). Why
haste you not? Off with him to the dungeon!

> [*All rush out in tumult.*

From

ACT IV, SCENE III

The mountains by moonlight. ALHADRA *alone in a Moorish dress.*

Alhadra. Yon hanging woods, that touched by autumn seem
As they were blossoming hues of fire and gold
The flower-like woods, most lovely in decay,
The many clouds, the sea, the rock, the sands,
Lie in the silent moonshine: and the owl,
(Strange! very strange!) the screech-owl only wakes!
Sole voice, sole eye of all this world of beauty!
Unless, perhaps, she sing her screeching song
To a herd of wolves, that skulk athirst for blood.
Why such a thing am I?—Where are these men?
I need the sympathy of human faces,
To beat away this deep contempt for all things,
Which quenches my revenge. O! would to Alla,
The raven, or the sea-mew, were appointed
To bring me food! or rather that my soul
Could drink in life from the universal air!
It were a lot divine in some small skiff
Along some Ocean's boundless solitude,
To float for ever with a careless course,
And think myself the only being alive!

From
ACT V, SCENE I
A Dungeon.

ALVAR (*alone*) *rises slowly from a bed of reeds.*

Alvar.   And this place my forefathers made for man!
This is the process of our love and wisdom
To each poor brother who offends against us—
Most innocent, perhaps—and what if guilty?
Is this the only cure? Merciful God!
Each pore and natural outlet shrivelled up
By ignorance and parching poverty,
His energies roll back upon his heart,
And stagnate and corrupt, till, changed to poison,
They break out on him, like a loathsome plague-spot!
Then we call in our pampered mountebanks:
And this is their best cure! uncomforted
And friendless solitude, groaning and tears,
And savage faces, at the clanking hour,
Seen through the steam and vapours of his dungeon
By the lamp's dismal twilight! So he lies
Circled with evil, till his very soul
Unmoulds its essence, hopelessly deformed
By sights of evermore deformity!
With other ministrations thou, O Nature!
Healest thy wandering and distempered child:
Thou pourest on him thy soft influences,
Thy sunny hues, fair forms, and breathing sweets;
Thy melodies of woods, and winds, and waters!
Till he relent, and can no more endure
To be a jarring and a dissonant thing
Amid this general dance and minstrelsy;
But, bursting into tears, wins back his way,
His angry spirit healed and harmonized
By the benignant touch of love and beauty.

I am chill and weary! Yon rude bench of stone,
In that dark angle, the sole resting-place!
But the self-approving mind is its own light
And life's best warmth still radiates from the heart
Where love sits brooding, and an honest purpose.

[*Retires out of sight.*
1812

From
ZAPOLYA
SONG

By GLYCINE

A SUNNY shaft did I behold,
    From sky to earth it slanted:
And poised therein a bird so bold—
    Sweet bird, thou wert enchanted!

He sank, he rose, he twinkled, he trolled
    Within that shaft of sunny mist;
His eyes of fire, his beak of gold,
    All else of amethyst!

And thus he sang: "Adieu! adieu!
Love's dreams prove seldom true.
The blossoms, they make no delay:
The sparkling dew-drops will not stay.
    Sweet month of May,
        We must away;
            Far, far away!
                To-day! to-day!"

1815

THE PICCOLOMINI

ACT I, SCENE IV

Octavio. My son, the nursling of the camp spoke in thee!
A war of fifteen years
Hath been thy education and thy school.
Peace hast thou never witnessed! There exists
A higher than the warrior's excellence.
In war itself war is no ultimate purpose.
The vast and sudden deeds of violence,
Adventures wild, and wonders of the moment,
These are not they, my son, that generate
The calm, the blissful, and the enduring mighty!
Lo there! the soldier, rapid architect!
Builds his light town of canvas, and at once
The whole scene moves and bustles momently,
With arms, and neighing steeds, and mirth and quarrel
The motley market fills; the roads, the streams
Are crowded with new freights, trade stirs and hurries!
But on some morrow morn, all suddenly,
The tents drop down, the horde renews its march.
Dreary, and solitary as a church-yard
The meadow and down-trodden seed-plot lie,
And the year's harvest is gone utterly.

Max. O let the Emperor make peace, my father!
Most gladly would I give the blood-stained laurel
For the first violet of the leafless spring,
Plucked in those quiet fields where I have journeyed!

Octavio. What ails thee? What so moves thee all at once?

Max. Peace have I ne'er beheld? I have beheld it.
From thence am I come hither: O! that sight,
It glimmers still before me, like some landscape
Left in the distance,—some delicious landscape!
My road conducted me through countries where

The war has not yet reached. Life, life, my father—
My venerable father, life has charms
Which we have ne'er experienced. We have been
But voyaging along its barren coasts,
Like some poor ever-roaming horde of pirates,
That, crowded in the rank and narrow ship,
House on the wild sea with wild usages,
Nor know aught of the main land, but the bays
Where safeliest they may venture a thieves' landing.
Whate'er in the inland dales the land conceals
Of fair and exquisite, O! nothing, nothing,
Do we behold of that in our rude voyage.
  Octavio. And so your journey has revealed this to you?
  Max. 'Twas the first leisure of my life. O tell me,
What is the meed and purpose of the toil,
The painful toil, which robbed me of my youth,
Left me a heart unsouled and solitary,
A spirit uninformed, unornamented.
For the camp's stir and crowd and ceaseless larum,
The neighing war-horse, the air-shattering trumpet,
The unvaried, still-returning hour of duty,
Word of command, and exercise of arms—
There's nothing here, there's nothing in all this
To satisfy the heart, the gasping heart!
Mere bustling nothingness, where the soul is not—
This cannot be the sole felicity,
These cannot be man's best and only pleasures.

            1800

POLITICAL
JOURNALISM

Coleridge was interested in, and emotionally concerned with, political questions all his life; but the years 1795-1802 represent the only time when, except for a few months in 1811, political journalism was one of his main occupations. His motives at the beginning and the end of these periods were different. To start with there were the political lecture-sermons at Bristol, when he believed in the salvation of society through a new economic and ethical order, such as Pantisocracy. This was followed by the "Watchman," his paper of 1796, which, though it was less ambitious and dwindled in the course of publication, started with equal enthusiasm. In 1800, on the other hand, he was an efficient independent journalist reporting for the "Morning Post," and contributing verses and articles, in an effort to support his family. Finally, in 1811, he was miserably doing hack-work for the "Courier," trying to support himself.

Sarah Coleridge's collection of her father's journalism ("Essays on His Own Times") fills nearly a thousand pages, but this section has been made the shortest, partly because most of it represents Coleridge working to order and therefore at his least expressive, and partly because nearly all his politics are to be found much less impersonally set forth elsewhere. For instance, we can only understand Pantisocracy from the Letters, and in the same section his views on factory children are better put than in the more formal "Remarks" on Sir Robert Peel's Bill.

No attempt therefore has been made in these few pages to trace his political evolution, the course of which seemed to antagonize radical men like Hazlitt. It may be said of Coleridge's attitude to politics that it gradually crystallized into the normal physiological antipathy to change which seemed to most of his contemporaries to be intellectually supported by the results of the French Revolution. But there was no complete reversal, no "handful of silver," no association with the governing classes, as was the case with Wordsworth and Southey. It seems that political questions became less and less important to him, though he agitated for social reform, at the same time inconsistently attacking the Reform Bill on the ground that it was associated with "mob rule" rather than the "will of the people."

POLITICAL
JOURNALISM

CONCIONES AD POPULUM
from
ON THE PRESENT WAR

WE will now take a rapid survey of the consequences of this unjust because unnecessary War. I mean not to describe the distressful stagnation of Trade and Commerce: I direct not your attention to the wretches that sadden every street in this City, the pale and meagre Troop, who in the bitterness of reluctant Pride, are forced to beg the Morsel, for which they would be willing to "work their fingers to the bone" in honest Industry: I will not frighten you by relating the distresses of that brave Army, which has been melted away on the Continent, nor picture to your imaginations the loathsome pestilence that has mocked our Victories in the West-Indies: I bid you not hear the screams of the deluded Citizens of Toulon—I will not press on your recollection the awful Truth, that in the course of this calamitous Contest more than a Million of men have perished—a *MILLION of men, of each of whom the mangled corse terrifies the dreams of her that loved him, and makes some mother, some sister, some widow start from slumber with a shriek! These arguments have been urged even to satiety—a British Senator has sneeringly styled them mere *common-place* against wars. I could weep for the criminal Patience of Humanity! These arguments are *hacknied;* yet *Wars* continue!

Horrors, the same in kind though perhaps not equal in degree, necessarily attend all wars: it was my intention to

---

*By the internal disturbances of France in La Vendée and other places, disturbances excited by English agents, and rendered obstinate by our Ministers' promises, more than *Three Hundred Thousand* have been butchered.

detail those only that are peculiar to the present. And first
and least—the loss of our National Character. At the commencement of the War the Government solemnly disclaimed
all intervention in the internal affairs of France: not six
months passed, ere with matchless insincerity the Restitution
of Monarchy became its avowed aim. This guilt however
may perhaps rest on its first authors, and fly unclaimed by
the People, unless it should be thought, that they, who permit, perpetrate. The depravation of private morals is a more
serious and less transient evil. All our happiness and the
greater part of our virtues depend on social confidence. This
beautiful fabric of Love the system of Spies and Informers
has shaken to the very foundation. There have been multiplied among us "Men who carry tales to shed blood!" Men
who resemble the familiar Spirits described by Isaiah, as
"dark ones, that peep and that mutter!" Men, who may
seem to have been typically shadowed out in the Frogs that
formed the second plague of Egypt: little low animals with
chilly blood and staring eyes, that "come up into our houses
and our bed-chambers!" These men are plenteously scattered among us: our very looks are decyphered into dis-
affection, and we cannot move without treading on some
political spring-gun. Nor here has the evil stopped. We
have breathed so long the atmosphere of Imposture and
Panic, that many honest minds have caught an aguish
disorder; in their cold fits they shiver at Freedom, in their
hot fits they turn savage against its advocates; and sacrifice
to party Rage what they would have scornfully refused to
Corruption. Traitors to friendship, that they may be faithful to the Constitution—Enemies of human nature, that
they may prove themselves the Adorers of the God of Peace—
they hide from themselves the sense of their crime by the
Merit of their motive. Thus every man begins to suspect his
neighbour, the warm ebullience of our hearts is stagnating:
and I dread, lest by long stifling the expressions of Patriotism, we may at last lose the Feeling. "Society is in every
state a blessing; Government even in its best state but a
necessary evil." We are subverting this Blessing in order to
support this Evil—or rather to support the desparate
Quacks who are administering it with a Life—or Death
Temerity.   1795

THE WATCHMAN

PROSPECTUS

That all may know the TRUTH;
And that the TRUTH may make us FREE!!

On Friday, the 5th *Day of February*
1 7 9 6
WILL BE PUBLISHED
Nº. 1.
(PRICE FOUR PENCE)
OF A
MISCELLANY, TO BE PUBLISHED EVERY
EIGHTH DAY,
UNDER THE NAME OF

"THE WATCHMAN"

═══════

BY
S. T. COLERIDGE,
AUTHOR OF
ADDRESSES TO THE PEOPLE,
A PLOT DISCOVERED, &c., &c.

═══════

The Publishers in the different Towns and Cities will be
specified in future Advertisements.

PROSPECTUS

IN AN ENSLAVED STATE THE RULERS FORM AND SUPPLY
THE OPINIONS OF THE PEOPLE.

This is the mark by which Despotism is distinguished: for
it is the power by which Despotism is begun and continued.

—— "*The abuses, that are rooted in all the old Governments of
Europe, give such numbers of men such a direct interest in supporting,
cherishing, and defending abuses, that no wonder advocates for tyranny of
every species are found in every country and almost in every company.
What a mass of People in every part of England are some way or other
interested in the present representation of the people, in tythes, charters,
corporations, monopolies, and taxation! and not merely in the things
themselves, but in all the abuses attending them; and how many are there
who derive their profit or their consideration in life, not merely from such
institutions, but from the evils they engender!*"

ARTHUR YOUNG'S TRAVELS

Among the most powerful advocates and auxiliaries of
abuses we must class (with a few honorable exceptions) the
weekly Provincial Newspapers, the Editors of which receive
the Treasury Prints gratis, and in some instances *with particular paragraphs marked out for their insertion.* —— These Papers
form the chief, and sometimes the only, reading of that large
and important body of men, who living out of towns and
cities have no opportunity of hearing calumnies exposed and
false statements detected. Thus are Administrations enabled
to steal away their Rights and Liberties, either so gradually
as to undermine their Freedom without alarming them: or
if it be necessary to carry any great point suddenly, to over-
throw their Freedom by alarming them against themselves.

A PEOPLE ARE FREE IN PROPORTION AS THEY FORM THEIR
OWN OPINIONS. In the strictest sense of the word KNOWLEDGE
IS POWER. Without previous illumination a change in the
forms of Government will be of no avail. These are but the
shadows, the virtue and rationality of the People at large
are the substance, of Freedom: and where Corruption and
Ignorance are prevalent, the best *forms* of Government are
but the "Shadows of a Shade!" We actually transfer the
Sovereignty to the People, when we make them susceptible
of it. In the present perilous state of our Constitution the
Friends of Freedom, of Reason, and of Human Nature,
must feel it their duty by every mean in their power to

supply or circulate political information. We ask not their patronage: It will be obtained in proportion as we shall be found to deserve it. —— Our Miscellany will be comprised in two sheets, or thirty-two pages, closely printed, the size and type the same as of this PROSPECTUS. —— The contents will be

I. An History of the domestic and foreign Occurrences of the preceding days.

II. The Speeches in both Houses of Parliament: and during the Recess, select Parliamentary Speeches, from the commencement of the reign of Charles the First to the present aera, with Notes historical and biographical.

III. Original Essays and Poetry, chiefly or altogether political.

It's chief objects are to co-operate (1) with the WHIG CLUB in procuring a repeal of Lord Grenville's and Mr. Pitt's bills, now passed into laws, and (2) with the PATRIOTIC SOCIETIES for obtaining a Right of Suffrage general and frequent.

In the cities of London, Bristol,   ,   , and   , it will appear as regularly as a News-paper, over which it will have these advantages:—

I. There being no advertisements, a greater quantity of original matter must be given.

II. From its form, it may be bound up at the end of the year, and become an Annual Register.

III. This last circumstance may induce Men of Letters to prefer this Miscellany to more perishable publi-cations, as the vehicle of their effusions.

It remains to say, that whatever powers or acquirements the Editor possesses, he will dedicate *entirely* to this work; and (which is of more importance to the Public) he has received promises of occasional assistance from literary men of eminence and established reputation. With such encouragement he offers himself to the Public as a faithful

WATCHMAN,

to proclaim the State of the Political Atmosphere, and preserve Freedom and her Friends from the attacks of Robbers and Assassins!!

From NO. III

MODERN PATRIOTISM.

IT is advisable that men should not deceive themselves, or their neighbours, by assuming titles which do not belong to them. Good Citizen ——! why do you call yourself a PATRIOT? You talk loudly and rapidly; but powers of vociferation do not constitute a PATRIOT. You wish to be distinguished from the herd; you like victory in an argument; you are the tongue-major of every company: therefore you love a Tavern better than your own fire-side. Alas! you hate power in others, because you love power yourself! You are not a PATRIOT! You have studied Mr Godwin's Essay on Political Justice; but to think filial affection folly, gratitude a crime, marriage injustice, and the promiscuous intercourse of the sexes right and wise, may class you among the despisers of vulgar prejudices, but cannot increase the probability that you are a PATRIOT. But you act up to your principles— So much the worse! Your principles are villainous ones! I would not entrust my wife or sister to you— Think you, I would entrust my country? The PATRIOT indulges himself in no comfort, which, if society were properly constituted, all men might not enjoy; but you get drunk on claret, and you frequent public dinners, where whole joints are stewed down into essences—and all for your country! You are a Gamester—*you* a Patriot!—— A very poor man was lately hovering round a Butcher's shop—he wanted to buy a sheep's liver; but your footman in livery outbid him, and your spaniel had it! I doubt your Patriotism. You harangue against the Slave-Trade; you attribute the present scarcity to the war—yet you wear powder, and eat pies and sugar! Your patriotism and philanthropy cost you very little. If I might presume so far, I would inform *how* you might become a Patriot. Your *heart* must believe, that the good of the whole is the greatest possible good of each individual: that *therefore* it is your *duty* to be just, because it is your *interest*. In the present state of society, taking away Hope and Fear, you cannot believe this—for it is not true; yet you cannot be a Patriot unless you do believe it. How shall we reconcile this apparent contradiction? You must give up your sensuality and your philosophy, the pimp of your sensuality; you must condescend to believe in a God, and in the existence of a Future State!

From NO. V

[ABOLITION.]

SINCE I have been capable of reasoning, I have beheld with compassion and indignation the state of the Slaves in the West-Indies.— I have longed for the abolition of the slave-trade, as the abolition of the Source of the evil, and for a system of laws which may finally lead to the emancipation of this oppressed race of Men— Latterly I have trembled on seeing intelligence from our Island, lest I should read that the Negroes had at length by some horrid act of Justice avenged themselves on their oppressors— One night, after having mused long on this subject, I retired to rest, when I dreamt that, removed far from the din of modern politics, I had been travelling through distant countries, and had at last arrived at the West-Indies— My heart throbbed as it approached that land, which, since its acquaintance with Europeans, had witnessed every extravagance that Souls the most deeply polluted could suggest— I called up all my fortitude to bear with steadiness those scenes which I antici-pated—abject and oppressed Slaves!—Masters in a state of disgusting luxury!—but how great was my amazement to find a People at once free and happy. On landing I was accosted with the utmost urbanity by a Negro, who with his Wife walking on the shore in a lovely evening, had been observing the approach of our vessel. I was delighted to see that some at least of these people were happy. He offered to conduct me to the neighbouring town; I thanked him, and on the way began to make those enquiries so natural, con-cerning the state of the slaves in that country— SLAVES! he cried, with a countenance of pity, indignation, and rapture,— we have no Slaves here,— The TIME IS PASSED— Almost suffocated, but yet incredulous, I asked a hundred questions without waiting for a reply— He saw that I was un-acquainted with the great revolution which had taken place during the few short years that I had been travelling among the isles of the southern ocean. He satisfied every interrogatory as quickly as I possibly could permit him. At length being in the town, he led me to a spacious square; in the midst of which, was placed on a magnificent pedestal, the statue of a Negroe. Behold, said he, our Hampden, our Tell, our Washington. At the foot of this statue were engraved these words:—

TO THE AVENGER OF THE NEW WORLD.

The head of the figure was naked, his arm stretched out, his eye sublime, the whole attitude noble, and commanding awe: the wrecks of twenty sceptres were scattered round him. I burst forth with renewed ecstasy. Yes, exclaimed my Conductor, with a warmth equal to my Transports, Nature at length produced that astonishing man, who was destined to rid the world of the most atrocious, the most insulting and the longest Tyranny;—his genius, his intrepidity, his patience and virtuous vengeance were recompensed;—he broke the chains of his countrymen—*human beings* oppressed under the most odious slavery, who wanted only the opportunity to form as many heroes; the torrent which breaks its dams, the thunder which strikes, have an effect less instantaneous, less violent:—at the same moment of time we shed the blood of *all* our tyrants—English, Spanish, Dutch—*all* were victims to fire, poison, and the sword—this earth drank greedily that blood after which it had long thirsted, and the bones of our ancestors, basely assassinated, seemed at that moment to rise anew and tremble with joy.

1796

*   *   *

[THE MORNING POST]
From
[THE CHARACTER OF MR. PITT]

As his reasonings, even so his eloquence. One character pervades his whole being. Words on words, finely arranged, and so dexterously consequent, that the whole bears the semblance of argument, and still keeps awake a sense of surprise; but when all is done, nothing remarkable has been said: no one philosophical remark, no one image, not even a pointed aphorism. Not a sentence of Mr. Pitt's has ever been quoted, or formed the favourite phrase of the day—a thing unexampled in any man of equal reputation. But while he speaks, the effect varies according to the character of his auditor. The man of no talent is swallowed up in surprise; and when the speech is ended, he remembers his feelings, but nothing distinct of that which produced them—(how opposite an effect to that of nature and genius, from whose works the idea still remains, when the feeling is passed away—remains to connect itself with the other feelings, and combine with new impressions!) The mere man of talent hears him with admiration—the mere man of genius with contempt—the philosopher neither admires nor contemns, but listens to him with a deep and solemn interest, tracing in the effects of his eloquence the power of words and phrases, and that peculiar constitution of human affairs in their present state, which so eminently favours this power.

Such appears to us to be the prime minister of Great Britain, whether we consider him as a statesman or as an orator. The same character betrays itself in his private life; the same coldness to realities, and to all whose excellence relates to reality. He has patronised no science, he has raised no man of genius from obscurity; he counts no one prime work of God among his friends. From the same source he has no attachment to female society, no fondness for children, no perceptions of beauty in natural scenery; but he is fond of convivial indulgencies, of that stimulation, which, keeping up the glow of self-importance and the sense of internal power, gives feelings without the mediation of ideas.

These are the elements of his mind; the accidents of his fortune, the circumstances that enabled such a mind to acquire and retain such a power, would form a subject of a philosophical history, and that too of no scanty size. We can scarcely furnish the chapter of contents to a work, which would comprise subjects so important and delicate, as the causes of the diffusion and intensity of secret influence; the machinery and state intrigue of marriages; the overbalance of the commercial interest; the panic of property struck by the late revolution; the short-sightedness of the careful; the carelessness of the far-sighted; and all those many and various events which have given to a decorous profession of religion, and a seemliness of private morals, such an unwonted weight in the attainment and preservation of public power. We are unable to determine whether it be more consolatory or humiliating to human nature, that so many complexities of event, situation, character, age, and country, should be necessary in order to the production of a Mr. Pitt.*

1800

---

*To-morrow of Bonaparte.

NOTEBOOKS

From 1795 at latest, Coleridge made continuous use of notebooks. More than fifty, according to E. H. Coleridge, are extant. It was not his practice to keep one book for his observations of nature, another for cooking recipes, another for plans of future work and first fragments of a growing poem: he would put down each entry on the first blank page he found, or beneath some quotation copied from whatever book he happened to be reading at the time. So that taken as they stand these pages (I have reproduced a few literatim *at the beginning of this Section) are as miscellaneous, as untidy, as illuminating and as obscure, as original and as allusive, as Coleridge himself. It is only in the last few folios—the "flycatchers" as he called them— that his preoccupation with theological questions brings about an unwelcome uniformity.*

Professor Lowes has shown how it is possible to thread this chaos by tracing through the notebooks the evolution of a poem or image, how by using them as a guide the strange process may be followed which welded whole stanzas out of scattered observations, and images found in the course of vast readings. They have another kind of autobiographical interest. "Since I left you, my pocket-books have been my sole confidants," Coleridge wrote to Wordsworth in 1812. With the letters, these memoranda are all that remain of certain periods in his life when he was unable to do any set work, and often, even when Coleridge was at his most prolific, the notebook entry is the most expressive, written as it was without any obligation to fill space, or ingratiate the writer with a hostile public. The non-philosophical notebooks represent the one great piece of Coleridge editing which remains to be done—though "Anima Poetae" is the best of selections.

NOTEBOOKS

["GUTCH MEMORANDUM BOOK"]

. . . Poem in ⟨three⟩ one Books in the manner of Dante on the excursion of Thor—

2 Satires in the manner of Donne.
1. Horace Walpole.
2. Monthly Reviewers [?] Bowles address to Poverty at the end of the

In early youth—Ωστραλ! Console my SARA— And grieve not, my son! that we &c: Tob.

Take a pound of Beef, Mutton, or Pork; cut it into small pieces; a pint of Peas; four Turnips sliced; six or seven Potatoes cut very small; four or five Onions; put to them three Quarts of Water, and let it boil about two hours and a half—⟨thick⟩—then thicken it with a pound of Rice—and boil it a quarter of an ⟨other⟩ hour more—after which season it with salt & pepper—

N.B. better season it at first—peppering & salting the Meat, &c—

1. An Essay on Tobit.
2. On the art of prolonging Life—by getting up in the morning.
3. On Marriage—in opposition to French Principles.
4. Jacob Böhmen.
5. Life of John Henderson.
6. Ode to a Looking Glass.
7. Burnet's de montibus: in English Blank Verse.
8. Escapes from Misery, a Poem—Halo round the Candle —sigh visible.
9. Cavern—candle.
10. Life of David—a Sermon.
11. Wild Poem on Maniac—Εραστου Γαληρος: ἁτ:
12. Ode on St. Withold.
13. Crotchets, by S. T. Coleridge.

14. Edition of Akenside.

15. of Collins & Gray—

16. Hymns to the Sun, the Moon, and the Elements—six hymns.

In one of them to introduce a dissection of Atheism— particularly the Godwinian system of Pride—Proud of what? an outcast of blind nature ruled by a fatal necessity—Slave of an ideot Nature!

17. Letters to Godwin.

18. Randolph consecrating D. of York's banners—

19. Ode to Southey.

*Deproeliantium e carcere nubium.

20. Egomist, a metaphysical Rhapsody—

21. Berkley's Maxims—Vol II, 345.

In the last Hymn a sublime enumeration of all the charms or Tremendities of Nature—then a bold avowal of Berkley's System!!!!! Ode to a Moth—against [?]

22. Adventures of CHRISTIAN the mutineer — —

23. Military anecdotes—(N.B. promised to be sergeants).

24. History of Phrases—ex. gr. The King must have men.

25. Hymn to Dr. Darwin—in the manner of the Orphics.

26. Addressed to the Clergy against the two Bills—

27. Satire addressed to a Young Man who intended to study medicine at Edingburgh—

The Earth feared and was still, then GOD arose to Judgement to save the meek of the Earth. Surely, the Wrath of Man shall praise thee—: the remainder of Wrath shalt thou restrain.—

God shall cut off the spirit of Princes—he is terrible to the Kings of the Earth.

Then shall the right-aiming Thunderbolt go abroad; & from the Clouds, as from a strong Bow, shall they fly to the mark.

There be Spirits that are created for Vengeance—in the time of Destruction they pour out their force and appease the Wrath of him that made them.

Men that run mad unto prosperity compared to cats on beds of Marum and Valerian — —

There is not a new or strange opinion— Truth returned from banishment— a river run under ground — — — fire beneath embers—

Men anxious for this world—Owls that watch all night to
catch mice—

Smooth, shining, & deceitful as thin Ice—

Wisdom, Mother of retired Thought,

> εστι τις θεος ενδον
>
> πολυν εσσαμενοι νουν.

Nature

Wrote Rascal on his face by chiliographic art

Our quaint metaphysical opinions in an hour of anguish
like playthings by the bedside of a child deadly sick.

* * *

Twas sweet to know it only possible—
Some *wishes* cross'd my mind & dimly cheer'd it,
And one or two poor melancholy Pleasures
In these, the pale unwavering light of Hope
Silvring their flimsy wing flew silent by,
Moths in the moonlight—

          —the prophetic soul
of the wide world dreaming on things to come.

                     Shak. sonnets.

    Most true it is, that I have look'd on Truth
    Askance & strangely.

                       Id.

        Behind the thin
    Grey cloud that cover'd but not hid the sky
    The round full moon look'd small.—

The subtle snow in every breeze rose curling from the
Grove, like pillars of cottage smoke.

The alligators terrible roar, like heavy distant thunder,
not only shaking the air & waters, but causing the earth to
tremble—& when hundreds & thousands are roaring at the
same time, you can scarcely be persuaded but that the whole
globe is dangerously agitated—

The eggs are layed in layers between a compost of mud,
grass, & herbage.—The female watches them.—When born,
she leads them about the shores, as a hen her chickens—&
when she is basking on the warm banks, with her brood
around, you may hear the young ones whining & barking,
like young Puppies.

20 feet long—lizard-shaped, plated—head vulnerable—tusked—eyes small & sunk—

Hartley fell down & hurt himself—I caught him up crying & screaming—& ran out of doors with him.—The Moon caught his eye—he ceased crying immediately—& his eyes & the tears in them, how they glittered in the Moonlight!

Some wilderness-plot, green & fountainous & unviolated by Man.

?1796-7

* * *

[ANIMA POETAE]

1797-1801

REAL pain can alone cure us of imaginary ills. We feel a thousand miseries till we are lucky enough to feel misery.

POETRY, like schoolboys, by too frequent and severe correction, may be cowed into dullness!

PECULIAR, not far-fetched; natural, but not obvious; delicate, not affected; dignified, not swelling; fiery, but not mad; rich in imagery, but not loaded with it—in short, a union of harmony and good sense, of perspicuity and conciseness. Thought is the body of such an ode, enthusiasm the soul, and imagery the drapery.

THE elder languages were fitter for poetry because they expressed only prominent ideas with clearness, the others but darkly. . . . Poetry gives most pleasure when only generally and not perfectly understood. It was so by me with Gray's "Bard" and Collins' Odes. The "Bard" once intoxicated me, and now I read it without pleasure. From this cause it is that what I call metaphysical poetry gives me so much delight.

A CHILD scolding a flower in the words in which he had been himself scolded and whipped, is poetry—passion past with pleasure.

HOT-HEADED men confuse, your cool-headed gentry jumble. The man of warm feelings only produces order and true connection. In what a jumble M. and H. write, every third paragraph beginning with "Let us now return," or "We come now to the consideration of such a thing"— that is, what *I said* I *would* come to in the contents prefixed to the chapter.

SOCINIANISM, moonlight; methodism, a stove. O for some sun to unite heat and light!

1799

ADVANTAGE of public schools. [They teach men to be] content with school praise when they publish. Apply this to Cottle and J. Jennings.

1799

THE sunny mist, the luminous gloom of Plato.

1799

NOTHING affects me much at the moment it happens. It either stupefies me, and I, perhaps, look at a merry-make and dance-the-hay of flies, or listen entirely to the loud click of the great clock, or I am simply indifferent, not without some sense of philosophical self-complacency. For a thing at the moment is but a thing of the moment; it must be taken up into the mind, diffuse itself through the whole multitude of shapes and thoughts, not one of which it leaves untinged, between [not one of] which and it some new thought is not engendered. Now this is a work of time, but the body feels it quicker with me.

1799

MATERIALISTS unwilling to admit the mysterious element of our nature make it all mysterious—nothing mysterious in nerves, eyes, &c., but that nerves think, &c.! Stir up the sediment into the transparent water, and so make all opaque.

To attempt to subordinate the idea of time to that of likeness.

EMPIRICS are boastful and egotists because they introduce real or apparent novelty, which excites great opposition, [while] personal opposition creates re-action (which is of course a consciousness of power) associated with the person re-acting. Paracelsus was a boaster, it is true; so were the French Jacobins, and Wolff, though not a boaster, was persecuted into a habit of egotism in his philosophical writings; so Dr. John Brown, and Milton in his prose works; and those, in similar circumstances, who, from prudence, abstain from egotism in their writings are still egotists among their friends. It would be unnatural effort not to be so, and egotism in such cases is by no means offensive to a kind and discerning man.

Some flatter themselves that they abhor egotism, and do not suffer it to appear *prima facie*, either in their writings or conversation, however much and however personally they or their opinions have been opposed. What now? Observe, watch those men; their habits of feeling and thinking are made up of *contempt*, which is the concentrated vinegar of egotism—it is *laetitia mixta cum odio*, a notion of the weakness of another conjoined with a notion of our own comparative strength, though that weakness is still strong enough to be troublesome to us, though not formidable.

> —and the deep power of Joy
> We see into the Life of Things.   1801

By deep feeling we make our *ideas dim*, and this is what we mean by our life, ourselves. I think of the wall—it is before me a distinct image. Here I necessarily think of the *idea* and the thinking *I* as two distinct and opposite things. Now let me think of *myself*, of the thinking being. The idea becomes dim, whatever it be—so dim that I know not what it is; but the feeling is deep and steady, and this I call *I*—identifying the percipient and the perceived.

> O Thou! whose fancies from afar are brought.

HARTLEY, looking out of my study window, fixed his eyes steadily and for some time on the opposite prospect and said, "Will yon mountains *always* be?" I shewed him the whole magnificent prospect in a looking-glass, and held it up, so that the whole was like a canopy or ceiling over his head, and he struggled to express himself concerning the difference between the thing and the image almost with convulsive effort. I never before saw such an abstract of *thinking* as a pure act and energy—of thinking as distinguished from thought.

1801

OBSERVED the great half moon setting behind the mountain ridge, and watched the shapes its various segments presented as it slowly sunk—first the foot of a boot, all but the heel—then a little pyramid △—then a star of the first magnitude—indeed, it was not distinguishable from the evening star at its largest—then rapidly a smaller, a small, a very small star—and, as it diminished in size, so it grew paler in tint. And now where is it? Unseen—but a little fleecy cloud hangs above the mountain ridge, and is rich in amber light.

September, 1801

I DO not wish you to act from those truths. No! still and always act from your feelings; but only meditate often on these truths, that sometime or other they may become your feelings.

QUAERE, whether or no too great definiteness of terms in any language may not consume too much of the vital and idea-creating force in distinct, clear, full-made images, and so prevent originality. For original might be distinguished from positive thought.

ALL the mountains black and tremendously obscure, except Swinside. At this time I saw, one after the other, nearly in the same place, two perfect moon-rainbows, the one foot in the field below my garden, the other in the field nearest but two to the church. It was grey-moonlight-mist-colour. Friday morning, Mary Hutchinson arrives.

Tuesday evening, ½ *past* 6, 22 *October,* 1801

1802-1803

METAPHYSICS make all one's thoughts equally corrosive on the body, by inducing a habit of making momently and common thought the subject of uncommon interest and intellectual energy.

GREAT injury has resulted from the supposed incompatibility of one talent with another, judgement with imagination and taste, good sense with strong feeling, &c. If it be false, as assuredly it is, the opinion has deprived us of a test which every man might apply. [Hence] Locke's opinions of Blackmore, Hume's of Milton and Shakspere.

IN natural objects we feel ourselves, or think of ourselves, only by *likenesses*—among men, too often by *differences*. Hence the soothing, love-kindling effect of rural nature—the bad passions of human societies. And why is difference linked with hatred?

WE imagine ourselves discoverers, and that we have struck a light, when, in reality, at most, we have but snuffed a candle.

INTENSELY hot day; left off a waistcoat and for yarn wore silk stockings. Before nine o'clock, had unpleasant chillness; heard a noise which I thought Derwent's in sleep, listened, and found it was a calf bellowing. Instantly came on my mind that night I slept out at Ottery, and the calf in the field across the river whose lowing so deeply impressed me. Chill + child and calf-lowing—probably the Rivers Greta and Otter.

Tuesday night, 19 *July,* 1803

A SMILE, as foreign or alien to, as detached from the gloom of the countenance, as I have seen a small spot of light travel slowly and sadly along the mountain's breast, when all beside has been dark with the storm.

October, 1803

NEVER to lose an opportunity of reasoning against the head-dimming, heart-damping principle of judging a work by its defects, not its beauties. Every work must have the former—we know it *a priori*—but every work has not the latter, and he, therefore, who discovers them, tells you something that you could not with certainty, or even with probability, have anticipated.

WITHOUT drawing, I feel myself but half invested with language. Music, too, is wanting to me. But yet, though one should unite poetry, draftsman's skill, and music, the greater and, perhaps, nobler, certainly *all* the subtler, parts of one's nature must be *solitary*. Man exists herein to himself and to God alone—yea! in how much only to God! how much lies *below* his own consciousness!

THE tree or sea-weed like appearance of the side of the mountain, all white with snow, made by little bits of snow loosened. Introduce this and the stones leaping rabbit-like down on my sopha of sods.

THOSE only who feel no originality, no consciousness of having received their thoughts and opinions from immediate inspiration are anxious to be thought original. The certainty, the feeling that he is right, is enough for the man of genius, and he rejoices to find his opinions plumed and winged with the authority of several forefathers.

EVEN among good and sensible men, how common it is that one attaches himself scrupulously to the rigid performance of some minor virtue or makes a point of carrying some virtue into all its minutiae, and is just as lax in a similar point, *professedly* lax. What this is depends, seemingly, on temperament. *A* makes no conscience of a little flattery in cases where he is certain that he is not acting from base or interested motives—in short, whenever his only motives are the amusement, the momentary pleasure given, &c., a medley of good nature, diseased proneness to sympathy, and a habit of *being wiser* behind the curtain than his own actions before it. *B* would die rather than deviate from truth and sincerity in this instance, but permits himself to utter, nay, publish the harshest censure of men as moralists and as *literati*, and that, too, on his simple *ipse dixit*, without assigning any reason, and often without having any, save that he himself *believes* it—believes it because he *dislikes* the man, and dislikes him probably for his looks, or, at best, for some one fault without any collation of the sum total of the man's qualities. Yet *A* and *B* are both good men, as the world goes. They do not act from conscious self-love, and are amenable to principles in their own minds.

October, 1803

A DRIZZLING rain. Heavy masses of shapeless vapour upon the mountains (O the perpetual forms of Borrowdale!) yet it is no unbroken tale of dull sadness. Slanting pillars travel across the lake at long intervals, the vaporous mass whitens in large stains of light—on the lakeward ridge of that huge arm-chair of Lodore fell a gleam of softest light, that brought out the rich hues of the late autumn. The woody Castle Crag between me and Lodore is a rich flower-garden of colours—the brightest yellows with the deepest crimsons and the infinite shades of brown and green, the *infinite* diversity of which blends the whole, so that the brighter colours seem to be colours upon a ground, not coloured things. Little woolpacks of white bright vapour rest on different summits and declivities. The vale is narrowed by the mist and cloud, yet through the wall of mist you can see into a bower of sunny light, in Borrowdale; the birds are singing in the tender rain, as if it were the rain of April, and the decaying foliage were flowers and blossoms. The pillar of smoke from the chimney rises up in the mist, and is just distinguishable from it, and the mountain forms in the gorge of Borrowdale consubstantiate with the mist and cloud, even as the pillar'd smoke—a shade deeper and a determinate form.

21 *October*, 1803, *Friday morning*

A MOST unpleasant dispute with Wordsworth and Hazlitt. I spoke, I fear, too contemptuously; but they spoke so irreverently, so malignantly of the Divine Wisdom that it overset me. Hazlitt, how easily raised to rage and hatred self-projected! but who shall find the force that can drag him up out of the depth into one expression of kindness, into the showing of one gleam of the light of love on his countenance. Peace be with him! But *thou*, dearest Wordsworth—and what if Ray, Durham, Paley have carried the observation of the aptitude of things too far, too habitually into pedantry? O how many worse pedantries! how few so harmless, with so much efficient good! Dear William, pardon pedantry in others, and avoid it in yourself, instead of scoffing and reviling at pedantry in good men and a good cause and *becoming* a pedant yourself in a bad cause—even by that very act becoming one. But, surely, always to look at the superficies of objects for the purpose of taking delight in their beauty, and sympathy with their real or imagined life, is as deleterious to the health and manhood of intellect as, always to be peering and unravelling contrivance may be to the simplicity of the affection and the grandeur and unity of the imagination. O dearest William! would Ray or Durham have spoken of God as you spoke of Nature?

26 *October*, 1803

Dozing, dreamt of Hartley as at his christening—how, as he was asked who redeemed him, and was to say, "God the Son," he went on humming and hawing in one hum and haw (like a boy who knows a thing and will not make the effort to recollect) so as to irritate me greatly. Awakening gradually, I was able completely to detect that it was the ticking of my watch, which lay in the pen-place in my desk, on the round table close by my ear, and which, in the diseased state of my nerves, had fretted on my ears. I caught the fact while Hartley's face and moving lips were yet before my eyes, and his hum and haw and the ticking of the watch were each the other, as often happens in the passing off of sleep—that curious modification of ideas by each other which is the element of *bulls*. I arose instantly and wrote it down. It is now ten minutes past five.

What is it that I employ my metaphysics on? To perplex our clearest notions and living moral instincts? To extinguish the light of love and of conscience, to put out the life of arbitrement, to make myself and others *worthless, soulless, Godless?* No, to expose the folly and the legerdemain of those who have thus abused the blessed organ of language, to support all old and venerable truths, to support, to kindle, to project, to make the reason spread light over our feelings, to make our feelings diffuse vital warmth through our reason—these are my objects and these my subjects. Is this the metaphysic that bad spirits in hell delight in?

Awoke, after long struggles, from a persecuting dream. The tale of the dream began in two *images*, in two sons of a nobleman, desperately fond of shooting, brought out by the footman to resign their property, and to be made believe that they had none. They were far too cunning for that, and as they struggled and resisted their cruel wrongers, and my interest for them, I suppose, increased, I became they—the duality vanished—Boyer and Christ's Hospital became concerned; yet, still, the former story was kept up, and I was conjuring him, as he met me in the street, to have pity on a nobleman's orphan, when I was carried up to bed, and was struggling up against some unknown impediment—when a noise of one of the doors awoke me. Drizzle; the sky uncouthly marbled with white vapours and large black clouds, their surface of a fine woolly grain, but in the height and key-stone of the arch a round space of sky with dim watery stars, like a friar's crown; the seven stars in the central seen through white vapour that, entirely shapeless, gave a whiteness to the circle of the sky, but stained with exceedingly thin and subtle flakes of black vapour, might be happily said in language of Boccace (describing Demogorgon, in his "Genealogia De Gli Dei") to be *vestito d'una pallidezza affumicata.*

10 *November,* ½ *past* 2 *o'clock, morning*

My nature requires another nature for its support, and reposes only in another from the necessary indigence of its being. Intensely similar yet not the same [must that other be]; or, may I venture to say, the same indeed, but dissimilar, as the same breath sent with the same force, the same pauses, and the same melody pre-imaged in the mind, into the flute and the clarion shall be the same *soul diversely incarnate.*

A BEAUTIFUL sunset, the sun setting behind Newlands across the foot of the lake. The sky is cloudless, save that there is a cloud on Skiddaw, one on the highest mountains in Borrowdale, some on Helvellyn, and that the sun sets in a glorious cloud. These clouds are of various shapes, various colours, and belong to their mountains and have nothing to do with the sky. N.B.—There is something metallic, silver playfully and imperfectly gilt and highly polished, or, rather, something mother-of-pearlish, in the sun-gleams on ice, thin ice.

I HAVE repeatedly said that I could make a volume if only I had noted down, as they occurred to my recollection, the instances of the proverb "Extremes Meet." This night, Sunday, December 11, 1803, half-past eleven, I have determined to devote the last nine pages of my pocket-book to a collection of the same.

1.   The parching Air
    Burns frore, and cold performs th' effect of Fire.

Paradise Lost, II, 594

2. Insects by their smallness, the mammoth by its hugeness, terrible.

3. In the foam-islands in a fiercely boiling pool, at the bottom of a waterfall, there is sameness from infinite change.

4. The excess of humanity and disinterestedness in polite society, the desire not to give pain, for example, not to talk of your own diseases and misfortunes, and to introduce nothing but what will give pleasure, destroy all humanity and disinterestedness, by making it intolerable, through desuetude, to listen to the complaints of our equals, or of any, where the listening does not gratify or excite some vicious pride and sense of superiority.

5. It is difficult to say whether a perfectly unheard-of subject or a *crambe bis cocta*, if chosen by a man of genius, would excite in the higher degree the sense of novelty. Take, as an instance of the latter, the "Orestes" of Sotheby.

6. Dark with excess of light.

7. Self-absorption and worldly-mindedness (N.B.—The latter a most philosophical word).

8. The dim intellect sees an absolute oneness, the perfectly clear intellect *knowingly perceives* it. Distinction and plurality lie in the betwixt.

9. The naked savage and the gymnosophist.

10. Nothing and intensest absolute being.

11. Despotism and ochlocracy.

1804

THIS evening, and indeed all this day, I ought to have been reading and filling the margins of Malthus.

I had begun and found it pleasant. Why did I neglect it? Because I *ought* not to have done this. The same applies to the reading and writing of letters, essays, &c. Surely this is well worth a serious analysis, that, by understanding, I may attempt to heal it. For it is a deep and wide disease in my moral nature, at once elm-and-oak-rooted. Is it love of liberty, of spontaneity or what? These all express, but do not explain the fact.

After I had got into bed last night I said to myself that I had been pompously enunciating as a difficulty, a problem of easy and common solution—viz., that it was the effect of association. From infancy up to manhood, under parents, schoolmasters, inspectors, etc., our pleasures and pleasant self-chosen pursuits (self-chosen because pleasant, and not originally pleasant because self-chosen) have been forcibly interrupted, and dull, unintelligible rudiments, or painful tasks imposed upon us instead. *Now* all duty is felt as a *command*, and every command *must offend*. Duty, therefore, by the law of association being felt as a command from without, would naturally call up the sensation of the pain roused from the commands of parents and schoolmasters. But I awoke with gouty suffocation this morning at half-past one, and as soon as disease permitted me to think at all, the shallowness and sophistry of this solution flashed upon me at once. I saw that the phenomenon occurred far, far too early: I have observed it in infants of two or three months old, and in Hartley I have seen it turned up and layed bare to the unarmed eye of the merest common sense. The fact is that interruption of itself is painful, because and as far as it acts as *disruption*. And thus without any reference to or distinct recollection of my former theory I saw great reason to attribute the effect, wholly, to the streamy nature of the associative faculty, and the more, as it is evident that they labour under this defect who are most reverie-ish and streamy—Hartley, for instance, and myself. This seems to me no common corroboration of my former thought on the origin of moral evil in general.

January, 1804

A TIME will come when passiveness will attain the dignity of worthy activity, when men shall be as proud within themselves of having remained in a state of deep tranquil emotion, whether in reading or in hearing or in looking, as they now are in having figured away for an hour. Oh! how few can transmute activity of mind into emotion! Yet there are as active as the stirring tempest and playful as the may-blossom in a breeze of May, who can yet for hours together remain with *hearts* broad awake, and the *understanding* asleep in all but its retentiveness and *receptivity*. Yea, and [in] the latter [state of mind] evince as great genius as in the former.

To J. Tobin, Esq., 10 April, 1804.

MEN who habitually enjoy robust health have, too gener-ally, the trick, and a very cruel one it is, of imagining that they discover the secret of all their acquaintances' ill health in some malpractice or other; and, sometimes, by gravely asserting this, here there and everywhere (as who likes his penetration [hid] under a bushel?), they not only do all they can, without intending it, to deprive the poor sufferer of that sympathy which is always a comfort and, in some degree, a support to human nature, but, likewise, too often implant serious alarm and uneasiness in the minds of the person's relatives and his nearest and dearest connections. Indeed (but that I have known its inutility, that I should be ridiculously sinning against my own law which I was pro-pounding, and that those who are most fond of advising are the least able to hear advice from others, as the passion to command makes men disobedient) I should often have been on the point of advising you against the two-fold rage of advising and of discussing character, both the one and the other of which infallibly generates presumption and blindness to our own faults. . . . Show me anyone made better by blunt advice, and I may abate of my dislike to it, but I have experienced the good effects of the contrary in Wordsworth's conduct to me; and, in Poole and others, have witnessed enough of its ill effects to be convinced that it does little else but harm both to the adviser and the advisee.

As I was gazing at a wall in Caernarvon Castle, I wished the guide fifty miles off that was telling me, In this chamber the Black Prince was born (or whoever it was). I am not certain whether I should have seen with any emotion the mulberry-tree of Shakspere. If it were a tree of no notice in itself, I am sure that I should feel by an effort—with self-reproach at the dimness of the feeling; if a striking tree, I fear that the pleasure would be diminished rather than increased, that I should have no unity of feeling, and find in the constant association of Shakspere having planted it an intrusion that prevented me from wholly (as a whole man) losing myself in the flexures of its branches and intertwining of its roots. . . .

But a Shakspere, a Milton, a Bruno, exist in the mind as pure *action*, defecated of all that is material and passive. And the great moments that formed them—it is a kind of impiety against a voice within us, not to regard them as predestined, and therefore things of now, for ever, and which were always. But it degrades the sacred feeling, and is to it what stupid superstition is to enthusiastic religion, when a man makes a pilgrimage to see a great man's shinbone found unmouldered in his coffin.

WHY do we so very, very often see men pass from one extreme to the other? στοδκαρδία [Stoddart, for instance]. Alas! they sought not the truth, but praise, self-importance, and above all [the sense of] something doing! Disappointed, they hate and persecute their former opinion, which no man will do who by meditation had adopted it, and in the course of unfeigned meditation gradually enlarged the circle and so got out of it. For in the perception of its falsehood he will form a perception of certain truths which had made the falsehood plausible, and can never cease to venerate his own sincerity of intention and Philalethie. For, perhaps, we never *hate* any opinion, or can do so, till we have *impersonated* it. We hate the persons because they oppose us, symbolize that opposition under the form and words of the opinion and then hate the person for the opinion and the opinion for the person.

[I HAVE no pity or patience for that] blindness which comes from putting out your own eyes and in mock humility refusing to form an opinion on the right and the wrong of a question. "If we say so of the Sicilians, why may not Buonaparte say this of the Swiss?" and so forth. As if England and France, Swiss and Sicilian were the x y z of Algebra, naked names of unknown quantities. [What is this but] to fix morals without morality, and [to allow] general rules to supersede all particular thought? And though it be never acted on in reality, yet the opinion is pernicious. It kills public spirit and deadens national effort.

O YOUNG man, who hast seen, felt and known the truth, to whom reality is a phantom and virtue and mind the sole actual and permanent being, do not degrade the truth in thee by disputing. Avoid it! do not by any persuasion be tempted to it! Surely not by vanity or the weakness of the pleasure of communicating thy thoughts and awaking sympathy, but not even by the always mixed hope of producing conviction. This is not the mode, this is not the time, not the place. [Truth will be better served] by modestly and most truly saying, "Your arguments are all consequent, if the foundation be admitted. I do not admit the foundation. But this will be a business for moments of thought, for a Sabbath-day of your existence. Then, perhaps, a voice from within will say to you, better, because [in a manner] more adapted to you, all I can say. But if I felt this to *be* that day or that moment, a sacred sympathy would at once compel and inspire me to the task of uttering the very truth. Till then I am right willing to bear the character of a mystic, a visionary, or self-important juggler, who nods his head and says, 'I could if I would.' But I cannot, I *may* not, bear the reproach of profaning the truth which is my life in moments when all passions heterogeneous to it are eclipsing it to the exclusion of its dimmest ray. I might lose my tranquillity, and in acquiring the *passion* of proselytism lose the *sense* of conviction. I might become *positive!* Now I am *certain!* I might have the heat and fermentation, now I have the warmth of life."

11 *Oct., Syracuse, Lecky's, midnight*

THE most common appearance in wintry weather is that of the sun under a sharp, defined level line of a stormy cloud, that stretches one-third or half round the circle of the horizon, thrice the height of the space that intervenes between it and the horizon, which last is about half again as broad as the sun. [At length] out comes the sun, a mass of brassy light, himself lost and diffused in his [own] strong splendour. Compare this with the beautiful summer *set* of colours without cloud.

So far from deeming it, in a religious point of view, criminal to spread doubts of God, immortality and virtue (that 3 = 1) in the minds of individuals, I seem to see in it a duty—lest man by taking the *words* for granted never attain the feeling or the true *faith*. They only forbear, that is, even to suspect that the idea is erroneous or the communicators deceivers, but do not *believe* the idea itself. Whereas to *doubt* has more of faith, nay even to disbelieve, than that blank negation of all such thoughts and feelings which is the lot of the herd of church-and-meeting-trotters.

I HAVE read with wonder and delight that passage of Reimarus in which he speaks of the immense multitude of plants, and the curious, regular *choice* of different herbivorous animals with respect to them, and the following pages in which he treats of the pairing of insects and the equally wonderful processes of egg-laying and so forth. All in motion! the sea-fish to the shores and rivers—the land crab to the seashore! I would fain describe all the creation thus agitated by the one or other of the three instincts—self-preservation, childing, and child-preservation. Set this by Darwin's theory of the maternal instinct—O mercy! the blindness of the man! and it is imagination, forsooth! that misled him—too much poetry in his philosophy! this abject deadness of all that sense of the obscure and indefinite, this superstitious fetish-worship of lazy or fascinated fancy! O this, indeed, deserves to be dwelt on.

THINK of all this as an absolute revelation, a real presence of Deity, and compare it with historical traditionary religion. There are two revelations—the material and the moral—and the former is not to be seen but by the latter. As St. Paul has so well observed: "By worldly wisdom no man ever arrived at God;" but having seen Him by the moral sense, then we *understand* the outward world. Even as with books, no book of itself teaches a language in the first instance; but having by sympathy of soul learnt it, we then understand the book—that is, the *Deus minor* in His work.

I SEE now that the eye refuses to decide whether it be surface or convexity, for the exquisite oneness of the flame makes even its angles so different from the angles of tangible substances. Its exceeding oneness added to its very subsistence in motion is the very *soul* of the loveliest curve—it does not need its body as it were. Its sharpest point is, however, rounded, and besides it is cased within its own penumbra.

ONE travels along with the lines of a mountain. Years ago I wanted to make Wordsworth sensible of this. How fine is Keswick vale! Would I repose, my soul lies and is quiet upon the broad level vale. Would it act? it darts up into the mountain-top like a kite, and like a chamois-goat runs along the ridge—or like a boy that makes a sport on the road of running along a wall or narrow fence!

IN the preface of my metaphysical works, I should say—"Once for all, read Kant, Fichte, &c., and then you will trace, or, if you are on the hunt, track me." Why, then, not acknowledge your obligations step by step? Because I could not do so in a multitude of glaring resemblances without a lie, for they had been mine, formed and full-formed, before I had ever heard of these writers, because to have fixed on the particular instances in which I have really been indebted to these writers would have been hard, if possible, to me who read for truth and self-satisfaction, and not to make a book, and who always rejoiced and was jubilant when I found my own ideas well expressed by others—and, lastly, let me say, because (I am proud, perhaps, but) I seem to know that much of the *matter* remains my own, and that the *soul* is mine. I fear not him for a critic who can confound a fellow-thinker with a compiler.

How flat and common-place! O that it were in my heart, nerves, and muscles! O that it were the *prudential* soul of all I love, of all who deserve to be loved, in every proposed action to ask yourself, To what end is this? and how is this the means? and not the means to something else foreign to or abhorrent from my purpose? *Distinct means to distinct ends!* With friends and beloved ones follow the heart. Better be deceived twenty times than suspect one-twentieth of once; but with strangers, or enemies, or in a quarrel, whether in the world's squabbles, as Dr. Stoddart's and Dr. Sorel in the Admiralty Court at Malta; or in moral businesses, as mine with Southey or Lloyd (O pardon me, dear and honoured Southey, that I put such a name by the side of yours . . . .)—in all those cases, write your letter, disburthen yourself, and when you have done it—even as when you have pared, sliced, vinegared, oiled, peppered and salted your plate of cucumber, you are directed to smell it, and then throw it out of the window—so, dear friend, vinegar, pepper and salt your letter—your cucumber argument, that is, cool reasoning previously sauced with passion and sharpness—then read it, eat it, drink it, smell it, with eyes and ears (a small catachresis but never mind), and then throw it into the fire—unless you can put down in three or four sentences (I cannot allow more than one side of a sheet of paper) the *distinct end* for which you conceive this letter (or whatever it be) to be the *distinct means!* How trivial! Would to God it were only *habitual!* O what is sadder than that the *crambe bis cocta* of the understanding should be and remain a foreign dish to the efficient *will*—that the best and loftiest precepts of wisdom should be trivial, and the worst and lowest modes of folly habitual.

1805

SEEING a nice bed of glowing embers with one junk of firewood well placed, like the remains of an old edifice, and another well-nigh mouldered one corresponding to it, I felt an impulse to put on three pieces of wood that exactly completed the perishable architecture, though it was eleven o'clock, though I was that instant going to bed, and there could be, in common ideas, no possible use in it. Hence I seem (for I write not having yet gone to bed) to suspect that this disease of totalising, of perfecting, may be the bottom impulse of many, many actions, in which it never is brought forward as an avowed or even agnized as a conscious motive.

Mem.—to collect facts for a comparison between a *wood* and a *coal* fire, as to sights and sounds and bodily feeling.

. . . deep sky is, of all visual impressions, the nearest akin to a feeling.

[THE] cause of the offence or disgust received by the *mean* in good poems when we are young, and its diminution and occasional evanescence when we are older in true taste [is] that, at first, we are from various causes delighted with *generalities* of nature which can all be expressed in dignified words; but, afterwards, becoming more intimately acquainted with Nature in her detail, we are delighted with *distinct*, vivid ideas, and with vivid ideas most when made distinct, and can most often forgive and sometimes be delighted with even a low image from art or low life when it gives you the very thing by an illustration, as, for instance, Cowper's stream "inlaying" the level vale as with silver, and even Shakspere's "shrill-tongued Tapster's answering shallow wits" applied to echoes in an *echofull* place.

16 *March,* 1805

"I WILL write," I said, "as truly as I can from experience, actual individual experience, not from book-knowledge." But yet it is wonderful how exactly the knowledge from good books coincides with the experience of men of the world. How often, when I was younger, have I noticed the deep delight of men of the world who have taken late in life to literature, on coming across a passage the force of which had either escaped me altogether, or which I knew to be true from books only and at second hand! Experience is necessary, no doubt, if only to give a light and shade in the mind, to give to some one idea a greater vividness than to others, and thereby to make it a *Thing* of *Time* and actual reality. For all ideas being equally vivid, the whole becomes a dream. But, notwithstanding this and other reasons, I yet believe that the saws against book-knowledge are handed down to us from times when books conveyed only abstract science or abstract morality and religion. Whereas, in the present day, what is there of real life, in all its goings on, trades, manufactures, high life, low life, animate and inanimate that is not to be found in books? In these days books are conversation. And this, I know, is for evil as well as good, but for good, too, as well as evil.

Midnight, 5 *April,* 1805

THERE are two sorts of talkative fellows whom it would be injurious to confound, and I, S. T. Coleridge, am the latter.

The first sort is of those who use five hundred words more than needs to express an idea—that is not my case. Few men, I will be bold to say, put more meaning into their words than I, or choose them more deliberately and discriminately. The second sort is of those who use five hundred more ideas, images, reasons, &c., than there is any need of to arrive at their object, till the only object arrived at is that the mind's eye of the bystander is dazzled with colours succeeding so rapidly as to leave one vague impression that there has been a great blaze of colours all about something. Now this is my case, and a grievous fault it is. My illustrations swallow up my thesis. I feel too intensely the omnipresence of all in each, platonically speaking; or, psychologically, my brain-fibres, or the spiritual light which abides in the brain-marrow, as visible light appears to do in sundry rotten mackerel and other *smashy* matters, is of too general an affinity with all things, and though it perceives the *difference* of things, yet is eternally pursuing the likenesses, or, rather, that which is common [between them]. Bring me two things that seem the very same, and then I am quick enough [not only] to show the difference, even to hair-splitting, but to go on from circle to circle till I break against the shore of my hearers' patience, or have my concentricals dashed to nothing by a snore. That is my ordinary mishap. At Malta, however, no one can charge me with one or the other. I have earned the general character of being a quiet well-meaning man, rather dull indeed! and who would have thought that he had been a *poet!* "O, a very wretched poetaster, ma'am! As to the reviews, 'tis well known he half-ruined himself in paying cleverer fellows than himself to write them," &c.

IT is as trite as it is mournful (but yet most instructive), and by the genius that can produce the strongest impressions of novelty by rescuing the stalest and most admitted truths from the impotence caused by the very circumstance of their universal admission—admitted so instantly as never to be *reflected* on, never by that sole key of reflection admitted into the effective, legislative chamber of the heart—so true that they lose all the privileges of Truth, and, as extremes meet by being *truisms*, correspond in utter inefficiency with universally acknowledged errors (in Algebraic symbols Truisms=Falsehoodisms=∞)—by that genius, I say, might good be worked in considering the old, old Methusalem saw that "evil produces evil." One error almost compels another. Tell one lie, tell a hundred. Oh, to show this, *a priori*, by bottoming it in all our faculties and by experience of touching examples!

In looking at objects of Nature while I am thinking, as at yonder moon dim-glimmering through the dewy window-pane, I seem rather to be seeking, as it were *asking* for, a symbolical language for something within me that already and for ever exists, than observing anything new. Even when that latter is the case, yet still I have always an obscure feeling as if that new phenomena were the dim awaking of a forgotten or hidden truth of my inner nature. It is still interesting as a word—a symbol. It is $\Lambda\acute{o}\gamma o\varsigma$ the Creator, and the Evolver! [Now] what is the right, the virtuous feeling, and consequent action when a man having long meditated on and perceived a certain truth, finds another, a foreign writer, who has handled the same with an approximation to the truth as he had previously conceived it? Joy! Let Truth make her voice audible! While I was preparing the pen to write this remark, I lost the train of thought which had led me to it. I meant to have asked something else now forgotten. For the above answers itself. It needed no answer, I trust, in my heart.

14 *April*, 1805

There are times when my thoughts—how like music! O that these times were more frequent! But how can they be, I being so hopeless, and for months past so incessantly employed in official tasks, subscribing, examining, administering oaths, auditing, and so forth?

John Tobin dead, and just after the success of his play! and Robert Allen dead suddenly!

O when we are young we lament for death only by sympathy, or with the general feeling with which we grieve for misfortunes in general, but there comes a time (and this year is the time that has come to me) when we lament for

death as death, when it is felt for itself, and as itself, aloof
from all its consequences. Then comes the grave-stone into
the heart with all its mournful names, then the bell-man's
or clerk's verses subjoined to the bills of mortality are no
longer common-place.

THE two characteristics which I have most observed in
Roman Catholic mummery processions, baptisms,&c., are,
first, the immense *noise* and jingle-jingle as if to frighten
away the daemon common-sense; and, secondly, the unmoved, stupid, uninterested faces of the conjurers. I have
noticed no exception. Is not the very nature of superstition
in general, as being utterly sensuous, *cold* except where it
is *sensual?* Hence the older form of idolatry, as displayed in
the Greek mythology, was, in some sense, even preferable to
the Popish. For whatever life did and could exist in superstition it brought forward and sanctified in its rites of
Bacchus, Venus, &c. The papist by pretence of suppression
warps and denaturalizes. In the pagan [ritual, superstition]
burnt with a bright flame, in the popish it consumes the
soul with a smothered fire that stinks in darkness and
smoulders like gum that burns but is incapable of light.

SCHILLER, disgusted with Kotzebuisms, deserts from Shakspere! What! cannot we condemn a counterfeit and yet
remain admirers of the original? This is a sufficient proof
that the first admiration was not sound, or founded on sound
distinct perceptions [or, if sprung from] a sound feeling, yet
clothed and manifested to the consciousness by false ideas.
And now the French stage is to be re-introduced. O Germany! Germany! why this endless rage for novelty? Why
this endless looking out of thyself? But stop, let me not fall
into the pit against which I was about to warn others. Let
me not confound the discriminating character and genius
of a nation with the conflux of its individuals in cities and
reviews. Let England be Sir Philip Sidney, Shakspere,
Milton, Bacon, Harrington, Swift, Wordsworth; and never
let the names of Darwin, Johnson, Hume, *fur* it over. If
these, too, must be England let them be another England; or,
rather, let the first be old England, the spiritual, Platonic
old England, and the second, with Locke at the head of the

philosophers and Pope [at the head] of the poets, together with the long list of Priestleys, Paleys, Hayleys, Darwins, Mr. Pitts, Dundasses, &c., &c., be the representatives of commercial Great Britain. These have [indeed] their merits, but are as alien to me as the Mandarin philosophers and poets of China. Even so Leibnitz, Lessing, Voss, Kant, shall be *Germany* to me, let whatever coxcombs rise up, and *shrill* it away in the grasshopper vale of reviews. And so shall Dante, Ariosto, Giordano Bruno, be my Italy; Cervantes my Spain; and O! that I could find a France for my love. But spite of Pascal, Madame Guyon and Molière, France is my Babylon, the mother of whoredoms in morality, philosophy and taste. The French themselves feel a foreignness in these writers. How indeed is it possible at once to *love* Pascal and Voltaire?

GOD knows! that at times I derive a comfort even from my infirmities, my sins of omission and commission, in the joy of the deep feeling of the opposite virtues in the two or three whom I love in my heart of hearts. Sharp, therefore, is the pain when I find faults in these friends opposite to my virtues. I find no comfort in the notion of average, for I wish to love even more than to be beloved, and am so haunted by the conscience of my many failings that I find an unmixed pleasure in esteeming and admiring, but, as the recipient of esteem or admiration, I feel as a man, whose good dispositions are still alive, feels in the enjoyment of a *darling* property on a doubtful title. My instincts are so far dog-like that I love beings superior to myself better than my equals. But the notion of inferiority is so painful to me that I never, in common life, feel a man my inferior except by after-reflection. What seems vanity in me is in great part attributable to this feeling. But of this hereafter. I will cross-examine myself.

THERE are actions which left undone mark the greater man; but to have done them does not imply a bad or mean man. Such, for instance, are Martial's compliments of Domitian. So may we praise Milton without condemning Dryden. By-the-bye, we are all too apt to forget that contemporaries have not the same *wholeness*, and *fixedness* in their notions of persons' characters, that we their posterity have. They can *hope* and *fear* and *believe* and *disbelieve*. We make up an ideal which, like the fox or lion in the fable, never changes.

MODERN poetry is characterized by the poets' *anxiety* to be always striking. There is the same march in the Greek and Latin poets. Claudian, who had powers to have been anything—observe in him this anxious, craving vanity! Every line, nay, every word, stops, looks full in your face, and asks and *begs* for praise! As in a Chinese painting, there are no distances, no perspective, but all is in the foreground; and this is nothing but vanity. I am pleased to think that, when a mere stripling, I had formed the opinion that true taste was virtue, and that bad writing was bad feeling.

THE desire of carrying things to a greater height of pleasure and admiration than, *omnibus trutinatis*, they are susceptible of, is one great cause of the corruption of poetry. Both to understand my own reasoning and to communicate it, ponder on Catullus' hexameters and pentameters, his "*numine abusum homines*" [and similar harsh expressions]. It is not whether or no the very same ideas expressed with the very same force and the very same naturalness and simplicity in the versification of Ovid and Tibullus, would not be still more delightful (though even that, for any number of poems, may well admit a doubt), but whether it is *possible* so to express them and whether, in every attempt, the result has not been to substitute manner for matter, and point that will not bear reflection (so fine that it breaks the moment you try it) for genuine sense and true feeling, and, lastly, to confine both the subjects, thoughts, and even words of poetry within a most beggarly cordon. *N.B.*—The same criticism applies to Metastasio, and, in Pope, to his quaintness, perversion, unnatural metaphors, and, still more, the cold-blooded use, for artifice or connection, of language justifiable only by enthusiasm and passion.

I CONFESS that it has cost, and still costs, my philosophy some exertion not to be vexed that I must admire, aye, greatly admire, Richardson. His mind is so very vile a mind, so oozy, hypocritical, praise-mad, canting, envious, concupiscent! But to understand and draw *him* would be to produce a work almost equal to his own; and, in order to do this, "*down, proud Heart, down*" (as we teach little children to say to themselves, bless them!), all hatred down! and, instead thereof, charity, calmness, a heart fixed on the good part, though the understanding is surveying all. Richardson felt truly the defect of Fielding, or what was not his excellence, and made that his *defect*—a trick of uncharitableness often played, though not exclusively, by contemporaries. Fielding's talent was observation, not meditation. But Richardson was not philosopher enough to know the difference—say, rather, to understand and develop it.

STODDART passes over a poem as one of those tiniest of tiny night-flies runs over a leaf, casting its shadow, three times as long as itself, yet only just shading one, or at most two letters at a time.

THE shattering of long and deep-rooted associations always places the mind in an angry state, and even when our own understandings have effected the revolution, it still holds good, only we apply the feeling to and against our former faith and those who still hold it—[a tendency] shown in modern infidels. Great good, therefore, of such revolution as alters, not by exclusion, but by an enlargement that includes the former, though it places it in a new point of view.

SEPTEMBER 1806—DECEMBER 1807

IN all processes of the understanding the shortest way will be discovered the last; and this, perhaps, while it constitutes the great advantage of having a teacher to put us on the shortest road at the first, yet sometimes occasions a difficulty in the comprehension, inasmuch as the longest way is more near to the existing state of the mind, nearer to what if left to myself, on starting the thought, I should have thought next. The shortest way gives me the *knowledge* best, but the longest makes me more *knowing*.

HAS every finite being (or only some) the temptation to become intensely and wholly conscious of its distinctness

and, as a result, to be betrayed into the wretchedness of
division? Grosser natures, wholly swallowed up in selfishness
which does not rise to self-love, never even acquire that
sense of distinctness, while, to others, love is the first step
to re-union. It is a by-word that religious enthusiasm borders on and tends to sensuality—possibly because all our
powers work together, and as a consequence of striding too
vastly up the ladder of existence, a great *round* of the ladder
is omitted, namely, love to some, *Eine verschiedene,* of our own
kind. Then let Religion love, else will it not only partake of,
instead of being partaken by, and so co-adunated with, the
summit of love, but will necessarily include the nadir of
love, that is, appetite. Hence will it tend to dissensualize
its nature into fantastic passions, the idolatry of Paphian
priestesses.

TIME, space, duration, action, active passion passive,
activeness, passiveness, reaction, causation, affinity—here
assemble all the mysteries known. All is known-unknown,
say, rather, *merely* known. All is unintelligible, and yet Locke
and the stupid adorers of that *fetish* earth-clod take all for
granted. By-the-bye, in poetry as well as metaphysics, that
which we first meet with in the dawn of our mind becomes
ever after *fetish,* to the many at least. Blessed he who first
sees the morning star, if not the sun, or purpling clouds his
harbingers. Thence is *fame* desirable to a great man, and
thence subversion of vulgar fetishes becomes a duty.

REST, motion! O ye strange locks of intricate simplicity,
who shall find the key? He shall throw wide open the por-
tals of the palace of sensuous or symbolical truth, and the
Holy of Holies will be found in the adyta. Rest=enjoyment
and death. Motion=enjoyment and life. O the depth of
the proverb, "Extremes meet"!

O FOR the power to persuade all the writers of Great
Britain to adopt the *ver, zer,* and *al* of the German! Why not
verboil, zerboil; verrend, zerrend? I should like the very
words *verflossen, zerflossen,* to be naturalised:

>   And as I looked now feels my soul creative throes,
>   And now all joy, all sense *zerflows.*

I do not know, whether I am in earnest or in sport while I recommend this *ver* and *zer;* that is, I cannot be sure whether I feel, myself, anything ridiculous in the idea, or whether the feeling that seems to imply this be not the effect of my anticipation of and sympathy with the ridicule of, perhaps, all my readers.

1808-1809

THE one mighty main defect of female education is that everything is taught but reason and the means of retaining affection. This—this—O! it is worth all the rest told ten thousand times:—how to greet a husband, how to receive him, how never to recriminate—in short, the power of pleasurable thoughts and feelings, and the mischief of giving pain, or (as often happens when a husband comes home from a party of old friends, joyous and full of heart) the love-killing effect of cold, dry, uninterested looks and manners.

LET me record the following important remark of Stuart, with whom I never converse but to receive some distinct and rememberable improvement (and if it be not remembered, it is the defect of my memory—which, alas! grows weaker daily—or a fault from my indolence in not noting it down, as I do this)—that there is a period in a man's life, varying in various men, from thirty-five to forty-five, and operating most strongly in bachelors, widowers, or those worst and miserablest widowers, unhappy husbands, in which a man finds himself at the *top of the hill*, and having attained, perhaps, what he wishes, begins to ask himself, What is all this for?—begins to feel the vanity of his pursuits, becomes half-melancholy, gives in to wild dissipation or self-regardless drinking; and some, not content with these (not *slow*) poisons, destroy themselves, and leave their ingenious female or female-minded friends to fish out some *motive* for an act which proceeded from a *motive-making* impulse, which would have acted even without a motive (even as the terror in nightmare is a bodily sensation, and though it most often calls up consonant images, yet, as I know by experience, can take effect equally without any); or, if not so, yet like gunpowder in a smithy, though it will not go off without a spark, is *sure* to receive one, if not this hour, yet the next. I had *felt* this truth, but never saw it before clearly: it came upon me at Malta under the melancholy, dreadful feeling of finding myself to be *man*, by a distinct division from boyhood, youth, and "young man." Dreadful was the feeling—till then life had flown so that I had always been a boy, as it were; and this sensation had blended in all my conduct, my willing acknowledgment of superiority, and, in truth, my meeting every person as a superior at the first moment. Yet if men survive this period, they commonly become cheerful again. That is a comfort for mankind, *not for me!*   18 *May*, 1808

EXPRESSIONS of honest self-esteem, in which *self* was only a diagram of the *genus*, will excite sympathy at the minute, and yet, even among persons who love and esteem you, be remembered and quoted as ludicrous instances of strange self-involution.

HE was grown, and solid from his infancy, like that most *useful* of domesticated animals, that never runs but with some prudent motive to the mast or the wash-tub and, at no time a slave to the present moment, never even grunts over the acorns before him without a scheming squint and the segment, at least, of its wise little eye cast toward those on one side, which his neighbour is or may be about to enjoy.

TREMENDOUS as a Mexican god is a strong sense of duty— separate from an enlarged and discriminating mind, and gigantically disproportionate to the size of the understanding; and, if combined with obstinacy of self-opinion and indocility, it is the parent of tyranny, a promoter of inquisitorial persecution in public life, and of inconceivable misery in private families. Nay, the very virtue of the person, and the consciousness that *it* is sacrificing its own happiness, increases the obduracy, and selects those whom it best loves for its objects. *Eoque immitior quia ipse tolerat* (not *toleraverat*) is its inspiration and watchword.

GREAT exploits and the thirst of honour which they inspire, enlarge states by enlarging hearts.

HEAVEN preserve me from the modern epidemic of a proud ignorance!

1810

THE *great change*—that in youth and early manhood we psychologize and with enthusiasm but all out of ourselves, and so far ourselves only as we descry therein some general law. Our own self is but the diagram, the triangle which represents all triangles. Afterward we psychologize out of others, and so far as they differ from ourselves. O how hollowly!

THE immense difference between being glad to find Truth *it*, and to find *it* TRUTH! O! I am ashamed of those who praise me! For I know that as soon as I tell them my mind on another subject, they will shrink and abhor me. For not because I enforced a truth were they pleased in the first instance, but because I had supported a favourite notion of theirs which they loved for its and their sake, and therefore would be glad to find it true—not that loving Truth they loved this opinion as one of its forms and consequences. The root! the root must be attacked!

THERE are, in every country, times when the few who know the truth have clothed it for the vulgar, and addressed the vulgar in the vulgar language and modes of conception, in order to convey any part of the truth. This, however, could not be done with safety, even to the *illuminati* themselves in the first instance; but to their successors habit gradually turned lie into belief, partial and *stagnate* truth into ignorance, and the teachers of the vulgar (like the Franciscan friars in the South of Europe) became a part of the vulgar— nay, because the laymen were open to various impulses and influences, which their instructors had built out (compare a brook in open air, liable to rainstreams and rills from new-opened fountains, to the same running through a mill guarded by sluice-gates and back-water), they became the vulgarest of the vulgar, till, finally, resolute not to detach themselves from the mob, the mob at length detaches itself from them, and leaves the mill-race dry, the moveless, rotten wheels as day-dormitories for bats and owls, and the old grindstones for wags and scoffers of the taproom to whet their wits on.

I WOULD strongly recommend Lloyd's "State Worthies" as the manual of every man who would rise in the world. In every twenty pages it recommends contradictions, but he who cannot reconcile them for himself, and discover which suits his plan, can never rise in the world. *N.B.*—I have a mind to draw a complete character of a worldly-wise man out of Lloyd. He would be highly-finished, useful, honoured, popular—a man revered by his children, his wife, and so forth. To be sure, he must not expect to be *beloved* by *one* proto-friend; and, if there be truth in reason or Christianity, he will go to hell—but, even so, he will doubtless secure himself a most respectable place in the devil's chimney-corner.

THE *thinking* disease is that in which the feelings, instead of embodying themselves in *acts*, ascend and become materials of general reasoning and intellectual pride. The dreadful consequences of this perversion [may be] instanced in Germany, *e.g.*, in Fichte *versus* Kant, Schelling *versus* Fichte and in Verbidigno [Wordsworth] *versus* S. T. C. Ascent where nature meant descent, and thus shortening the process—viz., *feelings* made the subjects and tangible substance of thought, instead of actions, realizations, *things done*, and as such externalized and remembered. On such meagre diet as feelings, evaporated embryos in their progress to *birth*, no moral being ever becomes healthy.

?1810

IN controversy it is highly useful to know whether you are really addressing yourself to an opponent or only to partisans, with the intention of preserving them firm. Either is well, but they should never be commingled.

WE understand Nature just as if, at a distance, we looked at the image of a person in a looking-glass, plainly and fervently discoursing, yet what he uttered we could decipher only by the motion of the lips or by his mien.

I WOULD say to a man who reminded me of a friend's unkind words or deeds which I had forgiven—Smoking is very well while we are all smoking, even though the head is made dizzy by it and the candle of reason burns red, dim and thick; but, for Heaven's sake, don't put an old pipe to my nose just at breakfast time, among dews and flowers and sunshine.

1811-1812

WHERE health is—at least, though pain be no stranger, yet when the breath can rise, and turn round like a comet at its perihelion in its ellipse, and again descend, instead of being a Sisiphus's stone; and the chest can expand as by its own volition and the head sits firm yet mobile aloft, like the vane of a tower on a hill shining in the blue air, and appropriating sunshine and moonlight whatever weight of clouds brood below—O when health and hope, and if not competence yet a debtless *unwealth, libera et laeta paupertas*, is his, a man may have and love many friends, but yet, if indeed they be friends, he lives with each a several and individual life.

ONE source of calumny (I say *source*, because *allophoby* from *hĕautopithygmy* is the only proper *cause*) may be found in this— every man's life exhibits two sorts of selfishness, those which are and those which are not objects of his own consciousness. *A* is thinking, perhaps, of some plan in which he may benefit another, and during this absorption consults his own little bodily comforts blindly—occupies the best place at the fire-side, or asks at once, "Where am I to sit?" instead of first inquiring after the health of another. Now the error lies here, that *B*, in complaining of *A*, first takes for granted either that these are acts of conscious selfishness in *A*, or, if he allows the truth, yet considers them just as bad (and so perhaps they may be in a certain sense), but *forgets* that his own life presents the same, judges of his own life exclusively by his own consciousness, that of another by conscious and unconscious in a lump. A monkey's anthropomorph attitudes we take for anthropic.

TRY not to become disgusted with active benevolence, or despondent because there is a *philanthropy-trade*. It is a sort of benefit-club of virtue, supported by the contributions of paupers in virtue, founded by genuine enthusiasts who gain a reputation for the thing—then slip in successors who know how to avail themselves of the influence and connections derived thereby—quite gratuitous, however, and bustling-active—but yet *bribe high* to become the unpaid physicians of the dispensary at St. Luke's Hospital, and bow and scrape and intrigue, Carlyleize and Knappize for it. And such is the [case with regard to] the slave trade. The first abolitionists were the good men who laboured when the thing seemed desperate—it was virtue for its own sake. Then the quakers, Granville Sharp, etc.—then the restless spirits who are under the action of tyrannical oppression from images, and, gradually, mixed vanity and love of power with it—the politicians+saints=Wilberforce. Last come the Scotchmen—and Brougham is now canvassing more successfully for the seat of Wilberforce, who retires with great honour and regret, from infirmities of age and *enoughness*. It is just as with the great original benefactors and founders of useful plans, Raleigh, Sir Hugh Middleton, etc.—men of genius succeeded by sharpers, but who often can better carry on what they never could have first conceived—and this, too, by their very want of those qualities and virtues which were necessary to the discovery.

THE sick and sleepless man, after the dawn of the fresh day, is fain to watch the smoke now from this and then from the other chimney of the town from his bed-chamber, as if willing to borrow from others that sense of a new day, of a discontinuity between the yesterday and the to-day, which his own sensations had not afforded.

1814-1818

THE first man of science was he who looked into a thing, not to learn whether it could furnish him with food, or shelter, or weapons, or tools, or ornaments, or *playwiths*, but who sought to know it for the gratification of *knowing;* while he that first sought to *know* in order to *be* was the first philosopher. I have read of two rivers passing through the same lake, yet all the way preserving their streams visibly distinct —if I mistake not, the Rhone and the Adar, through the Lake of Geneva. In a far finer distinction, yet in a subtler union, such, for the contemplative mind, are the streams of knowing and being. The lake is formed by the two streams in man and nature as it exists in and for man; and up this lake the philosopher sails on the junction-line of the constituent streams, still pushing upward and sounding as he goes, towards the common fountain-head of both, the mysterious source whose being is knowledge, whose knowledge is being—the adorable I AM IN THAT I AM.

I THOUGHT I expressed my thoughts well when I said, "There is no superstition but what has a religion as its base, and religion is only reason, seen perspectively by a finite intellect."

23 *February*, 1816

REFLECTIONS on my four gaudy flower-pots, compared with the former flower-poems. After a certain period, crowded with counterfeiters of poetry, and illustrious with true poets, there is formed for common use a vast *garden* of language, all the showy and all the odorous words and clusters of words are brought together, and to be plucked by mere mechanic and passive memory. In such a state, any man of common poetical reading, having a strong desire (to be?—O no! but—) to be thought a poet will present a flower-pot gay and gaudy, but the *composition!* That is wanting. We carry on judgement of times and circumstances into our pleasures. A flower-pot which would have enchanted us before flower gardens were common, for the very beauty of the component flowers, will be rightly condemned as commonplace, out of place (for such is a common-place poet)—it involves a contradiction both in terms and thought. So Homer's Juno, Minerva, &c., are read with delight—but Blackmore? This is the reason why the judgement of those who are newlings in poetic reading is not to be relied on. The positive, which belongs to all, is taken as the comparative, which is the individual's praise. A good ear which had never heard music—with what raptures would it praise one of Shield's or Arne's Pasticcios and Centos! But it is the human mind it praises, not the individual. Hence it may happen (I believe has happened) that fashionableness may produce popularity. "The Beggar's

Petition" is a fair instance, and what if I dared to add Gray's "Elegy in a Country Churchyard"?

30 *April*, 1816

THE merry little gnats (*Tipulidae minimae*) I have myself often watched in an April shower, evidently "dancing the hayes" in and out between the falling drops, unwetted, or, rather, un-down-dashed by rocks of water many times larger than their whole bodies.

WE all look up to the blue sky for comfort, but nothing appears there, nothing comforts, nothing answers us, and so we die.

THE revival of classical literature, like all other revolutions, was not an unmixed good. One evil was the passion for pure Latinity, and a consequent contempt for the barbarism of the scholastic style and terminology. For awhile the schoolmen made head against their assailants; but, alas! all the genius and eloquence of the world was against them, and by an additional misfortune the scholastic logic was professed by those who had no other attainments, namely, the monks, and these, from monkishness, were the enemies of all genius and liberal knowledge. They were, of course, laughed out of the field as soon as they lost the power of aiding their logic by the post-predicaments of dungeon, fire, and faggot. Henceforward speculative philosophy must be written classically, that is, without technical terms—therefore popularly—and the inevitable consequence was that those sciences only were progressive which were permitted by the apparent as well as real necessity of the case to have a scientific terminology—as mathesis, geometry, astronomy and so forth—while metaphysic sank and died, and an empirical highly superficial psychology took its place. And so it has remained in England to the present day. A man must have felt the pain of being compelled to express himself either laxly or paraphrastically (which latter is almost as great an impediment in intellectual construction as the translation of letters and symbols into the thought they represent would be in Algebra), in order to understand how much a metaphysician suffers from not daring to adopt the *ivitates* and *eitates* of the schoolmen as objectivity, subjectivity, negativity, positivity.

29 *April*, 1817, *Tuesday night*

IF a man could pass through Paradise in a dream, and have a flower presented to him as a pledge that his soul had really been there, and if he found that flower in his hand when he awoke—Aye! and what then?

FOR compassion a human heart suffices; but for full, adequate sympathy with joy, an angel's.

1819-1828

THERE is a species of applause scarcely less genial to a poet, whether bard, musician, or artist, than the vernal warmth to the feathered songsters during their nest-building or incubation—a sympathy, an expressed hope, that is the open air in which the poet breathes, and without which the sense of power sinks back on itself like a sigh heaved up from the tightened chest of a sick man. Alas! alas! alas!

THE defect of Archbishop Leighton's reasoning is the taking eternity for a sort of time, a *baro major*, a baron of beef or quarter of lamb, out of which and off which time is cut, as a brisket or shoulder—while, even in common discourse, without any design of sounding the depth of the truth or of weighing the words expressing it in the hair-balance of metaphysics, it would be more convenient to consider eternity the *simul et totum*—as the *antitheton* of time.

FOUND Mr. G. with Hartley in the garden, attempting to explain to himself and to Hartley a feeling of a something not present in Milton's works, that is, in "Paradise Lost," "Paradise Regained," and "Samson Agonistes," which he *did* feel delightedly in the "Lycidas," and (as I added afterwards) in the Italian sonnets compared with the English. And this appeared to me to be the *poet* appearing and wishing to appear as the poet, and, likewise, as the man, as much as, though more rare than, the father, the brother, the preacher, and the patriot. Compare with Milton, Chaucer's "Fall of the Leaf" and Spenser throughout, and you cannot but *feel* what Gillman meant to convey. What is the solution? This, I believe—but I must premise that there is a *synthesis* of intellectual insight including the mental object, the organ of the correspondent being indivisible, and this (O deep truth!) because the objectivity consists in the universality of its subjectiveness—as when it *sees*, and millions *see* even so, and the seeing of the millions is what constitutes to *A* and to each of the millions the *objectivity* of the sight, the equivalent to a common object—a synthesis of *this*, I say, and of proper external object which we call *fact*. Now, this it is which we find in religion. It is more than philosophical truth—it is other and more than historical fact; it is not made up by the addition of the one to the other, but it is the *identity* of both, the co-inherence.

Now, this being understood, I proceed to say, using the term objectivity (arbitrarily, I grant), for this identity of truth and fact, that Milton hid the poetry in or transformed (not trans-substantiated) the poetry into this objectivity, while Shakspere, in all things, the divine opposite or antithetic correspondent of the divine Milton, transformed the objectivity into poetry.

Mr. G. observed as peculiar to the "Hamlet," that it alone, of all Shakspere's plays, presented to him a moving along *before* him; while in others it was a moving, indeed, but with which he himself moved equally in all and with all, and without any external something by which the motion was manifested, even as a man would move in a balloon—a sensation of motion, but not a sight of moving and having been moved. And why is this? Because of all the characters of Shakspere's plays Hamlet is the only character with which, by contra-distinction from the rest of the *dramatis personae*, the fit and capable reader identifies himself as the representation of his own contemplative and strictly proper and very own being (action, &c., belongs to others, the moment we call it our own)—hence the events of the play, with all the characters, move because you stand still. In the other plays, your identity is equally diffused over all. Of no parts can you say, as in "Hamlet," they are moving. But ever it is *we*, or that period and portion of human action, which is unified into a dream, even as in a dream the personal unity is diffused and severalized (divided to the sight though united in the dim feeling) into a sort of reality. Even so [it is with] the styles of Milton and Shakspere—the same weight of effect from the exceeding *felicity* (subjectively) of Shakspere, and the exceeding *propriety* (*extra arbitrium*) of Milton.

THE best plan, I think, for a man who would wish his mind to continue growing is to find, in the first place, some means of ascertaining for himself whether it does or no; and I can think of no better than early in life, say after three-and-twenty, to procure gradually the works of some two or three great writers—say, for instance, Bacon, Jeremy Taylor, and Kant, with the "De Republica," "De Legibus," the "Sophistes" and "Politicus" of Plato, and the "Poetics," "Rhetorics," and "Politics" of Aristotle—and amidst all other reading, to make a point of reperusing some one, or some weighty part of some one of these every four or five years, having from the beginning a separate note-book for each of these writers, in which your impressions, suggestions, conjectures, doubts and judgements are to be recorded with date of each, and so worded as to represent most sincerely the exact state of your convictions at the time, such as they would be if you did not (which this plan will assuredly make you do sooner or later) anticipate a change in them from increase of knowledge. "It is possible that I am in the wrong, but so it now appears to me, after my best attempts; and I must therefore put it down in order that I may find myself so, if so I am." It would make a little volume to give in detail all the various moral as well as intellectual advantages that would result from the systematic observation of the plan. Diffidence and hope would reciprocally balance and excite each other. A continuity would be given to your being, and its progressiveness ensured. All your knowledge otherwise obtained, whether from books or conversation or experience, would find centres round which it would organize itself. And, lastly, the habit of confuting your past self, and detecting the causes and occasions of your having mistaken or overlooked the truth, will give you both a quickness and a winning kindness, resulting from sympathy, in exposing the errors of others, as if you were an *alter ego*, of his mistake. And such, indeed, will your antagonist appear to you, another past self—in all points in which the falsity is not too plainly a derivation from a corrupt heart and the predominance of bad passion or worldly interests overlaying the love of truth as truth. And even in this case the liveliness with which you will so often have expressed yourself in your private note-books, in which the words, unsought for and untrimmed because intended for your own eye, exclusively, were the first-born of your first impressions, when you were either enkindled by admiration of your writer, or excited by a humble disputing with him reimpersonated in his book, will be of no mean rhetorical advantage to you, especially in public and extemporary debate or animated conversation.

I SHOULD like to know whether or how far the delight I feel, and have always felt, in adages or aphorisms of universal or very extensive application is a general or common feeling with men, or a peculiarity of my own mind. I cannot describe how much pleasure I have derived from "Extremes meet," for instance, or "Treat everything according to its nature," and, the last, "Be"! In the last I bring all inward rectitude to its test, in the former all outward morality to its rule, and in the first all problematic results to their solution, and reduce apparent contraries to correspondent opposites. How many hostile tenets has it enabled me to contemplate as fragments of truth, false only by negation and mutual exclusion?

N.B.—The injurious manner in which men of genius are treated, not only as authors, but even when they are in social company. *A* is believed to be, or talked of as, a man of unusual talent. People are anxious to meet him. If he says little or nothing, they wonder at the report, never considering whether they themselves were fit either to excite, or if self-excited to receive and comprehend him. But with the simplicity of genius he attributes more to them than they have, and they put questions that cannot be answered but by a return to first principles, and then they complain of him as not conversing, but lecturing. "He is quite intolerable," "Might as well be hearing a sermon." In short, in answer to some objection, *A* replies, "Sir, this rests on the distinction between an *idea* and an *image*, and, likewise, its

difference from a perfect *conception*." "Pray, sir, explain."
Because he does not and cannot [state the case as concisely
as if he had been appealed to about a hand at] whist, 'tis
"Lord! how long he talks," and they never ask themselves,
Did this man force himself into your company? Was he not
dragged into it? What is the practical result? That the
man of genius should live as much as possible with beings
that simply love him, from relationship or old association,
or with those that have the same feelings with himself; but
in all other company he will do well to cease to be the man of
genius, and make up his mind to appear dull or common-
place as a companion, to be the most silent except upon the
most trivial subjects of any in the company, to turn off
questions with a joke or a pun as not suiting a wine-table,
and to trust only to his writings.

Few die of a *broken heart*, and these few (the surgeons tell
us) know nothing of it, and, dying suddenly, leave to the
dissector the first discovery. O this is but the shallow remark
of a hard and unthinking prosperity! Have you never seen
a stick broken in the middle, and yet cohering by the rind?
The fibres, half of them actually broken and the rest
sprained and, though tough, unsustaining? O many, many
are the broken-hearted for those who know what the moral
and practical heart of the man is!

Now the breeze through the stiff and brittle-becoming
foliage of the trees counterfeits the sound of a rushing stream
or water-flood suddenly sweeping by. The sigh, the modu-
lated continuousness of the murmur is exchanged for the
confusion of overtaking sounds—the self-evolution of the
One, for the clash or stroke of ever-commencing contact of
the multitudinous, without interspace, by confusion. The
short gusts rustle and the ear feels the unlithesome dryness,
before the eye detects the coarser, duller, though deeper
green, deadened and not [yet] awakened into the hues of
decay—echoes of spring from the sepulchral vault of winter.
The aged year, conversant with the forms of its youth and
forgetting all the intervals, feebly reproduces them, [as it
were, from] memory.

H   30 *September*, 1824

THE sweet prattle of the chimes—counsellors pleading in
the court of Love—then the clock, the solemn sentence of the
mighty Judge—long pause between each pregnant, inappellable word, too deeply weighed to be reversed in the High-
Justice-Court of Time and Fate. A more richly solemn
sound than this eleven o'clock at Antwerp I never heard—
dead enough to be opaque as central gold, yet clear enough
to be the mountain air.

1 August, 1828

OMNIANA

INWARD BLINDNESS

Talk to a blind man—he knows he wants the sense of sight,
and willingly makes the proper allowances. But there are
certain internal senses which a man may want, and yet be
wholly ignorant that he wants them. It is most unpleasant
to converse with such persons on subjects of taste, philosophy, or religion. Of course, there is no *reasoning* with them,
for they do not possess the facts, on which the reasoning
must be grounded. Nothing is possible but a naked dissent,
which implies a sort of unsocial contempt; or—what a man
of kind dispositions is very likely to fall into—a heartless
tacit acquiescence, which borders too nearly on duplicity.

TEXT SPARRING

When I hear (as who now can travel twenty miles in a
stage coach without the probability of hearing!) an ignorant
religionist quote an unconnected sentence of half a dozen
words from any part of the Old or New Testament, and
resting on the literal sense of these words the eternal misery
of all who reject, nay, even of all those countless myriads
who have never had the opportunity of accepting, this, and
sundry other articles of faith conjured up by the same
textual magic; I ask myself what idea these persons form of
the Bible, that they should use it in a way which they themselves use no other book in? They deem the whole written
by inspiration. Well! but is the very essence of rational
discourse, *i.e.* connection and dependency, done away,
because the discourse is infallibly rational? The mysteries,
which these spiritual Lynxes detect in the simplest texts,

remind me of the 500 nondescripts, each as large as his own
black cat, which Dr. Katterfelto, by aid of his solar microscope, discovered in a drop of transparent water.

But to a contemporary who has not thrown his lot in the
same helmet with them, these fanatics think it a crime to
listen. Let them then, or far rather, let those who are in
danger of infection from them, attend to the golden aphorisms of the old and orthodox divines. "Sentences in scripture
(says Dr. Donne), like hairs in horse-tails, concur in one
root of beauty and strength; but being *plucked out, one by one,
serve only for springes and snares.*"

SIR GEORGE ETHEREGE, ETC.

Often and often had I *read* Gay's "Beggar's Opera," and
always delighted with its poignant wit and original satire,
and if not without noticing its immorality, yet without any
offence from it. Some years ago, I for the first time saw it
represented in one of the London theatres; and such were
the horror and disgust with which it impressed me, so
grossly did it outrage all the best feelings of my nature, that
even the angelic voice and perfect science of Mrs. Billington
lost half their charms, or rather increased my aversion to the
piece by an additional sense of incongruity. Then I learned
the immense difference between reading and seeing a play—
no wonder, indeed. For who has not passed over with his
eye a hundred passages without offence which he could not
have even *read* aloud, or have heard so read by another
person, without an inward struggle? In mere passive silent
reading the thoughts remain mere thoughts, and these too
not our own,—phantoms with no attribute of place, no sense
of appropriation, that flit over the consciousness as shadows
over the grass or young corn in an April day. But even the
sound of our own or another's voice takes them out of
that lifeless, twilight realm of idea, which is the confine,
the *intermundium*, as it were, of existence and non-existence.
Merely that the thoughts have become audible, by blending
with them a sense of *outness*, gives them a sort of reality.
What then when by every contrivance of scenery, appropriate dresses, accordant and auxiliary looks and gestures,
and the variety of persons on the stage, realities are employed to carry the imitation of reality as near as possible to

perfect delusion? If a manly modesty shrinks from uttering an indecent phrase before a wife or sister in a private room, what must be the effect when a repetition of such treasons (for all gross and libidinous allusions are emphatically treasons against the very foundations of human society, against all its endearing charities, and all the mother virtues,) is hazarded before a mixed multitude in a public theatre? When every innocent female must blush at once with pain at the thoughts she rejects, and with indignant shame at those, which the foul hearts of others may attribute to her!

Thus too with regard to the comedies of Wycherly, Vanburgh, and Etherege, I used to please myself with the flattering comparison of the manners universal at present among all classes above the lowest with those of our ancestors even of the highest ranks. But if for a moment I think of those comedies as having been acted, I lose all sense of comparison in the shame, that human nature could at any time have endured such outrages to its dignity; and if conjugal affection and the sweet name of sister were too weak, that yet Filial Piety, the gratitude for a Mother's holy love, should not have risen and hissed into infamy these traitors to their own natural gifts, who lampooned the noblest passions of humanity in order to pander for its lowest appetites.

RELIGIOUS CEREMONIES

A man may look at glass, or through it, or both. Let all earthly things be unto thee as glass to see heaven through! Religious ceremonies should be pure glass, not dyed in the gorgeous crimsons and purple blues and greens of the drapery of saints and saintesses.

DECEMBER MORNING

The giant shadows sleeping amid the wan yellow light of the December morning, looked like wrecks and scattered ruins of the long, long night.

ARCHBISHOP LEIGHTON

Next to the inspired Scriptures,—yea, and as the vibration of that once struck hour remaining on the air, stands Leighton's Commentary on the first Epistle of Peter.

CHRISTIAN HONESTY

"O! that God," says Carey, in his "Journal in Hindostan," "would make the Gospel successful among them! That would undoubtedly make them honest men, and I fear nothing else ever will." Now this is a fact,—spite of infidels and psilosophizing Christians, a fact. A perfect explanation of it would require and would show the psychology of faith, —the difference between the whole soul's modifying an action, and an action enforced by modifications of the soul amid prudential motives or favouring impulses. Let me here remind myself of the absolute necessity of having my whole faculties awake and imaginative, in order to illustrate this and similar truths—otherwise my writings will be no other than pages of algebra.

RATIONALISM IS NOT REASON

. . . O! place before your eyes the island of Britain in the reign of Alfred, its unpierced woods, its wide morasses and dreary heaths, its blood-stained and desolated shores, its untaught and scanty population; behold the monarch listening now to Bede, and now to John Erigena; and then see the same realm, a mighty empire, full of motion, full of books, where the cotter's son, twelve years old, has read more than archbishops of yore, and possesses the opportunity of reading more than our Alfred himself; and then finally behold this mighty nation, its rulers and its wise men listening to —— Paley and to —— Malthus! It is mournful, mournful.

LIMITATION OF LOVE OF POETRY

A man may be, perhaps, exclusively a poet, a poet most exquisite in his kind, though the kind must needs be of inferior worth; I say, may be; for I cannot recollect any one instance in which I have a right to suppose it. But, surely, to have an exclusive pleasure in poetry, not being yourself a poet—to turn away from all effort, and to dwell wholly on the images of another's vision, is an unworthy and effeminate thing. A jeweller may devote his whole time to jewels unblamed; but the mere amateur, who grounds his taste on no chemical or geological idea, cannot claim the same

exemption from despect. How shall he fully enjoy Wordsworth, who has never meditated on the truths which Wordsworth has wedded to immortal verse?

NEGATIVE THOUGHT

On this calm morning of the 13th of November, 1809, it
occurs to me, that it is by a negation and voluntary act of
no thinking that we think of earth, air, water, &c. as dead.
It is necessary for our limited powers of consciousness, that
we should be brought to this negative state, and that this
state should pass into custom; but it is likewise necessary
that at times we should awake and step forward; and this
is effected by those extenders of our consciousness—sorrow,
sickness, poetry, and religion. The truth is, we stop in the
sense of life just when we are not forced to go on, and then
adopt a permission of our feelings for a precept of our
reason.

HATRED OF INJUSTICE

It is the mark of a noble nature to be more shocked with
the unjust condemnation of a bad man than of a virtuous
one; as in the instance of Strafford. For in such cases the
love of justice, and the hatred of the contrary, are felt more
nakedly, and constitute a strong passion *per se*, not only
unaided by, but in conquest of, the softer self-repaying
sympathies. A wise foresight too inspires jealousy, that so
may principles be most easily overthrown. This is the
virtue of a wise man, which a mob never possesses, even as
a mob never, perhaps, has the malignant *finis ultimus*, which
is the vice of a man.

A GOOD HEART

. . . There is in the heart of all men a working principle—
call it ambition, or vanity, or desire of distinction, the in-
separable adjunct of our individuality and personal nature,
and flowing from the same source as language—the instinct
and necessity in each man of declaring his particular existence, and thus of singling or singularizing himself. In some
this principle is far stronger than in others, while in others
its comparative dimness may pass for its non-existence. But

in thoughts at least, and secret fancies, there is in all men (idiocy of course excepted) a wish to remain the same and yet to be something else, and something more, or to exhibit what they are, or imagine they might be, somewhere else and to other spectators. Now, though this desire of distinction, when it is disproportionate to the powers and qualities by which the individual is indeed distinguished, or when it is the governing passion, or taken as the rule of conduct, is but a "knavish sprite," yet as an attendant and subaltern spirit, it has its good purposes and beneficial effects: and is not seldom

> — Sent with broom before,
> To sweep the dust behind the door.

Though selfish in its origin, it yet tends to elevate the individual from selfishness into self-love, under a softer and perhaps better form than that of self-interest, the form of self-respect. Whatever other objects the man may be pursuing, and with whatever other inclinations, he is still by this principle impelled and almost compelled to pass out of himself in imagination, and to survey himself at a sufficient distance, in order to judge what figure he is likely to make in the eyes of his fellow men. But in thus taking his station as at the apex of a triangle, while the self is at one angle of the base, he makes it possible at least that the image of his neighbour may appear at the other, whether by spontaneous association, or placed there for the purposes of comparison; and so both be contemplated at equal distance. But this is the first step towards disinterestedness; and though it should never be reached, the advantage of the appearance is soon learnt, and the necessity of avoiding the appearance of the contrary. But appearances cannot be long sustained without some touch of the reality. At all events there results a control over our actions; some good may be produced, and many a poisonous or offensive fruit will be prevented. Courtesy, urbanity, gallantry, munificence,—the outward influence of the law shall I call it, or rather fashion of honour,—these are the handsome hypocrisies that spring from the desire of distinction. I ask not the genius of a Machiavel, a Tacitus, or a Swift; it needs only a worldly experience and an observing mind, to convince a man of forty that there is no medium between the creed of misanthropy and that of the gospel.

LITERARY
CRITICISM

Coleridge was a literary critic all his life, associated with books and criticism and writers from his schooldays. He used to say that he had read "almost everything," and it was usually his habit to write comments in the margins and on the fly-leaves of the books he owned or borrowed. Through the libraries and private collections of the world are scattered volumes made valuable by these annotations, which, with the published criticism, make this division of Coleridge's work the largest.

The middle part of his life must be called the literary criticism "period." His first lecture-course was in 1805, his last in 1818, the year after the publication of "Biographia Literaria." The best reported and most important lectures were those of 1811-2. Almost equally important and more financially successful were those of 1818, but these lead on to other activities, to the Highgate conversations and speculations, and the philosophic leadership of some of the young men who were then first attracted to him.

It was difficult to know whether to include the "Biographia Literaria" here or in the section which follows. Having set himself to compose two volumes on literature, Coleridge could not restrain his impulse to write about philosophy and religion. The presence of the Wordsworth chapters decides it, though some of these now seem, unlike the Shaksperian criticism, to have more historical than permanent value; certain main issues, such as poetic diction, were finally dealt with by Coleridge and are now therefore the common and familiar foundation from which all such criticism starts.

Coleridge's earliest opinions, a few of which I have quoted first, contain strange enthusiasms which he soon grew out of. But as the later extracts show, his attitude never became "critical" in the sense of "scientific." The last thing Coleridge wanted to do was to withdraw himself to some height of observation remote from his subject. His nature needed the support of another's, and he was capable of inspiration from such contact. He longed for, and was capable of, influence. This explains the strength and tangibility of his praise, just as it partly explains his attack on the Review school of criticism and his own determination "always to reason against the head-dimming, heart-damping principle of judging a work by its defects, not its beauties."

The "Miscellaneous" Section consists of extracts from lecture notes, lecture reports, marginalia, and "Literary Remains." In spite of the difference in dependability between all the different texts concerned, I have thought it better to arrange them under subject headings. The reader who wants to gauge the authenticity of individual passages must use the Notes.

*"The Mysteries of Udolpho," a Romance; interspersed with some
Pieces of Poetry. By Ann Radcliffe, Author of the "Romance
of the Forest," &c.* 4 Vols. Robinsons. 1794.

> Thine too these golden keys, immortal **Boy!**
> This can unlock the gates of Joy,
> Of Horrour, that, and thrilling Fears,
> Or ope the sacred source of sympathetic **Tears.**

SUCH were the presents of the Muse to the infant Shakspere, and though perhaps to no other mortal has she been
so lavish of her gifts, the keys referring to the third line Mrs.
Radcliffe must be allowed to be completely in possession of.
This, all who have read the "Romance of the Forest" will
willingly bear witness to. Nor does the present production
require the name of its author to ascertain that it comes from
the same hand. The same powers of description are displayed, the same predilection is discovered for the wonderful
and the gloomy—the same mysterious terrors are continually
exciting in the mind the idea of a supernatural appearance,
keeping us, as it were, upon the very edge and confines of the
world of spirits, and yet are ingeniously explained by familiar causes; curiosity is kept upon the stretch from page to
page, and from volume to volume, and the secret, which the
reader thinks himself every instant on the point of penetrat-
ing, flies like a phantom before him, and eludes his eagerness
till the very last moment of protracted expectation. This art
of escaping the guesses of the reader has been improved and
brought to perfection along with the reader's sagacity; just
as the various inventions of locks, bolts, and private drawers,
in order to secure, fasten, and hide, have always kept pace
with the ingenuity of the pickpocket and house breaker,
whose profession is to unlock, unfasten, and lay open what
you have taken so much pains to conceal. In this contest of

curiosity on one side, and invention on the other, Mrs. Radcliffe has certainly the advantage. She delights in concealing her plan with the most artificial contrivance, and seems to amuse herself with saying, at every turn and doubling of the story, "Now you think you have me, but I shall take care to disappoint you." This method is, however, liable to the following inconvenience, that in the search of what is new, an author is apt to forget what is natural; and, in rejecting the more obvious conclusions, to take those which are less satisfactory. The trite and the extravagant are the Scylla and Charybdis of writers who deal in fiction. With regard to the work before us, while we acknowledge the extraordinary powers of Mrs. Radcliffe, some readers will be inclined to doubt whether they have been exerted in the present work with equal effect as in the "Romance of the Forest." Four volumes cannot depend entirely on terrific incidents and intricacy of story. They require character, unity of design, a delineation of the scenes of real life, and the variety of well supported contrast. "The Mysteries of Udolpho" are indeed relieved by much elegant description and picturesque scenery; but in the descriptions there is too much of sameness: the pine and the larch tree wave, and the full moon pours its lustre through almost every chapter. Curiosity is raised oftener than it is gratified; or rather, it is raised so high that no adequate gratification can be given it; the interest is completely dissolved when once the adventure is finished, and the reader, when he is got to the end of the work, looks about in vain for the spell which had bound him so strongly to it. There are other little defects, which impartiality obliges us to notice. The manners do not sufficiently correspond with the aera the author has chosen; which is the latter end of the sixteenth century. There is, perhaps, no direct anachronism, but the style of accomplishments given to the heroine, a country young lady, brought up on the banks of the Garonne; the mention of botany; of little circles of infidelity, &c. give so much the air of modern manners, as is not counter-balanced by Gothic arches and antique furniture.

1794

[WORDSWORTH: A FOOTNOTE]

I mark the glow-worm, as I pass,
Move with "green radiance"* through the grass,
Lines at Shurton Bars.

---

*The expression "green radiance" is borrowed from Mr. Wordsworth, a Poet whose versification is occasionally harsh and his diction too frequently obscure; but whom I deem unrivalled among the writers of the present day in manly sentiment, novel imagery, and vivid colouring.

1795

[BOWLES]

IN a Sonnet then we require a development of some lovely feeling, by whatever cause it may have been excited; but those Sonnets appear to me the most exquisite, in which moral Sentiments, Affections, or Feelings, are deduced from, and associated with, the Scenery of Nature. Such compositions generate a kind of thought highly favorable to delicacy of character. They create a sweet and indissoluble union between the intellectual and the material world. Easily remembered from their briefness, and interesting alike to the eye and the affections, these are the poems which we can "lay up in our heart and our soul," and repeat them "when we walk by the way, and when we lie down, and when we rise up." Hence the Sonnets of BOWLES derive their marked superiority over all other Sonnets; hence they domesticate with the heart, and become, as it were, a part of our identity.

1796

BIOGRAPHIA
LITERARIA

CHAPTER I

The motives of the present work—Reception of the Author's first publication—The discipline of his taste at school—The effect of contemporary writers on youthful minds—Bowles's sonnets—Comparison between the Poets before and since Mr. Pope.

It has been my lot to have had my name introduced, both in conversation, and in print, more frequently than I find it easy to explain, whether I consider the fewness, unimportance, and limited circulation of my writings, or the retirement and distance in which I have lived, both from the literary and political world. Most often it has been connected with some charge which I could not acknowledge, or some principle which I had never entertained. Nevertheless, had I had no other motive or incitement, the reader would not have been troubled with this exculpation. What my additional purposes were, will be seen in the following pages. It will be found, that the least of what I have written concerns myself personally. I have used the narration chiefly for the purpose of giving a continuity to the work, in part for the sake of the miscellaneous reflections suggested to me by particular events, but still more as introductory to the statement of my principles in Politics, Religion, and Philosophy, and an application of the rules, deduced from philosophical principles, to poetry and criticism. But of the objects, which I proposed to myself, it was not the least important to effect, as far as possible, a settlement of the long continued controversy concerning the true nature of poetic diction; and at the same time to define with the utmost impartiality the real *poetic* character of the poet, by whose writings this controversy was first kindled, and has been since fuelled and fanned.

In 1794, when I had barely passed the verge of manhood, I published a small volume of juvenile poems. They were received with a degree of favor, which, young as I was, I well know was bestowed on them not so much for any positive merit, as because they were considered buds of hope, and promises of better works to come. The critics of that day, the most flattering equally with the severest, concurred in objecting to them obscurity, a general turgidness of diction, and a profusion of new coined double epithets.* The first is the fault which a writer is the least able to detect in his own compositions: and my mind was not then sufficiently disciplined to receive the authority of others, as a substitute for my own conviction. Satisfied that the thoughts, such as they were, could not have been expressed otherwise, or at least more perspicuously, I forgot to enquire, whether the thoughts themselves did not demand a degree of attention unsuitable to the nature and objects of poetry. This remark however applies chiefly, though not exclusively, to the "Religious Musings." The remainder of the charge I admitted to its full extent, and not without sincere

---

*The authority of Milton and Shakspere may be usefully pointed out to young authors. In the "Comus," and other early Poems of Milton there is a superfluity of double epithets; while in the "Paradise Lost" we find very few, in the "Paradise Regained" scarce any. The same remark holds almost equally true of the "Love's Labour 's Lost," "Romeo and Juliet," "Venus and Adonis," and "Lucrece," compared with the "Lear," "Macbeth," "Othello," and "Hamlet" of our great Dramatist. The rule for the admission of double epithets seems to be this: either that they should be already denizens of our Language, such as blood-stained, terror-stricken, self-applauding: or when a new epithet, or one found in books only, is hazarded, that it, at least, be one word, not two words made one by mere virtue of the printer's hyphen. A language which, like the English, is almost without cases, is indeed in its very genius unfitted for compounds. If a writer, every time a compounded word suggests itself to him, would seek for some other mode of expressing the same sense, the chances are always greatly in favor of his finding a better word. *Tanquam scopulum sic vites insolens verbum*, is the wise advice of Caesar to the Roman Orators, and the precept applies with double force to the writers in our own language. But it must not be forgotten, that the same Caesar wrote a grammatical treatise for the purpose of reforming the ordinary language by bringing it to a greater accordance with the principles of Logic or universal Grammar.

acknowledgments both to my private and public censors for their friendly admonitions. In the after editions, I pruned the double epithets with no sparing hand, and used my best efforts to tame the swell and glitter both of thought and diction; though in truth, these parasite plants of youthful poetry had insinuated themselves into my longer poems with such intricacy of union, that I was often obliged to omit disentangling the weed, from the fear of snapping the flower. From that period to the date of the present work I have published nothing, with my name, which could by any possibility have come before the board of anonymous criticism. Even the three or four poems, printed with the works of a friend, as far as they were censured at all, were charged with the same or similar defects, though I am persuaded not with equal justice: with an EXCESS OF ORNA- MENT, in addition to STRAINED AND ELABORATE DICTION. (*Vide the criticisms on the "Ancient Mariner" in the Monthly and Critical Reviews of the first volume of the Lyrical Ballads.*) May I be permitted to add, that, even at the early period of my juvenile poems, I saw and admitted the superiority of an austerer and more natural style, with an insight not less clear, than I at present possess. My judgement was stronger, than were my powers of realizing its dictates; and the faults of my language, though indeed partly owing to a wrong choice of subjects, and the desire of giving a poetic colouring to abstract and metaphysical truths, in which a new world then seemed to open upon me, did yet, in part likewise, originate in unfeigned diffidence of my own comparative talent.—During several years of my youth and early man- hood, I reverenced those, who had re-introduced the manly simplicity of the Greek, and of our own elder poets, with such enthusiasm as made the hope seem presumptuous of writing successfully in the same style. Perhaps a similar process has happened to others; but my earliest poems were marked by an ease and simplicity, which I have studied, perhaps with inferior success, to impress on my later compositions.

At school I enjoyed the inestimable advantage of a very sensible, though at the same time a very severe master. He*

---

*The Rev. James Bowyer, many years Head Master of the Grammar School, Christ's Hospital.

early moulded my taste to the preference of Demosthenes to Cicero, of Homer and Theocritus to Virgil, and again of Virgil to Ovid. He habituated me to compare Lucretius, (in such extracts as I then read) Terence, and above all the chaster poems of Catullus, not only with the Roman poets of the, so called, silver and brazen ages; but with even those of the Augustan era: and on grounds of plain sense and universal logic to see and assert the superiority of the former in the truth and nativeness, both of their thoughts and diction. At the same time that we were studying the Greek Tragic Poets, he made us read Shakspere and Milton as lessons: and they were the lessons too, which required most time and trouble to *bring up*, so as to escape his censure. I learnt from him, that Poetry, even that of the loftiest and, seemingly, that of the wildest odes, had a logic of its own, as severe as that of science; and more difficult, because more subtle, more complex, and dependent on more, and more fugitive causes. In the truly great poets, he would say, there is a reason assignable, not only for every word, but for the position of every word; and I well remember that, availing himself of the synonimes to the Homer of Didymus, he made us attempt to show, with regard to each, *why* it would not have answered the same purpose; and *wherein* consisted the peculiar fitness of the word in the original text.

In our own English compositions, (at least for the last three years of our school education), he showed no mercy to phrase, metaphor, or image, unsupported by a sound sense, or where the same sense might have been conveyed with equal force and dignity in plainer words. Lute, harp, and lyre, muse, muses, and inspirations, Pegasus, Parnassus, and Hippocrene were all an abomination to him. In fancy I can almost hear him now, exclaiming *"Harp? Harp? Lyre? Pen and ink, boy, you mean! Muse, boy, Muse? Your Nurse's daughter, you mean! Pierian spring? Oh aye! the cloister-pump, I suppose!"* Nay, certain introductions, similes, and examples, were placed by name on a list of interdiction. Among the similes, there was, I remember, that of the Manchineel fruit, as suiting equally well with too many subjects; in which however it yielded the palm at once to the example of Alexander and Clytus, which was equally good and apt, whatever might be the theme. Was it

ambition? Alexander and Clytus!—Flattery? Alexander
and Clytus!—Anger? Drunkenness? Pride? Friendship?
Ingratitude? Late repentance? Still, still Alexander and
Clytus! At length, the praises of agriculture having been
exemplified in the sagacious observation, that, had Alexander been holding the plough, he would not have run his
friend Clytus through with a spear, this tried and serviceable
old friend was banished by public edict *in secula seculorum*.
I have sometimes ventured to think, that a list of this kind,
or an index expurgatorius of certain well known and ever
returning phrases, both introductory, and transitional, including a large assortment of modest egoisms, and flattering
illeisms, &c., &c., might be hung up in our law-courts, and
both houses of parliament, with great advantage to the
public, as an important saving of national time, an incal-
culable relief to his Majesty's ministers, but above all, as
insuring the thanks of country attornies, and their clients,
who have private bills to carry through the house.

Be this as it may, there was one custom of our master's,
which I cannot pass over in silence, because I think it imitable and worthy of imitation. He would often permit our
exercises, under some pretext of want of time, to accumulate, till each lad had four or five to be looked over. Then
placing the whole number *abreast* on his desk, he would ask
the writer, why this or that sentence might not have found
as appropriate a place under this or that other thesis: and if
no satisfying answer could be returned, and two faults of the
same kind were found in one exercise, the irrevocable verdict followed, the exercise was torn up, and another on the
same subject to be produced, in addition to the tasks of the
day. The reader will, I trust, excuse this tribute of recollection to a man, whose severities, even now, not seldom
furnish the dreams, by which the blind fancy would fain
interpret to the mind the painful sensations of distempered
sleep; but neither lessen nor dim the deep sense of my moral
and intellectual obligations. He sent us to the University
excellent Latin and Greek scholars, and tolerable Hebraists.
Yet our classical knowledge was the least of the good gifts,
which we derived from his zealous and conscientious tutor-
age. He is now gone to his final reward, full of years, and
full of honors, even of those honors, which were dearest to

his heart, as gratefully bestowed by that school, and still binding him to the interests of that school, in which he had been himself educated, and to which during his whole life he was a dedicated thing.

From causes, which this is not the place to investigate, no models of past times, however perfect, can have the same vivid effect on the youthful mind, as the productions of contemporary genius. The Discipline, my mind had undergone, *Ne falleretur rotundo sono et versuum cursu, concinnis et floribus; sed ut inspiceret quidnam subesset, quae sedes, quod firmamentum, quis fundus verbis; an figurae essent mera ornatura et orationis fucus; vel sanguinis e materiae ipsius corde effluentis rubor quidam nativus et incalescentia genuina;* removed all obstacles to the appreciation of excellence in style without diminishing my delight. That I was thus prepared for the perusal of Mr. Bowles's sonnets and earlier poems, at once increased *their* influence, and *my* enthusiasm. The great works of past ages seem to a young man things of another race, in respect to which his faculties must remain passive and submiss, even as to the stars and mountains. But the writings of a contemporary, perhaps not many years older than himself, surrounded by the same circumstances, and disciplined by the same manners, possess a *reality* for him, and inspire an actual friendship as of a man for a man. His very admiration is the wind which fans and feeds his hope. The poems themselves assume the properties of flesh and blood. To recite, to extol, to contend for them is but the payment of a debt due to one, who exists to receive it.

There are indeed modes of teaching which have produced, and are producing, youths of a very different stamp; modes of teaching, in comparison with which we have been called on to despise our great public schools, and universities

in whose halls are hung
Armoury of the invincible knights of old—

modes, by which children are to be metamorphosed into prodigies. And prodigies with a vengeance have I known thus produced! Prodigies of self-conceit, shallowness, arrogance, and infidelity! Instead of storing the memory, during the period when the memory is the predominant faculty, with facts for the after exercise of the judgement; and instead of awakening by the noblest models the fond and unmixed LOVE and ADMIRATION, which is the natural and graceful temper of early youth; *these* nurselings of improved pedagogy are taught to dispute and decide; to suspect all, but their own and their lecturer's wisdom; and to hold nothing sacred from their contempt, but their own contemptible arrogance: boy-graduates in all the technicals, and in all the dirty passions and impudence of anonymous criticism. To such dispositions alone can the admonition of Pliny be requisite, *Neque enim debet operibus ejus obesse, quod vivit. An si inter eos, quos nunquam vidimus, floruisset, non solum libros ejus, verum etiam imagines conquireremus, ejusdem nunc honor praesentis, et gratia quasi satietate languescit? At hoc pravum, malignumque est, non admirari hominem admiratione dignissimum, quia videre, complecti, nec laudare tantum, verum etiam amare contingit.*   *Plin. Epist., Lib.* I

I had just entered on my seventeenth year, when the sonnets of Mr. Bowles, twenty in number, and just then published in a quarto pamphlet, were first made known and presented to me, by a schoolfellow who had quitted us for the University, and who, during the whole time that he was in our first form (or in our school language a GRECIAN,) had been my patron and protector. I refer to Dr. Middleton, the truly learned, and in every way excellent Bishop of Calcutta:

> *qui laudibus amplis*
> *Ingenium celebrare meum, calamumque solebat,*
> *Calcar agens animo validum. Non omnia terrae*
> *Obruta; vivit amor, vivit dolor; ora negatur*
> *Dulcia conspicere; at flere et meminisse* relictum est.*
>
>   *Petr. Epist., Lib.* I, *Ep.* i

It was a double pleasure to me, and still remains a tender recollection, that I should have received from a friend so revered the first knowledge of a poet, by whose works, year after year, I was so enthusiastically delighted and inspired. My earliest acquaintances will not have forgotten the undisciplined eagerness and impetuous zeal, with which I laboured to make proselytes, not only of my companions, but of all

---

*I am most happy to have the necessity of informing the reader that, since this passage was written, the report of Dr. Middleton's death on his voyage to India has been proved erroneous. He lives and long may he live; for I dare prophecy, that with his life only will his exertions for the temporal and spiritual welfare of his fellow men be limited.

with whom I conversed, of whatever rank, and in whatever place. As my school finances did not permit me to purchase copies, I made, within less than a year and a half, more than forty transcriptions, as the best presents I could offer to those, who had in any way won my regard. And with almost equal delight did I receive the three or four following publications of the same author.

Though I have seen and known enough of mankind to be well aware, that I shall perhaps stand alone in my creed, and that it will be well, if I subject myself to no worse charge than that of singularity; I am not therefore deterred from avowing, that I regard, and ever have regarded the obligations of intellect among the most sacred of the claims of gratitude. A valuable thought, or a particular train of thoughts, gives me additional pleasure, when I can safely refer and attribute it to the conversation or correspondence of another. My obligations to Mr. Bowles were indeed important, and for radical good. At a very premature age, even before my fifteenth year, I had bewildered myself in metaphysicks, and in theological controversy. Nothing else pleased me. History, and particular facts, lost all interest in my mind. Poetry (though for a school-boy of that age, I was above par in English versification, and had already produced two or three compositions which, I may venture to say, without reference to my age, were somewhat above mediocrity, and which had gained me more credit than the sound, good sense of my old master was at all pleased with,) poetry itself, yea, novels and romances, became insipid to me. In my friendless wanderings on our *leave-days*,* (for I was an orphan, and had scarcely any connections in London,) highly was I delighted, if any passenger, especially if he were drest in black, would enter into conversation with me. For I soon found the means of directing it to my favorite subjects

> Of providence, fore-knowledge, will, and fate,
> Fixed fate, free will, fore-knowledge absolute,
> And found no end in wandering mazes lost.

This preposterous pursuit was, beyond doubt, injurious both

---

*The Christ's Hospital phrase, not for holidays altogether, but for those on which the boys are permitted to go beyond the precincts of the school.

to my natural powers, and to the progress of my education. It would perhaps have been destructive, had it been continued; but from this I was auspiciously withdrawn, partly indeed by an accidental introduction to an amiable family, chiefly however, by the genial influence of a style of poetry, so tender and yet so manly, so natural and real, and yet so dignified and harmonious, as the sonnets &c. of Mr. Bowles! Well were it for me, perhaps, had I never relapsed into the same mental disease; if I had continued to pluck the flower and reap the harvest from the cultivated surface, instead of delving in the unwholesome quicksilver mines of metaphysic depths. But if in after time I have sought a refuge from bodily pain and mismanaged sensibility in abstruse researches, which exercised the strength and subtlety of the understanding without awakening the feelings of the heart; still there was a long and blessed interval, during which my natural faculties were allowed to expand, and my original tendencies to develope themselves: my fancy, and the love of nature, and the sense of beauty in forms and sounds.

The second advantage, which I owe to my early perusal, and admiration of these poems, (to which let me add, though known to me at a somewhat later period, the Lewsdon Hill of Mr. Crow) bears more immediately on my present subject. Among those with whom I conversed, there were, of course, very many who had formed their taste, and their notions of poetry, from the writings of Mr. Pope and his followers: or to speak more generally, in that school of French poetry, condensed and invigorated by English understanding, which had predominated from the last century. I was not blind to the merits of this school, yet as from inexperience of the world, and consequent want of sympathy with the general subjects of these poems, they gave me little pleasure, I doubtless undervalued the *kind*, and with the presumption of youth withheld from its masters the legitimate name of poets. I saw that the excellence of this kind consisted in just and acute observations on men and manners in an artificial state of society, as its matter and substance: and in the logic of wit, conveyed in smooth and strong epigrammatic couplets, as its *form*. Even when the subject was addressed to the fancy, or the intellect, as in the "Rape of the Lock," or the "Essay on Man"; nay, when it was a consecutive narration, as in that astonishing product of matchless talent and ingenuity, Pope's Translation of the Iliad; still a *point* was looked for at the end of each second line, and the whole was as it were a sorites, or, if I may exchange a logical for a grammatical metaphor, a *conjunction disjunctive*, of epigrams. Meantime the matter and diction seemed to me characterized not so much by poetic thoughts, as by thoughts *translated* into the language of poetry. On this last point, I had occasion to render my own thoughts gradually more and more plain to myself, by frequent amicable disputes concerning Darwin's "BOTANIC GARDEN," which, for some years, was greatly extolled, not only by the *reading* public in general, but even by those, whose genius and natural robustness of understanding enabled them afterwards to act foremost in dissipating these "painted mists" that occasionally rise from the marshes at the foot of Parnassus. During my first Cambridge vacation, I assisted a friend in a contribution for a literary society in Devonshire: and in this I remember to have compared Darwin's work to the Russian palace of ice, glittering, cold and transitory. In the same essay, too, I assigned sundry reasons, chiefly drawn from a comparison of passages in the Latin poets with the original Greek, from which they were borrowed, for the preference of Collins' odes to those of Gray; and of the simile in Shakspere

> How like a younker or a prodigal,
> The skarfed bark puts from her native bay,
> Hugged and embraced by the strumpet wind!
> How like the prodigal doth she return,
> With over-weathered ribs and ragged sails,
> Lean, rent, and beggared by the strumpet wind!

to the imitation in the Bard;

> Fair laughs the morn, and soft the zephyr blows,
> While proudly riding o'er the azure realm
> In gallant trim the gilded vessel goes,
> YOUTH at the prow and PLEASURE at the helm;
> Regardless of the sweeping whirlwind's sway,
> That hushed in grim repose, expects its evening prey.

(In which, by the bye, the words "realm" and "sway" are rhymes dearly purchased.) I preferred the original on the ground, that in the imitation it depended wholly on the compositor's putting, or not putting, a *small Capital*, both in this, and in many other passages of the same poet, whether

the words should be personifications, or mere abstractions.
I mention this, because, in referring various lines in Gray to
their original in Shakspere and Milton; and in the clear
perception how completely all the propriety was lost in the
transfer; I was, at that early period, led to a conjecture,
which, many years afterwards was recalled to me from the
same thought having been started in conversation, but far
more ably, and developed more fully, by Mr. Wordsworth;
namely, that this style of poetry, which I have characterized
above, as translations of prose thoughts into poetic language,
had been kept up by, if it did not wholly arise from, the
custom of writing Latin verses, and the great importance
attached to these exercises, in our public schools. Whatever
might have been the case in the fifteenth century, when the
use of the Latin tongue was so general among learned men,
that Erasmus is said to have forgotten his native language;
yet in the present day it is not to be supposed, that a youth
can *think* in Latin, or that he can have any other reliance on
the force or fitness of his phrases, but the authority of the
writer from whence he has adopted them. Consequently he
must first prepare his thoughts, and then pick out, from
Virgil, Horace, Ovid, or perhaps more compendiously from
his* Gradus, halves and quarters of lines, in which to
embody them.

I never object to a certain degree of disputatiousness in a
young man from the age of seventeen to that of four or five
and twenty, provided I find him always arguing on one side
of the question. The controversies, occasioned by my unfeigned zeal for the honor of a favorite contemporary, then
known to me only by his works, were of great advantage in
the formation and establishment of my taste and critical
opinions. In my defence of the lines running into each
other, instead of closing at each couplet, and of natural

---

*In the "Nutricia" of Politian there occurs this line:
  Pura coloratos interstrepit unda lapillos.

Casting my eye on a University prize-poem, I met this line:
  Lactea purpureos interstrepit unda lapillos.

Now look out in the Gradus for *Purus*, and you find as the first
synonime, *lacteus;* for *coloratus*, and the first synonime is *purpureus*.
I mention this by way of elucidating one of the most ordinary
processes in the *ferrumination* of these centos.

language, neither bookish, nor vulgar, neither redolent of
the lamp, nor of the kennel, such as *I will remember thee;* instead of the same thought tricked up in the rag-fair finery of

> ———Thy image on her wing
> Before my FANCY's eye shall MEMORY bring,

I had continually to adduce the metre and diction of the
Greek Poets from Homer to Theocritus inclusive; and still
more of our elder English poets from Chaucer to Milton.
Nor was this all. But as it was my constant reply to authorities brought against me from later poets of great name, that
no authority could avail in opposition to TRUTH, NATURE,
LOGIC, and the LAWS of UNIVERSAL GRAMMAR; actuated
too by my former passion for metaphysical investigations;
I labored at a solid foundation, on which permanently to
ground my opinions, in the component faculties of the
human mind itself, and their comparative dignity and importance. According to the faculty or source, from which
the pleasure given by any poem or passage was derived, I
estimated the merit of such poem or passage. As the result
of all my reading and meditation, I abstracted two critical
aphorisms, deeming them to comprise the conditions and
criteria of poetic style; first, that not the poem which we
have *read*, but that to which we *return*, with the greatest pleasure, possesses the genuine power, and claims the name of
essential poetry. Second, that whatever lines can be translated
into other words of the same language, without diminution
of their significance, either in sense, or association, or in any
worthy feeling, are so far vicious in their diction. Be it
however observed, that I excluded from the list of worthy
feelings, the pleasure derived from mere novelty in the
reader, and the desire of exciting wonderment at his powers
in the author. Oftentimes since then, in perusing French
tragedies, I have fancied two marks of admiration at the end
of each line, as hieroglyphics of the author's own admiration
at his own cleverness. Our genuine admiration of a great
poet is a continuous *under-current* of feeling; it is everywhere
present, but seldom anywhere as a separate excitement. I
was wont boldly to affirm, that it would be scarcely more
difficult to push a stone out from the pyramids with the
bare hand, than to alter a word, or the position of a word,
in Milton or Shakspere, (in their most important works at

least,) without making the author say something else, or something worse, than he does say. One great distinction, I appeared to myself to see plainly, between, even the characteristic faults of our elder poets, and the false beauty of the moderns. In the former, from DONNE to COWLEY, we find the most fantastic out-of-the-way thoughts, but in the most pure and genuine mother English; in the latter, the most obvious thoughts, in language the most fantastic and arbitrary. Our faulty elder poets sacrificed the passion and passionate flow of poetry, to the subtleties of intellect, and to the starts of wit; the moderns to the glare and glitter of a perpetual, yet broken and heterogeneous imagery, or rather to an amphibious something, made up, half of image, and half of abstract* meaning. The one sacrificed the heart to the head; the other both heart and head to point and drapery.

The reader must make himself acquainted with the general style of composition that was at that time deemed poetry, in order to understand and account for the effect produced on me by the "SONNETS," the "MONODY at MATLOCK," and the "HOPE," of Mr. Bowles; for it is peculiar to original genius to become less and less *striking*, in proportion to its success in improving the taste and judgement of its contemporaries. The poems of WEST, indeed, had the merit of chaste and manly diction, but they were cold, and, if I may so express it, only *dead-coloured;* while in the best of Warton's there is a stiffness, which too often gives them the appearance of imitations from the Greek. Whatever relation therefore of cause or impulse Percy's collection of Ballads may bear to the most *popular* poems of the present day; yet in the more sustained and elevated style, of the then living poets, Bowles and Cowper† were, to the best of my knowledge,

---

*I remember a ludicrous instance in the poem of a young tradesman:

> No more will I endure love's pleasing pain,
> Or round my *heart's leg* tie his galling chain.

† Cowper's "Task" was published some time before the "Sonnets" of Mr. Bowles; but I was not familiar with it till many years afterwards. The vein of satire which runs through that excellent poem, together with the sombre hue of its religious opinions, would probably, *at that time*, have prevented its laying any strong hold on my affections. The love of nature seems to have led

the first who combined natural thoughts with natural diction; the first who reconciled the heart with the head.

It is true, as I have before mentioned, that from diffidence in my own powers, I for a short time adopted a laborious and florid diction, which I myself deemed, if not absolutely vicious, yet of very inferior worth. Gradually, however, my practice conformed to my better judgement; and the compositions of my twenty-fourth and twenty-fifth years (*ex. gr.* the shorter blank verse poems, the lines, which are now adopted in the introductory part of the "VISION" in the present collection, in Mr. Southey's "Joan of Arc," 2nd book, 1st edition, and the Tragedy of "REMORSE") are not more below my present ideal in respect of the general tissue of the style than those of the latest date. Their faults were at least a remnant of the former leaven, and among the many who have done me the honour of putting my poems in the same class with those of my betters, the one or two, who have pretended to bring examples of affected simplicity from my volume, have been able to adduce but one instance, and that out of a copy of verses half ludicrous, half splenetic. which I intended, and had myself characterized, as *sermoni propriora*.

Every reform, however necessary, will by weak minds be carried to an excess, that itself will need reforming. The reader will excuse me for noticing, that I myself was the first to expose *risu honesto* the three sins of poetry, one or the other of which is the most likely to beset a young writer. So long ago as the publication of the second number of the monthly magazine, under the name of NEHEMIAH HIGGIN-BOTTOM, I contributed three sonnets, the first of which had for its object to excite a good-natured laugh at the spirit of *doleful egotism*, and at the recurrence of favorite phrases, with the double defect of being at once trite and licentious. The second, on low, creeping language and thoughts, under the pretence of *simplicity*. And the third, the phrases of

---

Thompson to a chearful religion; and a gloomy religion to have led Cowper to a love of nature. The one would carry his fellow-men along with him into nature; the other flies to nature from his fellow-men. In chastity of diction however, and the harmony of blank verse, Cowper leaves Thompson immeasurably below him; yet still I feel the latter to have been the *born poet*.

which were borrowed entirely from my own poems, on the indiscriminate use of elaborate and swelling language and imagery. The reader will find them in the note* below, and

---

*   SONNET I

PENSIVE at eve, on the *hard* world I mused,
And *my poor* heart was sad; so at the MOON
I gazed, and sighed, and sighed; for ah how soon
Eve saddens into night! mine eyes perused
With tearful vacancy the *dampy* grass
That wept and glittered in the *paly* ray:
And I *did pause me* on my lonely way
And *mused me* on the *wretched ones* that pass
O'er the bleak heath of sorrow. But alas!
Most of *myself* I thought! when it befel,
That the *soothe* spirit of the *breezy* wood
Breathed in mine ear: "All this is very well,
But much of ONE thing, is for NO thing good."
Oh *my poor heart's* INEXPLICABLE SWELL!

                    SONNET II

OH I do love thee, meek SIMPLICITY!
For of thy lays the lulling simpleness
Goes to my heart, and soothes each small distress,
Distress though small, yet haply great to me.
'Tis true on Lady Fortune's gentlest pad
I amble on; and yet I know not why
So sad I am! but should a friend and I
Frown, pout and part, then I am *very* sad.
And then with sonnets and with sympathy
My dreamy bosom's mystic woes I pall;
Now of my false friend plaining plaintively,
Now raving at mankind in general;
But whether sad or fierce, 'tis simple all,
All very simple, meek SIMPLICITY!

                    SONNET III

AND this reft house is that, the which he built,
Lamented Jack! and here his malt he piled,
Cautious in vain! these rats, that squeak so wild,
Squeak not unconscious of their father's guilt.
Did he not see her gleaming through the glade!
Belike 'twas she, the maiden all forlorn.
What though she milk no cow with crumpled horn,
Yet, *aye* she haunts the dale where *erst* she strayed:
And *aye*, beside her stalks her amorous knight!
Still on his thighs their wonted brogues are worn,
And through those brogues, still tattered and betorn,
His hindward charms gleam an unearthly white.
Ah! thus through broken clouds at night's high Noon
Peeps in fair fragments forth the full-orbed harvest moon!

will I trust regard them as reprinted for biographical purposes, and not for their poetic merits. So general at that time, and so decided was the opinion concerning the characteristic vices of my style, that a celebrated physician (now, alas! no more) speaking of me in other respects with his usual kindness to a gentleman, who was about to meet me at a dinner party, could not however resist giving him a hint not to mention the *"House that Jack built"* in my presence, for "that I was *as sore as a boil* about that sonnet"; he not knowing, that I was myself the author of it.

From

CHAPTER II

[*My Critics*]

INDIGNATION at literary wrongs I leave to men born under happier stars. I cannot *afford it*. But so far from condemning those who can, I deem it a writer's duty, and think it creditable to his heart, to feel and express a resentment proportioned to the grossness of the provocation, and the importance of the object. There is no profession on earth, which requires an attention so early, so long, or so unintermitting as that of poetry; and indeed as that of literary composition in general, if it be such as at all satisfies the demands both of taste and of sound logic. How difficult

---

The following anecdote will not be wholly out of place here, and may perhaps amuse the reader. An amateur performer in verse expressed to a common friend a strong desire to be introduced to me, but hesitated in accepting my friend's immediate offer, on the score that "he was, he must acknowledge, the author of a confounded severe epigram on my *ancient mariner*, which had given me great pain." I assured my friend that, if the epigram was a good one, it would only increase my desire to become acquainted with the author, and begged to hear it recited: when, to my no less surprise than amusement, it proved to be one which I had myself some time before written and inserted in the "Morning Post."

To the author of the "Ancient Mariner."

> Your poem must eternal be,
> Dear sir! it cannot fail,
> For 'tis incomprehensible,
> And without head or tail.

and delicate a task even the mere mechanism of verse is, may be conjectured from the failure of those, who have attempted poetry late in life. Where then a man has, from his earliest youth, devoted his whole being to an object, which by the admission of all civilized nations in all ages is honorable as a pursuit, and glorious as an attainment; what of all that relates to himself and his family, if only we except his moral character, can have fairer claims to his protection, or more authorize acts of self-defence, than the elaborate products of his intellect and intellectual industry? Prudence itself would command us to *show*, even if defect or diversion of natural sensibility had prevented us from *feeling*, a due interest and qualified anxiety for the offspring and representatives of our nobler being. I know it, alas! by woeful experience! I have laid too many eggs in the hot sands of this wilderness, the world, with ostrich carelessness and ostrich oblivion. The greater part indeed have been trod under foot, and are forgotten; but yet no small number have crept forth into life, some to furnish feathers for the caps of others, and still more to plume the shafts in the quivers of my enemies, of them that unprovoked have lain in wait against my soul.

Sic vos, non vobis, mellificatis, apes!

From

CHAPTER III

*The Author's obligations to critics, and the probable occasion—
Principles of modern criticism—Mr. Southey's works and character.*

To anonymous critics in reviews, magazines, and news-journals of various name and rank, and to satirists with or without a name in verse or prose, or in verse-text aided by prose-comment, I do seriously believe and profess, that I owe full two thirds of whatever reputation and publicity I happen to possess. For when the name of an individual has occurred so frequently, in so many works, for so great a length of time, the readers of these works (which with a shelf or two of BEAUTIES, ELEGANT EXTRACTS and ANAS, form nine-tenths of the reading of the reading public) cannot but be familiar with the name, without distinctly remembering whether it was introduced for an eulogy or for censure. And this becomes the more likely, if (as I believe) the habit of perusing periodical works may be properly added to Averrhoe's* catalogue of ANTI-MNEMONICS, or weakeners of the memory. But where this has not been the case, yet the reader will be apt to suspect, that there must be something more than usually strong and extensive in a reputation, that could either require or stand so merciless and long-continued a cannonading. Without any feeling of *anger* therefore (for which indeed, on my own account, I have no pretext) I may yet be allowed to express some degree of *surprize*, that, after having run the critical gauntlet for a certain class of faults which I *had*, nothing having come before the judgement-seat in the interim, I should, year after year, quarter after quarter, month after month (not to mention sundry petty periodicals of still quicker revolution, "or weekly or diurnal") have been, for at least 17 years consecutively dragged forth by them into the foremost ranks of the *proscribed*, and forced to abide the brunt of abuse, for faults directly opposite, and which I certainly had not. How shall I explain this?

Whatever may have been the case with others, I certainly cannot attribute this persecution to personal dislike, or to envy, or to feelings of vindictive animosity. Not to the former, for with the exception of a very few who are my intimate friends, and were so before they were known as authors, I have had little other acquaintance with literary characters, than what may be implied in an accidental introduction, or casual meeting in a mixt company. And, as far as words and looks can be trusted, I must believe that, even in these instances, I had excited no unfriendly

---

Ex. gr. *Pediculos e capillis excerptos in arenam jacere incontusos:* eating of unripe fruit; gazing on the clouds, and (*in genere*) on moveable things suspended in the air; riding among a multitude of camels; frequent laughter; listening to a series of jests and humorous anecdotes, as when (so to modernize the learned Saracen's meaning) one man's droll story of an Irishman inevitably occasions another's droll story of a Scotchman, which again, by the same sort of conjunction disjunctive, leads to some *étourderie* of a Welshman, and that again to some sly hit of a Yorkshireman; the habit of reading tombstones in church-yards, &c. By the bye, this catalogue, strange as it may appear, is not insusceptible of a sound psychological commentary.

disposition.* Neither by letter, or in conversation, have I ever had dispute or controversy beyond the common social interchange of opinions. Nay, where I had reason to suppose my convictions fundamentally different, it has been my habit, and I may add, the impulse of my nature, to assign the grounds of my belief, rather than the belief itself; and not to express dissent, till I could establish some points of complete sympathy, some grounds common to both sides, from which to commence its explanation.

Still less can I place these attacks to the charge of envy. The few pages which I have published, are of too distant a date; and the extent of their sale a proof too conclusive against their having been popular at any time; to render probable, I had almost said possible, the excitement of envy

---

*Some years ago, a gentleman, the chief writer and conductor of a celebrated review, distinguished by its hostility to Mr. Southey, spent a day or two at Keswick. That he was, without diminution on this account, treated with every hospitable attention by Mr. Southey and myself, I trust I need not say. But one thing I may venture to notice; that at no period of my life do I remember to have received so many, and such high coloured compliments in so short a space of time. He was likewise circumstantially informed by what series of accidents it had happened, that Mr. Wordsworth, Mr. Southey, and I had become neighbours; and how utterly unfounded was the supposition, that we considered ourselves, as belonging to any common school, but that of good sense confirmed by the long-established models of the best times of Greece, Rome, Italy, and England; and still more groundless the notion, that Mr. Southey (for as to myself I have published so little, and that little of so little importance, as to make it ludicrous to mention my name at all) could have been concerned in the formation of a poetic sect with Mr. Wordsworth, when so many of his works had been published not only previously to any acquaintance between them; but before Mr. Wordsworth himself had written anything but in a diction ornate, and uniformly sustained; when too the slightest examination will make it evident, that between those and the after writings of Mr. Southey, there exists no other difference than that of a progressive degree of excellence from progressive developement of power, and progressive facility from habit and increase of experience. Yet among the first articles which this man wrote after his return from Keswick, we were characterized as "the School of whining and hypochondriacal poets that haunt the Lakes." In reply to a letter from the same gentleman, in which he had asked me, whether I was in earnest in preferring the style of Hooker to that of Dr. Johnson; and Jeremy Taylor to Burke; I stated, somewhat at large, the comparative excellences and defects, which characterized our

on *their* account; and the man who should envy me on any *other*, verily he must be *envy-mad!*

Lastly, with as little semblance of reason, could I suspect any animosity towards me from vindictive feelings as the cause. I have before said, that my acquaintance with literary men has been limited and distant; and that I have had neither dispute nor controversy. From my first entrance into life, I have, with few and short intervals, lived either abroad or in retirement. My different essays on subjects of national interest, published at different times, first in the "Morning Post" and then in the "Courier," with my courses of lectures on the principles of criticism as applied to Shakspere and Milton, constitute my whole publicity; the only occasions on which I *could* offend any member of the

---

best prose writers, from the reformation, to the first half of Charles 2nd; and that of those who had flourished during the present reign, and the preceding one. About twelve months afterwards, a review appeared on the same subject, in the concluding paragraph of which the reviewer asserts, that his chief motive for entering into the discussion was to separate a rational and qualified admiration of our elder writers, from the indiscriminate enthusiasm of a recent school, who praised what they did not understand, and caricatured what they were unable to imitate. And, that no doubt might be left concerning the persons alluded to, the writer annexes the names of Miss BAILIE, W. SOUTHEY, WORDSWORTH and COLERIDGE. For that which follows, I have only hearsay evidence; but yet such as demands my belief; *viz.* that on being questioned concerning this apparently wanton attack, more especially with regard to Miss Bailie, the writer had stated as his motives, that this lady, when at Edinburgh had declined a proposal of introducing him to her; that Mr. Southey had written against him; and Mr. Wordsworth had talked contemptuously of him; but that as to *Coleridge*, he had noticed him merely because the names of Southey and Wordsworth and Coleridge always went together. But if it were worth while to mix together, as ingredients, half the anecdotes which I either myself know to be true, or which I have received from men incapable of intentional falsehood, concerning the characters, qualifications, and motives of our anonymous critics, whose decisions are oracles for our reading public, I might safely borrow the words of the apocryphal Daniel, "*Give me leave*, O SOVEREIGN PUBLIC, *and I shall slay this dragon without sword or staff.*" For the compound would be as the "Pitch, and fat, and hair which Daniel took, and did seethe them together, and made lumps thereof, and put into the dragon's mouth, and so the dragon burst in sunder; and Daniel said, 'Lo, THESE ARE THE GODS YE WORSHIP.' "

I

republic of letters. With one solitary exception in which my words were first misstated and then wantonly applied to an individual, I could never learn, that I had excited the displeasure of any among my literary contemporaries. Having announced my intention to give a course of lectures on the characteristic merits and defects of English poetry in its different aeras; first, from Chaucer to Milton; second, from Dryden inclusive to Thompson; and third, from Cowper to the present day; I changed my plan, and confined my disquisition to the two former aeras, that I might furnish no possible pretext for the unthinking to misconstrue, or the malignant to misapply my words, and having stampt their own meaning on them, to pass them as current coin in the marts of garrulity or detraction.

Praises of the unworthy are felt by ardent minds as robberies of the deserving; and it is too true, and too frequent, that Bacon, Harrington, Machiavel, and Spinosa, are *not* read, because Hume, Condillac, and Voltaire *are*. But in promiscuous company no prudent man will oppugn the merits of a contemporary in his own supposed department; contenting himself with praising in his turn those whom *he* deems excellent. If I should ever deem it my duty at all to oppose the pretensions of individuals, I would oppose them in books which could be weighed and answered, in which I could evolve the whole of my reasons and feelings, with their requisite limits and modifications; not in irrecoverable conversation, where however strong the reasons might be, the feelings that prompted them would assuredly be attributed by some one or other to envy and discontent. Besides I well know, and I trust, have acted on that knowledge, that it must be the ignorant and injudicious who extol the unworthy; and the eulogies of critics without taste or judgement are the natural reward of authors without feeling or genius. *Sint unicuique sua praemia.*

How then, dismissing, as I do, these three causes, am I to account for attacks, the long continuance and inveteracy of which it would require all three to explain? The solution may seem to have been given, or at least suggested, in a note to a preceding page. *I was in habits of intimacy with Mr. Wordsworth and Mr. Southey!* This, however, transfers, rather than removes the difficulty. Be it, that, by an unconscionable extension of the old adage, *noscitur a socio*, my literary friends are never under the water-fall of criticism, but I must be wet through with the spray; yet how came the torrent to descend upon *them?*

First then, with regard to Mr. Southey. I well remember the general reception of his earlier publications: *viz.* the poems published with Mr. Lovell under the names of "Moschus" and "Bion"; the two volumes of poems under his own name, and the "Joan of Arc." The censures of the critics by profession are extant, and may be easily referred to:—careless lines, inequality in the merit of the different poems, and (in the lighter works) a predilection for the strange and whimsical; in short, such faults as might have been anticipated in a young and rapid writer, were indeed sufficiently enforced. Nor was there at that time wanting a party spirit to aggravate the defects of a poet, who with all the courage of uncorrupted youth had avowed his zeal for a cause, which he deemed that of liberty, and his abhorrence of oppression by whatever name consecrated. But it was as little objected by others, as dreamt of by the poet himself, that he *preferred* careless and prosaic lines on rule and of forethought, or indeed that he pretended to any other art or theory of poetic diction, besides that which we may all learn from Horace, Quinctilian, the admirable dialogue de Causis Corruptae Eloquentiae, or Strada's Prolusions; if indeed natural good sense and the early study of the best models in his own language had not infused the same maxims more securely, and, if I may venture the expression, more vitally. All that could have been fairly deduced was, that in his taste and estimation of writers Mr. Southey agreed far more with Warton, than with Johnson. Nor do I mean to deny, that at all times Mr. Southey was of the same mind with Sir Philip Sidney in preferring an excellent ballad in the *humblest* style of poetry to twenty indifferent poems that strutted in the *highest*. And by what have his works, published since then, been characterized, each more strikingly than the preceding, but by greater splendor, a deeper pathos, profounder reflections, and a more sustained dignity of language and of metre? Distant may the period be, but whenever the time shall come, when all his works shall be collected by some editor worthy to be his biographer,

I trust that an excerpta of all the passages, in which his writings, name, and character have been attacked, from the pamphlets and periodical works of the last twenty years, may be an accompaniment. Yet that it would prove medicinal in after times I dare not hope; for as long as there are readers to be delighted with calumny, there will be found reviewers to calumniate. And such readers will become in all probability more numerous, in proportion as a still greater diffusion of literature shall produce an increase of sciolists, and sciolism bring with it petulance and presumption. In times of old, books were as religious oracles; as literature advanced, they next became venerable preceptors; they then descended to the rank of instructive friends; and, as their numbers increased, they sunk still lower to that of entertaining companions; and at present they seem degraded into culprits to hold up their hands at the bar of every self-elected, yet not the less peremptory, judge, who chuses to write from humour or interest, from enmity or arrogance, and to abide the decision (in the words of Jeremy Taylor) "of him that reads in malice, or him that reads after dinner."

* * *

From
CHAPTER IV
. . . Mr. Wordsworth's earlier poems—On fancy and imagination . . .

DURING the last year of my residence at Cambridge, I became acquainted with Mr. Wordsworth's first publication entitled "Descriptive Sketches"; and seldom, if ever, was the emergence of an original poetic genius above the literary horizon more evidently announced. In the form, style, and manner of the whole poem, and in the structure of the particular lines and periods, there is an harshness and acerbity connected and combined with words and images all a-glow, which might recall those products of the vegetable world, where gorgeous blossoms rise out of the hard and thorny rind and shell, within which the rich fruit was elaborating. The language was not only peculiar and strong, but at times knotty and contorted, as by its own impatient strength; while the novelty and struggling crowd of images, acting in conjunction with the difficulties of the style, demanded always a greater closeness of attention, than poetry, (at all events, than descriptive poetry) has a right to claim. It not seldom therefore justified the complaint of obscurity. In the following extract I have sometimes fancied, that I saw an emblem of the poem itself, and of the author's genius as it was then displayed.

> 'Tis storm; and hid in mist from hour to hour,
> All day the floods a deepening murmur pour;
> The sky is veiled, and every cheerful sight:
> Dark is the region as with coming night;
> And yet what frequent bursts of overpowering light!
> Triumphant on the bosom of the storm,
> Glances the fire-clad eagle's wheeling form;
> Eastward, in long perspective glittering, shine
> The wood-crowned cliffs that o'er the lake recline;
> Wide o'er the Alps a hundred streams unfold,
> At once to pillars turned that flame with gold;
> Behind his sail the peasant strives to shun
> The West, that burns like one dilated sun,
> Where in a mighty crucible expire
> The mountains, glowing hot, like coals of fire.

The poetic PSYCHE, in its process to full development, undergoes as many changes as its Greek name-sake, the butterfly.* And it is remarkable how soon genius clears and purifies itself from the faults and errors of its earliest products; faults which, in its earliest compositions, are the more obtrusive and confluent, because as heterogeneous elements, which had only a temporary use, they constitute the very *ferment*, by which themselves are carried off. Or we may compare them to some diseases, which must work on the humors, and be thrown out on the surface, in order to secure the patient from their future recurrence. I was in

---

*The fact, that in Greek Psyche is the common name for the soul, and the butterfly, is thus alluded to in the following stanzas from an unpublished poem of the author:

> The butterfly the ancient Grecians made
> The soul's fair emblem, and its only name—
> But of the soul, escaped the slavish trade
> Of mortal life! For in this earthly frame
> Our's is the reptile's lot, much toil, much blame,
> Manifold motions making little speed,
> And to deform and kill the things, whereon we feed.

S.T.C.

my twenty-fourth year, when I had the happiness of knowing Mr. Wordsworth personally, and while memory lasts, I shall hardly forget the sudden effect produced on my mind, by his recitation of a manuscript poem, which still remains unpublished, but of which the stanza, and tone of style, were the same as those of the "Female Vagrant," as originally printed in the first volume of the "Lyrical Ballads." There was here no mark of strained thought, or forced diction, no crowd or turbulence of imagery; and, as the poet hath himself well described in his lines "on re-visiting the Wye," manly reflection, and human associations had given both variety, and an additional interest to natural objects, which in the passion and appetite of the first love they had seemed to him neither to need or permit. The occasional obscurities, which had risen from an imperfect controul over the resources of his native language, had almost wholly disappeared, together with that worse defect of arbitrary and illogical phrases, at once hackneyed, and fantastic, which hold so distinguished a place in the *technique* of ordinary poetry, and will, more or less, alloy the earlier poems of the truest genius, unless the attention has been specifically directed to their worthlessness and incongruity.* I did not perceive anything particular in the mere style of the poem alluded to during its recitation, except indeed such difference as was not separable from the thought and manner; and the Spenserian stanza, which always, more or less, recalls to

---

*Mr. Wordsworth, even in his two earliest, "The Evening Walk" and the "Descriptive Sketches," is more free from this latter defect than most of the young poets his contemporaries. It may however be exemplified, together with the harsh and obscure construction, in which he more often offended, in the following lines:—

'Mid stormy vapours ever driving by,
Where ospreys, cormorants, and herons cry;
Where hardly given the hopeless waste to cheer,
Denied the bread of life, the foodful ear,
Dwindles the pear on autumn's latest spray,
And *apple sickens* pale in summer's ray;
*Ev'n here content has fixed her smiling reign
With independence, child of high disdain.*

I hope, I need not say, that I have quoted these lines for no other purpose than to make my meaning fully understood. It is to be regretted that Mr. Wordsworth has not republished these two poems entire.

the reader's mind Spenser's own style, would doubtless have authorized, in my then opinion, a more frequent descent to the phrases of ordinary life, than could without an ill effect have been hazarded in the heroic couplet. It was not however the freedom from false taste, whether as to common defects, or to those more properly his own, which made so unusual an impression on my feelings immediately, and subsequently on my judgement. It was the union of deep feeling with profound thought; the fine balance of truth in observing, with the imaginative faculty in modifying the objects observed; and above all the original gift of spreading the tone, the *atmosphere*, and with it the depth and height of the ideal world around forms, incidents, and situations, of which, for the common view, custom had bedimmed all the lustre, had dried up the sparkle and the dew drops. "To find no contradiction in the union of old and new; to contemplate the ANCIENT of days and all his works with feelings as fresh, as if all had then sprung forth at the first creative fiat; characterizes the mind that feels the riddle of the world, and may help to unravel it. To carry on the feelings of childhood into the powers of manhood; to combine the child's sense of wonder and novelty with the appearances, which every day for perhaps forty years had rendered familiar;

With sun and moon and stars throughout the year,
And man and woman;

this is the character and privilege of genius, and one of the marks which distinguish genius from talents. And therefore is it the prime merit of genius and its most unequivocal mode of manifestation, so to represent familiar objects as to awaken in the minds of others a kindred feeling concerning them and that freshness of sensation which is the constant accompaniment of mental, no less than of bodily, convalescence. Who has not a thousand times seen snow fall on water? Who has not watched it with a new feeling, from the time that he has read Burns' comparison of sensual pleasure

To snow that falls upon a river
A moment white—then gone for ever!

In poems, equally as in philosophic disquisitions, genius produces the strongest impressions of novelty, while it

rescues the most admitted truths from the impotence caused
by the very circumstance of their universal admission.
Truths of all others the most awful and mysterious, yet being
at the same time of universal interest, are too often considered as *so* true, that they lose all the life and efficiency of
truth, and lie bed-ridden in the dormitory of the soul, side
by side with the most despised and exploded errors."—THE
FRIEND,* p. 76, No. 5.

This excellence, which in all Mr. Wordsworth's writings
is more or less predominant, and which constitutes the
character of his mind, I no sooner felt, than I sought to
understand. Repeated meditations led me first to suspect,
(and a more intimate analysis of the human faculties, their
appropriate marks, functions, and effects matured my conjecture into full conviction,) that fancy and imagination
were two distinct and widely different faculties, instead
of being, according to the general belief, either two names
with one meaning, or, at furthest, the lower and higher
degree of one and the same power. It is not, I own, easy
to conceive a more opposite translation of the Greek *Phan-
tasia* than the Latin *Imaginatio;* but it is equally true
that in all societies there exists an instinct of growth, a
certain collective, unconscious good sense working pro-
gressively to desynonymize those words originally of the
same meaning, which the conflux of dialects had supplied
to the more homogeneous languages, as the Greek and
German: and which the same cause, joined with accidents
of translation from original works of different countries,
occasion in mixt languages like our own. The first and
most important point to be proved is, that two conceptions
perfectly distinct are confused under one and the same
word, and (this done) to appropriate that word exclusively
to one meaning, and the synonyme (should there be one)
to the other. But if (as will be often the case in the arts
and sciences) no synonyme exists, we must either invent or
borrow a word. In the present instance the appropriation
has already begun, and been legitimated in the derivative

*As the "Friend" was printed on stampt sheets, and sent only by
the post to a very limited number of subscribers, the author has
felt less objection to quote from it, though a work of his own. To
the public at large indeed it is the same as a volume in manuscript.

adjective: Milton had a highly *imaginative*, Cowley a very *fanciful* mind. If therefore I should succeed in establishing the actual existences of two faculties generally different, the nomenclature would be at once determined. To the faculty by which I had characterized Milton, we should confine the term *imagination;* while the other would be contra-distinguished as *fancy*. Now were it once fully ascertained, that this division is no less grounded in nature, than that of delirium from mania, or Otway's

Lutes, lobsters, seas of milk, and ships of amber,

from Shakspere's

What! have his daughters brought him to this pass?

or from the preceding apostrophe to the elements; the theory of the fine arts, and of poetry in particular, could not, I thought, but derive some additional and important light. It would in its immediate effects furnish a torch of guidance to the philosophical critic; and ultimately to the poet himself. In energetic minds, truth soon changes by domestication into power; and from directing in the discrimination and appraisal of the product, becomes influencive in the production. To admire on principle, is the only way to imitate without loss of originality.

It has been already hinted, that metaphysics and psychology have long been my hobby-horse. But to have a hobby-horse, and to be vain of it, are so commonly found together, that they pass almost for the same. I trust therefore, that there will be more good humour than contempt, in the smile with which the reader chastises my self-complacency, if I confess myself uncertain, whether the satisfaction from the perception of a truth new to myself may not have been rendered more poignant by the conceit, that it would be equally so to the public.

From

CHAPTER X

*A chapter of digression and anecdotes, as an interlude preceding that
on the nature and genesis of the imagination or plastic power—
. . . Various anecdotes of the Author's literary life, and the
progress of his opinions in religion and politics.*

"*Esemplastic. The word is not in Johnson, nor have I met with
it elsewhere.*" Neither have I. I constructed it myself from
the Greek words, εἰς ἓν πλάττειν, to shape into one; because, having to convey a new sense, I thought that a new
term would both aid the recollection of my meaning, and
prevent its being confounded with the usual import of the
word, imagination. "*But this is pedantry!*" Not necessarily
so, I hope. If I am not misinformed, pedantry consists
in the use of words unsuitable to the time, place, and
company. The language of the market would be in the
schools as *pedantic*, though it might not be reprobated by
that name, as the language of the schools in the market.
The mere man of the world, who insists that no other terms
but such as occur in common conversation should be employed in a scientific disquisition, and with no greater
precision, is as truly a *pedant* as the man of letters, who
either over-rating the acquirements of his auditors, or misled
by his own familiarity with technical or scholastic terms, con-
verses at the wine-table with his mind fixed on his musaeum
or laboratory; even though the latter pedant instead of
desiring his wife to *make the tea* should bid her add to the
quant. suff. of thea Sinensis the oxyd of hydrogen saturated
with caloric. To use the colloquial (and in truth somewhat
vulgar) metaphor, if the pedant of the cloyster, and the
pedant of the lobby, both *smell equally of the shop*, yet the
odour from the Russian binding of good old *authentic-looking*
folios and quartos is less annoying than the steams from the
tavern or bagnio. Nay, though the pedantry of the scholar
should betray a little ostentation, yet a well-conditioned
mind would more easily, methinks, tolerate the *fox brush*
of learned vanity, than the *sans culotterie* of a contemptuous

ignorance, that assumes a merit from mutilation in the self-consoling sneer at the pompous incumbrance of tails.

The first lesson of philosophic discipline is to wean the student's attention from the DEGREES of things, which alone form the vocabulary of common life, and to direct it to the KIND abstracted from *degree*. Thus the chemical student is taught not to be startled at disquisitions on the heat in ice, or on latent and fixible light. In such discourse the instructor has no other alternative than either to use old words with new meanings (the plan adopted by Darwin in his Zoonomia;) or to introduce new terms, after the example of Linnaeus, and the framers of the present chemical nomenclature. The latter mode is evidently preferable, were it only that the former demands a twofold exertion of thought in one and the same act. For the reader, or hearer, is required not only to learn and bear in mind the new definition; but to unlearn, and keep out of his view, the old and habitual meaning; a far more difficult and perplexing task, and for which the mere *semblance* of eschewing pedantry seems to me an inadequate compensation. Where, indeed, it is in our power to recall an unappropriate term that had without sufficient reason become obsolete, it is doubtless a less evil to restore than to coin anew. Thus to express in one word, all that appertains to the perception, considered as passive, and merely recipient, I have adopted from our elder classics the word *sensuous;* because *sensual* is not at present used, except in a bad sense, or at least as a *moral* distinction; while *sensitive* and *sensible* would each convey a different meaning. Thus too I have followed Hooker, Sanderson, Milton, &c., in designating the *immediateness* of any act or object of knowledge by the word *intuition*, used sometimes subjectively, sometimes objectively, even as we use the word, thought, now as *the* thought, or act of thinking, and now as *a* thought, or the object of our reflection; and we do this without confusion or obscurity. The very words, *objective* and *subjective*, of such constant recurrence in the schools of yore, I have ventured to re-introduce, because I could not so briefly or conveniently by any more familiar terms distinguish the percipere from the percipi. Lastly, I have cautiously discriminated the terms, THE REASON, and THE UNDERSTANDING, encouraged and confirmed by the

authority of our genuine divines and philosophers, before
the revolution.

> ————both life, and sense,
> Fancy, and *understanding;* whence the soul
> *Reason* receives, and REASON is her *being*,
> DISCURSIVE or INTUITIVE: discourse*
> Is oftest your's, the latter most is our's,
> Differing but in *degree*, in *kind* the same.
> *Paradise Lost, Book V*

I say, that I was *confirmed* by authority so venerable: for
I had previous and higher motives in my own conviction
of the importance, nay, of the necessity of the distinction,
as both an indispensable condition and a vital part of all
sound speculation in metaphysics, ethical or theological.
To establish this distinction was one main object of THE
FRIEND; if even in a biography of my own literary life I can
with propriety refer to a work, which was printed rather
than published, or so published that it had been well for the
unfortunate author, if it had remained in manuscript!

. . . With equal lack of worldly knowledge, I was a far
more than equal sufferer for it, at the very outset of my
authorship. Toward the close of the first year from the time,
that in an inauspicious hour I left the friendly cloysters, and
the happy grove of quiet, ever honored Jesus College, Cambridge, I was persuaded by sundry Philanthropists and
Anti-polemists to set on foot a periodical work, entitled
THE WATCHMAN, that, (according to the general motto of the
work,) *all might know the truth, and that the truth might make us
free!* In order to exempt it from the stamp-tax, and likewise
to contribute as little as possible to the supposed guilt of a
war against freedom, it was to be published on every eighth
day, thirty-two pages, large octavo, closely printed, and
price only FOUR-PENCE. Accordingly with a flaming prospectus, "*Knowledge is Power*" &c., *to cry the state of the political
atmosphere*, and so forth, I set off on a tour to the North, from

---

*But for sundry notes on Shakspere, &c., and other pieces
which have fallen in my way, I should have deemed it unnecessary to observe, that *discourse* here, or elsewhere, does not
mean what we *now* call discoursing; but the *discursion* of the *mind*,
the processes of generalization and subsumption, of deduction
and conclusion. Thus, Philosophy has *hitherto* been DISCURSIVE;
while Geometry is *always* and *essentially* INTUITIVE.

Bristol to Sheffield, for the purpose of procuring customers, preaching by the way in most of the great towns, as an hireless volunteer, in a blue coat and white waistcoat, that not a rag of the woman of Babylon might be seen on me. For I was at that time and long after, though a Trinitarian (*i.e. ad normam Platonis*) in philosophy, yet a zealous Unitarian in Religion; more accurately, I was a *psilanthropist*, one of those who believe our Lord to have been the real son of Joseph, and who lay the main stress on the resurrection rather than on the crucifixion. O! never can I remember those days with either shame or regret. For I was most sincere, most disinterested! My opinions were indeed in many and most important points erroneous; but my heart was single. Wealth, rank, life itself then seemed cheap to me, compared with the interests of (what I believed to be) the truth, and the will of my maker. I cannot even accuse myself of having been actuated by vanity; for in the expansion of my enthusiasm I did not think of *myself* at all.

My campaign commenced at Birmingham; and my first attack was on a rigid Calvinist, a tallow-chandler by trade. He was a tall dingy man, in whom length was so predominant over breadth, that he might almost have been borrowed for a foundery poker. O that face! a face $κατ'$ $ἔμφασιν$! I have it before me at this moment. The lank, black, twine-like hair, *pingui-nitescent*, cut in a straight line along the black stubble of his thin gunpowder eye-brows, that looked like a scorched *after-math* from a last week's shaving. His coat collar behind in perfect unison, both of colour and lustre, with the coarse yet glib cordage, that I suppose he called his hair, and which with a *bend* inward at the nape of the neck, (the only approach to flexure in his whole figure,) slunk in behind his waistcoat; while the countenance lank, dark, very *hard*, and with strong perpendicular furrows, gave me a dim notion of some one looking at me through a *used* gridiron, all soot, grease, and iron! But he was one of the *thorough-bred*, a true lover of liberty, and, (I was informed,) had proved to the satisfaction of many, that Mr. Pitt was one of the horns of the second beast in the Revelations, that *spoke like a dragon*. A person, to whom one of my letters of recommendation had been

addressed, was my introducer. It was a new event in my
life, my first *stroke* in the new business I had undertaken of an
author, yea, and of an author trading on his own account.
My companion after some imperfect sentences and a multitude of hums and haas abandoned the cause to his client;
and I commenced an harangue of half an hour to Phileleu-
theros, the tallow-chandler, varying my notes, through the
whole gamut of eloquence, from the ratiocinative to the
declamatory, and in the latter from the pathetic to the
indignant. I argued, I described, I promised, I prophesied;
and beginning with the captivity of nations I ended with the
near approach of the millennium, finishing the whole with
some of my own verses describing that glorious state out of
the "Religious Musings":

> ———————————— Such delights
> As float to earth, permitted visitants!
> When in some hour of solemn jubilee
> The massive gates of Paradise are thrown
> Wide open: and forth come in fragments wild
> Sweet echoes of unearthly melodies,
> And odors snatched from beds of Amaranth,
> And they, that from the chrystal river of life
> Spring up on freshened wing, ambrosial gales!
>
> *Religious Musings*, l. 356

My taper man of lights listened with perseverant and
praise-worthy patience, though, (as I was afterwards told, on
complaining of certain gales there were not altogether ambrosial,) it was a *melting* day with him. And what, Sir,
(he said, after a short pause,) might the cost be? *Only*
FOUR-PENCE, (O! how I felt the anti-climax, the abysmal
bathos of that *four-pence!*)only *four-pence, Sir, each number,
to be published on every eighth day.* That comes to a deal of
money at the end of a year. And how much, did you say,
there was to be for the money? *Thirty-two pages, Sir! large
octavo, closely printed.* Thirty and two pages? Bless me!
why except what I does in a family way on the Sabbath,
that's more than I ever reads, Sir! all the year round. I
am as great a one, as any man in Brummagem, Sir! for
liberty and truth and all them sort of things, but as to this,
(no offence, I hope, Sir!) I must beg to be excused.

So ended my first canvass: from causes that I shall
presently mention, I made but one other application in

person. This took place at Manchester to a stately and opulent wholesale dealer in cottons. He took my letter of introduction, and, having perused it, measured me from head to foot and again from foot to head, and then asked if I had any bill or invoice of the thing; I presented my prospectus to him; he rapidly skimmed and hummed over the first side, and still more rapidly the second and concluding page; crushed it within his fingers and the palm of his hand; then most deliberately and *significantly* rubbed and smoothed one part against the other; and lastly putting it into his pocket turned his back on me with an "*over-run* with these articles!" and so without another syllable retired into his counting-house. And, I can truly say, to my unspeakable amusement.

This, I have said, was my second and last attempt. On returning baffled from the first, in which I had vainly essayed to repeat the miracle of Orpheus with the Brummagem patriot, I dined with the tradesman who had introduced me to him. After dinner he importuned me to smoke a pipe with him, and two or three other illuminati of the same rank. I objected, both because I was engaged to spend the evening with a minister and his friends, and because I had never smoked except once or twice in my lifetime, and then it was herb tobacco mixed with Oronooko. On the assurance, however, that the tobacco was equally mild, and seeing too that it was of a yellow colour; (not forgetting the lamentable difficulty, I have always experienced, in saying, "No," and in abstaining from what the people about me were doing,) I took half a pipe, filling the lower half of the bole with salt. I was soon however compelled to resign it, in consequence of a giddiness and distressful feeling in my eyes, which, as I had drunk but a single glass of ale, must, I knew, have been the effect of the tobacco. Soon after, deeming myself recovered, I sallied forth to my engagement; but the walk and the fresh air brought on all the symptoms again, and, I had scarcely entered the minister's drawing-room, and opened a small pacquet of letters, which he had received from Bristol for me; ere I sunk back on the sofa in a sort of swoon rather than sleep. Fortunately I had found just time enough to inform him of the confused state of my feelings, and of the occasion. For here and thus I lay, my face like a wall that is white-washing, *deathy* pale and with the cold drops of perspiration running down it from my forehead, while one after another there dropt in the different gentlemen, who had been invited to meet, and spend the evening with me, to the number of from fifteen to twenty. As the poison of tobacco acts but for a short time, I at length awoke from insensibility, and looked round on the party, my eyes dazzled by the candles which had been lighted in the interim. By way of relieving my embarrassment one of the gentlemen began the conversation, with *"Have you seen a paper to-day, Mr. Coleridge?"* "Sir!" (I replied, rubbing my eyes,) "I am far from convinced, that a christian is permitted to read either newspapers or any other works of merely political and temporary interest." This remark so ludicrously inapposite to, or rather, incongruous with, the purpose, for which I was known to have visited Birmingham, and to assist me in which they were all then met, produced an involuntary and general burst of laughter; and seldom indeed have I passed so many delightful hours, as I enjoyed in that room from the moment of that laugh to an early hour the next morning. Never, perhaps, in so mixed and numerous a party have I since heard conversation sustained with such animation, enriched with such variety of information, and enlivened with such a flow of anecdote.

* * *

In part from constitutional indolence, which in the very hey-day of hope had kept my enthusiasm in check, but still more from the habits and influences of a classical education and academic pursuits, scarcely had a year elapsed from the commencement of my literary and political adventures before my mind sank into a state of thorough disgust and despondency, both with regard to the disputes and the parties disputant. With more than *poetic* feeling I exclaimed:

> The sensual and the dark rebel in vain,
> Slaves by their own compulsion! In mad game
> They break their manacles, to wear the *name*
> Of freedom, graven on a heavier chain.
> O liberty! with profitless endeavour
> Have I pursued thee many a weary hour;
> But thou nor swell'st the victor's pomp, nor ever
> Didst breathe thy soul in forms of human power!

Alike from all, howe'er they praise thee,
(Nor prayer nor boastful name delays thee)
From superstition's harpy minions
And factious blasphemy's obscener slaves,
Thou speedest on thy cherub pinions,
The guide of homeless winds and playmate of the waves!

FRANCE, *a Palinodia*

I retired to a cottage in Somersetshire at the foot of Quantock, and devoted my thoughts and studies to the foundations of religion and morals. Here I found myself all afloat. Doubts rushed in; broke upon me "*from the fountains of the great deep*," and fell "*from the windows of heaven*." The fontal truths of natural religion and the books of Revelation alike contributed to the flood; and it was long ere my ark touched on an Ararat, and rested. The *idea* of the Supreme Being appeared to me to be as necessarily implied in all particular modes of being as the idea of infinite space in all the geometrical figures by which space is limited. I was pleased with the Cartesian opinion, that the idea of God is distinguished from all other ideas by involving its *reality;* but I was not wholly satisfied. I began then to ask myself, what proof I had of the outward *existence* of anything? Of this sheet of paper for instance, as a thing in itself, separate from the phaenomenon or image in my perception. I saw, that in the nature of things such proof is impossible; and that of all modes of being, that are not objects of the senses, the existence is *assumed* by a logical necessity arising from the constitution of the mind itself, by the absence of all motive to doubt it, not from any absolute contradiction in the supposition of the contrary. Still the existence of a being, the ground of all existence, was not yet the existence of a moral creator, and governor. "In the position, that all reality is either contained *in* the necessary being as an *attribute,* or exists *through* him, as its *ground,* it remains undecided whether the properties of intelligence and will are to be referred to the Supreme Being in the former or only in the latter sense; as inherent attributes, or only as *consequences* that have existence in other things *through* him. Thus organization, and motion, are regarded, as *from* God, not *in* God. Were the latter the truth, then notwithstanding all the pre-eminence which must be assigned to the ETERNAL FIRST from the sufficiency, unity, and independence of his being, as the dread ground of the universe, his nature would yet fall far short of that, which we are bound to comprehend in the idea of GOD. For, without any knowledge or determining resolve of its own, it would only be a blind necessary ground of other things and other spirits; and thus would be distinguished from the FATE of certain ancient philosophers in no respect, but that of being more definitely and intelligibly described." KANT's "Einzig möglicher Beweisgrund: vermischte Schriften," zweiter Band, §102 and 103.

For a very long time, indeed, I could not reconcile personality with infinity; and my head was with Spinoza, though my whole heart remained with Paul and John. Yet there had dawned upon me, even before I had met with the "Critique of the Pure Reason," a certain guiding light. If the mere intellect could make no certain discovery of a holy and intelligent first cause, it might yet supply a demonstration, that no legitimate argument could be drawn from the intellect *against* its truth. And what is this more than St. Paul's assertion, that by wisdom, (more properly translated by the powers of reasoning) no man ever arrived at the knowledge of God? What more than the sublimest, and probably the oldest, book on earth has taught us,

> Silver and gold man searcheth out:
> Bringeth the ore out of the earth, and darkness into light.
> But where findeth he wisdom? [&c.]

JOB, Chap. 28th

I become convinced, that religion, as both the corner-stone and the key-stone of morality, must have a *moral* origin; so far at least, that the evidence of its doctrines could not, like the truths of abstract science, be wholly independent of the will. It were therefore to be expected, that its *fundamental* truth would be such as MIGHT be denied; though only by the fool, and even by the fool from the madness of the *heart* alone!

*　*　*

From

CHAPTER XII

A Chapter of requests and premonitions concerning the perusal or omission of the chapter that follows.

IN the perusal of philosophical works I have been greatly benefited by a resolve, which, in the antithetic form and with the allowed quaintness of an adage or maxim, I have been accustomed to word thus: "*until you understand a writer's ignorance, presume yourself ignorant of his understanding.*" This *golden rule* of mine does, I own, resemble those of Pythagoras in its obscurity rather than in its depth. If however the reader will permit me to be my own Hierocles, I trust, that he will find its meaning fully explained by the following instances. I have now before me a treatise of a religious fanatic, full of dreams and supernatural *experiences*. I see clearly the writer's grounds, and their hollowness. I have a complete insight into the causes, which through the medium of his body has acted on his mind; and by application of received and ascertained laws I can satisfactorily explain to my own reason all the strange incidents, which the writer records of himself. And this I can do without suspecting him of any intentional falsehood. As when in broad daylight a man tracks the steps of a traveller, who had lost his way in a fog or by a treacherous moonshine, even so, and with the same tranquil sense of certainty, can I follow the traces of this bewildered visionary. I UNDERSTAND HIS IGNORANCE.

On the other hand, I have been re-perusing with the best energies of my mind the Timaeus of PLATO. Whatever I comprehend, impresses me with a reverential sense of the author's genius; but there is a considerable portion of the work, to which I can attach no consistent meaning. In other treatises of the same philosopher, intended for the average comprehensions of men, I have been delighted with the masterly good sense, with the perspicuity of the language, and the aptness of the inductions. I recollect likewise, that numerous passages in this author, which I thoroughly comprehend, were formerly no less unintelligible to me, than the passages now in question. It would, I am aware, be quite *fashionable* to dismiss them at once as Platonic Jargon. But this I cannot do with satisfaction to my own mind, because I have sought in vain for causes adequate to the solution of the assumed inconsistency. I have no insight into the possibility of a man so eminently wise using words with such half-meanings to himself, as must perforce pass into no-meaning to his readers. When in addition to the motives thus suggested by my own reason, I bring into distinct remembrance the number and the series of great men, who after long and zealous study of these works had joined in honoring the name of PLATO with epithets, that almost transcend humanity, I feel, that a contemptuous verdict on my part might argue want of modesty, but would hardly be received by the judicious, as evidence of superior penetration. Therefore, utterly baffled in all my attempts to understand the ignorance of Plato, I CONCLUDE MYSELF IGNORANT OF HIS UNDERSTANDING.

In lieu of the various requests which the anxiety of authorship addresses to the unknown reader, I advance but this one; that he will either pass over the following chapter altogether, or read the whole connectedly. The fairest part of the most beautiful body will appear deformed and monstrous, if dissevered from its place in the organic Whole. Nay, on delicate subjects, where a seemingly trifling difference of more or less may constitute a difference in *kind*, even a *faithful* display of the main and supporting ideas, if yet they are separated from the forms by which they are at once cloathed and modified, may perchance present a skeleton indeed; but a skeleton to alarm and deter. Though I might find numerous precedents, I shall not desire the reader to strip his mind of all prejudices, or to keep all prior systems out of view during his examination of the present. For in truth, such requests appear to me not much unlike the advice given to hypochondriacal patients in Dr. Buchan's domestic medicine; *videlicet*, to preserve themselves uniformly tranquil and in good spirits. Till I had discovered the art of destroying the memory *a parte post*, without injury to its future operations, and without detriment to the judgement, I should suppress the request as premature; and therefore, however much I may *wish* to be read with an unprejudiced mind, I do not presume to state it as a necessary condition.

The extent of my daring is to suggest one criterion, by which it may be rationally conjectured before-hand, whether or no a reader would lose his time, and perhaps his temper, in the perusal of this, or any other treatise constructed on similar principles. But it would be cruelly misinterpreted, as implying the least disrespect either for the moral or intellectual qualities of the individuals thereby precluded. The criterion is this: if a man receives as fundamental facts, and therefore of course indemonstrable and incapable of further analysis, the general notions of matter, spirit, soul, body, action, passiveness, time, space, cause, and effect, consciousness, perception, memory and habit; if he feels his mind completely at rest concerning all these, and is satisfied, if only he can analyse all other notions into some one or more of these supposed elements with plausible subordination and apt arrangement: to such a mind I would as courteously as possible convey the hint, that for him the chapter was not written.

*　*　*

I say then, that it is neither possible or necessary for all men, or for many, to be PHILOSOPHERS. There is a *philosophic* (and inasmuch as it is actualized by an effort of freedom, an *artificial*) *consciousness*, which lies beneath or (as is were) *behind* the spontaneous consciousness natural to all reflecting beings. As the elder Romans distinguished their northern provinces into Cis-Alpine and Trans-Alpine, so may we divide all the objects of human knowledge into those on this side, and those on the other side of the spontaneous consciousness; *citra et trans conscientiam communem.* The latter is exclusively the domain of PURE philosophy, which is therefore properly entitled *transcendental,* in order to discriminate it at once, both from mere reflection and *re*-presentation on the one hand, and on the other from those flights of lawless speculation which, abandoned by *all* distinct consciousness, because transgressing the bounds and purposes of our intellectual faculties, are justly condemned, as *transcendent.**

*   *   *

From
CHAPTER XIII
[Conclusion of Vol. I]

THE IMAGINATION then, I consider either as primary, or secondary. The primary IMAGINATION I hold to be the living Power and prime Agent of all human Perception, and as a repetition in the finite mind of the eternal act of creation in the infinite I AM. The secondary Imagination I consider as an echo of the former, co-existing with the conscious will, yet still as identical with the primary in the *kind* of its agency, and differing only in *degree*, and in the *mode* of its operation. It dissolves, diffuses, dissipates, in order to re-create; or where this process is rendered impossible, yet still at all events it struggles to idealize and to unify. It is essentially *vital*, even as all objects (*as* objects) are essentially fixed and dead.

FANCY, on the contrary, has no other counters to play with, but fixities and definites. The Fancy is indeed no other than a mode of Memory emancipated from the order of time and space; while it is blended with, and modified by that empirical phenomenon of the will, which we express by the word CHOICE. But equally with the ordinary memory the Fancy must receive all its materials ready made from the law of association.

Whatever more than this, I shall think it fit to declare concerning the powers and privileges of the imagination in

---

*This distinction between transcendental and transcendent is observed by our elder divines and philosophers, whenever they express themselves *scholastically*. Dr. Johnson indeed has confounded the two words; but his own authorities do not bear him out. Of this celebrated dictionary I will venture to remark once for all, that I should suspect the man of a morose disposition who should speak of it without respect and gratitude as a most instructive and entertaining *book*, and hitherto, unfortunately, an indispensable book; but I confess, that I should be surprized at hearing from a philosophic and thorough scholar any but very qualified praises of it, as a *dictionary*.

the present work, will be found in the critical essay on the uses of the Supernatural in poetry, and the principles that regulate its introduction: which the reader will find prefixed to the poem of 𝔗𝔥𝔢 𝔄𝔫𝔠𝔦𝔢𝔫𝔱 𝔐𝔞𝔯𝔦𝔫𝔢𝔯.

CHAPTER XIV

Occasion of the "Lyrical Ballads," and the objects originally proposed—Preface to the second edition—The ensuing controversy, its causes and acrimony—Philosophic definitions of a poem and poetry with scholia.

DURING the first year that Mr. Wordsworth and I were neighbours, our conversations turned frequently on the two cardinal points of poetry, the power of exciting the sympathy of the reader by a faithful adherence to the truth of nature, and the power of giving the interest of novelty by the modifying colors of imagination. The sudden charm, which accidents of light and shade, which moon-light or sun-set diffused over a known and familiar landscape, appeared to represent the practicability of combining both. These are the poetry of nature. The thought suggested itself (to which of us I do not recollect) that a series of poems might be composed of two sorts. In the one, the incidents and agents were to be, in part at least, supernatural; and the excellence aimed at was to consist in the interesting of the affections by the dramatic truth of such emotions, as would naturally accompany such situations, supposing them real. And real in *this* sense they have been to every human being who, from whatever source of delusion, has at any time believed himself under supernatural agency. For the second class, subjects were to be chosen from ordinary life; the characters and incidents were to be such, as will be found in every village and its vicinity, where there is a meditative and feeling mind to seek after them, or to notice them, when they present themselves.

In this idea originated the plan of the "Lyrical Ballads"; in which it was agreed, that my endeavours should be directed to persons and characters supernatural, or at least romantic; yet so as to transfer from our inward nature a

human interest and a semblance of truth sufficient to procure for these shadows of imagination that willing suspension
of disbelief for the moment, which constitutes poetic faith.
Mr. Wordsworth, on the other hand, was to propose to himself as his object, to give the charm of novelty to things of
every day, and to excite a feeling analogous to the supernatural, by awakening the mind's attention from the lethargy
of custom, and directing it to the loveliness and the wonders
of the world before us; an inexhaustible treasure, but for
which, in consequence of the film of familiarity and selfish
solicitude we have eyes, yet see not, ears that hear not, and
hearts that neither feel nor understand.

With this view I wrote "The Ancient Mariner," and was
preparing among other poems, "The Dark Ladie," and the
"Christabel," in which I should have more nearly realized
my ideal, than I had done in my first attempt. But Mr.
Wordsworth's industry had proved so much more successful,
and the number of his poems so much greater, that my compositions, instead of forming a balance, appeared rather
an interpolation of heterogeneous matter. Mr. Wordsworth
added two or three poems written in his own character, in
the impassioned, lofty, and sustained diction, which is characteristic of his genius. In this form the "Lyrical Ballads"
were published; and were presented by him, as an *experiment*, whether subjects, which from their nature rejected
the usual ornaments and extra-colloquial style of poems in
general, might not be so managed in the language of ordinary life as to produce the pleasureable interest, which it is
the peculiar business of poetry to impart. To the second
edition he added a preface of considerable length; in which,
notwithstanding some passages of apparently a contrary
import, he was understood to contend for the extension of
this style to poetry of all kinds, and to reject as vicious and
indefensible all phrases and forms of style that were not
included in what he (unfortunately, I think, adopting an
equivocal expression) called the language of *real* life. From
this preface, prefixed to poems in which it was impossible to
deny the presence of original genius, however mistaken
its direction might be deemed, arose the whole long-continued controversy. For from the conjunction of perceived
power with supposed heresy I explain the inveteracy and in

some instances, I grieve to say, the acrimonious passions, with which the controversy has been conducted by the assailants.

Had Mr. Wordsworth's poems been the silly, the childish things, which they were for a long time described as being; had they been really distinguished from the compositions of other poets merely by meanness of language and inanity of thought; had they indeed contained nothing more than what is found in the parodies and pretended imitations of them; they must have sunk at once, a dead weight, into the slough of oblivion, and have dragged the preface along with them. But year after year increased the number of Mr. Wordsworth's admirers. They were found too not in the lower classes of the reading public, but chiefly among young men of strong sensibility and meditative minds; and their admiration (inflamed perhaps in some degree by opposition) was distinguished by its intensity, I might almost say, by its *religious* fervor. These facts, and the intellectual energy of the author, which was more or less consciously felt, where it was outwardly and even boisterously denied, meeting with sentiments of aversion to his opinions, and of alarm at their consequences, produced an eddy of criticism, which would of itself have borne up the poems by the violence, with which it whirled them round and round. With many parts of this preface, in the sense attributed to them, and which the words undoubtedly seem to authorize, I never concurred; but on the contrary objected to them as erroneous in principle, and as contradictory (in appearance at least) both to other parts of the same preface, and to the author's own practice in the greater number of the poems themselves. Mr. Wordsworth in his recent collection has, I find, degraded this prefatory disquisition to the end of his second volume, to be read or not at the reader's choice. But he has not, as far as I can discover, announced any change in his poetic creed. At all events, considering it as the source of a controversy, in which I have been honored more than I deserve by the frequent conjunction of my name with his, I think it expedient to declare once for all, in what points I coincide with his opinions, and in what points I altogether differ. But in order to render myself intelligible I must previously, in as few words as possible, explain my ideas, first, of a POEM; and secondly, of POETRY itself, in *kind*, and in *essence*.

The office of philosophical *disquisition* consists in just *distinction;* while it is the priviledge of the philosopher to preserve himself constantly aware, that distinction is not division. In order to obtain adequate notions of any truth, we must intellectually separate its distinguishable parts; and this is the technical *process* of philosophy. But having so done, we must then restore them in our conceptions to the unity, in which they actually co-exist; and this is the *result* of philosophy. A poem contains the same elements as a prose composition; the difference therefore must consist in a different combination of them, in consequence of a different object being proposed. According to the difference of the object will be the difference of the combination. It is possible, that the object may be merely to facilitate the recollection of any given facts or observations by artificial arrangement; and the composition will be a poem, merely because it is distinguished from prose by metre, or by rhyme, or by both conjointly. In this, the lowest sense, a man might attribute the name of a poem to the well-known enumeration of the days in the several months;

> Thirty days hath September,
> April, June, and November, &c.

and others of the same class and purpose. And as a particular pleasure is found in anticipating the recurrence of sounds and quantities, all compositions that have this charm superadded, whatever be their contents, *may* be entitled poems.

So much for the superficial *form*. A difference of object and contents supplies an additional ground of distinction. The immediate purpose may be the communication of truths; either of truth absolute and demonstrable, as in works of science; or of facts experienced and recorded, as in history. Pleasure, and that of the highest and most permanent kind, may *result* from the *attainment* of the end; but it is not itself the immediate end. In other works the communication of pleasure may be the immediate purpose; and though truth, either moral or intellectual, ought to be the *ultimate* end, yet this will distinguish the character of the author, not the class to which the work belongs. Blest indeed is that state of society, in which the immediate purpose would be baffled by the perversion of the proper ultimate end; in which no charm of diction or imagery could exempt the Bathyllus even of an Anacreon, or the Alexis of Virgil, from disgust and aversion!

But the communication of pleasure may be the immediate object of a work not metrically composed; and that object may have been in a high degree attained, as in novels and romances. Would then the mere superaddition of metre, with or without rhyme, entitle *these* to the name of poems? The answer is, that nothing can permanently please, which does not contain in itself the reason why it is so, and not otherwise. If metre be superadded, all other parts must be made consonant with it. They must be such, as to justify the perpetual and distinct attention to each part, which an exact correspondent recurrence of accent and sound are calculated to excite. The final definition then, so deduced, may be thus worded. A poem is that species of composition, which is opposed to works of science, by proposing for its *immediate* object pleasure, not truth; and from all other species (having *this* object in common with it) it is discriminated by proposing to itself such delight from the *whole*, as is compatible with a distinct gratification from each component *part*.

Controversy is not seldom excited in consequence of the disputants attaching each a different meaning to the same word; and in few instances has this been more striking, than in disputes concerning the present subject. If a man chooses to call every composition a poem, which is rhyme, or measure, or both, I must leave his opinion uncontroverted. The distinction is at least competent to characterize the writer's intention. If it were subjoined, that the whole is likewise entertaining or affecting, as a tale, or as a series of interesting reflections, I of course admit this as another fit ingredient of a poem, and an additional merit. But if the definition sought for be that of a *legitimate* poem, I answer, it must be one, the parts of which mutually support and explain each other; all in their proportion harmonizing with, and supporting the purpose and known influences of metrical arrangemer.t. The philosophic critics of all ages coincide with the ultimate judgement of all countries, in equally denying the praises of a just poem, on the one hand, to a series of striking lines or distiches, each of which, absorbing the whole attention of the reader to itself, disjoins it from its context, and makes it a separate whole, instead of an harmonizing part; and on the other hand, to an unsustained composition, from which the reader collects rapidly the general result, unattracted by the component parts. The reader should be carried forward, not merely or chiefly by the mechanical impulse of curiosity, or by a restless desire to arrive at the final solution; but by the pleasureable activity of mind excited by the attractions of the journey itself. Like the motion of a serpent, which the Egyptians made the emblem of intellectual power; or like the path of sound through the air; at every step he pauses and half recedes, and from the retrogressive movement collects the force which again carries him onward. "*Praecipitandus est liber spiritus*," says Petronius Arbiter most happily. The epithet, *liber*, here balances the preceding verb; and it is not easy to conceive more meaning condensed in fewer words.

But if this should be admitted as a satisfactory character of a poem, we have still to seek for a definition of poetry. The writings of PLATO, and Bishop TAYLOR, and the "Theoria Sacra" of BURNET, furnish undeniable proofs that poetry of the highest kind may exist without metre, and even without the contra-distinguishing objects of a poem. The first chapter of Isaiah (indeed a very large portion of the whole book) is poetry in the most emphatic sense; yet it would be not less irrational than strange to assert, that pleasure, and not truth, was the immediate object of the prophet. In short, whatever *specific* import we attach to the word, poetry, there will be found involved in it, as a necessary consequence, that a poem of any length neither can be, or ought to be, all poetry. Yet if an harmonious whole is to be produced, the remaining parts must be preserved *in keeping* with the poetry; and this can be no otherwise effected than by such a studied selection and artificial arrangement, as will partake of *one*, though not a *peculiar* property of poetry. And this again can be no other than the property of exciting a more continuous and equal attention than the language of prose aims at, whether colloquial or written.

My own conclusions on the nature of poetry, in the strictest use of the word, have been in part anticipated in the preceding disquisition on the fancy and imagination. What is poetry? is so nearly the same question with, what is a poet? that the answer to the one is involved in the solution of the other. For it is a distinction resulting from the poetic genius itself, which sustains and modifies the images, thoughts, and emotions of the poet's own mind.

The poet, described in *ideal* perfection, brings the whole soul of man into activity, with the subordination of its faculties to each other, according to their relative worth and dignity. He diffuses a tone and spirit of unity, that blends, and (as it were) *fuses*, each into each, by that synthetic and magical power, to which we have exclusively appropriated the name of imagination. This power, first put in action by the will and understanding, and retained under their irremissive, though gentle and unnoticed, controul (*laxis effertur habenis*) reveals itself in the balance or reconciliation of opposite or discordant qualities: of sameness, with difference; of the general, with the concrete; the idea, with the image; the individual, with the representative; the sense of novelty and freshness, with old and familiar objects; a more than usual state of emotion, with more than usual order; judgement ever awake and steady self-possession, with enthusiasm and feeling profound or vehement; and while it blends and harmonizes the natural and the artificial, still subordinates art to nature; the manner to the matter; and our admiration of the poet to our sympathy with the poetry. "Doubtless," as Sir John Davies observes of the soul (and his words may with slight alteration be applied, and even more appropriately, to the poetic IMAGINATION)

> Doubtless this could not be, but that she turns
> Bodies to spirit by sublimation strange,
> As fire converts to fire the things it burns,
> As we our food into our nature change.

> From their gross matter she abstracts their forms,
> And draws a kind of quintessence from things;
> Which to her proper nature she transforms,
> To bear them light on her celestial wings.

> Thus does she, when from individual states
> She doth abstract the universal kinds;
> Which then re-clothed in divers names and fates
> Steal access through our senses to our minds.

Finally, GOOD SENSE is the BODY of poetic genius, FANCY its DRAPERY, MOTION its LIFE, and IMAGINATION the SOUL that is everywhere, and in each; and forms all into one graceful and intelligent whole.

CHAPTER XV

The specific symptoms of poetic power elucidated in a critical analysis of Shakspere's "Venus and Adonis," and "Lucrece."

IN the application of these principles to purposes of practical criticism as employed in the appraisal of works more or less imperfect, I have endeavoured to discover what the qualities in a poem are, which may be deemed promises and specific symptoms of poetic power, as distinguished from general talent determined to poetic composition by accidental motives, by an act of the will, rather than by the inspiration of a genial and productive nature. In this investigation, I could not, I thought, do better, than keep before me the earliest work of the greatest genius, that perhaps human nature has yet produced, our *myriad-minded** Shakspere. I mean the "Venus and Adonis," and the "Lucrece"; works which give at once strong promises of the strength, and yet obvious proofs of the immaturity, of his genius. From these I abstracted the following marks, as characteristics of original poetic genius in general.

1. In the "Venus and Adonis," the first and most obvious excellence is the perfect sweetness of the versification; its adaptation to the subject; and the power displayed in varying the march of the words without passing into a loftier and more majestic rhythm than was demanded by the thoughts, or permitted by the propriety of preserving a sense of melody predominant. The delight in richness and sweetness of sound, even to a faulty excess, if it be evidently original, and not the result of an easily imitable mechanism, I regard as a highly favourable promise in the compositions

---

*'Ανὴρ μυριόνους, a phrase which I have borrowed from a Greek monk, who applies it to a Patriarch of Constantinople. I might have said, that I have *reclaimed*, rather than borrowed it: for it seems to belong to Shakspere, *de jure singulari, et ex privilegio naturae.*

of a young man. "The man that hath not music in his soul" can indeed never be a genuine poet. Imagery (even taken from nature, much more when transplanted from books, as travels, voyages, and works of natural history); affecting incidents; just thoughts; interesting personal or domestic feelings; and with these the art of their combination or intertexture in the form of a poem; may all by incessant effort be acquired as a trade, by a man of talents and much reading, who, as I once before observed, has mistaken an intense desire of poetic reputation for a natural poetic genius; the love of the arbitrary end for a possession of the peculiar means. But the sense of musical delight, with the power of producing it, is a gift of imagination; and this together with the power of reducing multitude into unity of effect, and modifying a series of thoughts by some one predominant thought or feeling, may be cultivated and improved, but can never be learned. It is in these that *poeta nascitur non fit.*

2. A second promise of genius is the choice of subjects very remote from the private interests and circumstances of the writer himself. At least I have found, that where the subject is taken immediately from the author's personal sensations and experiences, the excellence of a particular poem is but an equivocal mark, and often a fallacious pledge, of genuine poetic power. We may perhaps remember the tale of the statuary, who had acquired considerable reputation for the legs of his goddesses, though the rest of the statue accorded but indifferently with ideal beauty; till his wife, elated by her husband's praises, modestly acknowledged that she herself had been his constant model. In the "Venus and Adonis" this proof of poetic power exists even to excess. It is throughout as if a superior spirit more intuitive, more intimately conscious, even than the characters themselves, not only of every outward look and act, but of the flux and reflux of the mind in all its subtlest thoughts and feelings, were placing the whole before our view; himself meanwhile unparticipating in the passions, and actuated only by that pleasureable excitement, which had resulted from the energetic fervor of his own spirit in so vividly exhibiting, what it had so accurately and profoundly contemplated. I think, I should have conjectured from these poems, that even then the great instinct, which impelled the poet to the drama,

was secretly working in him, prompting him by a series and never broken chain of imagery, always vivid and, because unbroken, often minute; by the highest effort of the picturesque in words, of which words are capable, higher perhaps than was ever realized by any other poet, even Dante not excepted; to provide a substitute for that visual language, that constant intervention and running comment by tone, look and gesture, which in his dramatic works he was entitled to expect from the players. His Venus and Adonis seem at once the characters themselves, and the whole representation of those characters by the most consummate actors. You seem to be told nothing, but to see and hear everything. Hence it is, that from the perpetual activity of attention required on the part of the reader; from the rapid flow, the quick change, and the playful nature of the thoughts and images; and above all from the alienation, and, if I may hazard such an expression, the utter *aloofness* of the poet's own feelings, from those of which he is at once the painter and the analyst; that though the very subject cannot but detract from the pleasure of a delicate mind, yet never was poem less dangerous on a moral account. Instead of doing as Ariosto, and as, still more offensively, Wieland has done, instead of degrading and deforming passion into appetite, the trials of love into the struggles of concupiscence; Shakspere has here represented the animal impulse itself, so as to preclude all sympathy with it, by dissipating the reader's notice among the thousand outward images, and now beautiful, now fanciful circumstances, which form its dresses and its scenery; or by diverting our attention from the main subject by those frequent witty or profound reflections, which the poet's ever active mind has deduced from, or connected with, the imagery and the incidents. The reader is forced into too much action to sympathize with the merely passive of our nature. As little can a mind thus roused and awakened be brooded on by mean and indistinct emotion, as the low, lazy mist can creep upon the surface of a lake, while a strong gale is driving it onward in waves and billows.

3. It has been before observed that images, however beautiful, though faithfully copied from nature, and as accurately represented in words, do not of themselves

characterize the poet. They become proofs of original genius only as far as they are modified by a predominant passion; or by associated thoughts or images awakened by that passion; or when they have the effect of reducing multitude to unity, or succession to an instant; or lastly, when a human and intellectual life is transferred to them from the poet's own spirit,

> Which shoots its being through earth, sea, and air.

In the two following lines for instance, there is nothing objectionable, nothing which would preclude them from forming, in their proper place, part of a descriptive poem:

> Behold yon row of pines, that shorn and bowed
> Bend from the sea-blast, seen at twilight eve.

But with a small alteration of rhythm, the same words would be equally in their place in a book of topography, or in a descriptive tour. The same image will rise into semblance of poetry if thus conveyed:

> Yon row of bleak and visionary pines,
> By twilight glimpse discerned, mark! how they flee
> From the fierce sea-blast, all their tresses wild
> Streaming before them.

I have given this as an illustration, by no means as an instance, of that particular excellence which I had in view, and in which Shakspere even in his earliest, as in his latest, works surpasses all other poets. It is by this, that he still gives a dignity and a passion to the objects which he presents. Unaided by any previous excitement, they burst upon us at once in life and in power.

> Full many a glorious morning have I seen
> *Flatter* the mountain tops with sovereign eye.
> > SHAKSPERE, *Sonnet* 33rd.

> Not mine own fears, nor the prophetic soul
> Of the wide world dreaming on things to come—

> *   *   *   *
> *   *   *   *

> The mortal moon hath her eclipse endured,
> And the sad augurs mock their own presage;
> Incertainties now crown themselves assured,
> And Peace proclaims olives of endless age.

K

Now with the drops of this most balmy time
My Love looks fresh, and DEATH to me subscribes!
Since spite of him, I'll live in this poor rhyme,
While he insults o'er dull and speechless tribes.
And thou in this shalt find thy monument,
When tyrants' crests, and tombs of brass are spent.

Sonnet 107

As of higher worth, so doubtless still more characteristic of poetic genius does the imagery become, when it moulds and colors itself to the circumstances, passion, or character, present and foremost in the mind. For unrivalled instances of this excellence, the reader's own memory will refer him to the "LEAR," "OTHELLO," in short to which not of the "*great, ever living, dead man's*" dramatic works? *Inopem me copia fecit.* How true it is to nature, he has himself finely expressed in the instance of love in Sonnet 98.

From you have I been absent in the spring,
When proud pied April drest in all its trim
Hath put a spirit of youth in every thing,
That heavy Saturn laughed and leaped with him.
Yet nor the lays of birds, nor the sweet smell
Of different flowers in odour and in hue,
Could make me any summer's story tell,
Or from their proud lap pluck them, where they grew:
Nor did I wonder at the lilies white,
Nor praise the deep vermilion in the rose;
They were, though sweet, but figures of delight,
Drawn after you, you pattern of all those.
Yet seemed it winter still, and, you away,
As with your shadow I with these did play!

Scarcely less sure, or if a less valuable, not less indispensable mark

Γονίμου μὲν ποιητοῦ—
——ὅστις ῥῆμα γενναῖον λάκοι,

will the imagery supply, when, with more than the power of the painter, the poet gives us the liveliest image of succession with the feeling of simultaneousness!

With this, he breaketh from the sweet embrace
Of those fair arms, that held him to her heart,
And homeward through the dark lawns runs apace:
Look! how a bright star shooteth from the sky,
So glides he in the night from Venus' eye.

4. The last character I shall mention, which would prove indeed but little, except as taken conjointly with the former; yet without which the former could scarce exist in a high degree, and (even if this were possible) would give promises only of transitory flashes and a meteoric power; is DEPTH, and ENERGY of THOUGHT. No man was ever yet a great poet, without being at the same time a profound philosopher. For poetry is the blossom and the fragrancy of all human knowledge, human thoughts, human passions, emotions, language. In Shakspere's *poems* the creative power and the intellectual energy wrestle as in a war embrace. Each in its excess of strength seems to threaten the extinction of the other. At length in the DRAMA they were reconciled, and fought each with its shield before the breast of the other. Or like two rapid streams, that, at their first meeting within narrow and rocky banks, mutually strive to repel each other and intermix reluctantly and in tumult; but soon finding a wider channel and more yielding shores blend, and dilate, and flow on in one current and with one voice. The "Venus and Adonis" did not perhaps allow the display of the deeper passions. But the story of Lucretia seems to favor and even demand their intensest workings. And yet we find in *Shakspere's* management of the tale neither pathos, nor any other *dramatic* quality. There is the same minute and faithful imagery as in the former poem, in the same vivid colors, inspirited by the same impetuous vigor of thought, and diverging and contracting with the same activity of the assimilative and of the modifying faculties; and with a yet larger display, a yet wider range of knowledge and reflection; and lastly, with the same perfect dominion, often *domination*, over the whole world of language. What then shall we say? even this; that Shakspere, no mere child of nature; no automaton of genius; no passive vehicle of inspiration possessed by the spirit, not possessing it; first studied patiently, meditated deeply, understood minutely, till knowledge, become habitual and intuitive, wedded itself to his habitual feelings, and at length gave birth to that stupendous power, by which he stands alone, with no equal or second in his own class; to that power which seated him on one of the two glory-smitten summits of the poetic mountain, with Milton as his compeer, not

rival. While the former darts himself forth, and passes into all the forms of human character and passion, the one Proteus of the fire and the flood; the other attracts all forms and things to himself, into the unity of his own IDEAL. All things and modes of action shape themselves anew in the being of MILTON; while SHAKSPERE becomes all things, yet for ever remaining himself. O what great men hast thou not produced, England! my country! truly indeed—

> Must *we* be free or die, who speak the tongue,
> Which SHAKSPERE spake; the faith and morals hold,
> Which MILTON held. In every thing we are sprung
> Of earth's first blood, have titles manifold!
>
> WORDSWORTH.

CHAPTER XVII

Examination of the tenets peculiar to Mr. Wordsworth—Rustic life (above all, low and rustic life) especially unfavorable to the formation of a human diction—The best parts of language the product of philosophers, not of clowns or shepherds—Poetry essentially ideal and generic—The language of Milton as much the language of real life, yea, incomparably more so than that of the cottager.

As far then as Mr. Wordsworth in his preface contended, and most ably contended, for a reformation in our poetic diction, as far as he has evinced the truth of passion, and the *dramatic* propriety of those figures and metaphors in the original poets, which, stripped of their justifying reasons, and converted into mere artifices of connection or ornament, constitute the characteristic falsity in the poetic style of the moderns; and as far as he has, with equal acuteness and clearness, pointed out the process by which this change was effected, and the resemblances between that state into which the reader's mind is thrown by the pleasureable confusion of thought from an unaccustomed train of words and images; and that state which is induced by the natural language of empassioned feeling; he undertook a useful task, and deserves all praise, both for the attempt and for the execution. The provocations to this remonstrance in behalf of truth and nature were still of perpetual recurrence before and after the publication of this preface. I cannot likewise but add, that the comparison of such poems of merit, as have been given to the public within the last ten or twelve years, with the majority of those produced previously to the appearance of that preface, leave no doubt on my mind, that Mr. Wordsworth is fully justified in believing his efforts to have been by no means ineffectual. Not only in the verses of those who have professed their admiration of his genius, but even of those who have distinguished themselves by hostility to his theory, and depreciation of his writings, are the impressions of his principles plainly visible. It is possible, that with these principles others may have been blended, which are not equally evident; and some which are unsteady and subvertible from the narrowness or imperfection of their basis. But it is more than possible, that these errors of defect or exaggeration, by kindling and feeding the controversy, may have conduced not only to the wider propagation of the accompanying truths, but that, by their frequent presentation to the mind in an excited state, they may have won for them a more permanent and practical result. A man will borrow a part from his opponent the more easily, if he feels himself justified in continuing to reject a part. While there remain important points in which he can still feel himself in the right, in which he still finds firm footing for continued resistance, he will gradually adopt those opinions, which were the least remote from his own convictions, as not less congruous with his own theory than with that which he reprobates. In like manner with a kind of instinctive prudence, he will abandon by little and little his weakest posts, till at length he seems to forget that they had ever belonged to him, or affects to consider them at most as accidental and "petty annexments," the removal of which leaves the citadel unhurt and unendangered.

My own differences from certain supposed parts of Mr. Wordsworth's theory ground themselves on the assumption, that his words had been rightly interpreted, as purporting that the proper diction for poetry in general consists altogether in a language taken, with due exceptions, from the mouths of men in real life, a language which actually constitutes the natural conversation of men under the influence of natural feelings. My objection is, first, that in *any* sense this rule is applicable only to *certain* classes of poetry; secondly, that even to these classes it is not applicable, except in such a sense, (as hath never by any one (as far as I know or have read) been denied or doubted; and lastly, that as far as, and in that degree in which it is *practicable*, yet as a *rule* it is useless, if not injurious, and therefore either need not, or ought not to be practised. The poet informs his reader, that he had generally chosen *low and rustic* life; but not *as* low and rustic, or in order to repeat that pleasure of doubtful moral effect, which persons of elevated rank and of superior refinement oftentimes derive from a happy *imitation* of the rude unpolished manners and discourse of their inferiors. For the pleasure so derived may be traced to three exciting causes. The first is the naturalness, in *fact*, of the things represented. The second is the apparent naturalness of the *representation*, as raised and qualified by an imperceptible infusion of the author's own knowledge and talent, which infusion does, indeed, constitute it an *imitation* as distinguished from a mere *copy*. The third cause may be found in the reader's conscious feeling of his superiority awakened by the contrast presented to him; even as for the same purpose the kings and great barons of yore retained sometimes *actual* clowns and fools, but more frequently shrewd and witty fellows in that *character*. These, however, were not Mr. Wordsworth's objects. *He* chose low and rustic life, "because in that condition the essential passions of the heart find a better soil, in which they can attain their maturity, are less under restraint, and speak a plainer and more emphatic language; because in that condition of life our elementary feelings coexist in a state of greater simplicity, and consequently may be more accurately contemplated, and more forcibly communicated; because the manners of rural life germinate from those elementary feelings; and from the necessary character of rural occupations are more easily comprehended, and are more durable; and lastly, because in that condition the passions of men are incorporated with the beautiful and permanent forms of nature."

Now it is clear to me, that in the most interesting of the poems, in which the author is more or less dramatic, as "The Brothers," "Michael," "Ruth," "The Mad Mother,"

&c., the persons introduced are by no means taken *from low or rustic life* in the common acceptation of those words; and it is not less clear, that the sentiments and language, as far as they can be conceived to have been really transferred from the minds and conversation of such persons, are attributable to causes and circumstances not necessarily connected with "their occupations and abode." The thoughts, feelings, language, and manners of the shepherd-farmers in the vales of Cumberland and Westmoreland, as far as they are actually adopted in those poems, may be accounted for from causes, which will and do produce the same results in *every* state of life, whether in town or country. As the two principal I rank that INDEPENDENCE, which raises a man above servitude, or daily toil for the profit of others, yet not above the necessity of industry and a frugal simplicity of domestic life; and the accompanying unambitious, but solid and religious, EDUCATION, which has rendered few books familiar, but the Bible, and the liturgy or hymn book. To this latter cause, indeed, which is so far *accidental*, that it is the blessing of particular countries and a particular age, not the product of particular places or employments, the poet owes the show of probability, that his personages might really feel, think, and talk with any tolerable resemblance to his representation. It is an excellent remark of Dr. Henry More's, ("Enthusiasmus triumphatus," Sec. XXXV), that "a man of confined education, but of good parts, by constant reading of the Bible will naturally form a more winning and commanding rhetoric than those that are learned; the intermixture of tongues and of artificial phrases debasing *their* style."

It is, moreover, to be considered that to the formation of healthy feelings, and a reflecting mind, *negations* involve impediments not less formidable than sophistication and vicious intermixture. I am convinced, that for the human soul to prosper in rustic life a certain vantage-ground is pre-requisite. It is not every man that is likely to be improved by a country life or by country labors. Education, or original sensibility, or both, must pre-exist, if the changes, forms, and incidents of nature are to prove a sufficient stimulant. And where these are not sufficient, the mind contracts and hardens by want of stimulants: and the man becomes selfish, sensual, gross, and hard-hearted. Let the management of the Poor Laws in Liverpool, Manchester, or Bristol be compared with the ordinary dispensation of the poor rates in agricultural villages, where the *farmers* are the overseers and guardians of the poor. If my own experience has not been particularly unfortunate, as well as that of the many respectable country clergymen with whom I have conversed on the subject, the result would engender more than scepticism concerning the desireable influences of low and rustic life in and for itself. Whatever may be concluded on the other side, from the stronger local attachments and enterprising spirit of the Swiss, and other mountaineers, applies to a particular mode of pastoral life, under forms of property that permit and beget manners truly republican, not to rustic life in general, or to the absence of artificial cultivation. On the contrary the mountaineers, whose manners have been so often eulogized, are in general better educated and greater readers than men of equal rank elsewhere. But where this is not the case, as among the peasantry of North Wales, the ancient mountains, with all their terrors and all their glories, are pictures to the blind, and music to the deaf.

I should not have entered so much into detail upon this passage, but here seems to be the point, to which all the lines of difference converge as to their source and centre. (I mean, as far as, and in whatever respect, my poetic creed *does* differ from the doctrines promulged in this preface.) I adopt with full faith the principle of Aristotle, that poetry as poetry is essentially* *ideal*, that it avoids and excludes all

---

*Say not that I am recommending abstractions; for these class-characteristics which constitute the instructiveness of a character, are so modified and particularized in each person of the Shaksperian Drama, that life itself does not excite more distinctly that sense of individuality which belongs to real existence. Paradoxical as it may sound, one of the essential properties of Geometry is not less essential to dramatic excellence; and Aristotle has accordingly required of the poet an involution of the universal in the individual. The chief differences are, that in Geometry it is the universal truth, which is uppermost in the consciousness; in poetry the individual form, in which the truth is clothed. With the ancients, and not less with the elder dramatists of England and France, both comedy and tragedy were considered as kinds of poetry. They neither sought in comedy to make us laugh merely; much less to make us laugh by wry faces, accidents of jargon, *slang*

accident; that its apparent individualities of rank, character, or occupation must be *representative* of a class; and that the *persons* of poetry must be clothed with *generic* attributes, with the *common* attributes of the class: not with such as one gifted individual might *possibly* possess, but such as from his situation it is most probable before-hand that he *would* possess. If my premises are right and my deductions legitimate, it follows that there can be no *poetic* medium between the swains of Theocritus and those of an imaginary golden age.

The characters of the vicar and the shepherd-mariner in the poem of "THE BROTHERS," that of the shepherd of Greenhead Ghyll in the "MICHAEL," have all the verisimilitude and representative quality, that the purposes of poetry can require. They are persons of a known and abiding class, and their manners and sentiments the natural product of circumstances common to the class. Take "MICHAEL" for instance:

> An old man stout of heart, and strong of limb:
> His bodily frame had been from youth to age
> Of an unusual strength: his mind was keen,
> Intense, and frugal, ... [&c.]

On the other hand, in the poems which are pitched at a lower note, as the "HARRY GILL," "IDIOT BOY," &c., the *feelings* are those of human nature in general; though the poet has judiciously laid the *scene* in the country, in order to place *himself* in the vicinity of interesting images, without

---

phrases for the day, or the clothing of common-place morals drawn from the shops or mechanic occupations of their characters. Nor did they condescend in tragedy to wheedle away the applause of the spectators, by representing before them facsimiles of their own mean selves in all their existing meanness, or to work on the sluggish sympathies by a pathos not a whit more respectable than the maudlin tears of drunkenness. Their tragic scenes were meant to *affect* us indeed; but yet within the bounds of pleasure, and in union with the activity both of our understanding and imagination. They wished to transport the mind to a sense of its possible greatness, and to implant the germs of that greatness, during the temporary oblivion of the worthless "thing we are," and of the peculiar state in which each man *happens* to be, suspending our individual recollections and lulling them to sleep amid the music of nobler thoughts.

"Friend," pages 251, 252.

the necessity of ascribing a sentimental perception of their beauty to the persons of his drama. In the "Idiot Boy," indeed, the mother's character is not so much a real and native product of a "situation where the essential passions of the heart find a better soil, in which they can attain their maturity and speak a plainer and more emphatic language," as it is an impersonation of an instinct abandoned by judgement. Hence the two following charges seem to me not wholly groundless: at least, they are the only plausible objections, which I have heard to that fine poem. The one is, that the author has not, in the poem itself, taken sufficient care to preclude from the reader's fancy the disgusting images of *ordinary morbid idiocy*, which yet it was by no means his intention to represent. He has even by the "burr, burr, burr," uncounteracted by any preceding description of the boy's beauty, assisted in recalling them. The other is, that the idiocy of the *boy* is so evenly balanced by the folly of the *mother*, as to present to the general reader rather a laughable burlesque on the blindness of anile dotage, than an analytic display of maternal affection in its ordinary workings.

In the "Thorn" the poet himself acknowledges in a note the necessity of an introductory poem, in which he should have pourtrayed the character of the person from whom the words of the poem are supposed to proceed: a superstitious man moderately imaginative, of slow faculties and deep feelings, "a captain of a small trading vessel, for example, who, being past the middle age of life, had retired upon an annuity, or small independent income, to some village or country town of which he was not a native, or in which he had not been accustomed to live. Such men having nothing to do become credulous and talkative from indolence." But in a poem, still more in a lyric poem (and the Nurse in Shakspere's "Romeo and Juliet" alone prevents me from extending the remark even to dramatic *poetry*, if indeed the Nurse itself can be deemed altogether a case in point) it is not possible to imitate truly a dull and garrulous discourser, without repeating the effects of dullness and garrulity. However this may be, I dare assert, that the parts (and these form the far larger portion of the whole) which might as well or still better have proceeded from the poet's own imagination, and have been spoken in his own character, are those which have given, and which will continue to give, universal delight; and that the passages exclusively appropriate to the supposed narrator, such as the last couplet of the third stanza;* the seven last lines of the tenth;† and the five following stanzas, with the exception of the four admirable lines at the commencement of the fourteenth, are felt by many unprejudiced and unsophisticated hearts, as sudden and unpleasant sinkings from the height to which the poet had previously lifted them, and to which he again re-elevates both himself and his reader.

If then I am compelled to doubt the theory, by which the choice of *characters* was to be directed, not only *a priori*,

---

* I've measured it from side to side;
  'Tis three feet long, and two feet wide.

† Nay, rack your brain—'tis all in vain,
  I'll tell you every thing I know;
  But to the Thorn, and to the Pond
  Which is a little step beyond,
  I wish that you would go:
  Perhaps when you are at the place,
  You something of her tale may trace.

  I'll give you the best help I can:
  Before you up the mountain go,
  Up to the dreary mountain-top,
  I'll tell you all I know.
  'Tis now some two-and-twenty years
  Since she (her name is Martha Ray)
  Gave, with a maiden's true good will,
  Her company to Stephen Hill;
  And she was blithe and gay,
  And she was happy, happy still
  Whene'er she thought of Stephen Hill.

  And they had fixed the wedding-day,
  The morning that must wed them both;
  But Stephen to another maid
  Had sworn another oath;
  And, with this other maid, to church
  Unthinking Stephen went—
  Poor Martha! on that woeful day
  A pang of pitiless dismay
  Into her soul was sent;
  A fire was kindled in her breast,
  Which might not burn itself to rest.

from grounds of reason, but both from the few instances in which the poet himself *need* be supposed to have been governed by it, and from the comparative inferiority of those instances; still more must I hesitate in my assent to the sentence which immediately follows the former citation; and which I can neither admit as particular fact, or as general rule. "The language too of these men is adopted (purified indeed from what appear to be its real defects, from all lasting and rational causes of dislike or disgust) because such men hourly communicate with the best objects from which the best part of language is originally derived; and because, from their rank in society and the sameness and narrow circle of their intercourse, being less under the action of social vanity, they convey their feelings and notions in simple and unelaborated expressions." To this I reply;

They say, full six months after this,
While yet the summer leaves were green,
She to the mountain-top would go,
And there was often seen.
'Tis said a child was in her womb,
As now to any eye was plain;
She was with child, and she was mad;
Yet often she was sober sad
From her exceeding pain.
Oh me! ten thousand times I'd rather
That he had died, that cruel father!

    *   *   *

Last Christmas when we talked of this,
Old farmer Simpson did maintain,
That in her womb the infant wrought
About its mother's heart, and brought
Her senses back again:
And, when at last her time drew near,
Her looks were calm, her senses clear.

No more I know, I wish I did,
And I would tell it all to you:
For what became of this poor child
There's none that ever knew:
And if a child was born or no,
There's no one that could ever tell;
And if 'twas born alive or dead,
There's no one knows, as I have said:
But some remember well,
That Martha Ray about this time
Would up the mountain often climb.

that a rustic's language, purified from all provincialism and grossness, and so far reconstructed as to be made consistent with the rules of grammar (which are in essence no other than the laws of universal logic, applied to psychological materials) will not differ from the language of any other man of common-sense, however learned or refined he may be, except as far as the notions, which the rustic has to convey, are fewer and more indiscriminate. This will become still clearer, if we add the consideration (equally important though less obvious) that the rustic, from the more imperfect developement of his faculties, and from the lower state of their cultivation, aims almost solely to convey *insulated facts*, either those of his scanty experience or his traditional belief; while the educated man chiefly seeks to discover and express those *connections* of things, or those relative *bearings* of fact to fact, from which some more or less general law is deducible. For *facts* are valuable to a wise man, chiefly as they lead to the discovery of the indwelling *law*, which is the true *being* of things, the sole solution of their modes of existence, and in the knowledge of which consists our dignity and our power.

As little can I agree with the assertion, that from the objects with which the rustic hourly communicates the best part of language is formed. For first, if to communicate with an object implies such an acquaintance with it, as renders it capable of being discriminately reflected on; the distinct knowledge of an uneducated rustic would furnish a very scanty vocabulary. The few things, and modes of action, requisite for his bodily conveniences, would alone be individualized; while all the rest of nature would be expressed by a small number of confused general terms. Secondly, I deny that the words and combinations of words derived from the objects, with which the rustic is familiar, whether with distinct or confused knowledge, can be justly said to form the *best* part of language. It is more than probable, that many classes of the brute creation possess discriminating sounds, by which they can convey to each other notices of such objects as concern their food, shelter, or safety. Yet we hesitate to call the aggregate of such sounds a language, otherwise than metaphorically. The best part of human language, properly so called, is derived from reflection on the acts of the mind itself. It is formed by a voluntary appropriation of fixed symbols to internal acts, to processes and results of imagination, the greater part of which have no place in the consciousness of uneducated man; though in civilized society, by imitation and passive remembrance of what they hear from their religious instructors and other superiors, the most uneducated share in the harvest which they neither sowed or reaped. If the history of the phrases in hourly currency among our peasants were traced, a person not previously aware of the fact would be surprised at finding so large a number, which three or four centuries ago were the exclusive property of the universities and the schools; and, at the commencement of the Reformation, had been transferred from the school to the pulpit, and thus gradually passed into common life. The extreme difficulty, and often the impossibility, of finding words for the simplest moral and intellectual processes of the languages of uncivilized tribes has proved perhaps the weightiest obstacle to the progress of our most zealous and adroit missionaries. Yet these tribes are surrounded by the same nature as our peasants are; but in still more impressive forms; and they are, moreover, obliged to *particularize* many more of them. When therefore, Mr. Wordsworth adds, "accordingly, such a language" (meaning, as before, the language of rustic life purified from provincialism)—"arising out of repeated experience and regular feelings, is a more permanent, and a far more philosophical language, than that which is frequently substituted for it by poets, who think they are conferring honor upon themselves and their art in proportion as they indulge in arbitrary and capricious habits of expression:" it may be answered, that the language, which he has in view, can be attributed to rustics with no greater right, than the style of Hooker or Bacon to Tom Brown or Sir Roger L'Estrange. Doubtless, if what is peculiar to each were omitted in each, the result must needs be the same. Further, that the poet, who uses an illogical diction, or a style fitted to excite only the low and changeable pleasure of wonder by means of groundless novelty, substitutes a language of *folly* and *vanity*, not for that of the *rustic*, but for that of *good sense* and *natural feeling*.

Here let me be permitted to remind the reader, that the

positions, which I controvert, are contained in the sentences
—"*a selection of the* REAL *language of men;*"—"*the language of
these men*" (*i.e.* men in low and rustic life) "*I propose to myself to imitate, and, as far as is possible, to adopt the very language
of men.*" "*Between the language of prose and that of metrical
composition, there neither is, nor can be any essential difference.*"
It is against these exclusively that my opposition is directed.

I object, in the very first instance, to an equivocation in
the use of the word "real." Every man's language varies,
according to the extent of his knowledge, the activity of his
faculties, and the depth or quickness of his feelings. Every
man's language has, first, its *individualities;* secondly, the
common properties of the *class* to which he belongs; and
thirdly, words and phrases of *universal* use. The language
of Hooker, Bacon, Bishop Taylor, and Burke differs from
the common language of the learned class only by the
superior number and novelty of the thoughts and relations
which they had to convey. The language of Algernon
Sidney differs not at all from that, which every well-educated
gentleman would wish to write, and (with due allowances
for the undeliberateness, and less connected train, of thinking natural and proper to conversation) such as he would
wish to talk. Neither one nor the other differ half so much
from the general language of cultivated society, as the
language of Mr. Wordsworth's homeliest composition differs
from that of a common peasant. For "real" therefore, we
must substitute *ordinary*, or *lingua communis*. And this, we
have proved, is no more to be found in the phraseology of
low and rustic life than in that of any other class. Omit the
peculiarities of each, and the result of course must be common to all. And assuredly the omissions and changes to
be made in the language of rustics, before it could be
transferred to any species of poem, except the drama or
other professed imitation, are at least as numerous and
weighty, as would be required in adapting to the same
purpose the ordinary language of tradesmen and manu-
facturers. Not to mention, that the language so highly
extolled by Mr. Wordsworth varies in every county, nay in
every village, according to the accidental character of the
clergyman, the existence or non-existence of schools; or
even, perhaps, as the exciseman, publican, or barber, happen

to be, or not to be, zealous politicians, and readers of the weekly newspaper *pro bono publico*. Anterior to cultivation, the *lingua communis* of every country, as Dante has well observed, exists every where in parts, and no where as a whole.

Neither is the case rendered at all more tenable by the addition of the words, *in a state of excitement*. For the nature of a man's words, where he is strongly affected by joy, grief, or anger, must necessarily depend on the number and quality of the general truths, conceptions and images, and of the words expressing them, with which his mind had been previously stored. For the property of passion is not to *create*; but to set in increased activity. At least, whatever new connections of thoughts or images, or (which is equally, if not more than equally, the appropriate effect of strong excitement) whatever generalizations of truth or experience, the heat of passion may produce; yet the terms of their conveyance must have pre-existed in his former conversations, and are only collected and crowded together by the unusual stimulation. It is indeed very possible to adopt in a poem the unmeaning repetitions, habitual phrases, and other blank counters, which an unfurnished or confused understanding interposes at short intervals, in order to keep hold of his subject, which is still slipping from him, and to give him time for recollection; or in mere aid of vacancy, as in the scanty companies of a country stage the same player pops backwards and forwards, in order to prevent the appearance of empty spaces, in the procession of Macbeth, or Henry VIIIth. But what assistance to the poet, or ornament to the poem, these can supply, I am at a loss to conjecture. Nothing assuredly can differ either in origin or in mode more widely from the *apparent* tautologies of intense and turbulent feeling, in which the passion is greater and of longer endurance than to be exhausted or satisfied by a single representation of the image or incident exciting it. Such repetitions I admit to be a beauty of the highest kind; as illustrated by Mr. Wordsworth himself from the song of Deborah. *"At her feet he bowed, he fell, he lay down; at her feet he bowed, he fell; where he bowed, there he fell down dead."*

From
CHAPTER XVIII

Language of metrical composition, why and wherein essentially different from that of prose—Origin and elements of metre—Its necessary consequences, and the conditions thereby imposed on the metrical writer in the choice of his diction.

I CONCLUDE, therefore, that the attempt is impracticable; and that, were it not impracticable, it would still be useless. For the very power of making the selection implies the previous possession of the language selected. Or where can the poet have lived? And by what rules could he direct his choice, which would not have enabled him to select and arrange his words by the light of his own judgement? We do not adopt the language of a class by the mere adoption of such words exclusively, as that class would use, or at least understand; but likewise by following the *order*, in which the words of such men are wont to succeed each other. Now this order, in the intercourse of uneducated men, is distinguished from the diction of their superiors in knowledge and power, by the greater *disjunction* and *separation* in the component parts of that, whatever it be, which they wish to communicate. There is a want of that prospectiveness of mind, that *surview*, which enables a man to foresee the whole of what he is to convey, appertaining to any one point; and by this means so to subordinate and arrange the different parts according to their relative importance, as to convey it at once, and as an organized whole.

Now I will take the first stanza, on which I have chanced to open, in the "Lyrical Ballads." It is one the most simple and the least peculiar in its language.

> In distant countries have I been,
> And yet I have not often seen
> A healthy man, a man full grown,
> Weep in the public roads alone.
> But such a one, on English ground,
> And in the broad highway, I met;
> Along the broad highway he came,
> His cheeks with tears were wet:
> Sturdy he seemed, though he was sad;
> And in his arms a lamb he had.

The words here are doubtless such as are current in all ranks of life; and of course not less so in the hamlet and cottage than in the shop, manufactory, college, or palace. But is this the *order*, in which the rustic would have placed the words? I am grievously deceived, if the following *less compact* mode of commencing the same tale be not a far more faithful copy. "I have been in a many parts, far and near, and I don't know that I ever saw before a man crying by himself in the public road; a grown man I mean, that was neither sick nor hurt," &c., &c. But when I turn to the following stanza in "The Thorn":

> At all times of the day and night
> This wretched woman thither goes,
> And she is known to every star,
> And every wind that blows:
> And there, beside the thorn, she sits,
> When the blue day-light's in the skies;
> And when the whirlwind's on the hill,
> Or frosty air is keen and still;
> And to herself she cries,
> Oh misery! Oh misery!
> Oh woe is me! Oh misery!

and compare this with the language of ordinary men; or with that which I can conceive at all likely to proceed, in *real* life, from *such* a narrator, as is supposed in the note to the poem; compare it either in the succession of the images or of the sentences; I am reminded of the sublime prayer and hymn of praise, which MILTON, in opposition to an established liturgy, presents as a fair *specimen* of common extemporary devotion, and such as we might expect to hear from every self-inspired minister of a conventicle! And I reflect with delight, how little a mere theory, though of his own workmanship, interferes with the processes of genuine imagination in a man of true poetic genius, who possesses, as Mr. Wordsworth, if ever man did, most assuredly does possess,

"THE VISION AND THE FACULTY DIVINE."

One point then alone remains, but that the most important; its examination having been, indeed, my chief inducement for the preceding inquisition. "*There neither is or can be any essential difference between the language of prose and metrical composition.*" Such is Mr. Wordsworth's assertion. Now prose itself, at least in all argumentative and consecutive works, differs, and ought to differ, from the language of conversation; even as *reading ought to differ from talking. Unless therefore the difference denied be that of the mere *words*, as materials common to all styles of writing, and not of the *style* itself in the universally admitted sense of the term, it might be naturally presumed that there must exist a still greater between the ordonnance of poetic composition and that of prose, than is expected to distinguish prose from ordinary conversation.

There are not, indeed, examples wanting in the history of literature, of apparent paradoxes that have summoned the public wonder as new and startling truths, but which on examination have shrunk into tame and harmless *truisms;* as the eyes of a cat, seen in the dark, have been mistaken for flames of fire. But Mr. Wordsworth is among the last

---

*It is no less an error in teachers, than a torment to the poor children, to inforce the necessity of reading as they would talk. In order to cure them of *singing* as it is called, that is, of too great a difference, the child is made to repeat the words with his eyes from off the book; and then, indeed, his tones resemble talking, as far as his fears, tears and trembling will permit. But as soon as his eye is again directed to the printed page, the spell begins anew; for an instinctive sense tells the child's feelings, that to utter its own momentary thoughts, and to recite the written thoughts of another, as of another, and a far wiser than himself, are two widely different things; and as the two acts are accompanied with widely different feelings, so must they justify different modes of enunciation. Joseph Lancaster, among his other sophistications of the excellent Dr. Bell's invaluable system, cures this fault of *singing*, by hanging fetters and chains on the child, to the music of which one of his school-fellows, who walks before, dolefully chaunts out the child's last speech and confession, birth, parentage, and education. And this soul-benumbing ignominy, this unholy and heart-hardening burlesque on the last fearful infliction of outraged law, in pronouncing the sentence to which the stern and familiarized judge not seldom bursts into tears, has been extolled as a happy and ingenious method of remedying—what? and how?—why, one extreme in order to introduce another, scarce less distant from good sense, and certainly likely to have worse moral effects, by enforcing a semblance of petulant ease and self-sufficiency, in repression, and possible after-perversion of the natural feelings. I have to beg Dr. Bell's pardon for this connection of the two names, but he knows that contrast is no less powerful a cause of association than likeness.

men, to whom a delusion of this kind would be attributed by anyone, who had enjoyed the slightest opportunity of understanding his mind and character. Where an objection has been anticipated by such an author as natural, his answer to it must needs be interpreted in some sense which either is, or has been, or is capable of being controverted. My object then must be to discover some other meaning for the term *"essential difference"* in this place, exclusive of the indistinction and community of the words themselves. For whether there ought to exist a class of words in the English, in any degree resembling the poetic dialect of the Greek and Italian, is a question of very subordinate importance. The number of such words would be small indeed, in our language; and even in the Italian and Greek, they consist not so much of different words, as of slight differences in the *forms* of declining and conjugating the same words; forms, doubtless, which having been, at some period more or less remote, the common grammatic flexions of some tribe or province, had been accidentally appropriated to poetry by the general admiration of certain master intellects, the first established lights of inspiration, to whom that dialect happened to be native.

Essence, in its primary signification, means the principle of *individuation*, the inmost principle of the possibility of any thing, as that particular thing. It is equivalent to the *idea* of a thing, when ever we use the word, idea, with philosophic precision. Existence, on the other hand, is distinguished from essence, by the superinduction of *reality*. Thus we speak of the essence, and essential properties of a circle; but we do not therefore assert, that any thing, which really exists, is mathematically circular. Thus too, without any tautology we contend for the *existence* of the Supreme Being; that is, for a reality correspondent to the idea. There is, next, a *secondary* use of the word essence, in which it signifies the point or ground of contra-distinction between two modifications of the same substance or subject. Thus we should be allowed to say, that the style of architecture of Westminster Abbey is *essentially* different from that of St. Paul's, even though both had been built with blocks cut into the same form, and from the same quarry. Only in this latter sense of the term must it have been *denied* by Mr. Wordsworth (for in this sense alone is it *affirmed* by the general opinion) that the language of poetry (*i.e.* the formal construction, or architecture, of the words and phrases) is *essentially* different from that of prose. Now the burthen of the proof lies with the oppugner, not with the supporters of the common belief. Mr. Wordsworth, in consequence, assigns as the proof of his position, "that not only the language of a large portion of every good poem, even of the most elevated character, must necessarily, except with reference to the metre, in no respect differ from that of good prose, but likewise that some of the most interesting parts of the best poems will be found to be strictly the language of prose, when prose is well written. The truth of this assertion might be demonstrated by innumerable passages from almost all the poetical writings even of Milton himself." He then quotes Gray's sonnet—

> In vain to me the smiling mornings shine,
> And reddening Phoebus lifts his golden fire;
> The birds in vain their amorous descant join,
> Or chearful fields resume their green attire.
> These ears, alas! for other notes repine;
> *A different object do these eyes require;*
> *My lonely anguish melts no heart but mine;*
> *And in my breast the imperfect joys expire.*
> Yet morning smiles the busy race to cheer,
> And newborn pleasure brings to happier men:
> The fields to all their wonted tribute bear,
> To warm their little loves the birds complain.
> *I fruitless mourn to him that cannot hear,*
> *And weep the more because I weep in vain.*

and adds the following remark:—"It will easily be perceived, that the only part of this Sonnet, which is of any value, is the lines printed in italics. It is equally obvious, that, except in the rhyme, and in the use of the single word 'fruitless' for 'fruitlessly,' which is so far a defect, the language of these lines does in no respect differ from that of prose."

An idealist defending his system by the fact, that when asleep we often believe ourselves awake, was well answered by his plain neighbour, "Ah, but when awake do we ever believe ourselves asleep?"—Things identical must be convertible. The preceding passage seems to rest on a similar sophism. For the question is not, whether there may not occur in prose an order of words, which would be equally

proper in a poem; nor whether there are not beautiful lines
and sentences of frequent occurrence in good poems, which
would be equally becoming as well as beautiful in good
prose; for neither the one nor the other has ever been either
denied or doubted by any one. The true question must be,
whether there are not modes of expression, a *construction*,
and an *order* of sentences, which are in their fit and natural
place in a serious prose composition, but would be disproportionate and heterogeneous in metrical poetry; and,
vice versa, whether in the language of a serious poem there
may not be an arrangement both of words and sentences,
and a use and selection of (what are called) *figures of speech*,
both as to their kind, their frequency, and their occasions,
which on a subject of equal weight would be vicious and
alien in correct and manly prose. I contend that in both
cases this unfitness of each for the place of the other frequently will and ought to exist.

And first from the *origin* of metre. This I would trace to
the balance in the mind effected by that spontaneous effort
which strives to hold in check the workings of passion. It
might be easily explained likewise in what manner this
salutary antagonism is assisted by the very state, which
it counteracts; and how this balance of antagonists became
organized into *metre* (in the usual acceptation of that term)
by a supervening act of the will and judgement, consciously
and for the foreseen purpose of pleasure. Assuming these
principles, as the data of our argument, we deduce from
them two legitimate conditions, which the critic is entitled
to expect in every metrical work. First, that, as the *elements*
of metre owe their existence to a state of increased excitement, so the metre itself should be accompanied by the
natural language of excitement. Secondly, that as these
elements are formed into metre *artificially*, by a *voluntary*
act, with the design and for the purpose of blending *delight*
with emotion, so the traces of present *volition* should
throughout the metrical language be proportionately discernible. Now these two conditions must be reconciled
and co-present. There must be not only a partnership, but
a union; an interpenetration of passion and of will, of
spontaneous impulse and of *voluntary* purpose. Again, this
union can be manifested only in a frequency of forms and

figures of speech (originally the offspring of passion, but now the adopted children of power) greater than would be desired or endured, where the emotion is not voluntarily encouraged and kept up for the sake of that pleasure, which such emotion, so tempered and mastered by the will, is found capable of communicating. It not only dictates, but of itself tends to produce, a more frequent employment of picturesque and vivifying language, than would be natural in any other case, in which there did not exist, as there does in the present, a previous and well understood, though tacit, *compact* between the poet and his reader, that the latter is entitled to expect, and the former bound to supply, this species and degree of pleasureable excitement. We may in some measure apply to this union the answer of POLIXENES, in the "Winter's Tale," to PERDITA's neglect of the streaked gilly-flowers, because she had heard it said,

> There is an art which, in their piedness, shares
> With great creating nature.
>   *Pol*.   Say there be;
> Yet nature is made better by no mean,
> But nature makes that mean; so, ev'n that art,
> Which, you say, adds to nature, is an art,
> That nature makes. You see, sweet maid, we marry
> *A gentler scyon to the wildest stock;*
> And make conceive a bark of ruder kind
> By bud of nobler race. This is an art,
> Which does mend nature—change it rather; but
> The art itself is nature.

Secondly, I argue from the EFFECTS of metre. As far as metre acts in and for itself, it tends to increase the vivacity and susceptibility both of the general feelings and of the attention. This effect it produces by the continued excitement of surprize, and by the quick reciprocations of curiosity still gratified and still re-excited, which are too slight indeed to be at any one moment objects of distinct consciousness, yet become considerable in their aggregate influence. As a medicated atmosphere, or as wine during animated conversation; they act powerfully, though themselves unnoticed. Where, therefore, correspondent food and appropriate matter are not provided for the attention and feelings thus roused, there must needs be a disappointment felt; like that of leaping in the dark from the last step of a stair-case, when we had prepared our muscles for a leap of three or four.

The discussion on the powers of metre in the preface is highly ingenious and touches at all points on truth. But I cannot find any statement of its powers considered abstractly and separately. On the contrary Mr. Wordsworth seems always to estimate metre by the powers, which it exerts during (and, as I think, in *consequence of*) its combination with other elements of poetry. Thus the previous difficulty is left unanswered, *what* the elements are, with which it must be combined in order to produce its own effects to any pleasureable purpose. Double and tri-syllable rhymes, indeed, form a lower species of wit, and, attended to exclusively for their own sake, may become a source of momentary amusement; as in poor Smart's distich to the Welsh 'Squire who had promised him a hare:

> Tell me, thou son of great Cadwallader!
> Hast sent the hare? or hast thou swallow'd her?

But for any *poetic* purposes, metre resembles (if the aptness of the simile may excuse its meanness) yeast, worthless or disagreeable by itself, but giving vivacity and spirit to the liquor with which it is proportionally combined.

The reference to the "Children in the Wood," by no means satisfies my judgement. We all willingly throw ourselves back for awhile into the feelings of our childhood. This ballad, therefore, we read under such recollections of our own childish feelings, as would equally endear to us poems, which Mr. Wordsworth himself would regard as faulty in the opposite extreme of gaudy and technical ornament. Before the invention of printing, and in a still greater degree, before the introduction of writing, metre, especially *alliterative* metre (whether alliterative at the beginning of the words, as in "Pierce Plouman," or at the end as in rhymes) possessed an independent value as assisting the recollection, and consequently the preservation, of *any* series of truths or incidents. But I am not convinced by the collation of facts, that the "Children in the Wood" owes either its preservation, or its popularity, to its metrical form. Mr. Marshal's repository affords a number of tales in prose inferior in pathos and general merit, some of as old a date, and many as widely popular. "Tom Hickathrift," "Jack the Giant-killer," "Goody Two-shoes," and "Little Red Riding-hood" are formidable rivals. And that they have continued in prose, cannot be fairly explained by the assumption, that the comparative meanness of their thoughts and images precluded even the humblest forms of metre. The scene of GOODY TWO-SHOES in the church is perfectly susceptible of metrical narration; and, among the Θαύματα θαυμαστότατα even of the present age, I do not recollect a more astonishing image than that of the "*whole rookery, that flew out of the giant's beard,*" scared by the tremendous voice, with which this monster answered the challenge of the heroic TOM HICKATHRIFT!

If from these we turn to compositions universally, and independently of all early associations, beloved and admired; would "THE MARIA," "THE MONK," or "THE POOR MAN'S ASS" of Sterne, be read with more delight, or have a better chance of immortality, had they without any change in the diction been composed in rhyme, than in their present state? If I am not grossly mistaken, the general reply would be in the negative. Nay, I will confess, that, in Mr. Wordsworth's own volumes, the "ANECDOTE FOR FATHERS," "SIMON LEE," "ALICE FELL," "THE BEGGARS," and "THE SAILOR'S MOTHER," notwithstanding the beauties which are to be found in each of them where the poet interposes the music of his own thoughts, would have been more delightful to me in prose, told and managed, as by Mr. Wordsworth they would have been, in a moral essay, or pedestrian tour.

Metre in itself is simply a stimulant of the attention, and therefore excites the question: Why is the attention to be thus stimulated? Now the question cannot be answered by the pleasure of the metre itself: for this we have shown to be *conditional*, and dependent on the appropriateness of the thoughts and expressions, to which the metrical form is superadded. Neither can I conceive any other answer that can be rationally given, short of this: I write in metre, because I am about to use a language different from that of prose. Besides, where the language is not such, how interesting soever the reflections are, that are capable of being drawn by a philosophic mind from the thoughts or incidents of the poem, the metre itself must often become feeble. Take the last three stanzas of "THE SAILOR'S MOTHER," for instance. If I could for a moment abstract from the effect

produced on the author's feelings, as a man, by the incident
at the time of its real occurrence, I would dare appeal to
his own judgement, whether in the *metre* itself he found a
sufficient reason for *their* being written *metrically?*

> And, thus continuing, she said,
> I had a son, who many a day
> Sailed on the seas; but he is dead;
> In Denmark he was cast away:
> And I have travelled far as Hull, to see
> What clothes he might have left, or other property.
>
> The bird and cage they both were his:
> 'Twas my son's bird; and neat and trim
> He kept it: many voyages
> This singing-bird hath gone with him;
> When last he sailed he left the bird behind;
> As it might be, perhaps, from bodings of his mind.
>
> He to a fellow-lodger's care
> Had left it, to be watched and fed,
> Till he came back again; and there
> I found it when my son was dead;
> And now, God help me for my little wit!
> I trail it with me, Sir! he took so much delight in it.

If disproportioning the emphasis we read these stanzas so
as to make the rhymes perceptible, even *tri-syllable* rhymes
could scarcely produce an equal sense of oddity and strangeness, as we feel here in finding *rhymes at all* in sentences so
exclusively colloquial. I would further ask whether, but
for that visionary state, into which the figure of the woman
and the susceptibility of his own genius had placed the poet's
imagination, (a state, which spreads its influence and coloring
over all, that co-exists with the exciting cause, and in which

> The simplest, and the most familiar things
> Gain a strange power of spreading awe around* them,)

---

*Altered from the description of Night-Mair in the "Remorse."

> Oh Heaven! 'twas frightful! Now run down and stared at
> By hideous shapes that cannot be remembered;
> Now seeing nothing and imagining nothing;
> But only being afraid—stifled with fear!
> While every goodly or familiar form
> Had a strange power of spreading terror round me!

N.B. Though Shakspere has, for his own *all-justifying* purposes, introduced the Night-*Mare* with her own foals, yet Mair
means a Sister, or perhaps a Hag.

I would ask the poet whether he would not have felt an abrupt downfall in these verses from the preceding stanza?

> The ancient spirit is not dead;
> Old times, thought I, are breathing there;
> Proud was I that my country bred
> Such strength, a dignity so fair:
> She begged an alms, like one in poor estate;
> I looked at her again, nor did my pride abate.

It must not be omitted, and is besides worthy of notice, that those stanzas furnish the only fair instance that I have been able to discover in all Mr. Wordsworth's writings, of an *actual* adoption, or true imitation, of the *real* and *very* language of *low and rustic life*, freed from provincialisms.

Thirdly, I deduce the position from all the causes elsewhere assigned, which render metre the proper form of poetry, and poetry imperfect and defective without metre. Metre therefore having been connected with *poetry* most often and by a peculiar fitness, whatever else is combined with *metre* must, though it be not itself *essentially* poetic, have nevertheless some property in common with poetry, as an intermedium of affinity, a sort (if I may dare borrow a well-known phrase from technical chemistry) of *mordaunt* between it and the super-added metre. Now poetry, Mr. Wordsworth truly affirms, does always imply PASSION: which word must be here understood in its general sense, as an excited state of the feelings and faculties. And as every passion has its proper pulse, so will it likewise have its characteristic modes of expression. But where there exists that degree of genius and talent which entitles a writer to aim at the honors of a poet, the very *act* of poetic composition *itself* is, and is *allowed* to imply and to produce, an unusual state of excitement, which of course justifies and demands a correspondent difference of language, as truly, though not perhaps in as marked a degree, as the excitement of love, fear, rage, or jealousy. The vividness of the descriptions or declamations in DONNE or DRYDEN is as much and as often derived from the force and fervor of the describer, as from the reflections, forms or incidents, which constitute their subject and materials. The wheels take fire from the mere rapidity of their motion. To what extent, and under what modifications, this may be admitted to act, I shall attempt to define in an after remark on Mr. Wordsworth's reply to this objection, or rather on his objection to this reply, as already anticipated in his preface.

Fourthly, and as intimately connected with this, if not the same argument in a more general form, I adduce the high spiritual instinct of the human being impelling us to seek unity by harmonious adjustment, and thus establishing the principle, that *all* the parts of an organized whole must be assimilated to the more *important* and *essential* parts. This and the preceding arguments may be strengthened by the reflection, that the composition of a poem is among the *imitative* arts; and that imitation, as opposed to copying, consists either in the interfusion of the SAME throughout the radically DIFFERENT, or of the different throughout a base radically the same.

Lastly, I appeal to the practice of the best poets, of all countries and in all ages, as *authorizing* the opinion (*deduced* from all the foregoing) that in every import of the word ESSENTIAL, which would not here involve a mere truism, there may be, is, and ought to be an *essential* difference between the language of prose and of metrical composition.

In Mr. Wordsworth's criticism of GRAY's Sonnet, the reader's sympathy with his praise or blame of the different parts is taken for granted rather perhaps too easily. He has not, at least, attempted to win or compel it by argumentative analysis. In *my* conception at least, the lines rejected as of no value do, with the exception of the two first, differ as much and as little from the language of common life, as those which he has printed in italics as possessing genuine excellence. Of the five lines thus honorably distinguished, two of them differ from prose, even more widely than the lines which either precede or follow, in the *position* of the words.

> *A different object do these eyes require;*
> My lonely anguish melts no heart but mine;
> *And in my breast the imperfect joys expire.*

But were it otherwise, what would this prove, but a truth, of which no man ever doubted? *Videlicet,* that there are sentences, which would be equally in their place both in verse and prose. Assuredly it does not prove the point, which alone requires proof; namely, that there are not passages, which would suit the one and not suit the other. The first line of this sonnet is distinguished from the ordinary language of men by the epithet to morning. (For we will set aside, at present, the consideration, that the particular word "*smiling*" is hackneyed and (as it involves a sort of personification) not quite congruous with the common and material attribute of *shining*). And, doubtless, this adjunction of epithets for the purpose of additional description, where no particular attention is demanded for the quality of the thing, would be noticed as giving a poetic cast to a man's conversation. Should the sportsman exclaim, "*Come boys! the rosy morning calls you up*," he will be supposed to have some song in his head. But no one suspects this, when he says, "A wet morning shall not confine us to our beds." This then is either a defect in poetry, or it is not. Whoever should decide in the *affirmative*, I would request him to re-peruse any one poem of any confessedly great poet from Homer to Milton, or from Aeschylus to Shakspere; and to strike out (in thought I mean) every instance of this kind. If the number of these fancied erasures did not startle him; or if he continued to deem the work improved by their total omission; he must advance reasons of no ordinary strength and evidence, reasons grounded in the essence of human nature. Otherwise, I should not hesitate to consider him as a man not so much *proof against* all authority, as *dead to* it.

The second line,

> And reddening Phoebus lifts his golden fire;

has indeed almost as many faults as words. But then it is a bad line, not because the language is distinct from that of prose; but because it conveys incongruous images, because it confounds the cause and the effect, the real *thing* with the personified *representative* of the thing; in short, because it differs from the language of GOOD SENSE! That the "Phoebus" is hackneyed, and a school-boy image, is an *accidental* fault, dependent on the age in which the author wrote, and not deduced from the nature of the thing. That it is part of an exploded mythology, is an objection more deeply grounded. Yet when the torch of ancient learning was re-kindled, so cheering were its beams, that our eldest poets, cut off by Christianity from all *accredited* machinery, and deprived of all *acknowledged* guardians and symbols of the great objects of nature, were naturally induced to adopt, as a *poetic* language, those fabulous personages, those forms of the supernatural in nature, which had given them such dear delight in the poems of their great masters. Nay, even at this day what scholar of genial taste will not so far sympathize with them, as to read with pleasure in PETRARCH, CHAUCER, or SPENSER, what he would perhaps condemn as puerile in a modern poet?

*   *   *

From

CHAPTER XXII

The characteristic defects of Wordsworth's poetry, with the principles from which the judgement, that they are defects, is deduced —Their proportion to the beauties—For the greatest part characteristic of his theory only.

. . . FIFTH and last [of these defects]; thoughts and images too great for the subject. This is an approximation to what might be called *mental* bombast, as distinguished from verbal: for, as in the latter there is a disproportion of the expressions to the thoughts, so in this there is a disproportion of thought to the circumstance and occasion. This, by the bye, is a fault of which none but a man of genius is capable. It is the awkwardness and strength of Hercules with the distaff of Omphale.

It is a well-known fact, that bright colors in motion both make and leave the strongest impressions on the eye. Nothing is more likely too, than that a vivid image or visual spectrum, thus originated, may become the link of association in recalling the feelings and images that had accompanied the original impression. But if we describe this in such lines, as

> They flash upon that inward eye,
> Which is the bliss of solitude !

in what words shall we describe the joy of retrospection, when the images and virtuous actions of a whole well-spent life, pass before that conscience which is indeed the *inward* eye: which is indeed "*the bliss of solitude*"? Assuredly we seem to sink most abruptly, not to say burlesquely, and almost as in a *medly*, from this couplet to—

> And then my heart with pleasure fills,
> And dances with the *daffodils*.   *Vol*. I, *p*. 320

The second instance is from Vol. II, page 12, where the poet, having gone out for a day's tour of pleasure, meets early in the morning with a knot of *gypsies*, who had pitched their blanket-tents and straw-beds, together with their children and asses, in some field by the road-side. At the close of the day on his return our tourist found them in the same place. "Twelve hours," says he,

> Twelve hours, twelve bounteous hours are gone, while I
> Have been a traveller under open sky,
> Much witnessing of change and cheer,
> Yet as I left I find them here!

Whereat the poet, without seeming to reflect that the poor tawny wanderers might probably have been tramping for weeks together through road and lane, over moor and mountain, and consequently must have been right glad to rest themselves, their children and cattle, for one whole day; and overlooking the obvious truth, that such repose might be quite as necessary for *them*, as a walk of the same continuance was pleasing or healthful for the more fortunate poet; expresses his indignation in a series of lines, the diction and imagery of which would have been rather above, than below the mark, had they been applied to the immense empire of China improgressive for thirty centuries:

> The weary SUN betook himself to rest:—
> —Then issued VESPER from the fulgent west,
> Outshining, like a visible God,
> The glorious path in which he trod!
> And now, ascending, after one dark hour,
> And one night's diminution of her power,
> Behold the mighty MOON! this way
> She looks, as if at them—but they
> Regard not her:—oh, better wrong and strife,
> Better vain deeds or evil than such life!
> The silent HEAVENS have goings on:
> The STARS have tasks!—but *these* have none!

The last instance of this defect (for I know no other than these already cited) is from the "Ode," page 351, Vol. II, where, speaking of a child, "a six years' darling of a pigmy size," he thus addresses him:

> Thou best philosopher, who yet dost keep
> Thy heritage! Thou eye among the blind,
> That, deaf and silent, read'st the eternal deep,
> Haunted for ever by the Eternal Mind,—
> Mighty Prophet! Seer blest!

On whom those truths do rest,
Which we are toiling all our lives to find!
Thou, over whom thy immortality
Broods like the day, a master o'er the slave,
A presence that is not to be put by!

Now here, not to stop at the daring spirit of metaphor which connects the epithets "deaf and silent," with the apostrophized *eye:* or (if we are to refer it to the preceding word, philosopher) the faulty and equivocal syntax of the passage; and without examining the propriety of making a "master *brood* o'er a slave," or the *day* brood *at all;* we will merely ask, what does all this mean? In what sense is a child of that age a *philosopher?* In what sense does he *read* "the eternal deep"? In what sense is he declared to be *"for ever haunted"* by the Supreme Being? or so inspired as to deserve the splendid titles of a *mighty prophet,* a *blessed seer?* By reflection? by knowledge? by conscious intuition? or by *any* form or modification of consciousness? These would be tidings indeed; but such as would pre-suppose an immediate revelation to the inspired communicator, and require miracles to authenticate his inspiration. Children at this age give us no such information of themselves; and at what time were we dipped in the Lethe, which has produced such utter oblivion of a state so godlike? There are many of us that still possess some remembrances, more or less distinct, respecting themselves at six years old; pity that the worthless straws only should float, while treasures, compared with which all the mines of Golconda and Mexico were but straws, should be absorbed by some unknown gulf into some unknown abyss.

But if this be too wild and exorbitant to be suspected as having been the poet's meaning; if these mysterious gifts, faculties, and operations, are *not* accompanied with consciousness; who *else* is conscious of them? or how can it be called the child, if it be no part of the child's conscious being? For aught I know, the thinking Spirit within me may be *substantially* one with the principle of life, and of vital operation. For aught I know, it might be employed as a secondary agent in the marvellous organization and organic movements of my body. But, surely, it would be strange language to say, that *I* construct my *heart!* or that

I propel the finer influences through my *nerves!* or that *I* compress my brain, and draw the curtains of sleep round my own eyes! SPINOZA and BEHMEN were, on different systems, both Pantheists; and among the ancients there were philosophers, teachers of the EN KAI ΠΑΝ, who not only taught that God was All, but that this All constituted God. Yet not even these would confound the *part, as* a part, with the Whole, *as* the whole. Nay, in no system is the distinction between the individual and God, between the Modification, and the one only Substance, more sharply drawn, than in that of SPINOZA. JACOBI indeed relates of LESSING, that, after a conversation with him at the house of the poet, GLEIM (the Tyrtaeus and Anacreon of the German Parnassus) in which conversation L. had avowed privately to Jacobi his reluctance to admit any *personal* existence of the Supreme Being, or the *possibility* of personality except in a finite Intellect, and while they were sitting at table, a shower of rain came on unexpectedly. Gleim expressed his regret at the circumstance, because they had meant to drink their wine in the garden: upon which Lessing in one of his half-earnest half-joking moods, nodded to Jacobi, and said, "It is *I*, perhaps, that am doing *that*," *i.e. raining!* and J. answered, "or perhaps I"; Gleim contented himself with staring at them both, without asking for any explanation.

So with regard to this passage. In what sense can the magnificent attributes, above quoted, be appropriated to a *child*, which would not make them equally suitable to a *bee*, or a *dog*, or a *field of corn:* or even to a ship, or to the wind and waves that propel it? The omnipresent Spirit works equally in them, as in the child; and the child is equally unconscious of it as they. It cannot surely be, that the four lines immediately following, are to contain the explanation?

> To whom the grave
> Is but a lonely bed without the sense or sight
> Of day or the warm light,
> A place of thought where we in waiting lie.

Surely, it cannot be that this wonder-rousing apostrophe is but a comment on the little poem, "We are Seven"(——)? that the whole meaning of the passage is reducible to the assertion, that a *child*, who by the bye at six years old would have been better instructed in most Christian families, has

L

no other notion of death than that of lying in a dark, cold place? And still, I hope, not as in a *place of thought!* not the frightful notion of lying *awake* in his grave! The analogy between death and sleep is too simple, too natural, to render so horrid a belief possible for children; even had they not been in the habit, as all Christian children are, of hearing the latter term used to express the former. But if the child's belief be only, that "he is not dead, but sleepeth:" wherein does it differ from that of his father and mother, or any other adult and instructed person? To form an idea of a thing's becoming nothing; or of nothing becoming a thing; is impossible to all finite beings alike, of whatever age, and however educated or uneducated. Thus it is with splendid paradoxes in general. If the words are taken in the common sense, they convey an absurdity; and if, in contempt of dictionaries and custom, they are so interpreted as to avoid the absurdity, the meaning dwindles into some bald truism. Thus you must at once understand the words *contrary* to their common import, in order to arrive at any *sense;* and *according* to their common import, if you are to receive from them any feeling of *sublimity* or *admiration.*

Though the instances of this defect in Mr. Wordsworth's poems are so few, that for themselves it would have been scarce just to attract the reader's attention toward them; yet I have dwelt on it, and perhaps the more for this very reason. For being so very few, they cannot sensibly detract from the reputation of an author, who is even characterized by the number of profound truths in his writings, which will stand the severest analysis; and yet few as they are, they are exactly those passages which his *blind* admirers would be most likely, and best able, to imitate. But WORDSWORTH, where he is indeed Wordsworth, may be mimicked by Copyists, he may be plundered by Plagiarists; but he can not be imitated, except by those who are not born to be imitators. For without his depth of feeling and his imaginative power his *sense* would want its vital warmth and peculiarity; and without his strong sense, his *mysticism* would become *sickly*—mere fog, and dimness!

To these defects which, as appears by the extracts, are only occasional, I may oppose, with far less fear of encountering the dissent of any candid and intelligent reader, the following (for the most part correspondent) excellencies. First, an austere purity of language both grammatically and logically; in short a perfect appropriateness of the words to the meaning. Of how high value I deem this, and how particularly estimable I hold the example at the present day, has been already stated: and in part too the reasons on which I ground both the moral and intellectual importance of habituating ourselves to a strict accuracy of expression. It is noticeable, how limited an acquaintance with the masterpieces of art will suffice to form a correct and even a sensitive taste, where none but master-pieces have been seen and admired: while on the other hand, the most correct notions, and the widest acquaintance with the works of excellence of all ages and countries, will not perfectly secure us against the contagious familiarity with the far more numerous offspring of tastelessness or of a perverted taste. If this be the case, as it notoriously is, with the arts of music and painting, much more difficult will it be to avoid the infection of multiplied and daily examples in the practice of an art, which uses words, and words only, as its instruments. In poetry, in which every line, every phrase, may pass the ordeal of deliberation and deliberate choice, it is possible, and barely possible, to attain that ultimatum which I have ventured to propose as the infallible test of a blameless style; its *untranslateableness* in words of the same language without injury to the meaning. Be it observed, however, that I include in the *meaning* of a word not only its correspondent object, but likewise all the associations which it recalls. For language is framed to convey not the object alone, but likewise the character, mood and intentions of the person who is representing it. In poetry it *is* practicable to preserve the diction uncorrupted by the affectations and misappropriations, which promiscuous authorship, and reading not promiscuous only because it is disproportionally most conversant with the compositions of the day, have rendered general. Yet even to the poet, composing in his own province, it is an arduous work: and as the result and pledge of a watchful good sense, of fine and luminous distinction, and of complete self-possession, may justly claim all the honor which belongs to an attainment equally difficult and valuable, and the more valuable for being rare.

It is at *all* times the proper food of the understanding; but in an age of corrupt eloquence it is both food and antidote.

In prose I doubt whether it be even possible to preserve our style wholly unalloyed by the vicious phraseology which meets us everywhere, from the sermon to the newspaper, from the harangue of the legislator to the speech from the convivial chair, announcing a *toast* or sentiment. Our chains rattle, even while we are complaining of them. The poems of Boetius rise high in our estimation when we compare them with those of his contemporaries, as Sidonius Apollinarius, &c. They might even be referred to a purer age, but that the prose, in which they are set, as jewels in a crown of lead or iron, betrays the true age of the writer. Much however may be effected by education. I believe not only from grounds of reason, but from having in great measure assured myself of the fact by actual though limited experience, that, to a youth led from his first boyhood to investigate the meaning of every word and the reason of its choice and position, Logic presents itself as an old acquaintance under new names.

On some future occasion, more especially demanding such disquisition, I shall attempt to prove the close connection between veracity and habits of mental accuracy; the beneficial after-effects of verbal precision in the preclusion of fanaticism, which masters the feelings more especially by indistinct watch-words; and to display the advantages which language alone, at least which language with incomparably greater ease and certainty than any other means, presents to the instructor of impressing modes of intellectual energy so constantly, so imperceptibly, and as it were by such elements and atoms, as to secure in due time the formation of a second nature. When we reflect, that the cultivation of the judgement is a positive command of the moral law, since the reason can give the *principle* alone, and the conscience bears witness only to the *motive*, while the application and effects must depend on the judgement: when we consider, that the greater part of our success and comfort in life depends on distinguishing the similar from the same, that which is peculiar in each thing from that which it has in common with others, so as still to select the most probable, instead of the merely possible or positively unfit, we shall learn to value earnestly and with a practical seriousness a mean, already prepared for us by nature and society, of teaching the young mind to think well and wisely by the same unremembered process and with the same never forgotten results, as those by which it is taught to speak and converse. Now how much warmer the interest is, how much more genial the feelings of reality and practicability, and thence how much stronger the impulses to imitation are, which a *contemporary* writer, and especially a contemporary *poet*, excites in youth and commencing manhood, has been treated of in the earlier pages of these sketches. I have only to add, that all the praise which is due to the exertion of such influence for a purpose so important, joined with that which must be claimed for the infrequency of the same excellence in the same perfection, belongs in full right to Mr. Wordsworth. I am far however from denying that we have poets whose *general* style possesses the same excellence, as Mr. Moore, Lord Byron, Mr. Bowles, and, in all his later and more important works, our laurel-honoring Laureate. But there are none, in whose works I do not appear to myself to find *more* exceptions, than in those of Wordsworth. Quotations or specimens would here be wholly out of place, and must be left for the critic who doubts and would invalidate the justice of this eulogy so applied.

The second characteristic excellence of Mr W.'s work is: a correspondent weight and sanity of the Thoughts and Sentiments, won—not from books, but—from the poet's own meditative observation. They are *fresh* and have the dew upon them. His muse, at least when in her strength of wing, and when she hovers aloft in her proper element,

> Makes audible a linked lay of truth,
> Of truth profound a sweet continuous lay,
> Not learnt, but native, her own natural notes!
>
> S. T. C.

Even throughout his smaller poems there is scarcely one, which is not rendered valuable by some just and original reflection.

See page 25, vol. 2nd.: or the two following passages in one of his humblest compositions.

> O Reader! had you in your mind
> Such stores as silent thought can bring,
> O gentle Reader! you would find
> A tale in every thing;

and I've heard of hearts unkind, kind deeds
With coldness still returning;
Alas! the gratitude of men
Has oftener left *me* mourning.

or in a still higher strain the six beautiful quatrains, page 134.

Thus fares it still in our decay:
And yet the wiser mind
Mourns less for what age takes away
Than what it leaves behind.

The Blackbird in the summer trees,
The Lark upon the hill,
Let loose their carols when they please,
Are quiet when they will.

With nature never do *they* wage
A foolish strife; they see
A happy youth, and their old age
Is beautiful and free!

But we are pressed by heavy laws;
And often, glad no more,
We wear a face of joy, because
We have been glad of yore.

If there is one, who need bemoan
His kindred laid in earth,
The household hearts that were his own,
It is the man of mirth.

My days, my Friend, are almost gone,
My life has been approved,
And many love me; but by none
Am I enough beloved.

or the sonnet on Buonaparte, page 202, Vol. II; or finally
(for a volume would scarce suffice to exhaust the instances)
the last stanza of the poem on the withered Celandine,
Vol. II, p. 312.

To be a prodigal's favorite—then, worse truth,
A miser's pensioner—behold our lot!
O man! that from thy fair and shining youth
Age might but take the things youth needed not.

Both in respect of this and of the former excellence, Mr.
Wordsworth strikingly resembles Samuel Daniel, one of the
golden writers of our golden Elizabethan age, now most
causelessly neglected: Samuel Daniel, whose diction bears
no mark of time, no distinction of age, which has been, and

as long as our language shall last, will be so far the language of the to-day and for ever, as that it is more intelligible to us, than the transitory fashions of our own particular age. A similar praise is due to his sentiments. No frequency of perusal can deprive them of their freshness. For though they are brought into the full day-light of every reader's comprehension; yet are they drawn up from depths which few in any age are priviledged to visit, into which few in any age have courage or inclination to descend. If Mr. Wordsworth is not equally with Daniel alike intelligible to all readers of average understanding in all passages of his works, the comparative difficulty does not arise from the greater impurity of the ore, but from the nature and uses of the metal. A poem is not necessarily obscure, because it does not aim to be popular. It is enough, if a work be perspicuous to those for whom it is written, and

> Fit audience find, though few.

To the "Ode on the intimation of immortality from recollections of early childhood" the poet might have prefixed the lines which Dante addresses to one of his own Canzoni—

> *Canzon, io credo, che saranno radi*
> *Che tua ragione intendan bene,*
> *Tanto lor sei faticoso ed alto.*

> O lyric song, there will be few, think I,
> Who may thy import understand aright:
> Thou art for *them* so arduous and so high!

But the ode was intended for such readers only as had been accustomed to watch the flux and reflux of their inmost nature, to venture at times into the twilight realms of consciousness, and to feel a deep interest in modes of inmost being, to which they know that the attributes of time and space are inapplicable and alien, but which yet can not be conveyed save in symbols of time and space. For such readers the sense is sufficiently plain, and they will be as little disposed to charge Mr. Wordsworth with believing the Platonic pre-existence in the ordinary interpretation of the words, as I am to believe, that Plato himself ever meant or taught it.

———Πολλά μοι ὑπ᾽ ἀγκῶ-
νος ὠκέα βέλη
ἔνδον ἐντὶ φαρέτρας
φωνᾶντα συνετοῖσιν· ἐς
δὲ τὸ πᾶν ἑρμηνέων
χατίζει. σοφὸς ὁ πολ-
λὰ εἰδὼς φυᾷ.
μαθόντες δέ, λάβροι
παγγλωσσίᾳ, κόρακες ὥς,
ἄκραντα γαρύετον
Διὸς πρὸς ὄρνιχα θεῖον.

Third (and wherein he soars far above Daniel) the sinewy
strength and originality of single lines and paragraphs: the
frequent *curiosa felicitas* of his diction, of which I need not
here give specimens, having anticipated them in a preceding
page. This beauty, and as eminently characteristic of Wordsworth's poetry, his rudest assailants have felt themselves
compelled to acknowledge and admire.

Fourth: the perfect truth of nature in his images and
descriptions, as taken immediately from nature, and proving
a long and genial intimacy with the very spirit which gives
the physiognomic expression to all the works of nature. Like
a green field reflected in a calm and perfectly transparent
lake, the image is distinguished from the reality only by its
greater softness and lustre. Like the moisture or the polish
on a pebble, genius neither distorts nor false-colours its
objects; but on the contrary brings out many a vein and
many a tint, which escapes the eye of common observation,
thus raising to the rank of gems what had been often kicked
away by the hurrying foot of the traveller on the dusty high
road of custom.

Let me refer to the whole description of skating, Vol. I,
page 42 to 47, especially to the lines

> So through the darkness and the cold we flew,
> And not a voice was idle: with the din
> Meanwhile the precipices rang aloud;
> The leafless trees and every icy crag
> Tinkled like iron; while the distant hills
> Into the tumult sent an alien sound
> Of melancholy, not unnoticed, while the stars
> Eastward were sparkling clear, and in the west
> The orange sky of evening died away.

Or to the poem on the green linnet, Vol. I, page 244.

What can be more accurate yet more lovely than the two concluding stanzas?

> Upon yon tuft of hazel trees,
> That twinkle to the gusty breeze,
> Behold him perched in ecstasies,
>   Yet seeming still to hover;
> There! where the flutter of his wings
> Upon his back and body flings
> Shadows and sunny glimmerings,
>   That cover him all over.

> While thus before my eyes he gleams,
> A brother of the leaves he seems;
> When in a moment forth he teems
>   His little song in gushes:
> As if it pleased him to disdain
> And mock the form which he did feign,
> While he was dancing with the train
>   Of leaves among the bushes.

Or the description of the blue-cap, and of the noon-tide silence, page 284; or the poem to the cuckoo, page 299; or, lastly, though I might multiply the references to ten times the number, to the poem, so completely Wordsworth's, commencing

> Three years she grew in sun and shower, &c.

Fifth: a meditative pathos, a union of deep and subtle thought with sensibility; a sympathy with man as man; the sympathy indeed of a contemplator, rather than a fellow-sufferer or co-mate, (spectator, *haud particeps*) but of a contemplator, from whose view no difference of rank conceals the sameness of the nature; no injuries of wind or weather, or toil, or even of ignorance, wholly disguise the human face divine. The superscription and the image of the Creator still remain legible to *him* under the dark lines, with which guilt or calamity had cancelled or cross-barred it. Here the man and the poet lose and find themselves in each other, the one as glorified, the latter as substantiated. In this mild and philosophic pathos, Wordsworth appears to me without a compeer. Such he *is:* so he *writes.* See Vol. I, page 134 to 136, or that most affecting composition, the "Affliction of Margaret —— of ——," page 165 to 168, which no mother, and, if I may judge by my own experience, no parent can read without a tear. Or turn to that genuine lyric, in the former edition, entitled "The Mad Mother," page 174 to 178, of which I cannot refrain from quoting two of the stanzas, both of them for their pathos, and the former for the fine transition in the two concluding lines of the stanza, so expressive of that deranged state, in which from the increased sensibility the sufferer's attention is abruptly drawn off by every trifle, and in the same instant plucked back again by the one despotic thought, bringing home with it, by the blending, *fusing* power of Imagination and Passion, the alien object to which it had been so abruptly diverted, no longer an alien but an ally and an inmate.

> Suck, little babe, oh suck again!
> It cools my blood; it cools my brain:
> Thy lips, I feel them, baby! they
> Draw from my heart the pain away.
> Oh! press me with thy little hand;
> It loosens something at my chest:
> About that tight and deadly band
> I feel thy little fingers prest.
> The breeze I see is in the tree!
> It comes to cool my babe and me.
>
> Thy father cares not for my breast,
> 'Tis thine, sweet baby, there to rest,
> 'Tis all thine own!—and, if its hue
> Be changed, that was so fair to view,
> 'Tis fair enough for thee, my dove!
> My beauty, little child, is flown,
> But thou wilt live with me in love;
> And what if my poor cheek be brown?
> 'Tis well for me, thou canst not see
> How pale and wan it else would be.

Last, and pre-eminently, I challenge for this poet the gift of IMAGINATION in the highest and strictest sense of the word. In the play of *Fancy*, Wordsworth, to my feelings, is not always graceful, and sometimes *recondite*. The *likeness* is occasionally too strange, or demands too peculiar a point of view, or is such as appears the creature of pre-determined research, rather than spontaneous presentation. Indeed his fancy seldom displays itself, as mere and unmodified fancy. But in imaginative power, he stands nearest of all modern writers to Shakspere and Milton; and yet in a kind perfectly unborrowed and his own. To employ his own words, which are at once an instance and an illustration, he does indeed to all thoughts and to all objects

—————————add the gleam,
The light that never was, on sea or land,
The consecration, and the poet's dream.

I shall select a few examples as most obviously manifesting this faculty; but if I should ever be fortunate enough to render my analysis of imagination, its origin and characters, thoroughly intelligible to the reader, he will scarcely open on a page of this poet's works without recognising, more or less, the presence and the influences of this faculty.

From the poem on the Yew Trees, Vol. I, page 303, 304.

But worthier still of note
Are those fraternal four of Borrowdale,
Joined in one solemn and capacious grove:
Huge trunks!—and each particular trunk a growth
Of intertwisted fibres serpentine
Up-coiling, and inveterately convolved,—
Not uninformed with phantasy, and looks
That threaten the profane;—a pillared shade,
Upon whose grassless floor of red-brown hue,
By sheddings from the pinal umbrage tinged
Perennially—beneath whose sable roof
Of boughs, as if for festal purpose decked
With unrejoicing berries, ghostly shapes
May meet at noontide—FEAR and trembling HOPE,
SILENCE and FORESIGHT—DEATH, the skeleton,
And TIME, the shadow—there to celebrate,
As in a natural temple scattered o'er
With altars undisturbed of mossy stone,
United worship; or in mute repose
To lie, and listen to the mountain flood
Murmuring from Glaramara's inmost caves.

The effect of the old man's figure in the poem of Resolution and Independence, Vol. II, page 33.

While he was talking thus, the lonely place,
The old man's shape, and speech, all troubled me:
In my mind's eye I seemed to see him pace
About the weary moors continually,
Wandering about alone and silently.

Or the 8th, 9th, 19th, 26th, 31st, and 33d, in the collection of miscellaneous sonnets—the sonnet on the subjugation of Switzerland, page 210, or the last ode, from which I especially select the two following stanzas or paragraphs, page 349 to 350.

Our birth is but a sleep and a forgetting;
The soul that rises with us, our life's star, [&c.]

And page 352 to 354 of the same ode.

> O joy that in our embers
> Is something that doth live, [&c.]

And since it would be unfair to conclude with an extract, which, though highly characteristic, must yet, from the nature of the thoughts and the subject, be interesting, or perhaps intelligible, to but a limited number of readers; I will add, from the poet's last published work, a passage equally Wordsworthian; of the beauty of which, and of the imaginative power displayed therein, there can be but one opinion, and one feeling. See White Doe, page 5, [Canto i].

> Fast the church-yard fills;—anon
> Look again and they are gone;
> The cluster round the porch, and the folk
> Who sate in the shade of the prior's oak!
> And scarcely have they disappeared,
> Ere the prelusive hymn is heard;—
> With one consent the people rejoice,
> Filling the church with a lofty voice!
> They sing a service which they feel,
> For 'tis the sun-rise of their zeal;
> And faith and hope are in their prime
> In great Eliza's golden time.
>   A moment ends the fervent din,
> And all is hushed, without and within;
> For though the priest, more tranquilly,
> Recites the holy liturgy,
> The only voice which you can hear
> Is the river murmuring near.
> When soft!—the dusky trees between,
> And down the path through the open green,
> Where is no living thing to be seen;
> And through yon gateway, where is found,
> Beneath the arch with ivy bound,
> Free entrance to the church-yard ground;
> And right across the verdant sod,
> Towards the very house of God;
> Comes gliding in with lovely gleam,
> Comes gliding in serene and slow,
> Soft and silent as a dream,
> A solitary doe!
> White she is as lily of June,
> And beauteous as the silver moon
> When out of sight the clouds are driven
> And she is left alone in heaven!

> Or like a ship some gentle day
> In sunshine sailing far away—
> A glittering ship, that hath the plain
> Of ocean for her own domain.
>
> *   *   *
>
> What harmonious pensive changes
> Wait upon her as she ranges
> Round and through this pile of state
> Overthrown and desolate!
> Now a step or two her way
> Is through space of open day,
> Where the enamoured sunny light
> Brightens her that was so bright;
> Now doth a delicate shadow fall,
> Falls upon her like a breath,
> From some lofty arch or wall,
> As she passes underneath.

The following analogy will, I am apprehensive, appear dim and fantastic, but in reading Bartram's "Travels" I could not help transcribing the following lines as a sort of allegory, or connected simile and metaphor of Wordsworth's intellect and genius.—"The soil is a deep, rich, dark mould, on a deep stratum of tenacious clay; and that on a foundation of rocks, which often break through both strata, lifting their back above the surface. The trees which chiefly grow here are the gigantic black oak; *magnolia magni-floria; fraxinus excelsior; platane;* and a few stately tulip trees." What Mr. Wordsworth *will* produce, it is not for me to prophecy: but I could pronounce with the liveliest convictions what he is capable of producing. It is the FIRST GENUINE PHILOSOPHIC POEM.

The preceding criticism will not, I am aware, avail to overcome the prejudices of those, who have made it a business to attack and ridicule Mr. Wordsworth's compositions.

Truth and prudence might be imaged as concentric circles. The poet may perhaps have passed beyond the latter, but he has confined himself far within the bounds of the former, in designating these critics, as too petulant to be passive to a genuine poet, and too feeble to grapple with him;—"men of palsied imaginations, in whose minds all healthy action is languid;—who, therefore, feed as the many direct them, or with the many are greedy after vicious provocatives."

Let not Mr. Wordsworth be charged with having expressed himself too indignantly, till the wantonness and the

systematic and malignant perseverance of the aggressions
have been taken into fair consideration. I myself heard
the commander in chief of this unmanly warfare make
a boast of his private admiration of Wordsworth's genius.
I have heard him declare, that whoever came into his room
would probably find the "Lyrical Ballads" lying open on his
table, and that (speaking exclusively of those written by
Mr. Wordsworth himself) he could nearly repeat the whole
of them by heart. *But* a Review, in order to be a saleable
article, must be *personal, sharp,* and *pointed:* and, *since then,*
the poet has made himself, and with himself all who were,
or were supposed to be, his friends and admirers, the object of the critic's revenge—how? by having spoken of a
work so conducted in the terms which it deserved! I once
heard a clergyman in boots and buckskin avow, that he
would cheat his own father *in a horse.* A moral system of
a similar nature seems to have been adopted by too many
anonymous critics. As we used to say at school, in reviewing they *make* being rogues: and he, who complains, is to
be laughed at for his ignorance of *the game.* With the pen
out of their hand they are *honorable men.* They exert indeed
power (which is to that of the injured party who should
attempt to expose their glaring perversions and misstate-
ments, as twenty to one) to write down, and (where the
author's circumstances permit) to *impoverish* the man, whose
learning and genius they themselves in private have repeatedly admitted. They knowingly strive to make it impossible for the man even to publish* any future work
without exposing himself to all the wretchedness of debt
and embarrassment. But this is all *in their vocation:* and,
bating what they do in their *vocation, "who can say that black
is the white of their eye?"*

So much for the detractors from Wordsworth's merits.
On the other hand, much as I might wish for their fuller
sympathy, I dare not flatter myself, that the freedom with

---

*Not many months ago an eminent bookseller was asked what
he thought of——? The answer was: "I have heard his powers
very highly spoken of by some of our first-rate men; but I would
not have a work of his if any one would give it to me: for he is
spoken but slightly of, or not at all, in the 'Quarterly Review':
and the 'Edinburgh,' you know, is decided to cut him up!"

which I have declared my opinions concerning both his theory and his defects, most of which are more or less connected with his theory, either as cause or effect, will be satisfactory or pleasing to *all* the poet's admirers and advocates. More indiscriminate than mine their admiration may be: deeper and more sincere it can not be. But I have advanced no opinion either for praise or censure, other than as texts introductory to the reasons which compel me to form it. Above all, I was fully convinced that such a criticism was not only wanted; but that, if executed with adequate ability, it must conduce, in no mean degree, to Mr. Wordsworth's *reputation*. His *fame* belongs to another age, and can neither be accelerated nor retarded. How small the proportion of the defects are to the beauties, I have repeatedly declared; and that no one of them originates in deficiency of poetic genius. Had they been more and greater, I should still, as a friend to his literary character in the present age, consider an analytic display of them as *pure gain;* if only it removed, as surely to all reflecting minds even the foregoing analysis must have removed, the strange mistake, so slightly grounded, yet so widely and industriously propagated, of Mr. Wordsworth's turn for SIMPLICITY! I am not half so much irritated by hearing his enemies abuse him for vulgarity of style, subject, and conception; as I am disgusted with the gilded side of the same meaning, as displayed by some affected admirers, with whom he is, forsooth, a *sweet, simple poet!* and *so* natural, that little master Charles and his younger sister are *so* charmed with them, that they play at "Goody Blake," or at "Johnny and Betty Foy!"

Were the collection of poems, published with these biographical sketches, important enough, (which I am not vain enough to believe), to deserve such a distinction; EVEN AS I HAVE DONE, SO WOULD I BE DONE UNTO.

For more than eighteen months have the volume of Poems, entitled "SIBYLLINE LEAVES," and the present volumes, up to this page, been printed, and ready for publication. But, ere I speak of myself in the tones, which are alone natural to me under the circumstances of late years, I would fain present myself to the Reader as I was in the first dawn of my literary life:

> When Hope grew round me, like the climbing vine,
> And fruits and foliage, not my own, seemed mine!

For this purpose I have selected from the letters, which I wrote home from Germany, those which appeared likely to be most interesting, and at the same time most pertinent to the title of this work.

From

SATYRANE'S LETTERS

[HAMBURG]

I walked onward at a brisk pace, enlivened not so much by anything I actually saw, as by the confused sense that I was for the first time in my life on the *continent* of our planet. I seemed to myself like a liberated bird that had been hatched in an aviary, who now after his first soar of freedom poises himself in the upper air. Very naturally I began to wonder at *all* things, some for being so like and some for being so unlike the things in England—Dutch women with large umbrella hats shooting out half a yard before them, with a prodigal plumpness of petticoat behind—the women of Hamburg with caps plaited on the caul with silver, or gold, or both, bordered round with stiffened lace, which *stood out* before their eyes, but not lower, so that the eyes sparkled through it—the Hanoverian women with the fore part of the head bare, then a stiff lace standing up like a wall perpendicular on the cap, and the cap behind *tailed* with an enormous quantity of ribbon which lies or tosses on the back:

> Their visnomies seemed like a goodly banner
> Spread in defiance of all enemies.
> SPENSER

—The ladies all in English dresses, all *rouged*, and all with bad teeth: which you notice instantly from their contrast to the almost *animal*, *too* glossy mother-of-pearl whiteness and the regularity of the teeth of the laughing, loud-talking country-women and servant-girls, who with their clean white stockings and with slippers without heel-quarters tripped along the dirty streets, as if they were secured by a charm from the dirt: with a lightness, too, which surprised me, who had always considered it as one of the annoyances of sleeping

in an Inn, that I had to clatter up stairs in a pair of them.
The streets narrow; to my English nose sufficiently offensive, and explaining at first sight the universal use of boots;
without any appropriate path for the foot-passengers; the
gable ends of the houses all towards the street, some in the
ordinary triangular form, and *entire*, as the botanists say, but
the greater number notched and scolloped with more than
Chinese grotesqueness. Above all, I was struck with the
profusion of windows, so large and so many, that the houses
look all glass. Mr. Pitt's Window Tax, with its pretty little
additionals sprouting out from it like young toadlets on the
back of a Surinam toad, would certainly improve the appearance of the Hamburg houses, which have a slight summer
look, not *in keeping* with their size, incongruous with the
climate, and precluding that feeling of retirement and self-
content, which one wishes to associate with a house in
a noisy city. But a conflagration would, I fear, be the
previous requisite to the production of any architectural
beauty in Hamburg: for verily it is a filthy town. I moved
on and crossed a multitude of ugly bridges, with huge black
deformities of water wheels close by them. The water inter-
sects the city every where, and would have furnished to the
genius of Italy the capabilities of all that is most beautiful
and magnificent in architecture. It might have been the
rival of Venice, and it is huddle and ugliness, stench and
stagnation.

[KLOPSTOCK]

Believe me, I walked with an impression of awe on my
spirits, as W—— and myself accompanied Mr. Klopstock
to the house of his brother, the poet, which stands about
a quarter of a mile from the city gate. It is one of a row of
little common-place summer-houses (for so they looked)
with four or five rows of young meagre elm trees before the
windows, beyond which is a green, and then a dead flat
intersected with several roads. Whatever beauty (thought
I) may be before the poet's eyes at present, it must certainly
be purely of his own creation. We waited a few minutes
in a neat little parlour, ornamented with the figures of two
of the Muses and with prints, the subjects of which were

from Klopstock's odes. The poet entered. I was much disappointed in his countenance, and recognised in it no likeness to the bust. There was no comprehension in the forehead, no weight over the eye-brows, no expression of peculiarity, moral or intellectual, on the eyes, no massiveness in the general countenance. He is, if anything, rather below the middle size. He wore very large half-boots, which his legs filled, so fearfully were they swoln. However, though neither W—— nor myself could discover any indications of sublimity or enthusiasm in his physiognomy, we were both equally impressed with his liveliness, and his kind and ready courtesy. He talked in French with my friend, and with difficulty spoke a few sentences to me in English. His enunciation was not in the least affected by the entire want of his upper teeth. The conversation began on his part by the expression of his rapture at the surrender of the detachment of French troops under General Humbert. Their proceedings in Ireland with regard to the committee which they had appointed, with the rest of their organizing system, seemed to have given the poet great entertainment. He then declared his sanguine belief in Nelson's victory, and anticipated its confirmation with a keen and triumphant pleasure. His words, tones, looks, implied the most vehement Anti-Gallicanism. The subject changed to literature, and I inquired in Latin concerning the history of German poetry and the elder German poets. To my great astonishment he confessed that he knew very little on the subject. He had indeed occasionally read one or two of their elder writers, but not so as to enable him to speak of their merits. Professor Ebeling, he said, would probably give me every information of this kind: the subject had not particularly excited his curiosity. He then talked of Milton and Glover, and thought Glover's blank verse superior to Milton's. W—— and myself expressed our surprise: and my friend gave his definition and notion of harmonious verse, that it consisted (the English iambic blank verse above all) in the apt arrangement of pauses and cadences, and the sweep of whole paragraphs,

> ——————with many a winding bout
> Of linked sweetness long drawn out,

and not in the even flow, much less in the prominence or

antithetic vigour, of single lines, which were indeed injurious
to the total effect, except where they were introduced for
some specific purpose. Klopstock assented, and said that
he meant to confine Glover's superiority to single lines. He
told us that he had read Milton, in a prose translation, when
he was fourteen.* I understood him thus myself, and W——
interpreted Klopstock's French as I had already construed
it. He appeared to know very little of Milton—or indeed
of our poets in general. He spoke with great indignation
of the English prose translation of his "Messiah." All the
translations had been bad, very bad—but the English was *no*
translation—there were pages on pages not in the original:
—and half the original was not to be found in the translation. W—— told him that I intended to translate a few of
his odes as specimens of German lyrics—he then said to me
in English, "I wish you would render into English some
select passages of the 'Messiah,' and *revenge* me of your
countryman!" It was the liveliest thing which he produced
in the whole conversation. He told us, that his first ode
was fifty years older than his last. I looked at him with
much emotion—I considered him as the venerable father
of German poetry; as a good man; as a Christian; seventy-
four years old; with legs enormously swoln; yet active,
lively, chearful, and kind, and communicative. My eyes
felt as if a tear were swelling into them. In the portrait of
Lessing there was a toupee perriwig, which enormously
injured the effect of his physiognomy—Klopstock wore the
same, powdered and frizzled. By the bye, old men ought
never to wear powder—the contrast between a large snow-
white wig and the colour of an old man's skin is disgusting,
and wrinkles in such a neighbourhood appear only channels
for dirt. It is an honor to poets and great men, that you
think of them as parts of nature; and anything of trick
and fashion wounds you in them, as much as when you
see venerable yews clipped into miserable peacocks.—The
author of the "Messiah" should have worn his own grey

---

*This was accidentally confirmed to me by an old German
gentleman at Helmstadt, who had been Klopstock's school and
bed-fellow. Among other boyish anecdotes, he related that the
young poet set a particular value on a translation of the "Paradise
Lost," and always slept with it under his pillow.

hair.—His powder and perriwig were to the eye what Mr. Virgil would be to the ear.

Klopstock dwelt much on the superior power which the German language possessed of concentrating meaning. He said, he had often translated parts of Homer and Virgil, line by line, and a German line proved always sufficient for a Greek or Latin one. In English you cannot do this. I answered, that in English we could commonly render one Greek heroic line in a line and a half of our common heroic metre, and I conjectured that this line and a half would be found to contain no more syllables than one German or Greek hexameter. He did not understand me: and, I, who wished to hear his opinions, not to correct them, was glad that he did not. . . .

The same day I dined at Mr. Klopstock's, where I had the pleasure of a third interview with the poet. We talked principally about indifferent things. I asked him what he thought of Kant. He said that his reputation was much on the decline in Germany. That for his own part he was not surprised to find it so, as the works of Kant were to him utterly incomprehensible—that he had often been pestered by the Kanteans, but was rarely in the practice of arguing with them. His custom was to produce the book, open it and point to a passage, and beg they would explain it. This they ordinarily attempted to do by substituting their own ideas. I do not want, I say, an explanation of your own ideas, but of the passage which is before us. In this way I generally bring the dispute to an immediate conclusion. He spoke of Wolf as the first Metaphysician they had in Germany. Wolf had followers; but they could hardly be called a sect, and luckily till the appearance of Kant, about fifteen years ago, Germany had not been pestered by any sect of philosophers whatsoever; but that each man had separately pursued his enquiries uncontrolled by the dogmas of a Master. Kant had appeared ambitious to be the founder of a sect; that he had succeeded: but that the Germans were now coming to their senses again. That Nicolai and Engel had in different ways contributed to disenchant the nation; but above all the incomprehensibility of the philosopher and his philosophy. He seemed pleased to hear, that as yet Kant's doctrines had not met with many admirers in England—did not doubt but that we had too much wisdom to be duped by a writer who set at defiance the common sense and common understandings of men. We talked of tragedy. He seemed to rate highly the power of exciting tears—I said that nothing was more easy than to deluge an audience, that it was done every day by the meanest writers.

I must remind you, my friend, first, that these notes are not intended as specimens of Klopstock's intellectual power, or even *"colloquial prowess,"* to judge of which by an accidental conversation, and this with strangers, and those too foreigners, would be not only unreasonable, but calumnious. Secondly, I attribute little other interest to the remarks than what is derived from the celebrity of the person who made them. Lastly, if you ask me, whether I have read the "Messiah," and what I think of it? I answer —as yet the first four books only: and as to my opinion (the reasons of which hereafter) you may guess it from what I could not help muttering to myself, when the good pastor this morning told me, that Klopstock was the German Milton——"a very *German* Milton indeed ! ! !"——Heaven preserve you, and   S. T. COLERIDGE

From
CHAPTER XXIV
CONCLUSION

With regard to the Unitarians, it has been shamelessly asserted, that I have denied them to be Christians. God forbid! For how should I know, what the piety of the Heart may be, or what Quantum of Error in the Understanding may consist with a saving faith in the intentions and actual dispositions of the whole moral Being in any one Individual? Never will God reject a soul that sincerely loves him: be his speculative opinions what they may: and whether in any given instance certain opinions, be they Unbelief, or Misbelief, are compatible with a sincere Love of God, God can only know.—But this I have said, and shall continue to say: that if the doctrines, the sum of which I *believe* to constitute the Truth in Christ, *be* Christianity, then Unitarianism is not, and *vice versa:* and that, in speaking theologically and *impersonally, i.e.* of PSILANTHROPISM and THEANTHROPISM as schemes of Belief, without reference to Individuals who profess either the one or the other, it will be absurd to use a different language as long as it is the dictate of common sense, that two opposites cannot properly be called by the same name. I should feel no offence if a Unitarian applied the same to me, any more than if he were to say, that 2 and 2 being 4, 4 and 4 must be 8.

——ἀλλὰ βροτῶν
τὸν μὲν κενεόφρονες αὖχαι
ἐξ ἀγαθῶν ἔβαλον·
τὸν δ' αὖ καταμεμφθέντ' ἄγαν
ἰσχὺν οἰκείων παρέσφαλεν καλῶν,
χειρὸς ἕλκων ὀπίσσω, θυμὸς ἄτολμος ἐών.

PINDAR, Nem. Ode xi

This has been my Object, and this alone can be my Defence—and O! that with this my personal   s well as my LITERARY LIFE might conclude! the unquenched desire I mean, not without the consciousness of having earnestly endeavoured, to kindle young minds, and to guard them against the temptations of Scorners, by showing that the Scheme of Christianity, as taught in the Liturgy and Homilies of our Church, though not discoverable by human Reason, is yet in accordance with it; that link follows link by necessary consequence; that Religion passes out of the ken of Reason only where the eye of Reason has reached its own Horizon; and that Faith is then but its continuation: even as the Day softens away into the sweet Twilight, and Twilight, hushed and breathless, steals into the Darkness. It is Night, sacred Night! the upraised Eye views only the starry Heaven which manifests itself alone: and the outward Beholding is fixed on the sparks twinkling in the aweful depth, though Suns of other Worlds, only to preserve the Soul steady and collected in its pure *Act* of inward adoration to the great I AM, and to the filial WORD that re-affirmeth it from Eternity to Eternity, whose choral Echo is the universe.

ΘΕΩι ΜΟΝΩι ΔΟΞΑ

FINIS

1815-17

GENERAL PRINCIPLES
[THE AGREEABLE AND THE BEAUTIFUL DISTINGUISHED]

Principle the First. That which has become, or which has been *made* agreeable to us, from causes not contained in its own nature, or in its original conformity to the human organs and faculties; that which is not pleasing for its own sake, but by connection or association with some other thing, separate or separable from it, is neither beautiful, nor capable of being a component part of Beauty: though it may greatly increase the sum of our pleasure, when it does not interfere with the beauty of the object, nay, even when it detracts from it. A moss-rose, with a sprig of myrtle and jasmine, is not more *beautiful* from having been plucked from the garden, or presented to us by the hand of the woman we love, but is abundantly more delightful. The total pleasure received from one of Mr. Bird's finest pictures may, without any impeachment of our taste, be the greater from his having introduced into it the portrait of one of our friends, or from our pride in him as our townsman, or from our knowledge of his personal qualities; but the amiable artist would rightly consider it a coarse compliment, were it affirmed, that the *beauty* of the piece, or its merit as a work of genius, was the more perfect on this account. I am conscious that I look with a stronger and more pleasureable emotion at Mr. Allston's large landscape, in the spirit of Swiss scenery, from its having been the occasion of my first acquaintance with him in Rome. This may or may not be a compliment to *him;* but the true compliment to the picture was made by a lady of high rank and cultivated taste, who declared, in my hearing, that she never stood before that landscape without seeming to feel the breeze blow out of it upon her. But the most striking instance is afforded by the portrait of a departed or absent friend or parent; which is endeared to us, and more delightful, from some awkward position of the limbs, which had defied the contrivances of art to render it picturesque, but which was the characteristic habit of the original.

Principle the Second.—That which is naturally agreeable and consonant to human nature, so that the exceptions may be attributed to disease or defect; that, the pleasure from which is contained in the immediate impression; cannot, indeed, with strict propriety, be called beautiful, exclusive of its relations, but one among the component parts of beauty, in whatever instance it is susceptible of existing as a part of a whole. This, of course, excludes the mere objects of the taste, smell, and feeling, though the sensation from these, especially from the latter when organized into touch, may secretly, and without our consciousness, enrich and vivify the perceptions and images of the eye and ear; which alone are true organs of sense, their sensations in a healthy or uninjured state being too faint to be noticed by the mind. We may, indeed, in common conversation, call purple a beautiful color, or the tone of a single note on an excellent piano-forte a beautiful tone; but if we were questioned, we should agree that a rich or delightful color; a rich, or sweet, or clear tone; would have been more appropriate— and this with less hesitation in the latter instance than in the former, because the single tone is more manifestly of the nature of a *sensation*, while color is the medium which seems to blend sensation and perception, so as to hide, as it were, the former in the latter; the direct opposite of which takes place in the lower senses of feeling, smell, and taste. (In strictness, there is even in these an ascending scale. The smell is less sensual and more sentient than mere feeling, the taste than the smell, and the eye than the ear: but between the ear and the taste exists the chasm or break, which divides the beautiful and the elements of beauty from the merely agreeable.) When I reflect on the manner in which smoothness, richness of sound, &c., enter into the formation of the beautiful, I am induced to suspect that they act negatively rather than positively. Something there must be to realize the form, something in and by which the *forma informans* reveals itself: and these, less than any that could be substituted, and in the least possible degree, distract the attention, in the least possible degree obscure the idea, of which they (composed into outline and surface) are the symbol. An illustrative hint may be taken from a pure crystal, as compared with an opaque, semi-opaque or clouded mass, on the one hand, and with a perfectly transparent body, such as the air, on the other. The crystal is lost in the light, which yet it contains, embodies, and gives a shape to; but which passes shapeless through the air, and, in the ruder body, is either quenched or dissipated.

Principle the Third.—The safest definition, then, of Beauty, as well as the oldest, is that of Pythagoras: THE REDUCTION OF MANY TO ONE—or, as finely expressed by the sublime disciple of Ammonius, τὸ ἄμερες ὄν, ἐν πολλοῖς φανταζόμενον, of which the following may be offered as both paraphrase and corollary. *The sense of beauty subsists in simultaneous intuition of the relation of parts, each to each, and of all to a whole: exciting an immediate and absolute complacency, without intervenence, therefore, of any interest, sensual or intellectual.* The BEAUTIFUL is thus at once distinguished both from the AGREEABLE, which is beneath it, and from the GOOD, which is above it: for both these have an interest necessarily attached to them: both act on the WILL, and excite a desire for the actual existence of the image or idea contemplated: while the sense of beauty rests gratified in the mere contemplation or intuition, regardless whether it be a fictitious Apollo, or a real Antinous.

1814

[DEFINITIONS OF POETRY]

Poetry is not the proper antithesis to prose, but to science. Poetry is opposed to science, and prose to metre. The proper and immediate object of science is the acquirement, or communication, of truth; the proper and immediate object of poetry is the communication of immediate pleasure. This definition is useful; but as it would include novels and other works of fiction, which yet we do not call poems, there must be some additional character by which poetry is not only divided from opposites, but likewise distinguished from disparate, though similar, modes of composition. Now how is this to be effected? In animated prose, the beauties of nature, and the passions and accidents of human nature, are often expressed in that natural language which the contemplation of them would suggest to a pure and benevolent mind; yet still neither we nor the writers call such a work a poem, though no work could deserve that name which did not include all this, together with something else. What is this? It is that pleasurable emotion, that peculiar state and degree of excitement, which arises in the poet himself in the act of composition;—and in order to understand this, we must combine a more than ordinary sympathy with the objects, emotions, or incidents contemplated by the poet, consequent on a more than common sensibility, with a more than ordinary activity of the mind in respect of the fancy and the imagination. Hence is produced a more vivid reflection of the truths of nature and of the human heart, united with a constant activity modifying and correcting these truths by that sort of pleasurable emotion, which the exertion of all our faculties gives in a certain degree; but which can only be felt in perfection under the full play of those powers of mind, which are spontaneous rather than voluntary, and in which the effort required bears no proportion to the activity enjoyed. This is the state which permits the production of a highly pleasurable whole, of which each part shall also communicate for itself a distinct and conscious pleasure; and hence arises the definition, which I trust is now intelligible, that poetry, or rather a poem, is a species of composition, opposed to science, as having intellectual pleasure for its object, and as attaining its end by the use of language natural to us in a state of excitement,—but distinguished from other species of composition, not excluded by the former criterion, by permitting a pleasure from the whole consistent with a consciousness of pleasure from the component parts;—and the perfection of which is, to communicate from each part the greatest immediate pleasure compatible with the largest sum of pleasure on the whole. This, of course, will vary with the different modes of poetry;—and that splendour of particular lines, which would be worthy of admiration in an impassioned elegy, or a short indignant satire, would be a blemish and proof of vile taste in a tragedy or an epic poem.

Milton, in three incidental words, has implied all which for the purposes of more distinct apprehension, which at first must be slow-paced in order to be distinct, I have endeavoured to develop in a precise and strictly adequate definition. Speaking of poetry, he says (as in a parenthesis), which is "simple, sensuous, passionate." How awful is the power of words! fearful often in their consequences when merely felt, not understood; but most awful when both felt and understood! Had these three words only been properly understood and present in the minds of general readers, not only almost a library of false poetry would have been either precluded or still-born, but, what is of more consequence, works truly excellent, and capable of enlarging the understanding, warming and purifying the heart, and placing in the centre of the whole being the germs of noble and manlike actions, would have been the common diet of the intellect instead. For the first condition—namely, simplicity,—while it distinguishes poetry from the arduous processes of science, laboring towards an end not yet arrived at, and supposes a smooth and finished road, on which the reader is to walk onward easily, with streams murmuring by his side, and trees and flowers and human dwellings to make his journey as delightful as the object of it is desirable, instead of having to toil with the pioneers and painfully make the road on which others are to travel, precludes every affectation and morbid peculiarity;—the second condition, sensuousness, insures that framework of objectivity, that definiteness and articulation of imagery, and that modification of the images themselves, without which poetry becomes flattened into mere didactics of practice or evaporated into a hazy, unthoughtful, day-dreaming; and the third condition, passion, provides that neither thought nor imagery shall be simply objective, but that the *passio vera* of humanity shall warm and animate both.

To return, however, to the previous definition, this most general and distinctive character of a poem originates in the poetic genius itself; and though it comprises whatever can with any propriety be called a poem, (unless that word be a mere lazy synonyme for a composition in metre) it yet becomes a just, and not merely discriminative, but full and adequate, definition of poetry in its highest and most peculiar sense, only so far as the distinction still results from the poetic genius, which sustains and modifies the emotions, thoughts, and vivid representations of the poem by the energy without effort of the poet's own mind,—by the spontaneous activity of his imagination and fancy, and by whatever else with these reveals itself in the balancing and reconciling of opposite or discordant qualities, sameness with difference, a sense of novelty and freshness with old or customary objects, a more than usual state of emotion with more than usual order, self-possession and judgement with enthusiasm and vehement feeling,—and which, while it blends and harmonizes the natural and the artificial, still subordinates art to nature, the manner to the matter, and our admiration of the poet to our sympathy with the images, passions, characters, and incidents of the poem:—

> Doubtless, this could not be, but that she turns
> Bodies to *spirit* by sublimation strange, [&c., see page 253]
> > ?1808

It is an art (or whatever better term our language may afford) of representing, in words, external nature and human thoughts and affections, both relatively to human affections, by the production of as much immediate pleasure in parts, as is compatible with the largest sum of pleasure in the whole.

Or, to vary the words, in order to make the abstract idea more intelligible:—

It is the art of communicating whatever we wish to communicate, so as both to express and produce excitement, but for the purpose of immediate pleasure; and each part is fitted to afford as much pleasure, as is compatible with the largest sum in the whole.

> 1811

[FALSE CATEGORIES]

We call, for we see and feel, the swan and the dove both transcendently beautiful. As absurd as it would be to institute a comparison between their separate claims to beauty from any abstract rule common to both, without reference to the life and being of the animals themselves—say rather if, having first seen the dove, we abstracted its outlines, gave

them a false generalization, called them principle or ideal of
bird-beauty and then proceeded to criticize the swan or the
eagle—not less absurd is it to pass judgement on the works of
a poet on the mere ground that they have been called by the
same class-name with the works of other poets of other times
and circumstances, or any ground indeed save that of their
inappropriateness to their own end and being, their want
of significance, as symbol and physiognomy.

O few have there been among the critics who have followed with the eye of the imagination the imperishable yet
ever wandering spirit of poetry through its various metem-
psychoses and consequent metamorphoses, or who have
rejoiced in the light of clear perception at beholding at each
new birth, at each rare avatar, the human race form itself a
new body by assimilating to itself the different materials of
nourishment out of the then circumstances, and new organs
of power and action appropriate to the new sphere of its
motion and activity.

[Watermark, 1810]

[THE PHENOMENON OF PROSE]

It has just struck my feelings that the Pherecydean origin
of prose being granted, prose must have struck men with
greater admiration than poetry. In the latter, it was the
language of passion and emotion: it is what they themselves
spoke and heard in moments of exultation, indignation, &c.
But to hear an evolving roll, or a succession of leaves, talk
continually the language of deliberate reason in a form of
continued preconception, of a Z already possessed when A
was being uttered,—this must have appeared godlike. I
feel myself in the same state, when in the perusal of a sober,
yet elevated and harmonious, succession of sentences and
periods, I abstract my mind from the particular passage,
and sympathize with the wonder of the common people
who say of an eloquent man:—"He talks like a book!"

[PROSE STYLE]

There is some truth in a remark, which I believe was made
by Sir Joshua Reynolds, that the greatest man is he who

forms the taste of a nation, and that the next greatest is he who corrupts it. The true classical style of Hooker and his fellows was easily open to corruption; and Sir Thomas Brown it was, who, though a writer of great genius, first effectually injured the literary taste of the nation by his introduction of learned words, merely because they were learned. It would be difficult to describe Brown adequately; exuberant in conception and conceit, dignified, hyperlatinistic, a quiet and sublime enthusiast; yet a fantast, a humourist, a brain with a twist; egotistic like Montaigne, yet with a feeling heart and an active curiosity, which, however, too often degenerates into a hunting after oddities. In his "Hydriotaphia" and, indeed, almost all his works the entireness of his mental action is very observable; he metamorphoses every thing, be it what it may, into the subject under consideration. But Sir Thomas Brown with all his faults had a genuine idiom; and it is the existence of an individual idiom in each, that makes the principal writers before the Restoration the great patterns or integers of English style. In them the precise intended meaning of a word can never be mistaken; whereas in the later writers, as especially in Pope, the use of words is for the most part purely arbitrary, so that the context will rarely show the true specific sense, but only that something of the sort is designed. A perusal of the authorities cited by Johnson in his dictionary under any leading word, will give you a lively sense of this declension in etymological truth of expression in the writers after the Restoration, or perhaps, strictly, after the middle of the reign of Charles II.

The general characteristic of the style of our literature down to the period which I have just mentioned, was gravity, and in Milton and some other writers of his day there are perceptible traces of the sternness of republicanism. Soon after the Restoration a material change took place, and the cause of royalism was graced, sometimes disgraced, by every shade of lightness of manner. A free and easy style was considered as a test of loyalty, or at all events, as a badge of the cavalier party; you may detect it occasionally even in Barrow, who is, however, in general remarkable for dignity and logical sequency of expression; but in L'Estrange, Collier, and the writers of that class, this easy manner was carried out to the utmost extreme of slang and ribaldry. Yet still the works, even of these last authors, have considerable merit in one point of view; their language is level to the understandings of all men; it is an actual transcript of the colloquialism of the day, and is accordingly full of life and reality. Roger North's life of his brother the Lord Keeper, is the most valuable specimen of this class of our literature; it is delightful, and much beyond any other of the writings of his contemporaries.

From the common opinion that the English style attained its greatest perfection in and about Queen Anne's reign I altogether dissent; not only because it is in one species alone in which it can be pretended that the writers of that age excelled their predecessors, but also because the specimens themselves are not equal, upon sound principles of judgment, to much that had been produced before. The classical structure of Hooker—the impetuous, thought-agglomerating, flood of Taylor—to these there is no pretence of a parallel; and for mere ease and grace, is Cowley inferior to Addison, being as he is so much more thoughtful and full of fancy? Cowley, with the omission of a quaintness here and there, is probably the best model of style for modern imitation in general. Taylor's periods have been frequently attempted by his admirers; you may, perhaps, just catch the turn of a simile or single image, but to write in the real manner of Jeremy Taylor would require as mighty a mind as his. Many parts of Algernon Sidney's treatises afford excellent exemplars of a good modern practical style; and Dryden in his prose works, is a still better model, if you add a stricter and purer grammar. It is, indeed, worthy of remark that all our great poets have been good prose writers, as Chaucer, Spenser, Milton; and this probably arose from their just sense of metre. For a true poet will never confound verse and prose; whereas it is almost characteristic of indifferent prose writers that they should be constantly slipping into scraps of metre. Swift's style is, in its line, perfect; the manner is a complete expression of the matter, the terms appropriate, and the artifice concealed. It is simplicity in the true sense of the word.

After the Revolution, the spirit of the nation became much more commercial, than it had been before; a learned body, or clerisy, as such, gradually disappeared, and literature in general began to be addressed to the common miscellaneous public. That public had become accustomed to, and required, a strong stimulus; and to meet the requisitions of the public taste, a style was produced which by combining triteness of thought with singularity and excess of manner of expression, was calculated at once to soothe ignorance and to flatter vanity. The thought was carefully kept down to the immediate apprehension of the commonest understanding, and the dress was as anxiously arranged for the purpose of making the thought appear something very profound. The essence of this style consisted in a mock antithesis, (that is, an opposition of mere sounds), in a rage for personification, the abstract made animate, far-fetched metaphors, strange phrases, metrical scraps—in every thing, in short, but genuine prose. Style is, of course, nothing else but the art of conveying the meaning appropriately and with perspicuity, whatever that meaning may be, and one criterion of style is that it shall not be translateable without injury to the meaning. Johnson's style has pleased many from the very fault of being perpetually translateable; he creates an impression of cleverness by never saying any thing in a common way. The best specimen of this manner is in Junius, because his antithesis is less merely verbal than Johnson's. Gibbon's manner is the worst of all; it has every fault of which this peculiar style is capable. Tacitus is an example of it in Latin; in coming from Cicero you feel the *falsetto* immediately.

In order to form a good style, the primary rule and condition is, not to attempt to express ourselves in language before we thoroughly know our own meaning;—when a man perfectly understands himself, appropriate diction will generally be at his command either in writing or speaking.

1818

[INFLUENCE OF PUBLIC TASTE]

Of this epidemic influence there are two forms of disease most preclusive of tragic worth. The first I have already alluded to, the necessary growth of a sense and love of the ludicrous, and a diseased sensibility of the assimilating power

—[an] inflammation from cold and weakness—that in the boldest bursts of passion will lie in wait, or at once kindle into jest, at any phrase which had an accidental coincidence *in the mere* words with something base or trivial. For instance, to express woods not on a plain, but clothing a hill that overlooks valley, or dell, or river, or sea, the trees rising each above each other, as the spectators in an ancient theatre, I know of no other word in our language (bookish and pedantic words out of the question) but "hanging" woods—the *sylvae superimpendentes* of Catullus. [But] let a wit's . . . [?] slang voice call out "the gallows," and a peal of laughter would damn the play. Hence it is that so many dull pieces have had a decent run, only because nothing unusual above or absurd below mediocrity furnished an occasion, a spark, for the explosive materials collected behind the orchestra.

[MEANINGS OF WORDS]

If a man discovers any new substance or combination of substances in nature, he claims and without opposition takes the right of giving a discriminate name to the same. Again, if he should discover that two very different bodies have from certain superficial resemblances been confounded under one name, he has a right to assign the original name to that which best deserves it, from reasons of general analogy, and to name the other according to the class which he has proved it belongs to. Nor will it be a fair objection that many persons who have not known the fact or not reflected on it, continue to use the word promiscuously. Now apply this to our intellectual and moral researches. To erect a firm bulwark against capricious and arbitrary innovation, if we have a right to demand first, that a certain distinct faculty or modification of the human mind has a real existence, which every reflecting individual may prove to himself by a cautious appeal to his own consciousness, and that another faculty exists, distinct from the former, in source and application—should there be a word in the language which nine times in ten is really used to express the first faculty, and another word which would with equal precision discriminate the second, there can surely be no doubt, that we ought to appropriate those words, however in careless conversation they may ordinarily be confounded. If in drinking choice wine from a goblet cast and adorned by Myron, a man should say, "A beautiful flavor from a beautiful bowl"; and a friend should observe that it would be better to say, "A delightful flavor from a beautiful vase," there are few even among the uneducated who would not feel the superior propriety. In a boat on the Lake of Keswick, at the time that recent rains had filled all the waterfalls, I was looking at the celebrated Cataract of Lodore, then in all its force and greatness; a lady of no mean rank observed that it was sublimely beautiful, and indeed absolutely *pretty*. I have never mentioned this without occasioning a laugh of a kind which I am convinced could not possibly have arisen, if some deeper source of absurdity had not existed than that of a merely unusual phrase; if instead of *beautiful*, a pompous word coined from the Latin, as *formose* for instance, had been used, we should certainly laugh at the pedantry, but with a very different feeling from that with which we laugh at the incongruity of ideas involved in the former. 1808

[CHOICE OF WORDS]

I adverted in my last lecture to the prevailing laxity in the use of terms: this is the principal complaint to which the moderns are exposed; but it is a grievous one, inasmuch as it inevitably tends to the misapplication of words, and to the corruption of language. I mentioned the word "taste," but the remark applies not merely to substantives and adjectives, to things and their epithets, but to verbs: thus, how frequently is the verb "indorsed" strained from its true signification, as given by Milton in the expression—"And elephants indorsed with towers." Again, "virtue" has been equally perverted: originally it signified merely strength; it then became strength of mind and valour, and it has now been changed to the class term for moral excellence in all its various species. I only introduce these as instances by the way, and nothing could be easier than to multiply them.

At the same time, while I recommend precision both of thought and expression, I am far from advocating a pedantic

niceness in the choice of language: such a course would only
render conversation stiff and stilted. Dr. Johnson used to
say that in the most unrestrained discourse he always sought
for the properest word,—that which best and most exactly
conveyed his meaning: to a certain point he was right, but
because he carried it too far, he was often laborious where he
ought to have been light, and formal where he ought to have
been familiar. Men ought to endeavour to distinguish
subtilely, that they may be able afterwards to assimilate
truly.   1811

[LANGUAGES COMPARED]

The language, that is to say the particular tongue, in which
Shakespeare wrote, cannot be left out of consideration. It
will not be disputed, that one language may possess advantages which another does not enjoy; and we may state with
confidence, that English excels all other languages in the
number of its practical words. The French may bear the
palm in the names of trades, and in military and diplomatic
terms. Of the German it may be said, that, exclusive of
many mineralogical words, it is incomparable in its metaphysical and psychological force: in another respect it nearly
rivals the Greek,

> The learned Greek, rich in fit epithets,
> Blest in the lovely marriage of pure words;

I mean in its capability of composition—of forming compound words. Italian is the sweetest and softest language;
Spanish the most majestic. All these have their peculiar
faults; but I never can agree that any language is unfit for
poetry, although different languages, from the condition and
circumstances of the people, may certainly be adapted to one
species of poetry more than to another.

Take the French as an example. It is, perhaps, the most
perspicuous and pointed language in the world, and therefore best fitted for conversation, for the expression of light
and airy passion, attaining its object by peculiar and felicitous
turns of phrase, which are evanescent, and, like the beautifully coloured dust on the wings of a butterfly, must not be
judged by the test of touch. It appears as if it were all
surface and had no substratum, and it constantly most

dangerously tampers with morals, without positively offending decency. As the language for what is called modern genteel comedy all others must yield to French.   1811

[ATROPHY OF METAPHORS]

All things that have been highly admired by mankind at any time, or which have gone into excess, must have been originally applicable to some part or other of our nature. They have become ridiculous only in the excess; but great geniuses having used them with the truth of nature and the force of passion, have extorted from all mankind praise, or, rather, won it by their instant sympathy. Men, afterwards, most desirous of the end, and mistaking the desire of the end for a capacity of the means, have mechanically, and devoid of that spirit of life, employed the terms. They enquired what pleased or struck us? It was this or that—and they imitated it without knowing what it was that made them excellent, or that, excellent as they were, they would be ridiculous in another form. Such was the nature of metaphors, apostrophes, and what were called conceits.   1811

[TRANSLATORS AS CRITICS]

A Translator stands connected with the original Author by a certain law of subordination, which makes it more decorous to point out excellencies than defects: indeed he is not likely to be a fair judge of either. The pleasure or disgust from his own labour will mingle with the feelings that arise from an afterview of the original. Even in the first perusal of a work in any foreign language which we understand, we are apt to attribute to it more excellence than it really possesses from our own pleasurable sense of difficulty overcome without effect [effort?]. Translation of poetry into poetry is difficult, because the Translator must give a brilliancy to his language without that warmth of original conception, from which such brilliancy would follow of its own accord.   1800

[ATTITUDE OF MODERN EDITORS]

Among the strange differences between our ancestors and their descendants of latter days was the wide difference between the feelings and language of commentators on great classical works. At the restoration of letters, when men discovered the MSS. of the great ancients, as some long hidden treasure, the editor of even the most trivial work was exuberant in phrases of panegyric, and superlatives of praise seemed to be almost their only terms. In the editing of modern writers, on the contrary, we found the commentator everywhere assuming a sort of critical superiority over the author he edited. Which of the two was to be blamed? [Coleridge confessed that] the former (even admitting him more deficient in judgement, which he was by no means prepared to allow) was more congenial with the moral feelings, and better suited to all purposes of instruction, for though too much love for an author was like a mist which magnified unduly, it brought forward objects that would otherwise have passed unnoticed.

Never would he cease to deprecate that haughty insolence of the modern critic whose name would pass unknown were it not for the great and awful being on whom he exercises his art—like a monkey who had seated himself on the top of a rock, it was the rock which enabled him to reach the eminence where he was making his grimaces. In the course of the lectures it would be necessary to point out many instances of this kind. 1811

[TYPES OF READERS]

Readers may be divided into four classes:

1. Sponges, who absorb all they read, and return it nearly in the same state, only a little dirtied.

2. Sand-glasses, who retain nothing, and are content to get through a book for the sake of getting through the time.

3. Strain-bags, who retain merely the dregs of what they read.

4. Mogul diamonds, equally rare and valuable, who profit by what they read, and enable others to profit by it also. 1811

[READING ALOUD]

Again, as to the proper mode of reading: why is a tone in reading to be visited as a criminal offence, especially when

the estimate of that offence arises out of the ignorance and
incompetence of the master? Every man who reads with
true sensibility, especially poetry, must read with a tone,
since it conveys, with additional effect, the harmony and
rhythm of the verse, without in the slightest degree obscuring
the meaning. That is the highest point of excellence in
reading, which gives to every thing, whether of thought or
language, its most just expression. There may be a wrong
tone, as a right, and a wrong tone is of course to be avoided;
but a poet writes in measure, and measure is best made
apparent by reading with a tone, which heightens the verse,
and does not in any respect lower the sense. I defy any man,
who has a true relish of the beauty of versification, to read a
canto of the "Faery Queene," or a book of "Paradise Lost,"
without some species of intonation.   1811

[BOOKS FOR CHILDREN]

Give me, [cried Coleridge, with enthusiasm,] the works
which delighted my youth. Give me the "History of St.
George" and the "Seven Champions of Christendom,"
which at every leisure moment I used to hide myself in a
corner to read. Give me the "Arabian Nights Entertainments," which I used to watch till the sun shining on the
bookcase approached it, and glowing full upon it gave me
courage to take it from the shelf. I heard of no little Billies,
and sought no praise for giving to beggars, and I trust that
my heart is not the worse, or the less inclined to feel sympathy for all men, because I first learnt the powers of my
nature, and to reverence that nature—for who can feel and
reverence the nature of man and not feel deeply for the
afflictions of others possessing like powers and like nature?

                                             1811

MEMORANDA

for a History of English Poetry, biographical, bibliographical, critical, & philosophical, in distinct Essays.

1. English Romances—compared with the Latin Hexameter
Romance on Attila—with the German metrical Romances,
&c.

2. CHAUCER—illustrated by the Minnesänger, and as in all that follows an endeavour to ascertain, first, the degree and sort of the merit of the *Poems* comprized in his works, & secondly, what and how much of this belonged strictly *et sibi proprium* to Chaucer himself, what must be given to his Contemporaries, Predecessors, &c. This will be abundantly *more* interesting in *Shakspere;* yet interesting & necessary to a philosophical critic in all.

3. SPENSER—with connecting Introduction.

4. ENGLISH BALLADS, illustrated by the [? my] Translations of the Volkslieder of all countries—Ossian—Welsh Poets—Series of true heroic Ballads from Ossian.

5. SHAKSPERE!!! {ALMIGHTY FATHER! if thou grantest me Life, grant me Health & Perseverance!

6. MILTON!!!

7. Dryden & the History of the witty Logicians; *Butler* (ought he not to have a distinct though short essay?)—B. Jonson, Donne, Cowley — — Pope.

8. MODERN POETRY—with introductory (or annexed?) characters of Cowper, Burns, Thomson, Collins, Akenside, & any real poet, *quod real* poet, & exclusively confined to their own Faults & Excellencies—To conclude with a philosophical Analysis of *Poetry, nempe ens=bonum,* & the fountains of its pleasures in the Nature of man: of the pain and disgust with which it may affect men in a vitiated state of thought & Feeling; though this will have been probably anticipated in the former Essay, Modern Poetry, *i.e.* Poetry= Not-poetry, *ut Lucus a non Lucendo,* & *mens a non movendo,* & the badness & impermanence demonstrated, & the sources detected of the pain given to the wise, & of the pleasures to the corrupted—illustrated by a History of bad Poetry in all ages of our Literature.— —

Milton carefully compared, & contrasted with Jerome Taylor—& [in the discussion] perhaps of his Controversy with Hall introduce a philosophical abstract of the History of English Prose: if only to cut Dr. J[ohnson] "*to the liver.*"

[Watermark, 1796]

DANTE

It is impossible to understand the genius of Dante, and difficult to understand his poem, without some knowledge of the characters, studies, and writings of the schoolmen of the twelfth, thirteenth, and fourteenth centuries. For Dante was the living link between religion and philosophy; he philosophized the religion and christianized the philosophy of Italy; and, in this poetic union of religion and philosophy, he became the ground of transition into the mixed Platonism and Aristotelianism of the Schools, under which, by numerous minute articles of faith and ceremony, Christianity became a craft of hair-splitting, and was ultimately degraded into a complete *fetisch* worship, divorced from philosophy, and made up of a faith without thought, and a credulity directed by passion. Afterwards, indeed, philosophy revived under condition of defending this very superstition; and, in so doing, it necessarily led the way to its subversion, and that in exact proportion to the influence of the philosophic schools. Hence it did its work most completely in Germany, then in England, next in France, then in Spain, least of all in Italy. We must, therefore, take the poetry of Dante as christianized, but without the further Gothic accession of proper chivalry. It was at a somewhat later period, that the importations from the East, through the Venetian commerce and the crusading armaments, exercised a peculiarly strong influence on Italy.

In studying Dante, therefore, we must consider carefully the differences produced, first, by allegory being substituted for polytheism, and secondly and mainly, by the opposition of Christianity to the spirit of pagan Greece, which receiving the very names of its gods from Egypt, soon deprived them of all that was universal. The Greeks changed the ideas into finites, and these finites into *anthropomorphi*, or forms of men. Hence their religion, their poetry, nay, their very pictures, became statuesque. With them the form was the end. The reverse of this was the natural effect of Christianity; in which finites, even the human form, must, in order to satisfy the mind, be brought into connexion with, and be in fact symbolical of, the infinite; and must be considered in some enduring, however shadowy and indistinct, point of view, as the vehicle or representative of moral truth.

Hence resulted two great effects: a combination of poetry with doctrine, and, by turning the mind inward on its own essence instead of letting it act only on its outward circumstances and communities, a combination of poetry with sentiment. And it is this inwardness or subjectivity, which principally and most fundamentally distinguishes all the classic from all the modern poetry. Compare the passage in the "Iliad" (VI, 119-236) in which Diomed and Glaucus change arms,—

Χεῖράς τ' ἀλλήλων λαβέτην καὶ πιστώσαντο—

They took each other by the hand and pledged friendship— with the scene in Ariosto ("Orlando Furioso," Canto i, St. xx-xxii), where Rinaldo and Ferrauto fight and afterwards make it up:—

> Al Pagan la proposta non dispiacque:
> Così fu differita la tenzone;
> E tal tregua tra lor subito nacque,
> Sì l' odio e l' ira va in oblivione,
> Che 'l Pagano al partir dalle fresche acque
> Non lasciò a piede il buon figliuol d' Amone;
> Con preghi invita, e alfin lo toglie in groppa,
> E per l' orme d' Angelica galoppa. [St. xxi]

Here Homer would have left it. But the Christian poet has his own feelings to express, and goes on:—

> Oh gran bontà de' cavalieri antiqui!
> Eran rivali, eran di fe' diversi,
> E si sentian degli aspri colpi iniqui
> Per tutta la persona anco dolersi;
> Eppur per selve oscure e calli obliqui
> Insieme van, senza sospetto aversi! [St. xxii]

And here you will observe, that the reaction of Ariosto's own feelings on the image or act is more fore-grounded (to use a painter's phrase) than the image or act itself.

The two different modes in which the imagination is acted on by the ancient and modern poetry, may be illustrated by the parallel effects caused by the contemplation of the Greek or Roman-Greek architecture, compared with the Gothic. In the Pantheon, the whole is perceived in a perceived harmony with the parts which compose it; and generally you will remember that where the parts preserve any distinct individuality, there simple beauty, or beauty simply, arises; but where the parts melt undistinguished into the whole, there majestic beauty, or majesty, is the result. In York Minster, the parts, the grotesques, are in themselves very sharply distinct and separate, and this distinction and separation of the parts is counterbalanced only by the multitude and variety of those parts, by which the attention is bewildered;—whilst the whole, or that there is a whole produced, is altogether a feeling in which the several thousand distinct impressions lose themselves as in a universal solvent. Hence in a Gothic cathedral, as in a prospect from a mountain's top, there is, indeed, a unity, an awful oneness; but it is, because all distinction evades the eye. And just such is the distinction between the "Antigone" of Sophocles and the "Hamlet" of Shakspere.

* * *

Consider the wonderful profoundness of the whole third canto of the "Inferno"; and especially of the inscription over Hell gate: *Per me si va, &c.—*
which can only be explained by a meditation on the true nature of religion; that is, reason *plus* the understanding. I say profoundness rather than sublimity; for Dante does not so much elevate your thoughts as send them down deeper. In this canto all the images are distinct, and even vividly distinct, but there is a total impression of infinity; the wholeness is not in vision or conception, but in an inner feeling of totality, and absolute being.   1818

RABELAIS

One cannot help regretting that no friend of Rabelais, (and surely friends he must have had), has left an authentic account of him. His buffoonery was not merely Brutus' rough stick, which contained a rod of gold; it was necessary as an amulet against the monks and bigots. Beyond a doubt, he was among the deepest as well as boldest thinkers of his age. Never was a more plausible, and seldom, I am persuaded, a less appropriate line than the thousand times quoted,   *Rabelais laughing in his easy chair—*
of Mr. Pope. The caricature of his filth and zanyism proves

how fully he both knew and felt the danger in which he
stood. I could write a treatise in proof and praise of the
morality and moral elevation of Rabelais' work which would
make the church stare and the conventicle groan, and yet
should be the truth and nothing but the truth. I class
Rabelais with the creative minds of the world, Shakspere,
Dante, Cervantes, &c.   1825

CERVANTES

[DON QUIXOTE]

Too uninformed, and with too narrow a sphere of power
and opportunity to rise into the scientific artist, or to be
himself a patron of art, and with too deep a principle and
too much innocence to become a mere projector, Don
Quixote has recourse to romances:—

His curiosity and extravagant fondness herein arrived at that
pitch, that he sold many acres of arable land to purchase books of
knight-errantry, and carried home all he could lay hands on of
that kind !   [Page 2]

The more remote these romances were from the language
of common life, the more akin on that very account were
they to the shapeless dreams and strivings of his own mind;—
a mind, which possessed not the highest order of genius
which lives in an atmosphere of power over mankind, but
that minor kind which, in its restlessness, seeks for a vivid
representative of its own wishes, and substitutes the movements of that objective puppet for an exercise of actual power
in and by itself. The more wild and improbable these romances were, the more were they akin to his will, which had
been in the habit of acting as an unlimited monarch over the
creations of his fancy ! Hence observe how the startling of
the remaining common sense, like a glimmering before its
death, in the notice of the impossible-improbable of Don
Belianis, is dismissed by Don Quixote as impertinent:—

He had some doubt as to the dreadful wounds which Don Belianis
gave and received: for he imagined, that notwithstanding the
most expert surgeons had cured him, his face and whole body
must still be full of seams and scars. *Nevertheless* he commended
in his author the concluding his book with a promise of that
unfinishable adventure !   [*Ibid.*]

Hence also his first intention to turn author; but who, with such a restless struggle within him, could content himself with writing in a remote village among apathists and ignorants? During his colloquies with the village priest and the barber surgeon, in which the fervour of critical controversy feeds the passion and gives reality to its object— what more natural than that the mental striving should become an eddy?—madness may perhaps be defined as the circling in a stream which should be progressive and adaptive: Don Quixote grows at length to be a man out of his wits; his understanding is deranged; and hence without the least deviation from the truth of nature, without losing the least trait of personal individuality, he becomes a substantial living allegory, or personification of the reason and the moral sense, divested of the judgement and the understanding. Sancho is the converse. He is the common sense without reason or imagination; and Cervantes not only shows the excellence and power of reason in Don Quixote, but in both him and Sancho the mischiefs resulting from a severance of the two main constituents of sound intellectual and moral action. Put him and his master together, and they form a perfect intellect; but they are separated and without cement; and hence each having a need of the other for its own completeness, each has at times a mastery over the other. For the common sense, although it may see the practical inapplicability of the dictates of the imagination or abstract reason, yet cannot help submitting to them. These two characters possess the world, alternately and interchangeably the cheater and the cheated. To impersonate them, and to combine the permanent with the individual, is one of the highest creations of genius, and has been achieved by Cervantes and Shakspere, almost alone.   1818

CHAUCER

Chaucer must be read with an eye to the Norman-French *Trouvères*, of whom he is the best representative in English. He had great powers of invention. As in Shakspere, his characters represent classes, but in a different manner; Shakspere's characters are the representatives of the interior nature of humanity, in which some element has become so

predominant as to destroy the health of the mind; whereas Chaucer's are rather representatives of classes of manners. He is therefore more led to individualize in a mere personal sense. Observe Chaucer's love of nature; and how happily the subject of his main work is chosen. When you reflect that the company in the "Decameron" have retired to a place of safety from the raging of a pestilence, their mirth provokes a sense of their unfeelingness; whereas in Chaucer nothing of this sort occurs, and the scheme of a party on a pilgrimage, with different ends and occupations, aptly allows of the greatest variety of expression in the tales.

1818

SPENSER

There is this difference, among many others, between Shakspere and Spenser:—Shakspere is never coloured by the customs of his age; what appears of contemporary character in him is merely negative; it is just not something else. He has none of the fictitious realities of the classics, none of the grotesquenesses of chivalry, none of the allegory of the middle ages; there is no sectarianism either of politics or religion, no miser, no witch—no common witch—no astrology—nothing impermanent of however long duration; but he stands like the yew tree in Lorton vale, which has known so many ages that it belongs to none in particular; a living image of endless self-reproduction, like the immortal tree of Malabar. In Spenser the spirit of chivalry is entirely predominant, although with a much greater infusion of the poet's own individual self into it than is found in any other writer. He has the wit of the southern with the deeper inwardness of the northern genius.

* * *

You will take especial note of the marvellous independence and true imaginative absence of all particular space or time in the "Faery Queene." It is in the domains neither of history or geography; it is ignorant of all artificial boundary, all material obstacles; it is truly in land of Faery, that is, of mental space. The poet has placed you in a dream, a charmed sleep, and you neither wish, nor have the power,

to inquire where you are, or how you got there. It reminds
me of some lines of my own:—

> Oh ! would to Alla,
> The raven, or the sea-mew, were appointed
> To bring me food ! [&c. *See* page 134]

Indeed Spenser himself, in the conduct of his great poem,
may be represented under the same image, his symbolizing
purpose being his mariner's compass:—

> As pilot well expert in perilous wave, [&c.]
> *Book II, Canto vii, St. i*

So the poet through the realms of allegory.

¶ You should note the quintessential character of Christian
chivalry in all his characters, but more especially in his
women. The Greeks, except, perhaps, in Homer, seem to
have had no way of making their women interesting, but by
unsexing them, as in the instances of the tragic Medea,
Electra, &c. Contrast such characters with Spenser's Una,
who exhibits no prominent feature, has no particulariza-
tion, but produces the same feeling that a statue does, when
contemplated at a distance:—

> From her faire head her fillet she undight,
> And layd her stole aside. Her angels face
> As the great eye of heaven shyned bright,
> And made a sunshine in the shadie place;
> Did never mortall eye behold such heavenly grace.
> *Book I, Canto iii, St. iv*

¶ In Spenser we see the brightest and purest form of
that nationality which was so common a characteristic of
our elder poets. There is nothing unamiable, nothing contemptuous of others, in it. To glorify their country—to
elevate England into a queen, an empress of the heart—this
was their passion and object; and how dear and important
an object it was or may be, let Spain, in the recollection of
her Cid, declare ! There is a great magic in national names.
What a damper to all interest is a list of native East Indian
merchants ! Unknown names are non-conductors; they stop
all sympathy. No one of our poets has touched this string
more exquisitely than Spenser; especially in his chronicle of
the British Kings (Book II, Canto x), and the marriage
of the Thames with the Medway (Book IV, Canto xi),
in both which passages the mere names constitute half the

pleasure we receive. To the same feeling we must in particular attribute Spenser's sweet reference to Ireland:—

> Ne thence the Irishe rivers absent were,
> Sith no lesse famous than the rest they bee, &c.
> > *Book IV, Canto xi, St. xl*
>
> And Mulla mine, whose waves I whilom taught to weep.
> > *Ibid., St. xli*

And there is a beautiful passage of the same sort in the "Colin Clout's Come Home Again":—

> One day, (quoth he) I sat, (as was my trade)
> Under the foote of Mole, &c.   [*l. 56*].

Lastly, the great and prevailing character of Spenser's mind is fancy under the conditions of imagination, as an ever present but not always active power. He has an imaginative fancy, but he has not imagination, in kind or degree, as Shakspere and Milton have; the boldest effort of his powers in this way is the character of Talus. Add to this a feminine tenderness and almost maidenly purity of feeling, and above all, a deep moral earnestness which produces a believing sympathy and acquiescence in the reader, and you have a tolerably adequate view of Spenser's intellectual being.   1818

CHAPMAN: Homer translated, *see* p. 715

SHAKSPERE
[HIS CHARACTERISTICS]

It seems to me that his plays are distinguished from those of all other dramatic poets by the following characteristics:

1. Expectation in preference to surprise. It is like the true reading of the passage;—"God said, Let there be light, and there was *light;*"—not there *was* light. As the feeling with which we startle at a shooting star, compared with that of watching the sunrise at the pre-established moment, such and so low is surprise compared with expectation.

2. Signal adherence to the great law of nature, that all opposites tend to attract and temper each other. Passion in Shakspere generally displays libertinism, but involves morality; and if there are exceptions to this, they are, independently of their intrinsic value, all of them indicative of individual character, and, like the farewell admonitions

of a parent, have an end beyond the parental relation. Thus the Countess's beautiful precepts to Bertram, by elevating her character, raise that of Helena her favorite, and soften down the point in her which Shakspere does not mean us not to see, but to see and to forgive, and at length to justify. And so it is in Polonius, who is the personified memory of wisdom no longer actually possessed. This admirable character is always misrepresented on the stage. Shakspere never intended to exhibit him as a buffoon; for although it was natural that Hamlet,—a young man of fire and genius, detesting formality, and disliking Polonius on political grounds, as imagining that he had assisted his uncle in his usurpation,—should express himself satirically, —yet this must not be taken as exactly the poet's conception of him. In Polonius a certain induration of character had arisen from long habits of business; but take his advice to Laertes, and Ophelia's reverence for his memory, and we shall see that he was meant to be represented as a statesman somewhat past his faculties,—his recollections of life all full of wisdom, and showing a knowledge of human nature, whilst what immediately takes place before him, and escapes from him, is indicative of weakness.

But as in Homer all the deities are in armour, even Venus; so in Shakspere all the characters are strong. Hence real folly and dullness are made by him the vehicles of wisdom. There is no difficulty for one being a fool to imitate a fool; but to be, remain, and speak like a wise man and a great wit, and yet so as to give a vivid representation of a veritable fool,—*hic labor, hoc opus est.* A drunken constable is not uncommon, nor hard to draw; but see and examine what goes to make up a Dogberry.

3. Keeping at all times in the high road of life. Shakspere has no innocent adulteries, no interesting incests, no virtuous vice;—he never renders that amiable which religion and reason alike teach us to detest, or clothes impurity in the garb of virtue, like Beaumont and Fletcher, the Kotzebues of his day. Shakspere's fathers are aroused by ingratitude, his husbands stung by unfaithfulness; in him, in short, the affections are wounded in those points in which all may, nay, must, feel. Let the morality of Shakspere be contrasted with that of the writers of his own, or the

succeeding, age, or of those of the present day, who boast their superiority in this respect. No one can dispute that the result of such a comparison is altogether in favour of Shakspere;—even the letters of women of high rank in his age were often coarser than his writings. If he occasionally disgusts a keen sense of delicacy, he never injures the mind; he neither excites, nor flatters, passion, in order to degrade the subject of it; he does not use the faulty thing for a faulty purpose, nor carries on warfare against virtue, by causing wickedness to appear as no wickedness, through the medium of a morbid sympathy with the unfortunate. In Shakspere vice never walks as in twilight; nothing is purposely out of its place;—he inverts not the order of nature and propriety, —does not make every magistrate a drunkard or glutton, nor every poor man meek, humane, and temperate; he has no benevolent butchers, nor any sentimental rat-catchers.

4. Independence of the dramatic interest on the plot. The interest in the plot is always in fact on account of the characters, not *vice versa*, as in almost all other writers; the plot is a mere canvas and no more. Hence arises the true justification of the same stratagem being used in regard to Benedict and Beatrice,—the vanity in each being alike. Take away from the "Much Ado About Nothing" all that which is not indispensable to the plot, either as having little to do with it, or, at best, like Dogberry and his comrades, forced into the service, when any other less ingeniously absurd watchmen and night-constables would have answered the mere necessities of the action;—take away Benedict, Beatrice, Dogberry, and the reaction of the former on the character of Hero,—and what will remain? In other writers the main agent of the plot is always the prominent character; in Shakspere it is so, or is not so, as the character is in itself calculated, or not calculated, to form the plot. Don John is the main-spring of the plot of this play; but he is merely shown and then withdrawn.

5. Independence of the interest on the story as the groundwork of the plot. Hence Shakspere never took the trouble of inventing stories. It was enough for him to select from those that had been already invented or recorded such as had one or other, or both, of two recommendations, namely, suitableness to his particular purpose, and their

being parts of popular tradition,—names of which we had often heard, and of their fortunes, and as to which all we wanted was, to see the man himself. So it is just the man himself, the Lear, the Shylock, the Richard, that Shakspere makes us for the first time acquainted with. Omit the first scene in "Lear," and yet every thing will remain; so the first and second scenes in the "Merchant of Venice." Indeed it is universally true.

6. Interfusion of the lyrical—that which in its very essence is poetical—not only with the dramatic, as in the plays of Metastasio, where at the end of the scene comes the *aria* as the *exit* speech of the character,—but also in and through the dramatic. Songs in Shakspere are introduced as songs only, just as songs are in real life, beautifully as some of them are characteristic of the person who has sung or called for them, as Desdemona's "Willow," and Ophelia's wild snatches, and the sweet carollings in "As You Like It." But the whole of the "Midsummer Night's Dream" is one continued specimen of the dramatized lyrical. And observe how exquisitely the dramatic of Hotspur;—

> Marry,
> And I am glad of it with all my heart:
> I had rather be a kitten and cry mew, &c.

melts away into the lyric of Mortimer;—

> I understand thy looks: that pretty Welsh
> Which thou pourest down from these swelling heavens
> I am too perfect in, &c.
>
> *1. Henry IV, III, i*

7. The characters of the *dramatis personae*, like those in real life, are to be inferred by the reader;—they are not told to him. And it is well worth remarking that Shakspere's characters, like those in real life, are very commonly misunderstood, and almost always understood by different persons in different ways. The causes are the same in either case. If you take only what the friends of the character say, you may be deceived, and still more so, if that which his enemies say; nay, even the character himself sees himself through the medium of his character, and not exactly as he is. Take all together, not omitting a shrewd hint from the clown or the fool, and perhaps your impression will be

right; and you may know whether you have in fact discovered the poet's own idea, by all the speeches receiving light from it, and attesting its reality by reflecting it.

Lastly, in Shakspere the heterogeneous is united, as it is in nature. You must not suppose a pressure or passion always acting on or in the character;—passion in Shakspere is that by which the individual is distinguished from others, not that which makes a different kind of him. Shakspere followed the main march of the human affections. He entered into no analysis of the passions or faiths of men, but assured himself that such and such passions and faiths were grounded in our common nature, and not in the mere accidents of ignorance or disease. This is an important consideration, and constitutes our Shakspere the morning star, the guide and the pioneer, of true philosophy. ?1817

In Shakspere's females the sweet yet dignified feeling of all that *continuates* society, as sense of ancestry, of sex, &c. A purity inassailable by sophistry, because it does not rest on the analytic processes—but in feeling may be misinterpreted to the worse purposes—but in that sane equipoise of the faculties during which the feelings are representative of all past experience, not of the individual but of all those by whom she has been educated and of their predecessors *usque ad Evam*.

1813

[HIS CONCEITS]

I have been induced to offer these remarks, in order to obviate an objection often made against Shakspere on the ground of the multitude of his conceits. I do not pretend to justify every conceit, and a vast number have been most unfairly imputed to him; for I am satisfied that many portions of scenes attributed to Shakspere were never written by him. I admit, however, that even in those which bear the strongest characteristics of his mind, there are some conceits not strictly to be vindicated. The notion against which I declare war is, that when ever a conceit is met with it is unnatural. People who entertain this opinion forget, that had they lived in the age of Shakspere, they would have deemed them natural. Dryden in his translation of Juvenal

has used the words "Look round the world," which are a
literal version of the original; but Dr. Johnson has swelled
and expanded this expression into the following couplet:—

> Let Observation with extensive View,
> Survey Mankind, from *China* to *Peru;*
>
> *Vanity of Human Wishes*

mere bombast and tautology; as much as to say, "Let
observation with extensive observation observe mankind
extensively."

Had Dr. Johnson lived in the time of Shakspere, or even
of Dryden, he would never have been guilty of such an
outrage upon common sense and common language; and if
people would, in idea, throw themselves back a couple of
centuries, they would find that conceits, and even puns, were
very allowable, because very natural. Puns often arise out
of a mingled sense of injury, and contempt of the person
inflicting it, and, as it seems to me, it is a natural way of
expressing that mixed feeling. I could point out puns in
Shakspere, where they appear almost as if the first openings
of the mouth of nature—where nothing else could so properly
be said. This is not peculiar to puns, but is of much wider
application: read any part of the works of our great dramatist, and the conviction comes upon you irresistibly, not
only that what he puts into the mouths of his personages
might have been said, but that it must have been said,
because nothing so proper could have been said.   1811

[HIS WIT]

The wit of Shakspere is, as it were, like the flourishing of
a man's stick, when he is walking, in the full flow of animal
spirits: it is a sort of exuberance of hilarity which disburdens,
and it resembles a conductor, to distribute a portion of
our gladness to the surrounding air. While, however, it
disburdens, it leaves behind what is weightiest and most
important, and what most contributes to some direct aim
and purpose.   1811

[FIRST SCENES]

But as of more importance, so more striking is the judgement displayed by our truly *dramatic* poet as well as *poet* of

the drama in the management of his first scenes. With the
single exception of "Cymbeline" they either place before us
in one glance both the past and the future in some effect
which implies the continuance and full agency of its cause,
as in the feuds and party spirit of the servants of the two
houses in the first scene of "Romeo and Juliet," or in the
degrading passion for shews and public spectacles, and the
overwhelming attachment for the newest successful war-
chief in the Roman people, already become a populace, contrasted with the jealousy of the nobles, in "Julius Caesar"; or
they at once commence the action so as to excite a curiosity
for the explanation in the following [scenes], as in the storm
of the wind, the waves, and the boatswain in the "Tempest,"
instead of anticipating our curiosity, as in most other first
scenes and in too many other first *acts;* or they act, by contrast of diction suited to the characters, at once to heighten
the effect and yet to give a naturalness to the language and
rhythm of the principal characters, either as that of Prospero
and Miranda, in the last instance, by the appropriate lowness
of the style, or as in "King John" by the equally appropriate
stateliness of state harangue or official narration, so that the
after blank verse seems to belong to the rank and quality of
the speakers and not to the poet; or they strike at once the
key-note, give the predominant spirit of the play, as in the
"Twelfth Night" and in "Macbeth"; or the first scene com-
prizes all these advantages at once, as in "Hamlet."   1818

[SHAKSPERE'S ADVANTAGES]

Shakspere had advantages as well as disadvantages in
forming the class of writing which he took, and it has been
truly said that it was a magic circle in which he himself could
only tread. This remark has been applied to his magic
characters only, and it has been added that in this alone
Shakespeare succeeded; but it will be found equally true
that in the whole scheme of his drama, he invented a work
which was peculiar to himself, and not to be compared with
the productions of any writer of any nation,—in which he
had neither follower nor second.

How was he able to effect this?

He lived in an age in which from the religious controversies, carried on in a way of which we have no conception, there was a general energy of thinking, a pleasure in hard thinking and an expectation of it from those who came forward to solicit public praise, of which, in this day, we are equally ignorant. Consequently the judges were real amateurs. The author had to deal with a learned public, and he had no idea of a mixed public; it was divided, in truth, between those who had no taste at all and who went merely to amuse themselves, and those who were deeply versed in the literature to which they gave encouragement.

Although the piety of the times narrowed the numbers of those who attended the theatre, it made those who did visit it especially conversant with what they ought to expect. The theatre itself had no artificial, extraneous inducements —few scenes, little music—and all that was to excite the senses in a high degree was wanting. Shakspere himself said, "We appeal to your imaginations; by your imagination you can conceive this round O to be a mighty field of monarchs, and if you do not, all must seem absurd."

The circumstances of acting were altogether different from ours; it was much more of recitation, or rather a medium between recitation and what we now call recitation. The idea of the poet was always present, not of the actors, not of the thing to be represented. It was at that time more a delight and employment for the intellect, than an amusement for the senses.   1811

[POSSIBILITIES OF THE THEATRE AS A VEHICLE FOR SHAKSPERE]

Even so [it is] in the language of man and that of nature. The sound, *sun*, or the figures, *S*, *U*, *N*, are pure arbitrary modes of recalling the object, and for visual mere objects not only sufficient, but have infinite advantages from their very nothingness *per se*. But the language of nature is a subordinate *Logos*, that was in the beginning, and was with the thing it represented, and it was the thing represented. Now the language of Shakspere (in his "Lear," for instance), is a something intermediate, or rather it is the former blended with the latter, the arbitrary not merely recalling the cold notion of the thing, but expressing the reality of it, and, as arbitary language is an heirloom of the human race, being itself a part of that which it manifests. What shall I deduce from this? Even from this the appropriate, the never to be [too much] valued advantage of the theatre, if only the actors were what we know they have been,—a delightful, yet most effectual remedy for this dead palsy of the public mind. What would appear mad or ludicrous in a book, presented to the senses under the form of reality and with the truth of nature, supplies a species of actual experience. This indeed is the grand privilege of a great actor above a great poet. No part was ever played in perfection but that nature justified herself in the hearts of all her children, in whatever state they were, short of absolute moral exhaustion or downright stupidity. There is no time given to ask questions, or pass judgements. He takes us by storm, and though in the histrionic art many a clumsy counterfeit by caricature exaggeration of one or two features may gain applause as a fine likeness, yet never was the *very thing* rejected as a counterfeit. O, when I think of the inexhaustible mine of virgin treasure in our Shakspere, that I have been almost daily reading him since I was ten years old, that the thirty intervening years have been not fruitlessly and unintermittingly employed in the study of Greek, Latin, English, Italian, Spanish, and German *belles lettrists*, and for the last fifteen years far more intensely to the analysis of the laws of life and reason as they exist in man, and that every step I have made forward in taste, number of facts, from history or my own observation, and in the knowledge of [the different laws] and the apparent exceptions [from] accidental collision [of] the disturbing forces of them, and know that at every new accession of knowledge, after every successful exercise of meditation, every fresh presentation of experience, I have unfailingly discovered a proportionate increase of wisdom and intuition in Shakspere—when I know this, and know too that by a conceivable and possible, though hardly to be expected, arrangement of the British theatres, so large—*not* all indeed—but so large a proportion of this indefinite *all* (which no comprehension has yet drawn the line of circumscription so as to say to itself, I have seen *the whole*), might be sent into the heads and hearts, into the very souls, of the mass of mankind, to whom except by this living comment and interpretation it must remain for ever a sealed-up volume, a deep well without a wheel or windlass—it seems to me a pardonable enthusiasm to steal away from sober likelihood and share so rich a feast in the faery world of possibility! Yet even in the sober cheerfulness of a circumspect hope, much, very much, might be done—enough, assuredly, to furnish a kind and strenuous nature with ample motives for the attempt to effect what may be effected.

[SHAKSPERE'S CRITICS]

It is humiliating to reflect that, as it were, because heaven has given us the greatest poet, it has inflicted upon that poet the most incompetent critics: none of them seem to understand even his language, much less the principles upon which he wrote, and the peculiarities which distinguish him from all rivals. I will not now dwell upon this point, because it is my intention to devote a lecture more immediately to the prefaces of Pope and Johnson. Some of Shakspere's contemporaries appear to have understood him, and imitated him in a way that does the original no small honour; but modern preface-writers and commentators, while they praise him as a great genius, when they come to publish notes upon his plays, treat him like a schoolboy; as if this great genius did not understand himself, was not aware of his own powers, and wrote without design or purpose. Nearly all they can do is to express the most vulgar of all feelings, wonderment—wondering at what they term the irregularity of his genius, sometimes above all praise, and at other times, if they are to be trusted, below all contempt. They endeavour to reconcile the two opinions by asserting that he wrote for the mob; as if a man of real genius ever wrote for the mob. Shakspere never consciously wrote what was below himself: careless he might be, and his better genius may not always have attended him; but I fearlessly say, that he never penned a line that he knew would degrade him. No man does anything equally well at all times; but because Shakspere could not always be the greatest of poets, was he therefore to condescend to make himself the least?   1812

[SHAKSPERE'S JUDGEMENT EQUAL TO HIS GENIUS]

The object which I was proceeding to attain in my last lecture was to prove that independently of his peculiar merits, which are hereafter to be developed, Shakspere appears, from his poems alone, apart from his great works, to have possessed all the conditions of a true poet, and by this proof to do away, as far as may be in my power, [with] the popular notion that he was a great dramatist by a sort of instinct, immortal in his own despite, and sinking below men of second or third-rate character when he attempted aught beside the drama—even as bees construct their cells and manufacture their honey to admirable perfection, but would in vain attempt to build a nest. Now this mode of reconciling a compelled sense of inferiority with a feeling of pride, began in a few pedants, who having read that Sophocles was the great model of tragedy, and Aristotle the infallible dictator, and finding that the "Lear," "Hamlet," "Othello," and the rest, were neither in imitation of Sophocles, nor in obedience to Aristotle—and not having (with one or two exceptions) the courage to affirm that the delight which their country received from generation to generation, in defiance of the alterations of circumstances and habits, was wholly groundless—it was a happy medium and refuge, to talk of Shakspere as a sort of beautiful *lusus naturae*, a delightful monster,—wild, indeed, without taste or judgement, but like the inspired idiots so much venerated in the East, uttering, amid the strangest follies, the sublimest truths. In nine places out of ten in which I find his aweful name mentioned, it is with some epithet of "wild," "irregular," "pure child of nature," &c., &c., &c. If all this be true, we must submit to it; though to a thinking mind it cannot but be painful to find any excellence, merely human, thrown out of all human analogy, and thereby leaving us neither rules for imitation, nor motives to imitate. But if false, it is a dangerous falsehood; for it affords a refuge to secret self-conceit,—enables a vain man at once to escape his reader's indignation by general swoln panegyrics on Shakspere, merely by his *ipse dixit* to treat what he has not intellect enough to comprehend, or soul to feel, as contemptible, without assigning any reason, or referring his opinion to any demonstrated principle; and so has left Shakspere as a sort of Tartarian Dalai Lama, adored indeed, and his very excrescences prized as relics, but with no authority, no real influence. I grieve that every late voluminous edition of his works would enable me to substantiate the present charge with a variety of facts one tenth of which would of themselves exhaust the time allotted to me. Every critic, who has or has not made a collection of black letter books—in itself a useful and respectable amusement—puts on the seven-league boots of self-opinion and strides at once from an illustrator into a supreme judge, and blind and deaf, fills his three-ounce phial at the waters of Niagara—and determines positively the greatness of the cataract to be neither more nor less than his three-ounce phial has been able to receive.   ?1808

[SHAKSPERE "OUT OF TIME"]

It is absolutely necessary to recollect, that the age in which Shakspere lived was one of great abilities applied to individual and prudential purposes, and not an age of high moral feeling and lofty principle, which gives a man of genius the power of thinking of all things in reference to all. If, then, we should find that Shakspere took these materials as they were presented to him, and yet to all effectual purposes produced the same grand result as others attempted to produce in an age so much more favourable, shall we not feel and acknowledge the purity and holiness of genius—a light, which, however it might shine on a dunghill, was as pure as the divine effluence which created all the beauty of nature?

One of the consequences of the idea prevalent at the period when Shakspere flourished, *viz.*, that persons must be men of talents in proportion as they were gentlemen, renders certain characters in his dramas natural with reference to the date when they were drawn: when we read them we are aware that they are not of our age, and in one sense they may be said to be of no age. A friend of mine well remarked of Spenser, that he is out of space: the reader never knows where he is, but still he knows, from the consciousness within him, that all is as natural and proper, as if the country where the action is laid were distinctly pointed out, and marked down in a map. Shakspere is as much out of time, as Spenser is out of space; yet we feel conscious, though we never knew that such characters existed, that they might exist, and are satisfied with the belief in their existence.

This circumstance enabled Shakspere to paint truly, and according to the colouring of nature, a vast number of personages by the simple force of meditation: he had only to imitate certain parts of his own character, or to exaggerate such as existed in possibility, and they were at once true to nature, and fragments of the divine mind that drew them. Men who see the great luminary of our system through various optical instruments declare that it seems either square, triangular, or round, when in truth it is still the sun, unchanged in shape and proportion. So with the characters of our great poet: some may think them of one form, and some of another; but they are still nature, still Shakspere, and the creatures of his meditation.

When I use the term meditation, I do not mean that our great dramatist was without observation of external circumstances: quite the reverse; but mere observation may be able to produce an accurate copy, and even to furnish to other men's minds more than the copyist professed; but what is produced can only consist of parts and fragments, according to the means and extent of observation. Meditation looks at every character with interest, only as it contains something generally true, and such as might be expressed in a philosophical problem. 1811

[THE *I* IN SHAKSPERE]

Shakspere shaped his characters out of the nature within; but we cannot so safely say, out of his own nature as an individual person. No! this latter is itself but a *natura naturata*,—an effect, a product, not a power. It was Shakspere's prerogative to have the universal, which is potentially in each particular, opened out to him, the *homo generalis*, not as an abstraction from observation of a variety of men, but as the substance capable of endless modifications, of which his own personal existence was but one, and to use this one as the eye that beheld the other, and as the tongue that could convey the discovery. There is no greater or more common vice in dramatic writers than to draw out of themselves. How I—alone and in the self-sufficiency of my study, as all men are apt to be proud in their dreams—should like to be talking *king!* Shakspere, in composing, had no I, but the *I* representative. In Beaumont and Fletcher you have descriptions of characters by the poet rather than the characters themselves; we are told, and impressively told, of their being; but we rarely or never feel that they actually are.

"LOVE'S LABOUR'S LOST"

I can never sufficiently admire the wonderful activity of thought throughout the whole of the first scene of the play, rendered natural, as it is, by the choice of the characters, and the whimsical determination on which the drama is founded. A whimsical determination certainly;—yet not altogether so very improbable to those who are conversant in the history of the middle ages, with their Courts of Love, and all that lighter drapery of chivalry, which engaged even mighty kings with a sort of serio-comic interest, and may well be supposed to have occupied more completely the smaller princes, at a time when the noble's or prince's court contained the only theatre of the domain or principality. This sort of story, too, was admirably suited to Shakspere's times, when the English court was still the foster-mother of the state and the muses; and when, in consequence, the courtiers, and men of rank and fashion, affected a display of wit, point, and sententious observation, that would be deemed intolerable at present,—but in which a hundred years of controversy, involving every great political, and every dear domestic, interest, had trained all but the lowest classes to participate. Add to this the very style of the sermons of the time, and the eagerness of the Protestants to distinguish themselves by long and frequent preaching, and it will be found that, from the reign of Henry VIII to the abdication of James II, no country ever received such a national education as England.

Hence the comic matter chosen in the first instance is a

ridiculous imitation or apery of this constant striving after logical precision, and subtle opposition of thoughts, together with a making the most of every conception or image, by expressing it under the least expected property belonging to it, and this, again, rendered specially absurd by being applied to the most current subjects and occurrences. The phrases and modes of combination in argument were caught by the most ignorant from the custom of the age, and their ridiculous misapplication of them is most amusingly exhibited in Costard; whilst examples suited only to the gravest propositions and impersonations, or apostrophes to abstract thoughts impersonated, which are in fact the natural language only of the most vehement agitations of the mind, are adopted by the coxcombry of Armado as mere artifices of ornament.

The same kind of intellectual action is exhibited in a more serious and elevated strain in many other parts of this play. Biron's speech at the end of the fourth act is an excellent specimen of it. It is logic clothed in rhetoric;—but observe how Shakspere, in his two-fold being of poet and philosopher, avails himself of it to convey profound truths in the most lively images,—the whole remaining faithful to the character supposed to utter the lines, and the expressions themselves constituting a further development of that character:—

> Other slow arts entirely keep the brain:
> And therefore finding barren practisers,
> Scarce shew a harvest of their heavy toil:
> But love, first learned in a lady's eyes, [&c.]

This is quite a study;—sometimes you see this youthful god of poetry connecting disparate thoughts purely by means of resemblances in the words expressing them,—a thing in character in lighter comedy, especially of that kind in which Shakspere delights, namely, the purposed display of wit, though sometimes, too, disfiguring his graver scenes;—but more often you may see him doubling the natural connection or order of logical consequence in the thoughts by the introduction of an artificial and sought-for resemblance in the words, as, for instance, in the third line of the play,—

> And then grace us in the disgrace of death;—

this being a figure often having its force and propriety, as justified by the law of passion, which, inducing in the mind an unusual activity, seeks for means to waste its superfluity, —when in the highest degree—in lyric repetitions and sublime tautology—(*at her feet he bowed, he fell, he lay down; at her feet he bowed, he fell; where he bowed, there he fell down dead*),—and, in lower degrees, in making the words themselves the subjects and materials of that surplus action, and for the same cause that agitates our limbs, and forces our very gestures into a tempest in states of high excitement.

The mere style of narration in "Love's Labour 's Lost," like that of Aegeon in the first scene of the "Comedy of Errors," and of the Captain in the second scene of "Macbeth," seems imitated with its defects and its beauties from Sir Philip Sidney; whose "Arcadia," though not then published, was already well known in manuscript copies, and could hardly have escaped the notice and admiration of Shakspere as the friend and client of the Earl of Southampton. The chief defect consists in the parentheses and parenthetic thoughts and descriptions, suited neither to the passion of the speaker, nor the purpose of the person to whom the information is to be given, but manifestly betraying the author himself,—not by way of continuous undersong, but —palpably, and so as to show themselves addressed to the general reader. However, it is not unimportant to notice how strong a presumption the diction and allusions of this play afford, that, though Shakspere's acquirements in the dead languages might not be such as we suppose in a learned education, his habits had, nevertheless, been scholastic, and those of a student. For a young author's first work almost always bespeaks his recent pursuits, and his first observations of life are either drawn from the immediate employments of his youth, and from the characters and images most deeply impressed on his mind in the situations in which those employments had placed him;—or else they are fixed on such objects and occurrences in the world, as are easily connected with, and seem to bear upon, his studies and the hitherto exclusive subjects of his meditation. Just as Ben Jonson, who applied himself to the drama after having served in Flanders, fills his earliest plays with true or pretended soldiers, the wrongs and neglects of the former, and the absurd boasts and knavery of their counterfeits. So

Lessing's first comedies are placed in the universities, and consist of events and characters conceivable in an academic life.

"ROMEO AND JULIET"

[*The Seventh Lecture of the 1811-12 Series*]

In a former lecture I endeavoured to point out the union of the Poet and the Philosopher, or rather the warm embrace between them, in the "Venus and Adonis" and "Lucrece" of Shakspere. From thence I passed on to "Love's Labour's Lost," as the link between his character as a Poet, and his art as a Dramatist; and I shewed that, although in that work the former was still predominant, yet that the germs of his subsequent dramatic power were easily discernible.

I will now, as I promised in my last, proceed to "Romeo and Juliet," not because it is the earliest, or among the earliest of Shakspere's works of that kind, but because in it are to be found specimens, in degree, of all the excellences which he afterwards displayed in his more perfect dramas, but differing from them in being less forcibly evidenced, and less happily combined: all the parts are more or less present, but they are not united with the same harmony.

There are, however, in "Romeo and Juliet" passages where the poet's whole excellence is evinced, so that nothing superior to them can be met with in the productions of his after years. The main distinction between this play and others is, as I said, that the parts are less happily combined, or to borrow a phrase from the painter, the whole work is less in keeping. Grand portions are produced: we have limbs of giant growth; but the production, as a whole, in which each part gives delight for itself, and the whole, consisting of these delightful parts, communicates the highest intellectual pleasure and satisfaction, is the result of the application of judgement and taste. These are not to be attained but by painful study, and to the sacrifice of the stronger pleasures derived from the dazzling light which a man of genius throws over every circumstance, and where we are chiefly struck by vivid and distinct images. Taste is an attainment after a poet has been disciplined by experience, and has added to genius that talent by which he knows what part of his genius he can make acceptable, and intelligible to the portion of mankind for which he writes.

In my mind it would be a hopeless symptom, as regards genius, if I found a young man with anything like perfect taste. In the earlier works of Shakspere we have a profusion of double epithets, and sometimes even the coarsest terms are employed, if they convey a more vivid image; but by degrees the associations are connected with the image they are designed to impress, and the poet descends from the ideal into the real world so far as to conjoin both—to give a sphere of active operations to the ideal, and to elevate and refine the real.

In "Romeo and Juliet" the principal characters may be divided into two classes: in one class passion—the passion of love—is drawn and drawn truly, as well as beautifully; but the persons are not individualised farther than as the actor appears on the stage. It is a very just description and development of love, without giving, if I may so express myself, the philosophical history of it—without shewing how the man became acted upon by that particular passion, but leading it through all the incidents of the drama, and rendering it predominant.

Tybalt is, in himself, a common-place personage. And here allow me to remark upon a great distinction between Shakspere, and all who have written in imitation of him. I know no character in his plays, (unless indeed Pistol be an exception) which can be called the mere portrait of an individual: while the reader feels all the satisfaction arising from individuality, yet that very individual is a sort of class character, and this circumstance renders Shakspere the poet of all ages.

Tybalt is a man abandoned to his passions—with all the pride of family, only because he thought it belonged to him as a member of that family, and valuing himself highly, simply because he does not care for death. This indifference to death is perhaps more common than any other feeling: men are apt to flatter themselves extravagantly, merely because they possess a quality which it is a disgrace not to have, but which a wise man never puts forward, but when it is necessary.

Jeremy Taylor in one part of his voluminous works,

speaking of a great man, says that he was naturally a coward, as indeed most men are, knowing the value of life, but the power of his reason enabled him, when required, to conduct himself with uniform courage and hardihood. The good bishop, perhaps, had in his mind a story, told by one of the ancients, of a Philosopher and a Coxcomb, on board the same ship during a storm: the Coxcomb reviled the Philosopher for betraying marks of fear: "Why are you so frightened? I am not afraid of being drowned: I do not care a farthing for my life."—"You are perfectly right," said the Philosopher, "for your life is not worth a farthing."

Shakspere never takes pains to make his characters win your esteem, but leaves it to the general command of the passions, and to poetic justice. It is most beautiful to observe, in "Romeo and Juliet," that the characters principally engaged in the incidents are preserved innocent from all that could lower them in our opinion, while the rest of the personages, deserving little interest in themselves, derive it from being instrumental in those situations in which the more important personages develope their thoughts and passions.

Look at Capulet—a worthy, noble-minded old man of high rank, with all the impatience that is likely to accompany it. It is delightful to see all the sensibilities of our nature so exquisitely called forth; as if the poet had the hundred arms of the polypus, and had thrown them out in all directions to catch the predominant feeling. We may see in Capulet the manner in which anger seizes hold of everything that comes in its way, in order to express itself, as in the lines where he reproves Tybalt for his fierceness of behaviour, which led him to wish to insult a Montague, and disturb the merriment:—

> Go to, go to;
> You are a saucy boy. Is't so, indeed?
> This trick may chance to scath you;—I know what.
> You must contrary me! marry, 'tis time.—
> Well said, my hearts!—You are a princox: go:
> Be quiet or—More light, more light!—For shame!
> I'll make you quiet.—What! cheerly, my hearts!
>
> *Act I, Scene v*

The line

> This trick may chance to scath you;—I know what.

was an allusion to the legacy Tybalt might expect; and then,

N

seeing the lights burn dimly, Capulet turns his anger against
the servants. Thus we see that no one passion is so predominant, but that it includes all the parts of the character,
and the reader never has a mere abstract of a passion, as of
wrath or ambition, but the whole man is presented to him—
the one predominant passion acting, if I may so say, as the
leader of the band to the rest.

It could not be expected that the poet should introduce
such a character as Hamlet into every play; but even in
those personages, which are subordinate to a hero so eminently philosophical, the passion is at least rendered instructive, and induces the reader to look with a keener eye, and
a finer judgement into human nature.

Shakspere has this advantage over all other dramatists
—that he has availed himself of his psychological genius to
develope all the *minutiae* of the human heart: shewing us the
thing that, to common observers, he seems solely intent
upon, he makes visible what we should not otherwise have
seen: just as, after looking at distant objects through a
telescope, when we behold them subsequently with the
naked eye, we see them with greater distinctness, and in
more detail, than we should otherwise have done.

Mercutio is one of our poet's truly Shaksperian characters; for throughout his plays, but especially in those of
the highest order, it is plain that the personages were drawn
rather from meditation than from observation, or to speak
correctly, more from observation, the child of meditation.
It is comparatively easy for a man to go about the world, as if
with a pocket-book in his hand, carefully noting down what
he sees and hears: by practice he acquires considerable
facility in representing what he has observed, himself frequently unconscious of its worth, or its bearings. This is
entirely different from the observation of a mind, which,
having formed a theory and a system upon its own nature,
remarks all things that are examples of its truth, confirming
it in that truth, and, above all, enabling it to convey the
truths of philosophy, as mere effects derived from, what we
may call, the outward watchings of life.

Hence it is that Shakspere's favourite characters are full
of such lively intellect. Mercutio is a man possessing all
the elements of a poet: the whole world was, as it were,

subject to his law of association. Whenever he wishes to impress anything, all things become his servants for the purpose: all things tell the same tale, and sound in unison. This faculty, moreover, is combined with the manners and feelings of a perfect gentleman, himself utterly unconscious of his powers. By his loss it was contrived that the whole catastrophe of the tragedy should be brought about: it endears him to Romeo, and gives to the death of Mercutio an importance which it could not otherwise have acquired.

I say this in answer to an observation, I think by Dryden, (to which indeed Dr. Johnson has fully replied) that Shakspere having carried the part of Mercutio as far as he could, till his genius was exhausted, had killed him in the third Act, to get him out of the way. What shallow nonsense! As I have remarked, upon the death of Mercutio the whole catastrophe depends; it is produced by it. The scene in which it occurs serves to show how indifference to any subject but one, and aversion to activity on the part of Romeo, may be overcome and roused to the most resolute and determined conduct. Had not Mercutio been rendered so amiable and so interesting, we could not have felt so strongly the necessity for Romeo's interference, connecting it immediately, and passionately, with the future fortunes of the lover and his mistress.

But what am I to say of the Nurse? We have been told that her character is the mere fruit of observation—that it is like Swift's "Polite Conversation," certainly the most stupendous work of human memory, and of unceasingly active attention to what passes around us, upon record. The Nurse in "Romeo and Juliet" has sometimes been compared to a portrait by Gerard Dow, in which every hair was so exquisitely painted, that it would bear the test of the microscope. Now, I appeal confidently to my hearers whether the closest observation of the manners of one or two old nurses would have enabled Shakespeare to draw this character of admirable generalization? Surely not. Let any man conjure up in his mind all the qualities and peculiarities that can possibly belong to a nurse, and he will find them in Shakspere's picture of the old woman: nothing is omitted. This effect is not produced by mere observation. The great prerogative of genius (and Shakspere felt and availed himself of it) is now to swell itself to the dignity of a god, and now to subdue and keep dormant some part of that lofty nature, and to descend even to the lowest character—to become everything, in fact, but the vicious.

Thus, in the Nurse you have all the garrulity of old age, and all its fondness; for the affection of old-age is one of the greatest consolations of humanity. I have often thought what a melancholy world this would be without children, and what an inhuman world without the aged.

You have also in the Nurse the arrogance of ignorance, with the pride of meanness at being connected with a great family. You have the grossness, too, which that situation never removes, though it sometimes suspends it; and, arising from that grossness, the little low vices attendant upon it, which, indeed, in such minds are scarcely vices.—Romeo at one time was the most delightful and excellent young man, and the Nurse all willingness to assist him; but her disposition soon turns in favour of Paris, for whom she professes precisely the same admiration. How wonderfully are these low peculiarities contrasted with a young and pure mind, educated under different circumstances!

Another point ought to be mentioned as characteristic of the ignorance of the Nurse:—it is, that in all her recollections, she assists herself by the remembrance of visual circumstances. The great difference, in this respect, between the cultivated and the uncultivated mind is this—that the cultivated mind will be found to recal the past by certain regular trains of cause and effect; whereas, with the uncultivated mind, the past is recalled wholly by coincident images, or facts which happened at the same time. This position is fully exemplified in the following passages put into the mouth of the Nurse:—

> Even or odd, of all days in the year,
> Come Lammas eve at night shall she be fourteen.
> Susan and she—God rest all Christian souls!—
> Were of an age.—Well, Susan is with God;
> She was too good for me. But, as I said,
> On Lammas eve at night shall she be fourteen;
> That shall she, marry: I remember it well.
> 'Tis since the earthquake now eleven years;
> And she was wean'd,—I never shall forget it,—
> Of all the days of the year, upon that day;
> For I had then laid wormwood to my dug.

Sitting in the sun under the dove-house wall:
My lord and you were then at Mantua.—
Nay, I do bear a brain:—but, as I said,
When it did taste the wormwood on the nipple
Of my dug, and felt it bitter, pretty fool,
To see it tetchy, and fall out with the dug!
Shake, quoth the dove-house: 'twas no need, I trow,
To bid me trudge.
And since that time it is eleven years;
For then she could stand alone.

Act I, Scene iii

She afterwards goes on with similar visual impressions, so true to the character.—More is here brought into one portrait than could have been ascertained by one man's mere observation, and without the introduction of a single incongruous point.

I honour, I love, the works of Fielding as much, or perhaps more, than those of any other writer of fiction of that kind: take Fielding in his characters of postillions, landlords, and landladies, waiters, or indeed, of any-body who had come before his eye, and nothing can be more true, more happy, or more humorous; but in all his chief personages, Tom Jones for instance, where Fielding was not directed by observation, where he could not assist himself by the close copying of what he saw, where it is necessary that something should take place, some words be spoken, or some object described, which he could not have witnessed, (his soliloquies for example, or the interview between the hero and Sophia Western before the reconciliation) and I will venture to say, loving and honouring the man and his productions as I do, that nothing can be more forced and unnatural: the language is without vivacity or spirit, the whole matter is incongruous, and totally destitute of psychological truth.

On the other hand, look at Shakspere: where can any character be produced that does not speak the language of nature? where does he not put into the mouths of his *dramatis personae,* be they high or low, Kings or Constables, precisely what they must have said? Where, from observation, could he learn the language proper to Sovereigns, Queens, Noblemen or Generals? yet he invariably uses it.— Where, from observation, could he have learned such lines as these, which are put into the mouth of Othello, when he is talking to Iago of Brabantio?

> Let him do his spite:
> My services, which I have done the signiory,
> Shall out-tongue his complaints. 'Tis yet to know,
> Which, when I know that boasting is an honour,
> I shall promulgate, I fetch my life and being
> From men of royal siege; and my demerits
> May speak, unbonneted, to as proud a fortune
> As this that I have reach'd: for know, Iago,
> But that I love the gentle Desdemona,
> I would not my unhoused free condition
> Put into circumscription and confine
> For the sea's worth.   *Act I, Scene ii*

I ask where was Shakspere to observe such language as
this? If he did observe it, it was with the inward eye of
meditation upon his own nature: for the time, he became
Othello, and spoke as Othello, in such circumstances, must
have spoken.

Another remark I may make upon "Romeo and Juliet"
is, that in this tragedy the poet is not, as I have hinted,
entirely blended with the dramatist,—at least, not in the
degree to be afterwards noticed in "Lear," "Hamlet,"
"Othello," or "Macbeth." Capulet and Montague not unfrequently talk a language only belonging to the poet, and
not so characteristic of, and peculiar to, the passions of
persons in the situations in which they are placed—a mistake,
or rather an indistinctness, which many of our later dramatists have carried through the whole of their productions.

When I read the song of Deborah, I never think that she
is a poet, although I think the song itself a sublime poem:
it is as simple a dithyrambic production as exists in any
language; but it is the proper and characteristic effusion of a
woman highly elevated by triumph, by the natural hatred of
oppressors, and resulting from a bitter sense of wrong: it is
a song of exultation on deliverance from these evils, a deliverance accomplished by herself. When she exclaims, "The
inhabitants of the villages ceased, they ceased in Israel, until
that I, Deborah, arose, that I arose a mother in Israel," it is
poetry in the highest sense: we have no reason, however,
to suppose that if she had not been agitated by passion, and
animated by victory, she would have been able so to express
herself; or that if she had been placed in different circumstances, she would have used such language of truth and
passion. We are to remember that Shakspere, not placed

under circumstances of excitement, and only wrought upon
by his own vivid and vigorous imagination, writes a language
that invariably, and intuitively becomes the condition and
position of each character.

On the other hand, there is a language not descriptive of
passion, not uttered under the influence of it, which is at the
same time poetic, and shows a high and active fancy, as when
Capulet says to Paris:—

> Such comfort as do lusty young men feel,
> When well-apparell'd April on the heel
> Of limping winter treads, even such delight
> Among fresh female buds, shall you this night
> Inherit at my house.
>
> *Act I, Scene ii*

Here the poet may be said to speak, rather than the
dramatist; and it would be easy to adduce other passages
from this play, where Shakspere, for a moment forgetting
the character, utters his own words in his own person.

In my mind, what have often been censured as Shakspere's conceits are completely justifiable, as belonging to
the state, age, or feeling of the individual. Sometimes, when
they cannot be vindicated on these grounds, they may well
be excused by the taste of his own and of the preceding age;
as for instance, in Romeo's speech,

> Here's much to do with hate, but more with love:—
> Why then, O brawling love! O loving hate!
> O anything, of nothing first created!
> O heavy lightness! serious vanity!
> Misshapen chaos of well-seeming forms!
> Feather of lead, bright smoke, cold fire, sick health!
> Still-waking sleep, that is not what it is!
>
> *Act I, Scene i*

I dare not pronounce such passages as these to be absolutely unnatural, not merely because I consider the author a
much better judge than I can be, but because I can understand and allow for an effort of the mind, when it would
describe what it cannot satisfy itself with the description of,
to reconcile opposites and qualify contradictions, leaving a
middle state of mind more strictly appropriate to the imagination than any other, when it is, as it were, hovering between
images. As soon as it is fixed on one image, it becomes
understanding; but while it is unfixed and wavering between

them, attaching itself permanently to none, it is imagination.
Such is the fine description of Death in Milton:—

> The other shape,
> If shape it might be call'd, that shape had none
> Distinguishable in member, joint, or limb,
> Or substance might be call'd, that shadow seem'd,
> For each seem'd either: black it stood as night;
> Fierce as ten furies, terrible as hell,
> And shook a dreadful dart: what seem'd his head
> The likeness of a kingly crown had on.
>
> *Paradise Lost, Book II*

The grandest efforts of poetry are where the imagination
is called forth, not to produce a distinct form, but a strong
working of the mind, still offering what is still repelled, and
again creating what is again rejected; the result being what
the poet wishes to impress, namely, the substitution of a
sublime feeling of the unimaginable for a mere image. I
have sometimes thought that the passage just read might be
quoted as exhibiting the narrow limit of painting, as compared with the boundless power of poetry: painting cannot
go beyond a certain point; poetry rejects all control, all confinement. Yet we know that sundry painters have attempted
pictures of the meeting between Satan and Death at the gates
of Hell; and how was Death represented? Not as Milton
has described him, but by the most defined thing that can be
imagined—a skeleton, the dryest and hardest image that it is
possible to discover; which, instead of keeping the mind in
a state of activity, reduces it to the merest passivity,—an
image, compared with which a square, a triangle, or any
other mathematical figure, is a luxuriant fancy.

It is a general but mistaken notion that, because some
forms of writing, and some combinations of thought, are not
usual, they are not natural; but we are to recollect that the
dramatist represents his characters in every situation of life
and in every state of mind, and there is no form of language
that may not be introduced with effect by a great and judicious poet, and yet be most strictly according to nature.
Take punning, for instance, which may be the lowest, but
at all events is the most harmless, kind of wit, because it
never excites envy. A pun may be a necessary consequence
of association: one man, attempting to prove something that
was resisted by another, might, when agitated by strong

feeling, employ a term used by his adversary with a directly contrary meaning to that for which that adversary had resorted to it: it might come into his mind as one way, and sometimes the best, of replying to that adversary. This form of speech is generally produced by a mixture of anger and contempt, and punning is a natural mode of expressing them.

It is my intention to pass over none of the important so-called conceits of Shakspere, not a few of which are introduced into his later productions with great propriety and effect. We are not to forget, that at the time he lived there was an attempt at, and an affectation of, quaintness and adornment, which emanated from the Court, and against which satire was directed by Shakspere in the character of Osrick in "Hamlet." Among the schoolmen of that age, and earlier, nothing was more common than the use of conceits: it began with the revival of letters, and the bias thus given was very generally felt and acknowledged.

I have in my possession a dictionary of phrases, in which the epithets applied to love, hate, jealousy, and such abstract terms, are arranged; and they consist almost entirely of words taken from Seneca and his imitators, or from the schoolmen, showing perpetual antithesis, and describing the passions by the conjunction and combination of things absolutely irreconcileable. In treating the matter thus, I am aware that I am only palliating the practice in Shakspere: he ought to have had nothing to do with merely temporary peculiarities: he wrote not for his own only, but for all ages, and so far I admit the use of some of his conceits to be a defect. They detract sometimes from his universality as to time, person, and situation.

If we were able to discover, and to point out the peculiar faults, as well as the peculiar beauties of Shakspere, it would materially assist us in deciding what authority ought to be attached to certain portions of what are generally called his works. If we met with a play, or certain scenes of a play, in which we could trace neither his defects nor his excellences, we should have the strongest reason for believing that he had had no hand in it. In the case of scenes so circumstanced we might come to the conclusion that they were taken from the older plays, which, in some instances, he reformed or altered, or that they were inserted afterwards by some underhand, in order to please the mob. If a drama by Shakspere turned out to be too heavy for popular audiences, the clown might be called in to lighten the representation; and if it appeared that what was added was not in Shakspere's manner, the conclusion would be inevitable, that it was not from Shakspere's pen.

It remains for me to speak of the hero and heroine, of Romeo and Juliet themselves; and I shall do so with unaffected diffidence, not merely on account of the delicacy, but of the great importance of the subject. I feel that it is impossible to defend Shakspere from the most cruel of all charges,—that he is an immoral writer—without entering fully into his mode of pourtraying female characters, and of displaying the passion of love. It seems to me, that he has done both with greater perfection than any other writer of the known world, perhaps with the single exception of Milton in his delineation of Eve.

When I have heard it said, or seen it stated, that Shakspere wrote for man, but the gentle Fletcher for women, it has always given me something like acute pain, because to me it seems to do the greatest injustice to Shakspere: when, too, I remember how much character is formed by what we read, I cannot look upon it as a light question, to be passed over as a mere amusement, like a game of cards or chess. I never have been able to tame down my mind to think poetry a sport, or an occupation for idle hours.

Perhaps there is no more sure criterion of refinement in moral character, of the purity of intellectual intention, and of the deep conviction and perfect sense of what our own nature really is in all its combinations, than the different definitions different men would give of love. I will not detain you by stating the various known definitions, some of which it may be better not to repeat: I will rather give you one of my own, which, I apprehend, is equally free from the extravagance of pretended Platonism (which, like other things which super-moralise, is sure to demoralise) and from its grosser opposite.

Consider myself and my fellow-men as a sort of link between heaven and earth, being composed of body and soul, with power to reason and to will, and with that perpetual aspiration which tells us that this is ours for a while, but it is not ourselves; considering man, I say, in this two-fold character yet united in one person, I conceive that there can be no correct definition of love which does not correspond with our being, and with that subordination of one part to another which constitutes our perfection. I would say therefore that—

"Love is a desire of the whole being to be united to some thing, or some being, felt necessary to its completeness, by the most perfect means that nature permits, and reason dictates."

It is inevitable to every noble mind, whether man or woman, to feel itself, of itself, imperfect and insufficient, not as an animal only, but as a moral being. How wonderfully, then, has Providence contrived for us, by making that which is necessary to us a step in our exaltation to a higher and nobler state! The Creator has ordained that one should possess qualities which the other has not, and the union of both is the most complete ideal of human character. In everything the blending of the similar with the dissimilar is the secret of all pure delight. Who shall dare to stand alone, and vaunt himself, in himself, sufficient? In poetry it is the blending of passion with order that constitutes perfection: this is still more the case in morals, and more than all in the exc usive attachment of the sexes.

True it is, that the world and its business may be carried on without marriage; but it is so evident that Providence intended man (the only animal of all climates, and whose reason is pre-eminent over instinct) to be the master of the world, that marriage, or the knitting together of society by the tenderest, yet firmest ties, seems ordained to render him capable of maintaining his superiority over the brute creation. Man alone has been privileged to clothe himself, and to do all things so as to make him, as it were, a secondary creator of himself, and of his own happiness or misery: in this, as in all, the image of the Deity is impressed upon him.

Providence, then, has not left us to prudence only; for the power of calculation, which prudence implies, cannot have existed, but in a state which pre-supposes marriage. If God has done this, shall we suppose that he has given us no moral sense, no yearning, which is something more than animal, to secure that, without which man might form a herd, but could not be a society? The very idea seems to breathe absurdity.

From this union arise the paternal, filial, brotherly and sisterly relations of life; and every state is but a family magnified. All the operations of mind, in short, all that distinguishes us from brutes, originate in the more perfect state of domestic life.—One infallible criterion in forming an opinion of a man is the reverence in which he holds women. Plato has said, that in this way we rise from sensuality to affection, from affection to love, and from love to the pure intellectual delight by which we become worthy to conceive that infinite in ourselves, without which it is impossible for man to believe in a God. In a word, the grandest and most delightful of all promises has been expressed to us by this practical state—our marriage with the Redeemer of mankind.

I might safely appeal to every man who hears me, who in youth has been accustomed to abandon himself to his animal passions, whether when he first really fell in love, the earliest symptom was not a complete change in his manners, a contempt and a hatred of himself for having excused his conduct by asserting, that he acted according to the dictates of nature, that his vices were the inevitable consequences of youth, and that his passions at that period of life could not be conquered? The surest friend of chastity is love: it leads us, not to sink the mind in the body, but to draw up the body to the mind—the immortal part of our nature. See how contrasted in this respect are some portions of the works of writers, whom I need not name, with other portions of the same works: the ebullitions of comic humour have at times, by a lamentable confusion, been made the means of debasing our nature, while at other times, even in the same volume, we are happy to notice the utmost purity, such as the purity of love, which above all other qualities renders us most pure and lovely.

Love is not, like hunger, a mere selfish appetite: it is an associative quality. The hungry savage is nothing but an animal, thinking only of the satisfaction of his stomach: what is the first effect of love, but to associate the feeling with every object in nature? the trees whisper, the roses exhale their perfumes, the nightingales sing, nay the very skies smile in unison with the feeling of true and pure love. It gives to every object in nature a power of the heart, without which it would indeed be spiritless.

Shakspere has described this passion in various states and stages, beginning, as was most natural, with love in the young. Does he open his play by making Romeo and Juliet in love at first sight—at the first glimpse, as any ordinary thinker would do? Certainly not: he knew what he was about, and how he was to accomplish what he was about: he was to develope the whole passion, and he commences with the first elements—that sense of imperfection, that yearning to combine itself with something lovely. Romeo became enamoured of the idea he had formed in his own mind, and then, as it were, christened the first real being of the contrary sex as endowed with the perfections he desired. He appears to be in love with Rosaline; but, in truth, he is in love only with his own idea. He felt that necessity of being beloved which no noble mind can be without. Then our poet, our poet who so well knew human nature, introduces Romeo to Juliet, and makes it not only a violent, but a permanent love—a point for which Shakespeare has been ridiculed by the ignorant and unthinking. Romeo is first represented in a state most susceptible of love, and then, seeing Juliet, he took and retained the infection.

This brings me to observe upon a characteristic of Shakspere, which belongs to a man of profound thought and high genius. It has been too much the custom, when anything that happened in his dreams could not easily be explained by the few words the poet has employed, to pass it idly over, and to say that it is beyond our reach, and beyond the power of philosophy—a sort of *terra incognita* for discoverers—a great ocean to be hereafter explored. Others have treated such passages as hints and glimpses of something now non-existent, as the sacred fragments of an ancient and ruined temple, all the portions of which are beautiful, although their particular relation to each other is unknown. Shakspere knew the human mind, and its most minute and intimate workings, and he never introduces a word, or a thought, in vain or out of place: if we do not understand him, it is our own fault or the fault of copyists and typographers; but study, and the possession of some small stock of the knowledge by which he worked, will enable us often to detect and explain his meaning. He never wrote at random, or hit upon points of character and conduct by chance; and the smallest fragment of his mind not unfrequently gives a clue to a most perfect, regular, and consistent whole.

As I may not have another opportunity, the introduction of Friar Laurence into this tragedy enables me to remark upon the different manner in which Shakspere has treated the priestly character, as compared with other writers. In Beaumont and Fletcher priests are represented as a vulgar mockery; and, as in others of their dramatic personages, the errors of a few are mistaken for the demeanour of the many: but in Shakspere they always carry with them our love and respect. He made no injurious abstracts: he took no copies from the worst parts of our nature; and, like the rest, his characters of priests are truly drawn from the general body.

It may strike some as singular, that throughout all his productions he has never introduced the passion of avarice. The truth is, that it belongs only to particular parts of our nature, and is prevalent only in particular states of society; hence it could not, and cannot, be permanent. The Miser of Molière and Plautus is now looked upon as a species of madman, and avarice as a species of madness. Elwes, of whom everybody has heard, was an individual influenced by an insane condition of mind; but, as a passion, avarice has disappeared. How admirably, then, did Shakspere foresee, that if he drew such a character it could not be permanent! he drew characters which would always be natural, and therefore permanent, inasmuch as they were not dependent upon accidental circumstances.

There is not one of the plays of Shakspere that is built upon anything but the best and surest foundation; the characters must be permanent—permanent while men continue men,—because they stand upon what is absolutely necessary to our existence. This cannot be said even of some of the most famous authors of antiquity. Take the capital tragedies of Orestes, or of the husband of Jocasta: great as was the genius of the writers, these dramas have an obvious fault, and the fault lies at the very root of the action. In

Oedipus a man is represented oppressed by fate for a crime of which he was not morally guilty; and while we read we are obliged to say to ourselves, that in those days they considered actions without reference to the real guilt of the persons.

There is no character in Shakspere in which envy is pourtrayed, with one solitary exception—Cassius, in "Julius Caesar"; yet even there the vice is not hateful, inasmuch as it is counterbalanced by a number of excellent qualities and virtues. The poet leads the reader to suppose that it is rather something constitutional, something derived from his parents, something that he cannot avoid, and not something that he has himself acquired; thus throwing the blame from the will of man to some inevitable circumstance, and leading us to suppose that it is hardly to be looked upon as one of those passions that actually debase the mind.

Whenever love is described as of a serious nature, and much more when it is to lead to a tragical result, it depends upon a law of the mind, which, I believe, I shall hereafter be able to make intelligible, and which would not only justify Shakspere, but show an analogy to all his other characters.

1811

[*Notes*]

We have had occasion to speak at large on the subject of the three unities, time, place, and action, as applied to the drama in the abstract, and to the particular stage for which Shakspere wrote, as far as he can be said to have written for any stage but that of the universal mind. We succeeded in demonstrating that the two former, instead of being rules, were mere inconveniences attached to the local peculiarities of the Athenian drama; that the last alone deserved the name of a principle, and that in this Shakspere stood pre-eminent. Yet instead of unity of action I should greatly prefer the more appropriate though scholastic and uncouth words—homogeneity, proportionateness, and totality of interest. The distinction, or rather the essential difference, betwixt the shaping skill of mechanical talent, and the creative, productive life-power of inspired genius: In the former each part is separately conceived and then by a succeeding act put together—not as watches are made for wholesale—for here each part supposes a preconception of the whole in *some* mind—but as the pictures on a motley screen (N.B.—I must seek for a happier illustration). Whence [arises] the harmony that strikes us in the wildest natural landscapes,—in the relative shapes of rocks, the harmony of colors in the heath, ferns, and lichens, the leaves of the beech and oak, the stems and rich chocolate brown branches of the birch and other mountain trees, varying from verging autumn to returning spring—compared with the visual effect from the greater number of artificial plantations? The former are effected by a single energy, modified *ab intra* in each component part. Now as this is the particular excellence of the Shaksperian dramas generally, so is it especially characteristic of the "Romeo and Juliet."

First, the groundwork of the tale is altogether in family life, and the events of the play have their first origin in family-feuds. Filmy as are the eyes of party spirit, at once dim and truculent, still there is commonly some real or supposed object in view, or principle to be maintained—and though but equal to the twisted wires on the plate of rosin in the preparation for electrical pictures, it is still a guide in some degree, an assimilation to an outline; but in family quarrels, which have proved scarcely less injurious to states, wilfulness and precipitancy and passion from the mere habit and custom can alone be expected. With his accustomed judgement Shakspere has begun by placing before us a lively picture of all the impulses of the play, like a prelude; and as human folly ever presents two sides, one for Heraclitus and one for Democritus, he has first given the laughable absurdity of the evil in the contagion of the servants. The domestic tale begins with domestics, that have so little to do that they are under the necessity of letting the superfluity of sensorial power fly off thro' the escape-valve of wit-combats and quarreling with weapons of sharper edge, all in humble imitation of their masters. Yet there is a sort of unhired fidelity, an *our*-ishness about it that makes it rest pleasant on one's feelings. And all that follows to [the conclusion of the Prince's speech] is a motley dance of all ranks and ages to one tune, as if the horn of Huon had been playing.

The character of the Nurse is the nearest of anything in Shakspere to borrowing observation. The reason is that, as in infancy and childhood, the individual in nature is a representative. Like larch trees, in describing one you generalize a grove. The garrulity of age is strengthened by the [prerogative of a] long-trusted servant, whose sympathy with the mother's affections gives her privileges and rank in the house. [Observe] the mode of connecting by accidents of time and place, and the childlike fondness of repetition in her child[ish] age—and that happy, humble ducking under, yet resurgence against the check—

> Yes, madam! *yet* I cannot choose but laugh
>
> *I, iii, 51*

Scene iv introduces Mercutio to us. O how shall I describe that exquisite ebullience and overflow of youthful life, wafted on over the laughing wavelets of pleasure and prosperity, waves of the sea like a wanton beauty that distorted a face on which she saw her lover gazing enraptured, had wrinkled her surface in the triumph of its smoothness. Wit ever wakeful, fancy busy and procreative, courage, an easy mind that, without cares of its own, was at once disposed to laugh away those of others and yet be interested in them,—these and all congenial qualities, melting into the common copula of all, the man of quality and the gentleman, with all its excellencies and all its faults.

[III, ii, 85-91.

> *Nurse.* There's no trust,
> No faith, no honesty in men; . . . .
> . . . .
> Shame come to Romeo!
> *Jul.* Blister'd be thy tongue
> For such a wish!]

The Nurse's mistake of the mind's audible struggles with itself for its decision *in toto.*

[III, iii, 24-30.

> *Fri. L.* O deadly sin! O rude unthankfulness!
> Thy fault our law calls death; but the kind prince,
> Taking thy part, hath rush'd aside the law,
> And turn'd that black word death to banishment:
> This is dear mercy, and thou seest it not.
> *Rom.* 'Tis torture, and not mercy: heaven is here,
> Where Juliet lives.]

All deep passions [are] a sort of atheists, that believe no future.

[IV, iii, 55-58. Juliet's speech:

> O, look! methinks I see my cousin's ghost
> Seeking out Romeo, that did spit his body
> Upon a rapier's point: stay, Tybalt, stay!
> Romeo, I come! this do I drink to thee.]

The taking the poison in a fit of fright—how Shakspere provides for the finest decencies! A girl of fifteen—too bold for her but for [this].

"RICHARD II"

The transitional state between the epic and the drama is the historic drama. In the epic a pre-announced fate gradually adjusts and employs the will and the incidents as its instruments (ἔπομαι, *sequor*), while the drama places fate and will in opposition [and is] then most perfect when the victory of fate is obtained in consequence of imperfections in the opposing will, so as to leave the final impression that the fate itself is but a higher and more intelligent Will.

From the length of the speeches, the number of long speeches, and that (with one exception) the events are all *historical*, presented in their *results*, not produced by acts seen, or that take place before the audience, this tragedy is ill-suited to our present large theatres. But in itself, and for the closet, I feel no hesitation in placing it the first and most admirable of all Shakspere's *purely* historical plays. For the two parts of "Henry IV" form a species of themselves, which may be named the *mixt* drama. The distinction does not depend on the quantity of historical events compared with the fictions, for there is as much *history* in "Macbeth" as in "Richard," but in the relation of the history to the plot. In the purely historical plays, the history *informs* the plot; in the mixt it *directs* it; in the rest, as "Macbeth," "Hamlet," "Cymbeline," "Lear," it subserves it.

But this "*Richard II.*" O God forbid that however unsuited for the stage yet even there it should fall dead on the hearts of jacobinized Englishmen. Then indeed *praeteriit gloria mundi*. The spirit of patriotic reminiscence is the all-permeating spirit of this drama.

[I, iv.] A striking conclusion of a first act—letting the reader into the secret [of Richard's weakness], having before impressed the dignified and kingly manners of Richard, yet by well managed anticipations leading to the full gratification of the auditor's pleasure in his own penetration.

In this scene a new light is thrown on Richard's character. Until now he has appeared in all the beauty of royalty; but here, as soon as he is left to himself, the inherent weakness of his character is immediately shown. It is a weakness, however, of a peculiar kind, not arising from want of personal courage, or any specific defect of faculty, but rather an intellectual feminineness which feels a necessity of ever leaning on the breast of others, and of reclining on those who are all the while known to be inferiors. To this must be attributed as its consequences all Richard's vices, his tendency to concealment, and his cunning, the whole operation of which is directed to the getting rid of present difficulties. Richard is not meant to be a debauchee; but we see in him that sophistry which is common to man, by which we can deceive our own hearts, and at one and the same time apologize for, and yet commit, the error. Shakspere has represented this character in a very peculiar manner. He has not made him amiable with counterbalancing faults; but has openly and broadly drawn those faults without reserve, relying on Richard's disproportionate sufferings and gradually emergent good qualities for our sympathy; and this was possible, because his faults are not positive vices, but spring entirely from defect of character.

[II, ii, 5-13.

> *Queen.* To please the king I did; to please myself
> I cannot do it; yet I know no cause
> Why I should welcome such a guest as grief,
> Save bidding farewell to so sweet a guest
> As my sweet Richard: yet again, methinks,
> Some unborn sorrow, ripe in fortune's womb,
> Is coming towards me, and my inward soul
> With nothing trembles: at some thing it grieves,
> More than with parting from my lord the king.]

It is clear that Shakspere never meant to represent Richard II as a vulgar debauchee, but merely [as a man with] a wantonness in feminine shew, feminine *friendism*, intensely woman-like love of those immediately about him, mistaking the delight of being loved by him for a love for him.

Tender superstitions [are] encouraged by Shakspere. *Terra incognita* of the human mind: and how sharp a line of distinction he commonly draws between these obscure forecastings of general experience in each individual, and the vulgar errors of mere tradition.

"MIDSUMMER NIGHT'S DREAM"

[II, i, 3, 5.   Theobald adopts the reading "through" (Q_2Ff) in preference to "thorough" (Q_1).

> Through bush, through briar.]

What a noble pair of ears this worthy Theobald must have had! The eight amphimacers,

> Over hill, over dale,
> Thoro' bush, thoro' briar,
> Over park, over pale,
> Thoro' flood, thoro' fire,

have so delightful an effect on the ear! and then the sweet transition to the trochaic—

> I do wander ev'ry where—

for "where" itself, as a rhyme, is almost a trochee.

"MERCHANT OF VENICE"

See the different language which strong feelings may justify in Shylock, and learn from Shakspere's conduct of that character the terrible force of very plain and calm diction, when known to proceed from a resolved and impassioned man.

"TWELFTH NIGHT"

[II, iv, 109-11.

> *Vio.* A blank, my lord. She never told her love,
> But let concealment, like a worm i' the bud,
> Feed on her damask cheek.]

After the first line (of which the last five words should

be spoken with, and drop down in, a deep sigh) the speaker should make a pause and then start afresh, from the activity of thought born of suppressed feelings, which thoughts had accumulated during the brief interval, as vital heat under the skin during a dip in cold water.

"JULIUS CAESAR"

[I, i, 12-19.

Mar. But what trade art thou? answer me directly.

Sec. Com. A trade, sir, that, I hope, I may use with a safe conscience; which is indeed, sir, a mender of bad soles.

Mar. What trade, thou knave? thou naughty knave, what trade?

Sec. Com. Nay, I beseech you, sir, be not out with me: yet, if you be out, sir, I can mend you.

Mar. What mean'st thou by that? mend me, thou saucy fellow!]

The speeches of Flavius and Marullus are in blank verse. Wherever regular metre can be rendered truly imitative of character, passion, or personal rank, Shakspere seldom, if ever, neglects it. Hence, [this line] should be printed

What mean'st by that? Mend *me*, thou saucy fellow.

N.B. I say, *regular* metre: for even the prose has in the highest and lowest *dramatis personae*, a cobbler or a Hamlet, a rhythm so felicitous and so severally appropriate, as to be a virtual metre.

[I, ii, 19.

Bru. A soothsayer bids you beware the ides of March.]

If my ear does not deceive me, the metre of this line was meant to express that sort of mild philosophic contempt characterizing Brutus even in his first casual speech. The line is a trimeter, each foot containing two accented and two unaccented syllables, but variously arranged.

Ă sōothsāyĕr ˈ bĭds yŏu bĕwāre ˈ thĕ īdĕs ŏf Mārch.

[II, ii, 76. Theobald reads,

She dreamt last night, she saw my statue.]

A modern tragic poet would have written,

Last night she dreamt, that she my statue saw, &c.,

but Shakspere never avails himself of the supposed licence of transposition merely for the metre. There is always some logic either of thought or passion to justify it. In the present line we must read "statue," "stătŭā," as in the same age they pronounced "heroes" more often "hērōĕs," than "hērōse."

[III, i, 205-09.

> Pardon me, Julius! Here wast thou bay'd, brave hart;
> Here didst thou fall, and here thy hunters stand,
> Sign'd in thy spoil and crimson'd in thy lethe.
> *O world, thou wast the forest to this hart;*
> *And this, indeed, O world, the heart of thee.*]

I doubt these [last two] lines: not because they are vile; but first, on account of the rhythm, which is not Shaksperian but just the very *tune* of some old play, from which the actor might have interpolated them; and secondly, because they interrupt not only the sense and connection, but likewise the flow both of the passion and (what is with me still more decisive) the Shaksperian link of association. As with the parenthesis or gloss slipt into the text concerning Jonah in the Gospel, we have only to read the passage without it to see that it never was in it. I venture to say there is no instance in Shakspere fairly like it. Conceits he has, but they not [only] rise out of some *word* in the lines before, but they *lead* to the thought in the lines following. Here it is a mere alien: Antony forgets an image, when he is even touching it; and then recollects it when the thought last in his mind must have led him away from it.

"HAMLET"

"Hamlet" was the play, or rather Hamlet himself was the character in the intuition and exposition of which I first made my turn for philosophical criticism, and especially for insight into the genius of Shakspere, *noticed;* first among my acquaintances, as Sir George Beaumont will bear witness, and as Mr. Wordsworth knows, though from motives which I do not know or impulses which I *cannot* know, he has thought proper to assert that Schlegel and the German critics *first* taught Englishmen to admire their own great countryman intelligently; and secondly, long before Schlegel had given at Vienna the lectures on Shakspere which he afterwards published, I had given eighteen lectures on the same subject, *substantially* the same, proceeding from the same, the *very* same point of view, and deducing the same conclusions, as far as I either then or now agree with him. I gave them at the Royal Institution, before from six to seven hundred auditors of rank and eminence, in the spring of the same year in which Sir Humphry Davy, a fellow-lecturer, made his great revolutionary discoveries in chemistry. Even in detail the coincidence of Schlegel with my lectures was so extraordinary that all at a later period who heard the same words (taken from my Royal Institution notes) concluded a borrowing on my part from Schlegel. Mr. Hazlitt, whose hatred of me is in such an inverse ratio to my zealous kindness toward him as to be defended by his warmest admirer, C. Lamb (who, besides his characteristic obstinacy of adherence to old friends, as long at least as they are at all down in the world, is linked as by a charm to Hazlitt's conversation), only under the epithet of *"frantic"*—Mr. Hazlitt himself replied to an assertion of my plagiarism from Schlegel in these words: "That is a lie; for I myself heard the very same character of Hamlet from Coleridge before he went to Germany and when he had neither read nor could read a page of German." Now Hazlitt was on a visit to my cottage at Nether Stowey, Somerset, in the summer of the year 1798, in the September of which (see my "Literary Life") I first was out of sight of the shores of Great Britain.

Recorded by me, S. T. Coleridge, Jany. 7, 1819. Highgate.

We will now pass to "Hamlet," in order to obviate some of the general prejudices against the author, in reference to the character of the hero. Much has been objected to, which ought to have been praised, and many beauties of the highest kind have been neglected, because they are somewhat hidden.

The first question we should ask ourselves is—What did Shakspere mean when he drew the character of Hamlet? He never wrote any thing without design, and what was his design when he sat down to produce this tragedy? My

belief is, that he always regarded his story, before he began
to write, much in the same light as a painter regards his
canvas, before he begins to paint—as a mere vehicle for his
thoughts—as the ground upon which he was to work. What
then was the point to which Shakspere directed himself
in "Hamlet"? He intended to pourtray a person, in whose
view the external world, and all its incidents and objects,
were comparatively dim, and of no interest in themselves,
and which began to interest only, when they were reflected
in the mirror of his mind. Hamlet beheld external things
in the same way that a man of vivid imagination, who shuts
his eyes, sees what has previously made an impression on
his organs.

The poet places him in the most stimulating circumstances
that a human being can be placed in. He is the heir apparent
of a throne; his father dies suspiciously; his mother excludes
her son from his throne by marrying his uncle. This is
not enough; but the Ghost of the murdered father is introduced, to assure the son that he was put to death by his
own brother. What is the effect upon the son?—instant
action and pursuit of revenge? No: endless reasoning and
hesitating—constant urging and solicitation of the mind
to act, and as constant an escape from action; ceaseless
reproaches of himself for sloth and negligence, while the
whole energy of his resolution evaporates in these reproaches.
This, too, not from cowardice, for he is drawn as one of the
bravest of his time—not from want of forethought or slowness of apprehension, for he sees through the very souls of all
who surround him, but merely from that aversion to action,
which prevails among such as have a world in themselves.

How admirable, too, is the judgement of the poet! Hamlet's own disordered fancy has not conjured up the spirit of
his father; it has been seen by others: he is prepared by
them to witness its re-appearance, and when he does see it,
Hamlet is not brought forward as having long brooded on
the subject. The moment before the Ghost enters, Hamlet
speaks of other matters: he mentions the coldness of the
night, and observes that he has not heard the clock strike,
adding, in reference to the custom of drinking, that it is

More honour'd in the breach than the observance.

Act I, Scene iv

Owing to the tranquil state of his mind, he indulges in some moral reflections. Afterwards, the Ghost suddenly enters.

Hor. Look, my lord! it comes.
Ham. Angels and ministers of grace defend us!

The same thing occurs in "Macbeth": in the dagger-scene, the moment before the hero sees it, he has his mind applied to some indifferent matters; "Go, tell thy mistress," &c. Thus, in both cases, the preternatural appearance has all the effect of abruptness, and the reader is totally divested of the notion, that the figure is a vision of a highly wrought imagination.

Here Shakspere adapts himself so admirably to the situation—in other words, so puts himself into it—that, though poetry, his language is the very language of nature. No terms, associated with such feelings, can occur to us so proper as those which he has employed, especially on the highest, the most august, and the most awful subjects that can interest a human being in this sentient world. That this is no mere fancy, I can undertake to establish from hundreds, I might say thousands, of passages. No character he has drawn, in the whole list of his plays, could so well and fitly express himself, as in the language Shakspere has put into his mouth.

There is no indecision about Hamlet, as far as his own sense of duty is concerned; he knows well what he ought to do, and over and over again he makes up his mind to do it. The moment the players, and the two spies set upon him, have withdrawn, of whom he takes leave with a line so expressive of his contempt,

Ay so; good bye you.—Now I am alone,

he breaks out into a delirium of rage against himself for neglecting to perform the solemn duty he had undertaken, and contrasts the factitious and artificial display of feeling by the player with his own apparent indifference;

What's Hecuba to him, or he to Hecuba,
That he should weep for her?

Yet the player did weep for her, and was in an agony of grief at her sufferings, while Hamlet is unable to rouse himself to action, in order that he may perform the command of his father, who had come from the grave to incite him to revenge:—

> This is most brave!
> That I, the son of a dear father murder'd,
> Prompted to my revenge by heaven and hell,
> Must, like a whore, unpack my heart with words,
> And fall a cursing like a very drab,
> A scullion.
>
> *Act II, Scene ii*

It is the same feeling, the same conviction of what is his duty, that makes Hamlet exclaim in a subsequent part of the tragedy:

> How all occasions do inform against me,
> And spur my dull revenge! What is a man,
> If his chief good, and market of his time,
> Be but to sleep and feed? A beast, no more.
> . . . . I do not know
> Why yet I live to say—"this thing's to do,"
> Sith I have cause and will and strength and means
> To do't.
>
> *Act IV, Scene iv*

Yet with all this strong conviction of duty, and with all this resolution arising out of strong conviction, nothing is done. This admirable and consistent character, deeply acquainted with his own feelings, painting them with such wonderful power and accuracy, and firmly persuaded that a moment ought not to be lost in executing the solemn charge committed to him, still yields to the same retiring from reality, which is the result of having, what we express by the terms, a world within himself.

Such a mind as Hamlet's is near akin to madness. Dryden has somewhere said,

> Great wit to madness nearly is allied,

and he was right; for he means by "wit" that greatness of genius, which led Hamlet to a perfect knowledge of his own character, which, with all strength of motive, was so weak as to be unable to carry into act his own most obvious duty.

With all this he has a sense of imperfectness, which becomes apparent when he is moralising on the skull in the churchyard. Something is wanting to his completeness— something is deficient which remains to be supplied, and he is therefore described as attached to Ophelia. His madness is assumed, when he finds that witnesses have been placed behind the arras to listen to what passes, and when the heroine has been thrown in his way as a decoy.

Another objection has been taken by Dr. Johnson, and Shakspere has been taxed very severely. I refer to the scene where Hamlet enters and finds his uncle praying, and refuses to take his life, excepting when he is in the height of his iniquity. To assail him at such a moment of confession and repentance, Hamlet declares,

> Why, this is hire and salary, not revenge.
>
> *Act III, Scene iii*

He therefore forbears, and postpones his uncle's death, until he can catch him in some act

> That has no relish of salvation in't.

This conduct, and this sentiment, Dr. Johnson has pronounced to be so atrocious and horrible, as to be unfit to be put into the mouth of a human being. The fact, however, is that Dr. Johnson did not understand the character of Hamlet, and censured accordingly: the determination to allow the guilty King to escape at such a moment is only part of the indecision and irresoluteness of the hero. Hamlet seizes hold of a pretext for not acting, when he might have acted so instantly and effectually: therefore, he again defers the revenge he was bound to seek, and declares his determination to accomplish it at some time,

> When he is drunk, asleep, or in his rage,
> Or in th' incestuous pleasures of his bed.

This, allow me to impress upon you most emphatically, was merely the excuse Hamlet made to himself for not taking advantage of this particular and favourable moment for doing justice upon his guilty uncle, at the urgent instance of the spirit of his father.

Dr. Johnson farther states, that in the voyage to England, Shakspere merely follows the novel as he found it, as if the poet had no other reason for adhering to his original; but Shakspere never followed a novel, because he found such and such an incident in it, but because he saw that the story, as he read it, contributed to enforce, or to explain some great truth inherent in human nature. He never could lack invention to alter or improve a popular narrative; but he did not wantonly vary from it, when he knew that, as it was related, it would so well apply to his own great purpose. He saw at once how consistent it was with the character of Hamlet, that after still resolving, and still deferring, still determining to execute, and still postponing execution, he should finally, in the infirmity of his disposition, give himself up to his destiny, and hopelessly place himself in the power, and at the mercy of his enemies.

Even after the scene with Osrick, we see Hamlet still indulging in reflection, and hardly thinking of the task he has just undertaken: he is all dispatch and resolution, as far as words and present intentions are concerned, but all hesitation and irresolution, when called upon to carry his words and intentions into effect; so that, resolving to do everything, he does nothing. He is full of purpose, but void of that quality of mind which accomplishes purpose.

Anything finer than this conception, and working out of a great character, is merely impossible. Shakspere wished to impress upon us the truth, that action is the chief end of existence—that no faculties of intellect, however brilliant, can be considered valuable, or indeed otherwise than as misfortunes, if they withdraw us from, or render us repugnant to action, and lead us to think and think of doing, until the time has elapsed when we can do anything effectually. In enforcing this moral truth, Shakspere has shown the fulness and force of his powers: all that is amiable and excellent in nature is combined in Hamlet, with the exception of one quality. He is a man living in meditation, called upon to act by every motive human and divine, but the great object of his life is defeated by continually resolving to do, yet doing nothing but resolve.

                                                              1812

[Notes]

Compare the easy language of common life in which this drama opens, with the wild wayward lyric of the opening of "Macbeth." The language is familiar: no poetic descriptions of night, no elaborate information conveyed by one speaker to another of what both had before their immediate perceptions (such as the first distich in Addison's "Cato," which is a translation into poetry of "Past four o'clock, and a damp morning")—yet nothing bordering on the comic on the one hand, and no striving of the intellect on the other. It is the language of *sensation* among men who feared no charge of effeminacy for feeling what they felt no want of resolution to bear. Yet the armour, the dead silence, the watchfulness that first interrupts it, the welcome relief of guard, the cold, the broken expressions as of a man's compelled attention to bodily feelings allowed no man,—all excellently accord with and prepare for the after gradual rise into tragedy—but above all into a tragedy the interest of which is eminently *ad et apud intra*, as "Macbeth" ... [?] is *ad extra*.

The preparation *informative* of the audience is just as much as was precisely necessary: how gradual first, and with the uncertainty appertaining to a question—

What, has *this thing* appeared *again* to-night.

Even the word "again" has its *credibilizing* effect. Then the representative of the ignorance of the audience, Horatio (not himself but [quoted by] Marcellus to Bernardo) anticipates the common solution, "'tis but our phantasy." But Marcellus rises secondly into "this dreaded sight." Then this "thing" becomes at once an "apparition," and that too an intelligent spirit that is to be *spoken* to.

Tush, tush! 'twill not appear.

Then the shivery feeling, at such a time, with two eyewitnesses, of sitting down to hear a story of a ghost, and this, too, a ghost that had appeared two nights before at about this very time. The effort of the narrator to master his own imaginative terrors; the consequent elevation of the style, itself a continuation of this effort; the turning off to an *outward* object, "yon same star." O heaven! words are wasted to those that feel and to those who do not feel the exquisite judgement of Shakspere.

Hume himself could not but have faith in *this* Ghost dramatically, let his anti-ghostism be as strong as Samson against ghosts less powerfully raised.

[I, i, 70-72.

> *Mar.* Good now, sit down, and tell me, he that knows,
> Why this same strict and most observant watch
> So nightly toils the subject of the land.]

The exquisitely natural transit into the narration retrospective. [When the Ghost re-appears, note] Horatio's increased courage from having translated the late individual spectre into thought and past experience, and Marcellus' and Bernardo's sympathy with it [Horatio's courage] in daring to strike, while yet the former feeling returns in

> We do it wrong [being so majestical,
> To offer it the show of violence.]

[I, i, 149-52.

> I have heard,
> The cock, that is the trumpet to the morn,
> Doth with his lofty and shrill-sounding throat
> Awake the god of day.]

No Addison more careful to be poetical in diction than Shakspere in providing the grounds and sources of its propriety. But *how* to elevate a thing almost mean by its familiarity, young poets may learn in the cock-crow.

[I, ii, 74.

> *Ham.* Ay, madam, it is common.]

Suppression prepares for overflow.

[I, iii, 115-17.

> *Pol.*   I do know,
> When the blood burns, how prodigal the soul
> Lends the tongue vows: these blazes, daughter, &c.]

A spondee has, I doubt not, dropt out of the text. After "vows" insert either "Go to" or "mark you!" If the latter be preferred, it might end the line.

> Lends the tongue vows. Go to! these blazes, daughter,

or

> Lends the tongue vows. These blazes, daughter, mark you.

N.B. Shakspere never introduces a catalectic line without intending an equivalent to the foot omitted, in the pauses, or the dwelling emphasis, or the diffused retardation. I do not, however, deny that a good actor might by employing the last mentioned, *viz.*, the retardation or solemn knowing drawl, supply the missing spondee with good effect. But I do not believe that in this or the foregoing speeches Shakspere meant to bring out the senility or weakness of Polonius's mind. In the great ever-recurring dangers and duties of life, where to distinguish the fit objects for the application of the maxims collected by the experience of a

long life requires no fineness of tact, as in the admonitions
to his son and daughter, Polonius is always made respectable. But if the actor were capable of catching these shades in
the character, the pit and gallery would be malcontent.

[II, i. Polonius and Reynaldo. Polonius and Ophelia.]

In all things dependent on, or rather made up of, fine
address, the *manner* is no more or otherwise rememberable
than the light motions, steps, and gestures of youth and
health. But this is almost everything; no wonder, therefore, if that which can be *put down by rule* in the memory
should appear mere poring, maudlin-eyed cunning, slyness
blinking through the watery eye of superannuation. So in
this admirable scene, Polonius, who is throughout the
skeleton of his own former skill and statecraft, hunts the trail
of policy at a dead scent, supplied by the weak fever-smell
in his own nostrils.

[III, ii, 100-103.

Pol. I did enact Julius Caesar: I was killed i' the Capitol;
Brutus killed me.
Ham. It was a brute part of him to kill so capital a calf there.]

In any direct form to have kept Hamlet's love for Ophelia
before the audience, would have made a breach in the unity
of the interest; but yet to the thoughtful reader it is suggested by his spite to poor Polonius, whom he cannot let
rest.

[IV, v, 120-21. The king faces Laertes:
There's such divinity doth hedge a king,
That treason can but peep to what it would.]

Proof, as indeed all else is, that Shakspere never intended
us to see the king with Hamlet's eyes, though, I suspect, the
managers have long done so.

[V, i.] The contrast between the clowns and Hamlet as
two extremes—the [clowns'] mockery of logic, the traditional
wit valued like truth for its antiquity, and treasured up,
like a tune, for use.

[V, i-ii.] Shakspere seems to mean *all* Hamlet's character
to be brought together before his final disappearance from
the scene — his meditative excess in the grave-digging
[scene], his yielding to passion, his love for Ophelia blazing
out, his tendency to generalize on all occasions in the

dialogue with Horatio, his fine gentlemanly manners with Osrick, and his and Shakspere's fondness for presentiment— "O my prophetic soul" and his "Most generous and free from all contriving" in his fencing-duel—and all at last done by . . . [?] and accident at the conclusion.

THE CHARACTER OF HAMLET

Shakspere's code of conceiving characters out of his own intellectual and moral faculties, by conceiving any one intellectual or moral faculty in morbid excess and then placing himself, thus mutilated and diseased, under given circumstances. This we shall have repeated occasion to re-state and enforce. In Hamlet I conceive him to have wished to exemplify the moral necessity of a due balance between our attention to outward objects and our meditation on inward thoughts—a due balance between the real and the imaginary world. In Hamlet this balance does not exist—his thoughts, images, and fancy being far more vivid than his perceptions, and his very perceptions instantly passing through the medium of his contemplations, and acquiring as they pass a form and color not naturally their own. Hence great, enormous, intellectual activity, and a consequent proportionate aversion to real action, with all its symptoms and accompanying qualities.

Action is transitory, a step, a blow, &c.

Then as in the first instance proceed with a cursory survey through the play, with comments, &c.

(1) The easy language of ordinary life, contrasted with the direful music and wild rhythm of the opening of "Macbeth." Yet the armour, the cold, the dead silence, all placing the mind in the state congruous with tragedy.

(2) The admirable judgement and yet confidence in his own marvellous powers in introducing the ghost twice, each rising in solemnity and awfulness before its third appearance to Hamlet himself.

(3) Shakspere's tenderness with regard to all innocent superstition: no Tom Paine declarations and pompous philosophy.

(4) The first words that Hamlet speaks—

A little more than kin, and less than kind.

He begins with that play of words, the complete absence of which characterizes "Macbeth" . . . [?]. No one can have heard quarrels among the vulgar but must have noticed the close connection of punning with angry contempt. Add too what is highly characteristic of superfluous activity of mind, a sort of playing with a thread or watch chain or snuff box.

(5) And note how the character develops itself in the next speech—the aversion to externals, the betrayed habit of brooding over the world within him, and the prodigality of beautiful words, which are, as it were, the half embodyings of thoughts, that make them more than thoughts, give them an outness, a reality *sui generis*, and yet retain their correspondence and shadowy approach to the images and movements within.

(6) The first soliloquy,

[O, that this too too solid flesh would melt.]

The reasons why *taedium vitae* oppresses minds like Hamlet's: the exhaustion of bodily feeling from perpetual exertion of mind; that all mental form being indefinite and ideal, realities must needs become cold, and hence it is the indefinite that combines with passion.

(7) And in this mood the relation is made [by Horatio, who tells Hamlet of his father's ghost], of which no more than that it is a perfect model of dramatic narration and dramatic style, the purest poetry and yet the most natural language, equally distant from the inkhorn and the provincial plough.

(8) Hamlet's running into long reasonings [while waiting for the ghost], carrying off the impatience and uneasy feelings of expectation by running away from the *particular* into the *general*. This aversion to personal, individual concerns, and escape to generalizations and general reasonings a most important characteristic.

Besides that, it does away with surprizing all the ill effects that the two former appearances of the ghost would have produced by rendering the ghost an expected phenomenon, and restores to it all the suddenness essential to the effect.

(9) The ghost is a superstition connected with the most [sacred?] truths of revealed religion and, therefore, O how contrasted from the withering and wild language of the [witches in] "Macbeth."

o

(10) The instant and over violent resolve of Hamlet—
how he wastes in the efforts of resolving the energies of
action. Compare this with the . . . [?] of Medea; and
note his quick relapse into the satirical and ironical vein
[after the ghost disappears].

(11) Now comes the difficult task, [interpreting the jests
of Hamlet when his companions overtake him].

The familiarity, comparative at least, of a brooding mind
with shadows is something. Still more the necessary alterna-
tion when one muscle long strained is relaxed; the antagonist comes into action of itself. Terror is closely connected
with the ludicrous; the latter is the common mode by which
the mind tries to emancipate itself from terror. The laugh
is rendered by nature itself the language of extremes, even
as tears are. Add too, Hamlet's wildness is but *half-false*.
O that subtle trick to pretend the *acting* only when we are
very near *being* what we act. And this explanation of the
same with Ophelia's vivid images [describing Hamlet's
desperation when he visits her]; nigh akin to, and productive
of, temporary mania. [See II, i, 75-100, the speeches of]
Ophelia, [which were just mentioned,] proved by [Hamlet's
wildness at Ophelia's grave, V, i, 248-78].

(12) Hamlet's character, as I have conceived it, is described by himself [in the soliloquy after the players leave
him—

O, what a rogue and peasant slave am I, &c.]

But previous to this, speak of the exquisite judgement in
the diction of the introduced play. Absurd to suppose it
extracted in order to be ridiculed from an old play. It is
in thought and even in the separate parts of the diction
highly poetical, so that this is its fault, that it is too poetical,
the language of lyric vehemence and epic pomp, not of the
drama. But what if Shakspere had made the language
truly dramatic? Where would have been the contrast
between "Hamlet" and the play of [within] "Hamlet"?

"TROILUS AND CRESSIDA"

To all [these aspects of constancy and inconstancy],
however, there is so little comparative projection given,—

nay, the masterly group of Agamemnon, Nestor, Ulysses, and still more in advance, of Achilles, Ajax, and Thersites, so manifestly occupy the foreground that the subservience and vassalage of strength and animal courage to intellect and policy seem to be the lesson most often in our poet's view, and which he has taken little pains to connect with the former more interesting moral impersonated in the titular hero and heroine of the drama. But I am half inclined to believe that Shakspere's main object, or shall I rather say, that his ruling impulse, was to translate the poetic heroes of paganism into the not less rude but more intellectually vigorous, more *featurely* warriors of Christian chivalry, to substantiate the distinct and graceful profiles or outlines of the Homeric epic into the flesh and blood of the romantic drama—in short, to give a grand history-piece in the robust style of Albert Dürer.

The character of Thersites well deserves a more particular attention, as the Caliban of demagogues' life—the admirable portrait of intellectual power deserted by all grace, all moral principle, all not momentary purpose; just wise enough to detect the weak head, and fool enough to provoke the armed fist of his betters; whom malcontent Achilles can inveigle from malcontent Ajax, under the condition that he shall be called on to do nothing but to abuse and slander and that he shall be allowed to abuse as much and as purulently as he likes—that is, as [he] can; in short, a mule, quarrelsome by the original discord of its nature, a slave by tenure of his own baseness, made to bray and be brayed, to despise and be despicable.—Ay, sir, but say what you will, he is a devilish clever fellow, though the best friends will fall out; but there was a time when Ajax thought he deserved to have a statue of gold erected to him, and handsome Achilles, at the head of the Myrmidons, gave no little credit to his "friend, Thersites."

"OTHELLO"

[I, iii, 319-20.
Iago. Virtue! a fig! 'tis in ourselves that we are thus or thus.]

Iago's passionless character, all *will* in intellect; therefore a bold partisan here of a truth, but yet of a truth converted into falsehood by absence of all the modifications by the frail nature of man. And the *last sentiment*—

> [. . . . our raging motions, our carnal stings, our unbitted lusts; whereof I take this, that you call love, to be a sect or scion—]

There lies the Iagoism of how many! And the repetition, "Go make money!"—a pride in it, of an anticipated dupe, stronger than the love of lucre.

[I, iii, 377-78. (Q₁)

Iago. Go to, farewell, put money enough in your purse:
Thus do I ever make my fool my purse.]

The triumph! Again, "put money," after the effect has been fully produced. The last speech, [Iago's soliloquy,] the motive-hunting of motiveless malignity—how awful! In itself fiendish; while yet he was allowed to bear the divine image, too fiendish for his own steady view. A being next to devil, only *not* quite devil—and this Shakspere has attempted—executed—without disgust, without scandal!

"LEAR"

Of all Shakspere's plays "Macbeth" is the most rapid, "Hamlet" the slowest, in movement. "Lear" combines length with rapidity,—like the hurricane and the whirlpool, absorbing while it advances. It begins as a stormy day in summer, with brightness; but that brightness is lurid, and anticipates the tempest.

[I, i, 1-6.

Kent. I thought the king had more affected the Duke of Albany than Cornwall.

Glou. It did always seem so to us: but now, in the division of the kingdom, it appears not which of the dukes he values most; for equalities are so weighed that curiosity in neither can make choice of either's moiety.]

It was [not] without forethought, and it is not without its due significance, that the triple division is stated here as already determined and in all its particulars, previously to the trial of professions, as the relative rewards of which the daughters were to be made to consider their several portions. The strange, yet by no means unnatural, mixture of selfishness, sensibility, and habit of feeling derived from and fostered by the particular rank and usages of the individual; the intense desire to be intensely beloved, selfish, and yet characteristic of the selfishness of a loving and kindly nature —a feeble selfishness, self-supportless and leaning for all pleasure on another's breast; the selfish craving after a sympathy with a prodigal disinterestedness, contradicted by its own ostentation and the mode and nature of its claims; the anxiety, the distrust, the jealousy, which more or less accompany all selfish affections, and are among the surest contradistinctions of mere fondness from love, and which originate Lear's eager wish to enjoy his daughter's violent professions, while the inveterate habits of sovereignty convert the wish into claim and positive right, and the incompliance with it into crime and treason;—these facts, these passions, these moral verities, on which the whole tragedy is founded, are all prepared for, and will to the retrospect be found implied in, these first four or five lines of the play. They let us know that the trial is but a trick; and that the grossness of the old king's rage is in part the natural result of a silly trick suddenly and most unexpectedly baffled and disappointed. This having been provided in the fewest words, in a natural reply to as natural a question, which yet answers a secondary purpose of attracting our attention to the difference or diversity between the characters of Cornwall and Albany; the premises and data, as it were, having been thus afforded for our after-insight into the mind and mood of the person whose character, passions, and sufferings are the main *subject-matter* of the play;—from Lear, the *persona patiens* of his drama, Shakspere passes without delay to the second in importance, to the main *agent* and prime mover—introduces Edmund to our acquaintance, and with the same felicity of judgement, in the same easy, natural way, prepares us for his character in the seemingly casual communication of its origin and occasion. From the first drawing up of the curtain he has stood before us in the united strength and beauty of earliest manhood. Our eyes have been questioning him. Gifted thus with high advantages of *person*, and further endowed by nature with a powerful intellect and a strong energetic will, even without any concurrence of circumstances and accident, pride will be the sin that most easily besets him. But he is the known and acknowledged son of the princely Gloster. Edmund, therefore, has both the germ of pride and the conditions best fitted to evolve and ripen it into a predominant feeling. Yet hitherto no reason appears why it should be other than the not unusual pride of person, talent, and birth, a pride auxiliary if not akin to many virtues, and the natural ally of honorable [impulses?]. But alas! in his own presence his own father takes shame to himself for the frank avowal that he is his father—has "blushed so often to acknowledge him that he is now braz'd to it." He hears his mother and the circumstances of his birth spoken of with a most degrading and licentious levity—described as a wanton by her own paramour, and the remembrance of the animal sting, the low criminal gratifications connected with her wantonness and prostituted beauty assigned as the reason why "the whoreson must be acknowledged." This, and the consciousness of its notoriety—the gnawing conviction that every shew of respect is an effort of courtesy which recalls while it represses a contrary feeling—this is the ever-trickling flow of wormwood and gall into the wounds of pride, the corrosive virus which inoculates pride with a venom not its own, with envy, hatred, a lust of that power which in its blaze of radiance would hide the dark spots on his disk, [with] pangs of shame personally undeserved and therefore felt as wrongs, and a blind ferment of vindictive workings towards the occasions and causes, especially towards a brother whose stainless birth and lawful honors were the constant remembrancers of *his* debasement, and were ever in the way to prevent all chance of its being unknown or overlooked and forgotten. Add to this that with excellent judgement, and provident for the claims of the moral sense, for that which relatively to the drama is called poetic justice; and as the fittest means for reconciling the feelings of the spectators to the horrors of Gloster's after sufferings,—at least, of rendering them somewhat less unendurable (for I will not disguise my conviction that in this one point the tragic has been urged beyond the outermost mark and *ne plus ultra* of the dramatic)—Shakspere has precluded all excuse and palliation of the guilt incurred by both the parents of the base-born Edmund by Gloster's confession that he was at the time a married man and already blest with a lawful heir of his fortunes. The mournful alienation of brotherly love occasioned by primogeniture in noble families, or rather by the unnecessary distinctions engrafted thereon, and this in children of the same stock, is still almost proverbial on the continent—especially, as I know from my own observation, in the south of Europe—and appears to have been scarcely less common in our own island before the Revolution of 1688, if we may judge from the characters and sentiments so frequent in our elder comedies—the younger brother, for instance, in Beaumont and Fletcher's "Scornful Lady," on one side and the Oliver in Shakspere's own "As You Like It," on the other. Need it be said how heavy an aggravation the stain of bastardy must have been, were it only that the younger brother was liable to hear his own dishonor and his mother's infamy related by his father with an excusing shrug of the shoulders, and in a tone betwixt waggery and shame.

By the circumstances here enumerated as so many predisposing causes, Edmund's character might well be deemed already sufficiently explained and prepared for. But in this tragedy the story or fable constrained Shakspere to introduce wickedness in an outrageous form, in Regan and Goneril. He had read nature too heedfully not to know that courage, intellect, and strength of character were the most impressive forms of power, and that to power in itself, without reference to any moral end, an inevitable admiration and complacency appertains, whether it be displayed in the conquests of a Napoleon or Tamerlane, or in the foam and thunder of a cataract. But in the display of such a character it was of the highest importance to prevent the guilt from passing into utter *monstrosity*—which again depends on the presence or absence of causes and temptations sufficient to *account* for the wickedness, without the necessity of recurring to a thorough fiendishness of nature for its origination. For such are the appointed relations of intellectual power to truth, and of truth to goodness, that it becomes both morally and poetically unsafe to present what is admirable—what our nature compels us to admire—in the mind, and what is most detestable in the heart, as co-existing in the same individual without any apparent connection, or any modification of the one by the other.

That Shakspere has in one instance, that of Iago, approached to this, and that he has done it successfully, **is** perhaps the most astonishing proof of his genius, and the opulence of its resources. But in the present tragedy, in which he [was] compelled to present a Goneril and Regan, it was most carefully to be avoided; and, therefore, the one only conceivable addition to the inauspicious influences on the preformation of Edmund's character is given in the information that all the kindly counteractions to the mischievous feelings of shame that might have been derived from co-domestication with Edgar and their common father, had been cut off by an absence from home and a foreign education from boyhood to the present time, and the prospect of its continuance, as if to preclude all risk of his interference with the father's views for the elder and legitimate son:

He hath been out nine years, and away he shall again.

It is well worthy notice, that "Lear" is the only serious performance of Shakspere the interest and situations of which are derived from the assumption of a gross improbability; whereas Beaumont and Fletcher's tragedies are, almost all, founded on some out-of-the-way accident or exception to the general experience of mankind. But observe the matchless judgement of Shakspere! First, improbable as the conduct of Lear is, in the first scene, yet it was an old story, rooted in the popular faith—a thing taken for granted already, and consequently without any of the *effects* of improbability. Secondly, it is merely the canvas to the characters and passions, a mere *occasion*—not (as in Beaumont and Fletcher) perpetually recurring, as the cause and *sine qua non* of the incidents and emotions. Let the first scene of "Lear" have been lost, and let it be only understood that a fond father had been duped by hypocritical professions of love and duty on the part of two daughters to disinherit a third, previously, and deservedly, more dear to him, and all the rest of the tragedy would retain its interest undiminished, and be perfectly intelligible. The *accidental* is nowhere the groundwork of the passions, but the καθολον, that which in all ages has been and ever will be close and native to the heart of man—parental anguish from filial ingratitude, the genuineness of worth, though coffered in bluntness, the vileness of smooth iniquity. Perhaps I ought to have added the "Merchant of Venice"; but here too the same remarks apply. It was an old tale; and substitute any other danger than that of the pound of flesh (the circumstance in which the improbability lies), yet all the situations and the emotions appertaining to them remain equally excellent and appropriate. Whereas take away from "The Mad Lover" the fantastic hypothesis of his engagement to cut out his own heart and have it presented to his mistress, and all the main scenes must go with it.

Kotzebue is the German Beaumont and Fletcher, without their poetic powers and without their *vis comica*. But like them he always deduces his situations and passions from marvellous accidents, and the trick of bringing one part of our moral nature to counteract another—as our pity for misfortune and admiration of generosity and courage to combat our condemnation of guilt, as in adultery, robbery, etc.; and like them too, he excels in his mode of telling a story clearly and interestingly, in a series of dramatic dialogues. Only the trick of making tragedy-heroes and heroines out of shopkeepers and barmaids was too ow for the age, and too unpoetic for the genius, of Beaumolnt and Fletcher, inferior in every respect as they are to their great predecessor and contemporary! *How* inferior would they have appeared, had not Shakspere existed for them to *imitate*—which in every play, more or less, they do, and in their tragedies most glaringly; and yet (O shame! shame!) miss no opportunity of sneering at the divine man and subdetracting from his merits!! S. T. Coleridge, 1 Jan^y., 1813. 71, Berner's St. Oxford Street.

[I, i, 84-92.

> *Lear.*   . . . . what can you say to draw
> A third more opulent than your sisters? Speak.
> *Cor.* Nothing, my lord.
> *Lear.* Nothing!
> *Cor.* Nothing.
> *Lear.* Nothing will come of nothing: speak again.
> *Cor.* Unhappy that I am, I cannot heave
> My heart into my mouth: I love your majesty
> According to my bond; nor more nor less.]

Something of disgust at the ruthless hypocrisy of her

sisters, some little faulty admixture of pride and sullenness
in Cordelia's "Nothing." It is well contrived to lessen the
glaring absurdity of Lear; but the surest plan is that of
forcing away the attention from the nursery-tale the moment
it has answered its purpose, that of supplying the canvas to
paint on. This is done by Kent—[his punishment] displaying Lear's *moral* incapability of resigning the sovereign
power in the very moment of disposing of it.

Kent is the nearest to perfect goodness of all Shakspere's
characters, and yet the most *individualized*. His passionate
affection and fidelity to Lear acts on our feelings in Lear's
own favor; virtue itself seems to be in company with him.

[I, ii, 9-14.

> *Edm.*   . . . . Why brand they us
> With base? with baseness? bastardy? base, base?
> Who in the lusty stealth of nature take
> More composition and fierce quality
> Than doth, within a dull, stale, tired bed,
> Go to the creating a whole tribe of fops.

Warburton cites these lines as characteristic of Edmund's
atheism and quotes the wish of the atheist Vanini that he
might have been born out of wedlock, for reasons similar
to those given by Edmund in defence of his own birth.]

Poor Vanini! Any one but Warburton would have
thought the quotation more characteristic of Mr. Shandy
than of atheism! If the fact really were so (which it not
only is not, but almost contrary) I do not see why the most
confirmed theist might not very rationally utter the same
wish. But it is proverbial that the youngest son in a large
family is commonly the man of the greatest talents of the
family *et incalescere in venerem ardentius, spei sobolis injuriosum.*

In this speech of Edmund you see, as soon as a man
cannot reconcile himself to reason, how his conscience flies
off by way of appeal to nature, who is sure upon such
occasions never to find fault, and also how shame sharpens
a predisposition in the heart to evil. For it is a profound
moral, that shame will naturally generate guilt; the oppressed will be vindictive, like Shylock, and in the anguish
of undeserved ignominy the delusion secretly springs up, of
getting over the moral quality of an action by fixing the
mind on the mere physical act alone.

[**I**, ii, 113-116.

Edm. This is the excellent foppery of the world, that when we are sick in fortune—often the surfeit of our own behaviour —we make guilty of our disasters the sun, the moon and the stars.]

Scorn and misanthropy are often the anticipations and mouth-pieces of wisdom in the detection of superstitions. Both individuals and nations may be free from superstition by being below it as well as by rising above it.

[I, iii, 13-22. Goneril authorizes the Steward to be rude to Lear.]

The Steward (as a contrast to Kent) is the only character of utter unredeemable *baseness* in Shakspere. [Observe] even in this the judgement and invention. What could the willing tool of a Goneril be? Not a vice but this of baseness was left open for him.

[I, iv.] Old age, like infancy, is itself a character. In Lear the natural imperfections are increased by life-long habits of being promptly obeyed. Any addition of individuality [would be] unnecessary and painful. The relations of others to him, of wondrous fidelity and frightful ingratitude, sufficiently distinguish him. Thus he is the open and ample play-room of *nature's* passions.

The Fool is no comic buffoon to make the groundlings laugh, no forced condescension of Shakspere's genius to the taste of his audiences. Accordingly, he is *prepared* for —brought into living connection with the pathos of the play, with the sufferings.

Since my young lady's going into France, sir, the fool hath much pined away.

The Fool is as wonderful a creation as the Caliban—an inspired idiot.

[Goneril quarrels with her father.]

The monster Goneril prepares what is *necessary*, while the character of Albany renders a still more maddening grievance possible: *viz.* Regan and Cornwall in perfect sympathy of monstrosity. Not a sentiment, not an image that can give pleasure on its own account is admitted. Pure horror when they are introduced, and they are brought forward as little as possible.

[I, iv, 259.

> Ingratitude, thou marble-hearted fiend.]

The *one* general sentiment, as the mainspring of the feelings throughout, in Lear's first speeches. In the early stage the outward object is the pressure; [the mind is] not yet sufficiently familiarized with the anguish for the imagination to work upon it.

[I, iv, 311-14.

> *Gon.* Do you mark that, my lord?
> *Alb.* I cannot be so partial, Goneril,
> To the great love I bear you,—
> *Gon.* Pray you, content.]

The baffled endeavour of Goneril to act on the fears of Albany—and yet his passiveness, inertia—not convinced, yet afraid of looking into the thing. Such characters yield to those who will take the trouble of governing them or for them. . . . The influence of a princess whose choice of him had so royalized his state is some little excuse for Albany.

[I, v, 43.

> *Lear.* O, let me not be mad, not mad, . . .]

The mind's own anticipation of madness.

The deepest tragic notes are often struck by a half sense of an impending blow. The Fool's conclusion of this act by a grotesque prattling seems to indicate the dislocation of feeling that has begun and is to be continued.

[II, i, 66-67.

> *Edm.* . . . . he replied,
> "Thou unpossessing bastard . . . ."]

"*Thou unpossessing bastard*"—the secret poison in Edmund's heart—and then poor Gloster's "Loyal and *natural* boy," as if praising the *crime* of his birth!

[II, i, 91-92.

> *Reg.* What, did my father's godson seek your life?
> He whom my father named? Your Edgar?]

Incomparable! "What, did *my father's*," &c., compared with the unfeminine violence of the "all vengeance comes too short"—and yet no reference to the guilt but to the accident.

[II, ii, 90-92.
    Corn.   This is some fellow,
Who, having been praised for bluntness, doth affect
A saucy roughness.]

In thus placing these profound general truths in such
mouths as Cornwall's, Edmund's, Iago's, &c., Shakspere
at once gives them and yet shews how indefinite their
application.

[II, iii.] Edgar's false madness taking off part of the shock
from the true, as well as displaying the profound difference.
Modern [attempts at representing madness] lightheadedness,
as Otway's, &c.

In Edgar's ravings Shakspere all the while lets you see
a fixed purpose, a practical end in view;—in Lear's, there is
only the brooding of the one anguish, an eddy without
progression.

[II, iv, 98-110.
    Lear. The king would speak with Cornwall . . . .
"Fiery," "the fiery duke?" Tell the hot duke that—
No, but not yet: may be he is not well, &c.]

The strong interest now felt by Lear to **try to** find
excuses for his daughter—most pathetic.

[II, iv, 13-38.
    Lear.   . . . . Beloved Regan,
Thy sister's naught: . . . .
    Reg. I pray you, sir, take patience. I have hope
You less know how to value her desert
Than she to scant her duty.]

Nothing so heart-cutting as a cold unexpected defence,
&c., of a cruelty complained of passionately, or so expressive
of hardheartedness; and the horror of [Regan's] "O, sir,
you are old"—and then drawing from that universal object
of reverence and indulgence the reason for "Say, you have
wronged her." All Lear's faults increase our pity. We
refuse to know them otherwise than as means and aggravations of his sufferings and his daughters' ingratitude.

[II, iv, 263-85.
    Lear. O, reason not the need: our basest beggars
Are in the poorest thing superfluous, &c.]

The tranquillity from the first *stun* permitting Lear to
reason. Recite this.

[III, iv. Lear's despair and growing madness in the storm.]

What a world's *convention* of agonies! Surely, never was such a scene conceived before or since. Take it but as a picture for the eye only, it is more terrific than any a Michael Angelo inspired by a Dante could have conceived, and which none but a Michael Angelo could have executed. Or let it have been uttered to the blind, the howlings of convulsed nature would seem converted into the voice of conscious humanity.

The scene ends with the first symptoms of positive derangement—here how judiciously interrupted [by the fifth scene] in order to allow an interval for Lear in full madness to appear.

[III, vii. The blinding of Gloucester.]

What can I say of this scene? My reluctance to think Shakspere wrong, and yet—

[Later.] Necessary to harmonise their [Goneril's and Regan's] cruelty to their father.

[IV, vi. Lear's milder madness near the camp of Cordelia.]

The thunder recurs, but still at a greater distance from our feelings.

[IV, vii, 52-54.

Lear. Where have I been? Where am I? Fair daylight?
I am mightily abused. I should e'en die with pity,
To see another thus.]

The affecting return of Lear to reason, and the mild pathos preparing the mind for the last sad yet sweet consolation of his death.

[V, i, 24-27. Theobald emends the passage, but in his note prints the "old quarto" text as follows:

.... for this business
It touches us, as France invades our land,
Not holds the King, with others whom I fear
Most just and heavy causes make oppose.]

Evidently the old reading is the right one, [not Theobald's]: "As to this business, however, I do feel myself honestly engaged; I mean as far as we are resisting *invasion*, not in relation to the good king and other justly provoked opponents of our own countrymen." S.T.C.

"MACBETH"

[I, v, 50-51.

> Nor heaven peep through the blanket of the dark,
> To cry "Hold, hold!"]

"Height" is often spelled in our oldest manuscripts "Het." I suspect that Shakspere wrote:

> Nor heaven peep thro' the blank height of the dark
> To cry, Hold, hold!

[II, iii.] This low porter soliloquy I believe written for the mob by some other hand, perhaps with Shakspere's consent—and that finding it take, he with the remaining ink of a pen otherwise employed just interpolated it with the sentence, "I'll devil-porter it no further" and what follows to "bonfire." Of the rest not one syllable has the ever-present being of Shakspere.

Macbeth—the superstition natural to victorious generals. [See] Harte's "Gustavus Adolphus," Preface. The causes of it. So much of chance, such vast events connected. [The general is] a representative of the efforts of myriads, and yet to the public, and doubtless in his own feelings, the aggregate of all. Hope is the master element of a commanding genius, meeting with an active and combining intellect, and an imagination of just that degree of vividness which disquiets and impels the soul to try to realize its images. Greatly increase this creative power, and the images become a satisfying world of themselves; *i.e.* we have the poet, or original philosopher; but hope fully gratified, and yet the elementary basis of the passion remaining, becomes fear; and indeed the general, who must often feel, even though he may hide it from his own consciousness, how great a share chance had in his successes, may very naturally become irresolute in a new scene, where *all* depends on his own act and election.

"ANTONY AND CLEOPATRA"

Shakspere can be complimented only by comparison with himself: all other eulogies are either heterogeneous

(*ex. gr.*, in relation to Milton, Spenser, &c.) or flat truisms
(*ex. gr.*, to prefer him to Racine, Corneille, or even his own
immediate successors, Fletcher, Massinger, &c.). The highest praise or rather form of praise, of this play which I
can offer in my own mind, is the doubt which its perusal
always occasions in me, whether it is not in all exhibitions
of a giant power in its strength and vigor of maturity, a
formidable rival of the "Macbeth," "Lear," "Othello," and
"Hamlet." *Feliciter audax* is the motto for its style comparatively with his other works, even as it is the general motto of
all his works compared with those of other poets. Be it
remembered too, that this happy valiancy of style is but the
representative and result of all the material excellencies so
exprest.

This play should be perused in mental contrast with
"Romeo and Juliet";—as the love of passion and appetite
opposed to the love of affection and instinct. But the art
displayed in the character of Cleopatra is profound in this,
especially, that the sense of criminality in her passion is
lessened by our insight into its depth and energy, at the very
moment that we cannot but perceive that the passion itself
springs out of the habitual craving of a licentious nature,
and that it is supported and reinforced by voluntary stimulus and sought-for associations, instead of blossoming out of
spontaneous emotion.

"CORIOLANUS"

[IV, vii, 28-57. The speech of Aufidius.
   All places yield to him ere he sits down; &c.]

I have always thought this in itself so beautiful speech
the least explicable from the mood and full intention of the
speaker of any in the whole works of Shakspere. I cherish
the hope that I am mistaken and, becoming wiser, shall
discover some profound excellence in what I now appear to
myself to detect an imperfection.

"WINTER'S TALE"

Altho' on the whole exquisitely respondent to its title,
and even in the fault I am about to mention, still a winter's

tale, yet it seems a mere indolence of the great bard not to have in the oracle provided some ground for Hermione's seeming death and fifteen years concealment, voluntary concealment. This might have been easily affected by some obscure sentence of the oracle, as, *ex. gr.*, "Nor shall he ever recover an heir if he have a wife before that recovery."

[IV, ii, 29-30.
. . . . for the life to come, I sleep
out the thought of it.]

Fine as this is, and delicately characteristic of one who had lived and been reared in the best society, and had been precipitated from it by "die and drab"; yet still it strikes against my feelings as a note out of time and as not coalescing with that *pastoral* tint which gives such a charm to this fourth act. It is too Macbeth-like in the "snapper-up of unconsidered trifles."

"TEMPEST"

It addresses itself entirely to the imaginative faculty; and although the illusion may be assisted by the effect on the senses of the complicated scenery and decorations of modern times yet this sort of assistance is dangerous. For the principal and only genuine excitement ought to come from within,—from the moved and sympathetic imagination; whereas, where so much is addressed to the mere external senses of seeing and hearing, the spiritual vision is apt to languish, and the attraction from without will withdraw the mind from the proper and only legitimate interest which is intended to spring from within.

The romance opens with a busy scene admirably appropriate to the kind of drama, and giving, as it were, the keynote to the whole harmony. It prepares and initiates the excitement required for the entire piece, and yet does not demand anything from the spectators, which their previous habits had not fitted them to understand. It is the bustle of a tempest, from which the real horrors are abstracted;— therefore it is poetical, though not in strictness natural—(the distinction to which I have so often alluded)—and is purposely restrained from concentering the interest on itself, but used merely as an induction or tuning for what is to follow.

In the second scene, Prospero's speeches, till the entrance of Ariel, contain the finest example I remember of retrospective narration for the purpose of exciting immediate interest, and putting the audience in possession of all the information necessary for the understanding of the plot. Observe, too, the perfect probability of the moment chosen by Prospero (the very Shakspere himself, as it were, of the tempest) to open out the truth to his daughter, his own romantic bearing, and how completely any thing that might have been disagreeable to us in the magician, is reconciled and shaded in the humanity and natural feelings of the father. In the very first speech of Miranda the simplicity and tenderness of her character are at once laid open;—it would have been lost in direct contact with the agitation of the first scene. The opinion once prevailed, but, happily, is now abandoned, that Fletcher alone wrote for women;— the truth is, that with very few, and those partial, exceptions, the female characters in the plays of Beaumont and Fletcher are, when of the light kind, not decent; when heroic, complete viragos. But in Shakspere all the elements of womanhood are holy, and there is the sweet, yet dignified feeling of all that *continuates* society, as sense of ancestry and of sex, with a purity unassailable by sophistry, because it rests not in the analytic processes, but in that sane equipoise of the faculties, during which the feelings are representative of all past experience,—not of the individual only, but of all those by whom she has been educated, and their predecessors even up to the first mother that lived. Shakspere saw that the want of prominence, which Pope notices for sarcasm, was the blessed beauty of the woman's character, and knew that it arose not from any deficiency, but from the more exquisite harmony of all the parts of the moral being constituting one living total of head and heart. He has drawn it, indeed, in all its distinctive energies of faith, patience, constancy, fortitude,—shown in all of them as following the heart, which gives its results by a nice tact and happy intuition, without the intervention of the discursive faculty,—sees all things in and by the light of the affections, and errs, if it ever err, in the exaggerations of love alone. In all the Shaksperian women there is essentially the same foundation and principle; the distinct individuality and variety are merely the result of the modification of circumstances, whether in Miranda the maiden, in Imogen the wife, or in Katharine the queen.

[I, i.] Before I go further, I may take the opportunity of explaining what is meant by mechanic and organic regularity. In the former the copy must appear as if it had come out of the same mould with the original; in the latter there is a law which all the parts obey, conforming themselves to the outward symbols and manifestations of the essential principle. If we look to the growth of trees, for instance, we shall observe that trees of the same kind vary considerably, according to the circumstances of soil, air, or position; yet we are able to decide at once whether they are oaks, elms, or poplars.

So with Shakspere's characters: he shows us the life and principle of each being with organic regularity. The Boatswain, in the first scene of "The Tempest," when the bonds of reverence are thrown off as a sense of danger impresses all, gives a loose to his feelings, and thus pours forth his vulgar mind to the old Counsellor:—

> Hence! What care these roarers for the name of King? To cabin: silence! trouble us not.

Gonzalo replies—

> Good; yet remember whom thou hast aboard.

To which the Boatswain answers—

> None that I more love than myself. You are a counsellor: if you can command these elements to silence, and work the peace of the present, we will not hand a rope more; use your authority: if you cannot, give thanks that you have lived so long, and make yourself ready in your cabin for the mischance of the hour, if it so hap.—Cheerly, good hearts!—Out of our way, I say.

An ordinary dramatist would, after this speech, have represented Gonzalo as moralizing, or saying something connected with the Boatswain's language; for ordinary dramatists are not men of genius: they combine their ideas by association, or by logical affinity; but the vital writer, who makes men on the stage what they are in nature, in a moment transports himself into the very being of each personage, and, instead of cutting out artificial puppets, he brings before us the men themselves. Therefore, Gonzalo soliloquizes,—

> I have great comfort from this fellow: methinks, he hath no drowning mark upon him; his complexion is perfect gallows. Stand fast, good fate, to his hanging! make the rope of his destiny our cable, for our own doth little advantage. If he be not born to be hanged, our case is miserable.

In this part of the scene we see the true sailor with his contempt of danger, and the old counsellor with his high feeling, who, instead of condescending to notice the words just addressed to him, turns off, meditating with himself, and drawing some comfort to his own mind, by trifling with the ill expression of the boatswain's face, founding upon it a hope of safety.

* * *

Many, indeed innumerable, beautiful passages might be quoted from this play, independently of the astonishing scheme of its construction. Every body will call to mind the grandeur of the language of Prospero in that divine speech, where he takes leave of his magic art; and were I to indulge myself by repetitions of the kind, I should descend from the character of a lecturer to that of a mere reciter. Before I terminate, I may particularly recal one short passage, which has fallen under the very severe, but inconsiderate, censure of Pope and Arbuthnot, who pronounce it a piece of the grossest bombast. Prospero thus addresses his daughter, directing her attention to Ferdinand:

> The fringed curtains of thine eye advance,
> And say what thou seest yond.
>
> *Act. I, Scene ii*

Taking these words as a periphrase of—"Look what is coming yonder," it certainly may to some appear to border on the ridiculous, and to fall under the rule I formerly laid down,—that whatever, without injury, can be translated into a foreign language in simple terms, ought to be in simple terms in the original language; but it is to be borne in mind, that different modes of expression frequently arise from difference of situation and education: a blackguard would use very different words, to express the same thing, to those a gentleman would employ, yet both would be natural and proper; difference of feeling gives rise to difference of language: a gentleman speaks in polished terms, with due regard to his own rank and position, while a blackguard, a person little better than half a brute, speaks like half a brute, showing no respect for himself, nor for others.

But I am content to try the lines I have just quoted by the introduction to them; and then, I think, you will admit, that nothing could be more fit and appropriate than such language. How does Prospero introduce them? He has just told Miranda a wonderful story, which deeply affected her, and filled her with surprise and astonishment, and for his own purposes he afterwards lulls her to sleep. When she wakes, Shakspere has made her wholly inattentive to the present, but wrapped up in the past. An actress, who understands the character of Miranda, would have her eyes cast down, and her eyelids almost covering them, while she was, as it were, living in her dream. At this moment Prospero sees Ferdinand, and wishes to point him out to his daughter, not only with great, but with scenic solemnity, he standing before her, and before the spectator, in the dignified character of a great magician. Something was to appear to Miranda on the sudden, and as unexpectedly as if the hero of a drama were to be on the stage at the instant when the curtain is elevated. It is under such circumstances that Prospero says, in a tone calculated at once to arouse his daughter's attention,

> The fringed curtains of thine eye advance,
> And say what thou seest yond.

Turning from the sight of Ferdinand to his thoughtful daughter, his attention was first struck by the downcast appearance of her eyes and eyelids; and, in my humble opinion, the solemnity of the phraseology assigned to Prospero is completely in character, recollecting his preternatural capacity, in which the most familiar objects in nature present themselves in a mysterious point of view. It is much easier to find fault with a writer by reference to former notions and experience, than to sit down and read him, recollecting his purpose, connecting one feeling with another, and judging of his words and phrases, in proportion as they convey the sentiments of the persons represented.　　1812

DONNE

To read Dryden, Pope, &c., you need only count syllables;
but to read Donne you must measure *Time*, and discover
the *Time* of each word by the sense of Passion.

* * *

If you would teach a scholar in the highest form how to
read, take Donne, and of Donne this [Third] Satire. When he
has learned to read Donne, with all the force and meaning
which are involved in the words, then send him to Milton,
and he will stalk on like a master, *enjoying* his walk.

* * *

He was an orthodox Christian only because he could
have been an infidel *more* easily; and therefore willed to be
a Christian.

BEN JONSON

A contemporary is rather an ambiguous term, when
applied to authors. It may simply mean that one man lived
and wrote while another was yet alive, however deeply the
former may have been indebted to the latter as his model.
There have been instances in the literary world that might
remind a botanist of a singular sort of parasite plant, which
rises above ground, independent and unsupported, an apparent original; but trace its roots, and you will find the
fibres all terminating in the root of another plant at an
unsuspected distance, which, perhaps, from want of sun
and genial soil, and the loss of sap, has scarcely been able to
peep above the ground.—Or the word may mean those
whose compositions were contemporaneous in such a sense
as to preclude all likelihood of the one having borrowed
from the other. In the latter sense I should call Ben Jonson
a contemporary of Shakspere, though he long survived him;
while I should prefer the phrase of immediate successors for
Beaumont and Fletcher, and Massinger, though they too
were Shakspere's contemporaries in the former sense.

Ben Jonson is original; he is, indeed, the only one of the great dramatists of that day who was not either directly produced, or very greatly modified, by Shakspere. In truth, he differs from our great master in every thing—in form and in substance—and betrays no tokens of his proximity. He is not original in the same way as Shakspere is original; but after a fashion of his own, Ben Jonson is most truly original.

The characters in his plays are, in the strictest sense of the term, abstractions. Some very prominent feature is taken from the whole man, and that single feature or humour is made the basis upon which the entire character is built up. Ben Jonson's *dramatis personae* are almost as fixed as the mask, of the ancient actors; you know from the first scene—sometimes from the list of names—exactly what every one of them is to be. He was a very accurately observing man; but he cared only to observe what was external or open to, and likely to impress, the senses. He individualizes, not so much, if at all, by the exhibition of moral or intellectual differences, as by the varieties and contrasts of manners, modes of speech and tricks of temper; as in such characters as Puntarvolo, Bobadil, &c.

I believe there is not one whim or affectation in common life noted in any memoir of that age which may not be found drawn and framed in some corner or other of Ben Jonson's dramas; and they have this merit, in common with Hogarth's prints, that not a single circumstance is introduced in them which does not play upon, and help to bring out, the dominant humour or humours of the piece. Indeed I ought very particularly to call your attention to the extraordinary skill shown by Ben Jonson in contriving situations for the display of his characters. In fact, his care and anxiety in this matter led him to do what scarcely any of the dramatists of that age did—that is, invent his plots. It is not a first perusal that suffices for the full perception of the elaborate artifice of the plots of the "Alchemist" and the "Silent Woman"; that of the former is absolute perfection for a necessary entanglement, and an unexpected, yet natural, evolution.

Ben Jonson exhibits a sterling English diction, and he has with great skill contrived varieties of construction; but his style is rarely sweet or harmonious, in consequence of his labour at point and strength being so evident. In all his works, in verse or prose, there is an extraordinary opulence of thought; but it is the produce of an amassing power in the author, and not of a growth from within. Indeed a large proportion of Ben Jonson's thoughts may be traced to classic or obscure modern writers, by those who are learned and curious enough to follow the steps of this robust, surly, and observing dramatist.

"VOLPONE"

This admirable, indeed, but yet more wonderful than admirable, play is from the fertility and vigour of invention, character, language, and sentiment the strongest proof, how impossible it is to keep up any pleasurable interest in a tale, in which there is no goodness of heart in any of the prominent characters. After the third act, this play becomes not a dead, but a painful, weight on the feelings. "Zeluco" is an instance of the same truth. Bonario and Celia should have been made in some way or other principals in the plot; which they might have been, and the objects of interest, without having been made characters. In novels, the person, in whose fate you are most interested, is often the least marked character of the whole. If it were possible to lessen the paramountcy of Volpone himself, a most delightful comedy might be produced, by making Celia the ward or niece of Corvino, instead of his wife, and Bonario her lover.

1818

BEAUMONT and FLETCHER

There is a kind of Comedy which whoever produces must be capable of Tragedy (Cervantes, Shakspere)—but there is another kind, and that too highly amusing, which is quite heterogeneous. Of this Latter Fletcher was a great master. The surface of all its flowers of open pleasures, serious or light, were his Property—all his eye could see, ear hear—nothing more.

"THE PROPHETESS"

Were I to choose a play that most realized the Ideal of Anti-Shaksperianism, I should fix, I think, on this· though

perhaps half a dozen others of the same writer might be
perilous competitors. A witch, professed of all powers and
comprising in herself all the gods; yet an every-day old aunt,
only a witch (but by whose powers no-one knows)—working
neither for good or for evil, but to secure her niece a reluctant husband—and all the rest, pasteboard puppets, ducking
head, lifting arms, sprawling legs, as she pulls the thread—
nothing from within, all from without—sincere conversions
and virtue produced in an instant by unmanly terrors—no
characters, no men, no women—but only mouthing Vices,
or interlocutory ENTIA [?] NARRATIONIS—Explanations personified by Hat, Coat, Waistcoat, and Breeches—of course,
no *Interest* (for a vulgar curiosity about—not what is to
happen next—but about what the witch will *do* next, whether
Thunder, or a Brimstone She Devil, or an Earthquake,
cannot be called *Interest*)—miserable parodies and thefts of
fine Lines in Shakspere—and the compound, a senseless
Day-dream, with all the wildness without any of the terror
of a Night-mair—in short, stupidity from malice (of self-
conceit) prepense aping Madness. The proper compliment
is to open one's mouth in *wonder* and lo! it was only a yawn!

PREFACE TO SEWARD'S EDITION: 1750

[The "King And No King," too, is extremely spirited in all its
Characters; Arbaces holds up a Mirror to all Men of Virtuous
Principles but violent Passions: hence he is, as it were, at once
Magnanimity and Pride, Patience and Fury, Gentleness and
Rigor, Chastity and Incest, and is one of the finest Mixtures of
Virtues and Vices that any Poet has drawn, &c.]

These are among the endless instances of the abject state
to which psychology had sunk from the reign of Charles I
to the middle of the present reign of George III; and even
now it is but just awaking.

"VALENTINIAN"

[III, i.] B. and F. always write as if virtue or goodness were
a sort of talisman, or strange something, that might be lost
without the least fault on the part of the owner. In short,
their chaste ladies value their chastity as a material thing,—

not as an act or state of being; and this mere thing being imaginary, no wonder that all their women are represented with the minds of strumpets, except a few irrational humorists, far less capable of exciting our sympathy than a Hindoo, who has had a bason of cow-broth thrown over him;—for this, though a debasing superstition, is still real, and we might pity the poor wretch, though we cannot help despising him. But B. and F.'s Lucinas are clumsy fictions. It is too plain that the authors had no one idea of chastity as a virtue, but only such a conception as a blind man might have of the power of seeing, by handling an ox's eye. In "The Queen of Corinth," indeed, they talk differently; but it is all talk, and nothing is real in it but the dread of losing a reputation. Hence the frightful contrast between their women (even those who are meant for virtuous) and Shakspere's. So, for instance, "The Maid in the Mill":—a woman must not merely have grown old in brothels, but have chuckled over every abomination committed in them with a rampant sympathy of imagination, to have had her fancy so drunk with the *minutiae* of lechery as this icy chaste virgin evinces hers to have been.

BARCLAY: ARGENIS, *see* p. 715

MASSINGER

With regard to Massinger, observe,

1. The vein of satire on the times; but this is not as in Shakspere, where the natures evolve themselves according to their incidental disproportions, from excess, deficiency, or mislocation, of one or more of the component elements; but is merely satire on what is attributed to them by others.

2. His excellent metre—a better model for dramatists in general to imitate than Shakspere's,—even if a dramatic taste existed in the frequenters of the stage, and could be gratified in the present size and management, or rather mismanagement, of the two patent theatres. I do not mean that Massinger's verse is superior to Shakspere's or equal to it. Far from it; but it is much more easily constructed and may be more successfully adopted by writers in the present

day. It is the nearest approach to the language of real life at all compatible with a fixed metre. In Massinger, as in all our poets before Dryden, in order to make harmonious verse in the reading, it is absolutely necessary that the meaning should be understood;—when the meaning is once seen, then the harmony is perfect. Whereas in Pope and in most of the writers who followed in his school, it is the mechanical metre which determines the sense.

* * *

5. There is an utter want of preparation in the decisive acts of Massinger's characters, as in Camiola and Aurelia in the "Maid of Honour." Why? Because the *dramatis personae* were all planned each by itself. Whereas in Shakspere, the play is *syngenesia;* each character has, indeed, a life of its own, and is an *individuum* of itself, but yet an organ of the whole, as the heart in the human body. Shakspere was a great comparative anatomist.

Hence Massinger and all, indeed, but Shakspere, take a dislike to their own characters, and spite themselves upon them by making them talk like fools or monsters; as Fulgentio in his visit to Camiola (Act II, Sc. ii). Hence too, in Massinger, the continued flings at kings, courtiers, and all the favourites of fortune, like one who had enough of intellect to see injustice in his own inferiority in the share of the good things of life, but not genius enough to rise above it and forget himself. Beaumont and Fletcher have the same vice in the opposite pole, a servility of sentiment and a spirit of partizanship with the monarchical faction.

* * *

10. The comic scenes in Massinger not only do not harmonize with the tragic, not only interrupt the feeling, but degrade the characters that are to form any part in the action of the piece, so as to render them unfit for any tragic interest. At least, they do not concern, or act upon, or modify, the principal characters. As when a gentleman is insulted by a mere blackguard,—it is the same as if any other accident of nature had occurred, a pig run under his legs, or his horse thrown him. There is no dramatic interest in it. 1818

SIR THOMAS BROWNE

Sir Thomas Browne is among my first favourites, rich in
various knowledge, exuberant in conceptions and conceits,
contemplative, imaginative; often truly great and magnificent in his style and diction, though doubtless too often
big, stiff, and hyperlatinistic: thus I might without admixture of falsehood, describe Sir T. Browne, and my description would have only this fault, that it would be equally,
or almost equally, applicable to half a dozen other writers,
from the beginning of the reign of Elizabeth to the end of
Charles II. He is indeed all this; and what he has more than
all this peculiar to himself, I seem to convey to my own mind
in some measure by saying,—that he is a quiet and sublime
enthusiast with a strong tinge of the fantast, the humourist
constantly mingling with, and flashing across, the philosopher, as the darting colours in shot silk play upon the main
dye. In short, he has brains in his head which is all the more
interesting for a little twist in the brains. He sometimes
reminds the reader of Montaigne, but from no other than
the general circumstances of an egotism common to both;
which in Montaigne is too often a mere amusing gossip,
a chit-chat story of whims and peculiarities that lead to
nothing, but which in Sir Thomas Browne is always the
result of a feeling heart conjoined with a mind of active
curiosity,—the natural and becoming egotism of a man, who,
loving other men as himself, gains the habit, and the privilege of talking about himself as familiarly as about other
men. Fond of the curious, and a hunter of oddities and
strangenesses, while he conceived himself, with quaint and
humorous gravity a useful inquirer into physical truth and
fundamental science,—he loved to contemplate and discuss
his own thoughts and feelings, because he found by comparison with other men's, that they too were curiosities; and
so with a perfectly graceful and interesting ease he put them
too into his museum and cabinet of varieties. In very truth
he was not mistaken—so completely does he see every thing
in a light of his own, reading nature neither by sun, moon,
nor candle light, but by the light of the faery glory around

his own head; so that you might say that nature had granted to him in perpetuity a patent and monopoly for all his thoughts. Read his "Hydriotaphia" above all, and in addition to the peculiarity, the exclusive Sir-Thomas-Browne-ness of all the fancies and modes of illustration, wonder at and admire his entireness in every subject, which is before him. He is *totus in illo;* he follows it; he never wanders from it—and he has no occasion to wander, for whatever happens to be his subject, he metamorphoses all nature into it. In that "Hydriotaphia" or Treatise on some Urns dug up in Norfolk—how earthy, how redolent of graves and sepulchres is every line! You have now dark mould, now a thigh-bone, now a scull, then a bit of mouldered coffin! a fragment of an old tombstone with moss in its *hic jacet*—a ghost or a winding-sheet—or the echo of a funeral psalm wafted on a November wind! and the gayest thing you shall meet with shall be a silver nail or gilt *Anno Domini* from a perished coffin top. The very same remark applies in the same force to the interesting, though the far less interesting, "Treatise on the Quincuncial Plantations of the Ancients." There is the same attention to oddities, to the remoteness and *minutiae* of vegetable terms—the same entireness of subject. You have quincunxes in heaven above, quincunxes in earth below, and quincunxes in the water beneath the earth; quincunxes in deity, quincunxes in the mind of man, quincunxes in bones, in the optic nerves, in roots of trees, in leaves, in petals, in every thing. In short, first turn to the last leaf of this volume, and read out aloud to yourself the last seven paragraphs of Chap. v beginning with the words "More considerable," &c. But it is time for me to be in bed, in the words of Sir Thomas, which will serve you, my dear, as a fair specimen of his manner.—
"But the quincunx of heaven [the Hyades or five stars about the horizon at midnight at that time] runs low, and 'tis time to close the five ports of knowledge. We are unwilling to spin out our awaking thoughts into the phantasmes of sleep, which often continueth praecogitations,—making cables of cobwebbes, and wildernesses of handsome groves. . . . To keep our eyes open longer were but to act our Antipodes. The huntsmen are up in America, and they are already past their first sleep in Persia." Think you, my dear

Friend, that there ever was such a reason given before for
going to bed at midnight;—to wit, that if we did not, we
should be acting the part of our Antipodes! And then "the
huntsmen are up in America."—What life, what fancy!—
Does the whimsical knight give us thus a dish of strong
green tea, and call it an opiate! I trust that you are quietly
asleep—

> And that all the stars hang bright above your dwelling,
> Silent as though they watched the sleeping earth!

1804

"RELIGIO MEDICI" I

Strong feeling and an active intellect conjoined, lead almost necessarily, in the first stage of philosophising, to Spino-
sism. Sir T. Browne was a Spinosist without knowing it.

If I have not quite all the faith that the author of the
"Religio Medici" possessed, I have all the inclination to it:
it gives me pleasure to believe.

The postscript at the very end of the book is well worth
reading. Sir K. Digby's observations, however, are those of a
pedant in his own system and opinion. He ought to have considered the "R.M." in a dramatic, and not in a metaphysical,
view, as a sweet exhibition of character and passion, and not
as an expression, or investigation, of positive truth. The
"R.M." is a fine portrait of a handsome man in his best
clothes; it is much of what he was at all times, a good deal of
what he was only in his best moments. I have never read a
book in which I felt greater similarity to my own make of
mind—active in inquiry, and yet with an appetite to believe
—in short an affectionate visionary! But then I should tell a
different tale of my own heart; for I would not only endeavour to tell the truth, (which I doubt not Sir T. B. has done),
but likewise to tell the whole truth, which most assuredly he
has not done. However, it is a most delicious book.   1802

"RELIGIO MEDICI" II, *see* p. 717
"RELIGIO MEDICI" III, *see* p. 717

MILTON

The reader of Milton must be always on his duty: he is
surrounded with sense; it rises in every line; every word is to

the purpose. There are no lazy intervals; all has been considered, and demands and merits observation. If this be called obscurity, let it be remembered that it is such an obscurity as is a compliment to the reader; not that vicious obscurity, which proceeds from a muddled head.   1796

In his mind itself there were purity and piety absolute; an imagination to which neither the past nor the present were interesting, except as far as they called forth and enlivened the great ideal, in which and for which he lived; a keen love of truth, which, after many weary pursuits, found a harbour in a sublime listening to the still voice in his own spirit, and as keen a love of his country, which, after a disappointment still more depressive, expanded and soared into a love of man as a probationer of immortality. These were, these alone could be, the conditions under which such a work as the "Paradise Lost" could be conceived and accomplished. By a life-long study Milton had known—

> What was of use to know,
> What best to say could say, to do had done.
> His actions to his words agreed, his words
> To his large heart gave utterance due, his heart
> Contain'd of good, wise, fair, the perfect shape;

and he left the imperishable total, as a bequest to the ages coming, in the "PARADISE LOST."

"PARADISE LOST"

The language and versification of the "Paradise Lost" are peculiar in being so much more necessarily correspondent to each than those in any other poem or poet. The connexion of the sentences and the position of the words are exquisitely artificial; but the position is rather according to the logic of passion or universal logic, than to the logic of grammar. Milton attempted to make the English language obey the logic of passion as perfectly as the Greek and Latin. Hence the occasional harshness in the construction.

Sublimity is the pre-eminent characteristic of the "Paradise Lost." It is not an arithmetical sublime like Klopstock's, whose rule always is to treat what we might think large as contemptibly small. Klopstock mistakes bigness for greatness. There is a greatness arising from images of effort and daring, and also from those of moral endurance; in Milton both are united. The fallen angels are human passions, invested with a dramatic reality.

The apostrophe to light at the commencement of the third book is particularly beautiful as an intermediate link between Hell and Heaven; and observe, how the second and third books support the subjective character of the poem. In all modern poetry in Christendom there is an under conscious-ness of a sinful nature, a fleeting away of external things, the mind or subject greater than the object, the reflective character predominant. In the "Paradise Lost" the sublim-est parts are the revelations of Milton's own mind, producing itself and evolving its own greatness; and this is so truly so, that when that which is merely entertaining for its objective beauty is introduced, it at first seems a discord.

In the description of Paradise itself you have Milton's sunny side as a man; here his descriptive powers are exer-cised to the utmost, and he draws deep upon his Italian resources. In the description of Eve, and throughout this part of the poem, the poet is predominant over the theo-logian. Dress is the symbol of the Fall, but the mark of intellect; and the metaphysics of dress are, the hiding what is not symbolic and displaying by discrimination what is. The love of Adam and Eve in Paradise is of the highest merit—not phantomatic, and yet removed from every thing degrading. It is the sentiment of one rational being towards another made tender by a specific difference in that which is essentially the same in both; it is a union of opposites, a giving and receiving mutually of the permanent in either, a completion of each in the other.   1818

"COMUS"

[From her cabin'd loop-hole peep.

Warton's note: We have LOOP-HOLES of the Indian fig-tree, *Parad. L., B. IX, 1110* . . . . Milton was a student in botany. He took his description of this multifarious tree from the account of it in Gerard's "HERBALL," many of whose expres-sions he literally repeats.]

If I wished to display the charm and *effect* of metre and the *art* of poetry, independent of the Thoughts and Images—

the superiority, in short, of *poematic* over *prose* Composition, the poetry or no-poetry being the same in both, I question whether a more apt and convincing instance could be found, than in these exquisite lines of Milton's compared with the passage in Gerard, of which they are the organised version. Shakspere's Cleopatra on the Cydnus compared with the original in North's "Plutarch" is another almost equally striking example. S.T.C. 22nd Octr. 1823. Ramsgate.

"ON THE MORNING OF CHRIST'S NATIVITY"

> [So when the sun in bed
> Curtain'd with cloudy red
> Pillows his chin upon an **orient** wave.

Warton's note: The words *pillows* and *chin*, throw an air of burlesque and familiarity over a comparison most exquisitely conceived and adapted.]

I have tried in vain to imagine, in what other way the Image could be given. I rather think, that it is one of the Hardinesses permitted to a great Poet. Dante would have written it: though it is most in the spirit of Donne.

PEPYS

[1st Nov., 1667.

To the King's play-house, and there saw a silly play and an old one, "The Taming of a Shrew."]

This is, I think, the fifth of Shakespeare's Plays which Pepys found silly, stupid trash, and among them Othello! Macbeth indeed he commends for the *shews* and music, but not to be compared with the " Five Hours' Adventures"!! This and the want of *wit* in the Hudibras is very amusing— nay, it is seriously instructive. Thousands of shrewd and intelligent men, in whom, as in S. Pepys, the understanding is *hypertrophied* to the necrosis or marasmus of the Reason and Imagination, while far-sighted (yet, ah! how short-sighted,) Self-interest fills the place of Conscience, would say the same, if they dared.   ? 1830

PEPYS II, *see* p. 718

P

DEFOE

ROBINSON CRUSOE

[But my ill fate pushed me on now with an obstinacy that nothing could resist; and though I had several times loud calls from my reason, and my more composed judgement to go home, yet I had no power to do it. I know not what to call this, nor will I urge that it is a secret over-ruling decree that hurries us on to be the instruments of our own destruction, even though it be before us, and that we rush upon it with our eyes open.]

The wise only possess ideas; the greater part of mankind are possessed by them. Robinson Crusoe was not conscious of the master impulse, even because it was his master, and had taken, as he says, full possession of him. When once the mind, in despite of the remonstrating conscience, has abandoned its free power to a haunting impulse or idea, then whatever tends to give depth and vividness to this idea or indefinite imagination, increases its despotism, and in the same proportion renders the reason and free will ineffectual. Now, fearful calamities, sufferings, horrors, and hairbreadth escapes will have this effect, far more than even sensual pleasure and prosperous incidents. Hence the evil consequences of sin in such cases, instead of retracting or deterring the sinner, goad him on to his destruction. This is the moral of Shakspere's "Macbeth," and the true solution of this paragraph,—not any overruling decree of divine wrath, but the tyranny of the sinner's own evil imagination, which he has voluntarily chosen as his master.

Compare the contemptuous Swift with the contemned De Foe, and how superior will the latter be found! But by what test?—Even by this; that the writer who makes me sympathize with his presentations with the whole of my being, is more estimable than he who calls forth, and appeals but to, a part of my being—my sense of the ludicrous, for instance. De Foe's excellence it is, to make me forget my specific class, character, and circumstances, and to raise me while I read him, into the universal man.

[I smiled to myself at the sight of this money: "O drug!" said I aloud, &c. *However, upon second thoughts, I took it away;* and wrapping all this in a piece of canvass, &c.]

Worthy of Shakspere!—and yet the simple semicolon after it, the instant passing on without the least pause of reflex consciousness, is more exquisite and masterlike than the touch itself. A meaner writer, a Marmontel, would have put an (!) after "*away*," and have commenced a fresh paragraph. 30th July, 1830

[The growing up of the corn, as is hinted in my Journal, had, at first, some little influence upon me, and began to affect me with seriousness, as long as I thought it had something mira-culous in it, &c.]

By far the ablest vindication of miracles which I have met with. It is indeed the true ground, the proper purpose and intention of a miracle.

* * *

One excellence of De Foe, amongst many, is his sacrifice of lesser interest to the greater because more universal. Had he (as without any improbability he might have done) given his Robinson Crusoe any of the turn for natural history, which forms so striking and delightful a feature in the equally uneducated Dampier; had he made him find out qualities and uses in the before (to him) unknown plants of the island, [and] discover, for instance, a substi-tute for hops, or describe birds, &c., many delightful pages and incidents might have enriched the book;—but then Crusoe would have ceased to be the universal representa-tive, the person, for whom every reader could substitute himself. But now [here?] nothing is done, thought, suffered, or desired, but what every man can imagine himself doing, thinking, feeling, or wishing for. Even so very easy a prob-lem as that of finding a substitute for ink, is with ex-quisite judgment made to baffle Crusoe's inventive faculties. And in what he does, he arrives at no excellence; he does not make basket work like Will Atkins; the carpentering, tailoring, pottery, &c., are all just what will answer his purposes, and those are confined to needs that all men have, and comforts that all men desire. Crusoe rises only to the point to which all men may be made to feel that they might, and that they ought to, rise in religion,—to resignation, dependence on, and thankful acknowledgment of, the divine mercy and goodness. 1830

SWIFT

In Swift's writing there is a false misanthropy grounded upon an exclusive contemplation of the vices and follies of mankind, and this misanthropic tone is also disfigured or brutalized by his obtrusion of physical dirt and coarseness. I think "Gulliver's Travels" the great work of Swift. In the voyages to Lilliput and Brobdingnag he displays the littleness and moral contemptibility of human nature; in that to the Houyhnhnms he represents the disgusting spectacle of man with the understanding only, without the reason or the moral feeling, and in his horse he gives the misanthropic ideal of man—that is, a being virtuous from rule and duty, but untouched by the principle of love.   1818

FIELDING: "JONATHAN WILD," *see* p. 718

STERNE

With regard to Sterne, and the charge of licentiousness which presses so seriously upon his character as a writer, I would remark that there is a sort of knowingness, the wit of which depends—first, on the modesty it gives pain to; or, secondly, on the innocence and innocent ignorance over which it triumphs; or, thirdly, on a certain oscillation in the individual's own mind between the remaining good and the encroaching evil of his nature—a sort of dallying with the devil—a fluxionary act of combining courage and cowardice, as when a man snuffs a candle with his fingers for the first time, or better still, perhaps, like that trembling daring with which a child touches a hot tea urn, because it has been forbidden; so that the mind has in its own white and black angel the same or similar amusement, as may be supposed to take place between an old debauchee and a prude,—she feeling resentment, on the one hand, from a prudential anxiety to preserve appearances and have a character, and, on the other, an inward sympathy with the enemy. We have only to suppose society innocent, and then nine-tenths of this sort of wit would be like a stone that falls in snow, making no sound because exciting no resistance; the remainder rests on its being an offence against the good manners of human nature itself.

This source, unworthy as it is, may doubtless be combined with wit, drollery, fancy, and even humour, and we have only to regret the misalliance; but that the latter are quite distinct from the former, may be made evident by abstracting in our imagination the morality of the characters of Mr. Shandy, my Uncle Toby, and Trim, which are all antagonists to this spurious sort of wit, from the rest of "Tristram Shandy," and by supposing, instead of them, the presence of two or three callous debauchees. The result will be pure disgust. Sterne cannot be too severely censured for thus using the best dispositions of our nature as the panders and condiments for the basest.

The excellencies of Sterne consist—

1. In bringing forward into distinct consciousness those *minutiae* of thought and feeling which appear trifles, yet have an importance for the moment, and which almost every man feels in one way or other. Thus is produced the novelty of an individual peculiarity, together with the interest of a something that belongs to our common nature. In short, Sterne seizes happily on those points, in which every man is more or less a humourist. And, indeed, to be a little more subtle, the propensity to notice these things does itself constitute the humourist, and the superadded power of so presenting them to men in general gives us the man of humour. Hence the difference of the man of humour, the effect of whose portraits does not depend on the felt presence of himself, as a humourist, as in the instances of Cervantes and Shakspere—nay, of Rabelais too—and of the humourist, the effect of whose works does very much depend on the sense of his own oddity, as in Sterne's case, and perhaps Swift's; though Swift again would require a separate classification.

* * *

3. In Mr. Shandy's character,—the essence of which is a craving for sympathy in exact proportion to the oddity and unsympathizability of what he proposes;—this coupled with an instinctive desire to be at least disputed with, or rather, both in one, to dispute and yet to agree—and, holding as worst of all—to acquiesce without either resistance or sympathy. This is charmingly, indeed, profoundly conceived, and is psychologically and ethically true of all

Mr. Shandies. Note, too, how the contrasts of character, which are always either balanced or remedied, increase the love between the brothers.

*   *   *

6. There is great physiognomic tact in Sterne. See it particularly displayed in his description of Dr. Slop, accompanied with all that happiest use of drapery and attitude, which at once give reality by individualizing and vividness by unusual, yet probable, combinations:—

> Imagine to yourself a little squat, uncourtly figure of a Doctor Slop, of about four feet and a half perpendicular height, with a breadth of back, and a sesquipedality of belly, which might have done honour to a sergeant in the horse-guards.

[*Vol. II, Chap. ix*]
1818

GRAY: "ON A DISTANT PROSPECT OF ETON COLLEGE," *see* p. 719
ROBERT ANDERSON: "LIFE OF PHINEAS FLETCHER," *see* p. 719
GEORGE DYER: POEMS, *see* p. 720
CHALMERS: "LIFE OF DANIEL," *see* p. 720

JUNIUS

It is impossible to detract from the merit of these "Letters": they are suited to their purpose, and perfect in their kind. They impel to action, not thought. Had they been profound or subtle in thought, or majestic and sweeping in composition, they would have been adapted for the closet of a Sidney, or for a House of Lords such as it was in the time of Lord Bacon; but they are plain and sensible whenever the author is in the right, and whether right or wrong, always shrewd and epigrammatic, and fitted for the coffee-house, the exchange, the lobby of the House of Commons, and to be read aloud at a public meeting. When connected, dropping the forms of connection, desultory, without abruptness or appearance of disconnection, epigrammatic and antithetical to excess, sententious and personal, regardless of right or wrong, yet well-skilled to act the part of an honest warm-hearted man, and even when he is in the right, saying the truth but never proving it, much less attempting to bottom it,—this is the character of Junius:—and on this

character, and in the mould of these writings must every
man cast himself, who would wish in factious times to be
the important and long remembered agent of a faction. I
believe that I could do all that Junius has done, and surpass
him by doing many things which he has not done: for
example,—by an occasional induction of startling facts, in
the manner of Tom Paine, and lively illustrations and witty
applications of good stories and appropriate anecdotes in
the manner of Horne Tooke. I believe I could do it if it
were in my nature to aim at this sort of excellence, or to be
enamoured of the fame, and immediate influence, which
would be its consequence and reward. But it is not in my
nature. I not only love truth, but I have a passion for the
legitimate investigation of truth. The love of truth conjoined with a keen delight in a strict and skilful yet impassioned argumentation, is my master-passion, and to it
are subordinated even the love of liberty and all my public
feelings—and to it whatever I labour under of vanity,
ambition, and all my inward impulses.   1807

SIR WALTER SCOTT:
    "THE HEART OF MIDLOTHIAN," *see* p. 721
    "QUENTIN DURWARD," *see* p. 721
JOHN GALT: "THE PROVOST," *see* p. 721
BARRY CORNWALL: DRAMATIC SCENES AND
    OTHER POEMS, *see* p. 722

CHARLES TENNYSON
"SONNET XIX"

[The things that own most motion and most sound
Are tranc'd and silent in a golden *swound:*]

Swound! od's wounds—such gipsy jargon suits my
"Ancient Mariner," but surely not this highly polished
classical diction.

[Sink deeply in my thought, surpassing *scene!*
And be thy memory clear, for I would live therein!]

Suffer me, dear young poet, to conjure you never to use
this Covent Garden and Drury Lane word, unless some
distinct allusion or reference be intended to a theatre—this
scene and *scenery* I class among the villainous slang fineries
of the last Century.   1830

S. T. COLERIDGE

"REMORSE"

[III, ii.

> *Ordonio.* There, where Ordonio likewise would fain lie!
> In the sleep-compelling earth, in unpierced darkness!
> For while we live—
> An inward day that never, never sets,
> Glares round the soul, and mocks the closing eyelids!
> Over his rocky grave the fir-grove sighs
> A lulling ceaseless dirge! 'Tis well with him.
> (*Strides off towards the altar.*)]

It was pleasing to observe, during the Rehearsal all the Actors and Actresses and even the Mechanics on the stage clustering round while these lines were repeating just as if it had been a favourite strain of Music. But from want of depth and volume of voice in Rae, they did not produce an equal effect on the Public till after the Publication—and *then* they (I understand) were applauded. I have never seen the Piece since the first Night.

"DESTINY OF NATIONS"

> ["Maid beloved of Heaven!"
> (To her the tutelary Power exclaimed)
> "Of Chaos the adventurous progeny
> Thou seest; foul missionaries of foul sire,
> Fierce to regain the losses of that hour
> When Love rose glittering," &c.
> *ll. 278 ff.*]

These are very fine Lines, though I say it, that should not: but, hang me, if I know or ever did know the meaning of them, though my own composition.   ?1828

"THE PICCOLOMINI"

[II, vi.

> *Thekla.* Are we not happy now? Art thou not mine?
> Am I not thine? There lives within my soul
> A lofty courage—'tis love gives it me!
> I ought to be less open—ought to hide
> My heart more from thee—so decorum dictates:]

What may not a man write and publish, who writes with the press waiting, and composes p. 86 while the printer is composing p. 85?

"THEOLOGICO-METAPHYSICAL"

This section contains extracts from what Coleridge called his "theologico-metaphysical" writings. Nearly all of them belong to the latest years of his life, and are further connected by a common origin. Coleridge considered each of them (including even the "Biographia Literaria") to be offshoots, introductory matter, disjecta membra, incidental to the gradual preparation of a magnum opus. The first reference to this is in a letter of 1803, where later schemes, discussed more frequently after 1814, are anticipated. It was to be a new Organon, the history and practical application of a new logic—an "Instrument of Practical Reasoning in the Business of Real Life" by means of which the reader was to "acquire not only knowledge, but likewise power." The book was never published. A strong sense of obligation to his own talents, and to such practical admirers as Wedgwood, though it kept the scheme alive, combined to form that very kind of "ought" which Coleridge found an insuperable barrier to action. The manuscript remains, which have been recently assessed and quoted, are of very uneven value, and the attempt of his disciple Green to work up these and other fragments into a "Spiritual Philosophy" was a disappointment.

In the last few years of his life Coleridge concentrated more and more on the correlation of his philosophy with his orthodox religious beliefs. This tendency is well represented in what he published. But I have made the section short chiefly because Coleridge's most pregnant thoughts under this heading are to be found outside those works which deal formally with the subject: and because, though it might have been possible, by carefully schematized selection, to illustrate such problems as the extent to which Coleridge, with his "un-English" idealism, forms a link between the Cambridge Platonists and our nineteenth century Hegelians, an unjustifiably large amount of space would be taken up in the process. Unjustifiable because Coleridge was never by nature or intention a philosopher of the schools. "What is it that I employ my metaphysics on?" he wrote in a notebook. "To perplex our dearest notions and living moral instincts?" I use it "to support old and venerable truths, to kindle, to project, to make the reason spread light over our feelings, to make our feelings diffuse vital warmth through our reason. . . ." As his critics have noticed, Coleridge's scheme was, where it existed, always of secondary importance. It is his philosophic attitude, the way in which he lived his philosophy, which is definite, concrete and truly original.

[A SERMON]

ON THE ORIGIN OF EVIL

IT was towards Morning, when the Brain begins to re-assume its waking state, and our dreams approach to the regular trains of Reality, that I found myself in a vast Plain, which I immediately knew to be the Valley of Life. It possessed a great diversity of soils, and here was a sunny spot and there a dark one—just such a mixture of sunshine and shade as we may have observed on the Hills in an April Day when the thin broken Clouds are scattered over the heaven. Almost in the very entrance of the Valley stood a large and gloomy pile into which I seemed constrained to enter: every part of the building was crowded with tawdry ornament and fantastic deformity—on every window was portrayed in elegant and glowing colours some horrible tale or preternatural action, so that not a ray of light could enter un-tinged by the medium through which it passed. The Place was full of People, some of them dancing about in strange ceremonies and antic merriment, while others seemed convulsed with horror or pining in mad melancholy. Intermingled with all these I observed a great number of men in Black Robes who appeared now marshalling the various Groups and now collecting with scrupulous care the Tenths of every Thing that grew within their reach. I stood wondering a while what these Things might be when one of these men approached me and with a reproachful Look bade me uncover my Head, for that the Place into which I had entered was the Temple of *Religion*, in the holier recesses of which the great Goddess resided. Awestruck by the name I bowed before the Priest and entreated him to conduct me into her Presence—he assented. Offerings he took from me, with mystic sparklings of Water he purified me, and then led me through many a dark and winding alley the dew damps of which chilled and its hollow echoes beneath my feet affrighted me till at last we entered a large Hall where not even a Lamp glimmered. Around its walls I observed a number of phosphoric Inscriptions—each one of the words separately I seemed to understand, but when I read them in sentences they were riddles incomprehensible and contradictory. "Read and believe," said my Guide—"These are mysteries." In the middle of the Hall the Goddess was placed—her features blended with darkness rose to my view terrible yet vacant. I prostrated myself before her and then retired with my guide wond'ring and dissatisfied. As I re-entered the body of the Temple I heard a deep Bur as of Discontent. A few whose Eyes were piercing, and whose Foreheads spoke Thought, amid a much larger number who were enraged by the serenity of the Priests in exacting their Truths, had collected in a group, and exclaiming "This is the Temple of Superstition," after much contumely and much maltreatment they rushed out of it. I joined them—we travelled from the Temple with hasty steps and had now nearly gone round half the Valley when we were addressed by a Woman clad in white garments of simplest texture. Her Air was mild yet majestic, and her countenance displayed deep Reflection animated by ardent Feelings. We enquired her name. "My name is Religion," she said. The greater part of our Company, affrighted by the sound, and sore from recent impostures, hurried onwards and examined no further. A few, struck by the difference of her form and manners, agreed to follow her, although with cautious circumspection. She led us to an Eminence in the midst of the Valley, on the Top of which we could command the whole Plain, and observe the Relation of its different Parts, each one to the other. She then gave us an optic Glass which assisted without contradicting our natural vision and enabled us to see far beyond the Valley—(and now with the rapid Transition of a dream I had . . . [manuscript broken]) of Superstition and went to sleep in the darkest cloisters—but there were many however who lost not the impression of Hatred towards their oppressors, and, never looking back, had in their eagerness to recede from Superstition completed almost the whole of the circle, and were already in the Precincts of the Temple, when they abruptly entered a vast and dusky Cave. At the mouth of it sate two Figures:—the first, a female, by her dress and gestures I knew to be Sensuality: the Second, from the fierceness of his Demeanour and the brutal Scornfulness of his Looks, declared himself to be the Monster Blasphemy. He uttered big words, yet ever and anon I observed that he turned pale at his own courage. We entered—the climate of the place was unnaturally cold. In the midst was an old, dim-eyed Man.

*   *   *

The Old Man was continually applying his microscope, and seemed greatly delighted in the Irregularities which were made visible by it on the polished surface of the Marble! He spoke in diverse Tongues and unfolded many Mysteries, and among other strange Things he talked much about an infinite Series of Causes—which he explained to be — — a string of blind men of which the last caught hold of the skirt of the one before him, he of the next, and so on till they were all out of sight; and that they all walked straight without making one false step. We enquired Who there is at the head to guide them? He answered No one, but that the string of blind men went on for ever without a beginning, for though one blind man could not move without stumbling, yet that infinite blindness supplies the want of sight. I burst into Laughter at this strange exposition and awoke—

1795

[PRIESTS: A FOOTNOTE]

Warriors, and Lords, and Priests—all the sore ills*
That vex and desolate our mortal life.

Religious Musings, l. 215

*I deem that the teaching of the gospel for hire is wrong; because it gives the teacher an improper bias in favour of particular opinions on a subject where it is of the last importance that the mind should be perfectly unbiassed. Such is my private opinion; but I mean not to censure all hired teachers, many among whom I know, and venerate as the best and wisest of men—God forbid that I should think of these, when I use the word PRIEST, a name, after which any other term of abhorrence would appear an anti-climax. By a Priest I mean a man who holding the scourge of power in his right hand and a bible (translated by authority) in his left, doth necessarily cause the bible and the scourge to be associated ideas, and so produces that temper of mind which leads to Infidelity—Infidelity which judging of Revelation by the doctrines and practices of established Churches honors God by rejecting Christ. See "Address to the People," p. 57, sold by Parsons, Paternoster Row. 1796

THE FRIEND: 1809

[ERASMUS AND VOLTAIRE]

Those who are familiar with the Works of Erasmus, and who know the influence of his Wit, as the pioneer of the Reformation; and who likewise know, that by his Wit, added to the vast variety of knowledge communicated in his Works, he had won over by anticipation so large a part of the polite and lettered World to the Protestant Party; will be at no loss in discovering the intended counterpart in the Life and Writings of the veteran Frenchman. They will see, indeed, that the knowledge of the one was solid through its whole extent, and that of the other extensive at a cheap rate, by its superficiality: that the Wit of the one is always bottomed on sound sense, peoples and enriches the mind of the Reader with an endless variety of distinct images and living interests; and that his broadest laughter is everywhere translateable into grave and weighty truth: while the wit of the Frenchman, without imagery, without character, and without that pathos which gives the magic charm to genuine humour, consists, when it is most perfect, in happy turns of phrase, but far too often in fantastic incidents, outrages of the pure imagination, and the poor low trick of combining the ridiculous with the venerable, where he, who does not laugh, abhors. Neither will they have forgotten, that the object of the one was to drive the Thieves and Mummers out of the Temple, while the other was propelling a worse banditti, first to profane and pillage, and ultimately to raze it. Yet not the less will they perceive, that the *effects* remain parallel, the *circumstances* analogous, and the *instruments* the same. In each case the *effects* extended over Europe, were attested and augmented by the praise and patronage of thrones and dignities, and are not to be explained but by extraordinary industry and a life of literature; in both instances the *circumstances* were supplied by an Age of Hopes and Promises—the Age of Erasmus restless from the first vernal influences of real knowledge, that of Voltaire from the hectic of imagined superiority. In the voluminous works of both, the *instruments* employed are chiefly those of wit and amusive erudition, and alike in both the Errors and Evils (real or imputed) in Religion and Politics are the objects of the Battery. And here we must stop. The two *Men* were *essentially* different. Exchange mutually their dates and spheres of action, yet Voltaire, had he been tenfold a Voltaire, could not have made up an Erasmus; and Erasmus must have emptied himself of half his greatness, and all his goodness, to have become a Voltaire.

[JACOBINISM AND PANTISOCRACY]

I was never myself, at any period of my life, a Convert to the System. From my earliest Manhood, it was an axiom in Politics with me, that in every Country where Property prevailed, Property must be the grand basis of the Government; and that that Government was the best, in which the Power or political Influence of the Individual was in proportion to his property, provided that the free circulation of Property was not impeded by any positive Laws or Customs, nor the tendency of Wealth to accumulate in abiding Masses unduly encouraged. I perceived, that if the People at large were neither ignorant nor immoral, there could be no motive for a sudden and violent change of Government; and if they were, there could be no hope but of a change for the worse. "The Temple of Despotism, like that of the Mexican god, would be rebuilt with human skulls, and more firmly, though in a different architecture."* Thanks to the excellent Education which I had received, my reason was too clear not to draw this "circle of Power" round me, and

---

*To the best of my recollection, these were Mr. Southey's words in the year 1794.

my spirit too honest to attempt to break through it. My feelings, however, and imagination did not remain unkindled in this general conflagration; and I confess I should be more inclined to be ashamed than proud of myself, if they had: I was a sharer in the general vortex, though my little World described the path of its Revolution in an orbit of its own. What I dared not expect from constitutions of Government and whole Nations, I hoped from Religion and a small company of chosen Individuals, and formed a plan, as harmless as it was extravagant, of trying the experiment of human Perfectibility on the banks of the *Susquehannah;* where our little Society, in its second Generation, was to have combined the innocence of the patriarchal Age with the knowledge and genuine refinements of European culture; and where I dreamt that in the sober evening of my life, I should behold the Cottages of Independence in the *undivided* Dale of Industry,

> And oft, soothed sadly by some dirgeful wind
> Muse on the sore ills I had left behind!

Strange fancies! and as vain as strange! yet to the intense interest and impassioned zeal which called forth and strained every faculty of my intellect for the organization and defence of this Scheme, I owe much of whatever I at present possess, my clearest insight into the nature of individual Man, and my most comprehensive views of his social relations, of the true uses of Trade and Commerce, and how far the *Wealth* and relative *Power* of nations promote or impede their *welfare* and inherent *strength.* Nor were they less serviceable in securing myself, and perhaps some others, from the pitfalls of Sedition; and when we alighted on the firm ground of common sense from the gradually exhausted Balloon of youthful Enthusiasm, though the air-built Castles which we had been pursuing had vanished with all their pageantry of shifting forms and glowing colours, we were yet free from the stains and impurities which might have remained upon us, had we been travelling with the crowd of less imaginative malcontents through the dark lanes and foul bye-roads of ordinary Fanaticism.

But Oh! there were thousands as young and as innocent as myself who, not like me, sheltered in the tranquil nook or inland cove of a particular Fancy, were driven along with the general current! Many there were, young Men of loftiest minds, yea, the prime stuff out of which manly Wisdom and practical Greatness is to be formed, who had appropriated their hopes and the ardour of their souls to Mankind at large, to the wide expanse of national interests, which then seemed fermenting in the French Republic as in the main Outlet and chief Crater of the revolutionary Torrents; and who confidently believed, that these Torrents, like the Lavas of Vesuvius, were to subside into a soil of inexhaustible fertility on the circumjacent Lands, the old divisions and mouldering edifices of which they had covered or swept away—Enthusiasts of kindliest temperament, who, to use the words of the Poet (having already borrowed the meaning and the metaphor) had approached

> the shield
> Of human nature from the golden side,
> And would have fought even to the death to attest
> The quality of the metal which they saw.

My honoured Friend has permitted me to give a value and relief to the present Essay by a quotation from one of his unpublished Poems, the length of which I regret only from its forbidding me to trespass on his kindness by making it yet longer. I trust there are many of my Readers of the same Age with myself, who will throw themselves back into the state of thought and feeling in which they were when France was reported to have solemnized her first sacrifice of error and prejudice on the bloodless altar of Freedom, by an Oath of Peace and Good-will to all Mankind.

> Oh! pleasant exercise of hope and joy!
> For mighty were the auxiliars, which then stood
> Upon our side, we who were strong in love!
> Bliss was it in that dawn to be alive,
> But to be young was very heaven! [&c.]

WORDSWORTH

[TAXATION]

Taxes may be indeed, and often are injurious to a Country: at no time, however, from their amount merely, but from the time or injudicious mode in which they are raised. A great Statesman, lately deceased, in one of his anti-ministerial harangues against some proposed impost, said: "the Nation has been already bled in every vein, and is faint with loss of blood." This Blood, however, was circulating in the mean time through the whole Body of the State, and what was received into one chamber of the Heart was instantly sent out again at the other Portal. Had he wanted a metaphor to convey the possible injuries of Taxation, he might have found one less opposite to the fact in the known disease of aneurism, or relaxation of the coats of particular vessels, by a disproportionate accumulation of Blood in them, which sometimes occurs when the circulation has been suddenly and violently changed, and causes Helplessness, or even mortal stagnation, though the total quantity of Blood remains the same in the System at large.

But a fuller and fairer symbol of Taxation, both in its possible good and evil Effects, is to be found in the evaporation of Waters from the surface of the Planet. The Sun may draw up the moisture from the River, the Morass, and the Ocean, to be given back in genial Showers to the Garden, the Pasture, and the Corn-field; but it may likewise force away the moisture from the fields of Tillage, to drop it on the stagnant Pool, the saturated Swamp, or the unprofitable Sand-waste. The Gardens in the south of Europe supply, perhaps, a not less apt illustration of a system of Finance judiciously conducted, where the Tanks or Reservoirs would represent the Capital of a Nation, and the hundred Rills hourly varying their channels and directions under the Gardener's spade, give a pleasing image of the dispersion of that capital through the whole Population, by the joint effect of Taxation and Trade. For Taxation itself is a part of Commerce, and the Government may be fairly considered as a great manufacturing house carrying on in different Places, by means of its Partners and Overseers, the Trades of the Ship-builder, the Clothier, the Iron-founder, &c., &c.

THE STATESMAN'S MANUAL

[INCREDULITY]

Not only may we expect that men of strong religious feelings, but little religious knowledge, will occasionally be tempted to regard such occurrences as supernatural visitations; but it ought not to surprise us if such dreams should sometimes be confirmed by the event, as though they had actually possessed a character of divination. For who shall decide how far a perfect reminiscence of past experiences (of many, perhaps, that had escaped our reflex consciousness at the time)—who shall determine to what extent this reproductive imagination, unsophisticated by the will, and undistracted by intrusions from the senses, may or may not be concentred and sublimed into foresight and presentiment? There would be nothing herein either to foster superstition on the one hand, or to justify contemptuous disbelief on the other. Incredulity is but credulity seen from behind, bowing and nodding assent to the habitual and the fashionable.

[THE READING PUBLIC]

WHEN I named this Essay a Sermon, I sought to prepare the inquirers after it for the absence of all the usual softenings suggested by worldly prudence, of all compromise between truth and courtesy. But not even as a sermon would I have addressed the present discourse to a promiscuous audience; and for this reason I likewise announced it in the title-page, as exclusively *ad clerum;* that is (in the old and wide sense of the word), to men of clerkly acquirements of whatever profession. I would that the greater part of our publications could be thus directed, each to its appropriate class of readers. But this cannot be. For among other odd burs and kecksies, the misgrowth of our luxuriant activity, we have now a Reading Public—as strange a phrase, methinks, as ever forced a splenetic smile on the staid countenance of meditation; and yet no fiction. For our readers have, in good truth, multiplied exceedingly, and have waxed proud. It would require the intrepid accuracy of a Colquhoun to venture at the precise number of that vast company only, whose heads and hearts are dieted at the two public ordinaries of literature, the circulating libraries and the periodical press. But what is the result? Does the inward man thrive on this regimen? Alas! if the average health of the consumers may be judged of by the articles of largest consumption; if the secretions may be conjectured from the ingredients of the dishes that are found best suited to their palates; from all that I have seen, either of the banquet or the guests, I shall utter my *profaccia* with a desponding sigh. From a popular philosophy and a philosophic populace, Good Sense deliver us!

[THE BIBLE A SCIENCE OF REALITIES]

My second purpose is after the same manner in a two-fold sense specific: for as this Sermon is nominally addressed to, so was it for the greater part exclusively intended for, the perusal of the learned: and its object likewise is to urge men so qualified to apply their powers and attainments to an especial study of the Old Testament as teaching the elements of political science.

It is asked, in what sense I use these words? I answer: in the same sense as the terms are employed when we refer to Euclid for the elements of the science of geometry, only with one difference arising from the diversity of the subject. With one difference only; but that one how momentous! All other sciences are confined to abstractions, unless when the term science is used in an improper and flattering sense.—Thus we may speak without boast of natural history; but we have not yet attained to a science of nature. The Bible alone contains a science of realities: and therefore each of its elements is at the same time a living germ, in which the present involves the future, and in the finite the infinite exists potentially. That hidden mystery in every the minutest form of existence, which contemplated under the relations of time presents itself to the understanding retrospectively, as an infinite ascent of causes, and prospectively as an interminable progression of effects;—that which contemplated in space is beholden intuitively as a law of action and re-action, continuous and extending beyond all bound;—this same mystery freed from the *phaenomena* of time and space, and seen in the depth of real being, reveals itself to the pure reason as the actual immanence or in-being of all in each. Are we struck with admiration at beholding the cope of heaven imaged in a dew-drop? The least of the *animalcula* to which that drop would be an ocean contains in itself an infinite problem of which God omni-present is the only solution. The slave of custom is roused by the rare and accidental alone; but the axioms of the unthinking are to the philosopher the deepest problems as being the nearest to the mysterious root and partaking at once of its darkness and its pregnancy.

Oh what a mine of undiscovered treasures, what a new world of power and truth would the Bible promise to our future meditation, if in some gracious moment one solitary text of all its inspired contents should but dawn upon us in the pure untroubled brightness of an idea, that most glorious birth of the God-like within us, which even as the light, its material symbol, reflects itself from a thousand surfaces, and flies homeward to its Parent Mind enriched with a thousand forms, itself above form and still remaining in its own simplicity and identity! Oh for a flash of that same light, in which the first position of geometric science that ever loosed itself from the generalisations of a groping and insecure experience, for the first time revealed itself to a human intellect in all its evidence and all its fruitfulness, transparence without *vacuum*, and plenitude without opacity! Oh that a single gleam of our own inward experience would make comprehensible to us the rapturous Eureka, and the grateful hecatomb, of the philosopher of Samos.   1816

THE FRIEND: 1818

[DANGER OF INDISTINCT CONCEPTIONS]

I had walked from Gottingen in the year 1799, to witness the arrival of the Queen of Prussia, on her visit to the Baron Von Hartzberg's seat, five miles from the University. The spacious outer court of the palace was crowded with men and women, a sea of heads, with a number of children rising out of it from their fathers' shoulders. After a buzz of two hours' expectation, the avant-courier rode at full speed into the Court. At the loud cracks of his long whip and the trampling of his horse's hoofs, the universal shock and thrill of emotion—I have not language to convey it—expressed as it was in such manifold looks, gestures, and attitudes, yet with one and the same feeling in the eyes of all! Recovering from the first inevitable contagion of sympathy, I involuntarily exclaimed, though in a language to myself alone intelligible, "O man! ever nobler than thy circumstances!

Spread but the mist of obscure feeling over any form, and even a woman incapable of blessing or of injury to thee shall be welcomed with an intensity of emotion adequate to the reception of the Redeemer of the world!"

To a creature so highly, so fearfully gifted, who, alienated as he is by a sorcery scarcely less mysterious than the nature on which it is exercised, yet like the fabled son of Jove in the evil day of his sensual bewitchment, lifts the spindles and distaffs of Omphale with the arm of a giant, truth is self-restoration: for that which is the correlative of Truth, the existence of absolute Life, is the only object which can attract toward it the whole depth and mass of his fluctuating being, and alone therefore can unite Calmness with Elevation. But it must be truth without alloy and unsophisticated. It is by the agency of indistinct conceptions, as the counterfeits of the Ideal and Transcendent, that evil and vanity exercise their tyranny on the feelings of man.

But though knowledge be not the only, yet that it is an indispensable and most effectual agent in the direction of our actions, one consideration will convince us. It is an undoubted fact of human nature, that the sense of impossibility quenches all will. Sense of utter inaptitude does the same. The man shuns the beautiful flame, which is eagerly grasped at by the infant. The sense of disproportion of a certain after-harm to present gratification produces effects almost equally uniform: though almost perishing with thirst, we should dash to the earth a goblet of wine in which we had seen a poison infused, though the poison were without taste or odour, or even added to the pleasures of both. Are not all our vices equally inapt to the universal end of human actions, the satisfaction of the agent? Are not their pleasures equally disproportionate to the after-harm? Yet many a maiden, who will not grasp at the fire, will yet purchase a wreath of diamonds at the price of her health, her honour, nay (and she herself knows it at the moment of her choice) at the sacrifice of her peace and happiness. The sot would reject the poisoned cup, yet the trembling hand with which he raises his daily or hourly draught to his lips, has not left him ignorant that this too is altogether a poison. I know it will be objected, that the consequences foreseen are less immediate; that they are diffused over a larger space of time; and that the slave of vice hopes where no hope is. This, however, only removes the question one step further: for why should the distance or diffusion of known consequences produce so great a difference? Why are men the dupes of the present moment? Evidently because the conceptions are indistinct in the one case, and vivid in the other; because all confused conceptions render us restless; and because restlessness can drive us to vices that promise no enjoyment, no, not even the cessation of that restlessness. This is indeed the dread punishment attached by nature to habitual vice, that its impulses wax as its motives wane. No object, not even the light of a solitary taper in the far distance, tempts the benighted mind from before; but its own restlessness dogs it from behind, as with the iron goad of destiny. What then is or can be the preventive, the remedy, the counteraction, but the habituation of the intellect to clear, distinct, and adequate conceptions concerning all things that are the possible objects of clear conception, and thus to reserve the deep feelings which belong, as by a natural right, to those obscure ideas that are necessary to the moral perfection of the human being, notwithstanding, yea, even in consequence, of their obscurity—to reserve these feelings, I repeat, for objects, which their very sublimity renders indefinite, no less than their indefiniteness renders them sublime: namely, to the ideas of being, form, life, the reason, the law of conscience, freedom, immortality, God! To connect with the objects of our senses the obscure notions and consequent vivid feelings, which are due only to immaterial and permanent things, is profanation relatively to the heart, and superstition in the understanding.

[SHAKSPERE AND THE SCIENCE OF METHOD]

"Ὁ δὲ δίκαιόν ἐστι ποιεῖν, ἄκουε πῶς χρὴ ἔχειν ἐμὲ καὶ σὲ πρὸς ἀλλήλους. Εἰ μὲν ὅλως φιλοσοφίας καταπεφρόνηκας, ἐᾶν χαίρειν· εἰ δὲ παρ' ἑτέρου ἀκήκοας ἢ αὐτὸς βελτίονα εὕρηκας τῶν παρ' ἐμοί, ἐκεῖνα τίμα· εἰ δ' ἄρα τὰ παρ' ἡμῶν σοὶ ἀρέσκει, τιμητέον καὶ ἐμὲ μάλιστα.

ΠΛΑΤΩΝΟΣ Διονυσίῳ ἐπιστολὴ δευτέρα

(*Translation.*)—*Hear then what are the terms on which you and I ought to stand toward each other. If you hold philosophy altogether in contempt, bid it farewell. Or if you have heard from any other person, or have yourself found out a better than mine, then give honour to that, which ever it be. But if the doctrine taught in these our works please you, then it is but just that you should honour me too in the same proportion.*

Plato's 2nd Letter to Dionysius

What is that which first strikes us, and strikes us at once, in a man of education; and which among educated men so instantly distinguishes the man of superior mind, that (as was observed with eminent propriety of the late Edmund Burke) "we cannot stand under the same archway during a shower of rain, without finding him out"? Not the weight or novelty of his remarks; not any unusual interest of facts communicated by him; for we may suppose both the one and the other precluded by the shortness of our intercourse and the triviality of the subjects. The difference will be impressed and felt, though the conversation should be confined to the state of the weather or the pavement. Still less will it arise from any peculiarity in his words and phrases. For if he be, as we now assume, a well-educated man as well as a man of superior powers, he will not fail to follow the golden rule of Julius Caesar, *Insolens verbum, tanquam scopulum, evitare.* Unless where new things necessitate new terms, he will avoid an unusual word as a rock. It must have been among the earliest lessons of his youth that the breach of this precept—at all times hazardous—becomes ridiculous in the topics of ordinary conversation. There remains but one other point of distinction possible, and this must be, and in fact is, the true cause of the impression made on us. It is the unpremeditated and evidently habitual *arrangement* of his words, grounded on the habit of foreseeing in each integral part, or (more plainly) in every sentence, the whole that he then intends to communicate. However irregular and desultory his talk, there is *method* in the fragments.

Listen, on the other hand, to an ignorant man, though perhaps shrewd and able in his particular calling, whether he be describing or relating. We immediately perceive, that his memory alone is called into action; and that the objects and events recur in the narration in the same order, and with the same accompaniments, however accidental or impertinent, as they had first occurred to the narrator. The necessity of taking breath, the efforts of recollection, and the abrupt rectification of its failures, produce all his pauses; and with exception of the "*and then,*" the "*and there,*" and the still less significant "*and so,*" they constitute likewise all his connections.

Our discussion, however, is confined to method as employed in the formation of the understanding, and in the constructions of science and literature. It would indeed be superfluous to attempt a proof of its importance in the business and economy of active or domestic life. From the cotter's hearth or the workshop of the artisan to the palace of the arsenal, the first merit, that which admits neither substitute nor equivalent, is, that *every thing is in its place.* Where this charm is wanting, every other merit either loses its name, or becomes an additional ground of accusation and regret. Of one by whom it is eminently possessed, we say, proverbially, he is like clock-work. The resemblance extends beyond the point of regularity, and yet falls short of the truth. Both do, indeed, at once divide and announce the silent and otherwise indistinguishable lapse of time. But the man of methodical industry and honourable pursuits does more; he realizes its ideal divisions, and gives a character and individuality to its moments. If the idle are described as killing time, he may be justly said to call it into life and moral being, while he makes it the distinct object not only of the consciousness but of the conscience. He organizes the hours and gives them a soul; and that, the very essence of which is to fleet away, and evermore *to have been,* he takes up into his own permanence, and communicates to it the imperishableness of a spiritual nature. Of the good and faithful servant, whose energies, thus directed, are thus methodized, it is less truly affirmed that he lives in time, than that time lives in him. His days, months, and years, as the stops and punctual marks in the records of duties performed, will survive the wreck of worlds, and remain extant when time itself shall be no more.

But as the importance of method in the duties of social life is incomparably greater, so are its practical elements proportionably obvious, and such as relate to the will far more than to the understanding. Henceforward, therefore, we contemplate its bearings on the latter.

The difference between the products of a well disciplined

and those of an uncultivated understanding, in relation to what we will now venture to call the *Science of Method*, is often and admirably exhibited by our great dramatist. We scarcely need refer our readers to the Clown's evidence, in the first scene of the second act of "Measure for Measure," or to the Nurse in "Romeo and Juliet." But not to leave the position, without an instance to illustrate it, we will take the "easy-yielding" Mrs. Quickly's relation of the circumstances of Sir John Falstaff's debt to her:—

> *Falstaff.* What is the gross sum that I owe thee?
> *Mrs. Quickly.* Marry, if thou wert an honest man, thyself and the money too. Thou didst swear to me upon a parcel-gilt goblet, sitting in my Dolphin chamber, at the round table, by a sea-coal fire, on Wednesday in Whitsun week, when the prince broke thy head for liking his father to a singing-man of Windsor—thou didst swear to me then, as I was washing thy wound, to marry me and make me my lady thy wife. Canst thou deny it? Did not goodwife Keech, the butcher's wife, come in then and call me gossip Quickly?—coming in to borrow a mess of vinegar: telling us she had a good dish of prawns—whereby thou didst desire to eat some—whereby I told thee they were ill for a green wound, &c., &c., &c.
>
> *Henry IV, 2nd pt., Act II, Sc. i*

And this, be it observed, is so far from being carried beyond the bounds of a fair imitation, that "the poor soul's" thoughts and sentences are more closely interlinked than the truth of nature would have required, but that the connections and sequence, which the habit of method can alone give, have in this instance a substitute in the fusion of passion. For the absence of method, which characterizes the uneducated, is occasioned by an habitual submission of the understanding to mere events and images as such, and independent of any power in the mind to classify or appropriate them. The general accompaniments of time and place are the only relations which persons of this class appear to regard in their statements. As this constitutes *their* leading feature, the contrary excellence, as distinguishing the well-educated man, must be referred to the contrary habit. METHOD, therefore, becomes natural to the mind which has been accustomed to contemplate not *things* only, or for their own sake alone, but likewise and chiefly the *relations* of things, either their relations to each other, or to the observer, or to the state and apprehension of the hearers. To enumerate and analyze these relations, with the conditions under which alone they are discoverable, is to teach the science of method.

The enviable results of this science, when knowledge has been ripened into those habits which at once secure and evince its possession, can scarcely be exhibited more forcibly as well as more pleasingly, than by contrasting with the former extract from Shakspere the narration given by Hamlet to Horatio of the occurrences during his proposed transportation to England, and the events that interrupted his voyage.

> *Ham.* Sir, in my heart there was a kind of fighting
> That would not let me sleep: methought I lay
> Worse than the mutines in the bilboes. Rashly,
> And prais'd be rashness for it—*Let us know,*
> *Our indiscretion sometimes serves us well,*
> *When our deep plots do pall: and that should teach us,*
> *There's a divinity that shapes our ends,*
> *Rough-hew them how we will.*
> *Hor.* That is most certain.
> *Ham.* Up from my cabin,
> My sea-gown scarf'd about me, in the dark
> Grop'd I to find out them; had my desire,
> Finger'd their packet; and, in fine, withdrew
> To mine own room again: making so bold,
> *My fears forgetting manners,* to unseal
> Their grand commission; where I found, Horatio,
> O royal knavery! an exact command,
> *Larded with many several sorts of reasons,*
> *Importing Denmark's health, and England's too,*
> With, ho! such bugs and goblins in *my* life,
> That on the supervise, no leisure bated,
> No, not to stay the grinding of the axe,
> My head should be struck off!
> *Hor.* Is't possible?
> *Ham.* Here's the commission.—Read it at more leisure.
>
> *Act V, Sc. ii*

Here the events, with the circumstances of time and place, are all stated with equal compression and rapidity, not one introduced which could have been omitted without injury to the intelligibility of the whole process. If any tendency is discoverable, as far as the mere facts are in question, it is the tendency to omission; and, accordingly, the reader will observe that the attention of the narrator is afterwards called back to one material circumstance, which he was hurrying by, by a direct question from the friend to whom the story is communicated, "How WAS THIS SEALED?" But by a trait which is indeed peculiarly characteristic of Hamlet's mind, ever disposed to generalize, and meditative to excess (but which, with due abatement and reduction, is distinctive of every powerful and methodizing intellect), all the digressions and enlargements consist of reflections, truths, and principles of general and permanent interest, either directly expressed or disguised in playful satire.

> I sat me down:
> Devis'd a new commission; wrote it fair.
> *I once did hold it, as our statists do,*
> *A baseness to write fair, and labour'd much*
> *How to forget that learning;* but, sir, now
> It did me yeoman's service. Wilt thou know
> The effect of what I wrote?
> *Hor.* Aye, good my lord.
> *Ham.* An earnest conjuration from the king,
> As England was his faithful tributary;
> *As love between them, like the palm, might flourish;*
> *As peace should still her wheaten garland wear,*
> *And many such like As'es of great charge—*
> That on the view and knowing of these contents
> He should the bearers put to sudden death,
> Not shriving time allowed.
> *Hor.* How was this seal'd?
> *Ham.* Why, even in that was heaven ordinant.
> I had my father's signet in my purse,
> Which was the model of that Danish seal:
> Folded the writ up in form of the other;
> Subscrib'd it; gave't the impression; plac'd it safely,
> The changeling never known. Now, the next day
> Was our sea-fight; and what to this was sequent,
> Thou knowest already.
> *Hor.* So Guildenstern and Rosencrantz go to't?
> *Ham.* Why, man, they did make love to this employment.
> They are not near my conscience: their defeat
> Doth by their own insinuation grow.
> *'Tis dangerous when the baser nature comes*
> *Between the pass and fell incensed points*
> *Of mighty opposites.*

It would, perhaps be sufficient to remark of the preceding

passage, in connection with the humorous specimen of narration,

Fermenting o'er with frothy circumstance,

in "Henry IV," that if overlooking the different value of *matter* in each, we considered the *form* alone, we should find both *immethodical;* Hamlet from the excess, Mrs. Quickly from the want, of reflection and generalization; and that method, therefore, must result from the due mean or balance between our passive impressions and the mind's own reaction on the same. (Whether this reaction does not suppose or imply a primary act positively *originating* in the mind itself, and prior to the object in order of nature, though co-instantaneous in its manifestation, will be hereafter discussed.) But we had a further purpose in thus contrasting these extracts from our "myriad-minded bard," (μυριονοῦς ἄνηρ). We wished to bring forward, each for itself, these two elements of method, or (to adopt an arithmetical term) its two main *factors.*

Instances of the want of generalization are of no rare occurrence in real life; and the narrations of Shakspere's Hostess and the Tapster differ from those of the ignorant and unthinking in general by their superior humour, the poet's own gift and infusion, not by their want of Method, which is not greater than we often meet with in that class of which they are the dramatic representatives. Instances of the opposite fault, arising from the excess of generalization and reflection in minds of the opposite class, will, like the minds themselves, occur less frequently in the course of our own personal experience. Yet they will not have been wanting to our readers, nor will they have passed unobserved, though the great poet himself (ὁ τὴν ἑαυτοῦ ψυχὴν ὡσεὶ ὕλήν τινα ἀσώματον μορφαῖς ποικιλαῖς μορφώσας*) has more conveniently supplied the illustrations. To complete, therefore, the purpose aforementioned, that of presenting each of the two components as separately as possible, we chose an instance in which, by the surplus of its own

---

*(*Translation.*)—He that moulded his own soul, as some incorporeal material, into various forms.

Themistius

activity, Hamlet's mind disturbs the arrangement, of which that very activity had been the cause and impulse.

Thus exuberance of mind, on the one hand, interferes with the *forms* of Method; but sterility of mind, on the other, wanting the spring and impulse to mental action, is wholly destructive of Method itself. For in attending too exclusively to the relations which the past or passing events and objects bear to general truth, and the moods of his own Thought, the most intelligent man is sometimes in danger of overlooking that other relation in which they are likewise to be placed to the apprehension and sympathies of his hearers. His discourse appears like soliloquy intermixed with dialogue. But the uneducated and unreflecting talker overlooks *all* mental relations, both logical and psychological; and consequently precludes all Method that is not purely accidental. Hence the nearer the things and incidents in time and place, the more distant, disjointed, and impertinent to each other, and to any common purpose, will they appear in his narration; and this from the want of a *staple*, or *starting-post*, in the narrator himself; from the absence of *the leading Thought*, which, borrowing a phrase from the nomenclature of legislation, we may not inaptly call the INITIATIVE. On the contrary, where the habit of Method is present and effective, things the most remote and diverse in time, place, and outward circumstance, are brought into mental contiguity and succession, the more striking as the less expected. But while we would impress the necessity of this habit, the illustrations adduced give proof that in undue preponderance, and when the prerogative of the mind is stretched into despotism, the discourse may degenerate into the grotesque or the fantastical.

With what a profound insight into the constitution of the human soul is this exhibited to us in the character of the Prince of Denmark, where flying from the sense of reality, and seeking a reprieve from the pressure of its duties in that ideal activity, the overbalance of which, with the consequent indisposition to action, is his disease, he compels the reluctant good sense of the high yet healthful-minded Horatio, to follow him in his wayward meditation amid the graves! "To what base uses we may return, Horatio! Why may not imagination trace the noble dust of Alexander, till he find **it** stopping a bung-hole? HOR. 'Twere to consider too curiously to consider so. HAM. No, faith, not a jot; but to follow him thither with modesty enough and likelihood to lead it. As thus: Alexander died, Alexander was buried, Alexander returneth to dust—the dust is earth; of earth we make loam: and why of that loam, whereto he was converted, might they not stop a beer-barrel?

> Imperial Caesar, dead and turn'd to clay,
> Might stop a hole to keep the wind away!"

But let it not escape our recollection, that when the objects thus connected are proportionate to the connecting energy, relatively to the real, or at least to the desirable sympathies of mankind; it is from the same character that we derive the genial method in the famous soliloquy, "To be? or not to be?" which, admired as it is, and has been, has yet received only the first-fruits of the admiration due to it.

We have seen that from the confluence of innumerable impressions in each moment of time the mere passive memory must needs tend to confusion—a rule, the seeming exceptions to which (the thunder-bursts in "Lear," for instance) are really confirmations of its truth. For, in many instances, the predominance of some mighty Passion takes the place of the guiding Thought, and the result presents the method of Nature, rather than the habit of the Individual. For Thought, Imagination (and we may add Passion), are, in their very essence, the first, connective, the latter, co-adunative; and it has been shown, that if the excess lead to Method misapplied, and to connections of the moment, the absence, or marked deficiency, either precludes Method altogether, both form and substance, or (as the following extract will exemplify) retains the outward form only.

> My liege and madam, to expostulate
> What majesty should be, what duty is,
> Why day is day, night night, and time is time,
> Were nothing but to waste night, day and time.
> Therefore—since brevity is the soul of wit,
> And tediousness the limbs and outward flourishes,
> I will be brief. Your noble son is mad:
> Mad call I it—for to define true madness,
> What is't, but to be nothing else but mad?
> But let that go.
>   *Queen.* More matter with less art.
>   *Pol.* Madam! I swear, I use no art at all

That he is mad, 'tis true: 'tis true, 'tis pity:
And pity 'tis, 'tis true (a foolish figure!
But farewell it, for I will use no art).
Mad let us grant him then: and now remains,
That we find out the cause of this effect,
Or rather say the cause of this defect:
For this effect defective comes by cause.
Thus it remains, and the remainder thus
Perpend!   *Hamlet, Act II, Sc. ii*

Does not the irresistible sense of the ludicrous in this
flourish of the soul-surviving body of Old Polonius's intellect,
not less than in the endless confirmations and most undeniable matters of fact, of Tapster Pompey or "the hostess
of the tavern" prove to our feelings, even before the word
is found which presents the truth to our understandings,
that confusion and formality are but the opposite poles of
the same null-point?

It is Shakspere's peculiar excellence, that throughout
the whole of his splendid picture gallery (the reader will
excuse the confessed inadequacy of this metaphor), we find
individuality everywhere, mere portrait nowhere. In all his
various characters, we still feel ourselves communing with
the same human nature, which is everywhere present as the
vegetable sap in the branches, sprays, leaves, buds, blossoms,
and fruits, their shapes, tastes, and odours. Speaking of the
effect, *i.e.* his works themselves, we may define the excellence of *their* method as consisting in that just proportion,
that union and interpenetration of the universal and the
particular, which must ever pervade all works of decided
genius and true science. For Method implies a *progressive
transition*, and it is the meaning of the word in the original
language. The Greek $M\acute{\epsilon}\theta o\delta o\varsigma$, is literally *a way*, or *path of
Transit*. Thus we extol the Elements of Euclid, or Socrates'
discourse with the slave in the Menon, as *methodical*, a term
which no one who holds himself bound to think or speak
correctly would apply to the alphabetical order or arrangement of a common dictionary. But as, without continuous
transition, there can be no Method, so without a pre-con-
ception there can be no transition with continuity. The
term, Method, cannot therefore, otherwise than by abuse,
be applied to a mere dead arrangement, containing in itself
no principle of progression.

AIDS TO REFLECTION

From

INTRODUCTORY APHORISMS

Aphorism I

In philosophy equally as in poetry, it is the highest and most useful prerogative of genius to produce the strongest impressions of novelty, while it rescues admitted truths from the neglect caused by the very circumstance of their universal admission. Extremes meet. Truths, of all others the most awful and interesting, are too often considered as *so* true, that they lose all the power of truth, and lie bed-ridden in the dormitory of the soul, side by side with the most despised and exploded errors.

Aphorism II

There is one sure way of giving freshness and importance to the most *common-place* maxims—that of *reflecting* on them in direct reference to our own state and conduct, to our own past and future being.

Aphorism III

To restore a common-place truth to its first *uncommon* lustre, you need only *translate* it into action. But to do this, you must have *reflected* on its truth.

Aphorism IX

Life is the one universal soul, which, by virtue of the enlivening BREATH, and the informing WORD, all organized bodies have in common, each *after its kind*. This, therefore, all animals possess, and man as an animal. But, in addition to this, God transfused into man a higher gift, and specially imbreathed:—even a living (that is, self-subsisting)

Q

soul, a soul having its life in itself. "And man became a living soul." He did not merely *possess* it, he *became* it. It was his proper *being*, his truest *self*, *the* man *in* the man. None then, not one of human kind, so poor and destitute, but there is provided for him, even in his present state, *a house not built with hands*. Aye, and spite of the philosophy (falsely so called) which mistakes the causes, the conditions, and the occasions of our becoming *conscious* of certain truths and realities for the truths and realities themselves—a house gloriously furnished. Nothing is wanted but the eye, which is the light of this house, the light which is the eye of this soul. This *seeing* light, this *enlightening* eye, is Reflection.* It is more, indeed, than is ordinarily meant by that word; but it is what a Christian ought to mean by it, and to know too, whence it first came, and still continues to come—of what light even this light is *but* a reflection. This, too, is THOUGHT; and all thought is but unthinking that does not flow out of this, or tend towards it.

Aphorism XI

An hour of solitude passed in sincere and earnest prayer, or the conflict with, and conquest over, a single passion or "subtle *bosom* sin," will teach us more of thought, will more effectually awaken the *faculty*, and form the *habit*, of reflection, than a year's study in the schools without them.

Aphorism XII

In a world, the opinions of which are drawn from outside shows, many things may be *paradoxical*, (that is, contrary to the common notion) and nevertheless true: nay, *because* they are true. How should it be otherwise, as long as the imagination of the Worldling is wholly occupied by surfaces, while the Christian's thoughts are fixed on the substance, that which *is* and abides, and which, *because* it

---

*The "*dianoia*" of St. John, I Ep. v, 20, inaccurately rendered "understanding" in our translation. To exhibit the full force of the Greek word, we must say, *a power of discernment by Reason*.

is the substance,* the outward senses cannot recognize. Tertullian had good reason for his assertion, that the simplest Christian (if indeed a Christian) knows more than the most accomplished irreligious philosopher.

Aphorism XIII

Never yet did there exist a full faith in the Divine Word (by whom *light*, as well as immortality, was brought into the world), which did not expand the intellect, while it purified the heart;—which did not multiply the aims and objects of the understanding, while it fixed and simplified those of the desires and passions.

Comment

If acquiescence without insight; if warmth without light; if an immunity from doubt, given and guaranteed by a resolute ignorance; if the habit of *taking for granted* the words of a catechism, remembered or forgotten; if a mere *sensation* of positiveness substituted—I will not say, for the *sense* of *certainty*; but—for that calm assurance, the very means and conditions of which it supersedes; if a belief that seeks the darkness, and yet strikes no root, immovable as the limpet from the rock, and like the limpet, fixed there by mere force of adhesion; if these suffice to make men Christians, in what sense could the apostle affirm that believers receive, not indeed worldly wisdom, that comes to nought, but the wisdom of God, that we might *know and comprehend* the things that are freely given to us of God? On what grounds could he denounce the sincerest *fervour* of spirit as *defective*, where it does not likewise bring forth fruits in the UNDERSTANDING?

Quod stat subtus, that which stands *beneath*, and (as it were) supports, the appearance. In a language like ours, where so many words are derived from other languages, there are few modes of instruction more useful or more amusing than that of accustoming young people to seek for the etymology, or primary meaning, of the words they use. There are cases, in which more knowledge of more value may be conveyed by the history of a *word*, than by the history of a campaign.

Aphorism XXV

Woe to the man, who will believe neither power, freedom, nor morality; because he nowhere finds either entire, or unmixed with sin, thraldom and infirmity. In the natural and intellectual realms, we distinguish what we cannot separate; and in the moral world, we must distinguish *in order to* separate. Yea, in the clear distinction of good from evil the process of separation commences.

Comment

It was customary with religious men in former times, to make a rule of taking every morning some text, or aphorism,* for their occasional meditation during the day, and thus to fill up the intervals of their attention to business. I do not point it out for imitation, as knowing too well, how apt these self-imposed rules are to degenerate into superstition or hollowness; otherwise I would have recommended the following as the first exercise.

Aphorism XXVI

It is a dull and obtuse mind, that must divide in order to distinguish; but it is a still worse, that distinguishes in order to divide. In the former, we may contemplate the

---

*In accordance with a preceding remark, on the use of etymology in disciplining the youthful mind to thoughtful habits, and as consistent with the title of this work, "Aids to Reflection," I shall offer no apology for the following and similar notes:

Aphorism, determinate position, from the Greek, *ap*, from; and *horizein*, to bound or limit; whence our horizon.—In order to get the full sense of a word, we should first present to our minds the visual image that forms its primary meaning. Draw lines of different colours round the different counties of England, and then cut out each separately, as in the common play-maps that children take to pieces and put together—so that each district can be contemplated apart from the rest, as a whole in itself. This twofold act of circumscribing, and detaching, when it is exerted by the mind on subjects of reflection and reason, is to *aphorize*, and the result an *aphorism*.

source of superstition and idolatry; in the latter, of schism, heresy, and a seditious and sectarian spirit.

From

REFLECTIONS . . . ON SENSIBILITY

Lastly, where Virtue is, Sensibility is the ornament and becoming Attire of Virtue. On certain occasions it may almost be said to *become* Virtue. But Sensibility and all the amiable qualities may likewise become, and too often *have* become, the panders of Vice and the instruments of Seduction.

So must it needs be with all qualities that have their rise only in *parts* and *fragments* of our nature. A man of warm passions may sacrifice half his estate to rescue a friend from prison; for he is naturally sympathetic, and the more social *part* of his nature happened to be uppermost. The same man shall afterwards exhibit the same disregard of money in an attempt to seduce that friend's wife or daughter.

All the evil achieved by Hobbes, and the whole School of Materialists will appear inconsiderable, if it be compared with the mischief effected and occasioned by the sentimental Philosophy of STERNE, and his numerous imitators. The vilest appetites and the most remorseless inconstancy towards their objects, acquired the titles of *the Heart, the irresistible Feelings, the too tender Sensibility;* and if the Frosts of Prudence, the icy chains of Human Law thawed and vanished at the genial warmth of Human *Nature,* who *could help it?* It was an amiable Weakness!

About this time, too, the profanation of the word Love, rose to its height. The French Naturalists, Buffon and others, borrowed it from the sentimental Novelists: the Swedish and English Philosophers took the contagion; and the Muse of Science condescended to seek admission into the Saloons of Fashion and Frivolity, *rouged* like a harlot, and with the harlot's wanton leer. I know not how the Annals of Guilt could be better forced into the service of Virtue, than by such a Comment on the present paragraph, as would be afforded by a selection from the sentimental correspondence produced in Courts of Justice within the last thirty years, fairly translated into the true meaning of the words, and the actual Object and Purpose of the infamous writers.

Do you in good earnest aim at Dignity of Character? By all the treasures of a peaceful mind, by all the charms of an open countenance, I conjure you, O youth! turn away from those who live in the Twilight between Vice and Virtue. Are not Reason, Discrimination, Law, and deliberate Choice, the distinguishing Characters of Humanity? Can aught, then, worthy of a human Being, proceed from a Habit of Soul, which would exclude all these and (to borrow a metaphor from Paganism) prefer the den of Trophonius to the Temple and Oracles of the God of Light? Can any thing *manly*, I say, proceed from those, who for Law and Light would substitute shapeless feelings, sentiments, impulses, which as far as they differ from the vital workings in the brute animals, owe the difference to their former connexion with the proper Virtues of Humanity; as dendrites derive the outlines, that constitute their value above other clay-stones, from the casual neighbourhood and pressure of the plants, the names of which they assume? Remember, that Love itself in its highest earthly Bearing, as the ground of the marriage union, becomes Love by an inward FIAT of the Will, by a completing and sealing act of Moral Election, and lays claim to permanence only under the form of DUTY.

From

MORAL AND RELIGIOUS APHORISMS

And would it were my lot to meet with a Critic, who, in the might of his own Convictions, and with arms of equal point and efficiency from his own forge, would come forth as my assailant; or who, as a friend to my purpose, would set forth the objections to the matter and pervading Spirit of these Aphorisms, and the accompanying Elucidations. Were it my task to form the mind of a young man of talent, desirous to establish his opinions and belief on solid principles, and in the light of distinct understanding,—I would commence his theological studies, or, at least, that most important part of them respecting the aids which Religion promises in our attempts to realize the ideas of Morality, by bringing together all the passages scattered throughout the writings of Swift and Butler, that bear on Enthusiasm, Spiritual Operations, and pretences to the Gifts of the Spirit, with the whole train of New Lights, Raptures, Experiences, and the like. For all that the richest Wit, in intimate union with profound Sense and steady Observation, can supply on these topics, is to be found in the works of these satirists; though unhappily alloyed with much that can only tend to pollute the imagination.

From

APHORISMS ON SPIRITUAL RELIGION

Aphorism VI

BISHOP HACKET

[When every man is his own end, all things will come to a bad end. Blessed were those days, when every man thought himself rich and fortunate by the good success of the public wealth and glory. We want public souls, we want them. I speak it with compassion: there is no sin and abuse in the world that affects my thought so much. Every man thinks, that he is a whole Commonwealth in his private family. *Omnes quae sua sunt quaerunt.* All seek their own.]

Comment

Selfishness is common to all ages and countries. In all ages Self-seeking is the Rule, and Self-sacrifice the Exception. But if to seek our private advantage in harmony with, and by the furtherance of, the public prosperity, and to derive a portion of our happiness from sympathy with the prosperity of our fellow-men—if this be Public Spirit, it would be morose and querulous to pretend that there is any want of it in this country and at the present time. On the contrary, the number of "public souls" and the general readiness to contribute to the public good, in science and in religion, in patriotism and in philanthropy, stand prominent among the characteristics of this and the preceding generation. The habit of referring actions and opinions to fixed laws; convictions rooted in principles; thought, insight, system;—these, had the good Bishop lived in our times, would have been his *desiderata*, and the theme of his complaints.—"We want *thinking* Souls, we *want them*."

From

ON THE DIFFERENCE IN KIND OF REASON
AND THE UNDERSTANDING

Scheme of the Argument

On the contrary, Reason is the Power of Universal and necessary Convictions, the Source and Substance of Truths above Sense, and having their evidence in themselves. Its presence is always marked by the *necessity* of the position affirmed: this necessity being *conditional*, when a truth of Reason is applied to Facts of Experience, or to the rules and maxims of the Understanding; but *absolute*, when the subject matter is itself the growth or offspring of the Reason. Hence arises a distinction in the Reason itself, derived from the different mode of applying it, and from the objects to which it is directed: accordingly as we consider one and the same gift, now as the ground of formal principles, and now as the origin of *ideas*. Contemplated distinctively in reference to *formal* (or abstract) truth, it is the *speculative* reason; but in reference to *actual* (or moral) truth, as the fountain of ideas, and the *light* of the conscience, we name it the *practical* reason. Whenever by self-subjection to this universal light, the will of the individual, the *particular* will, has become a will of reason, the man is regenerate: and reason is then the *spirit* of the regenerated man, whereby the person is capable of a quickening inter-communion with the Divine Spirit. And herein consists the mystery of Redemption, that this has been rendered possible for us. *And so it is written: the first man Adam was made a living soul, the last Adam a quickening Spirit.* (1 Cor. xv, 45.) We need only compare the passages in the writings of the Apostles Paul and John, concerning the *spirit* and spiritual Gifts, with those in the Proverbs and in the Wisdom of Solomon respecting *reason*, to be convinced that the terms are synonymous. In this at once most comprehensive and most appropriate acceptation of the word, reason is pre-eminently spiritual, and a spirit, even *our* spirit, through an effluence of the same grace by which we are privileged to say Our Father!

On the other hand, the Judgements of the Understanding are binding only in relation to the objects of our Senses, which we *reflect* under the forms of the Understanding. It is, as Leighton rightly defines it, "the faculty judging according to sense." Hence we add the epithet *human*, without tautology: and speak of the *human* understanding, in disjunction from that of beings higher or lower than man. But there is, in this sense, no *human* reason. There neither is nor can be but one reason, one and the same: even the light that lighteth every man's individual Understanding (*Discursus*), and thus maketh it a reasonable understanding, *discourse of reason—one only*, yet *manifold: it goeth through all understanding, and remaining in itself regenerateth all other powers*. The same writer calls it likewise *an influence from the Glory of the Almighty*, this being one of the names of the Messiah, as the *Logos*, or co-eternal Filial Word. And most noticeable for its coincidence is a fragment of Heraclitus, as I have indeed already noticed elsewhere;—"To discourse rationally it behoves us to derive strength from that which is common to all men: for all human Understandings are nourished by the one DIVINE WORD."

Beasts, we have said, partake of understanding. If any man deny this, there is a ready way of settling the question. Let him give a careful perusal to Hüber's two small volumes, on bees and ants (especially the latter), and to Kirby and Spence's Introduction to Entomology; and one or other of two things must follow. He will either change his opinion as irreconcilable with the facts; or he must deny the facts, which yet I cannot suppose, inasmuch as the denial would be tantamount to the no less extravagant than uncharitable assertion, that Hüber, and the several eminent naturalists, French and English, Swiss, German, and Italian, by whom Hüber's observations and experiments have been repeated and confirmed, had all conspired to impose a series of falsehoods and fairy-tales on the world. I see no way at least, by which he can get out of this dilemma, but by over-leaping the admitted rules and fences of all legitimate discussion, and either transferring to the word, Understanding, the definition already appropriated to Reason, or defining Understanding *in genere* by the *specific* and *accessional* perfections which the *human* understanding derives from its co-existence with reason and free-will in the same individual person; in plainer words, from its being exercised by a self-conscious and responsible creature. And, after all, the supporter of Harrington's position would have a right to ask him, by what other name he would designate the faculty in the instances referred to? If it be not Understanding, what is it?

In no former part of this volume has the author felt the same anxiety to obtain a patient attention. For he does not hesitate to avow, that on his success in establishing the validity and importance of the distinction between Reason and Understanding, he rests his hopes of carrying the reader along with him through all that is to follow. . . .

Understanding

1. Understanding is discursive.

2. The Understanding in all its judgments refers to some other Faculty as its ultimate Authority.

3. Understanding is the Faculty of *Reflection*.

Reason

1. Reason is fixed.

2. The Reason in all its decisions appeals to itself, as the ground and *substance* of their truth. (Hebrews vi, 13.)

3. Reason of Contemplation. Reason indeed is much nearer to SENSE than to Understanding: for Reason (says our great HOOKER) is a direct aspect of Truth, an inward Beholding, having a similar relation to the Intelligible or Spiritual, as SENSE has to the Material or Phenomenal.

*   *   *

[POPULAR LITERATURE]

But above all, the whole world almost of minds, as far as we regard intellectual efforts, may be divided into two classes of the Busy-Indolent and Lazy-Indolent. To both alike all Thinking is painful, and all attempts to rouse them to think, whether in the re-examination of their existing convictions, or for the reception of new light, are irritating. "It *may* all be very deep and clever; but really one ought to be quite sure of it before one wrenches one's brain to find out what it is. I take up a Book as a Companion, with whom I can have an easy cheerful chit-chat on what we both know beforehand, or else matters of fact. In our leisure hours we have a right to relaxation and amusement."

Well! but in their *studious* hours, when their bow is to be bent, when they are *apud Musas*, or amidst the Muses? Alas! it is just the same! The same craving for *amusement*, that is, to be away from the Muses! for relaxation, that is, the unbending of a bow which in fact had never been strung! There are two ways of obtaining their applause. The first is: Enable them to reconcile in one and the same occupation the love of Sloth and the hatred of Vacancy! Gratify indolence, and yet save them from *ennui*—in plain English, from themselves! For, spite of their antipathy to *dry* reading, the keeping company with themselves is, after all, the insufferable annoyance: and the true secret of their dislike to a work of thought and inquiry lies in its tendency to make them acquainted with their own permanent Being. The other road to their favour is, to introduce to them their own thoughts and predilections, tricked out in the *fine* language, in which it would gratify their vanity to express them in their own conversation, and with which they can imagine themselves *showing off*: and this (as has been elsewhere remarked) is the characteristic difference between the second-rate writers of the last two or three generations, and the same class under Elizabeth and the Stuarts. In the latter we find the most far-fetched and singular thoughts in the simplest and most native language; in the former, the most obvious and common-place thoughts in the most far-fetched and motley language. But lastly, and as the *sine qua non* of their patronage, a sufficient arc must be left for the Reader's mind to *oscillate* in—freedom of choice,

> To make the shifting cloud be what you please,

save only where the attraction of curiosity determines the line of motion. The attention must not be fastened down: and this every work of genius, not simply narrative, must do before it can be justly appreciated.

In former times a *popular* work meant one that adapted the *results* of studious meditation or scientific research to the capacity of the people, presenting in the concrete, by instances and examples, what had been ascertained in the abstract and by discovery of the Law. *Now*, on the other hand, that is a popular work which gives back to the people their own errors and prejudices, and flatters the many by creating them, under the title of THE PUBLIC, into a supreme and inappellable Tribunal of intellectual Excellence. PS. In a continuous work, the frequent insertion and length of Notes would need an Apology: in a book like this of Aphorisms and detached Comments none is necessary, it being understood beforehand, that the sauce and the garnish are to occupy the greater part of the dish.

[LANGUAGE]

I would not lose any opportunity of impressing on the mind of my youthful readers the important truth that language (as the embodied and articulated Spirit of the Race, as the growth and emanation of a People, and not the work of any individual wit or will) is often inadequate, sometimes deficient, but never false or delusive. We have only to master the true origin and original import of any native and abiding word, to find in it, if not the *solution* of the facts expressed by it, yet a finger-mark pointing to the road on which this solution is to be sought.

From

THE CONCLUSION

I have, I am aware, in this present work furnished occasion for a charge of having expressed myself with slight and irreverence of celebrated Names, especially of the late Dr. Paley. O, if I were fond and ambitious of literary honour, of public applause, how well content should I be to excite but one third of the admiration which, in my inmost being, I feel for the head and heart of Paley! And how gladly would I surrender all hope of contemporary praise, could I even approach to the incomparable grace, propriety, and persuasive facility of his writings! But on this very account I believe myself bound in conscience to throw the whole force of my intellect in the way of this triumphal car, on which the tutelary genius of modern Idolatry is borne, even at the risk of being crushed under the wheels! I have at this moment before my eyes the eighteenth of his Posthumous Discourses: the amount of which is briefly this,—that all the words and passages in the New Testament which express and contain the *peculiar* doctrines of Christianity, the paramount objects of the Christian Revelation, all those which speak so strongly of the value, benefit, and efficacy, of the death of Christ, assuredly mean *something;* but *what* they mean, nobody, it seems can tell! But doubtless we shall discover it, and be convinced that there is a substantial sense belonging to these words—in a future state! Is there an enigma, or an absurdity, in the Koran or the Vedas which might not be defended on the same pretence? A similar impression, I confess, was left on my mind by Dr. Magee's statement or exposition (*ad normam Grotianam*) of the doctrine of Redemption; and deeply did it disappoint the high expectations, sadly did it chill the fervid sympathy, which his introductory chapter, his manly and masterly disquisition on the sacrificial rites of Paganism, had raised in my mind.

And yet I cannot read the pages of Paley, here referred to, aloud, without the liveliest sense, how plausible and popular they will sound to the great majority of readers. Thousands of sober, and in their way pious, Christians, will echo the words, together with Magee's kindred interpretation of the death of Christ, and adopt the doctrine for their *Make-faith;* and why? It is feeble. And whatever is feeble is always plausible: for it favours mental indolence. It is feeble: and feebleness, in the disguise of confessing and condescending strength, is always popular. It flatters the reader by removing the apprehended distance between him and the superior author; and it flatters him still more by enabling him to transfer to himself, and to appropriate, this superiority; and thus to make his very weakness the mark and evidence of his strength. Ay, quoth the *rational* Christian —or with a sighing, self-soothing sound between an Ay and an Ah!—*I* am content to think, with the great Dr. Paley, and the learned Archbishop of Dublin——

Man of Sense! Dr. Paley *was* a great man, and Dr. Magee *is* a learned and exemplary prelate; but You do not *think* at all!   1823-5

CONFESSIONS OF AN INQUIRING
SPIRIT

(*Letters on the Inspiration of the Scriptures*)

From

LETTER III

Yet one other instance, and let this be the crucial test of the Doctrine. Say that the Book of Job throughout was dictated by an infallible Intelligence. Then re-peruse the book, and still, as you proceed, try to apply the tenet: try if you can even attach any sense or semblance of meaning to the speeches which you are reading. What! were the hollow truisms, the unsufficing half-truths, the false assumptions and malignant insinuations of the supercilious bigots, who corruptly defended the truth:—were the impressive facts, the piercing outcries, the pathetic appeals, and the close and powerful reasoning with which the poor sufferer —smarting at once from his wounds, and from the oil of vitriol which the orthodox *liars for God* were dropping into them—impatiently, but uprightly and holily, controverted this truth, while in will and in spirit he clung to it;—were both dictated by an infallible Intelligence?—Alas! if I may judge from the manner in which both indiscriminately are recited, quoted, appealed to, preached upon, by the *routiniers* of desk and pulpit, I cannot doubt that they think so,—or rather, without thinking, take for granted that so they are to think;—the more readily, perhaps, because the so thinking supersedes the necessity of all after-thought.

Farewell.

?1824

[NOTES ON ENGLISH DIVINES]

DONNE

Sermon xvii

O! compare this manhood of our Church divinity with the feeble dotage of the Paleyan school, the "natural" theology, or watchmaking scheme, that knows nothing of the maker but what can be proved out of the watch, the unknown nominative case of the verb impersonal *fit—et natura est;* the "it," in short, in "it rains," "it snows," "it is cold," and the like. When, after reading the biographies of Walton and his contemporaries, I reflect on the crowded congregations, on the thousands, who with intense interest came to their hour and two hour long sermons, I cannot but doubt the fact of any true progression, moral or intellectual, in the mind of the many. The tone, the matter, the anticipated sympathies in the sermons of an age form the best moral criterion of the character of that age.

FULLER

Next to Shakspere, I am not certain whether Thomas Fuller, beyond all other writers, does not excite in me the sense and emotion of the marvellous;—the degree in which any given faculty or combination of faculties is possessed and manifested, so far surpassing what one would have thought possible in a single mind, as to give one's admiration the flavour and quality of wonder! Wit was the stuff and substance of Fuller's intellect. It was the element, the earthen base, the material which he worked in, and this very circumstance has defrauded him of his due praise for the practical wisdom of the thoughts, for the beauty and variety of the truths, into which he shaped the stuff. Fuller was incomparably the most sensible, the least prejudiced, great man of an age that boasted a galaxy of great men.

He is a very voluminous writer, and yet in all his numerous volumes on so many different subjects, it is scarcely too much to say, that you will hardly find a page in which some one sentence out of every three does not deserve to be quoted for itself—as motto or as maxim. God bless thee, dear old man! may I meet with thee!—which is tantamount to—may I go to heaven!

July, 1829

JEREMY TAYLOR

Apology for Authorised and Set Forms of Liturgy
section xcii

Now here dear Jeremy Taylor begins to be himself again; for with all his astonishing complexity, yet versatile agility, of powers, he was too good and of too catholic a spirit to be a good polemic. Hence he so continually is now breaking, now varying, the thread of the argument: and hence he is so again and again forgetting that he is reasoning against an antagonist, and falls into conversation with him as a friend,—I might almost say, into the literary chit-chat and unwithholding frankness of a rich genius whose sands are seed-pearl. Of his controversies, those against Popery are the most powerful, because there he had subtleties and obscure reading to contend against; and his wit, acuteness, and omnifarious learning found stuff to work on. Those on Original Sin are the most eloquent. But in all alike it is the digressions, overgrowths, parenthetic *obiter et in transitu* sentences, and, above all, his anthropological reflections and experiences—(for example, the inimitable account of a religious dispute, from the first collision to the spark, and from the spark to the world in flames, in his Dissuasive from Popery),—these are the costly gems which glitter, loosely set, on the chain armour of his polemic Pegasus, that expands his wings chiefly to fly off from the field of battle, the stroke of whose hoof the very rock cannot resist, but beneath the stroke of which the opening rock sends forth a Hippo-crene. The work in which all his powers are confluent, in which deep, yet gentle, the full stream of his genius winds onward, and still forming peninsulas in its winding course— distinct parts that are only not each a perfect whole—or in less figurative style—(yet what language that does not partake of poetic eloquence can convey the characteristics of a poet and an orator?)—the work which I read with most admiration, but likewise with most apprehension and regret, is the "Liberty of Prophesying." If indeed, like some Thessalian drug, or the strong herb of Anticyra,

> that helps and harms,
> Which life and death have sealed with counter charms—

it could be administered by special prescription, it might do good service as a narcotic for zealotry, or a solvent for bigotry.

WATERLAND

A Vindication of Christ's Divinity

In initio.

It would be no easy matter to find a tolerably competent individual who more venerates the writings of Waterland than I do, and long have done. But still in how many pages do I not see reason to regret, that the total idea of the $4=3=1$,—of the adorable Tetractys, eternally self-manifested in the Triad, Father, Son, and Spirit,—was never in its cloudless unity present to him. Hence both he and Bishop Bull too often treat it as a peculiarity of positive religion, which is to be cleared of all contradiction to reason, and then, thus negatively qualified, to be actually received by an act of the mere will; *sit pro ratione voluntas.* Now, on the other hand, I affirm, that the article of the Trinity is religion, is reason, and its universal *formula;* and that there neither is, nor can be, any religion, any reason, but what is, or is an expansion of the truth of the Trinity; in short, that all other pretended religions, pagan or *pseudo*-Christian (for example, Sabellian, Arian, Socinian), are in themselves Atheism; though God forbid, that I should call or even think the men so denominated Atheists. I affirm a heresy often, but never dare denounce the holder a heretic.

On this ground only can it be made comprehensible how any honest and commonly intelligent man can withstand the proofs and sound logic of Bull and Waterland, that they failed in the first place to present the idea itself of the great doctrine which they so ably advocated. Take myself,

S.T.C., as a humble instance. I was never so befooled as to think that the author of the fourth Gospel, or that St. Paul, ever taught the Priestleyan Psilanthropism, or that Unitarianism (presumptuously, nay, absurdly so called), was the doctrine of the New Testament generally. But during the sixteen months of my aberration from the Catholic Faith, I presumed that the tenets of the divinity of Christ, the Redemption, and the like, were irrational, and that what was contradictory to reason could not have been revealed by the Supreme Reason. As soon as I discovered that these doctrines were not only consistent with reason, but themselves very reason, I returned at once to the literal interpretation of the Scriptures, and to the Faith.

As to Dr. Samuel Clarke, the fact is, every generation has its one or more over-rated men. Clarke was such in the reign of George I; Dr. Johnson eminently so in that of George III; Lord Byron being the star now in the ascendant.

ON THE CONSTITUTION OF
CHURCH AND STATE

[SELF-EDUCATION]

And now, friend! for the practical rules which I promised, or the means by which you may educate in yourself that state of mind which is most favourable to a true knowledge of both the worlds that *now are*, and to a right faith in the *world to come*.

I. Remember that whatever *is*, *lives*. A thing absolutely lifeless is inconceivable, except as a thought, image, a fancy, in some other being.

II. In every living form, the conditions of its *existence* are to be sought for in that which is *below* it; the grounds of its *intelligibility* in that which is *above* it.

III. Accustom your mind to distinguish the relations of things from the things themselves. Think often of the latter as independent of the former, in order that you may never think of the former apart from the latter, *i.e.* mistake mere relations for true and enduring realities: and with regard to *these* seek the solution of each in some higher reality. The contrary process leads demonstrably to atheism, and though you may not get quite so far, it is not well to be seen travelling on the road with your face towards it.

[VALUE OF THE ESTABLISHED CHURCH]

That the maxims of a pure morality, and those sublime truths of the divine unity and attributes, which a Plato found it hard to learn, and more difficult to reveal; that these should have become the almost hereditary property of childhood and poverty, of the hovel and the workshop; that even to the unlettered they sound as *common-place;* this is a phenomenon which must withhold all but minds of the most vulgar cast from undervaluing the services even of the pulpit and the reading-desk. Yet he who should *confine* the efficiency of an Established Church to these, can hardly be placed in a much higher rank of intellect. That to every parish throughout the kingdom there is transplanted a germ of civilisation; that in the remotest villages there is a nucleus, round which the capabilities of the place may crystallise and brighten; a model sufficiently superior to excite, yet sufficiently near to encourage and facilitate imitation; *this* unobtrusive, continuous agency of a Protestant Church Establishment, *this* it is, which the patriot and the philanthropist, who would fain unite the love of peace with the faith in the progressive amelioration of mankind, cannot estimate at too high a price. "It cannot be valued with the gold of Ophir, with the precious onyx, or the sapphire. No mention shall be made of coral or of pearls: for the price of wisdom is above rubies."

1830

HINTS TOWARDS THE FORMATION OF A MORE COMPREHENSIVE THEORY OF LIFE

[TENDENCY TO INDIVIDUATION]

Exclusively, therefore, for the purposes of *illustration,* I would take as an instance of the first step, the metals, those, namely, that are capable of permanent reduction. For, by the established laws of nomenclature, the others (as sodium, potassium, calcium, silicium, &c.) would be entitled to a class of their own, under the name of *bases*. It is long since the chemists have despaired of decomposing this class of bodies. They still remain, one and all, as elements or simple bodies, though, on the principles of the corpuscularian philosophy, nothing can be more improbable than that they really are such; and no reason has or can be assigned on the grounds of that system, why, in no one instance, the contrary has not been proved. But this is at once explained, if we assume them as the simplest form of unity, namely, the unity of powers and properties. For these, it is evident, may be endlessly modified, but can never be decomposed. If I were asked by a philosopher who had previously extended the attribute of Life to the *Byssus speciosa*, and even to the crustaceous matter, or outward bones of a lobster, &c., whether the ingot of gold expressed *life*, I should answer without hesitation, as the *ingot* of gold assuredly not, for its form is accidental and *ab extra;* it may be added to or detracted from without in the least affecting the nature, state, or properties in the specific matter of which the ingot consists: but as *gold*, as that special union of absolute and of relative gravity, ductility, and hardness, which, wherever they are found, constitute *gold*, I should answer no less fearlessly, in the affirmative. But I should further add, that of the two counteracting tendencies of nature, namely, that of *detachment* from the universal life, which universality is represented to us by gravitation, and that of *attachment* or reduction into it, this and the other noble metals represented the units in which the latter tendency, namely, that of identity with the life of nature, subsisted in the greatest overbalance over the former. It is the form of unity with the least degree of tendency to individuation.

Rising in the ascent, I should take, as illustrative of the second step, the various forms of crystals as a union, not of powers only, but of parts, and as the simplest forms of composition in the next narrowest sphere of affinity. Here the form, or apparent *quantity*, is manifestly the result of the *quality*, and the chemist himself not seldom admits them as infallible characters of the substances united in the whole of a given crystal.

In the first step, we had Life, as the mere *unity* of powers; in the second we have the simplest forms of *totality* evolved. The third step is presented to us in those vast formations, the tracing of which generically would form the science of Geology, or its history in the strict sense of the word, even as their description and diagnostics constitute its preliminaries.

*   *   *

In the lowest forms of the vegetable and animal world we perceive totality dawning into *individuation*, while in man, as the highest of the class, the individuality is not only perfected in its corporeal sense, but begins a new series beyond the appropriate limits of physiology. The tendency to individuation, more or less obscure, more or less obvious, constitutes the common character of all classes, as far as they maintain for themselves a distinction from the universal life of the planet; while the degrees, both of intensity and extension, to which this tendency is realized, form the species, and their ranks in the great scale of ascent and expansion.

[MAGNUM OPUS]

[EVOLUTION]

And here once for all, I beg leave to remark that I attach neither belief nor respect to the Theory, which supposes the human Race to have been gradually perfecting itself from the darkest Savagery, or still more boldly tracing us back to the bestial as to our Larva, contemplates Man as the last metamorphosis, the gay *Image*, of some lucky species of Ape or Baboon. Of the two hypotheses I should, indeed, greatly prefer the Lucretian of the Parturiency of our Mother Earth, some score thousands years ago, when the venerable Elder was yet in her Teens, and her human Litter sucked the milk then oozing from countless Breasts of warm and genial Mud. For between an hypothetical ἁπαξγινόμενον or single Incident or Event in a state and during an epoch if the Planet presumed in all respects different from its present condition, and the laws of Nature appropriate to the same, a difference, for the historic verity of which in a smaller extent the metals and their positions have been [thought?] to furnish a plausible argument—between a single and temporary Event, anterior of necessity to all actual experience, and an assertion of a universal process of Nature now existing (since there is the same reason for asserting the progression of every other race of animal from some lower species as of the human race) in contradiction to all experience, I can have no hesitation in preferring the former, that, for which Nothing can be said, to that *against* which Everything may be said. The History I find in my Bible is in perfect coincidence with the opinions which I should form on Grounds of Experience and Common Sense. But our belief that Man first appeared with all his faculties perfect and in full growth, the anticipation exercised by virtue of the supernatural act of Creation, in nowise contravenes or weakens the assertion that these faculties . . . in each succeeding Individual, born according to nature, must be preceded by a process of growth, and consequently a state of involution or latency, correspondent to each successive Moment of Development. A rule abstracted from uniform Results, or the Facet of a Sum put by the Master's indulgence at the head of the sum to be worked, may not only render the Boy's Task shorter and easier, but without such assistance he might never have mastered it or attained the experience, from which the Rule might [have been derived?].

TABLE TALK

Coleridge's voice "*like some great river*" swept "*into a continuous stream of eloquent dissertation, certainly the most novel, the most finely illustrated, and traversing the most spacious fields of thought by transitions the most just and logical, that it was possible to conceive.*" De Quincey's account—he is describing his first meeting with Coleridge in 1807 ("*Works,*" II, p. 54)—agrees with most of the earlier and later accounts, from Hazlitt's impressions and those of Wordsworth—"*like a majestic river*" again—to those of the young men who came to listen to the voice on Thursday evenings at Highgate thirty years later. It is a tragedy that this kind of monologue, first published with the ironical title of "*Table Talk,*" is the most difficult to memorize and preserve: and it is a great pity that his nephew's notes, the only record on a large scale, should have been mostly collected in the last few years of Coleridge's life. Nor was H. N. Coleridge an ideal editor for this purpose, since he tended to end off the sentences in his own very characteristic style, with round and easily foreseen terminations, whereas his uncle's periods were unfinished, or followed an unexpected course.

A number of more casual records exist. Some of these are represented first.

TABLE TALK

Recorded by

H. CRABB ROBINSON

[SHAKSPERE]

[COLERIDGE'S] remarks on Shakspere were singularly ingenious. S., he said, delighted in portraying characters
in which the intellectual powers were found in a pre-
eminent degree, while the moral faculties were wanting, at
the same time that he taught the superiority of moral greatness. Such is the contrast exhibited in Iago and Othello.
Iago's most marked feature is his delight in governing by
fraud and superior understanding the noble minded and
generous Moor. In Richard the 3ᵈ. cruelty is less the prominent trait than pride, to which a sense of personal
deformity gave a deadly venom. C., however, asserted his
belief that S. wrote hardly anything of this play besides
the character of Richard. He found the piece a stock play
and rewrote the parts which developed the hero's character.
He certainly did not write the scenes in which Lady Anne
yielded to the usurper's solicitations.—He considered "Peri-
cles" as illustrating the way in which S. handled a piece
he had to refit for representation. At first he proceeded with
indifference, now and then only troubling himself to put in
a thought or an image, but as he advanced he interested
himself in his employment, and the last two acts are almost
altogether by him.   1810

*

C. as we walked talked on Shakspere, particularly his
Fools. These he considered as supplying the place of the
ancient chorus. The ancient drama, he observed, is distinguished from the Shaksperian in this, that it exhibits
a sort of abstraction, not of character, but of idea. A certain
sentiment or passion was exhibited in all its purity, unmixed

with any thing that could interfere with its effect. Shakspere imitates life, mingled as we find it with joy and sorrow. We meet with characters who are, as it were, unfeeling spectators of the most passionate situations, constantly in life. The Fool serves to supply the place of some such uninterested person where all the characters besides have interest. The most genuine and real of S.'s Fools is in "Lear." In "Hamlet" the Fool is, as it were, divided into several parts, dispersed through the piece.   1811

[JOB]

This incomparable poem has been absurdly interpreted. Job, far from being the most patient, was the most impatient of men. He was rewarded for his impatience. His integrity and sincerity had their recompense because he was superior to the hypocrisy of his friends.   1812

Recorded by

MR. JUSTICE COLERIDGE

[EIGHTEENTH CENTURY POETS]

As we walked up Mr. Cambridge's meadows towards Twickenham, he criticised Johnson and Gray as poets, and did not seem to allow them high merit. The excellence of verse, he said, was to be untranslatable into any other words without detriment to the beauty of the passage;— the position of a single word could not be altered in Milton without injury. Gray's personifications, he said, were mere printer's devils' personifications—persons with a capital letter, abstract qualities with a small one. He thought Collins had more genius than Gray, who was a singular instance of a man of taste, poetic feeling, and fancy, without imagination.

*

Young, he said, was not a poet to be read through at once. His love of point and wit had often put an end to his pathos and sublimity; but there were parts in him which must be immortal. He [Mr. C.] loved to read a page of Young, and walk out to think of him.   1811

Recorded by

J. P. COLLIER

For my part I freely own that I have no title to the name of poet, according to my own definition of poetry. Many years ago a small volume of verses came out with my name: it was not my doing, but Cottle offered me £20, when I much wanted it, for some short pieces I had written at Cambridge, and I sold the manuscripts to him, but I declare that I had no notion, at the time, that they were meant for publication; my poverty, and not my will, consented. Cottle paid my poverty, and I was dubbed poet, almost before I knew whether I was in Bristol or in London. I met people in the streets who congratulated me upon being a poet, and that was the first notice I had of my new rank and dignity. I was to have had £20 for what Cottle bought, but I never received more than £15, and for this paltry sum I was styled poet by the reviewers, who fell foul of me for what they termed my bombast and buckram. Nevertheless 500 copies were sold, and a new edition being called for, I pleaded guilty to the charge of inflation and grandiloquence. But now, only see the contrast! Wordsworth has printed two poems of mine, but without my name, and again the reviewers have laid their claws upon me, and for what? Not for bombast and buckram—not for inflation and grandiloquence, but for mock simplicity; and now I am put down as the master of a school for the instruction of grown children in nursery rhymes.   1811

Recorded by

T. ALLSOP

[HANDICAP OF LANGUAGE]

I believe that processes of thought might be carried on independent and apart from spoken or written language. I do not in the least doubt, that if language had been denied or withheld from man, or that he had not discovered and improved that mode of intercommunication, thought, as thought, would have been a process more simple, more easy, and more perfect than the present, and would both have included and evolved other and better means for its own manifestations, than any that exist now.

[SUPERIORITY OF MEN OF LETTERS]

All men in power are jealous of the pre-eminence of men of letters; they feel, as towards them, conscious of inferior power, and a sort of misgiving that they are, indirectly, and against their own will, mere instruments and agents of higher intellects.

Men in power, for instance Lord Castlereagh, are conscious of inferiority, and are yet ashamed to own, even to themselves, the fact, which is only the more evident by their neglect of men of letters. So entirely was Mr. Pitt aware of this, that he would never allow of any intercourse with literary men of eminence; fearing, doubtless, that the charm which spell-bound his political adherents would, at least for the time, fail of its effect.

*

A single thought is that which it is from other thoughts, as a wave of the sea takes its form and shape from the waves which precede and follow it.

[LAISSEZ-FAIRE]

It is not uncommon for 100,000 *operatives* (mark this word, for words *in this sense* are things) to be out of employment at once in the cotton districts, and, thrown upon parochial relief, to be dependent upon hard-hearted taskmasters for food. The Malthusian doctrine would indeed afford a certain means of relief, if this were not a twofold question. If, when you say to a man,—"You have no claim upon me: you have your allotted part to perform in the world, so have I. In a state of nature, indeed, had I food, I should offer you a share from sympathy, from humanity; but in this advanced and artificial state of society, I cannot afford you relief; you must starve. You came into the world when it could not sustain you." What would be this man's answer? He would say,—"You disclaim all connection with me; I have no claims upon you? I can then have no duties towards you, and this pistol shall put me in possession of your wealth. You may leave a law behind you which shall hang me, but what man who saw assured starvation before him, ever feared hanging." It is this accursed practice of ever considering *only* what seems *expedient* for the occasion, disjoined from all principle or enlarged systems of action, of never listening to the true and unerring impulses of our better nature, which has led the colder-hearted men to the study of political economy, which has turned our Parliament into a real committee of public safety. In it is all power vested; and in a few years we shall either be governed by an aristocracy, or, what is still more likely, by a contemptible democratical oligarchy of glib economists, compared to which the worst form of aristocracy would be a blessing.

[AN UNSATISFACTORY PROFESSION]

Teachers of youth are, by a necessity of their present condition, either unsound or uncongenial. If they possess that buoyancy of spirit, which best fits them for communicating to those under their charge the knowledge it is held useful for them to acquire, they are deemed unsound. If they possess a subdued sobriety of disposition, the result of a process compared to which the course of a horse in a mill is positive enjoyment, they of necessity become ungenial. Is this a fitting condition, a meet and just return for the class, Instructors? And yet have I not truly described them? Has any one known a teacher of youth who, having attained any repute as such, has also retained any place in society as an individual? Are not all such men "Dominie Sampsons" in what relates to their duties, interests, and feelings as citizens; and, with respect to females, do they not all possess a sort of mental odour? Are not all masters, all those who are held in estimation, not scholars, but always masters, even in their sports; and are not the female teachers always teaching and setting right? whilst both not only lose the freshness of youth, both of mind and body, but seem as though they never had been young. They who have to teach, can never afford to learn; hence their improgression.

To the above remarks, true as they are in themselves, I am desirous to draw your particular attention. Those who have to teach, a duty which if ably discharged is the highest and most important which society imposes, are placed in a position in which they necessarily acquire a general or generic character, and this, for the most part, unfits them for mixing in society with ease to themselves or to others. Is this just, is it for the advantage of the community, that those to whom the highest and most responsible trusts are confided, should be rendered unfit to associate with their fellow men, by something which is imposed upon them, or which they are made to acquire, as teachers? Does not Society owe it to this meritorious class, to examine into the causes of these peculiarities with a view to remove ascertained evils, or by developing them to bring constantly before our eyes the necessity, in their case, of results which at present have such evil influences upon the more genial feelings of so large, and every way estimable and intelligent, a portion of our fellow-men?

[MARRIAGE]

There is no condition (evil as it may be in the eye of reason), which does not include, or seem to include when it has become familiar, some good, some redeeming or reconciling qualities. I agree, however, that marriage is not one of these. Marriage has, as you say, no *natural* relation to love. Marriage belongs to society; it is a social contract. It should not merely include the conditions of esteem and friendship, it should be the ratification of their manifestation. Still I do not know how it can be replaced; *that* belongs to the future, and it is a question which the future only can solve. I however quite agree that we can now, better than at any former time, say what *will not*, what *cannot* be.

*

Men are not more generous than women. Men desire the happiness of women apart from themselves, chiefly, if not only, *when and where* it would be an imputation upon a woman's affections for her to be [?un]happy; and women, on their part, seldom cordially carry their wish for their husband's happiness and enjoyment beyond the threshold. Whether it is that women have a passion for nursing, or from whatever cause, they invariably discourage all attempts to seek for health itself, beyond their own abode. When balloons, or those new roads upon which they say it will be possible to travel fifteen miles an hour for a day together, shall become the common mode of travelling, women will become more locomotive;—the health of all classes will be materially benefited. Women will then spend less time in attiring themselves—will invent some more simple head gear, or dispense with it altogether.

Thousands of women, attached to their husbands by the most endearing ties, and who would deplore their death for months, would oppose a separation for a few weeks in search of health, or assent so reluctantly, and with so much dissatisfaction, as to deprive the remedy of all value—rather make it an evil. I speak of affectionate natures and of the various, but always selfish, guises of self-will.

Caresses and endearment on this side of sickening *fondness*, and affectionate interest in all that concerns himself, from a wife freely chosen, are what every man loves, whether he be communicative or reserved, staid or sanguine. But affection, where it exists, will always prompt or discover its own most appropriate manifestation. All men, even the most surly, are influenced by affection, even when little fitted to excite it.

*

I have shown in the "Biographia Literaria" the great evil of too entire domestication. My after-experience would confirm, nay, even extend, this. I incline to think that, unless the husband is abroad the whole day, and therefore only a partaker of his wife's social parties, that in the choice of their associates they should be independent. To exclude all that a woman or a man might wish to exclude from his or her help-mate's society, might leave the rest of little value, and lead to mutual discomfort. The Turkish method is good: they have no difference of opinion in that fine country; but, as our own habits and customs are different, we should seek to make arrangements in harmony with them; and this I think may be accomplished. Why insist upon a married pair—paired not matched—agreeing in the choice of their visitors?

[BURKE]

Burke possessed and had sedulously sharpened that eye which sees all things, actions, and events, in relation to the laws which determine their existence and circumscribe their possibility. He referred habitually to principles: he was a scientific statesman, and therefore a Seer. For every principle contains in itself the germs of a prophecy; and, as the prophetic power is the essential privilege of science, so the fulfilment of its oracles supplies the outward, and (to men in general) the only test, of its claim to the title. There is not one word I would add or withdraw from this, scarcely one which I would substitute. I can read Burke, and apply everything not merely temporary to the present most fearful condition of our country. I cannot conceive a time or a state of things in which the writings of Burke will not have the highest value. 1819-1823

Recorded by

J. H. FRERE

[KEATS]

F. You have not read much of Keats, Sir, I think.

C. No, I have not. I have seen two Sonnets which I think showed marks of a great genius had he lived. I have also read a poem with a classical name—I forget what. Poor Keats, I saw him once. Mr. Green, whom you have heard me mention, and I were walking out in these parts, and we were overtaken by a young man of a very striking countenance whom Mr. Green recognised and shook hands with, mentioning my name; I wish Mr. Green had introduced me, for I did not know who it was. He passed on, but in a few moments sprung back and said, "Mr. Coleridge, allow me the honour of shaking your hand."

I was struck by the energy of his manner, and gave him my hand.

He passed on and we stood still looking after him, when Mr. Green said,

"Do you know who that is? That is Keats, the poet."

"Heavens!" said I, "when I shook him by the hand there was death!" This was about two years before he died.

F. But what was it?

C. I cannot describe it. There was a heat and a dampness in the hand. To say that his death was caused by the Review is absurd, but at the same time it is impossible adequately to conceive the effect which it must have had on his mind.

It is very well for those who have a place in the world and are independent to talk of these things, they can bear such a blow, so can those who have a strong religious principle; but all men are not born Philosophers, and all men have not those advantages of birth and education.

Poor Keats had not, and it is impossible I say to conceive the effect which such a Review must have had upon him, knowing as he did that he had his way to make in the world by his own exertions, and conscious of the genius within him.

[FAUST], *see* p. 723

[SHELLEY]

F. Did you ever see Shelley's translation of the chorus in "Faust" you were just mentioning?

C. I have, and admire it very much. Shelley was a man of great power as a poet, and could he only have had some notion of order, could you only have given him some plane whereon to stand, and look down upon his own mind, he would have succeeded. There are flashes of the true spirit to be met with in his works. Poor Shelley, it is a pity I often think that I never met with him. I could have done him good. He went to Keswick in order to see me and unfortunately fell in with Southey instead. There could have been nothing so unfortunate: Southey had no understanding for a toleration of such principles as Shelley's.

I should have laughed at his Atheism. I could have sympathised with him and shown him that I did so. I could have shown him that I had once been in the same state

R

myself, and I could have guided him through it. I have often bitterly regretted in my heart of hearts that I did never meet with Shelley.   1830

Recorded by

H. N. COLERIDGE

Schiller has the material Sublime; to produce an effect, he sets you a whole town on fire, and throws infants with their mothers into the flames, or locks up a father in an old tower. But Shakspere drops a handkerchief, and the same or greater effects follow.

*

Lear is the most tremendous effort of Shakspere as a poet; Hamlet as a philosopher or meditator; and Othello is the union of the two. There is something gigantic and unformed in the former two; but in the latter, everything assumes its due place and proportion, and the whole mature powers of his mind are displayed in admirable equilibrium.

*   1822

This is not a logical age. A friend lately gave me some political pamphlets of the times of Charles I and the Cromwellate. In them the premisses are frequently wrong, but the deductions are almost always legitimate; whereas, in the writings of the present day, the premisses are commonly sound, but the conclusions false. I think a great deal of commendation is due to the University of Oxford for preserving the study of logic in the schools. It is a great mistake to suppose geometry any substitute for it.

*

Plagiarists are always suspicious of being stolen from,— as pickpockets are observed commonly to walk with their hands in their breeches' pockets.

*

St. John's logic is Oriental, and consists chiefly in position and parallel; whilst St. Paul displays all the intricacies of the Greek system.   *

Kean is original; but he copies from himself. His rapid descents from the hyper-tragic to the infra-colloquial, though sometimes productive of great effect, are often unreasonable. To see him act, is like reading Shakspere by flashes of lightning. I do not think him thorough-bred gentleman enough to play Othello.

[MYSELF AND LORD DARNLEY]

I have the honour of being slightly known to my Lord Darnley. In 1808-9, I met him accidentally, when, after a few words of salutation, he said to me, "Are you mad, Mr. Coleridge?" "Not that I know, my lord," I replied; "what have I done which argues any derangement of mind?" "Why, I mean," said he, "those letters of yours in the 'Courier,' 'On the Hopes and Fears of a People invaded by foreign Armies.' The Spaniards are absolutely conquered; it is absurd to talk of their chance of resisting."—"Very well, my lord," I said, "we shall see. But will your lordship permit me, in the course of a year or two, to retort your question upon you, if I should have grounds for so doing?" "Certainly!" said he; "that is fair!" Two years afterwards, when affairs were altered in Spain, I met Lord Darnley again, and, after some conversation, ventured to say to him, "Does your lordship recollect giving me leave to retort a certain question upon you about the Spaniards? Who is mad now?" "Very true, very true, Mr. Coleridge," cried he: " you are right. It is very extraordinary. It was a very happy and bold guess." Upon which I remarked, "I think '*guess*' is hardly a fair term. For, has anything happened that has happened, from any other causes, or under any other conditions, than such as I laid down beforehand?" Lord Darnley, who was always very courteous to me, took this with a pleasant nod of his head.   1823

*

If you take from Virgil his diction and metre, what do you leave him?
                    *

You will observe, that there is no mention of rain previously to the Deluge. Hence it may be inferred, that the rainbow was exhibited for the first time after God's covenant with Noah. However, I only suggest this.

If the matter were quite open, I should incline to disapprove the intermarriage of first cousins; but the church has decided otherwise on the authority of Augustine, and that seems enough upon such a point. 1824

[THE JEWS]

The people of all other nations but the Jewish seem to look backwards and also to exist for the present: but in the Jewish scheme everything is prospective and preparatory; nothing, however trifling, is done for itself alone, but all is typical of something yet to come.

["GOOD LEAVE, GOOD PHILIP"]

For an instance of Shakspere's power *in minimis*, I generally quote James Gurney's character in "King John." How individual and comical he is with the four words allowed to his dramatic life! And pray look at Skelton's Richard Sparrow also!

[HAMLET]

Hamlet's character is the prevalence of the abstracting and generalizing habit over the practical. He does not want courage, skill, will, or opportunity; but every incident sets him thinking; and it is curious, and at the same time strictly natural, that Hamlet, who all through the play seems reason itself, should be impelled, at last, by mere accident to effect his object. I have a smack of Hamlet myself, if I may say so.

[MAXIMS]

A Maxim is a conclusion upon observation of matters of fact, and is merely retrospective: an Idea, or, if you like, a Principle, carries knowledge within itself, and is prospective. Polonius is a man of maxims. Whilst he is descanting on matters of past experience, as in that excellent speech to Laertes before he sets out on his travels, he is admirable; but when he comes to advise or project, he is a mere dotard. You see Hamlet, as the man of ideas, despises him.

A man of maxims only is like a Cyclops with one eye, and that eye placed in the back of his head.

[THE ATHANASIAN]

The author of the Athanasian Creed is unknown. It is, in my judgement, heretical in the omission, or implicit denial, of the Filial subordination in the Godhead, which is the doctrine of the Nicene Creed, and for which Bull and Waterland have so fervently and triumphantly contended; and by not holding to which, Sherlock staggered to and fro between Tritheism and Sabellianism. This creed is also tautological, and, if not persecuting, which I will not discuss, certainly containing harsh and ill-conceived language.

[CANT]

How much I regret that so many religious persons of the present day think it necessary to adopt a certain cant of manner and phraseology as a token to each other. They must *improve* this and that text, and they must do so and so in a *prayerful* way; and so on. Why not use common language? A young lady the other day urged upon me that such and such feelings were the *marrow* of all religion; upon which I recommended her to try to walk to London upon her marrow-bones only.

*

Burke's Essay on the Sublime and Beautiful seems to me a poor thing; and what he says upon Taste is neither profound nor accurate.

*

The Reformation in the sixteenth century narrowed Reform. As soon as men began to call themselves names, all hope of further amendment was lost.

*

Berkeley can only be confuted, or answered, by one sentence. So it is with Spinoza. His premiss granted, the deduction is a chain of adamant.   1827

[MR. CHARLES TENNYSON]

In the present age it is next to impossible to predict from specimens, however favourable, that a young man will turn out a great poet, or rather a poet at all. Poetic taste, dexterity in composition, and ingenious imitation, often produce poems that are very promising in appearance. But genius, or the power of doing something new, is another thing. Mr. Tennyson's sonnets, such as I have seen, have many of the characteristic excellencies of those of Wordsworth and Southey.

*

Good and bad men are each less so than they seem.

[THE SCHOOLMEN]

It is remarkable that two-thirds of the eminent schoolmen were of British birth. It was the schoolmen who made the languages of Europe what they now are. We laugh at the quiddities of those writers now, but, in truth, these quiddities are just the parts of their language which we have rejected; whilst we never think of the mass which we have adopted, and have in daily use.

[PLATO]

Plato's works are preparatory exercises for the mind. He leads you to see that propositions involving in themselves contradictory conceptions are nevertheless true; and which, therefore, must belong to a higher logic—that of ideas. They are contradictory only in the Aristotelian logic, which is the instrument of the understanding. I have read most of the works of Plato several times with profound attention, but not all his writings. In fact, I soon found that I had read Plato by anticipation. He was a consummate genius.

*

A fall of some sort or other—the creation, as it were, of the non-absolute—is the fundamental postulate of the moral history of Man. Without this hypothesis, Man is unintelligible; with it, every phenomenon is explicable. The mystery itself is too profound for human insight.

[MADNESS: BESTIALITY]

Madness is not simply a bodily disease. It is the sleep of the spirit with certain conditions of wakefulness—that is to say, lucid intervals. During this sleep, or recession of the spirit, the lower or bestial states of life rise up into action and prominence. It is an awful thing to be eternally tempted by the perverted senses. The reason may resist— it does resist—for a long time; but too often, at length, it yields for a moment, and the man is mad for ever. An act of the will is, in many instances, precedent to complete insanity. I think it was Bishop Butler who said, that he was all his life struggling against the devilish suggestions of his senses, which would have maddened him, if he had relaxed the stern wakefulness of his reason for a single moment.

*

The dog alone, of all brute animals, has a στοργή, or affection *upwards* to man.

*

If an inscription be put upon my tomb, it may be that I was an enthusiastic lover of the church; and as enthusiastic a hater of those who have betrayed it, be they who they may.

*

I never could get much information out of the biblical commentators. Cocceius has told me the most; but he, and all of them, have a notable trick of passing *siccissimis pedibus* over the parts which puzzle a man of reflection.

[HORNE TOOKE]

Horne Tooke was pre-eminently a ready-witted man. He had that clearness which is founded on shallowness. He doubted nothing; and, therefore, gave you all that he himself knew, or meant, with great completeness. His voice was very fine, and his tones exquisitely discriminating. His mind had no progression or development. All that is worth anything (and that is but little) in the "Diversions of Purley" is contained in a short pamphlet-letter which he addressed to Mr. Dunning; then it was enlarged to an octavo, but there was not a foot of progression beyond the pamphlet; at last, a quarto volume, I believe, came out; and yet, verily, excepting newspaper lampoons and political insinuations, there was no addition to the argument of the pamphlet. It shows a base and unpoetical mind to convert so beautiful, so divine a subject as language into the vehicle or makeweight of political squibs.

Horne Tooke was always making a butt of Mr. Godwin; who, nevertheless, had that in him which Tooke could never have understood. I saw a good deal of Tooke at one time: he left upon me the impression of his being a keen, iron man.

*

I wish the Psalms were translated afresh; or, rather, that the present version were revised. Scores of passages are utterly incoherent as they now stand. If the primary visual images had been oftener preserved, the connection and force of the sentences would have been better perceived.

[MORAL OF THE "ANCIENT MARINER"]

Mrs. Barbauld once told me that she admired the "Ancient Mariner" very much, but that there were two faults in it,—it was improbable, and had no moral. As for the probability, I owned that that might admit some question; but as to the want of a moral, I told her that in my own judgement the poem had too much; and that the only, or chief fault, if I might say so, was the obtrusion of the moral sentiment so openly on the reader as a principle or cause of action in a work of such pure imagination. It ought to have had no more moral than the "Arabian Nights'" tale of the merchant's sitting down to eat dates by the side of a well, and throwing the shells aside, and lo! a genie starts up, and says he *must* kill the aforesaid merchant, *because one* of the date shells had, it seems, put out the eye of the genie's son.

I took the thought of *"grinning for joy,"* in that poem, from my companion's remark to me, when we had climbed to the top of Plinlimmon, and were nearly dead with thirst. We could not speak from the constriction, till we found a little puddle under a stone. He said to me, —"You grinned like an idiot!" He had done the same.

["PILGRIM'S PROGRESS"]

The wood-cut of Slay-good is admirable, to be sure; but this new edition of the "Pilgrim's Progress" is too fine a book for it. It should be much larger, and on sixpenny coarse paper.

The "Pilgrim's Progress" is composed in the lowest style of English, without slang or false grammar. If you were to polish it, you would at once destroy the reality of the vision. For works of imagination should be written in very plain language; the more purely imaginative they are the more necessary it is to be plain.

This wonderful work is one of the few books which may be read over repeatedly at different times, and each time with a new and different pleasure. I read it once as a theologian—and let me assure you, that there is great theological acumen in the work—once with devotional feelings—and once as a poet. I could not have believed beforehand that Calvinism could be painted in such exquisitely delightful colours.

[SOUTHEY'S "BUNYAN"]

Southey's Life of Bunyan is beautiful. I wish he had illustrated that mood of mind which exaggerates, and still more, mistakes, the inward depravation, as in Bunyan, Nelson, and others, by extracts from Baxter's Life of himself. What genuine superstition is exemplified in that bandying of texts and half-texts, and demi-semi-texts, just as memory happened to suggest them, or chance brought them before Bunyan's mind!

[RABELAIS: SWIFT]

Rabelais is a most wonderful writer. Pantagruel is the Reason; Panurge the Understanding,—the pollarded man, the man with every faculty except the reason. I scarcely know an example more illustrative of the distinction between the two. Rabelais had no mode of speaking the truth in those days but in such a form as this; as it was, he was indebted to the King's protection for his life. Some of the commentators talk about his book being all political; there are contemporary politics in it, of course, but the real scope is much higher and more philosophical. It is in vain to look about for a hidden meaning in all that he has written; you will observe that, after any particularly deep thrust, as the Papimania, for example, Rabelais, as if to break the blow, and to appear unconscious of what he has done, writes a chapter or two of pure buffoonery. He, every now and then, flashes you a glimpse of a real face from his magic lantern, and then buries the whole scene in mist. The morality of the work is of the most refined and exalted kind; as for the manners, to be sure, I cannot say much.

Swift was *anima Rabelaisii habitans in sicco*,—the soul of Rabelais dwelling in a dry place.

Yet Swift was rare. Can anything beat his remark on King William's motto,—*Recepit, non rapuit*,—"that the receiver was as bad as the thief"?

[PAINTING]

Painting went on in power till, in Raffael, it attained the zenith, and in him too it showed signs of a tendency downwards by another path. The painter began to think of overcoming difficulties. After this the descent was rapid, till sculptors began to work inveterate likenesses of perriwigs in marble,—as see Algarotti's tomb in the cemetery at Pisa—and painters did nothing but copy, as well as they could, the external face of nature. Now, in this age, we have a sort of reviviscence,—not, I fear, of the power, but of a taste for the power, of the early times.

*

You may get a motto for every sect in religion, or line of thought in morals or philosophy, from Seneca; but nothing is ever thought *out* by him.

[THE ONLY VALID CATEGORY]

Every man is born an Aristotelian, or a Platonist. I do not think it possible that any one born an Aristotelian can become a Platonist; and I am sure no born Platonist can ever change into an Aristotelian. They are the two classes of men, beside which it is next to impossible to conceive a third. The one considers reason a quality, or attribute; the other considers it a power. I believe that Aristotle never could get to understand what Plato meant by an idea. There is a passage, indeed, in the Eudemian Ethics which looks like an exception; but I doubt not of its being spurious, as that whole work is supposed by some to be. With Plato ideas are constitutive in themselves.

Aristotle was, and still is, the sovereign lord of the understanding; the faculty judging by the senses. He was a conceptualist, and never could raise himself into that higher state which was natural to Plato, and has been so to others, in which the understanding is distinctly contemplated, and, as it were, looked down upon from the throne of actual ideas, or living, inborn, essential truths.

[WELLINGTON]

I sometimes fear the Duke of Wellington is too much disposed to imagine that he can govern a great nation by word of command, in the same way in which he governed a highly disciplined army. He seems to be unaccustomed to, and to despise, the inconsistencies, the weaknesses, the bursts of heroism followed by prostration and cowardice, which invariably characterize all popular efforts. He forgets that, after all, it is from such efforts that all the great and noble institutions of the world have come; and that, on the other hand, the discipline and organization of armies have been only like the flight of the cannon-ball, the object of which is destruction.

[THE YOUNGER GENERATION]

I do not know whether I deceive myself, but it seems to me that the young men, who were my contemporaries, fixed certain principles in their minds, and followed them out to their legitimate consequences, in a way which I rarely witness now. No one seems to have any distinct convictions, right or wrong; the mind is completely at sea, rolling and pitching on the waves of facts and personal experiences. Mr. —— is, I suppose, one of the rising young men of the day; yet he went on talking, the other evening, and making remarks with great earnestness, some of which were palpably irreconcilable with each other. He told me that facts gave birth to, and were the absolute ground of, principles; to which I said, that unless he had a principle of selection, he would not have taken notice of those facts upon which he grounded his principle. You must have a lantern in your hand to give light, otherwise all the materials in the world are useless, for you cannot find them; and if you could, you could not arrange them. "But then," said Mr. ——, "*that* principle of selection came from facts!"—"To be sure!" I replied; "but there must have been again an antecedent light to see those antecedent facts. The relapse may be carried in imagination backwards for ever,—but go back as you may, you cannot come to a man without a previous aim or principle." He then asked me what I had to say to Bacon's induction: I told him I had a good deal to say, if need were; but that it was perhaps enough for the occasion to remark, that what he was evidently taking for the Baconian *in*duction was mere *de*duction —a very different thing.

[? CHARLES LAMB]

Nothing ever left a stain on that gentle creature's mind, which looked upon the degraded men and things around him like moonshine on a dunghill, which shines and takes no pollution. All things are shadows to him, except those which move his affections.

[THE TWO LOGICS]

There are two kinds of logic: 1. Syllogistic. 2. Criterional. How any one can by any spinning make out more than ten or a dozen pages about the first, is inconceivable to me; all those absurd forms of syllogisms are one half pure sophisms, and the other half mere forms of rhetoric.

The object of rhetoric is persuasion; of logic, conviction; of grammar, significancy. A fourth term is wanting—the rhematic, or logic of sentences.

[ENGLISH INDIFFERENCE TO ART]

The darkest despotisms on the Continent have done more for the growth and elevation of the fine arts than the English government. A great musical composer in Germany and Italy is a great man in society, and a real dignity and rank are universally conceded to him. So it is with a sculptor, or painter, or architect. Without this sort of encouragement and patronage such arts as music and painting will never come into great eminence. In this country there is no general reverence for the fine arts; and the sordid spirit of a money-amassing philosophy would meet any proposition for the fostering of art, in a genial and extended sense, with the commercial maxim,—*Laissez faire*. Paganini, indeed, will make a fortune, because he can actually sell the tones of his fiddle at so much a scrape; but Mozart himself might have languished in a garret for anything that would have been done for him here.

The Italian masters differ from the Dutch in this—that in their pictures ages are perfectly ideal. The infant that Raffael's Madonna holds in her arms cannot be guessed of any particular age; it is Humanity in infancy. The babe in the manger in a Dutch painting is a fac-simile of some real new-born bantling; it is just like the little rabbits we fathers have all seen with some dismay at first burst.

[PAGAN GOOD-NATURE]

The superstition of the peasantry and lower orders generally in Malta, Sicily, and Italy exceeds common belief. It is unlike the superstition of Spain, which is a jealous fanaticism, having reference to the catholicism, and always glancing on heresy. The popular superstition of Italy is the offspring of the climate, the old associations, the manners, and the very names of the places. It is pure paganism, undisturbed by any anxiety about orthodoxy, or animosity against heretics. Hence, it is much more good-natured and pleasing to a traveller's feelings, and certainly not a whit less like the true religion of our dear Lord than the gloomy idolatry of the Spaniards.

[MY SYSTEM]

My system, if I may venture to give it so fine a name, is the only attempt I know ever made to reduce all knowledges into harmony. It opposes no other system, but shows what was true in each; and how that which was true in the particular, in each of them became error, *because* it was only half the truth. I have endeavoured to unite the insulated fragments of truth, and therewith to frame a perfect mirror. I show to each system that I fully understand and rightfully appreciate what that system means; but then I lift up that system to a higher point of view, from which I enable it to see its former position, where it was, indeed, but under another light and with different relations; so that the fragment of truth is not only acknowledged, but explained. Thus the old astronomers discovered and maintained much that was true; but, because they were placed on a false ground, and looked from a wrong point of view, they never did, they never could, discover the truth—that is, the whole truth. As soon as they left the earth, their false centre, and took their stand in the sun, immediately they saw the whole system in its true light, and their former station remaining, but remaining as a part of the prospect. I wish, in short, to connect by a moral *copula* natural history with political history; or, in other words, to make history scientific, and science historical—to take from history its accidentality, and from science its fatalism.

*

Illness never in the smallest degree affects my intellectual powers. I can *think* with all my ordinary vigour in the midst of pain: but I am beset with the most wretched and unmanning reluctance and shrinking from action. I could not upon such occasions take the pen in hand to write down my thoughts for all the wide world.

[AN ADVOCATE'S LEISURE]

Still I think that, upon the whole, the advocate is placed in a position unfavourable to his moral being, and, indeed, to his intellect also, in its higher powers. Therefore I would recommend an advocate to devote a part of his leisure time to some study of the metaphysics of the mind, or metaphysics of theology; something, I mean, which shall call forth all his powers, and centre his wishes in the investigation of truth alone, without reference to a side to be supported. No studies give such a power of distinguishing as metaphysical, and in their natural and unperverted tendency they are ennobling and exalting. Some such studies are wanted to counteract the operation of legal studies and practice, which sharpen, indeed, but, like a grinding-stone, narrow whilst they sharpen.

[WICKEDNESS OF REFORM MINISTERS]

The present ministers have, in my judgement, been guilty of two things pre-eminently wicked, *sensu politico*, in their conduct upon this Reform Bill. First, they have endeavoured to carry a fundamental change in the material and mode of action of the government of the country by so exciting the passions, and playing upon the necessary ignorance of the numerical majority of the nation, that all freedom and utility of discussion, by competent heads, in the proper place, should be precluded. In doing this they have used, or sanctioned the use of, arguments which may be applied with equal or even greater force to the carrying of any measure whatever, no matter how atrocious in its character or destructive in its consequences. They have appealed directly to the argument of the greater number of voices, no matter whether the utterers were drunk or sober, competent or not competent; and they have done the utmost in their power to rase out the sacred principle in politics of a representation of interests, and to introduce the mad and barbarizing scheme of a delegation of individuals. And they have done all this without one word of thankfulness to God for the manifold blessings of which the constitution, as settled at the Revolution, imperfect as it may be, has been the source or vehicle or condition to this great nation,—without one honest statement of the manner in which the anomalies in the practice grew up, or any manly declaration of the inevitable necessities of government which those anomalies have met. With no humility, nor fear, nor reverence, like Ham the accursed, they have beckoned, with grinning faces, to a vulgar mob, to come and insult over the nakedness of a parent; when it had become them, if one spark of filial patriotism had burnt within their breasts, to have marched with silent steps and averted faces to lay their robes upon his destitution!

Secondly, they have made the *king* the prime mover in all this political wickedness: they have made the *king* tell his people that they were deprived of their rights, and, by direct and necessary implication, that they and their ancestors for a century past had been slaves; they have made the king vilify the memory of his own brother and father. Rights! There are no rights whatever without corresponding duties. Look at the history of the growth of our constitution, and you will see that our ancestors never upon any occasion stated, as a ground for claiming any of their privileges, an abstract right inherent in themselves; you will nowhere in our parliamentary records find the miserable sophism of the Rights of Man. No! they were too wise for that. They took good care to refer their claims to custom and prescription, and boldly—sometimes very impudently—asserted them upon traditionary and constitutional grounds. The Bill is bad enough, God knows; but the arguments of its advocates, and the manner of their advocacy, are a thousand times worse than the Bill itself; and you will live to think so.

I am far, very far, from wishing to indulge in any vulgar abuse of the vulgar. I believe that the feeling of the multitude will, in most cases, be in favour of something good; but this it is which I perceive, that they are always under the domination of some one feeling or view;—whereas truth, and above all, practical wisdom, must be the result of a wide comprehension of the more and the less, the balance and the counterbalance.   1831

*

How inimitably graceful children are in general before they learn to dance!
*

[? Wordsworth's] face is almost the only exception I know to the observation, that something feminine—not *effeminate*, mind—is discoverable in the countenances of all men of genius. Look at that face of old Dampier, a rough sailor, but a man of exquisite mind. How soft is the air of his countenance, how delicate the shape of his temples!

[LAW OF POLARITY]

It is curious to trace the operation of the moral law of polarity in the history of politics, religion, &c. When the maximum of one tendency has been attained, there is no gradual decrease, but a direct transition to its minimum, till the opposite tendency has attained its maximum; and then you see another corresponding revulsion. With the Restoration came in all at once the mechanico-corpuscular philosophy, which, with the increase of manufactures, trade, and arts, made everything in philosophy, religion, and poetry objective; till, at length, attachment to mere external worldliness and forms got to its maximum,—when out burst the French revolution: and with it everything became immediately subjective, without any object at all. The Rights of Man, the Sovereignty of the People, were subject and object both. We are now, I think, on the turning point again. This Reform seems the *ne plus ultra* of that tendency of the public mind, which substitutes its own undefined notions or passions for real objects and historical actualities. There is not one of the ministers—except the one or two revolutionists among them—who has ever given us a hint, throughout this long struggle, as to *what* he really does believe will be the product of the Bill; what sort of House of Commons it will make for the purpose of governing this empire soberly and safely. No; they have actualized for a moment a wish, a fear, a passion, but not an idea.

[ASTROLOGY: ALCHEMY]

It is curious to mark how instinctively the reason has always pointed out to men the ultimate end of the various sciences, and how immediately afterwards they have set to work, like children, to realise that end by inadequate means. Now they applied to their appetites, now to their passions, now to their fancy, now to the understanding, and lastly, to the intuitive reason again. There is no doubt but that astrology of some sort or other would be the last achievement of astronomy: there must be chemical relations between the planets; the difference of their magnitudes compared with that of their distances is not explicable otherwise; but this, though, as it were, blindly and unconsciously seen, led immediately to fortune-telling and other nonsense. So alchemy is the theoretic end of chemistry: there must be a common law, upon which all can become each, and each all; but then the idea was turned to the coining of gold and silver.

*

There have been three silent revolutions in England:—first, when the professions fell off from the church; secondly, when literature fell off from the professions; and, thirdly, when the press fell off from literature.

[SUBJECT FOR AN EPIC]

The destruction of Jerusalem is the only subject now remaining for an epic poem; a subject which, like Milton's Fall of Man, should interest all Christendom, as the Homeric

War of Troy interested all Greece. There would be difficulties, as there are in all subjects; and they must be miti-
gated and thrown into the shade, as Milton has done with
the numerous difficulties in the "Paradise Lost." But there
would be a greater assemblage of grandeur and splendour
than can now be found in any other theme. As for the old
mythology, *incredulus odi;* and yet there must be a mythology, or a *quasi*-mythology, for an epic poem. Here there
would be the completion of the prophecies—the termination
of the first revealed national religion under the violent
assault of Paganism, itself the immediate forerunner and
condition of the spread of a revealed mundane religion;
and then you would have the character of the Roman and
the Jew, and the awfulness, the completeness, the justice.
I schemed it at twenty-five; but, alas! *venturum expectat.*

[LATIN LITERATURE]

Much as the Romans owed to Greece in the beginning,
whilst their mind was, as it were, tuning itself to an after-
effort of its own music, it suffered more in proportion by
the influence of Greek literature subsequently, when it was
already mature and ought to have worked for itself. It
then became a superfetation upon, and not an ingredient
in, the national character. With the exception of the stern
pragmatic historian and the moral satirist, it left nothing
original to the Latin Muse.

[THE GERMAN LANGUAGE]

It is hardly possible to conceive a language more perfect
than the Greek. If you compare it with the modern
European tongues, in the points of the position and relative
bearing of the vowels and consonants on each other, and
of the variety of terminations, it is incalculably before all
in the former particulars, and only equalled in the last by
German. But it is in variety of termination alone that the
German surpasses the other modern languages as to sound;
for, as to position, Nature seems to have dropped an acid
into the language when a-forming, which curdled the vowels
and made all the consonants flow together. The Spanish

is excellent for variety of termination; the Italian, in this particular, the most deficient. Italian prose is excessively monotonous.

It is extraordinary that the Germans should not have retained or assumed the two beautifully discriminated sounds of the soft and hard *theta;* as in *thy thoughts—the thin ether that,* &c. How particularly fine the hard *theta* is in an English termination, as in that grand word—Death—for which the Germans gutturize a sound that puts you in mind of nothing but a loathsome toad.

[A NEOLOGISM]

I regret to see that vile and barbarous vocable *talented,* stealing out of the newspapers into the leading reviews and most respectable publications of the day. Why no, *shillinged, farthinged, tenpenced,* &c.? The formation of a participle passive from a noun, is a licence that nothing but a very peculiar felicity can excuse. If mere convenience is to justify such attempts upon the idiom, you cannot stop till the language becomes, in the proper sense of the word, corrupt. Most of these pieces of slang come from America.

*

The want of adverbs in the Iliad is very characteristic. With more adverbs there would have been some subjectivity, or subjectivity would have made them.

The Greeks were then just on the verge of the bursting forth of individuality.

[VERSE DIALOGUES]

Can dialogues in verse be defended? I cannot but think that a great philosophical poet ought always to teach the reader himself as from himself. A poem does not admit argumentation, though it does admit development of thought. In prose there may be a difference; though I must confess that, even in Plato and Cicero, I am always vexed that the authors do not say what they have to say at once in their own persons. The introductions and little urbanities, are, to be sure, very delightful in their way; I would not lose them; but I have no admiration for the practice of ventriloquizing through another man's mouth.

[INDIVIDUALS OR ORGANIZATIONS?]

I have no faith in act of parliament reform. All the great—the permanently great—things that have been achieved in the world, have been so achieved by individuals, working from the instinct of genius or of goodness. The rage now-a-days is all the other way: the individual is supposed capable of nothing; there must be organization, classification, machinery, &c., as if the capital of national morality could be increased by making a joint stock of it. Hence you see these infant schools so patronized by the bishops and others, who think them a grand invention. Is it found that an infant-school child, who has been bawling all day a column of the multiplication-table, or a verse from the Bible, grows up a more dutiful son or daughter to its parents? Are domestic charities on the increase amongst families under this system? In a great town, in our present state of society, perhaps such schools may be a justifiable expedient—a choice of the lesser evil; but as for driving these establishments into the country villages, and breaking up the cottage home education, I think it one of the most miserable mistakes which the well-intentioned people of the day have yet made; and they have made, and are making, a good many, God knows.

[DRYDEN: POPE]

You will find this a good gage or criterion of genius,— whether it progresses and evolves, or only spins upon itself. Take Dryden's Achitophel and Zimri,—Shaftesbury and Buckingham; every line adds to or modifies the character, which is, as it were, a-building up to the very last verse; whereas, in Pope's Timon, &c., the first two or three couplets contain all the pith of the character, and the twenty or thirty lines that follow are so much evidence or proof of overt acts of jealousy, or pride, or whatever it may be that is satirised. In like manner compare Charles

Lamb's exquisite criticisms on Shakspere with Hazlitt's round and round imitations of them.

[DON QUIXOTE]

Don Quixote is not a man out of his senses, but a man in whom the imagination and the pure reason are so powerful as to make him disregard the evidence of sense when it opposed their conclusions. Sancho is the common sense of the social man-animal, unenlightened and unsanctified by the reason. You see how he reverences his master at the very time he is cheating him.

*

A philosopher's ordinary language and admissions, in general conversation or writings *ad populum*, are as his watch compared with his astronomical timepiece. He sets the former by the town-clock, not because he believes it right, but because his neighbours and his cook go by it.

1832

[PREACHING]

Every attempt, in a sermon, to cause emotion, except as the consequence of an impression made on the reason, or the understanding, or the will, I hold to be fanatical and sectarian.

No doubt preaching, in the proper sense of the word, is more effective than reading; and, therefore, I would not prohibit it, but leave a liberty to the clergyman who feels himself able to accomplish it. But, as things now are, I am quite sure I prefer going to church to a pastor who reads his discourse: for I never yet heard more than one preacher without book, who did not forget his argument in three minutes' time; and fall into vague and unprofitable declamation, and generally, very coarse declamation too. These preachers never progress; they eddy round and round. Sterility of mind follows their ministry.

[MY "FAUST," AND GOETHE'S]

Before I had ever seen any part of Goethe's "Faust," (though, of course, when I was familiar enough with

Marlowe's), I conceived and drew up the plan of a work, a drama, which was to be, to my mind, what the "Faust" was to Goethe's. My Faust was old Michael Scott; a much better and more likely original than Faust. He appeared in the midst of his college of devoted disciples, enthusiastic, ebullient, shedding around him bright surmises of discoveries fully perfected in after-times, and inculcating the study of nature and its secrets as the pathway to the acquisition of power. He did not love knowledge for itself—for its own exceeding great reward—but in order to be powerful. This poison-speck infected his mind from the beginning. The priests suspect him, circumvent him, accuse him; he is condemned, and thrown into solitary confinement: this constituted the *prologus* of the drama. A pause of four or five years takes place, at the end of which Michael escapes from prison, a soured, gloomy, miserable man. He will not, cannot study; of what avail had all his study been to him? His knowledge, great as it was, had failed to preserve him from the cruel fangs of the persecutors; he could not command the lightning or the storm to wreak their furies upon the heads of those whom he hated and contemned, yet feared. Away with learning! away with study! to the winds with all pretences to knowledge! We *know* nothing; we are fools, wretches, mere beasts. Anon I began to tempt him. I made him dream, gave him wine, and passed the most exquisite of women before him, but out of his reach. Is there, then, no knowledge by which these pleasures can be commanded? *That way* lay witchcraft, and accordingly to witchcraft Michael turns with all his soul. He has many failures and some successes; he learns the chemistry of exciting drugs and exploding powders, and some of the properties of transmitted and reflected light; his appetites and his curiosity are both stimulated, and his old craving for power and mental domination over others revives. At last Michael tries to raise the Devil, and the Devil comes at his call. My Devil was to be, like Goethe's, the universal humourist, who should make all things vain and nothing worth, by a perpetual collation of the great with the little in the presence of the infinite. I had many a trick for him to play, some better, I think, than any in the "Faust." In the mean time, Michael is miserable; he has power, but no peace, and he every day more keenly feels the tyranny of hell surrounding him. In vain he seems to himself to assert the most absolute empire over the Devil, by imposing the most extravagant tasks; one thing is as easy as another to the Devil. "What next, Michael?" is repeated every day with more imperious servility. Michael groans in spirit; his power is a curse: he commands women and wine! but the women seem fictititious and devilish, and the wine does not make him drunk. He now begins to hate the Devil, and tries to cheat him. He studies again, and explores the darkest depths of sorcery for a receipt to cozen hell; but all in vain. Sometimes the Devil's finger turns over the page for him, and points out an experiment, and Michael hears a whisper—"Try *that*, Michael!" The horror increases; and Michael feels that he is a slave and a condemned criminal. Lost to hope, he throws himself into every sensual excess, in the mid career of which he sees Agatha, my Margaret, and immediately endeavours to seduce her. Agatha loves him; and the Devil facilitates their meetings; but she resists Michael's attempts to ruin her, and implores him not to act so as to forfeit her esteem. Long struggles of passion ensue, in the result of which his affections are called forth against his appetites, and, love-born, the idea of a redemption of the lost will dawns upon his mind. This is instantaneously perceived by the Devil; and for the first time the humourist becomes severe and menacing. A fearful succession of conflicts between Michael and the Devil takes place, in which Agatha helps and suffers. In the end, after subjecting him to every imaginable horror and agony, I made him triumphant, and poured peace into his soul in the conviction of a salvation for sinners through God's grace.

The intended theme of the "Faust" is the consequences of a misology, or hatred and depreciation of knowledge caused by an originally intense thirst for knowledge baffled. But a love of knowledge for itself, and for pure ends, would never produce such a misology, but only a love of it for base and unworthy purposes. There is neither causation nor progression in the Faust; he is a ready-made conjuror from the very beginning; the *incredulus odi* is felt from the first line. The sensuality and the thirst after knowledge

are unconnected with each other. Mephistopheles and
Margaret are excellent; but Faust himself is dull and
meaningless. The scene in Auerbach's cellars is one of
the best, perhaps the very best; that on the Brocken is
also fine; and all the songs are beautiful. But there is
no whole in the poem; the scenes are mere magic-lantern
pictures, and a large part of the work is to me very flat.
The German is very pure and fine.

[GOETHE: SCHILLER: LESSING]

The young men in Germany and England, who admire
Lord Byron, prefer Goethe to Schiller; but you may depend
upon it, Goethe does not, nor ever will, command the
common mind of the people of Germany as Schiller does.
Schiller had two legitimate phases in his intellectual character:—the first as author of the "Robbers"—a piece which
must not be considered with reference to Shakspere, but
as a work of the mere material sublime, and in that line
it is undoubtedly very powerful indeed. It is quite genuine,
and deeply imbued with Schiller's own soul. After this
he outgrew the composition of such plays as the "Robbers,"
and at once took his true and only rightful stand in the
grand historical drama—the "Wallenstein";—not the intense drama of passion,—he was not master of that—but the
diffused drama of history, in which alone he had ample
scope for his varied powers. The "Wallenstein" is the
greatest of his works; it is not unlike Shakspere's historical
plays—a species by itself. You may take up any scene,
and it will please you by itself; just as you may in "Don
Quixote," which you read *through* once or twice only, but
which you read *in* repeatedly. After this point it was, that
Goethe and other writers injured by their theories the
steadiness and originality of Schiller's mind; and in every
one of his works after the "Wallenstein" you may perceive
the fluctuations of his taste and principles of composition.
He got a notion of re-introducing the characterlessness of
the Greek tragedy with a chorus, as in the "Bride of
Messina," and he was for infusing more lyric verse into it.
Schiller sometimes affected to despise the "Robbers" and
the other works of his first youth; whereas he ought to have

spoken of them as of works not in a right line, but full of excellence in their way. In his ballads and lighter lyrics Goethe is most excellent. It is impossible to praise him too highly in this respect. I like the "Wilhelm Meister" the best of his prose works. But neither Schiller's nor Goethe's prose style approaches to Lessing's, whose writings, for *manner*, are absolutely perfect.

Although Wordsworth and Goethe are not much alike, to be sure, upon the whole; yet they both have this peculiarity of utter non-sympathy with the subjects of their poetry. They are always, both of them, spectators *ab extra*,—feeling *for*, but never *with*, their characters. Schiller is a thousand times more *hearty* than Goethe.

I was once pressed—many years ago—to translate the "Faust"; and I so far entertained the proposal as to read the work through with great attention, and to revive in my mind my own former plan of Michael Scott. But then I considered with myself whether the time taken up in executing the translation might not more worthily be devoted to the composition of a work which, even if parallel in some points to the "Faust," should be truly original in motive and execution, and therefore more interesting and valuable than any version which I could make; and, secondly, I debated with myself whether it became my moral character to render into English—and so far, certainly, lend my countenance to language—much of which I thought vulgar, licentious, and blasphemous. I need not tell you that I never put pen to paper as a translator of "Faust."

I have read a good deal of Mr. Hayward's version, and I think it done in a very manly style; but I do not admit the argument for prose translations. I would in general rather see verse attempted in so capable a language as ours. The French cannot help themselves, of course, with such a language as theirs.

*

All is an endless fleeting abstraction; *the whole* is a reality.

[A NAÏVE CONFIDENCE IN ADMINISTRATORS]

I never was much subject to violent political humours or accesses of feelings. When I was very young, I wrote and spoke very enthusiastically; but it was always on subjects connected with some grand general principle, the violation of which I thought I could point out. As to mere details of administration, I honestly thought that ministers, and men in office, must, of course, know much better than any private person could possibly do; and it was not till I went to Malta, and had to correspond with official characters myself, that I fully understood the extreme shallowness and ignorance with which men of some note too were able, after a certain fashion, to carry on the government of important departments of the empire. I then quite assented to Oxenstiern's saying, *Nescis, mi fili, quam parva sapientia regitur mundus.*

[FUTURE OF THE UNITED STATES]

The possible destiny of the United States of America,— as a nation of a hundred millions of freemen,—stretching from the Atlantic to the Pacific, living under the laws of Alfred, and speaking the language of Shakspere and Milton, is an august conception. Why should we not wish to see it realised? America would then be England viewed through a solar microscope; Great Britain in a state of glorious magnification! How deeply to be lamented is the spirit of hostility and sneering which some of the popular books of travels have shown in treating of the Americans! They hate us, no doubt, just as brothers hate; but they respect the opinion of an Englishman concerning themselves ten times as much as that of a native of any other country on earth. A very little humouring of their prejudices, and some courtesy of language and demeanour on the part of Englishmen, would work wonders, even as it is, with the public mind of the Americans.

[THE TRUE INTERPRETATION OF HISTORY]

You must, therefore, commence with the philosophic idea of the thing, the true nature of which you wish to find out and manifest. You must carry your rule ready made, if you wish to measure aright. If you ask me how I can know that this idea—my own invention—is the truth, by which the phenomena of history are to be explained, I answer, in the same way exactly that you know that your eyes were made to see with; and that is, because you *do* see with them. If I propose to you an idea or self-realizing theory of the constitution, which shall manifest itself as in existence from the earliest times to the present,—which shall comprehend within it *all* the facts which history has preserved, and shall give them a meaning as interchangeably causals or effects;—if I show you that such an event or reign was an obliquity to the right hand, and how produced, and such other event or reign a deviation to the left, and whence originating,—that the growth was stopped here, accelerated there,—that such a tendency is, and always has been, corroborative, and such other tendency destructive, of the main progress of the idea towards realization;—if this idea, not only like a kaleidoscope, shall reduce all the miscellaneous fragments into order, but shall also minister strength, and knowledge, and light to the true patriot and statesman for working out the bright thought, and bringing the glorious embryo to a perfect birth;—then, I think, I have a right to say that the idea which led to this is not only true, but the truth, the only truth. To set up for a statesman upon historical knowledge only, is about as wise as to set up for a musician by the purchase of some score flutes, fiddles, and horns. In order to make music, you must know how to play; in order to make your facts speak truth, you must know what the truth is which *ought* to be proved,—the ideal truth,—the truth which was consciously or unconsciously, strongly or weakly, wisely or blindly, intended at all times.

[MR. ALFRED TENNYSON]

I have not read through all Mr. Tennyson's poems, which have been sent to me; but I think there are some things of a good deal of beauty in what I have seen. The misfortune is, that he has begun to write verses without very well understanding what metre is. Even if you write in a known and approved metre, the odds are, if you are not a metrist yourself, that you will not write harmonious verses; but to deal in new metres without considering what metre means and requires, is preposterous. What I would, with many wishes for success, prescribe to Tennyson,—indeed without it he can never be a poet in act,—is to write for the next two or three years in none but one or two well known and strictly defined metres, such as the heroic couplet, the octave stanza, or the octo-syllabic measure of the "Allegro" and "Penseroso." He would, probably, thus get imbued with a sensation, if not a sense, of metre without knowing it, just as Eton boys get to write such good Latin verses by conning Ovid and Tibullus. As it is, I can scarcely scan some of his verses.

[MAN'S LOVE FOR MAN: THE "SONNETS"]

I believe it possible that a man may, under certain states of the moral feeling, entertain something deserving the name of love towards a male object—an affection beyond friendship, and wholly aloof from appetite. In Elizabeth's and James's time it seems to have been almost fashionable to cherish such a feeling; and perhaps we may account in some measure for it by considering how very inferior the women of that age, taken generally, were in education and accomplishment of mind to the men. Of course there were brilliant exceptions enough; but the plays of Beaumont and Fletcher—the most popular dramatists that ever wrote for the English stage—will show us what sort of women it was generally pleasing to represent. Certainly the language of the two friends, Musidorus and Pyrocles, in the "Arcadia," is such as we could not now use except to women; and in Cervantes the same tone is sometimes adopted, as in the novel of the "Curious Impertinent." And I think there is a passage in the "New Atlantis" of Lord Bacon, in which he speaks of the possibility of such a feeling, but hints the extreme danger of entertaining it, or allowing it any place in a moral theory. I mention this with reference to Shakspere's sonnets, which have been supposed, by some, to be addressed to William Herbert, Earl of Pembroke, whom Clarendon calls the most beloved man of his age, though his licentiousness was equal to his virtues. I doubt this. I do not think that Shakspere, merely because he was an actor, would have thought it necessary to veil his emotions towards Pembroke under a disguise, though he might probably have done so, if the real object had perchance been a Laura or a Leonora. It seems to me that the sonnets could only have come from a man deeply in love, and in love with a woman; and there is one sonnet which, from its incongruity, I take to be a purposed blind.

[CONCEPTIONAL KNOWLEDGE]

There is now no reverence for anything; and the reason is, that men possess conceptions only, and all their knowledge is conceptional only. Now, as to conceive is a work of the mere understanding, and as all that can be conceived may be comprehended, it is impossible that a man should reverence that, to which he must always feel something in himself superior. If it were possible to conceive God in a strict sense, that is, as we conceive a horse or a tree, even God himself could not excite any reverence, though he might excite fear or terror, or perhaps love, as a tiger or a beautiful woman. But reverence, which is the synthesis of love and fear, is only due from man, and, indeed, only excitable in man, towards ideal truths, which are always mysteries to the understanding, for the same reason that the motion of my finger behind my back is a mystery to you now—your eyes not being made for seeing through my body. It is the reason only which has a sense by which ideas can be recognised, and from the fontal light of ideas only can a man draw intellectual power.

[ST. PAUL]

I think St. Paul's Epistle to the Romans the most profound work in existence; and I hardly believe that the writings of the old Stoics, now lost, could have been deeper. Undoubtedly it is, and must be, very obscure to ordinary readers; but some of the difficulty is accidental, arising from the form in which the Epistle appears. If we could now arrange this work in the way in which we may

be sure St. Paul would himself do, were he now alive and
preparing it for the press, his reasoning would stand out
clearer. His accumulated parentheses would be thrown
into notes, or extruded to the margin. You will smile,
after this, if I say that I think I understand St. Paul; and
I think so, because, really and truly, I recognize a cogent
consecutiveness in the argument—the only evidence I know
that you understand any book. How different is the style of
this intensely passionate argument from that of the catholic
circular charge called the Epistle to the Ephesians!—and
how different that of both from the style of the Epistles to
Timothy and Titus, which I venture to call ἐπιστολαὶ
Παυλοειδεῖς.

[A DANGEROUS BILL]

Have you been able to discover any principle in this
Emancipation Bill for the Slaves, except a principle of
fear of the abolition party struggling with a dread of causing
some monstrous calamity to the empire at large? Well! I
will not prophesy; and God grant that this tremendous
and unprecedented act of positive enactment may not do
the harm to the cause of humanity and freedom which I
cannot but fear! But yet, what can be hoped, when all
human wisdom and counsel are set at nought, and religious
faith—the only miraculous agent among men—is not invoked or regarded! and that most unblest phrase—the
Dissenting *interest*—enters into the question!

[GREEK TRAGIC POETS]

When I was a boy, I was fondest of Aeschylus; in youth
and middle age, I preferred Euripides; now, in my declining
years, I admire Sophocles. I can now at length see that
Sophocles is the most perfect. Yet he never rises to the
sublime simplicity of Aeschylus—simplicity of design, I
mean—nor diffuses himself in the passionate outpourings
of Euripides. I understand why the ancients called Euripides the most tragic of their dramatists: he evidently
embraces within the scope of the tragic poet many passions,—love, conjugal affection, jealousy, and so on, which

Sophocles seems to have considered as incongruous with the ideal statuesqueness of the tragic drama.

[NOTES ON STYLE]

A good lecture upon style might be composed, by taking, on the one hand, the slang of L'Estrange, and perhaps even of Roger North, which became so fashionable after the Restoration as a mark of loyalty; and, on the other, the Johnsonian magniloquence or the balanced metre of Junius; and then showing how each extreme is faulty, upon different grounds.

It is quite curious to remark the prevalence of the Cavalier slang style in the divines of Charles the Second's time. Barrow could not, of course, adopt such a mode of writing throughout, because he could not in it have communicated his elaborate thinkings and lofty rhetoric; but even Barrow not unfrequently lets slip a phrase here and there, in the regular Roger North way,—much to the delight, no doubt, of the largest part of his audience and contemporary readers. See particularly, for instances of this, his work on the Pope's supremacy. South is full of it.

The style of Junius is a sort of metre, the law of which is a balance of thesis and antithesis. When he gets out of this aphorismic metre into a sentence of five or six lines long, nothing can exceed the slovenliness of the English. Horne Tooke and a long sentence seem the only two antagonists that were too much for him. Still the antithesis of Junius is a real antithesis of images or thought; but the antithesis of Johnson is rarely more than verbal.

The definition of good prose is—proper words in their proper places; of good verse—the most proper words in their proper places. The propriety is in either case relative. The words in prose ought to express the intended meaning, and no more; if they attract attention to themselves, it is, in general, a fault. In the very best styles, as Southey's, you read page after page, understanding the author perfectly, without once taking notice of the medium of communication; it is as if he had been speaking to you all the while. But in verse you must do more: there the words, the *media*, must be beautiful, and ought to attract your

notice—yet not so much and so perpetually as to destroy
the unity which ought to result from the whole poem. This
is the general rule, but, of course, subject to some modifications, according to the different kinds of prose or verse.
Some prose may approach towards verse, as oratory, and
therefore a more studied exhibition of the *media* may be
proper; and some verse may border more on mere narrative,
and there the style should be simpler. But the great thing
in poetry is, *quocunque modo*, to effect a unity of impression
upon the whole; and a too great fulness and profusion of
point in the parts will prevent this. Who can read with
pleasure more than a hundred lines or so of "Hudibras"
at one time? Each couplet or quatrain is so whole in itself,
that you can't connect them. There is no fusion,—just as
it is in Seneca.

[DR. JOHNSON]

Dr. Johnson's fame now rests principally upon Boswell.
It is impossible not to be amused with such a book. But
his *bow-wow* manner must have had a good deal to do with
the effect produced—for no one, I suppose, will set Johnson
before Burke, and Burke was a great and universal talker:
yet now we hear nothing of this except by some chance
remarks in Boswell. The fact is, Burke, like all men of
genius who love to talk at all, was very discursive and
continuous; hence he is not reported; he seldom said the
sharp short things that Johnson almost always did, which
produce a more decided effect at the moment, and which
are so much more easy to carry off. Besides, as to Burke's
testimony to Johnson's powers, you must remember that
Burke was a great courtier; and after all, Burke said and
wrote more than once that he thought Johnson greater in
talking than writing, and greater in Boswell than in real
life.

[WHY I TALK AT LENGTH]

You must not be surprised at my talking so long to you—
I pass so much of my time in pain and solitude, yet everlastingly thinking, that, when you or any other persons call
on me, I can hardly help easing my mind, by pouring forth

some of the accumulated mass of reflection and feeling, upon an apparently interested recipient.

[MUSIC]

Some music is above me; most music is beneath me. I like Beethoven and Mozart—or else some of the aërial compositions of the elder Italians, as Palestrina and Carissimi ——And I love Purcell.

The best sort of music is what it should be—sacred; the next best, the military, has fallen to the lot of the Devil.

Good music never tires me, nor sends me to sleep. I feel physically refreshed and strengthened by it, as Milton says he did.

I could write as good verses now as ever I did, if I were perfectly free from vexations, and were in the *ad libitum* hearing of fine music, which has a sensible effect in harmonising my thoughts, and in animating and, as it were, lubricating my inventive faculty. The reason of my not finishing "Christabel" is not, that I don't know how to do it—for I have, as I always had, the whole plan entire from beginning to end in my mind; but I fear I could not carry on with equal success the execution of the idea, an extremely subtle and difficult one. Besides, after this continuation of "Faust," which they tell me is very poor, who can have courage to attempt a reversal of the judgement of all criticism against continuations? Let us except "Don Quixote," however, although the second part of that transcendent work is not exactly *uno flatu* with the original conception.

[PHILANTHROPISTS]

I have never known a trader in philanthropy who was not wrong in heart somewhere or other. Individuals so distinguished are usually unhappy in their family relations, —men not benevolent or beneficent to individuals, but almost hostile to them, yet lavishing money and labour and time on the race, the abstract notion. The cosmopolitism which does not spring out of, and blossom upon, the deep-rooted stem of nationality or patriotism, is a spurious and rotten growth.

[GIBBON]

The difference between the composition of a history in modern and ancient times is very great; still there are certain principles upon which the history of a modern period may be written, neither sacrificing all truth and reality, like Gibbon, nor descending into mere biography and anecdote.

Gibbon's style is detestable, but his style is not the worst thing about him. His history has proved an effectual bar to all real familiarity with the temper and habits of imperial Rome. Few persons read the original authorities, even those which are classical; and certainly no distinct knowledge of the actual state of the empire can be obtained from Gibbon's rhetorical sketches. He takes notice of nothing but what may produce an effect; he skips on from eminence to eminence, without ever taking you through the valleys between: in fact, his work is little else but a disguised collection of all the splendid anecdotes which he could find in any book concerning any persons or nations from the Antonines to the capture of Constantinople. When I read a chapter in Gibbon I seem to be looking through a luminous haze or fog:—figures come and go, I know not how or why, all larger than life, or distorted or discoloured; nothing is real, vivid, true; all is scenical, and, as it were, exhibited by candlelight. And then to call it a "History of the Decline and Fall of the Roman Empire"! Was there ever a greater misnomer? I protest I do not remember a single philosophical attempt made throughout the work to fathom the ultimate causes of the decline or fall of that empire. How miserably deficient is the narrative of the important reign of Justinian! And that poor scepticism, which Gibbon mistook for Socratic philosophy, has led him to misstate and mistake the character and influence of Christianity in a way which even an avowed infidel or atheist would not and could not have done. Gibbon was a man of immense reading; but he had no philosophy; and he never fully understood the principle upon which the best of the old historians wrote. He attempted to imitate their artificial construction of the whole work—their dramatic ordonnance of the parts—without seeing that their histories were intended more as documents illustrative of the truths of political philosophy than as mere chronicles of events.

The true key to the declension of the Roman empire—which is not to be found in all Gibbon's immense work—may be stated in two words:—the *imperial* character over-laying, and finally destroying, the *national* character. Rome under Trajan was an empire without a nation.

[THE ART OF RHETORIC]

It is Irving's error to use declamation, high and passionate rhetoric, not introduced and pioneered by calm and clear logic, which is—to borrow a simile, though with a change in the application, from the witty-wise, but not always wisely-witty, Fuller—like knocking a nail into a board, without wimbling a hole for it, and which then either does not enter, or turns crooked, or splits the wood it pierces.

[THE ART OF DIPLOMACY]

The sure way to make a foolish ambassador is to bring him up to it. What can an English minister abroad really want but an honest and bold heart, a love for his country and the ten commandments? Your art diplomatic is stuff: —no truly great man now would negociate upon any such shallow principles.

[DR. JOHNSON'S CONVERSATION]

Dr. Johnson seems to have been really more powerful in discoursing *viva voce* in conversation than with his pen in hand. It seems as if the excitement of company called something like reality and consecutiveness into his reasonings, which in his writings I cannot see. His antitheses are almost always verbal only; and sentence after sentence in the "Rambler" may be pointed out to which you cannot attach any definite meaning whatever. In his political pamphlets there is more truth of expression than in his other works, for the same reason that his conversation is better than his writings in general. He was more excited and in earnest.

*

When I am very ill indeed, I can read Scott's novels, and they are almost the only books I can then *read*. I cannot at such times read the Bible; my mind reflects on it, but I can't bear the open page.   1833

[EDITOR'S ARRANGEMENTS]

After all you can say, I still think the chronological order the best for arranging a poet's works. All your divisions are in particular instances inadequate, and they destroy the interest which arises from watching the progress, maturity, and even the decay of genius.

[MODERN PRAYER]

How much the devotional spirit of the church has suffered by that necessary evil, the Reformation, and the sects which have sprung up subsequently to it! All our modern prayers seem tongue-tied. We appear to be thinking more of avoiding an heretical expression or thought than of opening ourselves to God. We do not pray with that entire, unsuspecting, unfearing, childlike profusion of feeling, which so beautifully shines forth in Jeremy Taylor and Andrewes and the writings of some of the older and better saints of the Romish church, particularly of that remarkable woman, St. Theresa.

[MERE FACT]

I am by the law of my nature a reasoner. A person who should suppose I meant by that word, an arguer, would not only not understand me, but would understand the contrary of my meaning. I can take no interest whatever in hearing or saying anything merely as a fact—merely as having happened. It must refer to something within me before I can regard it with any curiosity or care. My mind is always energic—I don't mean energetic; I require in everything what, for lack of another word, I may call *pro-priety*,—that is, a reason, why the thing *is* at all, and why it is *there* or *then* rather than elsewhere or at another time.

[CRABBE AND SOUTHEY]

I think Crabbe and Southey are something alike; but Crabbe's poems are founded on observation and real life—Southey's on fancy and books. In facility they are equal, though Crabbe's English is of course not upon a level with Southey's, which is next door to faultless. But in Crabbe there is an absolute defect of the high imagination; he gives me little or no pleasure: yet, no doubt, he has much power of a certain kind, and it is good to cultivate, even at some pains, a catholic taste in literature. I read all sorts of books with some pleasure, except modern sermons and treatises on political economy.

[CHAUCER]

I take unceasing delight in Chaucer. His manly cheerfulness is especially delicious to me in my old age. How exquisitely tender he is, and yet how perfectly free from the least touch of sickly melancholy or morbid drooping! The sympathy of the poet with the subjects of his poetry is particularly remarkable in Shakspere and Chaucer; but what the first effects by a strong act of imagination and mental metamorphosis, the last does without any effort, merely by the inborn kindly joyousness of his nature. How well we seem to know Chaucer! How absolutely nothing do we know of Shakspere!

[ESSENCE OF MALICIOUS COMPARISONS]

Lord Byron, as quoted by Lord Dover, says, that the "Mysterious Mother" raises Horace Walpole above every author living in his, Lord Byron's, time. Upon which I venture to remark, first, that I do not believe that Lord Byron spoke sincerely; for I suspect that he made a tacit exception in favour of himself at least; secondly, that it is a miserable mode of comparison which does not rest on difference of kind. It proceeds of envy and malice and detraction to say that A is higher than B, unless you show that they are *in pari materia;*—thirdly, that the "Mysterious Mother" is the most disgusting, vile, detestable composition that ever came from the hand of man. No one with a spark of true manliness, of which Horace Walpole had none, could have written it. As to the blank verse, it is indeed better than Rowe's and Thomson's, which was execrably bad:—any approach, therefore, to the manner of the old dramatists was, of course, an improvement; but the loosest lines in Shirley are superior to Walpole's best.

[GERMAN BLANK VERSE]

Schiller's blank verse is bad. He moves in it as a fly in a glue bottle. His thoughts have their connection and variety, it is true, but there is no sufficiently corresponding movement in the verse. How different from Shakspere's endless rhythms!

There is a nimiety—a too-muchness—in all Germans. It is the national fault. Lessing had the best notion of blank verse. The trochaic termination of German words renders blank verse in that language almost impracticable. We have it in our dramatic hendecasyllable; but then we have a power of interweaving the iambic close *ad libitum.*

[MY SYSTEM]

You may not understand my system, or any given part of it,—or by a determined act of wilfulness, you may, even though perceiving a ray of light, reject it in anger and disgust. But this I will say, that if you once master it, or any part of it, you cannot hesitate to acknowledge it as the truth. You cannot be sceptical about it.

[MY INCREASED PROFUNDITY]

The metaphysical disquisition at the end of the first volume of the "Biographia Literaria" is unformed and immature;—it contains the fragments of the truth, but it is not fully thought out. It is wonderful to myself to think how infinitely more profound my views now are, and yet how much clearer they are withal. The circle is completing; the idea is coming round to, and to be, the common sense.

[A NEW "CRUSOE"]

It would require a very peculiar genius to add another tale, *ejusdem generis*, to "Robinson Crusoe" and "Peter Wilkins." I once projected such a thing; but the difficulty of a pre-occupied ground stopped me. Perhaps La Motte Fouqué might effect something; but I should fear that neither he, nor any other German, could entirely understand what may be called the "*desert island*" feeling. I would try the marvellous line of "Peter Wilkins," if I attempted it, rather than the *real* fiction of "Robinson Crusoe."

[THE THREE BEST PLOTS]

What a master of composition Fielding was! Upon my word I think the "Oedipus Tyrannus," the "Alchemist," and "Tom Jones," the three most perfect plots ever planned. And how charming, how wholesome, Fielding always is! To take him up after Richardson, is like emerging from a sick room heated by stoves, into an open lawn, on a breezy day in May.

[10TH JULY, 1834]

I am dying, but without expectation of a speedy release. Is it not strange that very recently bygone images, and scenes of early life, have stolen into my mind, like breezes blown from the spice-islands of Youth and Hope—those twin realities of this phantom world! I do not add Love,— for what is Love but Youth and Hope embracing, and so seen as *one?* I say *realities;* for reality is a thing of degrees, from the Iliad to a dream; καὶ γὰρ τ᾽ ὄναρ ἐκ Διὸς ἐστι. Yet, in a strict sense, reality is not predicable at all of aught below Heaven. "*Es enim* in coelis, *Pater noster, qui tu vere es!*" Hooker wished to live to finish his Ecclesiastical Polity:—so I own I wish life and strength had been spared to me to complete my Philosophy. For, as God hears me, the originating, continuing, and sustaining wish and design in my heart were to exalt the glory of his name; and, which is the same thing in other words, to promote the improvement of mankind. But *visum aliter Deo*, and his will be done.

1834

LETTERS

As in other things, Coleridge was voluminous in his correspondence, judged even by the standards of his time; and though hundreds of letters are known to have been lost, hundreds more exist. Not least when he was a young man did his friends think that these letters might be worth preserving. At an early period we find Lamb remonstrating with him because he had not written to Lloyd, as if both of them were dependent on the stimulus of Coleridge's correspondence. At first it was the same with the Wordsworths and Southey, until the elements of preaching, or of self-abasement, became distasteful to them. Later, of course, admiring disciples treasured the letters carefully. The result is that the whole sequence, when Mr. E. L. Griggs has collected his complete edition, will be found to represent fully almost every year of Coleridge's life from Cambridge onwards. The gaps when Coleridge was too miserable even to write letters, as in the years after his return from Malta, are few.

If this does not seem sufficient to justify the amount of space given to this section here, it may once more be pointed out that though a small selection might possibly be made presenting Coleridge as a fair exponent of the literary letter of the kind Charles Lamb excelled in; though he would occasionally write such "good letters" to friends whom he wished to please, such as, in early life, the Evans family, or, later on, benefactors like the Wedgwoods and the Gillmans; yet this would be entirely to mistake the real value of his correspondence, which lies in the fact that much more often he wrote not for publication but in passionate, uncontrollable sincerity, the overflow of his own experience and suffering. His lack of reserve seems almost infinite. He apologises—"we are soothed by communications": and yet in these "communications" he presents a new kind of autobiography. Not all the letters are thus crucial, but in selecting this kind of correspondence it is necessary to make some attempt to show the steps leading to the successive crises of which Coleridge's life seems to have been composed, and to demonstrate the character which gave rise to them.

Many of the letters are printed in full, but more, unfortunately, have had to be curtailed. If the sense of what is retained is affected by what has been left out, an explanation will be found in the Notes. Generally I have tried to confine omissions to irrelevancies, repetitions, or to detailed accounts of "symptoms," already sufficiently represented in other parts of the section.

LETTERS

I

Monday, February, 1797

MY DEAR POOLE,—I could inform the dullest author how he might write an interesting book. Let him relate the events of his own life with honesty, not disguising the feelings that accompanied them. I never yet read even a Methodist's Experience in the "Gospel Magazine" without receiving instruction and amusement; and I should almost despair of that man who could peruse the "Life of John Woolman" without an amelioration of heart. As to my Life, it has all the charms of variety,—high life and low life, vices and virtues, great folly and some wisdom. However, what I am depends on what I have been; and you, *my best Friend!* have a right to the narration. To me the task will be a useful one. It will renew and deepen my reflections on the past; and it will perhaps make you behold with no unforgiving or impatient eye those weaknesses and defects in my character, which so many untoward circumstances have concurred to plant there. . . .

II

TO THE SAME

Sunday, March, 1797

MY DEAR POOLE,—My father (Vicar of, and Schoolmaster at, Ottery St. Mary, Devon) was a profound mathematician, and well versed in the Latin, Greek, and Oriental Languages. He published, or rather attempted to publish, several works; 1st, Miscellaneous Dissertations arising from the 17th and 18th Chapters of the Book of Judges; 2d, *Sententiae excerptae*, for the use of his own school; and 3d, his best work, a Critical Latin Grammar; in the preface to which he proposes a bold innovation in the names of the cases. My father's new nomenclature was not likely to become popular, although it must be allowed to be both sonorous and expressive. *Exempli gratia*, he calls the ablative the *quippe-quare-quale-quia-quidditive case!* My father made the world his confidant with respect to his learning and ingenuity, and the world seems to have kept the secret very faithfully. His various works, uncut, unthumbed, have been preserved free from all pollution. This piece of good luck promises to be hereditary; for all *my* compositions have the same amiable *home-studying* propensity. The truth is, my father was not a first-rate genius; he was, however, a first-rate Christian. I need not detain you with his character. In learning, good-heartedness, absentness of mind, and excessive ignorance of the world, he was a perfect Parson Adams.

My mother was an admirable economist, and managed exclusively. My eldest brother's name was John. He went over to the East Indies in the Company's service; he was a successful officer and a brave one, I have heard. He died of a consumption there about eight years ago. My second brother was called William. He went to Pembroke College, Oxford, and afterwards was assistant to Mr. Newcome's School, at Hackney. He died of a putrid fever the year before my father's death, and just as he was on the eve of marriage with Miss Jane Hart, the eldest daughter of a very wealthy citizen of Exeter. My third brother, James, has been in the army since the age of sixteen, has married a woman of fortune, and now lives at Ottery St. Mary, a respectable man. My brother Edward, the wit of the family, went to Pembroke College, and afterwards to Salisbury, as assistant to Dr. Skinner. He married a woman twenty years older than his mother. She is dead, and he now lives at Ottery St. Mary. My fifth brother, George, was educated at Pembroke College, Oxford, and from there went to Mr. Newcome's, Hackney, on the death of William. He stayed there fourteen years, when the living of Ottery St. Mary was given him. There he has now a fine school, and has lately married Miss Jane Hart, who with beauty and wealth had remained a faithful widow to the memory of William for sixteen years. My brother George is a man of reflective mind and elegant genius. He possesses learning in a greater degree than any of the family, excepting myself. His manners are grave and hued over with a tender sadness. In his moral character he approaches every way nearer to perfection thar any man I ever yet knew; indeed, he is worth the whole family in a lump. My sixth brother, Luke (indeed, the seventh, for one brother, the second, died in his infancy, and I had forgot to mention him), was bred as a medical man. He married Miss Sara Hart, and died at the age of twenty-two, leaving one child, a lovely boy, still alive. My brother Luke was a man of uncommon genius, a severe student, and a good man. The eighth child was a sister, Anne. She died a little after my brother Luke, aged twenty-one;

> Rest, gentle Shade! and wait thy Maker's will;
> Then rise *unchanged*, and be an Angel still!

The ninth child was called Francis. He went out as a midshipman, under Admiral Graves. His ship lay on the Bengal coast, and he accidentally met his brother John, who took him to land, and procured him a commission in the Army. He died from the effects of a delirious fever brought on by his excessive exertions at the siege of Seringapatam, at which his conduct had been so gallant, that Lord Cornwallis paid him a high compliment in the presence of the army, and presented him with a valuable gold watch, which my mother now has. All my brothers are remarkably handsome; but they were as inferior to Francis as I am to them. He went by the name of "the handsome Coleridge." The tenth and last child was S. T. Coleridge, the subject of these epistles, born (as I told you in my last) October 20, 1772. . . .

III

TO THE SAME

October 9, 1797

MY DEAREST POOLE,—From March to October—a long silence! But [as] it is possible that I may have been preparing materials for future letters, the time cannot be considered as altogether subtracted from you.

From October, 1775, to October, 1778. These three years I continued at the Reading School, because I was too little to be trusted among my father's schoolboys. After breakfast I had a halfpenny given me, with which I bought three cakes at the baker's close by the school of my old mistress; and these were my dinner on every day except Saturday and Sunday, when I used to dine at home, and wallowed in a beef and pudding dinner. I am remarkably fond of beans and bacon; and this fondness I attribute to my father having given me a penny for having eat a large quantity of beans on Saturday. For the other boys did not like them, and as it was an economic food, my father thought that my attachment and penchant for it ought to be encouraged. My father was very fond of me, and I was my mother's darling: in consequence I was very miserable. For Molly, who had nursed my brother Francis, and was immoderately fond of him, hated me because my mother took more notice of me than of Frank, and Frank hated me because my mother gave me a bit of cake now and then a bit of cake, when he had none,—quite forgetting that for one bit of cake which I had and he had not, he had twenty sops in the pan, and pieces of bread and butter with sugar on them from Molly, from whom I received only thumps and ill names.

So I became fretful and timorous, and a tell-tale; and the schoolboys drove me from play, and were always tormenting me, and hence I took no pleasure in boyish sports, but read incessantly. My father's sister kept an *everything* shop at Crediton, and there I read through all the gilt-cover little books that could be had at that time, and likewise all the uncovered tales of Tom Hickathrift, Jack the Giant-killer, &c., &c., &c., &c. And I used to lie by the wall and *mope*, and my spirits used to come upon me suddenly; and in a flood of them I was accustomed to race up and down the churchyard, and act over all I had been reading, on the docks, the nettles, and the rank grass. At six years old I remember to have read Belisarius, Robinson Crusoe, and Philip Quarles; and then I found the Arabian Nights' Entertainments, one tale of which (the tale of a man who was compelled to seek for a pure virgin) made so deep an impression on me (I had read it in the evening while my mother was mending stockings), that I was haunted by spectres, whenever I was in the dark: and I distinctly remember the anxious and fearful eagerness with which I used to watch the window in which the books lay, and whenever the sun lay upon them, I would seize it, carry it by the wall, and bask and read. My father found out the effect which these books had produced, and burnt them.

So I became a *dreamer*, and acquired an indisposition to all bodily activity; and I was fretful, and inordinately passionate, and as I could not play at anything, and was slothful, I was despised and hated by the boys; and because I could read and spell and had, I may truly say, a memory and understanding forced into almost an unnatural ripeness, I was flattered and wondered at by all the old women. And so I became very vain, and despised most of the boys that were at all near my own age, and before I was eight years old I was a *character*. Sensibility, imagination, vanity, sloth, and feelings of deep and bitter contempt for all who traversed the orbit of my understanding, were even then prominent and manifest.

From October, 1778, to 1779. That which I began to be from three to six I continued from six to nine. In this year (1778) I was admitted into the Grammar School, and soon outstripped all of my age. I had a dangerous putrid fever this year. My brother George lay ill of the same fever in the next room. My poor brother Francis, I remember, stole up in spite of orders to the contrary, and sat by my bedside and read Pope's Homer to me. Frank had a violent love of beating me; but whenever that was superseded by any humour or circumstances, he was always very fond of me, and used to regard me with a strange mixture of admiration and contempt. Strange it was not, for he hated books, and loved climbing, fighting, playing and robbing orchards, to distraction.

My mother relates a story of me, which I repeat here, because it must be regarded as my first piece of wit. During my fever, I asked why Lady Northcote (our neighbour) did not come and see me. My mother said she was afraid of catching the fever. I was piqued, and answered, "Ah, Mamma! the four Angels round my bed an't afraid of catching it!" I suppose you know the prayer:—

> Matthew! Mark! Luke and John!
> God bless the bed which I lie on.
> Four angels round me spread,
> Two at my foot, and two at my head.

This prayer I said nightly, and most firmly believed the truth of it. Frequently have I (half-awake and half-asleep, my body diseased and fevered by my imagination) seen armies of ugly things bursting in upon me, and these four angels keeping them off. In my next I shall carry on my life to my father's death.

God bless you, my dear Poole, and your affectionate

S. T. COLERIDGE.

IV

TO THE SAME

October 16, 1797

DEAR POOLE,—From October, 1779, to October, 1781. I had asked my mother one evening to cut my cheese entire, so that I might toast it. This was no easy matter, it being a *crumbly* cheese. My mother, however, did it. I went into the garden for something or other, and in the mean time my brother Frank *minced* my cheese "to disappoint the favorite." I returned, saw the exploit, and in an agony of passion flew at Frank. He pretended to have been seriously hurt by my blow, flung himself on the ground, and there lay with outstretched limbs. I hung over him moaning, and in a great fright; he leaped up, and with a horse-laugh gave me a severe blow in the face. I seized a knife, and was running at him, when my mother came in and took me by the arm. I expected a flogging, and struggling from her I ran away to a hill at the bottom of which the Otter flows, about one mile from Ottery. There I stayed; my rage died away, but my obstinacy vanquished my fears, and taking out a little shilling book which had, at the end, morning and evening prayers, I very devoutly repeated them—thinking at the *same time* with inward and gloomy satisfaction how miserable my mother must be! I distinctly remember my feelings when I saw a Mr. Vaughan pass over the bridge, at about a furlong's distance, and how I watched the calves in the fields beyond the river. It grew dark and I fell asleep. It was towards the latter end of October, and it proved a dreadful stormy night. I felt the cold in my sleep, and dreamt that I was pulling the blanket over me, and actually pulled over me a dry thorn bush which lay on the hill. In my sleep I had rolled from the top of the hill to within three yards of the river, which flowed by the unfenced edge at the bottom. I awoke several times, and finding myself wet and stiff and cold, closed my eyes again that I might forget it.

In the mean time my mother waited about half an hour, expecting my return when the *sulks* had evaporated. I not returning, she sent into the churchyard and round the town. Not found! Several men and all the boys were sent to ramble about and seek me. In vain! My mother was almost distracted; and at ten o'clock at night I was *cried* by the crier in Ottery, and in two villages near it, with a reward offered for me. No one went to bed; indeed, I believe half the town were up all the night. To return to myself. About five in the morning, or a little after, I was broad awake, and attempted to get up and walk; but I could not move. I saw the shepherds and workmen at a distance, and cried, but so faintly that it was impossible to hear me thirty yards off. And there I might have lain and died; for I was now almost given over, the ponds and even the river, near where I was lying, having been dragged. But by good luck, Sir Stafford Northcote, who had been out all night, resolved to make one other trial, and came so near that he heard me crying. He carried me in his arms for near a quarter of a mile, when we met my father and Sir Stafford's servants. I remember and never shall forget my father's face as he looked upon me while I lay in the servant's arms—so calm, and the tears stealing down his face; for I was the child of his old age. My mother, as you may suppose, was outrageous with joy. [Meantime] in rushed a *young lady*, crying out, "I hope you'll whip him, Mrs. Coleridge!" This woman still lives in Ottery; and neither philosophy or religion have been able to conquer the antipathy which I *feel* towards her whenever I see her. I was put to bed and recovered in a day or so, but I was certainly injured. For I was weakly and subject to the ague for many years after.

My father (who had so little of parental ambition in him, that he had destined his children to be blacksmiths, &c., and had accomplished his intention but for my mother's pride and spirit of aggrandizing her family)—my father had, however, resolved that I should be a parson. I read every book that came in my way without distinction; and my father was fond of me, and used to take me on his knee and hold long conversations with me. I remember that at eight years old I walked with him one winter evening from a farmer's house, a mile from Ottery, and he told me the names of the stars and how Jupiter was a thousand times larger than our world, and that the other twinkling stars were suns that had worlds rolling round them; and when I came home he shewed me how they rolled round. I heard him with a profound delight and admiration: but without the least mixture of wonder or incredulity. For from my early reading of fairy tales and genii, &c., &c., my mind had been habituated *to the Vast*, and I never regarded *my senses* in any way as the criteria of my belief. I regulated all my creeds by my conceptions, not by my *sight*, even at that age. Should children be permitted to read romances, and relations of giants and magicians and genii? I know all that has been said against it; but I have formed my faith in the affirmative. I know no other way of giving the mind a love of the Great and the Whole. Those who have been led to the same truths step by step, through the constant testimony of their senses, seem to me to want a sense which I possess. They contemplate nothing but *parts*, and all *parts* are necessarily little. And the universe to them is but a mass of *little things*. It is true, that the mind *may* become credulous and prone to superstition by the former method; but are not the experimentalists credulous even to madness in believing any absurdity, rather than believe the grandest truths, if they have not the testimony of their own senses in their favour? I have known some who have been *rationally* educated, as it is styled. They were marked by a microscopic acuteness, but when they looked at great things, all became a blank and they saw nothing, and denied (very illogically) that anything could be seen, and uniformly put the negation of a power for the possession of a power, and called the want of imagination judgement and the never being moved to rapture philosophy!

Towards the latter end of September, 1781, my father went to Plymouth with my brother Francis, who was to go as midshipman under Admiral Graves, who was a friend of my father's. My father settled my brother, and returned

October 4, 1781. He arrived at Exeter about six o'clock, and was pressed to take a bed there at the Harts', but he refused, and, to avoid their entreaties, he told them, that he had never been superstitious, but that the night before he had had a dream which had made a deep impression. He dreamt that Death had appeared to him as he is commonly painted, and touched him with his dart. Well, he returned home, and all his family, I excepted, were up. He told my mother his dream; but he was in high health and good spirits, and there was a bowl of punch made, and my father gave a long and particular account of his travel, and that he had placed Frank under a religious captain, &c. At length he went to bed, very well and in high spirits. A short time after he had lain down he complained of a pain in his bowels. My mother got him some peppermint water, and, after a pause, he said, "I am much better now, my dear!" and lay down again. In a minute my mother heard a noise in his throat, and spoke to him, but he did not answer; and she spoke repeatedly in vain. Her *shriek* awaked me, and I said, "Papa is dead!" I did not know of my father's return, but I knew that he was expected. How I came to think of his death I cannot tell; but so it was. Dead he was. Some said it was the gout in the heart;—probably it was a fit of apoplexy. He was an Israelite without guile, simple, generous, and taking some Scripture texts in their literal sense, he was conscientiously indifferent to the good and the evil of this world.

God love you and   S. T. COLERIDGE.

V

TO GEORGE COLERIDGE

[Undated, from Christ's Hospital, before 1790]

DEAR BROTHER,—You will excuse me for reminding you that, as our holidays commence next week, and I shall go out a good deal, a good pair of breeches will be no inconsiderable accession to my appearance. For though my present pair are excellent for the purposes of drawing mathematical figures on them, and though a walking thought, sonnet, or epigram would appear on them in very *splendid* type, yet they are not altogether so well adapted for a female

eye—not to mention that I should have the charge of vanity
brought against me for wearing a looking-glass. I hope
you have got rid of your cold—and I am your affectionate
brother,

SAMUEL TAYLOR COLERIDGE.

P.S. Can you let me have them time enough for re-
adaptation before Whitsunday? I mean that they may be
made up for me before that time.

VI

TO THE SAME

[October, 1791]

DEAR BROTHER,—As I am now settled in my rooms, and
as College Business is commenced, I shall be able to give
you some little account of matters. We go to Chapel twice
a day. Every time we miss, we pay twopence, and fourpence
on Surplice days, *id est*, Sundays, Saints' days and the eves
of Saints' days. I am remarkably religious on an economical
plan.

We have mathematical lectures, once a day, Euclid and
Algebra alternately. I read Mathematics three hours a day,
by which means I am always considerably before the lectures,
which are very good ones. Classical lectures we have had
none yet, nor shall I be often *bored* with them. They are
seldom given, and when given, very thinly attended. After
tea (N.B. sugar is very dear) I read classics till I go to bed,
viz., eleven o'clock. If I were to read on as I do now, there
is not the least doubt, that I should be classical medallist
and a very high Wrangler; but *freshmen* always *begin* very
furiously. I am reading Pindar, and composing Greek verse
like a mad dog. I am very fond of Greek verse, and shall
try hard for the Brown's Prize Ode. At my leisure hours I
translate Anacreon. I have translated the first, the second,
the 28th, the 32nd, the 43rd and the 46th Odes. Middleton
thinks I have translated the 32nd ἄγε ζωγράφων ἄριστε
very well. I think between us both we might translate him
entirely. You *have* translated six or 7, have you not?

Dr. Piarce is not come up to College yet. The Rustat
Scholarship will be worth to me 27 pound a year. There is

a new regulation at our College, they tell me, that, without any exception, the man who takes the highest honours in his year of the candidates, is to be elected Fellow. This will be a bit of a stimulus to my exertions.

There is no such thing as *discipline* at our College. There was once, they say, but so long ago that no one remembers it. Dr. Piarce, if I am not very much misinformed, will introduce it with a vengeance this year. We have had so very large an admittance that it will be absolutely necessary.

We do one declamation every term—two are spoken in a week, one English, one Latin. Consequently, when the college was very thin, the men were pestered with two or three in a term. Themes and verses are in disuse at our College. Whether the doctor intends to reintroduce them or no, I cannot tell.

I have a most violent cold in my head, a favour which I owe to the dampness of my rooms. The Rustat Scholarship depends in some measure upon residence; otherwise it would be worth thirty pound a year to me. But I should lose by this gain; while in the country, I can be at no expence; but unnecessary residence is a very *costly* thing.

Le Grice will send me a parcel in a few days. Pray let me hear from you.

My compliments to Mr. and Mrs. Sparrow and believe me with love and gratitude

Yours

S. T. COLERIDGE.

VII

TO THE SAME

[Postmark Nov. 28, 1791]

MY DEAR BROTHER,—I am very much distrest on account of your illness: I can form some idea of your sufferings from what I have seen my brother James suffer, when spasmodically affected. I hope to God, the spitting of blood has ceased. You should not take much animal food, nor any violent exercise. I should have written you on the receipt of your letter, had it not found me nailed to my bed with a fit of the rheumatism. Yesterday I exhibited my first resurrexit. I am very weak and have a disagreeable *tearing* pain in my head, when I move. I was very unwell, when I wrote last to you; but the day after I grew so much worse, that I was obliged to take to my bed. Cambridge is a damp place—the very palace of the winds: so without very great care one is sure to have a violent cold. I am not however certain, that I do not owe my rheumatism to the dampness of my rooms. Opium never used to have any disagreeable effects on me—but it has on many. . . .

VIII

TO MARY EVANS

Jesus College, Cambridge, February 7, 1793

I would to Heaven, my dear Miss Evans, that the god of wit, or news, or politics would whisper in my ear something that might be worth sending fifty-four miles—but alas! I am so closely blocked by an army of misfortunes that really there is no passage left open for mirth or anything else. Now, just to give you a few articles in the large inventory of my calamities. Imprimis, a gloomy, uncomfortable morning. Item, my head aches. Item, the Dean has set me a swinging imposition for missing morning chapel. Item, of the two only coats which I am worth in the world, both have holes in the elbows. Item, Mr. Newton, our mathematical lecturer, has recovered from an illness. But the story is rather a laughable one, so I must tell it you. Mr. Newton (a tall, thin man with a little, tiny, blushing face) is a great botanist. Last Sunday, as he was strolling out with a friend of his, some curious plant suddenly caught his eye. He turned round his head with great eagerness to call his companion to a participation of discovery, and unfortunately continuing to walk forward he fell into a pool, deep, muddy, and full of chickweed. I was lucky enough to meet him as he was entering the college gates on his return (a sight I would not have lost for the Indies), his best black clothes all green with duckweed, he shivering and dripping, in short a perfect river god. I went up to him (you must understand we hate each other most cordially) and sympathized with him in all the tenderness of condolence. The consequence of his misadventure was a violent cold attended with fever, which confined him to his room, prevented him from giving lectures, and freed me from the necessity of attending them; but this misfortune I supported with truly Christian fortitude. However, I constantly asked after his health with filial anxiety, and this morning, making my usual inquiries, I was informed, to my infinite astonishment and vexation, that he was perfectly recovered and intended to give lectures this very day!!! Verily, I swear that six of his duteous pupils—myself as their general—sallied forth to the apothecary's house with a fixed determination to thrash him for having performed so speedy a cure, but, luckily for himself, the rascal was not at home. But here comes my fiddling master, for (but this is a secret) I am learning to play on the violin. Twit, twat, twat, twit! "Pray, M. de la Penche, do you think I shall ever make anything of this violin? Do you think I have an ear for music?" "Un magnifique! Un superbe! Par honneur, sir, you be a ver great genius in de music. Good morning, monsieur!" This M. de la Penche is a better judge than I thought for.

This new whim of mine is partly a scheme of self-defence. Three neighbours have run music-mad lately—two of them fiddle-scrapers, the third a flute-tooter—and are perpetually annoying me with their vile performances, compared with which the gruntings of a whole herd of sows would be seraphic melody. Now I hope, by frequently playing myself, to render my ear callous. Besides, the evils of life are crowding upon me, and music is "the sweetest assuager of cares." It helps to relieve and soothe the mind, and is a sort of refuge from calamity, from slights and neglects and censures and insults and disappointments; from the warmth of real enemies and the coldness of pretended friends; from your *well wishers* (as they are justly called, in opposition, I suppose, to *well doers*), men whose inclinations to serve you always decrease in a most mathematical proportion as their opportunities to do it increase; from the

> Proud man's contumely, and the spurns
> Which patient merit of th' unworthy takes;

from grievances that are the growth of all times and places and not peculiar to *this age*, which authors call this *critical* age, and divines this *sinful age*, and politicians *this age of revolutions.* An acquaintance of mine calls it this *learned age* in due reverence to his own abilities, and like Monsieur Whatd'yecallhim, who used to pull off his hat when he spoke of himself. The poet laureate calls it "*this golden age,*" and with good reason,—

> For *him* the fountains with Canary flow,
> And, best of fruit, spontaneous guineas grow.

Pope, in his "Dunciad," makes it *this leaden age,* but I choose to call it without an epithet, *this* age. Many things we must expect to meet with which it would be hard to bear, if a compensation were not found in honest endeavours to do well, in virtuous affections and connections, and in harmless and reasonable amusements. And why should *not* a man amuse himself sometimes? *Vive la bagatelle!*

I received a letter this morning from my friend Allen. He is up to his ears in business, and I sincerely congratulate him upon it—occupation, I am convinced, being the great secret of happiness. "Nothing makes the temper so fretful as indolence," said a young lady who, beneath the soft surface of feminine delicacy, possesses a mind acute by nature, and strengthened by habits of reflection. 'Pon my word, Miss Evans, I beg your pardon a thousand times for bepraising you to your face, but, really, I have written so long that I had forgot to whom I was writing.

Have you read Mr. Fox's letter to the Westminster electors? It is quite the political *go* at Cambridge, and has converted many souls to the Foxite faith.

Have you seen the Siddons this season? or the Jordan? An acquaintance of mine has a tragedy coming out early in the next season, the principal character of which Mrs. Siddons will act. He has importuned me to write the prologue and epilogue, but, conscious of my inability, I have excused myself with a jest, and told him I was too good a Christian to be accessory to the damnation of anything.

There is an old proverb of a river of words and a spoonful of sense, and I think this letter has been a pretty good proof of it. But as nonsense is better than blank paper, I will fill this side with a song I wrote lately. My friend, Charles Hague the composer, will set it to wild music. I shall sing it, and accompany myself on the violin. *Ça ira!*

Cathloma, who reigned in the Highlands of Scotland

about two hundred years after the birth of our Saviour, was defeated and killed in a war with a neighbouring prince, and Nina Thoma his daughter (according to the custom of those times and that country) was imprisoned in a cave by the seaside. This is supposed to be her complaint:—

How long will ye round me be swelling,
    O ye blue-tumbling waves of the sea?
Not always in caves was my dwelling,
    Nor beneath the cold blast of the Tree;

Thro' the high sounding Hall of Cathloma
    In the steps of my beauty I strayed,
The warriors beheld Nina Thoma,
    And they blessed the dark-tressed Maid!

By my Friends, by my Lovers discarded,
    Like the Flower of the Rock now I waste,
That lifts its fair head unregarded,
    And scatters its leaves on the blast.

A Ghost! by my cavern it darted!
    In moonbeams the spirit was drest—
For lovely appear the Departed,
    When they visit the dreams of my rest!

But dispersed by the tempest's commotion,
    Fleet the shadowy forms of Delight;
Ah! cease, thou shrill blast of the Ocean!
    To howl thro' my Cavern by night.

Are you asleep, my dear Mary? I have administered rather a strong dose of opium; however, if in the course of your nap you should chance to dream that I am, with ardor of eternal friendship, your affectionate

S. T. COLERIDGE,

you will never have dreamt a truer dream in all your days.

IX

TO GEORGE COLERIDGE, HACKNEY

Sunday night, Feb. 23, 1794

My Brother would have heard from me long ere this had I not been unwell, unwell indeed—I verily thought, that

I was hastening to that quiet Bourne, where grief is hush'd—
And when my recovered strength would have enabled me to
have written to you, so utterly dejected were my spirits, that
my letter would have displayed such a hopelessness of all
future comfort, as would have approached to ingratitude—

Pardon me, my more than Brother! if it be the sickly
jealousy of a mind sore in the "self-contracted miseries,"
but was your last letter written in the same tone of tenderness with your former! Ah me! what awaits me from within
and without, after the first tumult of Pity shall have subsided— Well were it, if the consciousness of having merited
it, could arm my heart to the patient endurance of it—

Sweet in the sight of God and celestial Spirits are the
tears of Penitance—the pearls of heaven—the wine of
Angels! Such has been the language of Divines, but Divines
have exaggerated. Repentance may bestow that tranquillity,
which will enable man to pursue a course of undeviating
harmlessness, but it cannot restore to the mind that inward
sense of Dignity, which is the Parent of every kindling energy!
I am not what I was:—*Disgust*—I *feel*, as if I had jaundiced
all my Faculties.

I laugh almost like an insane person when I cast my eye
backward on the prospect of my past two years. What a
gloomy *Huddle* of eccentric actions, and dim-discovered
motives! To real happiness I bade adieu from the moment
I received my first "Tutors' Bill"; since that time, since
that period my mind has been irradiated by Bursts only of
sunshine, at all other times gloomy with clouds, or turbulent
with tempests. Instead of manfully disclosing the disease,
I concealed it with a shameful cowardice of sensibility, till it
cankered my very Heart. I became a proverb to the University for Idleness. The time, which I should have bestowed
on the academic studies, I employed in dreaming out wild
schemes of impossible extrication. It had been better for
me, if my Imagination had been less vivid. I could not with
such facility have shoved aside Reflection! How many and
how many hours have I stolen from the bitterness of Truth
in these soul-enervating Reveries—in building magnificent
edifices of Happiness on some fleeting shadow of Reality!
My affairs became more and more involved. I fled to
Debauchery; fled pure silent and solitary Anguish to all the

uproar of senseless mirth. Having, or imagining that I had, no *stock* of Happiness to which I could look forward, I seized the empty gratifications of the moment, and snatched at the Foam, as the wave passed by me. I feel a painful blush on my cheek, while I write it, but even for the Un. Scholarship, for which I affected to have read so severely, I did not read three days uninterruptedly—for the whole six weeks, that preceded the examination, I was almost constantly intoxicated! My Brother! you shudder as you read.

When the state of my affairs became known to you and by your exertions and my Brothers' generous Confidence a fair Road seemed open to extrication, Almighty God! what a sequel! I loitered away more money on the road, and in town than it was possible for me to justify to my Conscience; and when I returned to Cambridge a multitude of petty embarrassments buzzed round me, like a nest of Hornets, Embarrassments, which in my wild carelessness I had forgotten, and many of which I had contracted almost without knowing it. So small a sum remained, that I could not mock my Tutor with it. My agitations were delirium— I formed a Party, dashed to London at eleven o'clock at night, and for three days lived in all the tempest of Pleasure—resolved on my return—but I will not shock your religious feelings. I again returned to Cambridge—staid a *week*—such a week! Where Vice has not annihilated sensibility, there is little need of a Hell! On Sunday night I packed up a few things, went off in the mail, staid about a week in a strange way, still looking forward with a kind of recklessness to the *dernier ressort* of misery—an accident of a very singular kind prevented me, and led me to adopt my present situation—where what I have suffered—but enough, may he, who in mercy dispenseth anguish be gracious to me.

Ulcera possessis alte suffusa medullis Non leviore manu, ferro sanantur et igni. Ne noceat frustra mox eruptura cicatrix. Ad vivum penetrant flammae, quo funditus humor. Defluat, et vacuis corrupto sanguine venis Exundet fons ille mali— Claud. [xx, 13]

I received a letter from Tiverton on Thursday full of wisdom, and tenderness and consolation. I answered it immediately. Let me have the comfort of hearing from you. I will write again to-morrow night.

S.T.C.

X

May 1, 1794

MY DEAR BROTHER,—I have been convened before the fellows. Dr. Piarce behaved with great asperity, Mr. Plampin with exceeding and most delicate kindness. My sentence is a reprimand (not a public one, but *implied* in the sentence), a month's confinement to the precincts of the College, and to translate the works of Demetrius Phalareus into English. It is a thin quarto of about ninety Greek pages. All the fellows tried to persuade the Master to greater leniency, but in vain. Without the least affectation I applaud his conduct, and think nothing of it. The confinement is nothing. I have the fields and grove of the College to walk in, and what can I wish more? What do I wish more? Nothing. The Demetrius is dry, and utterly untransferable to *modern* use, and yet from the Doctor's words I suspect that he wishes it to be a publication, as he has more than once sent to know how I go on, and pressed me to exert erudition in some notes, and to write a preface. Besides this, I have had a declamation to write in the routine of college business, and the Rustat examination, at which I got credit. I get up every morning at five o'clock.

Every one of my acquaintance I have dropped solemnly and forever, except those of my College with whom before my departure I had been least of all connected—who had always remonstrated against my imprudences, yet have treated me with almost fraternal affection, Mr. Caldwell particularly. I thought the most *decent* way of dropping acquaintances was to express my intention, openly and irrevocably.

I find I must either go out at a by-term or degrade to the Christmas after next; but more of this to-morrow. I have been engaged in finishing a Greek ode. I mean to write for all the prizes. I have had no time upon my hands. I shall aim at correctness and perspicuity, not *genius*. My last ode was so *sublime* that nobody could understand it. *If* I should be so *very lucky* as to win one of the prizes, I could *comfortably* ask the Doctor advice concerning the *time* of my degree. I will write to-morrow.

God bless you, my brother! my father!

S. T. COLERIDGE.

XI

TO ROBERT SOUTHEY

Gloucester, Sunday morning, July 6, 1794

. . . It is *wrong*, Southey! for a little girl with a half-famished sickly baby in her arms to put her head in at the window of an inn—"Pray give me a bit of bread and meat!" from a party dining on lamb, green peas, and salad. Why? Because it is *impertinent* and *obtrusive!* "I am a gentleman! and wherefore the clamorous voice of woe intrude υpon mine ear?" My companion is a man of cultivated, though not vigorous understanding; his feelings are all on the side of humanity; yet such are the unfeeling remarks, which the lingering remains of aristocracy occasionally prompt. When the pure system of pantisocracy shall have *aspheterized*—from ἀ, non, and σφέτερος, proprius (we really *wanted* such a word), instead of travelling along the circuitous, dusty, beaten highroad of diction, you thus cut across the soft, green, pathless field of novelty! Similes for ever! Hurrah! I have bought a little blank book, and portable ink horn; [and] as I journey onward, I ever and anon pluck the wild flowers of poesy, "inhale their odours awhile," then throw them away and think no more of them. I will not do so! Two lines of mine:—

> And o'er the sky's unclouded blue
> The sultry heat *suffused* a *brassy* hue.

The cockatrice is a foul dragon with a *crown* on its head. The Eastern nations believe it to be hatched by a viper on a cock's egg. Southey, dost thou not see wisdom in her *Coan* vest of allegory? The cockatrice is emblematic of monarchy, a *monster* generated by *ingratitude* or *absurdity*. When serpents *sting*, the only remedy is to kill the *serpent*, and *besmear* the *wound* with the *fat*. Would you desire better sympathy?

Description of heat from a poem I am manufacturing, the title: "Perspiration. A Travelling Eclogue."

> The dust flies smothering, as on clatt'ring wheel
> Loathed aristocracy careers along;
> The distant track quick vibrates to the eye,
> And white and dazzling undulates with heat,
> Where scorching to the unwary travellers' touch,
> The stone fence flings its narrow slip of shade;
> Or, where the worn sides of the chalky road
> Yield their scant excavations (sultry grots!),
> Emblem of languid patience, we behold
> The fleecy files faint-ruminating lie.

Farewell, sturdy Republican! . . .

XII

TO THE SAME

Wrexham, Sunday, July 16, 1794

. . . Monday, 11 o'clock. Well, praised be God! here I am. *Videlicet*, Ruthin, sixteen miles from Wrexham. At Wrexham Church I glanced upon the face of a Miss E. Evans, a young lady with [whom] I had been in habits of fraternal correspondence. She turned excessively pale; she thought it my ghost, I suppose. I retreated with all possible speed to our inn. There, as I was standing at the window, passed by Eliza Evans, and with her to my utter surprise her sister, Mary Evans, *quam efflictim et perdite amabam*. I apprehend she is come from London on a visit to her grandmother, with whom Eliza lives. I turned sick, and all but fainted away! The two sisters, as H. informs me, passed by the window anxiously several times afterwards; but I had retired.

> *Vivit, sed mihi non vivit—nova forte marita,*
> *Ah dolor! alterius cara a cervice pependit.*
> *Vos, malefida valete accensae insomnia mentis,*
> *Littora amata valete! Vale, ah! formosa Maria!*

My fortitude would not have supported me, had I *recognized* her—I mean *appeared* to do it! I neither ate nor slept yesterday. But love is a local anguish; I am sixteen miles distant, and am not half so miserable. I must endeavour to forget it amid the terrible graces of the wild wood scenery that surround me. I never durst even in a

whisper avow my passion, though I knew she loved me.
Where were my fortunes? and why should I make her
miserable! Almighty God bless her! Her image is in the
sanctuary of my heart, and never can it be torn away
but with the strings that grapple it to life. Southey! there
are few men of whose delicacy I think so highly as to
have written all this. I am glad I have so deemed of you.
We are soothed by communications. . . .

XIII

TO THE SAME

London, Monday morning
[Postmark, September 6, 1794]

. . . Every night since my arrival I have spent at an Ale-
house, by courtesy called a Coffee-house: the "Salutation
and Cat" in Newgate St.—We have a comfortable Room to
ourselves, and drink Porter and *Punch* round a good fire. My
motive for all this is that every night I meet a most intelligent
young man who has spent the last five years of his life in
America—and is lately come from thence as an Agent to sell
Land. He was of our School—I had been kind to him—he
remembered it—and comes regularly every evening to
"benefit by conversation" he says. He says two thousand
pound will do—that he doubts not we can contract for our
Passage under £400—that we shall buy this Land a great
deal cheaper when we arrive at America, than we could do
in England—or why (adds he) am I sent over here? That
twelve men can *easily* clear *three hundred* Acres in 4 or 5
months—and that for six hundred Dollars a thousand Acres
may be cleared, and houses built upon them. He recommends the Susquehannah from its excessive Beauty, and its
security from hostile Indians—Every possible assistance will
be given us. We may get credit for the Land for ten years
or more as we settle upon it—That literary characters make
money there, that &c., &c. He never saw a Byson in his life,
but has heard of them. They are quite backwards. The
Mosquitos are not so bad as our Gnats—and after you have
been there a little while, they don't trouble you much. He
says the Women's *teeth* are bad there—but not the men's—

T

at least not nearly so much—attributes it to neglect—to particular foods—is by no means convinced it is the necessary effect of Climate. . . .

XIV

TO THE SAME

10 o'clock, Thursday morning, September 18, 1794

Well, my dear Southey! I am at last arrived at Jesus. My God! how tumultuous are the movements of my heart. Since I quitted this room what and how important events have been evolved! America! Southey! Miss Fricker! Yes, Southey, you are right. Even Love is the creature of strong motive. I certainly love her. I *think* of her incessantly and with unspeakable tenderness,—with that inward melting away of soul that symptomatizes it.

Pantisocracy! Oh, I shall have such a scheme of it! My head, my heart, are all alive. I have drawn up my arguments in battle array; they shall have the *tactician* excellence of the mathematician with the enthusiasm of the poet. The head shall be the mass; the heart the fiery spirit that fills, informs, and agitates the whole. Harwood—pish! I say nothing of him.

SHAD GOES WITH US. HE IS MY BROTHER! I am longing to be with you. Make Edith my sister. Surely, Southey, we shall be *frendotatoi meta frendous*—most friendly where all are friends. She must, therefore, be more emphatically my sister.

Brookes and Berdmore, as I suspected, have spread my opinions in mangled forms at Cambridge. Caldwell, the most pantisocratic of aristocrats, has been laughing at me. Up I arose, terrible in reasoning. He fled from me, because "he could not answer for his own sanity, sitting so near a madman of genius." He told me that the strength of my imagination had intoxicated my reason, and that the acuteness of my reason had given a directing influence to my imagination. Four months ago the remark would not have been more elegant than just. Now it is nothing.

I like your sonnets exceedingly—the best of any I have yet seen. "Though to the eye fair is the extended vale" should

be "to the eye though fair the extended vale." I by no means
disapprove of discord introduced to produce *effect*, nor is my
ear so fastidious as to be angry with it where it could not
have been avoided without weakening the sense. But discord
for discord's sake is rather too licentious.

"Wild wind" has no other but alliterative beauty; it
applies to a storm, not to the autumnal breeze that makes
the trees rustle mournfully. Alter it to "That rustle to the
sad wind moaningly."

" 'T was a long way and tedious," and the three last
lines are marked beauties—unlaboured strains poured sooth-
ingly along from the feeling simplicity of heart. The next
sonnet is altogether exquisite,—the circumstance common
yet new to poetry, the moral accurate and full of soul. "I
never saw," etc., is most exquisite. I am almost ashamed to
write the following, it is so inferior. Ashamed? No, Southey!
God knows my heart! I am *delighted* to feel you superior to
me in genius as in virtue.

> No more my visionary soul shall dwell
> On joys that were; no more endure to weigh
> The shame and anguish of the evil day.
> Wisely forgetful! O'er the ocean swell
> Sublime of Hope, I seek the cottaged dell
> Where Virtue calm with careless step may stray,
> And, dancing to the moonlight roundelay,
> The wizard Passions weave an holy spell.
> Eyes that have ached with sorrow! ye shall weep
> Tears of doubt-mingled joy, like theirs who start
> From precipices of distempered sleep,
> On which the fierce-eyed fiends their revels keep,
> And see the rising sun, and feel it dart
> New rays of pleasance trembling to the heart. . . .

XV

TO THE SAME

October 21, 1794

. . . No name was signed,—it was from Mary Evans. I
received it about three weeks ago. I loved her, Southey,
almost to madness. Her image was never absent from
me for three years, for *more* than three years. My resolution has not faltered, but I want a comforter. I have

done nothing, I have gone into company, I was constantly at the theatre here till they left us, I endeavoured to be perpetually with Miss Brunton, I even hoped that her exquisite beauty and uncommon accomplishments might have cured one passion by another. The latter I could easily have dissipated in her absence, and so have restored my affections to her whom I do not love, but whom by every tie of reason and honour I ought to love. I am resolved, but wretched! But time shall do much. You will easily believe that with such feelings I should have found it no easy task to write to ——. I should have detested myself, if after my first letter I had written coldly—how could I write *as warmly?* I was vexed too and alarmed by your letter concerning Mr. and Mrs. Roberts, Shad, and little Sally. I was wrong, very wrong, in the affair of Shad, and have given you reason to suppose that I should assent to the innovation. I will most assuredly go with you to America, on this plan, but remember, Southey, this is *not our plan*, nor can I defend it. "Shad's children will be educated as ours, and the education we shall give them will be such as to render them incapable of blushing at the want of it in their parents"—*Perhaps!* With this one word would every Lilliputian reasoner demolish the system. Wherever men *can* be vicious, some *will* be. The leading idea of pantisocracy is to make men *necessarily* virtuous by removing all motives to evil—all possible temptation. "Let them dine with us and be treated with as much equality as they would wish, but perform that part of labour for which their education has fitted them." *Southey* should not have written this sentence. My friend, my noble and high-souled friend should have said to his dependents, "Be my slaves, and ye shall be my equals;" to his wife and sister, "Resign the *name* of Ladyship and ye shall retain the *thing*." Again. Is every family to possess one of these unequal equals, these Helot Egalités? Or are the few you have mentioned, "with more toil than the peasantry of England undergo," to do for all of us "that part of labour which their education has fitted them for"? If your remarks on the other side are just, the inference is that the scheme of pantisocracy is impracticable, but I hope and believe that it is not a *necessary* inference. Your remark of the physical evil in the long infancy of men would indeed puzzle a Pangloss—puzzle him to account for the wish of a benevolent heart like yours to discover malignancy in its Creator. Surely every eye but an eye jaundiced by habit of peevish scepticism must have seen that the mothers' cares are repaid even to rapture by the mothers' endearments, and that the long helplessness of the babe is the *means* of our superiority in the filial and maternal affection and duties to the same feelings in the brute creation. It is likewise among other causes the *means* of society, that thing which makes them a little lower than the angels. If Mrs. S. and Mrs. F. go with us, they can at least prepare the food of simplicity for us. Let the married women do only what is absolutely convenient and customary for pregnant women or nurses. Let the husband do all the rest, and what will that all be? Washing with a machine and cleaning the house. One hour's addition to our daily labor, and *pantisocracy* in its most perfect sense is practicable. That the greater part of our female companions should have the task of maternal exertion at the same time is very *improbable;* but, though it were to happen, an infant is almost always sleeping, and during its slumbers the mother may in the same room perform the little offices of ironing clothes or making shirts. But the hearts of the women are not *all* with us. I do believe that Edith and Sarah are exceptions, but do even they know the bill of fare for the day, every duty that will be incumbent upon them?

All necessary knowledge in the branch of ethics is comprised in the word justice: that the good of the whole is the good of each individual, that, of course, it is each individual's *duty* to be just, *because* it is his *interest*. To perceive this and to assent to it as an abstract proposition is easy, but it requires the most wakeful attentions of the most reflective mind in all moments to bring it into practice. It is not enough that we have once swallowed it. The *heart* should have *fed* upon the *truth*, as insects on a leaf, till it be tinged with the colour, and show its food in every the minutest fibre. In the book of pantisocracy I hope to have comprised all that is good in Godwin, of whom and of whose book I will write more fully in my next letter (I think not so highly of him as you do, and I have read him with the greatest attention). This will be an advantage to the *minds* of our women. . . .

XVI

TO THE SAME

Autumn, 1794

Last night, dear Southey, I received a special invitation from Dr. Edwards (the great Grecian of Cambridge and heterodox divine) to drink tea and spend the evening. I there met a councillor whose name is Lushington, a democrat, and a man of the most powerful and Briarean intellect. I was challenged on the subject of pantisocracy, which is, indeed, the universal topic at the University. A discussion began and continued for six hours. In conclusion, Lushington and Edwards declared the system impregnable, supposing the assigned quantum of virtue and genius in the first individuals. I came home at one o'clock this morning in the honest consciousness of having exhibited closer argument in more elegant and appropriate language than I had ever conceived myself capable of. Then my heart smote me, for I saw your letter on the propriety of taking servants with us. I had answered that letter, and feel conviction that you will *perceive* the error into which the tenderness of your nature had led you. But other queries obtruded themselves on my understanding. The more perfect our system is, supposing the necessary premises, the more eager in anxiety am I that the necessary premises exist. O for that Lyncean eye that can discover in the acorn of Error the rooted and widely spreading oak of Misery! *Quaere:* should not all who mean to become members of our community be incessantly meliorating their temper and elevating their understandings? *Qu.:* whether a very respectable quantity of *acquired* knowledge (History, Politics, above all, *Metaphysics,* without which no man *can* reason but with women and children) be not a prerequisite to the improvement of the head and heart? *Qu.:* whether our Women have not been taught by us habitually to contemplate the littleness of individual comforts and a passion for the *novelty* of the scheme rather than a generous enthusiasm of Benevolence? Are they saturated with the Divinity of Truth sufficiently to be always wakeful? In the present state of their minds, whether it is not probable that the *Mothers* will tinge the minds of the infants with prejudication? The questions are meant merely as motives to you, Southey, to the strengthening the minds of the Women, and stimulating them to literary acquirements. But, Southey, there are *Children* going with us. Why did I never dare in my disputations with the unconvinced to hint at this circumstance? Was it not because I knew, even to certainty of conviction, that it is subversive of *rational* hopes of a permanent system? These children,—the little Frickers, for instance, and your brothers,—are they not already deeply tinged with the prejudices and errors of society? Have they not learned from their schoolfellows *Fear* and *Selfishness*, of which the necessary offsprings are Deceit and desultory Hatred? How are we to prevent them from infecting the minds of *our* children? By reforming their judgements? At so early an age, *can* they have *felt* the ill consequences of their errors in a manner sufficiently vivid to make this reformation practicable? How can we insure their silence concerning God, etc.? Is it possible *they* should enter into our *motives* for this silence? If not, we must produce their *Obedience* by *Terror. Obedience? Terror?* The repetition is sufficient. I need not inform you that they are as inadequate as inapplicable. I have told you, Southey, that I will accompany you on an *imperfect* system. But must our system be thus necessarily imperfect? I ask the question that I may know whether or not I should write the Book of Pantisocracy. . . .

XVII

TO MARY EVANS

[(?) December, 1794]

Too long has my heart been the torture house of suspense. After infinite struggles of irresolution, I will at last dare to request of you, Mary, that you will communicate to me whether or no you are engaged to Mr. ——. I conjure you not to consider this request as presumptuous indelicacy. Upon mine honour, I have made it with no other design or expectation than that of arming my fortitude by total hopelessness. Read this letter with benevolence—and consign it to oblivion.

For four years I have *endeavoured* to smother a very ardent attachment; in what degree I have succeeded you must know better than I can. With quick perceptions of moral beauty, it was impossible for me not to admire in you your sensibility regulated by judgement, your gaiety proceeding from a cheerful heart acting on the stores of a strong understanding. At first I voluntarily invited the recollection of these qualities into my mind. I made them the perpetual object of my reveries, yet I entertained no one sentiment beyond that of the immediate pleasure annexed to the thinking of you. At length it became a habit. I awoke from the delusion, and found that I had unwittingly harboured a passion which I felt neither the power nor the courage to subdue. My associations were irrevocably formed, and your image was blended with every idea. I thought of you incessantly; yet that spirit (if spirit there be that condescends to record the lonely beatings of my heart), that spirit knows that I thought of you with the purity of a brother. Happy were I, had it been with no more than brother's ardour!

The man of dependent fortunes, while he fosters an attachment, commits an act of suicide on his happiness. I possessed no establishment. My views were very distant; I saw that you regarded me merely with the kindness of a sister. What expectations could I form? I formed no expectations. I was ever resolving to subdue the disquieting passion; still some inexplicable suggestion palsied my efforts, and I clung with desperate fondness to this phantom of love, its mysterious attractions and hopeless prospects. It was a faint and rayless hope! Yet it soothed my solitude with many a delightful day-dream. It was a faint and rayless hope! Yet I nursed it in my bosom with an agony of affection, even as a mother her sickly infant. But these are the poisoned luxuries of a diseased fancy. Indulge, Mary, this my first, my last request, and restore me to *reality*, however gloomy. Sad and full of heaviness will the intelligence be; my heart will die within me. I shall, however, receive it with steadier resignation from yourself, than were it announced to me (haply on your marriage day!) by a stranger. Indulge my request; I will not disturb your peace by even a *look* of discontent, still less will I offend your ear by the whine of selfish sensibility. In a few months I shall enter at the Temple and there seek forgetful calmness, where only it can be found, in incessant and useful activity.

Were you not possessed of a mind and of a heart above the usual lot of women, I should not have written you sentiments that would be unintelligible to three fourths of your sex. But our feelings are congenial, though our attachment is doomed not to be reciprocal. You will not deem so meanly of me as to believe that I shall regard Mr. —— with the jaundiced eye of disappointed passion. God forbid! He whom you honour with your affections becomes sacred to me. I shall love him for *your* sake; the time may perhaps come when I shall be philosopher enough not to envy him for *his own*.   S. T. COLERIDGE.

I return to Cambridge to-morrow morning.

XVIII

TO THE SAME

December 24, 1794

I have this moment received your letter, Mary Evans. Its firmness does honour to your understanding, its gentleness to your humanity. You condescend to accuse yourself—most unjustly! You have been altogether blameless. In my wildest day-dream of vanity, I never supposed that you entertained for me any other than a common friendship.

To love you, habit has made unalterable. This passion, however, divested as it now is of all shadow of hope, will lose its disquieting power. Far distant from you I shall journey through the vale of men in calmness. He cannot long be wretched, who dares be actively virtuous.

I have burnt your letters—forget mine; and that I have pained you, forgive me!

May God infinitely love you!   S. T. COLERIDGE.

XIX

TO GEORGE DYER

[1795]
No. 25 College Street, Bristol

MY DEAR SIR,—Intending to return from day to day I postponed writing to you—I will however delay it no longer.

I am anxious and perturbed beyond measure concerning my proposed expedition to Scotland—I will pour out my heart before you as water. In the Autumn of last year, you know, we formed our American Plan and with precipitance that did credit to our hearts rather than heads, fixed on the coming April as the time of our embarkation. *This* following circumstances have rendered impracticable—but there are other engagements not so dissoluble. In expectation of emigrating on the Pantisocratic Plan I payed my addresses to a young Lady, whom *"οὔτ' αἰνεῖν ἐστι κακοῖσι θέμις"*! Independently of the Love and Esteem which her Person, and polished understanding may be supposed to have inspired into a young Man, I consider myself as under particular Ties of Gratitude to her—since in confidence of my Affection she has rejected the Addresses of two Men, one of them of large Fortune—and by her perseverant Attachment to me disobliged her Relations in a very uncomfortable Degree. Perpetually obliged to resist the entreaties and to endure the reproachful admonitions of her Uncle etc., she vainly endeavors to conceal from me how heavy her heart is with anxiety, how disquieted by Suspense— To leave her for two or three years would, I fear, be sacrificing her health and happiness— In short, why should I write circuitously to you? So commanding are the requests of her Relations, that a short Time must decide whether she marries me whom she loves with an affection to the ardor of which my Deserts bear no proportion—or a man whom she strongly dislikes, in spite of his fortune and solicitous attentions to her. These peculiar circumstances she had with her usual Delicacy concealed from me till my arrival at Bristol. . . .

XX

TO ROBERT SOUTHEY

Friday morning, November 13, 1795

Southey, I *have* lost friends—friends who still cherish for me sentiments of high esteem and unextinguished tenderness. For the sum total of my misbehaviour, the Alpha and Omega of their accusations, is epistolary neglect. I never speak of them without affection, I never think of them without reverence. Not "to this catalogue," Southey, have I "added *your* name." You are *lost* to *me*, because you are lost to Virtue. As this will probably be the last time I shall have occasion to address you, I will begin at the beginning and regularly retrace your conduct and my own. In the month of June, 1794, I first became acquainted with your person and character. Before I quitted Oxford, we had struck out the leading features of a pantisocracy. While on my journey through Wales you invited me to Bristol with the full hopes of realising it. During my abode at Bristol the plan was matured, and I returned to Cambridge hot in the anticipation of that happy season when we should remove the *selfish* principle from ourselves, and prevent it in our children, by an abolition of property; or, in whatever respects this might be impracticable, by such similarity of property as would amount to a *moral* sameness, and answer all the purposes of *abolition*. Nor were you less zealous, and thought and expressed your opinion, that if any man embraced our system he must comparatively disregard "his father and mother and wife and children and brethren and sisters, yea, and his own life also, or he could not be our disciple." In one of your letters, alluding to your mother's low spirits and situation, you tell me that "I cannot suppose any *individual* feelings will have an undue weight with you," and in the same letter you observe (alas! your recent conduct has made it a prophecy!), "God forbid that the *ebullience* of *schematism* should be over. It is the Promethean fire that animates my soul, and when *that* is gone *all will be darkness*. I have *devoted* myself!"

Previously to my departure from Jesus College, and during my melancholy detention in London, what convulsive struggles of feeling I underwent, and what sacrifices I made, you know. The liberal proposal from my family affected me no further than as it pained me to wound a revered brother by the positive and immediate refusal which duty compelled me to return. But there was a— I need not be particular; you remember what a fetter I burst, and that it snapt as if it had been a sinew of my heart. However, I returned to Bristol, and my addresses to Sara, which I at first paid from principle, not feeling, from feeling and from principle I renewed; and I met a reward more than proportionate to the greatness of the effort. I love and I am beloved, and I am happy!

Your letter to Lovell (two or three days after my arrival at Bristol), in answer to some objections of mine to the Welsh scheme, was the first thing that alarmed me. Instead of "It is our duty," "Such and such are the reasons," it was "I and I" and "will and will,"—sentences of gloomy and self-centering resolve. I wrote you a friendly reproof, and in my own mind attributed this unwonted style to your earnest desires of realising our plan, and the angry pain which you felt when any appeared to oppose or defer its execution. However, I came over to your opinions of the utility, and, in course, the duty of rehearsing our scheme in Wales, and, so, rejected the offer of being established in the Earl of Buchan's family. To this period of our connection I call your more particular attention and remembrance, as I shall revert to it at the close of my letter.

We commenced lecturing. Shortly after, you began to recede in your conversation from those broad principles in which pantisocracy originated. I opposed you with vehemence, for I well knew that no notion of morality or its motives could be without consequences. And once (it was just before we went to bed) you confessed to me that you had acted wrong. But you relapsed; your manner became cold and gloomy, and pleaded with increased pertinacity for the wisdom of making Self an undiverging Center. . . .

XXI

TO THE REV. T. EDWARDS

[Feb. 4, 1796]

Your spells, my dear Sir! might have been *Prosper-like;* but they are not like to prosper—so that both orthographically and heterographically, like Ashur, I must abide in these *Breaches.* As Harwood's form possesses such lubric and gregarious qualities, I presume you must, *thumb him* before you can safely exclaim "You're him!" Great Goddess of Grinnosity! what infernal nonsense will not your true* *Carthagian* squitter, rather than not *let* a *pun!*

---

*"*Homo punicus,*" S.T.C.

I preached on Sunday to very good purpose, as far as the plate went. Indeed (altogether) my sermon was the best composition I have ever been guilty of. I can give you but faint ideas of the kindness and hospitality, with which I was treated at Nottingham. I arrived at Sheffield Monday night —on Tuesday morning called on Mr. Kirkby with the letter from Bristol, the only letter I had from Bristol for Sheffield. Mr. Kirkby is journeying. I then called on Mr. Naylor. He too was absent. But finding that he was on a visit to a friend's house only four miles off, I trudged thither over hill and dale, thro' a worse road than ever Flibbertigibbet led poor Tom. This friend proved to be Mr. Meanly—that tobacco-toothed Parson with a majestic periphery of guts, whom we met (together with Scofield) at Mr. Coates'. Mr. Naylor received me politely—Mrs. Naylor with kindliness (N.B. she is an engaging little girl). Naylor declined interesting himself in my "Watchman," or even procuring me a Publisher—his motives were such as I could not but enter into and approve. He had formerly been joint-proprietor (with poor Montgomery) of the "Iris": and now that poor Montgomery is in prison, of course could not without great indelicacy promote a work which might injure the Sale of his Paper. However he recommended me to call on Mr. Smith, a bookseller, and gave me a letter to a Mr. Shore, a man of fortune who lives at Mearsbrook, two miles from Sheffield. I left him—it was now dark: and into pits and out of pits, and against stones and over stones I contrived to stumble some mile and a half out of my way. I enquired my road at a cottage—and on lifting up the latch beheld a tall old Hag, whose soul-gelding ugliness would chill to eternal chastity a cantharidized Satyr. However an Angel of Light could not have been more civil, and she sent her Son to conduct me home. Yesterday morning I called on Mr. Shore—who behaved civilly to me and promised to recommend my work as far as he was able, and offered me three guineas towards it's expenses, which (of course) I declined (N.B. The Governess of the Charity at Nottingham offered me three guineas for my charity, which I positively declined; but this morning I have received by Nottingham coach a parcel (without letter or name) containing eight pairs of silk stockings, ribbed, striped, and plain—and a sealed parcel for Mrs. Coleridge, containing I know not what—it being sealed). On my return from Mr. Shore's I called on Smith, the Bookseller— I opened my business, left my prospectus, and called on him a second time to receive the answer an hour after. "Sir! (said he) I have frequently heard of you; and the very motives, why I ought to publish and promote your work, are the motives that make me hesitate to do it— I am afraid that from the superiority of it's plan and your known abilities it will interfere with, and perhaps greatly lessen, the sale of poor Montgomery's paper—which I edit during his confinement—without pay or profit, I assure you, but he is my particular friend." I answered him—"I hope you do me the justice to believe, that I entirely enter into your feelings and approve of them; and if it cannot be published without injuring Montgomery, I will apply to [no] other Bookseller, but give it up altogether." He thanked me for my etc., in the name of Montgomery and said he would advise with a few *friends*. This morning he returned me a final answer—that to advertise and publicly disperse the work here would certainly injure Montgomery; but that he thought that 20 or 30 might be disposed of among friends—and so the matter rests. . . .

XXII

TO JOSEPH COTTLE

Redcliffe Hill, February 22, 1796

MY DEAR SIR,—It is my duty and business to thank God for all his dispensations, and to believe them the best possible; but, indeed, I think I should have been more thankful, if he had made me a journeyman shoemaker, instead of an author by trade. I have left my friends; I have left plenty; I have left that ease which would have secured a literary immortality, and have enabled me to give the public works conceived in moments of inspiration, and polished with leisurely solicitude; and alas! for what have I left them? for —— who deserted me in the hour of distress, and for a scheme of virtue impracticable and romantic! So I am forced to write for bread; write the flights of poetic enthusiasm, when every minute I am hearing a groan from my wife. Groans, and complaints, and sickness! The present hour I am in a quick-set hedge of embarrassment, and whichever way I turn a thorn runs into me! The future is cloud and thick darkness! Poverty, perhaps, and the thin faces of them that want bread, looking up to me! Nor is this all. My happiest moments for composition are broken in upon by the reflection that I must make haste. I am too late! I am already months behind! I have received my pay beforehand! Oh, wayward and desultory spirit of genius! Ill canst thou brook a taskmaster! The tenderest touch from the hand of obligation wounds thee like a scourge of scorpions.

I have been composing in the fields this morning, and came home to write down the first rude sheet of my prefaec, when I heard that your man had brought a note from you. I have not seen it, but I guess its contents. I am writing as fast as I can. Depend on it you shall not be out of pocket for me! I feel what I owe you, and independently of this I love you as a friend; indeed, so much, that I regret, seriously regret, that you have been my copyholder.

If I have written petulantly, forgive me. God knows I am sore all over. God bless you, and believe me that, setting gratitude aside, I love and esteem you, and have your interest at heart full as much as my own.

S. T. COLERIDGE.

XXIII

TO THE REV. T. EDWARDS

Sunday Morning, March 20, 1796

DEAR EDWARDS,—Believe me grateful for your communications which appear this week. Erskine's speech is excellent—the quotation happy beyond anything I ever read. I see by the "Star" that Binns is taken up by an order from the Secretary of State: if there be any particulars which have not appeared in the "Star" I beseech you, to be so kind as *immediately* to transmit them.

The Essay on Fasting has not promoted my work—indeed altogether I am sorry that I wrote it. What so many men wiser and better than myself think a solemn subject ought not to have been treated ludicrously. But it is one of the disadvantages attendant on my undertaking, that I am obliged to *publish* extempore as well as compose. My last number pleased beyond those which preceded it. From Birmingham I received an invocation to Liberty far above mediocrity; but I do not understand the word "Evanid" as there used. You will see the verses in the next "Watchman." The letters from Liverpool I have received—poor Meanly! His mountains shalt melt beneath the fervent heat! I have received several *trimming* letters from anonymous correspondents—one of them written with great elegance. It begins thus.—"Alas! alas! *Coleridge* the digito-monstratus of Cambridge, [. . . ? . . .] Political Newsmonger, News-paper-paragraph-thief, Re-retailer of retarded Scurrility, keeper of an asylum of old, poor and decayed jokes" &c.—then follow friendly admonitions, heartfelt condolences, and other *exacerbating Sugar-confits*—all that oil of Vitriol which these Pseudo-Samaritans pour into the wounds of misery. But I am perfectly callous except where Disapprobation tends to diminish Profit—there indeed I am all one tremble of Sensibility, marriage having taught me the wonderful uses of the vulgar article of life *Bread*. My wife, my wife's Mother and little Brother, and George Burnett—five mouths opening and shutting as I pull the string! Dear Edwards I know you do not altogether approve of direct Petitions to Deity—but in case there *should* be any efficacy in them, out of pity to the Guts of others pray for the Brains of your friend. Formerly I could select a fine morning, chuse my road and take my airing upon my Pegasus right leisurely but now I am in stirrups all day, pen and sheet *are* my spurs. But so the World wags, and what is the use of complaining? Misery is an article which every market is so glutted with that it can nowhere be encouraged as an Import.

Yesterday Mrs. Coleridge miscarried—but without danger and with little pain. From the first fortnight of pregnancy she has been so very ill with the Fever, that she could afford no nourishment to the Thing which might have been a Newton or an Hartley—it has wasted and melted away. I think the subject of Pregnancy the most obscure of all God's dispensations—it seems coercive against Immaterial-ism—it starts uneasy doubts respecting Immortality and the pangs which the Woman suffers seem inexplicable in the system of [Nature]. Other pains are only friendly admonitions that we are not acting as Nature requires—but here are pains most horrible in consequence of having obeyed Nature-Queen. How is it that Dr. Priestly is not an atheist? He asserts in three different places that God not only *does*, but *is* everything—But if God be everything, everything is God: which is all the Atheists assert. An eating, drinking, lustful God with no unity of *consciousness*—these appear to me the unavoidable Inferences from his philosophy— Has not Dr. Priestly forgotten that Incomprehensibility is as necessary an attribute of the First Cause as Love, or Poems, or Intelligence?

The Bishop of Llandaff has answered Payne—I mean to arrange all Payne's arguments in one column, and Watson's answers in another—it will do good. Estlin's sermon has some good points in it; Mr. Estlin hath not the Catenulating faculty. We want the silk-thread that ought to run through the Pearl Chain of Ratiocination.

Who and what is Bisset? and do you know where E.W. is? The Birminghamites are my best Friends—

God help you and believe me

Gratefully and affectionately

Your's   S. T. COLERIDGE.

P.S. In the last "Watchman" instead of "New hope and joy," read "New life and joy th' expanding Flowret feels"— did you like the verse?

XXIV

TO JOHN THELWALL

May 13, 1796

. . . Your remarks on my poems are, I think, just in general; there is a rage and affectation of double epithets. "Unshuddered, unaghasted" is, indeed, *truly* ridiculous. But why so violent against *metaphysics* in poetry? Is not Akenside's a metaphysical poem? Perhaps you do not like Akenside? Well, but *I do*, and so do a great many others. Why pass an act of *uniformity* against poets? I received a letter from a very sensible friend abusing love verses; another blaming the introduction of politics, "as wider from true poetry than the equator from the poles." "Some for each" is my motto. That poetry pleases which interests. My religious poetry interests the *religious*, who read it with rapture. Why? Because it awakes in them all the associations connected with a love of future existence, etc. A very dear friend of mine, who is, in my opinion, the best poet of the age (I will send you his poem when published), thinks that the lines from 364 to 375 and from 403 to 428 the best in the volume,—indeed, worth all the rest. And this man is a republican, and, at least a *semi*-atheist. Why do you object to "shadowy of truth"? It is, I acknowledge, a Grecism, but, I think, an elegant one. Your remarks on the della-crusca place of emphasis are just in part. Where we wish to point out the *thing*, and the *quality* is mentioned merely as a decoration, this mode of emphasis is indeed absurd; therefore, I very patiently give up to critical vengeance "*high* tree," "*sore* wounds," and "*rough* rock;" but when you wish to dwell chiefly on the *quality* rather than the *thing*, then this mode is proper, and, indeed, is used in common conversation. Who says good *man?* Therefore, "*big* soul," "*cold* earth," "*dark* womb," and "*flamy* child" are all right, and introduce a variety into the versification, [which is] an advantage where you can attain it without any sacrifice of sense. As to harmony, it is all *association*. Milton is *harmonious* to me, and I absolutely nauseate Darwin's poem.

Yours affectionately,

S. T. COLERIDGE.

XXV

TO THOMAS POOLE

Saturday, September 24, 1796

. . . On Tuesday morning I was surprised by a letter from Mr. Maurice, our medical attendant, informing me that Mrs. Coleridge was delivered on Monday, September 19, 1796, half past two in the morning, of a SON, and that both she and the child were uncommonly well. I was quite annihilated with the suddenness of the information, and retired to my own room to address myself to my Maker, but I could only offer up to Him the silence of stupefied feelings. I hastened home, and Charles Lloyd returned with me. When I first saw the child, I did not feel that thrill and overflowing of affection which I expected. I looked on it with a melancholy gaze; my mind was intensely contemplative and my heart only sad. But when two hours after I saw it at the bosom of its mother, on her arm, and her eye tearful and watching its little features, then I was thrilled and melted, and gave it the KISS of a *father*. . . . The baby seems strong, and the old nurse has over-persuaded my wife to discover a likeness of me in its face—no great compliment to me, for, in truth, I have seen handsomer babies in my lifetime. Its name is David Hartley Coleridge. I hope that ere he be a man, if God destines him for continuance in this life, his head will be convinced of, and his heart saturated with, the truths so ably supported by that great master of *Christian* Philosophy. . . .

XXVI

TO CHARLES LAMB

[September 28, 1796]

Your letter, my friend, struck me with a mighty horror. It rushed upon me and stupefied my feelings. You bid me write you a religious letter. I am not a man who would attempt to insult the greatness of your anguish by any other consolation. Heaven knows that in the easiest fortunes there is much dissatisfaction and weariness of spirit; much that calls for the exercise of patience and resignation; but in storms like these, that shake the dwelling and make the heart tremble, there is no middle way between despair and the yielding up of the whole spirit unto the guidance of faith. And surely it is a matter of joy that your faith in Jesus has been preserved; the Comforter that should relieve you is not far from you. But as you are a Christian, in the name of that Saviour, who was filled with bitterness and made drunken with wormwood, I conjure you to have recourse in frequent prayer to "his God and your God;" the God of mercies, and father of all comfort. Your poor father is, I hope, almost senseless of the calamity; the unconscious instrument of Divine Providence knows it not, and your mother is in heaven. It is sweet to be roused from a frightful dream by the song of birds and the gladsome rays of the morning. Ah, how infinitely more sweet to be awakened from the blackness and amazement of a sudden horror by the glories of God manifest and the hallelujahs of angels.

As to what regards yourself, I approve altogether of your abandoning what you justly call vanities. I look upon you as a man called by sorrow and anguish and a strange desolation of hopes into quietness, and a soul set apart and made peculiar to God! We cannot arrive at any portion of heavenly bliss without in some measure imitating Christ; and they arrive at the largest inheritance who imitate the most difficult parts of his character, and, bowed down and crushed underfoot, cry in fulness of faith, "Father, thy will be done."

I wish above measure to have you for a little while here; no visitants shall blow on the nakedness of your feelings; you shall be quiet, and your spirit may be healed. I see no possible objection, unless your father's helplessness prevent you, and unless you are necessary to him. If this be not the case, I charge you write me that you will come.

I charge you, my dearest friend, not to dare to encourage gloom or despair. You are a temporary sharer in human miseries that you may be an eternal partaker of the Divine nature. I charge you, if by any means it be possible, come to me.

I remain your affectionate

S. T. COLERIDGE.

XXVII

TO THOMAS POOLE

Saturday night, November 5, 1796

. . . I wanted such a letter as yours, for I am very unwell. On Wednesday night I was seized with an intolerable pain from my right temple to the tip of my right shoulder, including my right eye, cheek, jaw, and that side of the throat. I was nearly frantic, and ran about the house naked, endeavouring by every means to excite sensations in different parts of my body, and so to weaken the enemy by creating division. It continued from one in the morning till half past five, and left me pale and fainting. It came on fitfully, but not so violently, several times on Thursday, and began severer threats towards night; but I took between sixty and seventy drops of laudanum, and *sopped* the Cerberus, just as his mouth began to open. On Friday it only *niggled*, as if the chief had departed from a conquered place, and merely left a small garrison behind, or as if he had evacuated the Corsica, and a few straggling pains only remained. But *this morning* he returned in full force, and his name is Legion. Giant-fiend of a hundred hands, with a shower of arrowy death-pangs he transpierced me, and then he became a wolf, and lay a-gnawing at my bones! I am not mad, most noble Festus, but in sober sadness I have suffered this day more bodily pain than I had before a conception of. My right cheek has certainly been placed with admirable exactness under the focus of some invisible burning-glass, which concentrated all the rays of a Tartarean sun. My medical attendant decides it to be altogether nervous, and that it originates either in severe application, or excessive anxiety. My beloved Poole! in excessive anxiety, I believe it might originate. I have a blister under my right ear, and I take twenty-five drops of laudanum every five hours, the ease and *spirits* gained by which have enabled me to write you this flighty but not exaggerated account. With a gloomy wantonness of imagination I had been coquetting with the hideous *possibles* of disappointment. I drank fears like wormwood, yea, made myself drunken with bitterness; for my ever-shaping and distrustful mind still mingled gall-drops, till out of the cup of hope I almost *poisoned* myself with despair. ....

XXVIII

TO JOHN THELWALL

Oxford Street, Bristol, Saturday, November 19, [1796]
. . . Your portrait of yourself interested me. As to me, my face, unless when animated by immediate eloquence, expresses great sloth, and great, indeed, almost idiotic goodnature. 'T is a mere carcass of a face; fat, flabby, and

expressive chiefly of inexpression. Yet I am told that my eyes, eyebrows, and forehead are physiognomically good; but of this the deponent knoweth not. As to my shape, 't is a good shape enough if measured, but my gait is awkward, and the walk of the whole man indicates *indolence capable of energies*. I am, and ever have been, a great reader, and have read almost everything—a library cormorant. I am *deep* in all out of the way books, whether of the monkish times, or of the puritanical era. I have read and digested most of the historical writers; but I do not *like* history. Metaphysics and poetry and "facts of mind," that is, accounts of all the strange phantasms that ever possessed "your philosophy"; dreamers, from Thoth the Egyptian to Taylor the English pagan, are my darling studies. In short, I seldom read except to amuse myself, and I am almost always reading. Of useful knowledge, I am a so-so chemist, and I love chemistry. All else is *blank;* but I *will* be (please God) an horticulturalist and a farmer. I compose very little, and I absolutely hate composition, and such is my dislike that even a sense of duty is sometimes too weak to overpower it.

I cannot breathe through my nose, so my mouth, with sensual thick lips, is almost always open. In conversation I am impassioned, and oppose what I deem error with an eagerness which is often mistaken for personal asperity; but I am ever so swallowed up in the *thing* that I perfectly forget my *opponent*. Such am I. I am just going to read Dupuis' twelve octavos, which I have got from London. I shall read only one octavo a week, for I cannot *speak* French at all and I read it slowly.

My wife is well and desires to be remembered to you and your *Stella* and little ones. N. B. Stella (among the Romans) was a man's name. All the *classics* are against you; but our Swift, I suppose, is authority for this unsexing.

Write on the receipt of this, and believe me as ever, with affectionate esteem,

Your sincere friend,

S. T. COLERIDGE.

P. S. I have enclosed a five-guinea note. The five shillings over please to lay out for me thus. In White's (of Fleet Street or the Strand, I forget which—O! the

Strand I believe, but I don't know which), well, in White's catalogue are the following books:—

4674. "Iamblichus," "Proclus," "Porphyrius," etc., one shilling and sixpence, one little volume.

4686. "Juliani Opera," three shillings: which two books you will be so kind as to purchase for me, and send down with the twenty-five pamphlets. But if they should un fortunately be sold, in the same catalogue are:—

2109. "Juliani Opera," 12s. 6d.

676. "Iamblichus de Mysteriis," 10s. 6d.

2681. "Sidonius Apollinaris," 6s.

And in the catalogue of Robson, the bookseller in New Bond Street, "Plotini Opera, a Ficino," £1.1.0, making altogether £2.10.0.

If you can get the two former little books, costing only four and sixpence, I will rest content with them; if they are gone, be so kind as to purchase for me the others I mentioned to you, amounting to two pounds, ten shillings; and, as in the course of next week I shall send a small parcel of books and manuscripts to my very dear Charles Lamb of the India House, I shall be enabled to convey the money to you in a letter, which he will leave at your house. I make no apology for this commission, because I feel (to use a vulgar phrase) that I would do as much for you.

P.P.S. Can you buy them time enough to send down with your pamphlets? If not, make a parcel *per se*. I hope your hurts from the fall are not serious; you have given a *proof* now that you are no *Ippokrite*, but I forgot that you are not a Greekist, and perchance you hate puns; but, in Greek, *Krites* signifies a judge and *hippos* a horse. Hippocrite, therefore, may mean a *judge of horses*. My dear fellow, I laugh more and talk more nonsense in a week than [most] other people do in a year. Farewell.

XXIX

TO THOMAS POOLE

Monday night, [December, 1796]

I wrote the former letter immediately on receipt of yours, in the first flutter of agitation. The tumult of my spirits has now subsided, but the Damp struck into my very heart; and there I feel it. O my God! my God! where am I to find rest? Disappointment follows disappointment, and Hope seems given me merely to prevent my becoming callous to Misery. Now I know not where to turn myself. I was on my way to the City Library, and wrote an answer to it there. Since I have returned I have been poring into a book, as a shew for not looking at my wife and the baby. By God, I dare not look at them. Acton! The very name makes me grind my teeth! What am I to do there?

"You will have a good garden; you may, I doubt not, have ground." But am I not ignorant as a child of everything that concerns the garden and the ground? and shall I have one human being there who will instruct me? The House too—what should I do with it? We want but two rooms, or three at the furthest. And the country around is intolerably flat. I would as soon live on the banks of a Dutch canal! And no one human being near me for whom I should, or could, care a rush! No one walk where the beauties of nature might endear solitude to me! There is one Ghost that I *am* afraid of; with that I should be perpetually haunted in this same cursed Acton—the hideous Ghost of departed Hope. O Poole! how could *you* make such a proposal to me? I have compelled myself to reperuse your letter, if by any means I may be able to penetrate into your motives. I find three reasons assigned for my not settling at Stowey. The first, the distance from my friends and the Press. This I answered in the former letter. As to my friends, what can they do for me? And as to the Press, even if Cottle had not promised to correct it for me, yet I might as well be fifty miles from it as twelve, for any purpose of correcting. Secondly, the expense of moving. Well, but I must move to Acton, and what will the difference be? Perhaps three guineas. . . . I would give three guineas that you had not assigned this reason. Thirdly, the wretchedness of that cottage, which alone we can get. But surely, in the house which I saw, *two* rooms may be found, which, by a little green list and a carpet, and a slight alteration in the fireplace, may be made to exclude the cold: and this is all we want. Besides, it will be but for a while. If Cruikshank cannot buy and repair Adscombe, I have no doubt that my friends here and at Birmingham would, some of them, purchase it. So much for the reasons: but these cannot be the real reasons. I was with you for a week, and then we talked over the whole scheme, and you approved of it, and I gave up Derby. More than nine weeks have elapsed since then, and you saw and examined the cottage, and you knew every other of these reasons, if reasons they can be called. Surely, surely, my friend, something has occurred which you have not mentioned to me. Your mother has manifested a strong dislike to our living near you—or something or other; for the reasons you have assigned tell me nothing except that there are reasons which you have not assigned.

Pardon, if I write vehemently. I meant to have written calmly; but bitterness of soul came upon me. Mrs. Coleridge has observed the workings of my face while I have been writing, and is entreating to know what is the matter. I dread to show her your letter. I dread it. My God! my God! What if she should dare to think that my most beloved friend has grown cold towards me! . . .

XXX

TO JOHN THELWALL

December 31, 1796

Enough, my dear Thelwall, of theology. In my book on Godwin, I compare the two systems, his and Jesus', and that book I am sure you will read with attention. I entirely accord with your opinion of Southey's "Joan." The ninth book is execrable, and the poem, though it frequently reach the *sentimental*, does not display the *poetical-sublime*. In language at once natural, perspicuous, and dignified in manly pathos, in soothing and sonnet-like description, and, above all, in character and *dramatic* dialogue, Southey is unrivalled; but as certainly he does not possess opulence of imaginative lofty-paced harmony, or that toil of thinking which is necessary in order to plan a *whole*. Dismissing mock humility, and hanging your mind as a looking-glass over my idea-pot, so as to image on the said mind all the bubbles that boil in the said idea-pot (there's a damned long-winded metaphor for you), I think that an admirable poet might be made by *amalgamating him* and *me*. I *think* too much for a *poet*, he too little for a *great* poet. But he abjures *feeling*. Now (as you say) they must go together. Between ourselves the *enthusiasm* of friendship is not with S. and me. We quarrelled and the quarrel lasted for a twelvemonth. We are now reconciled; but the cause of the difference was solemn, and "the blasted oak puts not forth its buds anew." We are *acquaintances*, and feel *kindliness* towards each other, but I do not *esteem* or *love* Southey, as I must esteem and love the man whom I dared call by the holy name of *friend:* and *vice versa* Southey of me. I say no more. It is a painful subject, and do you say nothing. I mention this for obvious reasons, but let it go no farther. It is a painful subject. Southey's direction at present is R. Southey, No. 8 West-gate Buildings, Bath, but he leaves Bath for London in the course of a week. You imagine that I know Bowles personally. I never saw him but once, and when I was a boy and in Salisbury market-place. . . .

XXXI

TO ROBERT SOUTHEY
NO. 8 WESTGATE BUILDINGS, BATH

Tuesday Morning, [1797]

I thank you, Robert Southey, for your poems, and by way of return present you with a collection of (what appear to me) the faults—"The Race of Banquo" and "To the Genius of Africa" ought to have rescued the ode from your very harsh censure. The latter is perfect, saving the last line which is one of James Hennings' *new thoughts;* and besides who after having been whirled along by such a tide of enthusiasm can endure to be impaled at last on the needle-point of an Antithesis? Of the Inscriptions I like the first and last the least: all the rest almost equally, and each very much. In the spirited and most original lines to your own miniature "wrong" *rhymes* with "solitary song." *You*, I doubt not, have associated feelings dear to you with the ideas "this little picture was for ornament designed" etc.—and therefore do right in retaining them. To me and, I suppose, most strangers the four last lines appear to drag excrementitiously—the Poem would conclude more satisfactorily at "Spirit of Spenser! was the Wanderer wrong?" The fault of the four lines *seems* to be that having digressed you do not *lead* yourself to your subject, but without ceremony take a huge *leap* back again. Now though it is always well to *leave* the subject on the mind, yet rather than use such means I would forego it. "The Poem on the Death of an old Spaniel" will, I doubt not, be set to music by angelic and archangelic dogs in their state of exaltation. It is a poem which will do good and that is saying a great deal. In the Ode to Contemplation "the smoke long shadowing play" is scarcely accurate—"the smoke's long shadow" would surely be more natural and perspicuous. "The Musings on a Landscape" is a delicious poem. The words *To Him* begin the line awkwardly to *my* ear. The final pause at the end of the first two syllables of a line is seldom tolerable, except when the first two syllables form a trochee. The reason, I apprehend, is that to the ear they with the line foregoing make an Alexandrine. I have animadverted on these poems only which are my particular favourites—and now for the Penates which if I were to abandon my judgement to the impulse of present Feelings I should pronounce the most interesting poem of its Length in our Language. I have detected two faults only,—that a man amid the Miseries of a struggling Life should look back on the quiet happiness of childhood bears no resemblance to a Persian Monarch leaving the Luxuries of a Palace to revisit the cot where he had been a shepherd. But the *five first lines* of the Poem—they are very, very *beautiful*, but (pardon my obtuseness) have they any meaning? "The Temple of Paean" does not, I presume, mean any real temple but is only an allegorical building expressing Poesy—Either ancient or modern. If modern how is its wall ruined? If ancient how do *you* hang up your silent harp on it? Does it allude to ancient poetry as expressing the subject of the Present Poem? yet you say, that you shall strike that "high and solemn strain" *ere* you hang it up. (Besides is *Paean* the God of *Poetry?* I think that the ancients religiously confined the name to Apollo in his capacity of Healer and *Python-killer* but of this I am not

certain.) However whether ancient or modern poesy be
indicated or whatever may be the import of each distinct
image your general meaning is clear—namely that after this
song you will intermit the writing of Poetry. Yet in the next
lines you say, these many strings make melancholy music—
i.e. This one song and then I will *discontinue* verse-writing—
during which discontinuance I will write verses! Is all
this only my obtuseness and frigidity? or have you not
faultily mixed spiritual with corporal, allegorical meanings
with meanings predicable only of catgut and rosin, bricks
and mortar? A tempest may shake an aged pile, but what
has a tempest to do with ancient poetry? If there were any
respectable God with a respectable name who presided over
the Law, or the affairs of active Life in general, you would
have acted wiselier, (I speak not dogmatically but merely
say I think you would have acted wiselier) if you had hung
up your harp on the walls of his Temple and added—yet
shall its strings (if any ruder storm is abroad) make melancholy music *i.e.* Tho' I intermit my Poetry in consequence
of the calls of Business yet if any particular occasion arrive,
I will *unhang* my harp. What if you *left* the harp in the fane
of Vacuna? If these observations strike you as just I shall be
sorry they did not strike me when you *read* the Poem. But
indeed the Lines sound so sweet, and *seem* so much like
sense, that it is no great matter. 'Tis a handsome and finely-
sculptured Tomb and few will break it open with the
sacrilegious spade and pick-ax of Criticism to discover
whether or no it be not a *Cenotaph*.

I have been in bed for these two days, the effect of a dire
cold and feverish complaint but I am better now and leave
Bristol on Thursday—

S. T. Coleridge.

XXXII

to joseph cottle

Spring, 1797

. . Tom Poole desires to be kindly remembered to you. I
see they have reviewed Southey's Poems and my Ode in the
"Monthly Review." Notwithstanding the Reviews, I, who
in the sincerity of my heart am *jealous* for Robert Southey's
fame, regret the publication of that volume. Wordsworth

complains, with justice, that Southey writes *too much at his ease*—that he seldom

> feels his burthened breast
> Heaving beneath th' incumbent Deity.

He certainly will make literature more *profitable to him* from the fluency with which he writes, and the facility with which he pleases himself. But I fear, that to posterity his wreath will look unseemly—here an ever living amaranth, and close by its side some weed of an hour, sere, yellow, and shapeless —his exquisite beauties will lose half their effect from the bad company they keep. Besides I am fearful that he will begin to rely too much on *story* and *event* in his poems, to the neglect of those *lofty imaginings,* that are peculiar to, and definitive of, the poet. The *story* of Milton might be told in two pages—it is this which distinguishes an *Epic Poem* from a *Romance in metre.* Observe the march of Milton—his severe application, his laborious polish, his deep metaphysical researches, his prayers to God before he began his great poem, all that could lift and swell his intellect, became his daily food. I should not think of devoting less than 20 years to an Epic Poem. Ten to collect materials and warm my mind with universal science. I would be a tolerable Mathematician, I would thoroughly know Mechanics, Hydrostatics, Optics, and Astronomy, Botany, Metallurgy, Fossilism, Chemistry, Geology, Anatomy, Medicine—then the *mind of man*—then the *minds* of *men*—in all Travels, Voyages and Histories. So I would spend ten years—the next five to the composition of the poem—and the five last to the correction of it.

So I would write haply not unhearing of that divine and rightly-whispering Voice, which speaks to mighty minds of predestinated Garlands, starry and unwithering. God love you,

S. T. COLERIDGE.

XXXIII

TO ROBERT SOUTHEY July, 1797

DEAR SOUTHEY,—You are acting kindly in your exertions for Chatterton's sister; but I doubt the success. Chatterton's or Rowley's poems were never popular. The very circumstance which made them so much talked of, their *ancientness,* prevented them from being generally read, in the degree, I mean, that Goldsmith's poems or even Rogers' thing upon memory has been. . . . I am almost inclined to think a *subscription* simply would be better. It is unpleasant to cast a damp on anything; but that benevolence alone is likely to be beneficent which *calculates*. If, however, you continue to entertain higher hopes than I, believe me, I will shake off my sloth, and use my best muscles in gaining subscribers. I will certainly write a preliminary essay, and I will *attempt* to write a poem on the life and death of Chatterton, but the "Monody" *must not be reprinted*. Neither this nor the "Pixies' Parlour" would have been in the second edition, but for dear Cottle's solicitous importunity. Excepting the last eighteen lines of the "Monody," which, though deficient in chasteness and severity of diction, breathe a pleasing spirit of romantic feeling, there are not five lines in either poem which might not have been written by a man who had lived and died in the self-same St. Giles' cellar, in which he had been first suckled by a drab with milk and gin. The "Pixies" is the least disgusting, because the subject leads you to expect nothing, but on a life and death so full of heart-going *realities* as poor Chatterton's, to find such shadowy nobodies as cherub-winged *Death*, Trees of *Hope*, bare-bosomed *Affection* and simpering *Peace*, makes one's blood circulate like ipecacuanha. But so it is. A young man by strong feelings is impelled to write on a particular subject, and this is all his feelings do for him. They set him upon the business and then they leave him. He has such a high idea of what poetry ought to be, that he cannot conceive that such things as his natural emotions may be allowed to find a place in it; his learning therefore, his fancy, or rather conceit, and all his powers of buckram are put on the stretch. It appears to me that strong feeling is not so requisite to an author's being profoundly pathetic as taste and good sense. . . .

XXXIV

TO JOSIAH WEDGWOOD

Shrewsbury, January 17, 1798

DEAR SIR,—Yesterday morning I received the letter which you addressed to me in your own and your brother's name.

Your benevolence appeared so strange and it came upon my mind with such suddenness, that for a while I sat and mused on it with scarce a reference to myself, and gave you a moral approbation almost wholly unmingled with those personal feelings which have since filled my eyes with tears—which do so even now while I am writing to you. What can I say? I accept your proposal not unagitated but yet, I trust, in the same worthy spirit in which you made it.—I return to Stowey in a few days. Disembarrassed from all pecuniary anxieties yet unshackled by any regular profession, with powerful motives and no less powerful propensities to honourable effort, it is my duty to indulge the hope that at some future period I shall have given a proof that as your intentions were eminently virtuous, so the action itself was not unbeneficent.

With great affection and esteem

I remain

Yours sincerely

S. T. COLERIDGE.

XXXV

TO GEORGE COLERIDGE

April, 1798

MY DEAR BROTHER,—An illness, which confined me to my bed, prevented me from returning an immediate answer to your kind and interesting letter. My indisposition originated in the stump of a tooth over which some matter had formed; this affected my eye, my eye my stomach, my stomach my head, and the consequence was a general fever, and the sum of pain was considerably increased by the vain attempts of our surgeon to extract the offending member. Laudanum gave me repose, not sleep; but you, I believe, know how divine that repose is, what a spot of enchantment, a green spot of fountain and flowers and trees in the very heart of a waste of sands! God be praised, the matter has been absorbed; and I am now recovering apace, and enjoy that newness of sensation from the fields, the air, and the sun which makes convalescence almost repay one for disease.

I collect from your letter that our opinions and feelings on political subjects are more nearly alike than you imagine them to be. . . .

I am prepared to suffer without discontent the consequences of my follies and mistakes; and unable to conceive how that which I am of Good could have been without that which I have been of evil, it is withheld from me to regret anything. I therefore consent to be deemed a Democrat and a Seditionist. A man's character follows him long after he has ceased to deserve it; but I have snapped my squeaking baby-trumpet of sedition, and the fragments lie scattered in the lumber-room of penitence. I wish to be a good man and a Christian, but I am no Whig, no Reformist, no Republican, and because of the multitude of fiery and undisciplined spirits that lie in wait against the public quiet under these titles, because of them I chiefly accuse the present ministers, to whose folly I attribute, in a great measure, their increased and increasing numbers. You think differently, and if I were called upon by you to prove my assertions, although I imagine I could make them appear plausible, yet I should feel the insufficiency of my data. The Ministers may have had in their possession facts which alter the whole state of the argument, and make my syllogisms fall as flat as a baby's card-house. And feeling this, my brother! I have for some time past withdrawn myself totally from the consideration of *immediate causes*, which are infinitely complex and uncertain, to muse on fundamental and general causes the *causae causarum*. I devote myself to such works as encroach not on the anti-social passions—in poetry, to elevate the imagination and set the affections in right tune by the beauty of the inanimate impregnated as with a living soul by the presence of life—in prose to the seeking with patience and a slow, very slow mind, *Quid sumus, et quidnam victuri gignimus*,—what our faculties are and what they are capable of becoming. I love fields and woods and mountains with almost a visionary fondness. And because I have found benevolence and quietness growing within me as that fondness has increased, therefore I should wish to be the means of implanting it in others, and to destroy the bad passions not by combating them but by keeping them in inaction. . . .

XXXVI

TO REV. JOHN P. ESTLIN

May [? 1798]

MY DEAR FRIEND,—I write from Cross, to which place I accompanied Mr. Wordsworth, who will give you this letter. We visited Cheddar, but his main business was to bring back poor Lloyd, whose infirmities have been made the instruments of another man's darker passions. But Lloyd (as we found by a letter that met us in the road) is off for Birmingham. Wordsworth proceeds, lest possibly Lloyd may not be gone, and likewise to see his own Bristol friends, as he is so near them. I have now known him a year and some months, and my admiration, I might say my awe, of his intellectual powers has increased even to this hour, and (what is of more importance) he is a tried good man. On one subject we are habitually silent; we found our data dissimilar, and never renewed the subject. It is his practice and almost his nature to convey all the truth he knows without any attack on what he supposes falsehood, if that falsehood be interwoven with virtues or happiness. He loves and venerates Christ and Christianity. I wish he did more, but it were wrong indeed if an incoincidence with one of our wishes altered our respect and affection to a man of whom we are, as it were, instructed by one great Master to say that not being against us he is for us. His genius is most *apparent* in poetry, and rarely, except to me in *tête-à-tête*, breaks forth in conversational eloquence. My best and most affectionate wishes attend Mrs. Estlin and your little ones, and believe me, with filial and fraternal friendship, your grateful

S. T. COLERIDGE.

XXXVII

TO HIS WIFE

Ratzeburg, Monday, January 14, 1799

. . . As the sun both rises and sets over the little lake by us, both rising and setting present most lovely spectacles. In October Ratzeburg used at sunset to appear completely

U

beautiful. A deep red light spread over all, in complete harmony with the red town, the brown-red woods, and the yellow-red reeds on the skirts of the lake and on the slip of land. A few boats, paddled by single persons, used generally to be floating up and down in the rich light. But when first the ice fell on the lake, and the whole lake was frozen one large piece of thick transparent glass—O my God! what sublime scenery I have beheld. Of a morning I have seen the little lake covered with mist; when the sun peeped over the hills the mist broke in the middle, and at last stood as the waters of the Red Sea are said to have done when the Israelites passed; and between these two walls of mist the sunlight burst upon the ice in a straight road of golden fire, all across the lake, intolerably bright, and the walls of mist partaking of the light in a *multitude* of colours. About a month ago the vehemence of the wind had shattered the ice; part of it, quite shattered, was driven to shore and had frozen anew; this was of a deep blue, and represented an agitated sea—the water that ran up between the great islands of ice shone of a yellow-green (it was at sunset), and all the scattered islands of *smooth* ice were *blood*, intensely bright *blood;* on some of the largest islands the fishermen were pulling out their immense nets through the holes made in the ice for this purpose, and the fishermen, the net-poles, and the huge nets made a part of the glory! O my God! how I wished you to be with me! In skating there are three pleasing circumstances—firstly, the infinitely subtle particles of ice which the skate cuts up, and which creep and run before the skater like a low mist, and in sunrise or sunset become coloured; second, the shadow of the skater in the water seen through the transparent ice; and thirdly, the melancholy undulating sound from the skate, not without variety; and, when very many are skating together, the sounds give an impulse to the icy trees, and the woods all round the lake *tinkle*. It is a pleasant amusement to sit in an ice stool (as they are called) and be driven along by two skaters, faster than most horses can gallop. As to the customs here, they are nearly the same as in England, except that [the men] never sit after dinner [and only] drink at dinner, which often lasts three or four hours, and in noble families is divided into three gangs, that is, walks.

When you have sat about an hour, you rise up, each lady takes a gentleman's arm, and you walk about for a quarter of an hour—in the mean time another course is put upon the table; and, this in great dinners, is repeated three times. A man here seldom sees his wife till dinner,—they take their coffee in separate rooms, and never eat at breakfast; only as soon as they are up they take their coffee, and about eleven o'clock eat a bit of bread and butter with the coffee. The men at least take a pipe. Indeed, a pipe at breakfast is a great addition to the comfort of life. I shall [smoke at] no other time in England. Here I smoke four times a day— 1 at breakfast, 1 half an hour before dinner, 1 in the after-noon at tea, and 1 just before bed-time—but I shall give it all up, unless, as before observed, you should happen to like the smoke of a pipe at breakfast. Once when I first came here I smoked a pipe immediately after dinner; the pastor expressed his surprise: I expressed mine that he could smoke before breakfast. "O Herr Gott!" (that is, Lord God) quoth he, "it is delightful; it invigorates the frame and *it clears out the mouth so.*" A common amusement at the German Universities is for a number of young men to smoke out a candle! that is, to fill a room with tobacco smoke till the candle goes out. Pipes are quite the rage—a pipe of a particular kind, that has been smoked for a year or so, will sell here for twenty guineas—the same pipe when new costs four or five. They are called Meerschaum.

God bless you, my dear Love! I will soon write again.

S. T. COLERIDGE.

Postscript. Perhaps you are in Bristol. However, I had better direct it to Stowey. My love to Martha and your mother and your other sisters. Once more, my dearest Love, God love and preserve us through this long absence! O my dear Babies! my Babies!

XXXVIII

TO THOMAS POOLE

May 6, 1799, Monday morn.

My dear Poole, my dear Poole!—I am homesick. Society is a burden to me; and I find relief only in labour. So

I read and transcribe from morning till night, and never in my life have I worked so hard as this last month, for indeed I must sail over an ocean of matter with almost spiritual speed, to do what I have to do in the time in which I *will* do it or leave it undone! O my God, how I long to be at home! My *whole Being* so yearns after you, that when I think of the moment of our meeting, I catch the fashion of German joy, rush into your arms, and embrace you. Methinks my hand would swell if the whole force of my feeling were crowded there. Now the Spring comes, the vital sap of my affections rises as in a tree! And what a gloomy Spring! But a few days ago all the new buds were covered with snow; and everything yet looks so brown and wintry, that yesterday the roses (which the ladies carried on the ramparts, their promenade), beautiful as they were, so little harmonized with the general face of nature, that they looked to me like silk and made roses. But these leafless Spring Woods! Oh, how I long to hear you whistle to the Rippers! There are a multitude of nightingales here (poor things! they sang in the snow). I thought of my own verses on the nightingale, only because I thought of Hartley, my *only* Child. Dear lamb! I hope he won't be dead before I get home. There are moments in which I have such a power of life within me, such a *conceit* of it, I mean, that I lay the blame of my child's death to my absence. *Not intellectually;* but I have a strange sort of sensation, as if, while I was present, none could die whom I entirely loved, and doubtless it was no absurd idea of yours that there may be unions and connections out of the visible world. . . .

XXXIX

TO HUMPHRY DAVY
THE PNEUMATIC INSTITUTION
BRISTOL

January 1, 1800

. . . Questions—

On dipping my foot and leg into very hot water, the first sensation was identical with that of having dipped it into very cold. This identity recurred as often as I took my leg out in order to pour in the hot water from the kettle, and put it in again. How is this explained in philosophical Language divested of corpuscular Theories? Define Disgust in philosophical Language. Is it not, speaking as a materialist, always a stomach-sensation conjoined with an idea? What is the cause of that sense of cold, which accompanies inhalation, after having eat peppermint Drops?

If you don't answer me these, I'll send them to the Lady's Diary—where you may find fifty Questions of the same Depth and Kidney. . . .

X L

TO THE SAME

Greta Hall, Keswick, Cumberland,
Friday Evening, July 25, 1800

MY DEAR DAVY,—Work hard, and if Success do not dance up like the bubbles in the Salt (with the Spirit Lamp under it) may the Devil and his Dame take success! Sdeath, my dear fellow! from the Window before me there is a great *Camp* of Mountains—Giants seem to have pitch'd their tents there—Each mountain is a Giant's tent—and how the light streams from them—and the shadows that travel upon them! Davy! I *ake* for you to be with us.

W. Wordsworth is such a lazy fellow that I bemire myself by making promises for him—the moment, I received your letter, I wrote to him. He will, I hope, immediately write to Biggs and Cottle—At all events those poems must not as yet be delivered up to them, because that beautiful Poem, "The Brothers," which I read to you in Paul Street, I neglected to deliver to you—and that must begin the volume. I trust however that I have invoked the sleeping Bard with a spell so potent, that he will awake and deliver up that Sword of Argantyr, which is to rive the Enchanter *Gaudyverse* from his Crown to his Fork.

What did you think of that case, I translated for you from the German? That I was a well-meaning *Sutor*, who had ultra-crepidated with more zeal than wisdom! I give myself credit for that word "ultra-crepidated,"* it started up

---

* *"Ne sutor ultra crepidam."* S. T. C.

in my Brain like a creation. I write to Tobin by this Post. Godwin is gone Ireland-ward, on a visit to Curran, says the "Morning Post"; to Grattan, writes C. Lamb.

We drank tea the night before I left Grasmere, on the Island in that lovely lake, our kettle swung over the fire hanging from the branch of a Fir-tree, and I lay and saw the woods, and mountains, and lake all trembling, and as it were *idealized* thro' the subtle smoke which rose up from the clear red embers of the fir-apples, which we had collected; afterwards, we made a glorious Bonfire on the margin, by some elder bushes, whose twigs heaved and sobbed in the up-rushing column of smoke—and the Image of the Bonfire, and of us that danced round it—ruddy laughing faces in the twilight—the Image of this in a Lake smooth as that sea, to whose waves the Son of God had said, *Peace!* May God and all his Sons, love you as I do—   S. T. COLERIDGE.

Sara desires her kind remembrances—Hartley is a spirit that dances on an aspen leaf—the air that yonder sallow-faced and yawning Tourist is breathing, is to my Babe a perpetual Nitrous Oxide. Never was more joyous creature born. Pain with him is so wholly trans-substantiated by the Joys that had rolled on before, and rushed in after, that oftentimes 5 minutes after his mother had whipt him, he has gone up and asked her to whip him again.

XLI

TO WILLIAM GODWIN

Monday [Sept., 1800]

DEAR GODWIN,—There are vessels every week from Dublin to Workington, which place is 16 miles from my house, through a divine country, but these are idle regrets. I know not the nature of your present pursuits, whether or no they are such as to require the vicinity of large and curious libraries. If you were engaged in any work of imagination or reasoning, not biographical, not historical, I should repeat and urge my invitation after my wife's confinement. Our house is situated on a rising ground, not two furlongs from Keswick, about as much from the Lake Derwentwater, and about two miles from the Lake Bassenthwaite—both lakes

and mountains we command. The river Greta runs behind
our house, and before it too, and Skiddaw is behind us—not
half a mile distant indeed just distant enough to enable us
to view it as a Whole. The garden, orchard, fields and
immediate country all delightful. I have, or have the use of,
no inconsiderable collection of books. In *my* Library you
will find all the Poets and Philosophers, and many of the
best old writers. Below, in our parlour, belonging to our
landlord, but in my possession, are almost all the usual trash
of Johnsons, Gibbons, Robertsons etc., with the "Encyclopaedia Britannica," etc. Sir Wilfred Lawson's magnificent
library is some eight or nine miles distant, and he is liberal
in the highest degree in the management of it. . . . Of
North Wales my recollections are faint, and as to Wicklow
I only know from the newspapers that it is a mountainous
country. As far as my memory will permit me to decide on
the grander parts of Carnarvonshire, I may say that the
single objects are superior to any which I have seen elsewhere, but there is a deficiency in combination. I know of
no mountain in the North equal to Snowdon, but then we
have an encampment of huge mountains, in no harmony
perhaps to the eye of the mere painter, but always interesting, various and, as it were nutritive. Height is assuredly an
advantage, as it connects the earth with the sky, by the
clouds that are ever skimming the summits or climbing up,
or creeping down the sides, or rising from the chasm, like
smoke from a cauldron, or veiling or bridging the higher
parts or lower parts of waterfalls. That you were less impressed by North Wales I can easily believe; it is possible
that the scenes of Wicklow may be superior, but it is certain
that you were in a finer irritability of spirit to enjoy them.
The first pause and silence after a return from a very
interesting visit is somewhat connected with langour in all
of us. Besides, as you have observed, mountains and mountainous scenery taken collectively and cursorily, must depend for their charms on their novelty. They put on their
immortal interest then first, when we have resided among
them, and learnt to understand their language, their written
character and intelligible sounds, and all their eloquence,
so various, so unwearied. Then you will hear no "twice-told
tale." I question if there be a room in England which

commands a view of mountains, and lakes, and woods and vales superior to that in which I am now sitting. I say this, because it is destined for your study, if you come. You are kind enough to say that you feel yourself more natural and unreserved with me than with others. I suppose that this in great measure arises from my own ebullient unreservedness. Something, too, I will hope may be attributed to the circumstance that my affections are deeply interested in my opinions. But here, too, you will meet with Wordsworth, "the latchet of whose shoes I am unworthy to unloose," and five miles from Wordsworth Charles Lloyd has taken a house. Wordsworth is publishing a second volume of the "Lyrical Ballads," which title is to be dropped, and his "Poems" substituted. Have you seen Sheridan since your return? How is it with your tragedy? Were you in town when Miss Bayley's tragedy was represented? How was it that it proved so uninteresting? Was the fault in the theatre, the audience, or the play? It must have excited a deeper feeling in you than that of mere curiosity, for doubtless the tragedy has great merit. Have you read the "Wallenstein"? Prolix and crowded and dragging as it is, it is yet quite a model for its judicious management of the sequence of the scenes, and such it is held in German theatres. Our English acting plays are many of them wofully deficient in this part of the dramatic trade and mystery.

Hartley is well, and all life and action—Yours with unfeigned esteem,

S. T. COLERIDGE.

Kisses for Mary and Fanny. God love them. I wish you would come and look out for a house for yourself here. You know "I wish" is privileged to have something silly to follow it.

XLII

TO THE SAME

Monday, Sep. 22, 1800

DEAR GODWIN,—I received your letter, and with it the enclosed note, which shall be punctually re-delivered to you on the 1st October.

Your tragedy to be exhibited at Christmas! I have indeed merely read your letter, so it is not strange that my heart still continues beating out of time. Indeed, indeed, Godwin, such a stream of hope and fear rushed in on me, when I read the sentence, as you would not permit yourself to feel. If there be anything yet undreamed of in our philosophy; if it be, or if it be possible, that thought can impel Thought out of the visual limit of a man's own skull and heart; if the clusters of ideas, which contribute our identity, do ever connect and unite with a greater whole; if feelings could ever propagate themselves without the servile ministrations of undulating air or reflected light—I seem to feel within myself a strength and a power of desire that might start a modifying, commanding impulse on a whole theatre. What does all this mean? Alas! that sober sense should know no other to construe all this, except by the tame phrase, I wish you success . . . [*sic*]

Your feelings respecting Baptism are, I suppose, much like mine! At times I dwell on man with such reverence, resolve all his follies and superstitions into such grand primary laws of intellect, and in such wise so contemplate them as ever-varying incarnations of the Eternal Life—that the Llama's dung-pellet, or the cow-tail which the dying Brahmin clutches convulsively become sanctified and sublime by the feelings which cluster round them. In that mood I exclaim, my boys shall be christened! But then another fit of moody philosophy attacks me. I look at my doted-on Hartley—he moves, he lives, he finds impulses from within and from without, he is the darling of the sun and of the breeze. Nature seems to bless him as a thing of her own. He looks at the clouds, the mountains, the living beings of the earth, and vaults and jubilates! Solemn looks and solemn words have been hitherto connected in his mind with great and magnificent objects only: with lightning, with thunder, with the waterfall blazing in the sunset. Then I say, shall I suffer him to see grave countenances and hear grave accents, while his face is sprinkled? Shall I be grave myself and tell a lie to him? Or shall I laugh, and teach him to insult the feelings of his fellowmen? Besides, are we not all in this present hour fainting beneath the duty of Hope? From such thoughts I stand up, and vow a book of severe analysis, in which I will tell *all* I believe to be truth in the nakedest language in which it can be told. . . .

XLIII

Jan. 11, 1801

MY DEAR DAVY,—

With legs astraddle and bebolstered back,
Alack! alack!

. . . Somewhat more than 3 weeks ago I walked to Grasmere, and was wet thro'—I changed immediately—but still the next day I was taken ill, and by the Lettre de catchet of a Rheumatic Fever sentenced to the Bed-bastille—the Fever left me, and on Friday before last I was well enough to be conveyed home in a chaise—but immediately took to my bed again—a most excruciating pain on the least motion, but not without motion, playing Robespierre and Marat in my left Hip and the small of my back—. . .—yet still my animal spirits bear me up, tho' I am so weak, that even from sitting up to write this note to you, I seem to sink in upon myself in a ruin, like a column of Sand, informed and animated only by a Whirl-blast of the Desart.

Pray, my dear Davy! did you rectify the red oil which rises over after the spirit of Hartshorn is gotten from the Horn so as to make that animal oil of Diphelius? and is it true what Hoffman asserts, that 15 or so drops will exert many times the power of opium both in degree and duration, without inducing any after fatigue?

You say W.'s "last poem is full of just pictures of what human life ought to be"—believe me, that such scenes and such characters really exist in this country—the superiority of the small Estates-men, such as W. paints in old Michael, is a God compared to our Peasants and small Farmers in the South: and furnishes important documents of the kindly ministrations of local attachment and hereditary descent. . . .

XLIV

February 3, 1801

MY DEAR DAVY,—I can scarcely reconcile it to my conscience to make you pay postage for another letter. Oh, what a fine unveiling of modern politics it would be if there were published a minute detail of all the sums received by government from the post establishment, and of all the outlets in which the sums so received flowed out again! and, on the other hand, all the domestic affections which had been stifled, all the intellectual progress that would have been, but is not, on account of the heavy tax, etc., etc. The letters of a nation ought to be paid for as an article of national expense. Well! but I did not take up this paper to flourish away in splenetic politics. A gentleman resident here, his name Calvert, an idle, good-hearted, and ingenious man, has a great desire to commence fellow-student with me and Wordsworth in chemistry. He is an intimate friend of Wordsworth's, and he has proposed to W. to take a house which he (Calvert) has nearly built, called Windy Brow, in a delicious situation, scarce half a mile from Greta Hall, the residence of S. T. Coleridge, Esq., and so for him (Calvert) to live with them, that is, Wordsworth and his sister. In this case he means to build a little laboratory, etc. Wordsworth has not quite decided, but is strongly inclined to adopt the scheme, because he and his sister have before lived with Calvert on the same footing, and are much attached to him; because my health is so precarious and so much injured by wet, and his health, too, is like little potatoes, no great things, and therefore Grasmere (thirteen miles from Keswick) is too great a distance for us to enjoy each other's society without inconvenience, as much as it would be profitable for us both; and, likewise, because he feels it more necessary for him to have some intellectual pursuit less closely connected with deep passion than poetry, and is of course desirous, too, not to be so wholly ignorant of knowledge so exceedingly important. However, whether Wordsworth come or no, Calvert and I have determined to begin and go on. Calvert is a man of sense and some originality, and is, besides, what is well called a handy man. He is a good practical mechanic, etc., and is desirous to lay out any sum of money that is necessary. You know how long, how ardently I have wished to initiate myself in chemical science, both for its own sake and in no small degree likewise, my beloved friend, that I may be able to sympathise with all that you do and think. Sympathise blindly with it all I do even *now*, God knows! from the very middle of my heart's heart, but I would fain sympathise with you in the light of knowledge. This opportunity is exceedingly precious to me, as on my own account I could not afford the least additional expense, having been already, by long and successive illnesses, thrown behindhand so much that for the next four or five months I fear, let me work as hard as I can, I shall not be able to do what my heart within me *burns* to do, that is, to *concentre* my free mind to the affinities of the feelings with words and ideas under the title of "Concerning Poetry, and the nature of the Pleasures derived from it." I have faith that I do understand the subject, and I am sure that if I write what I ought to do on it, the work would supersede all the books of metaphysics, and all the books of morals too. To whom shall a young man utter *his pride*, if not to a young man whom he loves?

I beg you, therefore, my dear Davy, to write me a long letter when you are at leisure, informing me: Firstly, What books it will be well for me and Calvert to purchase. Secondly, Directions for a convenient little laboratory. Thirdly, To what amount apparatus would run in expense, and whether or no you would be so good as to superintend its making at Bristol. Fourthly, Give me your advice how to *begin.* And, fifthly, and lastly, and mostly, do send a *drop* of hope to my parched tongue, that you will, if you can, come and visit me in the spring. Indeed, indeed, you ought to see this country, this beautiful country, and then the joy you would send into me!

The shape of this paper will convince you with what eagerness I began this letter; I really did not see that it was not a sheet. . . .

XLV

TO THOMAS POOLE

Monday, March 16, 1801

MY DEAR FRIEND,—The interval since my last letter has been filled up by me in the most intense study. If I do not greatly delude myself, I have not only *completely extricated the notions of time and space*, but have overthrown the doctrine of association, as taught by Hartley, and with it all the irreligious metaphysics of modern infidels—

especially the doctrine of necessity. This I have *done;* but I trust that I am about to do more—namely, that I shall be able to evolve all the five senses, that is, to deduce them from one sense, and to state their growth and the causes of their difference, and in this evolvement to solve the process of life and consciousness. *I write this to you only, and I pray you, mention what I have written to no one.* At Wordsworth's advice, or rather fervent entreaty, I have intermitted the pursuit. The intensity of thought, and the number of minute experiments with light and figure, have made me so nervous and feverish that I cannot sleep as long as I ought and have been used to do; and the sleep which I have is made up of ideas so connected, and so little different from the operations of reason, that it does not afford me the due refreshment. I shall therefore take a week's respite, and make "Christabel" ready for the press; which I shall publish by itself, in order to get rid of all my engagements with Longman. My German Book I have suffered to remain suspended chiefly because the thoughts which had employed my sleepless nights during my illness were imperious over me; and though poverty was staring me in the face, yet I dared behold my image miniatured in the pupil of her hollow eye, so steadily did I look her in the face; for it seemed to me a suicide of my very soul to divert my attention from truths so important, which came to me almost as a revelation. Likewise, I cannot express to you, dear Friend of my heart! the loathing which I once or twice felt when I attempted to write, merely for the bookseller, without any sense of the moral utility of what I was writing. I shall, therefore, as I said, immediately publish my "Christabel," with two essays annexed to it, on "the Preternatural" and on "Metre."—This done, I shall propose to Longman, instead of my Travels (which, though nearly done, I am exceedingly anxious not to publish, because it brings me forward in a *personal* way, as a man who relates little adventures of himself to *amuse* people, and thereby exposes me to sarcasm and the malignity of anonymous critics, and is, besides, *beneath me*, . . .) I shall propose to Longman to accept instead of these Travels a work on the originality and merits of Locke, Hobbes, and Hume, which work I mean as a *pioneer* to my greater work, and as exhibiting a proof that I have not formed opinions without an attentive perusal of the works of my predecessors, from Aristotle to Kant. . . .

XLVI

TO THE SAME   March 23, 1801

. . . My opinion is thus: that deep thinking is attainable only by a man of deep feeling, and that all truth is a species of revelation. The more I understand of Sir Isaac Newton's works, the more boldly I dare utter to my own mind, and therefore to *you*, that I believe the souls of five hundred Sir Isaac Newtons would go to the making up of a Shakspere or a Milton. But if it please the Almighty to grant me health, hope, and a steady mind (always the three clauses of my hourly prayers), before my thirtieth year I will thoroughly understand the whole of Newton's works. At present I must content myself with endeavouring to make myself entire master of his easier work, that on Optics. I am exceedingly delighted with the beauty and neatness of his experiments, and with the accuracy of his *immediate* deductions from them; but the opinions founded on these deductions, and indeed his whole theory is, I am persuaded, so exceedingly superficial as without impropriety to be deemed false. Newton was a mere materialist. *Mind*, in his system, is always *passive*,—a lazy *Looker-on* on an external world. If the mind be not *passive*, if it be indeed made in God's Image, and that, too, in the sublimest sense, the *Image of the Creator*, there is ground for suspicion that any system built on the passiveness of the mind must be false, as a system. I need not observe, my dear friend, how unutterably silly and contemptible these opinions would be if written to any but to another self. I assure you, solemnly assure you, that you and Wordsworth are the only men on earth to whom I would have uttered a word on this subject. . . .

XLVII

TO WILLIAM GODWIN

Greta Hall, Keswick, March 25, 1801

DEAR GODWIN,—I fear your tragedy will find me in a very unfit state of mind to sit in judgement on it. I have been, during the last three months, undergoing a process of intellectual exsiccation. In my long illness I had compelled into hours of delight many a sleepless, painful hour of darkness by chasing down metaphysical game—and since then I have continued the hunt, till I found myself unaware at the root of Pure Mathematics—and up the tall, smooth tree, whose few poor branches are all at its very summit, am I climbing by pure adhesive strength of arms and thighs, still slipping down, still renewing my ascent. You would not know me! All sounds of similitude keep at such a distance from each other in my mind that I have *forgotten* how to make a rhyme. I look at the mountains (that visible God Almighty that looks in at all my windows), I look at the mountains only for the curves of their outlines; the stars, as I behold them, form themselves into triangles; and my hands are scarred with scratches from a cat, whose back I was rubbing in the dark in order to see whether the sparks in it were refrangible by a prism. The Poet is dead in me. My imagination (or rather the Somewhat that had been imaginative) lies like a cold snuff on the circular rim of a brass candlestick, without even a stink of tallow to remind you that it was once clothed and mitred with flame. That is past by! I was once a volume of gold leaf, rising and riding on every breath of Fancy, but I have beaten myself back into weight and density, and now I sink in quicksilver, yea, remain squat and square on the earth, amid the hurricane that makes oaks and straws join in one dance, fifty yards high in the element. . . .

XLVIII

TO THOMAS POOLE
NETHER STOWEY, BRIDGEWATER
SOMERSET

Keswick, Sunday, July 7, 1801

. . . I wrote to Tobin in the first gloomy moments of a sudden and severe Relapse: on the three following nights I had three sharp paroxysms of decided Gout which left me in apparent health and good spirits: and under these influences

I wrote a very chearful answer to Mr. Wedgwood, and informed him, that I had postponed, and I hoped relinquished the scheme of passing the Winter at St. Michael's; but that I meant to try a course of Horse Exercise. Within two Hours after I had dispatched this letter I was again taken ill with fever and the most distressing stomach-attacks—on Friday Evening and night I was very ill—only a little better on Saturday—and I am still very sick and *somewhat* sad. I can bear pain, my dear Poole! I can bear even violent pain with the meek patience of a woman; but nausea and giddiness are far worse than pain—for they insult and threaten the steadiness of our moral Being and there is one thing yet more deplorable than these—it is the direful Thought of being inactive and useless. Nine dreary months—and oh me! have I had even a fortnight's full and continuous health? I have hardly gained the Rock, ere a new wave has overtaken and carried me back again. When I am well and employed as I ought to be, I cannot describe to you how independent a Being I seem to myself to be. My connection with the Wedgwoods I feel to be an honor to myself, and I hope, and *almost feel*, that it will hereafter be even something like an honor to them too—but—oh Poole! you know my heart and I need not reverse the picture. Now what am I to do? Mr. Wedgwood says "From all I have heard of the part of England where you are, I think it is very likely that you may have suffered from the wetness of the climate, and that you might probably derive great benefit from merely changing your place of abode in England." To this I make two remarks which I shall make into two paragraphs—a trick, I have learnt by writing for Booksellers at so much *per sheet*. Blank spaces are a Relief to the Reader's eye and the Author's Brain—and the Printers too call them *Fat*.

First then, that beastly Bishop, that blustering Fool, Watson, a native of this vicinity, a pretty constant Resident here, and who has for many years kept a Rain-gage, considers it as a vulgar Error that the climate of this County is particularly wet. He says, the opinion originates in this— that the Rain here falls more certainly in certain months, and these happen to be the months, in which the Tourists visit us. William Coates said to me at Bristol—"Keswick,

Sir! is said to be the rainiest place in the Kingdom—it always rains there, Sir! I was there myself three Days, and it rained the whole of the Time." Men's memories are not much to be relied on in cases of weather; but judging from what I remember of Stowey and Devon, Keswick has not been, since I have been here, wetter than the former, and not so wet as Devonshire.

Secondly, whither am I to go? *Nota bene,* Poole! I have now no furniture: and no means whatever to buy any. . . .

XLIX

TO ROBERT SOUTHEY

Oct. 21. 1801—The day after my birthday—29 years of age! *Who on earth can say that without a sigh!*

DEAR SOUTHEY,—You did not stay long enough with us to *love* the mountains and this wonderful vale. Yesterday the snow fell—and today—O that you were here—Lodore full—the mountains snow-crested, misty, howling weather! After your arrival I move southward in the hopes that warm rooms and deep tranquillity may build me up anew, and that I may be able to return in the Spring without the necessity of going abroad. I propose to go with you and Edith to London and then to Stowey—or Wedgwood's as circumstances direct. My knee is no longer swoln, and this frosty weather agrees with me—but O Friend! I am sadly shattered. The least agitation brings on bowel complaints, and within the last week *twice* with an ugly symptom—namely of sickness even to vomiting—and Sara—alas! we are not suited to each other. But the months of my absence I devote to *self*-discipline, and to the attempt to draw her nearer to me by a regular development of all the sources of our unhappiness—then for another trial *fair* as I hold the love of good men dear to me—*patient* as I myself love my own dear children. I will go believing that it will end happily— if not, if our mutual unsuitableness continues, and (as it assuredly will do, if it continue) increases and strengthens— why then, it is better for her and my children that I should live apart, than that she should be a widow and they orphans. Carefully have I *thought thro'* the subject of marriage and deeply am I convinced of its indissolubleness. If I separate, I do it in the earnest desire to provide for her and them, that while I live she may enjoy the comforts of life and that when I die, something may have been accumulated that may secure her from degrading dependence. When I least love her, then most do I feel anxiety for her peace, comfort and welfare. Is she not the mother of my children? And am I the man not to know and feel this? Enough of this. But dear Southey! much as we differ in our habits, you do possess my esteem and affection in a degree that makes it uncomfortable to me not to tell you what I have told you. I once said, that I *missed* no body. I only enjoyed the *present*. At that moment my heart misgave me, and had no one been present I should have said to you—that you were the only exception—for my mind is full of visions and you had been so long connected with the fairest of all fair dreams, that I feel your absence more than I enjoy your society: tho' that I do not enjoy your society so much, as I anticipated that I should do, is wholly or almost wholly owing to the nature of my domestic feelings, and the fear or the consciousness that you did not and could not sympathize with them. Now my heart is a little easy—God bless you!

Dear Davy! If I have not overrated his intellectual powers, I have little fear for his moral character—

Metaphysician! Do, Southey, keep to your own most excellent word (for the insertion of which you deserve a pension far more than Johnson for his Dictionary) and always say *Metapothecaries*. There does not exist the instance of a *deep* metaphysician who was not led by his speculations to an austere system of morals. What can be more austere than the ethics of Aristotle? than the system of Zeno, St. Paul, Spinoza (in the ethical books of his ethics), Hartley, Kant and Fichte. As to Hume, were he not—*ubi non fur, ibi stultus*, and often thief and blockhead at the same time? It is not *thinking* that will disturb a man's morals or confound the distinctions which to *think makes*. But it is *talking, talking, talking* that is the cause of the poison. I defy Davy to *think* half of what he *talks;* if indeed he talk what has been attributed to him. But I must see with my own eyes, and hear with my own ears. Till then I will be to Davy what Max was to Wallenstein. Yet I do agree with you that chemistry tends in its present state to turn its priests into sacrifices. The way in which it does it (this however is an opinion that would make Rickman laugh at me if you told it to him) is this—it prevents or tends to prevent a young man from falling in love. We all have obscure feelings, that must be connected with something or other—the miser with a guinea —Lord Nelson with a blue ribbon, Wordsworth's old Molly with her washing tub—Wordsworth with the hills, Lakes and trees, (all men are poets in their way, tho' for the most part their ways are *damned bad ones*). Now Chemistry makes a young man associate these feelings with inanimate objects—and that without any moral revulsion, but on the contrary with complete self-approbation, and his distant views of benevolence or his sense of immediate beneficences attach themselves either to man as the whole human race, or to man, as a sick man, as a painter, as a manufacturer etc., and in no way to man as a husband, son, brother, daughter, wife, friend, etc., etc. That to be in love is simply to confine the feelings prospective of animal enjoyment to one woman is a gross mistake—it is to associate a large proportion of all our obscure feelings with a real form. A miser is *in love* with a guinea, and a virtuous young man with a woman, in the same sense without figure or metaphor. A young poet may do without being in love with a woman—it is enough if he loves—but to a young chemist it would be salvation to be downright romantically in love—and unfortunately so far from the poison and antidote growing together, they are like the wheat and Barberry. . . .

L

TO THOMAS POOLE

October 21, 1801

MY DEAR POOLE,—Was my society then *useless* to you during my abode at Stowey? Yet I do not remember, that I ever once offered you *advice!* If indeed under this word you chuse to comprehend all that free communication of thought and feeling, which distinguished our intercourse, I have nothing to do but to subscribe to your *meaning,* referring you to the Dictionary for the better wording thereof. By the "quiet influences of the great Being" I wished to convey all that all things do from natural impulse, rather than direct and prospective Volition: not that I meant to interdict the latter—on the contrary, in that very letter I felt it my duty to give you *plump advice;* nay, I admit that man is an *advising* animal, even as he is a concupiscent one— Now as Religion has directed it's main attacks against Concupiscence, because we are too much inclined to it, so does Prudence against *Advice*-giving, and for the same reason. In short, I meant no more than that it is well to have a general *suspicion* of ourselves in the moment of an inclination to advise—this suspicion, not as a ham-stringer to cripple, but as a curb-rein to check. As to myself, advice from almost anybody gives me pleasure, because it informs me of the mind and heart of the adviser—but from a very, very dear Friend it has occasionally given me great pain—but, so help me Heaven, as I *believe* at least that I speak truly—on *his* account alone—or *if* on my own, on my own only as a disruption of that sympathy, in which Friendship has it's being. A thousand people might have advised all that you did, and I might have been pleased; but it is the *you, you* part of the Business that afflicted me—tho' by what figure of speech any part of my letter could be called outrageous, I can discover by the science of metaphysics, rather than by any hitherto published Art of Rhetoric. And here ends, I trust, the controversial—from which I have seldom seen much good come even in conversation—and never anything but evil when letters have been the vehicle. . . .

Mackintosh, (who is a large tall man) spent two days with me at Keswick, and was very entertaining and pleasant. He is every inch the Being, I had conceived him to be, from what I saw of him at Cote House. We talked of all and every thing—on some very affecting subjects, in which he represented himself by words as affected; on some subjects that called forth his verbal indignation—or exultation: but in no one moment did any particle of his face from the top of his forehead to the half of his neck, *move.* His face has no *lines* like that of a man—no softness, like that of a woman—it is smooth, *hard,* motionless—*a flesh-mask!* As to his conversation, it was all uncommonly well-worded: but not a thought in it worthy of having been worded at all— He *was* however entertaining to me *always;* and to all around him then chiefly, when he talked of Parr, Fox, Addington, etc., etc. When I asked him concerning Davy—he answered *Oh! little* Davy—Dr. Beddoes' Eleve, you mean? This was an excellent trait of character. . . .

L I

TO HIS WIFE [1802]

[MS mutilated] . . .—as to what is thought or said of me by persons, whom I do not particularly esteem or love, and by whom I am not esteemed or loved. 4. An independence of, and contempt for, all advantages of external fortune, that are not immediately connected with bodily comforts, or moral pleasures. I love warm Rooms, comfortable fires, and food, books, natural scenery, music, etc.; but I do not care what *binding* the Books have, whether they are dusty or clean—and I *dislike* fine furniture, handsome cloathes, and all the ordinary symbols and appendages of artificial superiority—or what is called, *Gentility.* In the same spirit, I dislike, at least I seldom like, Gentlemen, gentlemanly manners, etc. I have no Pride, as far as Pride means a desire to be *thought* highly of by others—if I have any sort of Pride, it consists *in an indolent* . . . So much for myself—and now I will endeavour to give a short sketch of what appears to be the nature of your character. As I seem to exist, as it were, almost wholly within myself, in *thoughts* rather than in *things,* in a particular warmth felt *all* over me, but chiefly felt about my head and breast; and am connected with *things without* me by the pleasurable sense of their immediate Beauty or Loveliness, and not at all by my knowledge of the average value in the minds of people in general; and with *persons without* me, by no ambition of their esteem, or of having rank and consequence in their minds, but with people in general by general kindliness of feeling, and with my especial friends, by an intense delight in fellow-feeling, by an intense perception of the Necessity of *Like* to *Like;* so you on the contrary exist almost wholly in the world *without* you—the Eye and the Ear are your great organs, and you depend upon the eyes and ears of others for a great part of your pleasures. . . . [MS. mutilated]

LII

King Street, Covent Garden, Feb. 24, 1802

. . . On Sunday I dined at Sir William Rush's, and on Monday likewise, and went with them to Mrs. Billington's Benefit. 'T was the "Beggar's Opera"; it was *perfection!* I seem to have acquired a new sense by hearing her. I wished you to have been there. I assure you I am quite a man of *fashion;* so many titled acquaintances and handsome carriages stopping at my door, and fine cards. And then I am such an exquisite judge of music and painting, and pass criticisms on furniture and chandeliers, and pay such very handsome compliments to all women of fashion, that I do verily believe that if I were to stay three months in town and have tolerable health and spirits, I should be a Thing in vogue,—the very *tonish* poet and Jemmy-Jessamy-fine-talker in town. If you were only to see the tender smiles that I occasionally receive from the Honourable Mrs. Damer! you would scratch her eyes out for jealousy! And then there's the *sweet* (N.B. musky) Lady Charlotte ——! Nay, but I won't tell you her name,—you might perhaps take it into your head to write an anonymous letter to her, and distrust our little innocent amour.

Oh that I were at Keswick with my darlings! My Hartley and my fat Derwent! God bless you, my dear Sarah! I shall return in love and cheerfulness, and therefore in pleasurable convalescence, if not in health. . . .

LIII

Greta Hall, Keswick, Tuesday, July 13, 1802

. . . I was much pleased with your description of Wordsworth's character as it appeared to you. It is in a few words, in half a dozen strokes, like one of Mortimer's figures, a fine portrait. The word "homogeneous" gave

me great pleasure, as most accurately and happily expressing him. I must set you right with regard to my
perfect coincidence with his poetic creed. It is most certain that the heads of our mutual conversations, etc., and
the passages, were indeed partly taken from note of mine;
for it was at first intended that the preface should be written
by me. And it is likewise true that I warmly accord with
Wordsworth in his abhorrence of these poetic licenses, as
they are called, which are indeed mere tricks of convenience
and laziness. *Ex. gr.* Drayton has these lines:—

> Ouse having Ouleney past, as she were waxed mad
> From her first stayder course immediately doth gad,
> And in meandered gyres doth whirl herself about,
> *That, this* way, here and there, backward in and out.
> And like a wanton girl oft doubling in her gait
> In labyrinthian turns and twinings intricate, *&c.*

The first poets, observing such a stream as this, would say
with truth and beauty, "it *strays*"; and now every stream
shall *stray*, wherever it prattles on its *pebbled way*, instead of
its bed or channel. And I have taken the instance from a
poet from whom as few instances of this vile, commonplace,
trashy style could be taken as from any writer [namely],
from Bowles' execrable translation of that lovely poem of
Dean Ogle's (Vol. II, p. 27). I am confident that Bowles
good-naturedly translated it in a hurry, merely to give him
an excuse for printing the admirable original. In my opinion,
every phrase, every metaphor, every personification, should
have its justifying clause in some *passion*, either of the poet's
mind or of the characters described by the poet. But metre
itself implies a passion, that is, a state of excitement both in
the poet's mind, and is expected, in part, of the reader; and,
though I stated this to Wordsworth, and he has in some
sort stated it in his preface, yet he has not done justice to
it, nor has he, in my opinion, sufficiently answered it. In
my opinion, poetry justifies as poetry, independent of any
other passion, some new combinations of language and
commands the omission of many others allowable in other
compositions. Now Wordsworth, *me saltem judice,* has in his
system not sufficiently admitted the former, and in his
practice has too frequently sinned against the latter. Indeed,
we have had lately some little controversy on the subject,

and we begin to suspect that there is somewhere or other a radical difference in our opinions. *Dulce est inter amicos rarissima dissensione condere plurimas consentiones*, saith St. Augustine, who said more good things than any saint or sinner that I ever read in Latin. . . .

TO ROBERT SOUTHEY, *see* p. 726

LIV

TO TOM WEDGWOOD,
EASTBURY, BLANDFORD

Greta Hall, Keswick, October 20, 1802

MY DEAR SIR,—This is my Birthday, my thirtieth. It will not appear wonderful to you therefore, when I tell you that before the arrival of your Letter I had been thinking with a great weight of different feelings concerning you and your dear Brother. For I have good reason to believe, that I should not now have been alive, if in addition to other miseries I had had immediate poverty pressing upon me. I will never again remain silent so long. It has not been altogether Indolence or my habits of Procrastination which have kept me from writing, but an eager wish, I may truly say, a Thirst of Spirit, to have something honourable to tell you of myself— At present I must be content to tell you something cheerful. My Health is very much better. I am stronger in every respect: and am not injured by study or the act of sitting at my writing Desk. But my eyes suffer if at any time I have been intemperate in the use of Candle-light. This account supposes another, namely, that my mind is calm and more at ease. My dear Sir! when I was last with you at Stowey, my heart was often full, and I could scarcely keep from communicating to you the tale of my distresses. But how could I add to your depression, when you were low? Or how interrupt, or cast a shade on your good spirits, that were so rare and so precious to you? After my return to Keswick, I was, if possible, more miserable than before. Scarce a day passed without such a scene of discord between me and Mrs. Coleridge, as quite incapacitated me for any worthy exertion of my faculties by degrading me in my own estimation. I found my temper impaired, and daily more so; the good and pleasurable thoughts, which had been the support of my moral character, departed from my solitude. I determined to go abroad—but alas! the less I loved my wife, the more dear and necessary did my children seem to me. I found no comfort except in the driest speculations—In the "Ode to Dejection," which you were pleased with, these lines in the original followed the line—My shaping spirit of Imagination—

> For not to think of what I needs must feel,
> But to be still and patient, all I can,
> And haply by abstruse Research to steal
> From my own Nature all the natural man—
> This was my sole resource, my only plan,
> And that which suits a part infects the whole
> And now is almost grown the Temper of my Soul.

I give you these lines for the Truth and not for the Poetry. However about two months ago after a violent quarrel I was taken suddenly ill with spasms in my stomach—I expected to die—Mrs. C. was, of course, shocked and frightened beyond measure—and two days after, I being still very weak and pale as death, she threw herself upon me, and made a solemn promise of amendment—and she has kept her promise beyond any hope, I could have flattered myself with: and I have reason to believe, that two months of tranquillity, and the sight of my now not colourless and cheerful countenance, have really made her feel as a Wife ought to feel. If any woman wanted an exact and copious Recipe, "How to make a Husband compleatly miserable," I could her furnish with one—with a *Probatum est,* tacked to it. Ill-tempered Speeches sent after me when I went out of the House, ill-tempered Speeches on my return, my friends received with freezing looks, the least opposition or contradiction occasioning screams of passion, and the sentiments which I held most base, ostentatiously avowed—all this added to the utter negation of all, which a Husband expects from a Wife—especially, living in retirement—and the consciousness that I was myself growing a worse man. O dear Sir! no one can tell what I have suffered. I can say with strict truth, that the happiest half-hours, I have had, were when all of a sudden, as I have been sitting alone in my Study I have burst into Tears. . . .

LV

St. Clears, Carmarthen,
Tuesday morning, ½ past 5 !!
Nov. 22, 1802

. . . Be assured, my dear Love, that I shall never write otherwise than *most* kindly to you, except after great *aggressions* on your part; and not then, unless my reason convinces me that some good end will be answered by my reprehensions—My dear Love! let me in the spirit of Love say two things. 1. I owe duties, and solemn ones to you, as my wife, but some equally solemn ones to Myself, to my children, to my friends and to society. When duties are at variance, dreadful as the case may be, there must be a choice. I can neither retain my happiness nor my faculties, unless I move, live and love in perfect freedom, limited only by my own purity and self-respect and by my incapability of loving any person, man or woman, unless at the same time I honor and esteem them. My love is made up of 9/10ths of fervent wishes for the permanent *peace* of mind of those whom I love, be it man or woman; and for their progression in purity, goodness, and true knowledge. Such being the nature of my love, no human being can have a right to be jealous. My nature is quick to love and retentive. Of those who are within the immediate sphere of my daily agency and bound to me by bonds of Nature or Neighbourhood I shall love each as they appear to me to deserve my love, and to be capable of returning it. More is not in my power. If I would do it, I could not. That we can love but one person is a miserable mistake and the cause of abundant unhappiness. I can and do love many people, dearly—so dearly, that I really scarcely know, which I love the best. Is it not so with every good mother who has a large number of children—and with many, many brothers and sisters in large and affectionate families? Why should it be otherwise with friends? Would any good and wise man, any warm and wide-hearted man marry at all, if it were part of the contract? Henceforth the woman is your only friend, the sole beloved! all the rest of mankind, however amiable and akin to you, must be only your *acquaintance!* It were well, if every woman wrote down before her marriage all, she thought, she had a *right* to from her husband and to examine each in this form. By what *Law* of God, of man, or of general reason, do I claim *this* right? I suspect, that this process would make a ludicrous quantity of blots and erasures in most of the first rude draughts of these Rights of Wives—infinitely however to their own advantage, and to the security of their true and genuine rights. 2. Permit me, my dear Sara, without offence to you, as Heaven knows! it is without any feeling of pride in myself, to say, that in six acquirements, and in the quantity and quality of natural endowments whether of feeling, or of intellect, you are the inferior. Therefore it would be preposterous to expect that I should see with your eyes, and dismiss my friends from *my* heart; but it is not preposterous in me, on the contrary I have a *right* to expect and demand that you should to a certain degree love and act kindly to those whom I deem worthy of my Love. If you read this letter with half the tenderness with which it is written, it will do you and both of us *good.* . . . [erasure]

You know Sally Pally! I must have a joke or it would not be me!

Over frightful roads we at last arrived at Crescelly about 3 o'clock—found a Captain and Mrs. Tyler there (a stupid Brace), Jessica, Emma, and Frances Allen—All simple, good, kind-hearted lasses, and Jessie the eldest uncommonly so. We dined at ½ past 4—just after dinner down came old Allen—O Christ! Old Nightmair! An ancient Incubus! Every face was saddened, every mouth pursed up! Most solemnly civil, like the Lord of a stately castle 500 years ago! Doleful and plaintive eke for I believe that the Devil *is* twitching him home. After tea he left us, and went again to bed, and the whole party recovered their spirits. I drank nothing but I eat sweet meats, and cream and some fruit and talked a great deal and sate up till 12, and did not go to sleep till near 2. In consequence of which I rose sickish at ½ past 7—my breakfast brought me about—and all the way from Crescelly I was in a very pleasurable state of feeling, but my feelings too tender, my thoughts too vivid—I was *deliciously* unwell. On my arrival at St. Clears, I received your letter, and had scarcely read it before a fluttering of the heart came on, which ended (as usual) in a sudden and violent diarrhoea. I could scarcely touch my dinner and was obliged at last to take 20 drops of Laudanum which now that I have for 10 days left off all stimulus of all kinds, excepting $\frac{1}{3}$rd of a grain of opium at night, acted upon me more powerfully than 80 or 100 drops would have done at Keswick. I slept sound while I did sleep; but I am not *quite* well this morning; but I shall get round again in the course of the day—You must see by this, what absolute necessity I am under of *dieting* myself, and if possible, the still greater importance of *tranquillity* to me. . . .

LVI

TO THE SAME

Crescelly, Thursday morning, 7 o'clock,
Dec. 16, 1802

MY DEAR LOVE,—I write with trembling—at what time or in what state my letter may find you, how can I tell? Small need is there for saying, how anxious I am, how full of terrors and prayers! I trust in God, that this letter which I write with a palpitating heart, you will read with a chearful one—the new baby at your breast—O may God Almighty preserve you!

We leave this place in less than an hour. Our route lies thro' St. Clears, Carmarthen, Llandilo, Llandovery, Trecastle, Brecon, Hay, Hereford, Worcester, Birmingham, Litchfield, Abbots Bromly, Uttoxeter, Ashborn, Newbury, Buxton, Stockport, Manchester, Bolton, Preston, Garstang, Lancaster, Burton, Kendal, Ambleside, Keswick—346 miles. From Keswick I must go with T. Wedgwood to Mr. Clarkson's, and so on to Luff's. I calculate that we shall not much exceed forty miles a day: and that we shall be at Ambleside, Thursday Evening, December 23rd—Mrs. Wilson will be so good as to have a fire kept in Peach's Parlour, and likewise in Peach's bedroom and great care taken that the bed and bedding shall be thoroughly warmed and aired.

I should think it would be advisable to order immediately a pair of bed blankets from Miss Crosthwaite's. My dearest Love! T.W. will not stay above a day or two in Keswick—and for God's sake do not let [him] be any weight or bustle on your mind—let him be entirely Mr. Jackson's visitor, and let a girl from the town come up for the time he stays—and Mrs. W. will probably accommodate you with a fowl or two—But above all, Mr. Jackson will be so good as immediately to write a line to be left for me at the Post Office, Kendal, informing me how you are—*and of all I am to know.* Any letters you may have written to Gunville will be sent back again to Keswick.

Mrs. Wilson will be so good as to procure a pound or so of the best salt potted butter which Mr. T. Wedgwood likes.

Again and again, my dear Love

God bless you

S. T. Coleridge.

If Mr. Jackson open this, he will, I am sure excuse the liberty I take with him, and accept of my best and kindest remembrances. And the same to dear Mrs. Wilson. I sent 50£ Monday before last.

LVII

TO TOM WEDGWOOD

Keswick, January 9, 1803

. . . I found Mrs. Coleridge not so well as I expected, but she is better to-day—and I, myself, write with difficulty, with all the fingers but one of my right hand very much swollen. Before I was half up *Kirkstone* the storm had wetted me through and through, and before I reached the top it was so wild and outrageous, that it would have been unmanly to have suffered the poor woman (guide) to continue pushing on, up against such a torrent of wind and rain; so I dismounted and sent her home with the storm to her back. I am no novice in mountain mischiefs, but such a storm as this was I never witnessed, combining the intensity of the cold with the violence of the wind and rain. The rain-drops were pelted or, rather, slung against my face by the gusts, just like splinters of flint, and I felt as if every drop *cut* my flesh. My hands were all shrivelled up like a washerwoman's, and so benumbed that I was obliged to carry my stick under my arm. Oh, it was a wild business! Such hurry-skurry of clouds, such volleys of sound! In spite of the wet and the cold, I should have had some pleasure in it but for two vexations: first, an almost intolerable pain came into my right eye, a *smarting* and *burning* pain; and secondly, in consequence of riding with such cold water under my seat, extremely uneasy and burthensome feelings attacked my groin, so that, what with the pain from the one, and the alarm from the other, I had *no enjoyment at all!*

Just at the brow of the hill I met a man dismounted, who could not sit on horseback. He seemed quite scared by the uproar, and said to me, with much feeling, "Oh, sir, it is a perilous buffeting, but it is worse for you than for me, for I have it at my back." However I got safely over, and, immediately, all was calm and breathless, as if it was some mighty fountain just on the summit of Kirkstone, that shot forth its volcano of air, and precipitated huge streams of invisible lava down the road to Patterdale. . . .

LVIII

TO ROBERT SOUTHEY

Monday evening, August 1, 1803

MY DEAR OLD FRIEND,—On whatever plan you determine I will be your faithful servant and fellow-errant. If you were with me and health were not far away, I could now rely on myself, but my health is a very weighty, perhaps insuperable objection. Else the sense of responsibility to my own mind is growing deeper and deeper with me from many causes, chiefly, from the knowledge that I am not of no significance, relatively to, comparatively with other men, my contemporaries. I was thought *vain*—if there be no better word to express what I was, so let it be; but if Cottle be *vain*, Dyer vain, J. Jennings be *vain*, the word is a vague one. It was

in me, the heat, bustle and overflowing of a mind, too vehemently pushed on from within to be regardful of the objects
upon which it was moving; an instinct to have my power
proved to me by transient evidences, arising from an inward
feeling of weakness, both the one and the other working in
me unconsciously; above all a faulty delight in the being
beloved without having examined my heart, whether if
beloved, I had anything to give in return beyond general
kindness, and general sympathy, both indeed unusually
warm, but which being still *general*, were not a return in
kind, for that which I was unconsciously desiring to inspire.
All this added together might possibly have been a somewhat far worse than vanity, but it would still have been
different from it; far worse if it had not existed in a nature
where better things were indigenous— A sense of weakness,
a haunting sense that I was an herbaceous plant, as large
as a large tree, with a trunk of the same girth, and branches
as large and shadowing, but with pith within the trunk,
not heart of wood—that I had power not strength, an involuntary impostor, that I had no real Genius, no real
depth. This on my honor is as fair a statement of my
habitual haunting, as I could give before the tribunal of
Heaven. How it arose in me, I have but lately discovered;
still it works within me, but only as a disease, the cause and
meaning of which I know. The whole History of this
feeling would form a curious page in a *nosologia spiritualis*. . . .

LIX

TO SIR GEORGE AND LADY BEAUMONT

Greta Hall, Keswick, Friday, Aug. 12, 1803
. . . It will give a lasting interest to the Drawing of the
Waterfall, that I first saw it through tears. I was indeed
unwell, and sadly nervous; and I must not be ashamed to
confess to you, my honoured friends, that I found a bodily
relief in weeping, and yielded to it. On Tuesday evening
Mr. R——, the author of "The . . . of . . .," drank tea
and spent the evening with us at Grasmere—and this had
produced a very unpleasant effect on my spirits. Wordsworth's mind and body are both of a stronger texture than

mine, and he has passions, that have made their Pandemonium in the crazy hovel of that poor man's heart—but I was downright melancholy at the sight. If to be a poet or a man of genius entailed on us the necessity of housing such company in our bosoms, I would pray the very flesh off my knees to have a head as dark and unfurnished as Wordsworth's old Molly has, if only I might have a heart as careless and as loving. But God be praised! these unhappy beings are neither poets nor men of sense. Enough of them! Forgive me, dear Sir George, but I could not help being pleased that the man disliked you, and your Lady, and he lost no time in letting us know it. If I believed it possible that the man liked me, upon my soul I should feel exactly as if I were tarred and feathered. I have a *cowardly* dread of being hated even by bad men; but in this instance disgust comes in to my assistance, and the greater dread of being called Friend. I do seriously believe that the chief cause of Wordsworth's and Southey's having been classed with me, as a *school*, originates entirely in our not hating or envying each other. It is so unusual that three professed Poets, in every respect unlike each other, should nevertheless take pleasure in each other's welfare and reputation. What a refreshment of heart did I not find last night in Cowper's Letters! Their very defects suited me. Had they been of a higher class, as exhibitions of intellect, they would have less satisfied the then craving of my mind. I had taken up the book merely as connected with you; and had I hunted through all the Libraries of Oxford and Cambridge I should have found no one that would have been so delightful on its own account. . . .

LX

TO TOM WEDGWOOD

12 PAPER BUILDINGS, TEMPLE, LONDON

Greta Hall, Keswick, September 16, Friday [1803]

MY DEAR WEDGWOOD,—I reached home on yesterday noon, and it was not a Post Day. William Hazlitt is a thinking, observant, original man, of great power as a Painter of Character Portraits, and far more in the manner of the old

Painters, than any living Artist, but the objects must be *before* him; he has no imaginative memory. So much for his Intellectuals. His manners are to 99 in 100 singularly repulsive—: brow-hanging, shoe-contemplative, *strange*. Sharp seemed to like him; but Sharp saw him only for half an hour, and that walking—he is, I verily believe, kindly-natured—is very fond of, attentive to, and patient with, children; but he is jealous, gloomy, and of an irritable Pride—and addicted to women, as objects of sexual Indulgence. With all this, there is much good in him—he is disinterested, an enthusiastic lover of the great men, who have been before us—he says things that are his own in a way of his own—and tho' from habitual Shyness and the outside and bearskin at least of misanthropy, he is strangely confused and dark in his conversation and delivers himself of almost all his conceptions with a Forceps, yet he says more than any man, I ever knew, yourself only excepted, that is his own in a way of his own—and oftentimes when he has warmed his mind, and the synovial juice has come out and spread over his joints, he will gallop for half an hour together with real Eloquence. He sends well-headed and well-feathered Thoughts straight forwards to the mark with a Twang of the Bow-string. If you could recommend him, as a Portrait-painter, I should be glad. To be your Companion he is, in my opinion, utterly unfit. His own Health is fitful. I have written, as I ought to do, to you most freely *imo ex corde;* you know me, both head and heart, and will make what deductions, your reason will dictate to you. I can think of no other person. What wonder? For the last years I have been shy of all mere acquaintances—

To live beloved is all, I need,
And when I love, I love indeed.

I never had any ambition; and now, I trust, I have almost as little Vanity.

For 5 months past my mind has been strangely shut up. I have taken the paper with the intention to write to you many times; but it has been all one blank Feeling, one blank idealess Feeling. I had nothing to say, I could say nothing. How dearly I love you, my very Dreams make known to me. I will not trouble you with the gloomy Tale of my Health. While I am awake, by patience, employment, effort of mind,

x

and walking I can keep the fiend at Arm's length; but the Night is my Hell, Sleep my tormenting Angel. Three nights out of four I fall asleep, struggling to lie awake—and my frequent Night-screams have almost made me a nuisance in my own House. Dreams with me are no Shadows, but the very Substances and foot-thick Calamities of my Life. . . .

LXI

TO RICHARD SHARP

King's Arms, Kendal,
Sunday morning, January 15, 1804

MY DEAR SIR,—I give you thanks—and, that I may make the best of so poor and unsubstantial a return, permit me to say, that they are such thanks as can only come from a nature unworldly by constitution and by habit, and now rendered more than ever impressible by sudden restoration—resurrection I might say—from a long, long sickbed. I had gone to Grasmere to take my farewell of William Wordsworth, his wife, and his sister, and thither your letters followed me. I was at Grasmere a whole month, so ill, as that till the last week I was unable to read your letters. Not that my inner being was disturbed; on the contrary, it seemed more than usually serene and self-sufficing; but the exceeding pain, of which I suffered every now and then, and the fearful distresses of my sleep, had taken away from me the connecting link of voluntary power, which continually combines that part of us by which we know ourselves to be, with that outward picture or hieroglyphic, by which we hold communion with our like—between the vital and the organic—or what Berkeley, I suppose, would call mind and its sensuous language. I had only just strength enough to smile gratefully on my kind nurses, who tended me with sister's and mother's love, and often, I well know, wept for me in their sleep, and watched for me even in their dreams. Oh, dear sir! it does a man's heart good, I will not say, to know such a family, but even to know that there *is* such a family. In spite of Wordsworth's occasional fits of hypochondriacal uncomfortableness,— from which, more or less, and at longer or shorter intervals,

he has never been wholly free from his very childhood,—
in spite of this hypochondriacal graft in his nature, as dear
Wedgwood calls it, his is the happiest family I ever saw,
and were it not in too great sympathy with my ill health—
were I in good health, and their neighbour—I verily believe
that the cottage in Grasmere Vale would be a proud sight
for Philosophy. It is with no idle feeling of vanity that I
speak of my importance to them; that it is *I*, rather than
another, is almost an accident; but being so very happy
within themselves they are too good, not the more, for
that very reason, to want a friend and common object of
love out of their household. I have met with several
genuine Philologists, Philonoists, Physiophilists, keen hun-
ters after knowledge and science; but truth and wisdom
are higher names than these—and *revering* Davy, I am
half angry with him for doing that which would make me
laugh in another man—I mean, for prostituting and profaning the name of "Philosopher," "great Philosopher,"
"eminent Philosopher," etc., etc., etc., to every fellow who
has made a lucky experiment, though the man should be
Frenchified to the heart, and though the whole Seine, with
all its filth and poison, flows in his veins and arteries.

Of our common friends, my dear sir, I flatter myself
that you and I should agree in fixing on T. Wedgwood
and on Wordsworth as genuine Philosophers—for I have
often said (and no wonder, since not a day passes but the
conviction of the truth of it is renewed in me, and with the
conviction, the accompanying esteem and love), often have
I said that T. Wedgwood's faults impress me with veneration for his moral and intellectual character more than
almost any other man's virtues; for under circumstances
like his, to have a fault only in that degree is, I doubt not,
in the eye of God, to possess a high virtue. Who does not
prize the Retreat of Moreau more than all the straw-blaze
of Bonaparte's victories? And then to make it (as Wedgwood really does) a sort of crime even to think of his faults
by so many virtues retained, cultivated, and preserved in
growth and blossom, in a climate—where now the gusts so
rise and eddy, that deeply rooted must *that* be which is not
snatched up and made a plaything of by them,—and, now,
"the parching air burns frore."

W. Wordsworth does not excite that almost painfully profound moral admiration which the sense of the exceeding difficulty of a given virtue can alone call forth, and which therefore I feel exclusively towards T. Wedgwood; but, on the other hand, he is an object to be contemplated with greater complacency, because he both deserves to be, and *is*, a happy man; and a happy man, not from natural temperament, for therein lies his main obstacle, not by enjoyment of the good things of this world—for even to this day, from the first dawn of his manhood, he has purchased independence and leisure for great and good pursuits by austere frugality and daily self-denials; nor yet by an accidental confluence of amiable and happy-making friends and relatives, for every one near to his heart has been placed there by choice and after knowledge and deliberation; but he is a happy man, because he is a Philosopher, because he knows the intrinsic value of the different objects of human pursuit, and regulates his wishes in strict subordination to that knowledge; because he feels, and with a *practical* faith, the truth of that which you, more than once, my dear sir, have with equal good sense and kindness pressed upon me, that we can do but one thing well, and that therefore we must make a choice. He has made that choice from his early youth, has pursued and is pursuing it; and certainly no small part of his happiness is owing to this unity of interest and that homogeneity of character which is the natural consequence of it, and which that excellent man, the poet Sotheby, noticed to me as the characteristic of Wordsworth.

Wordsworth is a poet, a most original poet. He no more resembles Milton than Milton resembles Shakspere— no more resembles Shakspere than Shakspere resembles Milton. He is himself and, I dare affirm that, he will hereafter be admitted as the first and greatest philosophical poet, the only man who has effected a complete and constant synthesis of thought and feeling and combined them with poetic forms, with the music of pleasurable passion, and with Imagination or the *modifying* power in that highest sense of the word, in which I have ventured to oppose it to Fancy, or the *aggregating* power—in that sense in which it is a dim analogue of creation—not all that we can *believe*, but all that we can *conceive* of creation.—Wordsworth is a poet, and I feel myself a better poet, in knowing how to honour *him* than in all my own poetic compositions, all I have done or hope to do; and I prophesy immortality to his "Recluse," as the first and finest philosophical poem, if only it be (as it undoubtedly will be) a faithful transcript of his own most august and innocent life, of his own habitual feelings and modes of seeing and hearing. . . .

LXII

TO SIR GEORGE AND LADY BEAUMONT

Weds., Feb. 1, 1804

. . . In explaining what I shall do with Shakspere, I explain the nature of the other five [projected Essays]. Each scene of each play I read as if it were the whole of Shakspere's works—the sole thing extant. I ask myself what are the characteristics, the diction, the cadences, and metre, the character, the passion, the moral or metaphysical inherencies and fitness for theatric effect, and in what sort of theatres. All these I write down with great care and precision of thought and language (and when I have gone through the whole, I then shall collect my papers, and observe how often such and such expressions recur), and thus shall not only know what the characteristics of Shakspere's plays are, but likewise what proportion they bear to each other. Then, not carelessly, though of course with far less care, I shall read through the old plays, just before Shakspere's time, Sir Philip Sidney's "Arcadia," Ben Jonson, Beaumont and Fletcher, and Massinger in the same way; so as to see, and to be able to prove, what of Shakspere belonged to his age, and was common to all *the first-rate men* of that true *saeculum aureum* of English poetry, and what is his own, and his only. Thus I shall both exhibit the characteristics of the plays and of the mind of Shakspere, and a philosophical analysis and justification of almost every character, at greater or less length, in the spirit of that analysis of the character of Hamlet, with which you were much pleased, and by being so, I solemnly assure, gave me heart and hope, and did me much good. For much as I loathe flattery from the bottom of my very

stomach, and much as I *wriggle* under the burden and discomfort of the praise of people, for whose heads, hearts, and
specific competence I have small respect, yet I own myself
no self-subsisting mind. I know, I feel, that I am weak,
apt to faint away, inwardly self-deserted, and bereft of the
confidence in my own powers; and that the approbation
and sympathy of good and intelligent men is my sea-breeze,
without which I should languish from morn to evening,—a
very trade-wind to me, in which my bark drives on regularly
and lightly.

An author of some celebrity, and more notoriety, was
with me all yesterday, and inflicted on me five acts of a
tragedy, and all to-day, with aching spirit, I am to be
employed in pencil-marking its thousand flatnesses and
incongruities of diction and sentiment, in addition to a
conversation of two hours yesterday, in which I persuaded
him to many essential alterations; and yet, do all I can, I
could as easily pray Caligula or (within a month after his
arrival in England) Buonaparte out of purgatory as help
this poor devil of a tragedy out of absolute damnation. It
will die the death of a red-hot poker in water—all one hiss.
But what can a decently good-natured man say to a brother
bard, who tells you that it is of importance to his happiness
and pecuniary circumstances? . . .

LXIII

TO ROBERT SOUTHEY
GRETA HALL, KESWICK

Crown Inn, Portsmouth,
Wednesday morning, 10 o'clock, March 28, 1804

. . . While I was writing, Mottley, a dashing bookseller, a
booted, buck-skin-breeched Jockey, to whom Stuart gave
me a letter of most urgent recommendation (he is their
Portsmouth correspondent) called—he is a man of wealth,
and influence here, and a knowing Fellow. He took me
thro' the Dock-yards, and I was lucky enough to be present
at a *Heat*, *i.e.* at the welding a huge *Faggot* of small latten of
red hot Iron into the Shafts of the Anchor of a man of war.
It was truly sublime—the enormous Blaze, the regular yet

complex intertwisted strokes of between 20 and 30 men, with their huge Flail-hammers, the astonishment how they could throw them about, with such seeming wildness without dashing out each other's brains, and how they saved their eyes amidst the shower of sparks—the Iron *dripping* like a millwheel from the intense white heat—verily it was an unforgettable scene. The poor men are pitiable slaves— from 4 in the morning they work till 9 at night, and yet are payed less than any other in the yard. They all become old men in the prime of manhood. So do the rope-makers who get only work from 7 till noon. The rope-room is a *very low* broad room, of a length far too great for the eye to see from one end to the other—it gave me a grand idea of an Hindustan Cavern. A fire machine has been lately introduced, after a rebellion among the men, and but for the same deplorable delusion two thirds of that labour might be done by machines, which now eats up the rope-men like a Giant in a fairy tale. . . .

LXIV

TO HIS WIFE

[Malta], June, 1804

[My dear Sara,]—[I wrote] to Southey from Gibraltar, directing you to open the letter in case Southey should be in town. You received it, I trust, and learnt from it that I had been pretty well, and that we had had a famous quick passage. At Gibraltar we stayed five days, and so lost our fair wind, and [during our] after-voyage to Malta [there] was [a] storm, that carried away our main yard, etc., long dead calms, every rope of the whole ship reflected in the bright, soft blue sea, and light winds, often varying every quarter of an hour, and more often against us than for us. We were the best sailing vessel in the whole convoy; but every day we had to lie by and wait for the laggards. This is very disheartening; likewise the frequent danger in light winds or calms, or in foggy weather of running foul of each other is another heavy inconvenience of convoy, and, in case of a deep calm in a narrow sea, as in the Gut of Gibraltar and in the Archipelago, etc., where calms are most common, a privateering or piratical row-boat might board you and make slaves of you under the very nose of the man-of-war, which would lie a lifeless hulk on the smooth water. For these row-boats, mounting from one to four or five guns, would instantly sink a man-of-war's boat, and one of them, last war, had very nearly made a British frigate *strike*. I mention these facts because it is a common notion that going under convoy you are "as snug as a bug in a rug." If I had gone without convoy on board the "Speedwell," we should have reached Malta in twenty days from the day I left Portsmouth, but, however, we were congratulated on having had a *very good* passage for the time of the year, having been only forty days including our stay at Gibraltar; and if there be inconvenience in a convoy, I have reason to know and to be grateful for its advantages. The whole of the voyage from Gibraltar to Malta, excepting the four or five last days, I was wretchedly unwell. . . . The harbour at Valetta is narrow as the neck of a bottle in the entrance; but instantly opens out into a lake with tongues of land, capes, one little island, etc., etc., where the whole navy of England might lie as in a dock in the worst of weather. All around its banks, in the form of an amphitheatre, rise the magnificent houses of Valetta, and its two over-the-water towns, Burmola and Flavia (which are to Valetta what the Borough is to London). The houses are all lofty and built of fine white freestone, something like Bath, only still whiter and *newer* looking, yet the windows, from the prodigious thickness of the walls, being all out of sight, the whole appeared to me as Carthage to Aeneas, a proud city, well nigh but not quite finished. I walked up a long street of good breadth, all a flight of stairs (no place for beast or carriage, each broad stair composed of a cement-sand of *terra pozzolana*, hard and smooth as the hardest pavement of smooth rock by the seaside and very like it). I soon found out Dr. Stoddart's house, which seemed a large pile of building. He was not at home, but I stayed for him, and in about two hours he came, and received me with an explosion of surprise and welcome—more *fun* than *affection* in the manner, but just as I wished it. . . . Yesterday and to-day I have been pretty well. In a hot climate, now that the glass is high as 80 in the shade, the healthiest persons are liable to fever on the least disagreement of food with the first passages, and my general health is, I would fain believe, better *on the whole*. . . . I will try the most scrupulous regimen of diet and exercise; and I rejoice to find that the heat, great as it is, does not at all annoy me. In about a fortnight I shall probably take a trip into Sicily, and spend the next two or three months in some cooler and less dreary place, and return in September. For eight months in the year the climate of Malta is delightful, but a drearier place eye never saw. No stream in the whole island, only one place of springs, which are conveyed by aqueducts and supply the island with about one third of its water; the other two thirds they depend for upon the rain. And the reservoirs under the houses, walls, etc., to preserve the rain are *stupendous!* The tops of all the houses are flat, and covered with that smooth, hard composition, and on these and everywhere where rain can fall are channels and pipes to conduct it to the reservoirs. Malta is about twenty miles by twelve— a mere rock of freestone. In digging out this they find large quantities of vegetable soil. They separate it, and with the stones they build their houses and garden and field walls, all of an enormous thickness. The fields are seldom so much as half an acre ⊏ one above another in that form, so that everything grows as in huge garden pots. The whole island looks like one monstrous fortification. Nothing *green* meets your eye—one dreary, grey-white,—and all the country towns from the retirement and invisibility of the windows look like towns burnt out and desolate. Yet the fertility is marvellous. You almost see things grow, and the population is, I suppose, unexampled. The town of Valetta itself contains about one hundred and ten streets, all at right angles to each other, each having from twelve to fifty houses; but many of them very steep—a few *staired* all across, and almost all, in some part or other, if not the whole, having the footway on each side so staired. The houses lofty, all looking new. The good houses are built with a court in the centre, and the rooms large and lofty, from sixteen to twenty feet high, and walls enormously thick, all necessary for coolness. The fortifications of Valetta are endless. When I first walked about them, I was struck all of a heap with their strangeness, and when I came to understand a little of their purpose, I was overwhelmed with wonder. Such vast masses—bulky mountain-breasted heights; gardens with pomegranate trees—the prickly pears in the fosses, and the caper (the most beautiful of flowers) growing profusely in the interstices of the high walls and on the battlements. The Maltese are a dark, light-limbed people. Of the women five tenths are ugly; of the remainder, four fifths would be ordinary but that they look so *quaint*, and one tenth, perhaps, may be called quaint-pretty. The prettiest resemble pretty Jewesses in England. They are the noisiest race under heaven, and Valetta the noisiest place. The [most] sudden shot-up, explosive bellows-cries you ever heard in London would give you the faintest idea of it. Even when you pass by a fruit stall the fellow will put his hand like a speaking trumpet to his mouth and shoot such a thunder-bolt of sound full at you. Then the endless jangling of those cursed bells, etc. Sir Alexander Ball and General Valette (the civil and military commanders) have been marvellously attentive—Sir A. B. even friendly and confidential to me. . . .

LXV

TO ROBERT SOUTHEY
KESWICK, CUMBERLAND

Wednesday, August 20, 1806

MY DEAR SOUTHEY,—I write to you rather than to Mrs. Coleridge because I can write more tranquilly—indeed it agitates me so much that if I could have settled any rational plan to have set off tomorrow or tonight I should not have written at all—but have let the information sent to Grasmere suffice. After as sore a heartwasting as I believe ever poor creature underwent, and which commenced at and continued without interval from April, 1806, I landed at lower Haslow, Halling, in Kent on Sunday afternoon last—a few hundred yards from a curious little chapel, which being open and no one in it I hurried to—and offered, I trust, as deep a prayer as ever without words or thoughts was sent up by a human Being. Very very ill I was at my setting off from Leghorn—not one meal in ten, little as I eat, could I retain on my stomach—and we had 55 days aboard ship, and what I suffered even to the last day, may the worst of men only ever feel. Had not the Captain loved me as he often said better than a brother, and performed all the offices of a nurse I could not have survived. . . . I detail these shocking circumstances to you and my wife, in order that you may feel part of the gratitude which I am ever to do. Tho' as proud and jealous an American as ever even America produced, he would come and even with tears in his eyes beg and pray me to have an enema, and strange it is! but tho' the pain is so trifling that it is almost a misnomer to call it pain, yet my dread of and antipathy increased each time. However, almost immediately after my landing health seemed to flow in upon me, like the mountain waters upon the dry stones of a vale-stream after rains. And I can safely say that for 16 months I have never enjoyed four *days* of such health as I have had since Sunday afternoon and my nights have been unusually good. My body is quite open, and tho' I do not respire freely, yet I respire with comparative ease. One night indeed I was awakened with the old *knock* of the head, and was very bad indeed for three hours, but I attribute this to a little imprudence in drinking off, from thirst I did not perceive it, some stale beer instead of porter, and its long continuance was entirely to my being without assistance, without hot water, or ether, or indeed anything but the water in the wash basin. With great care, meat, potatoes, porter, and dissolved meat once an hour so as always to keep off faintness, I shall do. But whether it does, I live or die at home. I am now going to Lamb's. Stuart is at Margate—all are out of town. I have no one to advise me—I am shirtless and almost penniless—but money I can get immediately. My MSS. are all, excepting two pocketbooks—either in the sea, or (as in the case of the $\frac{9}{10}$ths) carried back to Malta. I will try to write again before night. I will come as soon as I can come—

S. T. COLERIDGE.

LXVI

TO HARTLEY COLERIDGE
April 3, 1807

MY DEAR BOY,—In all human beings good and bad qualities are not only found together, side by side, as it were, but they actually tend to produce each other; at least they must be considered as twins of a common parent, and the amiable propensities too often sustain and foster their unhandsome sisters. (For the old Romans personified virtues and vices both as women.) This is a sufficient proof that mere natural qualities, however pleasing and delightful, must not be deemed virtues until they are broken in and yoked to the plough of *Reason*. Now to apply this to your own case—I could equally apply it to myself—but you know yourself more accurately than you can know me, and will therefore understand my argument better when the facts on which it is built exist in your own consciousness. You are by nature very kind and forgiving, and wholly free from revenge and sullenness; you are likewise gifted with a very active and self-gratifying fancy, and such a high tide and flood of pleasurable feelings, that all unpleasant and painful thoughts and events are hurried away upon it, and neither remain in the surface of your memory nor sink to the bottom of your heart. So far all seems right and matter of thanksgiving to your Maker; and so all really *is* so, and will be so, if you exert your reason and free will. But on the other hand the very same disposition makes you less impressible both to the censure of your anxious friends and to the whispers of your conscience. Nothing that gives you pain dwells long enough upon your mind to do you any good, just as in some diseases the medicines pass so quickly through the stomach and bowels as to be able to exert none of their healing qualities. In like manner, this power which you possess of shoving aside all disagreeable reflections, or losing them in a labyrinth of day-dreams, which saves you from some present pain, has, on the other hand, interwoven with your nature habits of procrastination, which, unless you correct them in time (and it will require all your best exertions to do it effectually), must lead you into lasting unhappiness.

You are now going with me (if God have not ordered it otherwise) into Devonshire to visit your Uncle G. Coleridge. He is a very good man and very kind; but his notions of right and of propriety are very strict, and he is, therefore, exceedingly shocked by any gross deviations from what is right and proper. I take, therefore, this means of warning you against those bad habits, which I and all your friends here have noticed in you; and, be assured, I am not writing in anger, but on the contrary with great love, and a comfortable hope that your behaviour at Ottery will be such as to do yourself and me and your dear mother *credit*.

First, then, I conjure you never to do anything of any kind when out of sight which you would not do in my presence. What is a frail and faulty father on earth compared with God, your heavenly Father? But God is always present. Specially, never pick at or snatch up anything, eatable or not. I know it is only an idle, foolish trick, but your Ottery relations would consider you as a little thief; and in the Church Catechism *picking* and *stealing* are both put together as two sorts of the same vice, "And keep my hands from picking and stealing." And besides, it is a dirty trick; and people of weak stomachs would turn sick at a dish which a young *filth-paw* had been fingering.

Next, when you have done wrong acknowledge it at once, like a man. Excuses may show your ingenuity, but they make your *honesty* suspected. And a grain of honesty is better than a pound of wit. We may admire a man for his cleverness; but we love and esteem him only for his goodness; and a strict attachment to truth, and to the whole truth, with openness and frankness and simplicity is at once the foundation stone of all goodness, and no small part of the superstructure. Lastly, do what you have to do at once, and put it out of hand. No procrastination; no self-delusion; no "I am sure I can say it, I need not learn it again," etc., which *sures* are such very unsure folks that nine times out of ten their sureships break their word and disappoint you.

Among the lesser faults I beg you to endeavour to remember not to stand between the half-opened door, either while you are speaking, or spoken to. But come *in* or go out, and always speak and listen with the door shut. Likewise, not to speak so loud, or abruptly, and never to interrupt your elders while they are speaking, and not to talk at all during meals. I pray you, keep this letter, and read it over every two or three days.

Take but a little trouble with yourself, and every one

will be delighted with you, and try to gratify you in all your reasonable wishes. And, above all, you will be at peace with yourself, and a double blessing to me, who am, my dear, my very dear Hartley, most anxiously, your fond father,

S. T. COLERIDGE.

P.S. I have not spoken about your mad passions and frantic looks and pout-mouthing; because I trust that is all over.

LXVII

TO JOHN J. MORGAN

March 17, 1808

I have observed indeed in more than one or two instances that lawyers in their careless hands write more unintelligibly than any other class of men. Jack Colston's letters look like a *copy* of a good flowing hand—and yet I could never read three lines together without boggling—and as his conceptions are not *all* too (as the Germans) logical, I never wholly decyphered any one of his epistles, to me, or to Mr. Poole. My dear Morgan! I am glad to be able to turn off to any subject from the mournful one of myself. The anecdote of Vixen is not only interesting but valuable—Similar facts are commonly believed; but it is rare indeed to have them so accurately stated and circumstanced. Were I even in tolerable strength of body and spirits I would go thro' it analytically, as a distinct *datum* for canine psychology. As you have rightly observed, the memory is the least part, and yet even that is important because it completely confutes the dogma of Aristotle, which has been adopted by almost all after-metaphysicians—that Beasts and Infants *remember*, man only *recollects*—i.e. that hearts only *recognise*, the object being presented anew. But here is a clear instance of reflective recollection, proved by all the passions of distinct anticipation. And now again Pain drags me back to my unfortunate self. It is my wish and the dictate of my reason to come to you, and instantly to put myself under Dr. Beddoes, and to open the whole of my case. But yet—forgive me, *dear* dear friends! but yet I cannot help again and again questioning myself, what *right* I have to make your house my hospital—how I am justified in bringing sickness and sorrow and all the disgusts and *troublesomenesses* of disease, into your quiet dwelling. Ah! whither else can I go? To Grasmere? They are still in their cottage, one of their rooms is proved untenantable from damp—and they have not room scarcely for a cat. Not to speak of the distance. And shall I stay here? Alas it is sad, it is very sad. The noises of the Pressmen at between 4 and 5 in the morning, and continued till 8—the continual running up stairs by my door to the Editor's room, which is above me, the frequent calls of persons who wish to see me, and whom I cannot see—the forced intrusion of some and the alarm in consequence of every knock at the private door—trifles in themselves—are yet no trifles to me. Saving a few hours at night, in order to let my bed be made, I have not been out of bed I scarce remember when. All this morning I was so bad, I thought it was all over with me —O what agony I suffered! Pray write to me by return of post—and in the meantime I will exert myself to the utmost. Be assured that I feel the intensest gratitude—I entreat dear Miss Brent to think of what I wrote as the mere lightheadedness of a diseased body, and a heart sore-stricken fearing all things from every one. I love her most dearly! O had I health and youth and were what I once was—but I played the fool and cut the throat of my own happiness, of my genius, of my utility, in compliment to the merest phantom of overstrained honor—O Southey, Southey, what an unthinking man were you, and an unjust!

S.T.C.

LXVIII

TO THOMAS DE QUINCEY
NO. 5 NORTHUMBERLAND STREET
MARYBONE

[1808]

. . . And now permit me, my dear young friend! to do justice to myself as to one part of a character which has not many *positive* bad points in it, tho' in a moral *marasmus* from negatives—from misdemeanours of Omission and from Weakness and moral cowardice of moral Pain—But I can affirm with a *sense* of *certainty*, intuitively distinguished from a mere delusive *feeling* of *Positiveness*, that no man, I have ever known, is less affected by partiality to his own productions or thoughts. It would have been indeed far, far better for me—in some little degree perhaps for society—if I could have attached more importance, greater warmth of feeling, to my own writings. But I have not been happy enough for that. So however it is, that the pleasure of receiving that proof of friendship—"I cannot say, that this or that satisfied me—I did not like this for such and such reasons—it appeared to me slight, not the genuine Stuff, etc."—has often blinded me so far as to believe at once, and for a long season, more meanly of what I had done than after-experience confirmed. I do therefore earnestly ask of you as a proof of Friendship, that you will so far get over your natural modesty and timidity, as without reserve or withholding to tell me exactly what you think and feel on the perusal of anything, I may submit to you—for even if it be only your feelings, they will be valuable to me far more indeed than those criticisms in which the feeling is not stated, and mere objections made, which being weak have in one or 2 instances prevented my perception of real defects which I should soon have discovered if it had been said to me, there is something amiss in this! I feel it—perhaps, it may be *so* and *so*—perhaps not; but something I feel amiss. God bless you! Be assured of my unfeigned esteem.

S. T. COLERIDGE.

When I am tolerably recovered, in case of no relapse, I will on the first opportunity make the Party, we spoke of.

LXIX

TO DANIEL STUART

Grasmere, Kendal, June 13, 1809

. . . I have just read Wordsworth's pamphlet, and more than fear that your friendly expectations of its sale and influence have been too sanguine. Had I not known the author I would willingly have travelled from St. Michael's Mount to Johnny Groat's House on a pilgrimage to see and reverence him. But from the public I am apprehensive, first, that it will be impossible to rekindle an exhausted interest respecting the Cintra Convention, and therefore that the long porch may prevent readers from entering the Temple. Secondly, that, partly from Wordsworth's own style, which represents the chain of his thoughts and the movements of his heart, admirably for me and a few others, but I fear does not possess the more profitable excellence of translating these down into that style which might easily convey them to the understandings of common readers, and partly from Mr. De Quincey's strange and most mistaken system of punctuation—(The periods are often alarmingly long, perforce of their construction, but De Quincey's punctuation has made several of them immeasurable, and perplexed half the rest. Never was a stranger whim than the notion that , ; : and . could be made logical symbols, expressing all the diversities of logical connection)—but, lastly, I fear that readers, even of judgement, may complain of a want of shade and background; that it is all foreground, all in hot tints; that the first note is pitched at the height of the instrument, and never suffered to sink; that such depth of feeling is so incorporated with depth of thought, that the attention is kept throughout at its utmost strain and stretch; and—but this for my own feeling. I could not help feeling that a considerable part is almost a self-robbery from some great philosophical poem, of which it would form an appropriate part, and be fitlier attuned to the high dogmatic eloquence, the oracular [tone] of impassioned blank verse. In short, cold readers, conceited of their supposed judgement, on the score of their possessing nothing else, and for that reason only, taking for granted that they *must* have judgement, will abuse the book as positive, violent, and "in a mad passion"; and readers of sense and feeling will have no other dread, than that the Work (if it should die) would die of a plethora of the highest qualities of combined philosophic and poetic genius. The Apple Pie they may say is made all of Quinces. I much admired our young friend's note on Sir John Moore and his despatch; it was excellently arranged and urged. I have had no opportunity, as yet, to speak a word to Wordsworth himself about it; I wrote to you as usual in full confidence. . . .

LXX

TO THOS. W. SMITH

Grasmere, Kendal, June 22, 1809

DEAR SIR,—The irregularity and circuitousness of our Grasmere Post is such, that I did not receive your letter till late on yesternight. Accept therefore this explanation of my apparently slow acknowledgement of your kindness, instead of an Apology. I was affected by your Present, and receive it with feelings correspondent to those, with which it was sent; and still more by your approbation of the Principle, on which I have grounded the "Friend." Believe me, nothing but a deep and habitual conviction of it's Truth absolutely, and of it's particular Importance in the present generation could have roused me from that dream of great internal activity, and outward inefficience, into which ill-health and a wounded spirit had gradually lulled me. Intensely studious by Habit, and languidly affected by motives of Interest or Reputation, I found in my Books and my own meditations a sort of high-walled Garden, which excluded the very sound of the World without. But the Voice within could not be thrust out—the sense of Duty unperformed, and the pain of Self-dissatisfaction, aided and enforced by the sad and anxious looks of Southey, and Wordsworth, and some few others most beloved by me and most worthy of my regard and affection. Assuredly much happier and more truly tranquil I have already found myself, and shall deem myself amply remunerated if in consequence of my exertions a Few only of those, who had formed their moral creed on Hume, Paley, and their Imitators, with or without a belief in the facts of mere historical Christianity, shall have learnt to value actions primarily as the language and natural effect of the state of the agent; if they shall consider what they *are* instead of *merely* what they do; so that the fig-tree may bring forth it's own fruit from it's own living principle, and not have the figs tied on to it's barren sprays by the hand of outward Prudence and Respect of Character. These indeed are aids and great ones to our frailty, and it behoves us to be grateful for them and to use them; but let not the confidence in the gardner or his manures render us careless as to the health and quality of the *seed*. "Would not the whole moral code remain the same on the principle of enlightened Selfishness, as on that of Conscience, or the unconditional obedience of the Will to the pure Reason?" has been asked more than once of me. My answer was: All possibly might remain the same, only not the men themselves for whom the moral Law was given. But in truth I admitted more than was necessary, as I shall have occasion to prove at large. Permit me to recommend to your Perusal a late Pamphlet written by my dear friend and housemate W. Wordsworth "Concerning the Relations of Great Britain, Spain and Portugal" as containing sentiments and principles matured in our understanding by common energies and twelve years' inter-communion. The effects of national enthusiasm in the Spanish People is somewhat too much *idealized*—the introductory part respecting the Convention of Cintra might with great advantage have been written in a more calm and argumentative *manner*—and throughout, the Note is pitched at the very height of the Instrument, and by the constant combination of deep thought with deep feeling the whole work, in order to be both understood and felt, requires more attention and more warmth of sensibility than can reasonably be expected from the Public Mind, effeminated, as it is, by the unremitted Action of great outward Events daily soliciting and daily gratifying the appetite of Curiosity. But still the defects are but the overflowings of Excellence. I have not often met with a book at once so profound and so eloquent.

After the third number of the "Friend" the Paper will go on secure—as far as the nature of any weekly Essay permits—from interruption. But my finances had been exhausted in the purchase of Types, Advertisements, Prospectuses, and the Paper for the first four numbers, each sheet costing me four pence halfpenny and a small fraction, and all at once I found myself with paper sufficient only for two Numbers more, so suddenly had the Whole of self-offered Services, which I had mistaken for an Island, plunged away from under me—and the carriage of the Paper from London takes up nearly a fortnight. I had therefore to arrange the whole anew, by the agency of my kind friends, Thomas Clarkson, and Basil Montagu. After the 20th number the Work will be able to move on it's own legs.

I have thought it right on my own account to mention this circumstance, to ward off suspicions of irregularity and (to *coin* a word) *unreliability* from myself, at least as far as relates to this instance.

If Choice or Chance should divert you hitherward, you will find both in this house at Grasmere, and with R. Southey at Keswick (13 miles from hence) house-room and heart-room, and a heaven without to those who have peace within. That your Health may be restored to you, and your present Blessings preserved, is, dear Sir, the wish and prayer of your obliged and sincere Friend

S. T. COLERIDGE.

LXXI

TO MR. T. J. STREET

Grasmere, September 19, [1809]

. . . I am hard at work, and feel a pleasure and eagerness in it, which I have not known for years—a consequence and reward of my courage in at length overcoming the fear of dying suddenly in my Sleep, which Heaven knows! alone seduced me into the fatal habit of taking enormous quantities of Laudanum, and latterly, of spirits too—the latter merely to keep the former on my revolting Stomach. I am still far enough from well—my lungs are slightly affected, as by asthma, and my bowels dreadfully irritable; but I am far better than I could have dared expect. I left it off *all at once;* and drink nothing but Toast and Water, or Lemonade made with Creme of Tartar. If I entirely recover, I shall deem it a sacred duty to publish my cure, tho' without my name, for the practice of taking opium is dreadfully spread. Throughout Lancashire and Yorkshire it is the common Dram of the lower orders of People—in the small Town of Thorpe the Druggist informed me, that he commonly sold on market days two or three Pound of opium, and a Gallon of Laudanum—all among the labouring Classes. Surely, this demands legislative interference.

If I can on any important subject render you service, I can now venture to offer my powers to you without fear of disappointing you. Your's affectionately and gratefully,

S. T. COLERIDGE.

LXXII

TO GEORGE COLERIDGE

Grasmere, Kendal, October 9, 1809

. . . I am and was at the very first number of the "Friend" sensible of my defect in facility of style, and more desirous to avoid *obscurity* than successful in the attempt. Habits of abstruse and continuous thought and the almost exclusive perusal of the Greek Historians and Philosophers, of the German Metaphysicians and Moralists, and of our English writers from Edward VI, to James II, have combined to render my sentences more *piled up* and *architectural,* than is endurable in so illogical an eye [?age] as the present, in which all the cements of style are dismissed, and a popular book is only a sequence of epigrams and aphorisms on one subject. Too often my Readers may justly complain of involution and *entortillage* in my style, *tristem nescio quam et inflexam antiquitatem.* But I flatter myself, that the numbers have already become less faulty in these respects, and that as I proceed, not only will the essays themselves become more and more interesting and even entertaining, but the style likewise more graceful, and equally remote from the long-winded periods of our thoughtful ancestors and the asthmatic *sententiolae* of the French School, *syllabis perpetuo ad eundem numerum distributis, modulationi similiores quam sermoni.* . . .

LXXIII

TO THOMAS POOLE

Grasmere, Kendal, January 28, 1810

. . . We will take for granted that the "Friend" can be continued. On this supposition I have lately studied the "Spectator" and with increasing pleasure and admiration. Yet it must be evident to you that there is a class of thoughts and feelings, and these, too, the most important, even practically, which it would be impossible to convey in the manner of Addison, and which, if Addison had possessed, he would not have been Addison. Read, for instance, Milton's prose tracts, and only *try* to conceive them translated into the style of the "Spectator," or the finest part of Wordsworth's pamphlet. It would be less absurd to wish that the serious Odes of Horace had been written in the same style as his Satires and Epistles. Consider, too, the very different objects of the "Friend," and of the "Spectator," and above all do not forget, that these are AWEFUL TIMES! that the love of reading as a refined pleasure, weaning the mind from GROSSER enjoyments, which it was one of the "Spectator's" chief objects to awaken, has by that work, and those that followed ("Connoisseur," "World," "Mirror," etc.), but still more, by Newspapers, Magazines, and Novels, been carried into excess: and the "Spectator" itself has innocently contributed to the general taste for unconnected writing, just as if "Reading made easy" should act to give men an aversion to words of more than two syllables, instead of drawing them *through* those words into the power of reading books in general. In the present age, whatever flatters the mind in its ignorance of its ignorance, tends to aggravate that ignorance, and, I apprehend, does on the whole do more harm than good. Have you read the debate on the Address? What a melancholy picture of the intellectual feebleness of the country! So much on the one side of the question. On the other (1) I will, preparatory to writing on any chosen subject, consider whether it *can* be treated popularly, and with that lightness and variety of illustration which form the charms of the "Spectator." If it can, I will do my best. If not, next, whether yet there may not be furnished by the *results* of such an Essay thoughts and truths that may be so treated, and form a second Essay. (3) I shall always, *besides* this, have at least one number in four of rational entertainment, such as "Satyrane's Letters," as instructive as I can, but yet making entertainment the chief object in my own mind. But, lastly, in the Supplement of the "Friend" I shall endeavour to include whatever of higher and more abstruse meditation may be needed as the foundations of all the work after it; and the difference between those who will read and master that Supplement, and those who decline the toil, will be simply this, that what to the former will be *demonstrated conclusions,* the latter must start from as from *postulates,* and (to all whose minds have not been sophisticated by a half-philosophy) *axioms.* For no two things, that are yet different, can be in closer harmony than the deductions of a profound philosophy, and the dictates of plain common sense. Whatever tenets are obscure in the one, and requiring the greatest powers of abstraction to reconcile, are the same which are held in manifest contradiction by the common sense, and yet held and firmly believed, without sacrificing A to —A, or —A to A. . . . After this work I shall endeavour to pitch my note to the idea of a common, well-educated, thoughtful man, of ordinary talents; and the exceptions to this rule shall not form more than one fifth of the work. If with all this it will not do, well! And *well* it will be, in its noblest sense: for *I* shall have done my best. Of parentheses I may be too fond, and will be on my guard in this respect. But I am certain that no work of impassioned and eloquent reasoning ever did or could subsist without them. They are the *drama* of reason, and present the thought growing, instead of a mere *Hortus siccus.* The aversion to them is one of the numberless symptoms of a feeble Frenchified Public. One other observation: I have reason to *hope* for contributions from strangers. Some from *you I rely* on, and these will give a variety which is highly desirable—so much so, that it would weigh with me even to the admission of many things from unknown correspondents, though but little above mediocrity, if they were proportionately short, and on subjects which I should not myself treat. . . .

May God bless you, and your affectionate

S. T. Coleridge.

LXXIV

TO H. CRABB ROBINSON
59 HATTON GARDEN

32 Southampton Buildings, [March, 1811]

. . . In short, I believe, that *Love* (as distinguished both from Lust and from that habitual attachment which may include many Objects, diversifying itself by *degrees* only) that that

Feeling (or whatever it may be more aptly called) that specific mode of Being, which one Object only can possess, and possesses totally, is always the abrupt creation of a moment—tho' years of *Dawning* may have preceded. I said *Dawning;* for often as I have watched the Sun-rising, from the thinning, diluting Blue to the Whitening, to the fawn-coloured, the pink, the crimson, the glory, yet still the Sun itself has always *started* up, out of the Horizon! between the brightest Hues of the Dawn and the first Rim of the Sun itself there is a *chasm*—all before were Differences of Degrees, passing and dissolving into each other—but there is a difference of *Kind*—a chasm of Kind in a continuity of Time. And as no man, who had never watched for the rise of the Sun, could understand what I mean, so can no man who has not been in Love, understand what Love is, tho' he will be sure to imagine and believe, that he does. Thus, Wordsworth is by nature incapable of being in Love, tho' no man more tenderly attached—hence he ridicules the existence of any other passion, than a compound of Lust with Esteem and Friendship, confined to one Object, first by accidents of association, and permanently, by the force of Habit and a sense of Duty. Now this will do very well—it will suffice to make a good Husband—it may be even desirable (if the largest sum of easy and pleasurable sensations in this Life be the right aim and end of human Wisdom) that we should have this, and no more—but still it is not *Love*—and there is such a passion, as Love—which is no more a compound, than Oxygen, tho' like Oxygen, it has an almost universal affinity, and a long and finely graduated Scale of elective attractions. It combines with Lust—but how? Does Lust call forth or occasion Love? Just as much as the reek of the Marsh calls up the Sun. The sun calls up the vapour—attenuates, lifts it—it becomes a cloud—and now it is the Veil of the Divinity—the Divinity transpiercing it at once hides and declares his presence. We *see*, we are conscious of *Light* alone, but it is Light embodied in the earthly nature, which that Light itself awoke and sublimated. What is the Body, but the fixture of the mind? the stereotype Impression? Arbitrary are the Symbols—yet Symbols they are. Is Terror in my Soul—my Heart beats against my side—Is Grief? *Tears* form in my eyes. In her homely way the Body tries to interpret all the movements of the Soul. Shall it not then imitate and symbolize that divinest movement of a *finite* Spirit—the yearning to compleat itself by Union? Is there not a Sex in Souls? We have all eyes, cheeks, Lips—but in a lovely woman are not the eyes womanly—yea, every form, in every motion, of her whole frame *womanly?* Were there not an Identity in the Substance, man and woman might *join*, but they could never *unify*—were there not throughout, in body and in soul, a corresponding and adapted Difference, there might be addition, but there could be no combination. One *and one*=2; but one cannot be multiplied into one. $1 \times 1 = 1$. At best, it would be an idle echo, the same thing needlessly repeated—as the Ideot told the Clock—one, one, one etc. **. . .**

LXXV

TO JOHN RICKMAN

Saturday Noon, [October, 1811]

DEAR SIR,—On Tuesday next Mr. Morgan and myself will avail ourselves of your kind invitation. I was (and am) in town on the arrival of your letter—and have this moment received it. My business has been to bring about a Lecture Scheme—the Prospectus of which I shall be able to bring with me on Tuesday. On the subject of dining with Lamb I had a long conversation with him yester-evening—and only blame myself, that having long felt the deepest convictions of the vital importance of his not being visited till after 8 o'clock, and this too, rarely except on his open night, I should yet have been led to take my friend M. there, at dinner, at his proposal, out of a foolish delicacy in telling him the plain truth—that *it must not be done.* I am right glad, that something effective is now done—tho' permit me to say to you in confidence, that as long as Hazlitt remains in town I dare not expect any amendment in Lamb's Health, unless luckily H. should grow moody and take offence at being desired not to come till 8 o'clock. It is seldom indeed, that I am with Lamb more than once in the week—and when at Hammersmith, most often not once in a fortnight— and yet I see what Harm has been done even by me—what then if Hazlitt—as probably he will—is with him 5 evenings in the Seven? Were it possible to wean C.L. from the Pipe, other things would follow with comparative ease for till he gets a Pipe, I have regularly observed that he is contented with Porter—and that the unconquerable Appetite for Spirit comes in with the Tobacco—the oil of which, especially in the gluttonous manner in which he *volcanises* it, acts as an instant Poison on his Stomach or Lungs.

Believe me, dear Sir,

Your's, with affectionate Esteem

S. T. COLERIDGE.

P.S. I return to Hammersmith this evening—

LXXVI

TO JOHN J. MORGAN
7 PORTLAND PLACE, HAMMERSMITH

Saturday Night, [Postmark, October 15, 1811]

DEAR MORGAN,—On the Tuesday night after I had returned from Mr. Godwin's and his party of Mr. Curran, his daughter and Peter Pindar, I found a letter or rather a letter found me, in addition to one received before. It is no odds what. Suffice it was such as made me desirous not to see you: for I knew I must either tell you falsehoods which would answer no end, could I have endured to tell a deliberate falsehood, and if I had told you the truth it would probably have made you restless to attempt for me what you could not do with prudence or justice to yourself, and what at all events, I could not have received from you. That this my disappearance from you, will have afforded sign and seal to all the unfavourable judgements prompted by feelings of *contempt* which, Heaven knows how! I have excited for the last 8 months or more in your wife and sister I am well aware. I say Heaven knows how! because I cannot torture my memory into a recollection of a single moment in which I ever spoke, thought, wished or felt anything that was not consistent with the most fondly cherished esteem and a personal and affectionate predilection for them rendered worthy to my own thoughts by a sense of gratitude. I dare affirm that few men have ever felt or regretted their own infirmities more deeply than myself—they have in truth *preyed* too deeply on my mind, and the hauntings of regret have injured me more than the things to be regretted. Yet such as I am, such was I, when I was first under your hospitable roof—and such, unfortunately when I revisited you at Portland Place. But so it is. Our feelings govern our notions. Love a man and his talking shall be eloquence— dislike him, and the same thing becomes preaching. His quickness of Feeling and the starting Tear, shall be at one time natural sensibility—for the Tears swelled into his eye not for his own pains, or misfortunes, but either for others or for some wound from unkindness—the same at another time—shall be loathsome maudlin unmanliness. Activity of thought, scattering itself in jests, puns, and sportive nonsense, shall in the bud and blossom of acquaintanceship be amiable playfulness and met or anticipated by a laugh or correspondent jest, in the wane of friendship an object of disgust and a ground of warning to those better-beloved *not to get into that way*. Such, however, is life. Some few may find their happiness out of themselves in the regard and sympathy of others; but most are driven back by repeated disappointments into themselves, there to find tranquillity, or (too often) sottish Despondency. There are not those Beings on earth who can truly say that having professed affection for them, I ever either did or spoke unkindly or unjustly of them—would to heaven—the same thing was true of the Wordsworth family towards me. My present distracting difficulties which have disenabled me from doing what might have alleviated them, I must get thro' or sink under, as it may happen. Some consolation—nay, a great consolation—it is that they have not fallen on me thro' any vice, any extravagance or self-indulgence; but only from having imprudently hoped too highly of men—that if I had been treated with common tradesmanlike honesty by those, with whom (ignorantly blending the author with the publisher) I had traded—or with common humanity by a *Maecenas* worth £50,000 who yet knows I have not received back—what he lent me on the prospect of my receiving in money what I sent out in paper and stamps. This could not have been. Meantime what with those clamorous letters, from —— [*sic*] and what with the never-closing festering wound of Wordsworth and his family, and other aggravations Fortune seems to be playing "more sacks on the Mill" with me—and who in the agonies of suffocation would not wish to breathe no more rather than to have his breath stifled?

I pray you, send my books and other *paucities* directed to No. 6 Southampton Buildings—for thither I have gotten—As to seeing you, if I could give comfort to you by receiving it from you, I would request it, but that is out of the question— Therefore think of me as one deceased who *had been* your sincere friend

S. T. COLERIDGE.

Burn this after you have read it.

Private. If I get thro' these difficulties (and that done I doubt not that tranquillity of mind will enable me to mend all the rest) it will be my first desire to meet you. Till then what is the use of it? Pray send the books etc.—for something I must make up in a hurry—for I have tried in vain to compose anything anew. To transcribe is the utmost in my power.

LXXVII

TO AN UNKNOWN CORRESPONDENT

[December, 1811]

SIR,—As I am bound to thank you for your good-will, and the high opinion, you have been pleased to express of my Genius, so I ask in return that you should give me credit for perfect sincerity in the motives and feelings, which I shall assign for my inability to comply with your request.

Excuse me, if I say that I have ever held parallelisms adduced in proof of plagiarism or even of intentional imitation, in the utmost contempt. There are two kinds of Heads in the world of literature. The one I would call, SPRINGS: the other, TANKS. The latter class, habituated to receiving only, full or low, according to the state of it's Feeders, attach[es] no distinct notion to living production as contra-distinguished from mechanical formation. If they find a fine passage in Thomson, they refer it to Milton; if in

Milton, to Euripides or Homer; and if in Homer, they take for granted it's pre-existence in the lost works of Linus or Musaeus. It would seem as if it was a part of their creed, that all Thoughts are traditional, and that not only the Alphabet was revealed to Adam, but all that was ever written in it that was worth writing. But I come to the point. I can scarcely call myself an Acquaintance of Mr. Walter Scott's; but I have met him twice or thrice in company. Those who hold that a man's nature is shewn in his Countenance would not need the confident assurance, which all his Friends and Acquaintances so unanimously give, that he is of the most frank and generous disposition, incapable of trick or concealment. The mere expression of his Features, and the Tones of his voice in conversation, independent of the matter, sufficiently attest the fervour and activity of his mind. The Proofs must be strong indeed, Sir! which could convince me that such a man could consciously make an unfair and selfish use of *any* manuscript that came by accident into his possession—least of all, one of a known Contemporary. What then are they, the Facts that are to weaken this presumption?

First, that the Fragment, entitled "Christabel," was composed many *years*, and known and openly admired by Mr. Scott some time, before the *publication* of the "Lay of the Last Minstrel." (For be pleased to observe, it is no part of the known *Fact* that the "Lay of the Last Minstrel," was not composed in part at least or at least *planned*, before Mr. S. had seen the Fragment in question.)

Secondly, that of those who had seen or heard the Fragment a large proportion were struck with certain lines the same or nearly the same in the "L.L.M.," with similar movements in the manner of narration and the arrangement of the Imagery, and lastly with that general resemblance which is exprest by the words—the one still reminded them of the other. Before I proceed to the arguments on the other side, I will examine these, and if I can rely on my own feelings at the present moment exactly as I would wish a friend of mine to do if I had been the fortunate author of the "Lay of the Last Minstrel" and the "Marmion," and Mr. W. S. the earlier writer of the "Christabel."

Now it must be obvious on the first calm reflection, that

Mr. W. S. could have had no previous intention of using the "Christabel," from the very fact, which has furnished the main strength of the contrary presumption. For before the appearance of the "Lay of the L.M." he not only mentioned the "Christabel" repeatedly to persons who had never before heard of it, not only praised it with warmth, but *recited* it. In order to evade or weaken this fact, we must make the arbitrary supposition, that he had not at that time planned his Poem as it now appears: and that the purpose was formed in his mind afterwards, and while he was composing. A purpose, of course, implies consciousness. Now this again is rendered in the highest degree improbable by another of the Facts above stated, and by one too that has assuredly had no small share in occasioning the suspicion—the existence, I mean of a number of lines the same or nearly the same in both authors. I have not the Poems by me; but I distinctly remember, that the greater part consisted of phrases, such as "Jesu Maria! shield thee well," etc.—which might have occurred to a score of writers who had been previously familiar with Poems and Romances written before the Reformation or translated from the Spanish—and the small Remainder contain nothing remarkable either in language, thought, feeling or imagery. From long disuse I cannot have the tenth part of the fluency in versification as Mr. Scott or Southey have: and yet I would undertake in a couple of Hours to alter every one of these lines or Couplets, without the least injury to the context, to retain the same meaning in words equally poetical and suitable, and yet entirely remove all the *appearance* of Likeness. And this, Sir! is what an intentional Plagiarist would have done. He would have *translated*, not transcribed.

If then there be any just ground for the Charge of "stolen feathers" (say rather, for an imitation of the mode of flying), it must be found in the supposed close likeness of the metre, the *movements*, the way of relating an event, in short, in the general resemblance of the great Features, which have given to the Physiognomy of Mr. W. S.'s late Poems their marked originality, in the public Feeling. Now that several persons, and those too persons of education, and liberal minds, at several times, and without any knowledge of each other's opinions, have been struck with this general resemblance, and have expressed themselves more or less strongly on the subject, I do not pretend to deny: for it is a fact of my own knowledge. But it would be most dishonorable in me if I did not add, that *if* I had framed my expectations exclusively by the opinions and assertions of others, those whose expressions were most limited, would have excited anticipations which my own after Perusal of the "Lay of the Last Minstrel" were far from verifying to my own mind. But I will admit that of this neither I or Mr. S. are or can be the proper Judges. A poet may be able to appreciate the merit of each particular Part of his own Poem as well, or (if he have a well-disciplined mind) better than any other can do; but of the *effect* of the whole as a whole, he cannot from the very nature of Things (from the fore-knowledge of each following part, from the parts having been written at different times, from the blending of the pleasures and disgusts of composing with the composition itself, etc.) have the same sensation, as the Reader or auditor to whom the whole is new and simultaneous. The case must then be thus stated. Put aside the fact of the previous acquaintance with the "Christabel"—suppose that no circumstances were known, that rendered it probable—would the resemblances in and of themselves have enforced, or at least have generally *suggested*, the suspicion that [the] later Poem was an intentional Imitation of the elder? In other words, is the general Likeness, or [anything] in the particular resemblances, such as a liberal and enlightened Reader could not with any probability consider, as the result of mere Coincidence between two writers of similar Pursuits, and (*argumenti causa loquor*) of nearly equal Talent. Coincidence is here used as a negative—not as implying, that the Likeness between the works is merely accidental, the effect of chance, but as asserting that it is not the effect of imitation. Now how far Coincidence in this sense and under the supposed Conditions is possible, I can myself supply an instance, which happened at my lectures in Flower de Luce Court only last week, and the accuracy of which does not rely on *my* evidence only, but can be proved by the separate testimony of some hundred individuals—that is, by as many as have attended and retained any distinct recollection of my lectures at the Royal Institution or at Fetter Lane.

After the close of my lecture on "Romeo and Juliet," a German gentleman, a Mr. Bernard Krusve, introduced himself to me, and after some courteous Compliments said, "Were it not almost impossible, I must have believed that you had either heard or read, my countryman Schlegel's lecture on this play, given at Vienna: the principles, thought, and the very illustrations are so nearly the same. But the lectures were but just published as I left Germany, scarcely more than a week since, and the only two copies of the work in England I have reason to think, that I myself have brought over. One I retain: the other is at Mr. Boosey's." I replied that I had not even heard of these lectures, nor had indeed seen any work of Schlegel's except a volume of Translations from Spanish Poetry, which the Baron Von Humboldt had lent me when I was at Rome—one piece of which, a translation of a Play of Calderon, I had compared with the original, and formed in consequence a high opinion of Schlegel's Taste and Genius. A Friend standing by me added, This cannot be a question of Dates, Sir; for if the gentleman, whose name you have mentioned, first gave his lectures at Vienna in 1810, I can myself bear witness, that I heard Mr. Coleridge deliver all the *substance* of to-night's lecture at the Royal Institution some years before. The next morning, Mr. Krusve called on me and made me a present of the book; and as much as the Resemblance of the "L. of L.M." fell below the anticipations which the accounts of others were calculated to excite, so much did this book transcend—not in one lecture, but in all the lectures that related to Shakespeare or to the stage in general, the Grounds, Train of Reasoning, etc., were different in language only—and often not even in that. The Thoughts too were so far peculiar, that to the best of my knowledge they did not exist in any prior work of criticism. Yet I was far more flattered, or to speak more truly, I was more confirmed, than surprised. For Schlegel and myself had both studied deeply and perseverantly the philosophy of Kant, the distinguishing feature of which [is] to treat every subject in reference to the operation of the mental Faculties, to which it specially appertains—and to commence by the cautious discrimination of what is essential, *i.e.* explicable by mere consideration of the Faculties in themselves, from what is empirical, *i.e.* the modifying or disturbing Forces of Time, Place, and Circumstances. Suppose myself and Schlegel (my argument not my vanity, leads to these seeming Self-flatteries) nearly equal in natural powers, of similar pursuits and acquirements, and it is only necessary for both to have mastered the spirit of Kant's "Critique of the Judgement" to render it morally certain, that writing on the same subject we should draw the same conclusions by the same brains, from the same principles, write to one purpose and with one spirit.

Now, Sir! apply this to Mr. W. Scott. If his Poem had been in any sense a borrowed thing, it's Elements likewise would surely be assumed, not nature. But no insect was ever more like in the color of it's skin and juices to the leaf it fed on, than Scott's Muse is to Scott himself. Habitually conversant with the antiquities of his Country, and of all Europe during the ruder periods of society, living as it were, in whatever is found in them imposing either to the Fancy or interesting to the Feelings, passionately fond of natural Scenery, abundant in local anecdote, and besides learned in

all the antique scrolls of Faery land,
Processions, Tournaments, Spells, Chivalry—

in all languages, from Apuleius to "Tam o' Shanter"—how else or what else could he have been expected to write? His Poems are evidently the indigenous Products of his mind and Habits.

But I have wearied myself, and shall weary you. I will only add that I have a volume of Poems now before me, compleately made up of gross plagiarisms from Akenside, Thomson, Bowles, Southey, and the "Lyrical Ballads"—it is curious to observe, how many artifices the poor author has used to disguise the theft, transpositions, dilutions, substitutions of Synonyms, etc., etc.,—and yet not the least resemblance to any one of the Poets whom he pillaged. He who can catch the spirit of an original, has it already. It will not [be] by Dates, that Posterity will judge of the originality of a Poem; but by the original spirit itself. This is to be found neither in a Tale however interesting, which is but the Canvas; no, nor yet in the Fancy or the Imagery— which are but Forms and Colors—it is a subtle Spirit, all in each part, reconciling and unifying all. Passion and

Y

Imagination are it's *most* appropriate names; but even these say little—for it must be not merely Passion but poetic Passion, poetic Imagination. [No conclusion or signature.]

LXXVIII

TO JOHN J. MORGAN

Keswick, Sunday, February 28, 1812

. . . I trust I need not say that I should have written on the second day if nothing had happened; but from the dreadful dampness of the house, worse than it was in the rudest state when I first lived in it, and the weather, too, all storm and rain, I caught a violent cold which almost blinded me by inflammation of both my eyes, and for three days bore all the symptoms of an ague or intermittent fever. Knowing I had no time to lose, I took the most Herculean remedies, among others a solution of arsenic, and am now as well as when I left you, and see no reason to fear a relapse. I passed through Grasmere; but did not call on Wordsworth. I hear from Mrs. C. that he treats the affair as a trifle, and only wonders at my resenting it, and that Dorothy Wordsworth before my arrival expressed her confident hope that I should come to them at once! I who "for years past had been an ABSOLUTE NUISANCE in the family." This illness has thrown me behindhand; so that I cannot quit Keswick till the end of the week. On Friday I shall return by way of Ambleside, probably spend a day with Charles Lloyd. . . . It will not surprise you that the statements respecting me and Montagu and Wordsworth have been grossly perverted: and yet, spite of all this, there is not a friend of Wordsworth's, I understand, who does not severely blame him, though they execrate the Montagus yet more heavily. But the tenth part of the truth is not known. Would you believe it possible that Wordsworth himself stated my *wearing powder* as a proof positive that I never could have suffered any pain of mind from the affair, and that it was all pretence!! God forgive him! At Liverpool I shall either give lectures, if I can secure a hundred pounds for them, or return immediately to you. At all events, I shall not remain there beyond a fortnight, so that I shall be with you before you have changed houses. Mrs. Coleridge seems quite satisfied with my plans, and abundantly convinced of my obligations to your and Mary's kindness to me. Nothing (she said) but the circumstance of my residing with you could reconcile her to my living in London. Southey is the *semper idem*. It is impossible for a good heart not to esteem and to love him; but yet the love is one fourth, the esteem all the remainder. His children are, 1. Edith, seven years; 2. Herbert, five; 3. Bertha, four; 4. Catharine, a year and a half.

I had hoped to have heard from you by this time. I wrote from Slough, from Liverpool, and from Kendal. Why need I send my kindest love to Mary and Charlotte? I would not return if I had a doubt that they believed me to be in the very inmost of my being their and your affectionate and grateful and constant friend,

S. T. COLERIDGE.

LXXIX

TO THE SAME

Penrith, Good Friday Night, March 27, 1812

O would to Heaven I were but once more by your fireside! I have received four letters in 3 days about my not having called on Wordsworth as I passed thro' Grasmere—and this morning a most impassioned one from Mrs. Clarkson—Good God! how could I? how can I? I have no resentment and unless grief and anguish be resentment I never had—but unless I meet him as of yore what use is there in it?— What but more pain? I am not about to be his enemy— I want no stimulus to serve him to the utmost whenever it should be in my power— And can any friend of mine wish me to go without apology received, and as to a man the best beloved and honoured, who had declared me a nuisance, an absolute nuisance—and this to such a creature as Montagu? and who since then has professed his determination to believe Montagu rather than me, as to my assertion to Southey that Montagu prefaced his discourse with the words "Nay but Wordsworth has *commissioned* me to tell you, first that he has no hope of you, etc.—etc.—etc.—"

A nuisance! and then a deliberate Liar! O Christ! if I dared after this crawl to the man, must I not plead guilty to these charges and be a Liar against my own Soul?

No more of this! and be assured, I will never hereafter trouble you with any recurrence to it.

Mention me affectionately to Mary and Charlotte and unless I am utterly ignorant of my own heart assure yourself that I am by every feeling both of choice and gratitude both your and their

sincere Friend and Brother

S. T. COLERIDGE.

P.S. Mrs. Southey and Mrs. Coleridge who have twice debated the matter with Wordsworth as well as with his sister, are most vehement against Wordsworth, and Mrs. C. says she never in her whole life saw her sister so vehement, or so completely overcome her natural timidity as when she answered Wordsworth's excuses. She would not suffer him to wander from the point—Never mind, Sir! Coleridge does not heed *what* was said—whatever is true his friends all knew, and he himself never made a secret of—but that *you*, that *you* should say all this, and to Montagu, and having never at any time during a 15 years friendship given him even a *hint* of the state of your opinions concerning him—it is *you* Sir, *you*, not the things said, true or false!

Southey never says anything but only "*that miscreant, Montagu!*" whereas? (I have nothing to complain of in Montagu) I think him in error—for—

LXXX

TO DANIEL STUART

Friday, August 7, 1812

DEAR STUART,—Since I last saw you, I have been confined to my bed with the alarming symptom of a swollen leg, ankle, and Foot, and a painful oppression on my chest which for three days rendered me unable to sit up even in bed and with the pillows behind me more than 10 or 15 minutes at a time. The Morgans were really alarmed, and I myself thought it the commencement of Dropsy on the Chest. I called in a Physician, and a man in whom I have the greatest confidence, who has dismissed these apprehensions in good part—and declared the whole of my immediate Disease to be Indigestion, and Erysypelatous Inflammation— Accordingly, the complaint on the Chest has already disappeared, and tho' my right leg is still visibly larger than the left, yet the swelling is greatly abated. I informed Dr. Gooch without the least concealment of the whole of my *general case*, and have put myself under his direction. The two evils produced by the use of narcotics on my constitution are, he says, a secretion of acid Bile from the Liver, and a relaxation of the extremities of the Blood-vessels—but without tormenting myself or imposing on my fortitude a burthen greater than it can bear, he entertains strong hopes that I shall either wholly emancipate myself, or, if not *that*, yet bring myself to such an arrangement as will not very materially affect my health or longevity. These prescriptions are—Mercury in very small quantities, in the form of Carbyn's Blue Pill— Nitric Acid, 10 Drops in a glass of water, twice a day—and a known and measured quantity of Stimulant, with an attempt to diminish the opiate part of it by little and little, if it were only a single Drop in two days. I have adopted this plan for the last four days, and find it not in the slightest degree burthensome: and were it not [for] the remaining Inflammation in my Leg, I should feel myself better, livelier, and with more steady appetite and more regular Digestion than for some time past. This I attribute, however, in great measure to the weight having been taken off my spirits by my having at length put a Physician in possession of the *whole* of my case with all it's symptoms, and all it's known, probable and suspected Causes. . . .

LXXXI

TO JOSIAH WEDGWOOD

71, Berners Street, Oxford Street,
December 1, 1812

DEAR SIR,—I should deem myself indeed unworthy of your and your revered Brother's past munificence, if I had had any other feeling than that of Grief from your letter: or if I looked forward to any other or higher Comfort, than the confident Hope that (if God extend my life another year) I shall have a claim to an acknowledgement from you, that I have not misemployed my past years, or wasted that leisure which I have owed to you, and for which I must cease to be before I can cease to feel most grateful. Permit me to assure you, that had the "Friend" succeeded instead of bringing on me embarrassment and a loss of more than 200£ from the non-payment of the Subscriptions, or had my lectures done more than merely pay my Board in town, it was my intention to have resigned my claims on your Bounty—and I am sure, that I shall have your good wishes in my behalf, when I tell you that I have had a Play accepted at Drury Lane, which is to come out at Christmas, and of the success of which both Manager, Comm.-Men, and actors speak sanguinely. If I succeed in this, it will not only open out a smooth and not dishonorable road to competence, but give me heart and spirits (still more necessary than time) to bring into shape the fruits of 20 years study and observation.

Cruelly, I well know, have I been calumniated: and even my faults (the sinking under the sense of which has been itself perhaps one of the greatest) have been attributed to dispositions absolutely opposite to the real ones—and—and I beseech you, interpret it as a burst of thankfulness and most unfeigned esteem, not of pride, when I declare that to have an annuity settled on me of three times or thrice three times the amount, would not afford me such pleasure, as the restoration of your esteem and Friendship

for your deeply obliged

S. T. COLERIDGE.

PS. Since the receipt of your letter I have been confined by illness, till last Tuesday, with a nervous depression that rendered me incapable of answering it, or rather fearful of trusting myself.

LXXXII

TO HIS WIFE

Wednesday afternoon [January 20,] 18[13]

MY DEAR SARA,—*Hitherto* the "Remorse" has met with *unexampled applause*, but whether it will *continue* to fill the *house*, that is quite another question, and of this, my friends are, in my opinion, far, far too sanguine. I have disposed not of the copyright but of edition by edition to Mr. Pople, on terms advantageous to me as an author and honourable to him as a publisher. The expenses of printing and paper (at the trade-price), advertising, etc., are to be deducted from the total produce, and the net profits to be divided into three equal parts, of which Pople is to have one, and I the other two. And at any future time, I may publish it in any volume of my poems *collectively*. Mr. Arnold (the manager) has just left me. He called to urge me to exert myself a little with regard to the daily press, and brought with him "The Times" of Monday as a specimen of the *infernal lies* of which a newspaper scribe can be capable. Not only is not *one* sentence in it true; but every one is in the direct face of a palpable truth. The misrepresentations must have been wilful. I must now, therefore, write to "The Times," and if Walter refuses to insert, I will then, recording the circumstance, publish it in the "Morning Post," "Morning Chronicle," and the "Courier." The dirty malice of Antony Pasquin in the "Morning Herald" is below notice. This, however, will explain to you why the shortness of this letter, the main business of which is to desire you to draw upon Brent and Co., No. 103 Bishopsgate Street Within, for an hundred pounds, at a month's date from the drawing, or, if that be objected to, for three weeks, only let me know which. In the course of a month I have no hesitation in promising you another hundred, and I hope likewise before Mid-summer, if God grant me life, to repay you whatever you have expended for the children.

My wishes and purposes concerning Hartley and Derwent I will communicate as soon as this bustle and endless rat-a-tat-tat at our door is somewhat over. I concluded my Lectures last night most triumphantly—with loud, long, and enthusiastic applauses at my entrance, and ditto in yet fuller chorus as, and for some minutes after I had retired. It was lucky that (as I never once thought of the Lecture till I had entered the Lecture Box), the two last were the most impressive and really the best. I suppose that no dramatic author ever had so large a number of unsolicited, unknown yet *predetermined* plauditors in the theatre, as I had on Saturday night. One of the malignant papers asserted that I had collected all the saints from Mile End turnpike to Tyburn Bar. With so many warm friends, it is impossible, in the present state of human nature, that I should not have many unprovoked and unknown enemies. You will have heard that on my entering the box on Saturday night, I was discovered by the pit, and that they all turned their faces towards our box, and gave a treble cheer of claps.

I mention these things because it will please Southey to hear that there is a large number of persons in London who hail with enthusiasm my prospect of the stage's being purified and rendered classical. My success, if I succeed (of which I assure you I entertain doubts in my opinion well founded, both from the want of a prominent actor for Ordonio, and from the want of vulgar pathos in the play itself—nay, there is not enough even of *true* dramatic pathos), but if I succeed, I succeed for others as well as myself. . . .

S. T. Coleridge.

LXXXIII

TO JOHN J. MORGAN

[1814]

My dear Morgan,—Tomorrow morning, I doubt not, I shall be of clear and collected Spirits; but tonight I feel that I should do nothing to any purpose, but and excepting Thinking, Planning, and Resolving to resolve—and praying to be able to execute.

S. T. Coleridge.

LXXXIV

TO MR. THOMAS CURNICK

Bristol, April 9th, 1814

Dear Sir,—I have been much affected by your letter and have perused, with considerable pleasure, the poems which accompanied it. But how can I serve you? Gold and silver have I none; but, on the contrary, I am myself sorely embarrassed. Mr. Southey and I married sisters; and I am on terms of intimacy with him. But it was not to Kirke White, but to his family, that Southey could make himself serviceable, by becoming his biographer and editor, after his premature death.

Many thoughts crowded on me during the perusal of your letter, which pressing engagements prevent me communicating at present; but within a short time I will endeavour to perform that most arduous duty of one sympathising Christian to another, that of telling what appears to him to be the truth. O that I could convey to you, in all its liveliness, the anguish of regret which I have a thousand times felt (while obliged, for the bread of the day, to be aiming at excellencies which in the most favoured natures require health, competence, tranquillity, and genial feelings), that I had not been taught to earn my subsistence mechanically, where, if my fingers were weary, my heart and brain at least were at rest !

From the time of Pope's translation of Homer, inclusive, so countless have been the poetic metamorphoses of almost all possible thoughts and connections of thought, that it is scarcely practicable for a man to write in the ornamental style on any subject without finding his poem, against his will and without his previous consciousness, a cento of lines that had pre-existed in other works; and this it is which makes poetry so very difficult, because so very easy, in the present day. I myself have for many years past given it up in despair.

There is much fire and spirit in your ode on Lord Wellington: the chief defect is a confusion of mythology. Cherubs have no connection with Mars; and the first stanza is obscure, because the reader does not know whether you mean Lord Wellington or an imaginary god of war. If the latter, the after introduction of the Almighty is irreverent; or (as the painter's phrase is), "out of keeping." If the former, the ponderous spear, etc., is not translatable into sense and fact. Poetry must be more than good sense, or it is not poetry; but it dare not be less, or dis[c]repant. Good sense is not, indeed, the superstructure; but it is the rock, not only on which the edifice is raised, but likewise the rock-quarry from which all its stones have been, by patient toil, dug out.

The whole of next week I am unfortunately pre-engaged,

day after day, and the whole of each day; but, after that, you will generally find me at No. 2, Queen Square, any time from seven in the evening to ten; and if you can point out any mode in which I can be really useful to you, be assured I shall be most ready to attempt it.

Will you forgive a man who has had repeated occasions for mourning that he had not himself pursued the profession of the law (a profession which needs only to be considered in the light of a manly philosophy to present many charms to a thinking mind, and which, beyond all others, gives an insight into the real state of society, the hearts, morals, and passions of our fellow-creatures) to ask you why a man of genius should despair of making genius effective and illustrious in the pursuit of the profession in which it has pleased Providence to place him? I do not know your age, but you inform me that you are an attorney's clerk. Even such was Garrow—such was Dunning.

Do I advise you to desert the Muses? No! I give no advice which, I know, would be vain, but my experience does warrant me, "with a warning and dolorous blast" (as Milton says) to exhort all men of genius to take care that they should rely on literature only for private pleasure and solace; or, at most, for the dessert to their dinner, not for the dinner itself.

I beg your acceptance of the enclosed ticket, which, should you have leisure or inclination, will admit yourself and a friend to my course of lectures.

With sincere good wishes, yours, dear sir,

S. T. COLERIDGE.

LXXXV

TO JOSEPH COTTLE
BRUNSWICK SQUARE

April 26, 1814

You have poured oil in the raw and festering Wound of an old friend's Conscience, Cottle! but it is oil of Vitriol! I but barely glanced at the middle of the first page of your Letter, and have seen no more of it—not from resentment

(God forbid!) but from the state of my bodily and mental sufferings, that scarcely permitted human fortitude to let in a new visitor of affliction. The object of my present reply is to state the case just as it is—first, that for years the anguish of my spirit has been indescribable, the sense of my danger *staring*, but the conscience of my *guilt* worse, far far worse than all!—I have prayed with drops of agony on my Brow, trembling not only before the Justice of my Maker, but even before the Mercy of my Redeemer. "I gave thee so many Talents. What hast thou done with them?"— Secondly—that it is false and cruel to say, (overwhelmed as I am with the sense of my direful Infirmity) that I attempt or ever have attempted to *disguise* or conceal the cause. On the contrary, not only to friends have I stated the whole case with tears and the very bitterness of shame; but in two instances I have warned young men, mere acquaintances who had spoken of having taken Laudanum, of the direful consequences, by an ample exposition of it's tremendous effects on myself—Thirdly, tho' before God I dare not lift up my eyelids, and only do not despair of his Mercy because to despair would be adding crime to crime; yet to my fellow-men I may say, that I was seduced into the *accursed* Habit ignorantly. I had been almost bed-ridden for many months with swellings in my knees—in a medical Journal I un-happily met with an account of a cure performed in a similar case (or what to me appeared so) by rubbing in of Laud-anum, at the same time taking a given dose internally. It acted like a charm, like a miracle! I recovered the use of my Limbs, of my appetite, of my Spirits—and this continued for near a fortnight— At length, the unusual stimulus subsided —the complaint returned—the supposed remedy was re-curred to—but I can not go thro' the dreary history—suffice it to say, that effects were produced, which acted on me by *Terror* and *Cowardice* of *Pain* and sudden Death, not (so help me God!) by any Temptation of Pleasure, or expectation or desire of exciting pleasurable sensations. On the very con-trary, Mrs. Morgan and her Sister will bear witness so far, as to say that the longer I abstained, the higher my spirits were, the keener my enjoyments—till the moment, the dire-ful moment, arrived, when my pulse began to fluctuate, my Heart to palpitate, and such a dreadful *falling-abroad*, as it were, of my whole frame, such intolerable Restlessness and incipient Bewilderment, that in the last of my several attempts to abandon the dire poison, I exclaimed in agony, what I now repeat in seriousness and solemnity—"I am too poor to hazard this! Had I but a few hundred Pounds, but 200£, half to send to Mrs. Coleridge, and half to place myself in a private madhouse, where I could procure nothing but what a Physician thought proper, and where a medical attendant could be constantly with me for two or three months (in less than that time Life or Death would be determined) then there might be Hope. Now there is none!"—O God! how willingly would I place myself under Dr. Fox in his Establishment—for my Case is a species of madness, only that it is a derangement, an utter impotence of the *Volition,* and not of the intellectual Faculties—You bid me rouse myself—go, bid a man paralytic in both arms rub them briskly together, and that will cure him. Alas! (he would reply) that I cannot move my arms is my complaint and my misery.—

My friend, Wade, is not at home—and I sent off all the little money, I had—or I would with this have included the 10£ received from you.

> May God bless you
> and
> Your affectionate and
> Most afflicted
> S. T. COLERIDGE.

Dr. Estlin, I found, is raising the city against me, as far as he and his friends can, for having stated a mere matter of fact, viz.—that Milton had represented Satan as a sceptical Socinian—which is the case, and I could not have explained the excellence of the sublimest single Passage in all his writings had I not previously informed the Audience, that Milton had represented Satan as knowing the prophetic and Messianic Character of Christ, but was sceptical as to any higher Claims—and what other definition could Dr. E. himself give of a sceptical Socinian? Now that M. has done so, please to consult, "Par. Regained," Book IV, from line 196.—and then the same book from line 500.

LXXXVI

TO JOHN J. MORGAN

2—Queen's Square, Saturday, May 14, 1814

MY DEAR MORGAN,—If it could be said with a little *appearance* of profaneness, as there is feeling or intention in my mind, I might affirm, that I had been crucified, dead, and buried, descended into *Hell*, and am now, I humbly trust, rising again, tho' slowly and gradually. I thank you from my heart for your far too kind letter to Mr. Hood—so much of it is true that such as you described I always wished to be. I know, it will be vain to attempt to persuade Mrs. Morgan or Charlotte, that a man, whose moral feelings, reason, understanding, and senses are perfectly sane and vigorous, may yet have been *mad*— And yet nothing is more true. By the long long Habit of the accursed Poison my Volition—by which I mean the faculty *instrumental* to the Will, and by which alone the Will can realize itself—(it's Hands, Legs, and Feet, as it were) was compleatly deranged, at times frenzied, dissevered itself from the Will, and became an independent faculty: so that I was perpetually in the state, in which you may have seen paralytic Persons, who attempting to push a step forward in one direction are violently forced round to the opposite. I was sure that no ease, much less pleasure, would ensue: and, was certain of an accumulation of pain. But tho' there was no prospect, no gleam of Light before, an indefinite indescribable Terror as with a scourge of ever restless, ever coiling and uncoiling serpents, drove me on from behind. The worst was, that in *exact proportion* to the *importance* and *urgency* of any Duty was it, as of a fatal necessity, sure to be neglected: because it added to the Terror above described. In exact proportion, as I *loved* any person or persons more than others, and would have sacrificed my Life for them, were *they* sure to be the most barbarously mistreated by silence, absence, or breach of promise. I used to think St. James's text, "He who offendeth in one point of the Law, offendeth in all," very harsh; but my own sad experience has taught me it's aweful, dreadful Truth. What crime is there scarcely which has not been included in or followed from the one guilt of taking opium? Not to speak of ingratitude to my Maker for the wasted Talents; of ingratitude to so many friends who have loved me I know not why; of barbarous neglect of my family; excess of cruelty to Mary and Charlotte, when at Box, and both ill—(a vision of Hell to me when I think of it!) I have in this one dirty business of Laudanum an hundred times deceived, tricked, nay, actually and consciously *lied*. And yet *all* these vices are so opposite to my nature, that but for this *free-agency-annihilating* Poison, I verily believe that I should have suffered myself to have been cut to pieces rather than have committed any one of them. At length, it became too bad. I used to take 4 to 5 ounces a day of Laudanum, once [?] ounces *i.e.* near a Pint—besides great quantities of opium. From the Sole of my foot to the Crown of my head there was not an Inch in which I was not continually in torture; for more than a fortnight no sleep ever visited my Eyelids—but the agonies of remorse were worse than all!— Letters past between Cottle, Hood, and myself—and our kind Friend, Hood, sent Mr. Daniel to me. At his second call I told him plainly (for I had sculked out the night before and got Laudanum) that while I was in my own power, all would be in vain—I should inevitably cheat and trick *him*, just as I had done Dr. Tuthill—that I must either be removed to a place of confinement, or at all events have a Keeper. Daniel saw the truth of my observations, and my most faithful excellent friend, Wade, procured a strong-bodied but decent, meek, elderly man, to superintend me, under the name of my Valet—all in the House were forbidden to fetch anything but by the Doctor's order—Daniel generally spends two or three hours a day with me and already from 4 and 5 ounces has brought me down to four tea-spoonfuls in the 24 Hours—the terror and the indefinite craving are gone—and he expects to drop it altogether by the middle of next week—Till a day or two after that I would rather not see you. [Autograph excised]

LXXXVII

TO JOSIAH WADE

Bristol, June 26, 1814

DEAR SIR,—For I am unworthy to call any good man friend—much less you, whose hospitality and love I have abused; accept, however, my intreaties for your forgiveness, and for your prayers.

Conceive a poor miserable wretch, who for many years has been attempting to beat off pain, by a constant recurrence to the vice that reproduces it. Conceive a spirit in hell. employed in tracing out for others the road to that heaven, from which his crimes exclude him! In short, conceive whatever is most wretched, helpless, and hopeless, and you will form as tolerable a notion of my state, as it is possible for a good man to have.

I used to think the text in St. James that "he who offended in one point, offends in all," very harsh; but I now feel the awful, the tremendous truth of it. In the one crime of OPIUM, what crime have I not made myself guilty of!—Ingratitude to my Maker! and to my benefactors—injustice! *and unnatural cruelty to my poor children!*—self-contempt for my repeated promise—breach, nay, too often, actual falsehood!

After my death, I earnestly entreat, that a full and unqualified narration of my wretchedness, and of its guilty cause, may be made public, that at least some little good may be effected by the direful example.

May God Almighty bless you, and have mercy on your still affectionate, and in his heart, grateful

S. T. COLERIDGE.

LXXXVIII

TO DANIEL STUART

Mr. Smith's, Ashley, Box, near Bath,
September 12, 1814.

MY DEAR SIR,—I wrote some time ago to Mr. Smith, earnestly requesting your address, and entreating him to inform you of the dreadful state in which I was, when your kind letter must have arrived, during your stay at Bath. . . . But let me not complain. I ought to be and I trust I am, grateful for what I am, having escaped with my intellectual powers, if less elastic, yet not less vigorous, and with ampler and far more solid materials to exert them on. We know nothing even of ourselves, till we know *ourselves* to be as nothing (a solemn truth, spite of point and antithesis, in which the thought has chanced to *word* itself)!

From this *word* of truth which the sore discipline of a sick bed has compacted into an indwelling reality, from this article, formerly, of *speculative belief*, but which [circumstances] have actualised into *practical faith*, I have learned to counteract calumny by self-reproach, and not only to rejoice (as indeed from natural disposition, from the very constitution of my heart, I should have done at all periods of my life) at the temporal prosperity, and increased and increasing reputation of my old fellow-labourers in philosophical, political, and poetical literature, but to bear their neglect, and even their detraction, *as if I had done nothing at all*, when it would have asked no very violent strain of recollection for one or two of them to have considered, whether some part of *their* most successful *somethings* were not among the *nothings* of my intellectual no-doings. But all strange things are less strange than the sense of intellectual obligations. Seldom do I ever see a Review, yet almost as often as that seldomness permits have I smiled at finding myself attacked in strains of thought which would never have occurred to the writer, had he not directly or indirectly learned them from myself. This is among the salutary effects, even of the dawn of actual religion on the mind, that we begin to reflect on our duties to God and to ourselves as permanent beings, and not to flatter ourselves by a superficial auditing of our negative duties to our neighbours, or mere acts *in transitu* to the transitory. I have too sad an account to settle between myself that is and has been, and myself that *can* not cease to be, to allow me a single complaint that, for all my labours in behalf of truth against the Jacobin party, then against military despotism abroad, against weakness and despondency and faction and factious goodiness at home, I have never received from those in power even a verbal acknowledgment; though by mere reference to dates, it might be proved that no small number of fine speeches in the House of Commons, and elsewhere, originated, directly or indirectly, in my Essays and conversations. I dare assert, that the science of reasoning and judging concerning the productions of literature, the characters and measures of public men, and the events of nations, by a systematic subsumption of them, under PRINCIPLES, deduced from the nature of MAN, and that of prophesying concerning the future (in contradiction to the hopes or fears of the majority) by a careful cross-examination of some period, the most analogous in past history, as learnt from contemporary authorities, and the proportioning of the ultimate event to the likenesses as modified or counteracted by the differences, was as good as unknown in the public prints, before the year 1795-96. Earl Darnley, on the appearance of my letters in the "Courier" concerning the Spaniards, bluntly asked me, whether I had lost my senses, and quoted Lord Grenville at me. If you should happen to cast your eye over my character of Pitt, my two letters to Fox, my Essays on the French Empire under Buonaparte, compared with the Roman, under the first Emperors; that on the probability of the restoration of the Bourbons, and those on Ireland, and Catholic Emancipation (which last unfortunately remain for the greater part in manuscript, Mr. Street not relishing them), and should add to them my Essays in the "Friend" on Taxation, and the supposed effects of war on our commercial prosperity; those on international law in defence of our siege of Copenhagen; and if you had before you the long letter which I wrote to Sir G. Beaumont in 1806, concerning the inevitableness of a war with America, and the specific dangers of that war, if not provided against by specific pre-arrangements; with a list of their Frigates, so called, with their size, number, and weight of metal, the characters of their commanders, and the proportion suspected of British seamen.—I have luckily a copy of it, a rare accident with me.—I dare amuse myself, I say, with the belief, that by far the better half of all these, would read to you now, AS HISTORY. And what have I got for all this? What for my first daring to blow the trumpet of sound philosophy against the Lancastrian faction? The answer is not complex. Unthanked, and left worse than defenceless, by the friends of the Government and the Establishment, to be undermined or outraged by all the malice, hatred, and calumny of its enemies; and to think and toil, with a patent for all the abuse, and a transfer to others of all the honours. In the "Quarterly" Review of the "Remorse" (delayed till it could by no possibility be of the least service to me, and the compliments in which are as senseless and silly as the censures;

every fault ascribed to it, being either no improbability at all, or from the very essence and end of the drama no DRAMATIC improbability, without noticing any one of the REAL faults, and there are many glaring, and one or two DEADLY sins in the tragedy)—in this Review, I am abused, and insolently reproved as a man, with reference to my supposed private habits, for NOT PUBLISHING. Would to heaven I never had! To this very moment I am embarrassed and tormented, in consequence of the non-payment of the subscribers to the "Friend." But I *could* rebut the charge; and not merely say, but prove, that there is not a man in England, whose thoughts, images, words, and erudition have been published in larger quantities than *mine;* though I must admit, not *by,* or *for,* myself. . . .

And now, having for the very first time in my whole life opened out my whole feelings and thoughts concerning my past fates and fortunes, I will draw anew on your patience, by a detail of my present operations. My medical friend is so well satisfied of my convalescence, and that nothing now remains, but to superinduce *positive* health on a system from which disease and its *removable* causes have been driven out, that he has not merely consented to, but advised my leaving Bristol, for some rural retirement. I could indeed pursue nothing uninterruptedly in that city. Accordingly, I am now joint tenant with Mr. Morgan, of a sweet little cottage, at Ashley, half a mile from Box, on the Bath road. I breakfast every morning before nine; work till one, and walk or read till three. Thence, till tea-time, chat or read some lounge book, or correct what I have written. From six to eight work again; from eight till bed-time, play whist, or the little mock billiard called bagatelle, and then sup, and go to bed. My morning hours, as the longest and most important division, I keep sacred to my most important Work, which is printing at Bristol; two of my friends having taken upon themselves the risk. It is so long since I have conversed with you, that I cannot say, whether the subject will, or will not be interesting to you. The title is "Christianity, the one true Philosophy; or, Five Treatises on the Logos, or Communicative Intelligence, natural, human, and divine." To which is prefixed a prefatory Essay, on the laws and limits of toleration and liberality, illustrated by fragments of

AUTO-biography. The first Treatise—Logos Propaideuticos, or the Science of systematic thinking in ordinary life. The *second*—Logos Architectonicus, or an attempt to apply the constructive or Mathematical process to Metaphysics and Natural Theology. The *third*—ὁ Λόγος ὁ θεάνθρωπος (the divine logos incarnate)—a full commentary on the Gospel of St. John, in development of St. Paul's doctrine of preach, ing Christ alone, and Him crucified. The *fourth*—on Spinoza and Spinozism, with a life of B. Spinoza. This entitled Logos Agonistes. The *fifth* and last, Logos Alogos (*i.e.*, Logos Illogicus), or on modern Unitarianism, its causes and effects. The whole will be comprised in two portly octavos, and the second treatise will be the only one which will, and from the nature of the subject must, be unintelligible to the great majority even of well educated readers. The purpose of the whole is a philosophical defence of the Articles of the Church, as far as they respect doctrine, as points of faith. If originality be any merit, this Work will have that, at all events, from the first page to the last. . . .

LXXXIX

TO JOHN KENYON

Mr. B. Morgan's, Bath, November 3 [1814]
. . . But to return, or turn off, to the good old Bishop. It would be worth your while to read Taylor's "Letter on Original Sin," and what follows. I compare it to an old statue of Janus, with one of the faces, that which looks towards his opponents, the controversial phiz in highest preservation,—the force of a mighty one, all power, all life,—the face of a God rushing on to battle, and, in the same moment, enjoying at once both contest and triumph; the other, that which should have been the countenance that looks toward his followers, that with which he sub-stitutes his own opinion, all weather eaten, dim, useless, a *Ghost* in *marble*, such as you may have seen represented in many of Piranesi's astounding engravings from Rome and the Campus Martius. Jer. Taylor's discursive intellect dazzle-darkened his intuition. The principle of becoming all things to all men, if by *any* means he might save *any*,

with him as with Burke, thickened the protecting epidermis of the tact-nerve of truth into something like a callus. But take him all in all, such a miraculous combination of erudition, broad, deep, and omnigenous; of logic subtle as well as acute, and as robust as agile; of psychological insight, so fine yet so secure! of public prudence and practical *sageness* that one ray of *creative Faith* would have lit up and transfigured into wisdom, and of genuine imagination, with its streaming face unifying all at one moment like that of the setting sun when through an interspace of blue sky no larger than itself, it emerges from the cloud to sink behind the mountain, but a face seen only at *starts*, when some breeze from the higher air scatters, for a moment, the cloud of butterfly fancies, which flutter around him like a morning-garment of ten thousand colours—(now how shall I get out of this sentence? the tail is too big to be taken up into the coiler's mouth)—well, as I was saying, I believe such a complete man hardly shall we meet again. . . .

X C

TO WILLIAM WORDSWORTH

Calne, May 30, 1815

. . . Whatever in Lucretius is poetry is not philosophical, whatever is philosophical is not poetry; and in the very pride of confident hope I looked forward to "The Recluse" as the *first* and *only* true Philosophical poem in existence. Of course, I expected the colours, music, imaginative life, and passion of *poetry;* but the matter and arrangement of *philosophy;* not doubting from the advantages of the subject that the totality of a system was not only capable of being harmonised with, but even calculated to aid, the unity (beginning, middle, and end) of a poem. Thus, whatever the length of the work might be, still it was a *determinate* length; of the subjects announced, each would have its own appointed place, and, excluding repetitions, each would re lieve and rise in interest above the other. I supposed you first to have meditated the faculties of man in the abstract, in their correspondence with his sphere of action, and, first in the feeling, touch, and taste, then in the eye, and last in the ear,—to have laid a solid and immovable foundation for the edifice by removing the sandy sophisms of Locke, and the mechanic dogmatists, and demonstrating that the senses were living growths and developments of the mind and spirit, in a much juster as well as higher sense, than the mind can be said to be formed by the senses. Next, I understood that you would take the human race in the concrete, have exploded the absurd notion of Pope's "Essay on Man," Darwin, and all the countless believers even (strange to say) among Christians of man's having progressed from an ourang-outang state—so contrary to all history, to all religion, nay, to all possibility—to have affirmed a Fall in some sense, as a fact, the possibility of which cannot be understood from the nature of the will, but the reality of which is attested by experience and conscience. Fallen men contemplated in the different ages of the world, and in the different states—savage, barbarous, civilized, the lonely cot, or borderer's wigwam, the village, the manufacturing town, seaport, city, universities, and, not disguising the sore evils under which the whole creation groans, to point out, however, a manifest scheme of redemption, of reconciliation from this enmity with Nature—what are the obstacles, the *Antichrist* that must be and already is—and to conclude by a grand didactic swell on the necessary identity of a true philosophy with true religion, agreeing in the results and differing only as the analytic and synthetic process, as discursive from intuitive, the former chiefly useful as perfecting the latter; in short, the necessity of a general revolution in the modes of developing and disciplining the human mind by the substitution of life and intelligence (considered in its different powers from the plant up to that state in which the difference of degree becomes a new kind (man, self-consciousness), but yet not by essential opposition) for the philosophy of mechanism, which, in everything that is most worthy of the human intellect, strikes *Death*, and cheats itself by mistaking clear images for distinct conceptions, and which idly demands conceptions where intuitions alone are possible or adequate to the majesty of the Truth. In short, facts elevated into theory—theory into laws—and laws into living and intelligent powers—true idealism necessarily perfecting itself in realism, and realism refining itself into idealism.

Such or something like this was the plan I had supposed that you were engaged on. Your own words will therefore explain my feelings, *viz.*, that your object "was not to convey recondite, or refined truths, but to place commonplace truths in an interesting point of view." Now this I suppose to have been in your two volumes of poems, as far as was desirable or possible, without an insight into the whole truth. How can common truths be made permanently interesting but by being *bottomed* on our common nature? It is only by the profoundest insight into numbers and quantity that a sublimity and even religious wonder become attached to the simplest operations of arithmetic, the most evident properties of the circle or triangle. I have only to finish a preface, which I shall have done in two, or, at farthest, three days; and I will then, dismissing all comparison either with the poem on the growth of your own support, or with the imagined plan of "The Recluse," state fairly my main objections to "The Excursion" as it is. But it would have been alike unjust both to you and to myself, if I had led you to suppose that any disappointment I may have felt arose wholly or chiefly from the passages I do not like, or from the poem considered irrelatively. . . .

XCI

TO LORD BYRON

TERRACE, PICCADILLY, LONDON

Calne, Wiltshire,
Thursday [Postmark February 17, 1816]

MY LORD,—I have to acknowledge the receipt of your Letter with the 100£ inclosed. What can I say? Till a Friend and House-mate addressed me at my bedside, with— "You have had a letter franked by Lord Byron? Is it from *him?*" I had, as it were, forgotten that I was myself the object of your kindness—so completely lost was I in thinking of the thing itself and the manner in which it was done.

Whether, my Lord! it shall be a Loan or not, depends on

circumstances not in my power tho' in my hope and expectation. Thank God! this is of the least importance—the debt
and the *pleasure* of Love and Gratitude stand unaffected by
anything accidental.

I trust, that I shall soon have the honor of waiting on
you—and now, my Lord, I am about to take a Liberty with
you. I hope, you will not be offended—it is a request, that
you will be so good as to make me a present of your works.
Your own kindness has put it completely in my power to
purchase them without inconvenience; but *from you* they
would be a Heir-loom in my Family: and as a family
anecdote interesting to my Son at least, I should be pleased
to write in the Blank Leaf, that the Poem in my Volume,
which I am a little proud of as a Poet, on your Lordship,
was written before I had any correspondence or chance of
correspondence with you—and that your kindness was shewn
to me while my name was known to you, only as a man of
Letters.

My Lord! I write with a painful effort to suppress my
feelings, and an anxiety lest they might lead me to say
something that might wound your delicacy.

I will therefore conclude—with affectionate Respect

Your Lordship's obliged

S. T. COLERIDGE.

XCII

TO JAMES GILLMAN

42 Norfolk Street, Strand,

Saturday noon [April 13, 1816]

MY DEAR SIR,—The very first half hour I was with you
convinced me that I should owe my reception into your
family exclusively to motives not less flattering to me than
honourable to yourself. I trust we shall ever in matters of
intellect be reciprocally serviceable to each other. Men of
sense generally come to the same conclusion; but they are
likely to contribute to each other's exchangement of view,
in proportion to the distance or even opposition of the points
from which they set out. Travel and the strange variety of
situations and employments on which chance has thrown me,

in the course of my life, might have made me a mere man of *observation*, if pain and sorrow and self-miscomplacence had not forced my mind in on itself, and so formed habits of *meditation*. It is now as much my nature to evolve the fact from the law, as that of a practical man to deduce the law from the fact.

With respect to pecuniary remuneration, allow me to say, I must not at least be suffered to make any addition to your family expenses—though I cannot offer anything that would be in any way adequate to my sense of the service; for that, indeed, there could not be a compensation, as it must be returned in kind, by esteem and grateful affection.

And now of myself. My ever wakeful reason, and the keenness of my moral feelings, will secure you from all unpleasant circumstances connected with me, save only one, *viz.*, the evasion of a specific madness. You will never *hear* anything but truth from me:—prior habits render it out of my power to tell an untruth, but unless carefully observed, I dare not promise that I should not, with regard to this detested poison, be capable of acting one. No sixty hours have yet passed without my having taken laudanum, though for the last week [in] comparatively trifling doses. I have full belief tihat your anxiety need not be extended beyond the first week, and for the first week I shall not, I must not, be permitted to leave your house, unless with you. Delicately or indelicately, this must be done, and both the servants and the assistant must receive absolute commands from you. The stimulus of conversation suspends the terror that haunts my mind; but when I am alone, the horrors I have suffered from laudanum, the degradation, the blighted utility, almost overwhelm me. If (as I feel for the *first time* a soothing confidence it will prove) I should leave you restored to my moral and bodily health, it is not myself only that will love and honour you; every friend I have (and thank God! in spite of this wretched vice, I have many and warm ones, who were friends of my youth and have never deserted me) will thank you with reverence. I have taken no notice of your kind apologies. If I could not be comfortable in your house, and with your family, I should deserve to be miserable. If you could make it convenient I should wish to be with you by Monday evening, as it would prevent the necessity of taking fresh lodgings in town.

With respectful compliments to Mrs. Gillman and her sister, I remain, dear sir, your much obliged

S. T. COLERIDGE.

XCIII

TO HUGH J. ROSE

Muddiford, Christ Church
September 25, 1816

DEAR SIR,—I have received the "Friend," which awaits only for your instructions, and of which I intreat your acceptance as corrected by my self. You are quite in the right. It is idle to attempt the service of God and Mammon at the same altar. Instead of popularizing, therefore, I shall do my best to improve the style, which is sometimes more intangled and parenthetic than need is: tho' a book of reasoning without parentheses must be the work either of adeptship or of a *pliable* intellect. The acquaintance with so many languages has likewise made me too often *polysyllabic*—for these are the words which are possessed in common by the English with the Latin and its south European offspring, and those into which, with the least *looking roundabout*, one can translate the *full* words of the Greek, German, etc. Still there are not so many as the work has been charged with, if it be judged by what I have tried to impose on myself as the ordeal—that is, to reject whatever can be translated into other words of the same language without loss of any meaning—*i.e.* without change either in the conception or the feeling appropriate to it—under which latter head I do *not* place the feeling of self-importance on the part of the Author or that of *wonderment* on the part of the Readers.

Dr. Johnson's

> Let observation with extensive view
> Survey mankind from China to Peru

i.e. Let observation with extensive observation observe mankind extensively (besides this ἀναιμόσαρκος, ἀπαθής printer's devil's *Person.—observation.*) contrasted with Dryden's

"Look round the world"—is a good instance. Compare this with Milton's "yet Virgin of Proserpina from Jove"—which you may indeed easily translate into simple English as far as the *Thought* is concerned, or Image, but not without loss of the delicacy, the sublimation of the ethereal part of the thought with a compleat detachment from the grosser *caput mortuum*. As to Hazlitt, I shall take no notice of him or his libels— at least with reference to myself. What could I say to readers who could believe that I believed in *Astrology* but not in the Newtonian Astronomy, and had an enthusiastic faith in the Athanasian creed and the 39 Articles, but no faith at all in the existence of the Supreme Being? The last time I had the misfortune of being in this man's company I distinctly remember that I pointed out the *causes* of the Ath. creed having been adopted by the compilers of our Liturgy, and at the same time enumerated the weighty reasons for wishing it to be removed. Among others, that it must either be interpreted laxly under the superior authority of the Nicene Creed, or it could not be cleared of a very dangerous approach to *Tritheism* in its omission of the subordination of the Son to the Father, not as Man merely, but as the Eternal Logos. But enough of this. Hazlitt possesses considerable Talent; but it is diseased by a morbid hatred of the Beautiful, and killed by the absence of Imagination, and alas! by a wicked Heart of embruted appetites. Poor wretch! he is a melancholy instance of the awful Truth—that man cannot be on a level with the Beasts—he must be above them or below them. Almost all the *Sparkles* and *originalities* of his Essays are, however, echoes from Poor Charles Lamb—and in his last libel the image of the Angel without hands or feet, was stolen from a letter of my own to Charles Lamb, which had been quoted to him.

I have no other objection to the republication of the character of the late Mr. Pitt with *a comment* (for I have never altered my political *principles*) but the dislike to give pain, and not to any one party—for from the same motive I feel reluctant to republish the 2 letters to Mr. Fox written during his residence at the court of Napoleon. Of this latter gentleman I shall certainly write a character—the Hint towards it you will see in the third article of the appendix to the Lay Sermon now printing.

Should it please the Almighty to restore me to an adequate state of health, and prolong my years enough, my aspirations are toward the concentrating my powers in 3 works. The First (for I am convinced that a true System of Philosophy —the Science of Life—is *best* taught in Poetry as well as most safely) Seven Hymns with a large preface or prose commentary to each—1. to the Sun. 2. Moon. 3. Earth. 4. Air. 5. Water. 6. Fire. 7. God. The second work, 5 Treatises on the Logos, or communicative and communicable Intellect, in God and Man. 1. Λόγος προπαιδευτής or Organum verè organum. 2. Λόγος ἀρχιτεκτονικός, or the principles of the Dynamic or Constructive Philosophy as opposed to the Mechanic. 3. Commentary in detail on the Gospel of St. John or Λόγος θεανοσωπος. 4. Λόγος ἀγωνιστής Biography and Critique on the System of Giordano Bruno, Behmen, and Spinoza. 5. Λόγος ἄλογος or the Sources and Consequences of Modern *Unicism* absurdly called Unitarianism.

The third, an epic poem on the destruction of Jerusalem under Titus.

I hope that the volumes of my literary work Sibylline Leaves will be out by the end of October.

I am very weak but the sea air agrees with me, and I exclaimed again at the first sight of it—

> God be with thee—gladsome ocean!
> How gladly greet I thee once more!
> Ships and waves and endless motion,
> And men rejoicing on thy shore!

I mean to stay 5 weeks longer at least—but O dear Sir! it is a hard hard thing to be compelled to turn away from such subjects to scribble essays for newspapers—too good to answer one purpose, and not good enough for another— But so it is! and God's will be done! Should you leave Cambridge at Christmas I shall be very glad to see you if you will take the trouble of writing to Highgate at J. Gillman's Esqre. Surgeon, Highgate.

I remain meantime with unfeigned anticipations of regard

Your obliged

S. T. COLERIDGE.

XCIV

[Postmark, March 22, 1817]

. . . What injudicious advisers must not Southey have had ! It vexes me to the quick. Never yet did any human being gain anything by self-desertion. I shall never forget the *disgust*, with which Mackintosh's "bear witness, I *recant, abjure*, and *abhor* the principles"—*i.e.* of his Vindiciae Gallicae—struck his auditors in Lincoln's Inn. Southey should have rested his defence on the time the Work ["Wat Tyler"] was written, both respecting himself and the events that happened afterwards. With the exception of one outrageously absurd and frantic passage (p. 67) the thing contains nothing that I can find that would not have been praised and thought very right, *forty years ago*, at all the public schools in England, had it been written by a lad in the first form as a *poem*. For who in the Devil's name, ever thought of reading poetry for any political or practical purposes till these Devil's times that we live in? The *publication* of the Work is the wicked thing. Briefly, my dear Sir, every one is in the right to make the best he can honorably of a bad business. But the truth is the truth. The root of the evil is *a public*, and take my word for it, this will wax more and more prolific of inconveniences, that at length it will scarcely be possible for the State to suffer any truth to be published, because it will be certain to convey dangerous falsehood to ninety-nine out of a hundred. Then we shall come round to the *esoteric* (interior, hidden) doctrine of the ancients, and learn to understand what Christ meant when He commanded us not to cast pearls before swine. Take four-fifths of the "Wat Tyler" for instance—'tis a wretched mess of pig's meat I grant—but yet take it—and reduce it to single assertions. How many of them, think you, would bear denying as *truths?* But if truth yelps and bites at the heels of a horse that cannot stop, Why—truth may think herself well off if she only gets her teeth knocked down her throat. It is for this reason, that I entertain toward Mr. . . . Cobbetts, Hursts, [?] and all these creatures—and to the Foxites, who have fostered the vipers—a feeling more like hatred than I ever bore to other Flesh and Blood. So clearly do I see and always have seen, that it must end in the Suspension of Freedom of all kind. Hateful under all names these wretches are most hateful to me as Liberticides. The Work attributed to Buonaparte says "liberty is for a few, equality for all." Alas! dear Sir, what is mankind but *the few* in all ages? Take *them* away, and how long would the rest, think you, differ from the Negroes or New Zealanders? Strip Washburn [?] for instance of every thing that he does and talks, as a Barrel Organ, without really *understanding* one word of what he says, one ultimate end of what he does—leave him for instance, on a South sea Island, with no other words to talk in but what the savages can supply him with—and I think, in what one respect would Washburn differ from one of these Savages in his inward Soul and in any reality of Being—but for the worse? Oh! that conscience permitted me to dare tell the whole truth! I would, methinks, venture to brave the fury of the great and little Vulgar as the Advocate of an insufferable Aristocracy. But either by an Aristocracy, or a fool-and-knave-ocracy man must be governed. . . .

XCV

TO THE REV. F. WRANGHAM

J. Gillman's, Esq., Highgate,
June 5, 1817

A bad *correspondent*, my dear Wrangham! I may be—say rather, ever have been; but I am not so bad a *man*, as to have suffered any papers sent to me by an old friend to remain unanswered. Indeed I have received none.

While writing the above sentence, I was called out: and on returning to my desk, I again reperused your letter, and see that I have misinterpreted the word "*Notes*"—an hallucination which (I doubt not) was occasioned by my having been very lately employed in revising and correcting some notes on Aristophanes, at the request of the commentator. I have therefore only to plead guilty to the fact of having received several kind remembrancings from you, and to the having suffered my answers to them to corporate in the *composition*. For I verily believe that I have composed half a dozen letters to you. But what I dare not defend I can with truth palliate—for both my health and my circumstances have been such that my powers of volition, constitutionally weak, have sunk utterly under the weight of embarrassments, disappointments, and infamous calumny. For instance, the author of the Articles in the "Edinburgh Review" and the "Examiner" (W. Hazlitt) after efforts of friendship on my part which a brother could not have demanded—my House, Purse, Influence—and all this, tho' his manners were dreadfully repulsive to me, because I was persuaded that he was a young man of great talent and utterly friendless—his very father and mother having despaired of him—after having baffled all these efforts at the very moment, when he had been put in the way of an honourable maintenance, by the most unmanly vices that almost threatened to communicate a portion of their infamy to my family and Southey's and Wordsworth's, in all of which he had been familiarized, and in mine and Southey's domesticated—after having been snatched from an infamous punishment by Southey and myself (there were not less than 2 or [*sic*] men on horses in search of him)—after having given him all the money I had in the world, and the very shoes off my feet to enable him to escape over the mountains—and since that time never, either of us, injured him in the least degree—unless the quiet withdrawing from any further connection with him (and this without any ostentation, or any mask of shyness when we accidentally met him) not merely or chiefly on account of his Keswick conduct, but from the continued depravity of his life—but why need I say more? This man Mr. Jeffrey has sought out, knowing all this, because the wretch is notorious for his avowed hatred to *me* and affected contempt of Southey. He has repeatedly boasted, that he wrote the very contrary of all he believed—because he was under heavy obligations, and therefore *hated* me. The praise or dispraise of Reviews or indeed of any one whom I do not personally love, is utterly indifferent to me, and always has been. But I cannot be indifferent to starvation; a very eminent Bookseller was consulted by a brother of the trade concerning me—and his answer was—these words (You may safely conclude that the exaggeration in the first part excited a strange sort of smile and stare on my part) "I have heard from several of our first rate men, Lord Byron was one, and Mr. W. Scott another, that taking him all in all, Mr. C. is the greatest man we have; but *I* would not have a work of his, if it were given me ready printed etc., for the 'Quarterly Review' takes no notice of his works or but in a half in half way that damns a man worse than anything: and *our* 'Review' (the 'Edinburgh') is decided to write him down"— Before the "Christabel" was published, Jeffrey wrote to Anacreon Moore, begging him, as a favour, to supply a grand quiz of the poem; and tho' purchased by Merry (*q.e.* Murray) Gifford would not let it be reviewed in the "Quarterly"! the consequence is that tho' I have devoted 20 years incessant thought and at least 10 years positive labour to the one in six volumes Logosophia or on the Logos in man and Deity forming a compleat and perfectly original system of Logic, Natural Philosophy, and Theology, and including a detailed commentary on the Gospel of St. John (the particulars you will soon see in the last leaves of the second volume of my "Literary Life," which after having been printed off 20 months ago is now alas! only coming out) while, by the villainy of men who called themselves my friends, this work I cannot even get a Bookseller to print! No not one volume even on trial. "Your works, Sir! have *never* covered the expences"— And to this I have no reply to make. I have never recovered the losses sustained by the "Friend"—not half of the subscribers having paid me. So at length I have been compelled to give up all thought and hope of doing anything of a permanent nature, either as a Poet or a Philosopher and have (not without a sigh of anguish) hired myself as a job writer, and compiler to a great House who are now engaging in a work that will, if it succeed at all, consume all the years I can expect to live. This is but a part and specimen of what I have suffered yet enough to explain fully to you the Chapters in the Literary Life concerning authorship, and the earnest advice to young men of genius to adopt a profession or even a trade —which Southey (to whom I had sent the "Literary Life") has adopted in the "Quarterly Review," last number— *thoughtlessly* in my opinion. Of the few copies which I can claim of the "Auto-Biographia Literaria," "Sibylline Leaves," and the "Rifacciamento" of the "Friend" (one half of which is new) in three volumes, I will reserve one for you and, if I knew how, I would send you immediately the two Lay Sermons corrected by myself. I need not add, that I shall receive and read your Memorials etc. with great interest—for I am, my dear Wrangham, with every kind wish your sincere friend

S. T. COLERIDGE.

PS. I received your's last night, I congratulate you on your appointment.

XCVI

TO THE EDITOR OF THE "MORNING CHRONICLE"

Highgate,
Sunday, January 25, 1818

DEAR SIR,—You will gratify me by your acceptance of the inclosed ticket for my Lectures, admitting a lady and gentleman, and will both flatter and serve me by the compliment of your occasional attendance.

Should it consist with your feelings to give the Lectures some little complimentary notice in the body of the "Morning Chronicle," it would prove of *great service* to me. Alas! dear Sir—how adversity tames us! While I had hope and heart, and feeling kindly to all men, never suspected that I had an enemy in the world, how I should have started at the thought of soliciting to *be praised!* But I have never been, and never can be, of any party and since I was five-and-twenty, never wrote a line of the truth of which I was not at the time convinced, and very few, if any, to the *principle* of which I could not at this moment subscribe. More than this, thinking that to tell truth *all on one side* was but a more artful way of telling a lie, I withdrew from all *periodical* political writing as soon as I found the *whole truth* not admitted. *Exempli gratia* I loathe parodies of all kinds, and hold even "To wed or not to wed," "To print or not to print," not altogether guiltless, as disturbing the simplicity of feeling and imagination; and parodies on religion still more. Yet I exult in Hone's acquittal and Lord Ellenborough's deserved humiliation, and I will not express the former unless I can, at the same time, say the latter with my reasons for it. Again I utterly disapprove of the late domestic measures of our Ministers, and of the whole spirit of our Castlereagh foreign politics; but I must *add*, that without grievous mistakes on the part of Opposition and still more grievous misconduct on the part of the Ultra-whigs, the Government could not have remained in the hands of such simpleton saints, as the Sidmouth Sect, or of such unprincipled adventurers as the Castlereagh Gang. I detest Jacobinism, and as to the French, Jacobins or Royalists, even as I love what's virtuous, *hate* I them! I see and lament a woful deterioration of the lower classes, spite of Bible Societies, and spite of our spinning jennies for the cheap and speedy manufacture of reading and writing; but I cannot conceal from myself, and dare not conceal it from others, that neither the whole blame, nor even the greatest, is with the lower orders. I see an unmanly spirit of alarm, and of self-convenience, under many a soft title, domestic comfort, etc., etc. in our gentry. The hardihood of English good sense in the shape of manly compromise (on which, by the bye, all our institutions are founded) seems to me decaying. In consequence, I have been abused or neglected by all parties; and to return to my present solicitation, what chance of tolerable success can a man have, if the rancour, envy, and wantonness of unprovoked enemies or (as has been too often my sad case) provoked only by acts of more than brotherly kindness, will load one scale, and the zeal of a friend not be permitted to place the least counterweight in the other?

A man of your kind disposition will easily pardon a little egotism from the unfortunate and the persecuted—in which, I trust I remain, dear Sir, with unfeigned respect and regard,

Your (long ago) obliged and ever grateful

S. T. COLERIDGE.

PS. It was in your paper that my *first* poetic efforts were brought before the public.

z

XCVII

TO THE REV. H. F. CARY
LITTLE HAMPTON, ARUNDEL, SUSSEX

Highgate, February 6, 1818

. . . PS. I have this morning been reading a strange publication—*viz.* Poems with very wild and interesting pictures, as swathing, etched (I suppose) but it is said printed and painted by the author, W. Blake. He is a man of Genius—and I apprehend a Swedenborgian—certainly a mystic *emphatically*. You perhaps smile at *my* calling another poet a *Mystic;* but verily I am in the very mire of common-place common-place compared with Mr. Blake, apo- or rather—ana-calyptic Poet, and Painter!

XCVIII

TO CHARLES AUGUSTUS TULK

Highgate, Thursday evening, 1818

. . . Blake's Poems.—I begin with my dyspathies that I may forget them, and have uninterrupted space for loves and sympathies. Title-page and the following emblem contain all the faults of the drawings with as few beauties as could be in the compositions of a man who was capable of such faults and such beauties. The faulty despotism in symbols amounting in the title-page to the μισητόν, and occasionally, irregular unmodified lines of the inanimate, sometimes as the effect of rigidity and sometimes of exos-sation like a wet tendon. So likewise the ambiguity of the drapery. Is it a garment or the body incised and scored out? The lumpness (the effect of vinegar on an egg) in the upper one of the two prostrate figures in the title-page, and the straight line down the waistcoat of pinky gold-beaters' skin in the next drawing, with the I don't-know-whatness of the countenance, as if the mouth had been formed by the habit of placing the tongue not contemptu-ously, but stupidly, between the lower gums and the lower jaw—these are the only *repulsive* faults I have noticed. The figure, however, of the second leaf, abstracted from the *expression* of the countenance given it by something about the mouth, and the interspace from the lower lip to the chin, is such as only a master learned in his art could produce.

N. B. I signifies "It gave me great pleasure." Ɨ, "Still greater." H, "And greater still." Θ, "In the highest degree." O, "In the lowest."

Shepherd, I; Spring, I (last stanza, Ɨ); Holy Thursday, H; Laughing Song, Ɨ; Nurse's Song, I; The Divine Image, Θ; The Lamb, Ɨ; The little black Boy, Θ, yea Θ+Θ; Infant Joy, H (N. B. For the three last lines I should write, "When wilt thou smile," or "O smile, O smile! I'll sing the while." For a babe two days old does not, cannot smile, and innocence and the very truth of Nature must go together. Infancy is too holy a thing to be ornamented). "The Echoing Green," I, (the figures Ɨ, and of the second leaf, H); "The Cradle Song," I; "The School Boy," H; Night, Θ; "On another's Sorrow," I; "A Dream,"?; "The little boy lost," I (the drawing, Ɨ); "The little boy found," I; "The Blossom," O; "The Chimney Sweeper," O; "The Voice of the Ancient Bard," O.

Introduction, Ɨ; Earth's Answer, Ɨ; Infant Sorrow, I; "The Clod and the Pebble," I; "The Garden of Love," Ɨ; "The Fly," I; "The Tyger," Ɨ; "A little boy lost," Ɨ; "Holy Thursday," I; [p. 13, O; "Nurse's Song," O?]; "The little girl lost and found" (the ornaments most exquisite! the poem, I); "Chimney Sweeper in the Snow," O; "To Tirzah, and the Poison Tree," I—and yet O; "A little Girl lost," O. (I would have had it omitted, not for the want of innocence in the poem, but from the too probable want of it in many readers.) "London," I; "The Sick Rose," I; "The little Vagabond," O. Though I cannot approve altogether of this last poem, and have been inclined to think that the error which is most likely to beset the scholars of Emanuel Swedenborg is that of utterly demerging the tremendous incompatibilities with an evil will that arise out of the essential Holiness of the abysmal A-seity in the love of the Eternal *Person*, and thus giving temptation to weak minds to sink this love itself into *Good Nature*, yet still I disapprove the mood of mind in this wild poem so much less than I do the servile blind-worm, wrap-rascal scurf-coat of *fear* of the *modern* Saint (whose whole being is a lie, to themselves as well as to their brethren), that I should laugh with good conscience in watching a Saint of the new stamp, one of the first stars of our eleemosynary advertisements, groaning in wind-pipe! and with the whites of his eyes upraised at the *audacity* of this poem! Anything rather than this degradation I of Humanity, and therein of the Incarnate Divinity!

S. T. C.

O means that I am perplexed and have no opinion.
I, with which how can we utter "Our Father"?

XCIX

TO JOSEPH HENRY GREEN

Spring Garden Coffee House [May 2, 1818]

. . . The Cotton-children Bill (an odd irony to children *bred up in cotton!*) which has passed the House of Commons, would not, I suspect, have been discussed at all in the House of Lords, but have been quietly assented to, had it not afforded that *Scotch* coxcomb, the plebeian Earl of Lauderdale, too tempting an occasion for displaying his muddy three inch depths in the gutter (? Guttur) of his Political Economy. Whether some half-score of rich capitalists are to be prevented from suborning suicide and perpetuating infanticide and soul-murder is, forsooth, the most perplexing question which has ever called forth his *determining* faculties, accustomed as they are *well known* to have been, to grappling with difficulties. In short, he wants to make a speech almost as much as I do to have a release signed by conscience from the duty of making or anticipating answers to such speeches.

> O when the heart is deaf and blind, how blear
> The lynx's eye! how dull the mould-warp's ear!

Verily the *World* is mighty! and for all but the few the orb of Truth labours under eclipse from the shadow of the world! . . .

C

J. Green's, Esq., St. Lawrence, nr. Maldon,
Wednesday, July 19, 1818

MY VERY DEAR SISTER AND FRIEND,—The distance from
the post and the extraordinary thinness of population in
this district (especially of men and women of letters) which
affords only two days in the seven for sending to or receiving
from Maldon, are the sole causes of your not hearing oftener
from me. The cross roads from Margretting Street to the
very house are excellent, and through the first gate we drove
up between two large gardens, that on the right a flower
and fruit garden not without kitchenery, and that on the
left, a kitchen garden not without fruits and flowers, and
both in a perfect *blaze* of roses. Yet so capricious is our, at
least my, nature, that I feel I do not receive the fifth part
of the delight from this miscellany of Flora, flowers at every
step, as from the economized glasses and flower-pots at
Highgate so tended and worshipped by me, and each the
gift of some kind friend or courteous neighbour. I actually
make up a flower-pot every night, in order to imitate my
Highgate pleasures. The country road is very beautiful.
About a quarter of a mile from the garden, all the way
through beautiful fields in blossom, we come to a wood, full
of birds and not uncharmed by the nightingales, and which
the old workman, to please his mistress, has *romanticized* with.
I dare say, fifty seats and honeysuckle bowers and green
arches made by twisting the branches of the trees across
the paths. The view from the hilly field above the wood
commanding the arm of the sea, and ending in the open sea,
reminded me very much of the prospects from Stowey and
Alfoxden, in Somersetshire. The cottagers seem to be and
are in possession of plenty of comfort. Poverty I have seen
no marks of, nor of the least servility, though they are
courteous and respectful. We have *abundance of cream.* The
Farm must, I should think, be a valuable estate; and the
parents are anxious to leave it as complete as possible for
Joseph, their only child (for it is Mrs. J. Green's sisters that
we have seen—G. himself has no sister). There is no society

hereabouts. I like it the better there*fore*. The clergyman, a young man, is lost in a gloomy vulgar Calvinism, will read no book but the Bible, converse on nothing but the state of the soul, or rather he will not converse at all, but visit each house once in two months, when he prays and admonishes, and gives a lecture every evening at his own rooms. On being invited to dine with us, the sad and modest youth returned for answer, that if Mr. Green and I should be here when he visited the house, he should have no objection to enter into the state of our souls with us, and if in the mean time we desired any *instruction* from him, we might attend at his daily evening lecture! Election, Reprobation, Children of the Devil, and all such flowers of rhetoric, and flour of brimstone, form his discourses both in church and parlour. But my folly in not filling the snuff canister is a subject of far more serious and awful regret with me, than the not being in the way of being thus led by the nose of this Pseudo-Evangelist. Nothing but Scotch; and that five miles off. O Anne! it was cruel in you not to have calculated the monstrous disproportion between the huge necessities of my nostrils, or rather of my thumb and forefinger, and that vile little vial three fourths empty of snuff! The flat of my thumb, yea, the nail of my forefinger is not only clean; it is white! white as the pale flag of famine!

Now for my health. . . . Ludicrous as it may seem, yet it is no joke for me, that from the marshiness of these sea marshes, and the number of unnecessary fish ponds and other stagnancies immediately around the house, the gnats are a very plague of Egypt, and suspicious, with good reason, of an erysipelatous tendency, I am anxious concerning the effects of the irritation produced by these canorous visitants. While awake (and two thirds of last night I was kept awake by their bites and trumpetings) I can so far command myself as to check the intolerable itching by a weak mixture of goulard and rosewater; but in my sleep I scratch myself as if old Scratch had lent me his best set of claws. This is the only drawback from my comforts here, for nothing can be kinder or more cordial than my treatment. I *like* Mrs. J. Green better and better; but feel that in twenty years it would never be above or beyond *liking*. She is good-natured, lively, innocent, but without a *soothingness*, or something I do not know what that is tender. As to my return, I do not think it will be possible, without great unkindness, to be with you before Tuesday evening or Wednesday, calculating *wholly* by the progress of the manuscript; and we have been hard at it. Do not take it as words, of course, when I say and solemnly assure you, that if I followed my own *wishes*, I should leave this place on Saturday morning: for I feel more and more that I can be well off nowhere away from you and Gillman. May God bless him! For a dear friend he is and has been to me. . . .

C I

TO WILLIAM BLACKWOOD
BOOKSELLER, EDINBURGH

Highgate [Postmark, April 12, 1819]

. . . The Scheme on which a Magazine should be conducted (—and *if so constructed*, would, I am convinced, outrun all present rivalry) shall be communicated first to Messrs. Cadell and Davies, and then to you—so that you may have the advantage of their *confidential* opinions in addition to your own Judgement. For I shall entreat Mr. Davies to communicate his opinion of it to *you* and not to me—in order that he may not be withheld by any feeling of delicacy from expressing the whole of his mind, should it be unfavorable to the Scheme, whether more or less. Of this Scheme part will, of course, be *private*, for your eye, not that of the Public; but the far larger portion will be continued in a sort of Letter or Essay on the Desiderata of a Magazine— and should you *approve* of the contents, I propose that you should annex to it a declaration of your perfect assent to the sentiments of your correspondent, and a sort of promise *that* the Proprietors are determined to conduct *their* Magazine on the same principles, to the best of their power. If either the Scheme be rejected, or my co-operation in the realizing of the same not agreed to, I then rely on your honor that no use shall be made of the same; but that it shall be sent back to me.

Let us then for a moment *suppose* the plan to have received your approbation and concurrence—and that I, first, supplied you monthly to the amount of two Sheets, *one* article at least of which shall be (*i.e.* as far as my *comparative* Talents and Genius render it possible and probable) equivalent to the *leading* Article in the "Edinburgh" and "Quarterly" Reviews—(by *leading* I mean that one article, which is expected to be much talked of, as for instance several of Mr. Southey's in the "Quarterly")—and that I shall be at all times prepared to give my best advice and opinion with regard to all the other parts of the Magazine, to be, as it were, your London Editor or Curator, and to exert my interest among my literary friends, not being professional Authors, to procure communications; to re-enliven, for this purpose, my correspondence abroad with several valued Friends of mine who are of highest rank among the Foreign Literati—in short, to give to the "Edinburgh Magazine" the whole weight of my interest, name, and character, whatever that may be—what shall you consider as a due remuneration? Suppose, that I start with the first of June—and that every 3 months you are at liberty to reconsider the terms, according as your experience may have been. You may either attach the whole to the *nominal* price of the sheet furnished, or make the remuneration depend part on the correspondence and part on my Editorial Labors. I neither do or shall propose any terms myself; but will not suffer you to wait a single day, beyond the time required for the mutual receipt of the Letters, without a decisive answer, yes or no. If in your own opinion you do not find yourself permitted to hazard any deviation, of consequence, from your common price—it will be better to let it drop at once: for I use the words in their *literal* sense when I say, that I *could* not assist you on such terms. For I dare not write what I cannot gladly own, and expect an increase of reputation from—others with other objects might compose three sheets in the same time and with far less exertion than I *could* produce one. I may adopt the words which Mr. Wordsworth once used to Longman—You pay others, Sir! for what they write; but you must pay *me* likewise for what I do *not* write: for it is this (*i.e.* the omissions, erasures, etc.) that cost me most both Time and Toil. You should receive my plan as soon after I hear from you as the Post can carry it—Sincerely, Dear Sir

S. T. COLERIDGE.

PS. I shall hope to hear from you as soon as possible.

CII

October 8, 1819

MY DEAR SIR,—What shall I say? or what do? When I first read your letter and noticed the inclosed, unsuspicious of the magnitude, I remained for some minutes reflecting—I might almost say, mentally *gazing*—on the act, the impulse and the accompanying sentiments, perfectly abstracted from the *persons*, alike from myself and from you. Having again read the letter and then opened the note, it was not *surprize*, I felt —nor yet was it any confusion of feelings. All that rendered the kindness peculiar, all that individualizes us both by Lot and by Nature, rose up in my mind—I seemed to *struggle* to retain and review my first impression, and the complacency and the hope and the faith in Human Nature which had accompanied them—but—why should I hesitate to tell you? I burst into a flood of Tears. Why indeed should I be ashamed to say this? for such tears and such only will be shed at the threshold of the Gate, within which all tears will be wiped away. I can say no more—only this. My dear young Friend! you would cruelly tho' most unintentionally wound me, if you have in this made any sacrifice of your future worldly well-doing— I have not said, your present *comforts*—because you have made me know that I can interpret your feelings by what my own would be. But if in the fervor of kindness you have at all distressed yourself, you cannot conceive how dearly I should *love* you—more than even as I do now—if you would say it in some way. From one I did not sincerely respect I would of course receive nothing—but from you—wanting it I would receive what you do not. I scarcely know what I am writing—perhaps, I had better have delayed answering till my spirits were somewhat tranquillized. I can barely collect myself sufficiently to convey to you—first, that I receive this proof of your filial kindness with feelings not unworthy of the same— that I dare not offend against the sincerity, which is the bond of friendship, by disguising that my circumstances are such as rendered such an assistance somewhat more than merely useful, inasmuch as it has saved me from the necessity of abandoning a work of permanent character in order to waste myself in Magazines and Newspapers—but that, whenever (if ever) my circumstances shall improve, you must permit me to remind you that what was, and *forever* under *all* conditions of fortune will be *felt* as a *gift*, has become a Loan— and lastly, that you must let me have you as a frequent friend on whose visits I may rely as often as convenience will permit you—

May God bless you, my dearest Sir,—and I humbly thank God, that I dare wish you to see and *know*,

Your obliged and affectionate

S. T. COLERIDGE.

CIII

TO AN UNKNOWN CORRESPONDENT

[1820]

MY DEAR SIR,—In a copy of verses entitled "A Hymn before Sunrise in the Vale of Chamouny" I described myself under the influence of strong devotional feelings gazing on the Mountain till as if it had been a Shape emanating from and sensibly representing her own essence my soul had become diffused thro' "the mighty Vision," and there

As in her natural Form, swelled vast to Heaven.

Mr. Wordsworth, I remember, censured the passage as strained and unnatural, and condemned the Hymn *in toto* (which nevertheless I ventured to publish in the "Sibylline Leaves") as a specimen of the Mock Sublime. It may be so for others; but it is impossible that I should find it myself unnatural, being conscious that it was the image and utterance of Thoughts and Emotions in which there was no Mockery. Yet on the other hand I could readily believe that the mood and Habit of mind out of which the Hymn rose, that differs from Milton's and Thomson's and from the Psalms, the source of all three, in the Author's addressing himself to *individual* objects actually present to his Senses, while his great Predecessors apostrophize *classes* of things, presented by the memory and generalized by the Understanding—I can readily believe, I say, that in this there may be too much of what the learned Med'ciners call the *Idiosyncratic* for true Poetry. For from my very childhood I

have been accustomed to *abstract* and as it were unrealize
whatever of more than common interest my eyes dwelt on;
and then by a sort of transference and transmission of my
consciousness to identify myself with the Object—and I have
often thought, within the last five or six years, that if ever
I should feel once again the genial warmth and stir of the
poetic impulse, and referred to my own experiences, I should
venture on a yet stranger and wilder Allegory than of yore—
that I should *allegorize* myself, as a rock with it's summit
just raised above the surface of some Bay or Strait in the
Arctic Sea "while yet the stern and solitary Night Brook'd
no alternate Sway"—all around me fixed and firm methought as my own Substance, and near me lofty Masses,
that might have seemed to "hold the moon and stars in fee,"
and often in such wild play with meteoric lights, or with the
Shine from above which they made rebound in sparkles or
disband in off-shoots and splinters and iridescent needle-
shafts of keenest Glitter, that it was a pride and a place of
Healing to lie, as in an Apostle's Shadow, within the Eclipse
and deep substance-seeming Gloom of "these dread Ambas-
sadors from Earth to Heaven, Great Hierarchs" and tho'
obscured yet to think myself obscured by consubstantial
Forms, based in the same Foundation as my own. I grieved
not to serve them—yea, lovingly and with gladsomeness I
abased myself in their presence: for they are, my Brothers, I
said, and the Mastery is their's by right of elder birth and
by right of the mightier strivings of the hidden Fire that
uplifteth them above me—   [No conclusion or signature.]

CIV

TO J. GOODEN

Highgate, January 14, [1820]

. . . With regard to Philosophy, there are half a dozen
things, good and bad that in this country are so nick-named,
but in the only accurate sense of the term, there neither are,
have been, or ever will be but two essentially different
Schools of Philosophy: the Platonic, and the Aristotelean.
To the latter, but with a somewhat nearer approach to the
Platonic, Emanuel Kant belonged; to the former Bacon and

Leibnitz and in his riper and better years Berkeley—And to this I profess myself an adherent—*nihil novum, vel inauditum audemus*, tho' as every man has a force of his own, without being more or less than a man, so is every true Philosopher an original, without ceasing to be an Inmate of Academies or of the Lyceum. But as to caution, I will just tell you how I proceeded myself, 20 years and more ago when I first felt a curiosity about Kant, and was fully aware that to master his meaning, as a system, would be a work of great Labor and long Time. First, I asked myself, have I the Labor and the Time in my power? Secondly, if so and if it would be of adequate importance to me if true, by what means can I arrive at a rational presumption for or against? I enquired after all the more popular writings of Kant—read them with delight—I then read the Prefaces to several of his Systematic Works, as the Prolegomena etc.—here too every part, I understood, and that was nearly the whole, was replete with sound and plain tho' bold and novel truths to me—and I followed Socrates's Adage respecting Heraclitus—All I understand is excellent; and I am bound to presume that the rest is at least worth the trouble of trying whether it be not equally so. In other words, until I understand a Writer's Ignorance, I presume myself ignorant of his understanding. Permit me to refer you to a chapter on this subject in my "Literary Life." Yet I by no means recommend to you an extension of your philosophic researches beyond Kant. In him is contained all that can be *learnt*—and as to the results, you have a firm Faith in God, the responsible Will of Man, and Immortality—and Kant will demonstrate to you, that this Faith is acquiesced in,—indeed, nay, confirmed by the Reason and Understanding, but grounded in Postulates authorized and Substantiated solely by the *Moral* Being— These are likewise *mine:* and whether the *Ideas* are regulative only, as Aristotle and Kant teach, or constitutive and actual as Pythagoras and Plato, is of living Interest to the Philosopher by Profession alone. Both systems are equally true, if only the former abstain from denying *universally* what is denied individually. He for whom Ideas are constitutive, will in effect be a Platonist—and in those, for whom they are regulative only, Platonism is but a hollow affectation. Dryden *could* not have been a Platonist—

Shakspere, Milton, Dante, Michael Angelo, and Rafael could not have been other than Platonists. Lord Bacon, who never read Plato's Works, Taught pure Platonism in his *great* Work, the "Novum Organum," and abuses his divine Predecessor for fantastic nonsense, which he had been the first to explode.

Accept my best respects as, dear Sir,

Your's most sincerely,

S. T. COLERIDGE.

CV

TO DERWENT COLERIDGE
EXETER COLLEGE, OXFORD

Monday, July 3, 1820

MY DEAR DERWENT,—I were, methinks, to be pardoned, if even on my own account I felt it an aggravation of my sore affliction that, your Brother without writing or any other mode of communication should have bent his course to the North as tho' I were not his Father nor he himself bound to Mr. and Mrs. Gillman by his own knowledge of the affectionate and scarcely less than parental anxiety with which they follow him thro' luck and unluck, good report and evil. Or am I to suppose, that having taken his resolutions he found or fancied that it would be less painful to him to imply by his absence than to tell me by word of mouth, that my advice would be to no purposes and my Wishes of the same stuff as my Tears? One thing at least is certain: that had it been his object to make it known and felt, that he considered me as having forfeited the interest and authority of a Father *per desuetudinem usus*, and as a Defaulter in the Duties, which I owed his Youth, he could not have chosen a more intelligible (God knows! on his own account too afflictive to be mortifying) way of realizing it! Ignorant of all the *detail* of the case, of the Persons, and their relative Bearings both on Hartley's present and his prior situation, I do not permit myself to form any positive Judgement on certain parts of your letter. But I conjecture, that it will differ from your's and Mr. Burton's: tho' neither of you will have grounded his opinion less on mere worldly prudence, or on self-interest in any lower sense than as it is the necessary Counterweight of self-indulgence. O! my dear Boy! never forget, that as there is a Self-willedness which drifts on from self-interest to finish it's course in the sucking eddy-pool of Selfishness, so there is a Self-interest which begins in Self-sacrifice, and ends in God. But deferring the whole question of your Brother's acquaintances and connections, I can only gather from your letter the ascertainment of which I had before supposed—that Hartley had converted difference of manners, views and opinions into positive dislike, and, I sadly fear, into settled enmity by his ungracious style of repelling the requests and admonitions of the fellows of Oriel—that then instead of fortifying himself against the hostility, so excited, by more than common guardedness of conduct he managed to put himself completely in their power by a succession of trifling (many of them perhaps, unconscious) indiscretions, irregularities and unpunctualities, which have been woven together into a Web, with that cruellest sophism of Calumny, which destroying the actual distances and interspaces gives a false context and interprets fault by fault—and that Hartley's mood of mind gives the one only thing wanting to secure their triumph! You have not said, whether Dr. Coplestone is at Oxford or not! and if not, where he is? The names and present addresses of the Fellows of Oriel you should likewise procure. And then if your Brother have left Birmingham or in disregard of my entreaties perseveres in going to Keswick, I expect you here with as little delay as possible.

My health is not worse, and during the day or as long as I am up, I am calm or at all events can manage what I feel. But I cannot tell why, as soon as my head is on my pillow, my thoughts become their own masters, spite of every effort to go to sleep, with indifferent trains of thinking, and tho' I do not go to bed till I am downright weary of holding myself up, and continue reading and trying to interest my intellect or my fancy in the subject to the last moment. Last night, however, I screamed out but once only in my sleep, and my stomach felt but in a very slight degree sore after I woke— the exceeding order and wild *Swedenborgian* rationality of the Images in my Dreams, whenever I have been in any great affliction, so that they haunt me for days—and the odd circumstance that these dreams are always accompanied with profuse weeping in my sleep towards morning, and probably not long before I wake—for my pillow is often quite wet: (or the screaming fits take place in the first sleep, and from dreams that are either frightful or mere imageless sensation of affright and leave no traces)—these are problems which I encourage myself in proposing and trying to solve, were it only to divert my attention from the occasion of them. O surely if Hartley knew or believed that I love him and [hunger] after him as I do and ever have done, he would have come to me. . . .

CVI

TO T. ALLSOP

January, 1821

. . . To the completion of these four works I have literally nothing more to do than *to transcribe;* but, as I before hinted, from so many scraps and *Sibylline* leaves, including margins of books and blank pages, that, unfortunately, I must be my own scribe, and not done by myself, they will be all but lost; or perhaps (as has been too often the case already) furnish feathers for the caps of others; some for this purpose, and some to plume the arrows of detraction, to be let fly against the luckless bird from whom they had been plucked or moulted.

In addition to these—of my GREAT WORK, to the preparation of which more than twenty years of my life have been devoted, and on which my hopes of extensive and permanent utility, of fame, in the noblest sense of the word, mainly rest—that by which I might,

> As now by thee, by all the good be known,
>   When this weak frame lies mouldered in the grave,
> Which self-surviving I might call my own,
>   Which Folly cannot mar, nor Hate deprave—
> The incense of those powers, which, risen in flame,
> Might make me dear to Him from whom they came—

of this work, to which all my other writings (unless I except my Poems, and these I can exclude in part only) are introductory and preparative; and the result of which (if the premises be, as I with the most tranquil assurance am convinced they are—insubvertible, the deductions legitimate,

and the conclusions commensurate, and only commensurate, with both), must finally be a revolution of all that has been called *Philosophy* or Metaphysics in England and France since the era of the commencing predominance of the mechanical system at the restoration of our second Charles, and with this the present fashionable views, not only of religion, morals, and politics, but even of the modern physics and physiology. You will not blame the earnestness of my expressions, nor the high importance which I attach to this work; for how, with less noble objects, and less faith in their attainment, could I stand acquitted of folly, and abuse of time, talents, and learning, in a labour of three-fourths of my *intellectual* life? Of this work, something more than a volume has been dictated by me, so as to exist fit for the press, to my friend and enlightened pupil, Mr. Green; and more than as much again would have been evolved and delivered to paper, but that, for the last six or eight months, I have been compelled to break off our weekly meeting, from the necessity of writing (alas! alas! of *attempting* to write) for purposes, and on the subjects of the passing day.—Of my poetic works, I would fain finish the "Christabel." Alas! for the proud time when I planned, when I had present to my mind, the materials, as well as the scheme, of the Hymns entitled Spirit, Sun, Earth, Air, Water, Fire, and Man: and the Epic Poem on—what still appears to me the one only fit subject remaining for an Epic Poem—Jerusalem besieged and destroyed by Titus.
. . .

CVII

TO CHARLES AUGUSTUS TULK

February 12, 1821

My DEAR SIR,—"They say, Coleridge! that you are a Swedenborgian!" "Would to God," I replied fervently, "that *they* were *anything*." I was writing a brief essay on the prospects of a country where it has become the *mind* of the nation to appreciate the evil of public acts and measures by their next consequences or immediate occasions, while the *principle* violated, or that *a* principle is thereby violated, is either wholly dropped out of the consideration,

or is introduced but as a garnish or ornamental common-
place in the peroration of a speech! The deep interest was
present to my thoughts of that distinction between the
Reason, as the source of principles, the true celestial influx
and *porta Dei in hominem aeternum*, and the *Understanding;* with
the clearness of the proof, by which this distinction is
evinced, *viz.* that vital or zoo-organic power, instinct, and
understanding fall all three under the same definition *in
genere*, and the very additions by which the definition is
applied from the first to the second, and from the second to
the third, are themselves expressive of degrees only, and in
degree only deniable of the preceding. (*Ex. gr.* 1. Reflect on
the *selective* power exercised by the stomach of the caterpillar
on the undigested miscellany of food, and, 2, the same
power exercised by the caterpillar on the outward plants,
and you will see the order of the conceptions.) 1. Vital
Power=the power by which *means are adapted* to proximate
ends. 2. Instinct=the power *which adapts* means to proximate ends. 3. Understanding=the power which adapts
means to proximate ends according *to varying circumstances*.
May I not safely challenge any man to peruse Hüber's
"Treatise on Ants," and yet deny their claim to be included
in the last definition. But try to apply the same definition,
with any extension of degree, to the reason, the absurdity
will flash upon the conviction. First, in reason there is and
can be no *degree*. *Deus introit aut non introit*. Secondly, in
reason there are no *means* nor ends, reason itself being one
with the ultimate end, of which it is *the* manifestation.
Thirdly, reason has no concern with *things* (that is, the
impermanent flux of particulars), but with the permanent
Relations; and is to be defined even in its lowest or theoretical
attribute, as the power which enables man to draw *necessary*
and *universal* conclusions from particular facts or forms,
ex. gr. from any three-cornered thing, that the two sides of a
triangle are and must be greater than the third. From the
understanding to the reason, there is no continuous *ascent*
possible; it is a metabasis εἰς ἄλλο γένος even as from the
air to the light. The true essential peculiarity of the human
understanding consists in its capability of being irradiated
by the reason, in its recipiency; and even this is *given* to it
by the presence of a higher power than itself. What then

must be the fate of a nation that substitutes Locke for logic, and Paley for morality, and one or the other for polity and theology, according to the predominance of Whig or Tory predilection. Slavery, or a commotion is at hand! But if the gentry and *clerisy* (including all the learned and educated) do this, then the nation does it, *or* a commotion is at hand. *Acephalum enim, aura quamvis et calore vitali potiatur, morientem rectius dicimus, quam quod vivit.* With these thoughts was I occupied when I received your very kind and most acceptable present, and the results I must defer to the next post. With best regards to Mrs. Tulk,

Believe me, in the brief interval, your obliged and grateful

S. T. COLERIDGE.

CVIII

TO DERWENT COLERIDGE

ST. JOHN'S COLLEGE, CAMBRIDGE

Jan. 11, 1822

MY DEAR DERWENT,—I sit with my pen only not touching the paper, and my head hanging over it; but *what* to write and with what purpose I write at all, I know not. What can I urge that would not be the mere repetition of counsels already urged with all the weight that my urgent entreaties could add to them, so often both before you went to Cambridge and since? What that would not be the echo of echoes, which of late have *volleyed* round you in a circle—admonitions, which Friends of all ages, of your own and even your Juniors have given you—and I trust, that wisest and most faithful of all Friends, your Conscience? To study to the injury of your health, and the undermining of your constitution—was *this* required of you? You have long known both my Judgement and my wishes in this respect; that a Senior Wranglership with the first Classical medal as it's appendage would be a poor compensation to *me* and in *my* thoughts for shattered nerves and diseased digestive organs. You cannot do without intermissions of study, without recreation and such as society only can afford you? Be it so!

But is dissipation of mind and spirit, the fit recreation of a student? or not rather the fever fit, of which your studies are like to be the cold, feeble and languid Intermittents? "I have known instances of Drinkers and Whore-mongers," said Mr. Montague to me a few weeks [since]; "but in all my long experience of Cambridge never did I see or hear of any one instance of a high wrangler with or without classical honors, who was a man of Pleasure, Dress, and Family Visiting." Even extra-collegiate Society, by preference and in a larger proportion than that of his own college, and the flaring about with distinguished Graduates etc.,—never yet made even if it left a man friends in his own College—who are after all from obvious causes the friends most likely to stick by us. But extra-academic society, Concerts, Balls, Dressing, and an hour and a half or two Hours not seldom devoted to so respectable a purpose— O God! even the disappointment as to your success in the University, mortifying as I feel it, arising from such causes and morally ominous, as it becomes in your particular case and with the claims, that *you* must recognize on your exertions, is not the worst. This accursed Coxcombry, like Deianira's gift, sends a ferment into the very life-blood of a young man's Sense and Genius—and ends in a schirrus of the Heart. I know by experience what the social recreation is that does an undergraduate good. In my first Term, and from October till March, I read hard, and systematically. I had no acquaintance much less suitable (*i.e.*) studious, companion in my own College. Six nights out of seven, as soon as Chapel was over, I went to Pembroke, to Middleton's (the present Bp. of Calcutta) Rooms—opened the door without speaking, made and poured out the Tea and placed his cup beside his Book— went on with my Aeschylus, or Thucydides, as he with his Mathematics, in silence till $\frac{1}{2}$ past 9—then closed our books at the same moment—the size and college Ale came in—and till 12 we had true Noctes Atticae which I cannot to this hour think of without a strong emotion. With what delight did I not resume my reading in my own Rooms at Jesus each following morning. Think you a Ball or a Concert or a Lady Party, or a Literary Club, would have left me in the same state—and your studies Mathematical? Were it possible even that it could be otherwise; yet your character must suffer. From ill-health or any other cause, if should your (I quote Middleton's sweet sonnet to me)

> young Ambition feel the wound
> Of blighted Hope and Laurels sought in vain—

what sort of *solution* will be the one current? He *trifled* away his success! . . . O Derwent would to God you would so act as to permit you to attribute all the kindness shewn to you to your own account, with some plausibility at least— I am not angry, Derwent! but it is calamitous that you do not know how anxiously and affectionately

I am your *Father*—

S. T. COLERIDGE.

PS. I hear that you are Premier or Secretary of a Literary Club—about old Books— If such things did not dissipate your time and thought, they *dissipate* and perplex your *character*. They are well maybe for B.A.s and M.A.s.

CIX

TO JOHN MURRAY

Highgate, January 18, 1822

. . . Briefly then, I feel strongly persuaded, perhaps because I strongly wish it, that the Beauties of Archbishop Leighton, selected and methodized, with a (better) Life of the Author, that is, a biographical and critical introduction as Preface, and Notes, would make not only a useful but an interesting POCKET VOLUME. "Beauties" in general are objectionable works—injurious to the original author, as disorganizing his productions, pulling to pieces the well-wrought *crown* of his glory to pick out the shining stones, and injurious to the reader, by indulging the taste for unconnected, and for that reason unretained single thoughts, till it fares with him as with the old gentleman at Edinburgh, who eat six kittywakes by way of *whetting* his appetite— "whereas" (said he) "it proved quite the contrary: I never sat down to a dinner with so little." But Leighton's principal work, that which fills two volumes and a half of the four, being a commentary on St. Peter's Epistles, verse by verse, and varying, of course, in subject, etc., with almost every paragraph, the volume, I propose, would not only bring together his finest passages, but these being afterwards arranged on a principle wholly independent of the accidental place of each in the original volumes, and guided by their relative bearings, it would give a connection or at least a propriety of *sequency*, that was before of necessity wanting. It may be worth noticing, that the editions, both the one in three, and the other in four volumes, are most grievously misprinted and otherwise disfigured. Should you be disposed to think this worthy your attention, I would even send you the proof *transcribed*, sheet by sheet, as it should be printed, though doubtless by sacrificing one copy of Leighton's works, it might be effected by references to volume, page, and line, I having first carefully corrected the copy. Or, should you think another more likely to execute the plan better, or that another name would better promote its sale, I should by no means resent the preference, nor feel any mortification for which, the having occasioned the existence of such a work, tastefully selected and judiciously arranged, would not be sufficient compensation for,

> Dear sir, your obliged,
>
> S. T. COLERIDGE.

C X

TO T. ALLSOP

June 29, 1822

. . . It is a great advantage both in respect of Temper, Manners, and the Quickening of the Faculties, for a Boy to have a Sister or Sisters a year or two older than himself. But I devote this brief scroll to Feeling: so no more of disquisition, except it be to declare the entire coincidence of my experience with yours as to the very rare occurrence of strong and deep Feeling in conjunction with free power and vivacity in the expression of it. The most eminent Tragedians, Garrick for instance, are known to have had their emotions as much at command, and almost as much on the surface, as the muscles of their countenances; and the French, who are all Actors, are proverbially heartless. Is it that it is a false and feverous state for the Centre to live in the Circumference? The vital warmth seldom rises to the surface in the form of sensible Heat, without becoming hectic and inimical to the Life within, the only source of real sensibility. Eloquence itself—I speak of it as habitual and at call—too often is, and is always like to engender, a species of histrionism.

In one of my juvenile poems (on a Friend who died in a Frenzy Fever), you will find that I was jealous of this in myself; and that it is (as I trust it is), otherwise, I attribute mainly to the following causes:—A naturally, at once searching and communicative disposition, the necessity of reconciling the restlessness of an ever-working Fancy with an intense craving after a resting-place for my Thoughts in some *principle* that was derived from experience, but of which all other knowledge should be but so many repetitions under various limitations, even as circles, squares, triangles, &c., &c., are but so many positions of space. And lastly, that my eloquence was most commonly excited by the desire of running away and hiding myself from my personal and inward feelings, *and not for the expression of them*, while doubtless this very effort of feeling gave a passion and glow to my thoughts and language on subjects of a general nature, that they otherwise would not have had. I fled in a Circle, still overtaken by the Feelings, from which I was evermore fleeing, with my back turned towards them; but above all, my growing deepening conviction of the *transcendency of the moral to the intellectual*, and the inexpressible comfort and inward strength which I experience myself to derive as often as I contemplate truth realized into Being by a human Will; so that, *as I cannot love without esteem, neither can I esteem without loving.* Hence I *love* but few, but those I love as my own Soul; for I feel that without them I should—not indeed cease to be kind and effluent, but by little and little become a soulless fixed Star, receiving no rays nor influences into my Being, *a Solitude which I so tremble at, that I cannot attribute it even to the Divine Nature. . . .*

CXI

TO THE REV. RICHARD CATTERMOLE

Grove, Highgate, March 16, 1824

. . . Ignorant of the way in which a more formal notification of my grateful Acceptance of the Honor of a Royal Associateship should be conveyed, and uncertain whether it is usual and regular to have a more distinct and explicit acknowledgement layed before the Council, than the present Letter can be considered, I must press on your kindness for the requisite information and likewise at what date from the Election of an Associate the "Essay" should be delivered. I observe too in the printed papers, which I owe to your kind attention, that every Associate is required to state the particular department of Letters, to which (relatively at least to the Society) he would be understood as being especially attached. For myself, I have chosen a double branch, but with a common stem, namely:

1. The reciprocal oppositions and conjunctions of Philosophy, Religion, and Poetry (the heroic and dramatic especially, the former comprizing both the homeric and hesiodic species, and the latter including the lyric) in the Gentile World, and in early Greece more particularly. To which, as an offset, I add, the differences between the Popular, the Sacerdotal and the—if I may hazard the word—*Mysterial*, Religion of civilized Paganism.

2. The influences of the Institutions and Theology of the Latin Church on Philosophy, Language, Science and the Liberal Arts from the VIIth to the XIVth Century.

In whatever point I am informal or deficient, I presume on your goodness to set me right: and shall receive every correction, your superior judgement and information shall suggest, as an additional ground and motive for the high respect, with which I am,

Reverend Sir,

Your obliged humble Servant,

S. T. COLERIDGE.

CXII

TO MR. DUNN

[1824?]

DEAR SIR,—I do not doubt that within a few days my settlement with my publishers will enable me to settle with you. In the meantime be so good as to accept the enclosed, in addition to the account, as fairly your dues. The Day I left Highgate for Ramsgate a letter arrived, contained a draft for the sum, £26; but it was accompanied with a request in relation to a late unfortunate Public Measure, and Controversy or Feud in this District, which (had the compliance been less repugnant to my own private and disinterested conviction) I could not but resent as compromising my independence. Meantime, for motives of great literary and not trifling pecuniary magnitude, I was under the necessity of changing at a heavy present loss, the whole . . . of the work I was engaged on, and of re-writing the whole. I mention these circumstances to you in confidence in justice to myself. For be assured, that few things have given me so much pain as this Delay has done. A few months' hard work will enable me hereafter to be beforehand with you rather than behind.

With true respect,

Your obliged,

S. T. C.

PS.—I entreat you, be careful not to have any note delivered to me unless I am alone and passing your door.

CXIII

TO THE REV. S. MENCE

Saturday, January 12th, 1825

MY DEAR SIR,—Miss Bradley, whom you met yesterday, is the Daughter of a very dear Friend of Mr. and Mrs.

Gillman's, and in fact little less than a Father in the love and veneration of the Latter. Of course to Miss B. as the sole Relic of her departed Friend, she feels the duties of a Sister. When in addition to this I say, that Miss B. is liable by any unsettling forces, bodily or circumstantial, to get into "a *low way*," commencing with extreme nervousness and disposition to *eddy* round and round any past event or act, that had distressed or perplexed her, and (if not cut short) passing into temporary Melancholia, I have told you all.

Now at present there are symptoms that give us reason to apprehend a coming-on of this complaint—and for a week past her thoughts have been running on some supposed omission or other, of which she fears to have been guilty, in her preparation for the last Sacrament, she received. My dear Sir! I cannot help thinking, that Jer. Taylor and other great and good men who wrote and preached treatises, "Way to the Altar" etc., etc.—commonly in the hands of Church-Members, were not sufficiently on their guard against the effects many passages in these books (not to say the *Spirit* of some of them) are calculated to produce on nervous females under the irritation of Debility. However, Miss B. has been importuning Mrs. Gillman to consent to her consulting *you*. She conceives that she ought not to suffer her mind to be quieted by any thing, I might say as I am not a Minister etc. But from you it possibly might be of medicinal effect to be told, what a sad perversion of the Eucharist it is to turn a means of grace, and comfort, an act of confidence in the promises and all-sufficient Death of the Redeemer, into a thorn-brake of Scruples and a Snare for the Conscience—that if there was any thing to be done or to be done otherwise, her duty is to do it for the future— and that brooding on the past, and fretting and perplexing herself about what cannot be recalled, is the way to consume the very strength of mind and purpose, requisite for the due performance of what she has to do—[and] shews a great ignorance of the true meaning of Christian Repentance, and argues a distrust in the Saviour's assurances.

I take the liberty of throwing out these hints, from the apprehension that the triflingness or mistaken nature of the Lady's Scruples might (Judging unfairly, perhaps, of you by what happened to myself) *put you out.*

As far as there is any thing more than what may be best attributed to the state of bodily health in these Scruples and Hauntings, I have most often found, that there is an *irresolution* at the bottom, a clinging at the *core* of the Heart to a somewhat, which they can neither resolve to eject or retain— and that such persons are sure to do the thing which, when done, they then set about repenting *of*. Rarely, I fear, do they repent *from* it.

> With great regard and respect,
> My dear Sir
> Your's truly
> S. T. COLERIDGE.

CXIV

TO THE REV. EDWARD COLERIDGE

[July, 1825]

. . . I was asked, some few months past, and by no ordinary man, what course of Reading I would recommend as most likely to store the mind with various information and to fit it for the use and application of the knowledge acquired. I answered without hesitation—Make a point of reading a certain portion of the Scriptures, beginning from the Beginning, every day—whether a chapter or 20 verses, or ten, must depend on the times which your other Duties permit you to allot to your private studies. Only read with the determination to leave no means untried, that are in your power, to understand *every Word*—Use as your general Help, the Crohis Sacri [?], or Po[o]le's Synopsis—to which you may add (if you can conveniently procure the Work) the Commentaries of Cocceius.

And by this direct your other reading (and even in your chance reading which I by no means discourage, bear this in mind—) Travels, Voyages, Antiquities etc., etc.—as the object, you have in view at the particular time, may suggest or require. Supposing you to have read only three chapters a week on an average, I dare anticipate that at the end of a year you will yourself be surprized at the quantity and variety of information, that you will have acquired, and which will hang together in your mind—so as literally to become a *memoria technica*, by it's unity of purpose, or convergence *ad idem*. The Hebrew Sages said: Three things were, before the World was: the Law, Messiah and the Last Judgement. With better taste and without a play on words, we may say—The World was made for the Gospel—or that Christianity is the final Cause of the World. If so, the Idea of the Redemption of the World must needs form the best central Reservoir for all our knowledges physical or personal. Every fact must find it's place as a component point in some one or other of the converging Radii.

The Bishop of London has been pleased to express a *most* favorable Opinion of my Work—in consequence of which the celebrated Mr. Blanco White procured the Volume, and a few days after the "Friend." He then procured an introduction to me from Sir George and Lady Beaumont, and yesterday he came from Chelsea in a Glass Coach for he is in very infirm health and spent the whole day from 1 o'clock till ½ past 9 with me. It was highly gratifying to me to find, that he had the "Aids to Reflection" at his fingers' ends: and it would scarcely become me to repeat the strong expressions, he used, respecting the effect produced on his mind and views of Christianity by the (paragraphs) p. 130-140, and the Disquisitions on Original Sin and Redemption, with that on the Diversity of Reason and Understanding. Have you seen White's answer to Catholic Butler? I am not surprized, that the Bishop regards it as one of the most Momentous Works that have appeared on the subject of the true character of the Romish Religion—Blanco White is by general admission a man of strong mind; and it is impossible to be with him and not feel that he is a very good man.

He was so anxious to have the Addenda, I intended for you, transcribed in order to be bound in his Copy, that I let him have them and shall bring them with me when I come.

And now let me conclude this prolix *Author's* Letter, and take another sheet for my immediate business—In the mean time, May God bless you, my dear Nephew! and all with whom your happiness and well-being are or are about to be intertwined.

S. T. COLERIDGE.

C X V

Friday, July 8, 1825

MY DEAR SIR,—The bad weather had so far damped my expectations, that, though I regretted, I did not feel any disappointment at your not coming. And yet I hope you will remember our Highgate Thursday conversation evenings on your return to town; because, if you come once, I flatter myself, you will afterwards be no unfrequent visitor.

At least, I have never been at any of the town conversazioni, literary, or artistical, in which the conversation has been more miscellaneous without degenerating into *pinches*, a pinch of this, and a pinch of that, without the least connection between the subjects, and with as little interest. You will like Irving as a companion and a converser even more than you admire him as a preacher. He has a vigorous and (what is always pleasant) a GROWING mind, and his character is MANLY throughout. There is one thing, too, that I cannot help considering as a recommendation to our evenings, that, in addition to a few ladies and pretty lasses, we have seldom more than five or six in company, and these generally of as many professions or pursuits. A few weeks ago we had present, two painters, two poets, one divine, an eminent chemist and naturalist, a major, a naval captain and voyager, a physician, a colonial chief justice, a barrister, and a baronet; and this was the most numerous meeting we ever had. . . .

Such has been the influence of the "Edinburgh Review" that in all Edinburgh not a single copy of Wordsworth's works or of any part of them could be procured a few months ago. The only copy Irving saw in Scotland belonged to a poor weaver at Paisley, who prized them next to his Bible, and had all the "Lyrical Ballads" by heart—a fact which would cut Jeffrey's conscience to the bone, if he had any. I give you my honour that Jeffrey himself told me that *he* was himself an enthusiastic admirer of Wordsworth's poetry, but it was necessary that a Review should have a character.

S. T. COLERIDGE.

CXVI

TO MR. HUNT
BOOKSELLER, RAMSGATE

[1827]

DEAR SIR,—The "Courier" sent and now returned contains only the same debate, as I had before in the "New Times." If there be a Thursday's Morning Paper at liberty, you would oblige me by letting me have it—and likewise, the 3rd and 4th Vol. of Bruce, a great and for a long time most ungratefully calumniated Man—His remarks on Polygamy, Vol. II, p—178-185 are curious; but if the facts are accurate, still I would rather deem them the *effect* of Polygamy than believe God by a law imposed on Nature the Author and Sanction of a Practice, evidently and notoriously incompatible with the development of our Moral Being—the source of such frightful depravity and degeneracy. "It was not so from the beginning." *i.e.* It does not result from any necessity of God's making, but from hardness of heart—*ex. gr.* predatory Wars, murder of male Captives, Sale of the females—then (avarice prevailing over Blood-thirstiness) sale of male and female, and that accursed Slave Trade which Bruce likewise vindicates!! These, however, are but specks in a Diamond. By the bye, the fact that Christianity in any genuine or ennobling form exists only in the Northern, or rather in the temperate climates, and degenerates in proportion to the increase of Heat—say from the 40 Deg. of N.L. to the Equator—is one of deep interest for a reflecting mind. [signature excised]

CXVII

TO THE REV. EDWARD COLERIDGE

[1827]

. . . On running my eye over this sheet, I see that I have been putting your patience to the Trial—but prosing and egotistic as it would appear, and indeed *be*, to [an]other, yet as a chapter in my Biographia Interior it will have an interest for You—were it but as a humble instance of an earnest desire on the part of an Individual to know what he is, and to be what he knows, in an age where beyond all former precedent (such at least is my belief) men seem to regulate their conduct by the Worldling's maxim—*viz.* to sacrifice the world to himself in all worldly concerns, and himself to the world in all spiritual ones. . . .

I have just received Henry's Book; and have read almost half—I have received both amusement and instruction from it; it cannot but have an extensive circulation—One fault there is, that I would fain have had removed, an imitation of Southey, especially in his Letters from Portugal and Spain in the frequent obtrusion of offensive images, Sweating etc., and again a little too much and too often of eating. Like Southey, too, his Levities border now and then on the *Odd*, and Grotesque—and he has not Southey's excuse. For I can venture to say to *you*, *sub rosa*, that all men of cold constitutions are naturally immodest, as far as their Notions of Morality will permit. So Southey—while he keeps clean of *one* outlet, he does not care what filth comes out of the other Orifices. But I could almost be angry with Henry for that very indiscreet and *ex omni parte* objectionable Episode on *Maria*, not to say a word of the infantile Silliness of "but you do not know Maria, nor me either." It is idle to suppose that the Author of so interesting a Book, the only one that supplies any real reliable information on the present state and manners of the West Indies should not be generally known; and that he was the Bishop's Cousin and Secretary— nor is it possible but that the Book will be read in Madeira— and I know too many melancholy instances of the trouble, nay, ruin brought on Individuals and whole Families in Naples, Sicily, and Minorca by the unthinking *Blab* of English Tourists and Travellers. Read, my dear Edward! the last paragraph—about carrying off a Nun, as a good Joke etc. not to say, that the impertinence and coxcombry of a perfect Stranger making love and asking a Young Lady— Are you happy? would have surprized me less from my own Derwent. I may be too severe—the Snows may have drifted from my head downwards and inwards—but believe me, the source of it is in affectionate apprehension of the consequences. Mr. Gillman who has read it already twice over, when he should have been in bed, pronounces it a *right* pleasant Book and with a deal of valuable information in it—but he too complains of the Southeianisms. I shall take my very first leisure evening, possibly tomorrow, to finish it, and shall then write to Henry. . . .

CXVIII

TO ALARIC WATTS

Grove, Highgate, Sunday Midnight, Sept. 14, 1828

MY DEAR SIR,—Your wish shall at all events be complied with—whether my suspicion be well or ill-grounded that you have not received what yet to the best of my recollection I left at your own door, two letter-sheets of verses. The first a pretended fragment of Lee, the tragic poet, containing a description of Limbo, and according to my own fancy containing some of the most forcible lines and with the most original imagery that my niggard Muse ever made me a present of—for to compare one's own with one's honor is I trust no offence against humility and may stand free of the adage, comparisons are odious. I likewise explained to you in what manner by false and lying pretences that the edition of my Poems so many years pretendedly in hand was only stopped through a miscalculation in the quantity, so that it could not come for want of two sheets more (observe, when against my own judgement I assented to Mr. Gillman's wish, that I place the poems at his disposal, it was expressly stated that there should be no unprinted poems—had I possessed any of any importance in a finished state there would have been still many and serious objections to their making their first appearance in a collection of poems written in youth and earliest manhood—and that all that was or should be required of me, was to give a list of my printed poems, marking those which, I thought ought to be omitted). Well—by pretences which I am entitled to call false—for at this very time the first volume was not put to the press, certainly not all printed, Mr. G.'s mind was so worked on as repeatedly to intreat me to give what I had. I persevered in returning a denial, accompanied with very clear and (as has been proved) correct anticipations of the reprehension, it would bring on me, for three weeks—and this to a man, who had never heard the word, No! from my mouth during the eleven years I had been as a brother in his family. At length, I could only say "Mrs. G. has the copies—do what you will"—and being asked whether they would not want correcting, I replied, "Of these I *must* have the *proofs*—and by that time I shall be in a fitter mood to supply the defects." Could it have been believed, that the true cause of these applications was to steal (it was no better) these original poems for a Work, I had never even *heard of*—and to aggravate this by an impudent paragraph, of "thanks to Mr. Coleridge for his great liberality"!! And the copies, the great part of which had been hastily transcribed from old and not very legible scraps in my own hand, were (as how should they be otherwise, no proof having been sent?) infamously incorrect! Not only no pecuniary acknowledgment was afterwards proffered, but to this hour I have never received a copy of the book which, indeed, I should have sent back—tho' 50£ was offered to me for less than the third part of them. Nay! this was not the worst. By dint of the most solemn assurances made by a Mr. Frazer, which had they been verified would not much have amended the matter, my friend (you will consider this letter as strictly *confidential*) at that time in weak health, and his mind heavily oppressed and disturbed by the unhappy state of his younger son and other causes, let out of his hands a sonnet addressed to me by the Revd. Blanco White in a friendly letter which containing a passage respecting his elder son in his first term at Oxford I had given to Mrs. Gillman—and this spite of his honor thrice deliberately pledged to the contrary Mr. Bijou published. What must have been, what were my feelings to whom all this was utterly unknown, when I received a letter from Mr. White mildly complaining of my having published his sonnet! And at the same hour I first heard of *your* letter!

But to make an end of this shameful business, after the publication of the "Bijou," a pretended half sheet proof of some of the additional poems were sent up, all in scraps, doubtless struck off for the purpose and so infamously incorrect that it was impossible to correct them, in the ordinary way. Accordingly, after various attempts I sent the scraps back; and in dry words desired Mr. Pickering to send up a more decent proof immediately. None came and I took the trouble to write out the poems neatly and expressly—ordered the omission of several, especially that article in half prose, and that the contribution under my name in the "Amulet" (that, which as perhaps the most polished of my compositions both the dialogue and the poem, was *my own* weakness and facility!) has occasioned me another embarrassment, as you will find below—No attention was paid to my request, no notice taken, no further proof sent, and to this [day] have I had not a single copy of my poems, except an imperfect one that had been brought up to our house by Mr. B. Montagu, to prove to Mr. G. that the volumes were really on the eve of being finished. Lastly Mr. Pickering has sent word to Mr. Gillman, that he has printed only 300 copies (for which we have *his* word), and therefore there can be no profit, as it will merely pay the expence of paper and printing. I have as good grounds as an author well can have, for believing that an edition of a thousand, properly advertised and befriended as it might have been, would have been sold within a twelve month. Had it been, as it should have been, in two volumes, there is scarce a doubt of it. As it is, neither I nor Mr. G. will ever receive a penny. I dare prophesy so much for Mr. Pickering and company. . . .

CXIX

TO WILLIAM SOTHEBY

9 Waterloo Plains, Ramsgate,
November 9, 1828

MY DEAR SIR,—It is a not unfrequent tragico-whimsical fancy with me to imagine myself as the survivor of

This breathing House not built with hands,
This body that does me grievous wrong—

and an Assessor at it's dissection—infusing, as spirits may be supposed to have the power of doing, this and that thought into the mind of the Anatomist. *Ex. gr.* Be so good as to give a cut just *there*, right across the umbilical region—there lurks the fellow that for so many years tormented me on my first waking! or—a stab *there*, I beseech you, it was the seat and source of that dreaded subsultus which so often threw my Book out of my hand, or drove my pen in a blur over the paper on which I was writing! But above all and over all has risen and hovered the strong half-wish, half-belief, that there would be found if not the justifying reason yet the more than the palliation and excuse—if not the necessitating *cause*, yet the originating occasion, of my heaviest—and in truth they are so bad that without vanity of self-delusion I might be allowed to call them my *only* offences against others, *viz.* Sins of Omission. O if in addition to the disturbing accidents and Taxes on my Time resulting from my almost constitutional pain and difficulty in uttering and in persisting to utter, NO! if in addition to the distractions of narrow and embarrassed Circumstances, and of a poor man constrained to be under obligation to generous and affectionate Friends only one degree richer than himself, the calls of the day forcing me away in my most genial hours from a work in which my very heart and soul were buried, to a five guinea task, which fifty persons might have done better, at least, more effectually for the purpose; if in addition to these, and half a score other intrusive Draw-backs, it were possible to convey without inflicting the sensations, which (suspended by the stimulus of earnest conversation or of rapid motion) annoy and at times overwhelm me as soon as I sit down alone, with my pen in my hand, and my head bending and body compressed, over my table (I cannot say, desk)—I dare believe that in the mind of a competent Judge what I have performed will excite more surprize than what I have omitted to do, or failed in doing. Enough of this— which I have written because I sincerely respect you as a good *man*, to whose merits as an accomplished Scholar and Man of Letters his Rank and Fortune give a moral worth, as rendering this dedication of his time and talents an act of free choice, and *exemplary*—and by the beneficial influence of such an example in that class of society, in which the cultivation of the Liberal Arts and Sciences affords the best, almost I had said the only, security against Languor, and a refined but enfeebling Sensuality—the more enfeebling, in proportion as it is diffused and inobtrusive. This is indeed the true meaning and etymon of the *Liberal* Studies—*digna libero viro*—those, which beseem a Gentleman, as containing in themselves and in their reflex effects on the students over

mind and character a sufficing motive and reward—and are
followed for Love not Hire. Because you possess my inward
respect, I would not stand in a worse light, than the knowledge of the whole truth would place me, or forfeit more
of your esteem than my conscience assents to. I need not
tell you, that pecuniary motives either do not act at all—
or are of that class of stimulants which act only as Narcotics:
and as to what *people* in *general* think about me, my mind
and spirit are too awefully occupied with the concerns of
another Tribunal, before which I stand momently, to be
much affected by it one way or other. . . .

CXX

TO JOSEPH HENRY GREEN
33 LINCOLN'S INN FIELDS

[Postmark, Highgate, March 29, 1832]

MY VERY DEAR FRIEND,—On Monday I had a sad trial
of intestinal fever and restlessness; but thro' God's mercy,
without any craving for the poison which for more than
30 years has been the great debasement, and misery of my
existence. I pray that God may have mercy on me—tho'
thro' unmanly impatiency of wretched sensations that produced a disruption of my mental continuity of productive
action I have for the better part of my life yearned towards
God, yet having recourse to the evil *Being* [. . . ? . . .] a
continued act of thirty years self-poisoning thro' cowardice
of pain, and without other motives—say rather without
motive—but solely thro' the goad *a tergo* of unmanly and
unchristian fear, God knows! I in my inmost soul acknowledge all my sufferings as the necessary effect of his Wisdom,
and all the alleviations as the unmerited graces of his Goodness. Since Monday I have been tranquil; but still, placing
the palm of my hand with its lower edge on the navel, I
feel with no intermission a death-grasp, sometimes relaxed,
sometimes tightened, but always present; and I am convinced, that if Medical Ethics permitted the production
of an Euthanasy, and a Physician convinced that at my
time of Life there was no rational hope of revalescence to
any useful purpose, should administer a score drops of the

purest Hydrocyanic acid, and I were immediately after opened (as is my earnest wish) the state of the mesenteric region would solve the problem. . . .

CXXI

TO HENRY NELSON COLERIDGE

May 9, 1832

MY DEAR HENRY,—Tho' with the most willing faith in the validity of the grounds for your esteem and regard and friendly and affectionate liking for the Revd. Milman, I cannot yet persuade myself that it was consistent with either the modesty of a much younger man, or with the delicacy of a gentleman and a scholar, to consent and undertake, at the instance and under the auspices of an Anthropoid like Murray of Albemarle Street, to select, omit, correct and by a few felicitous interpolations improve and adapt my poetic works in a very abridged form, a sort of a half-brew between "Rifacciamento" and portable soup, to the correct taste of the age—I say, I cannot without hypocrisy pretend to acquiesce in the right feeling of this—first, because as aforesaid, Mr. Milman tho' a fellow of Brasenose, was yet my junior—and secondly, because (God forgive me if I speak the truth in a spirit of arrogance) at 5 and 20 I had not forgotten but thrown aside or precipitated more than the Revd. Milman had or ever will have the chance of possessing—and nathless he may be not a whit the less respectable Being in his eyes, in whose alone it is of any importance. Do not, my dear Henry! so utterly misunderstand me as to infer that I feel, much less cherish any dislike or resentment toward Milman. . . .

CXXII

TO MISS ANNE R. SCOTT
PRECINCTS, CANTERBURY

Grove, Highgate,
Monday, August 26, 1833

. . . Dorothy Wordsworth, the Sister of our great Poet, is a Woman of Genius, as well as manifold acquirements; and

but for the absorption of her whole Soul in her Brother's
fame and writings would, perhaps, in a different style have
been as great a Poet as Himself. Once, she being present,
I told one of these good stories, the main drollery of which
rests on their utter *unbelievability as actual fact*—viz.—of a
Surgeon, who having restored to life two or three persons
who had attempted to hang or drown themselves; and
having been afterwards importuned by them for Help and
Maintenance on the plea, that having forced life upon them
against their own will and wish, he was bound to support it;
had ventured, that he would never interfere in any such
accidents without having first ascertained whether the individual wished it or no. On a summer day while on a
water-party, one of the Rowers in some unaccountable way
fell over-board and disappeared. But on his re-emersion the
Surgeon caught hold of his Hair and lifting his head and
chest above the water said—Now, my good Fellow! did
you really mean to drown yourself! What is your own
wish?—O—O. O—! (sobbed out the man)—a sickly *Wife*—
and seven small children!—"Ha! *poor* Fellow! No Wonder
Then!"—exclaimed the Surgeon, and instantly popped him
under again. The party were all on the brink of a loud
Laugh, when Dorothy Wordsworth, with tears sparkling in
her eyes, cried out—Bless me! but was not that very *inhuman!*—This stroke of exquisite Simplicity and true single-
ness of heart, made us almost roll off our chairs; but was
there one of the Party, that did not love Dorothy the more
for it? I trust, not one. . . .

CXXIII

TO T. E. FINDEN

November 6, 1833

Mr. S. T. Coleridge presents his respects to Mr. Finden.
There are two pen or pencil Drawings of him at Highgate,
the one (and in point of something like expression, the
best) taken off hand, some 15 years ago, by Mr. Leslie,—
another, done very recently, by a young German Artist,—
a likeness certainly; but with such unhappy pensity of the

Nose and idiotic Drooping of the Lip, with a certain pervading *Woodeness* of the whole countenance, that it has not been thought guilty of any great Flattery by Mr. Coleridge's Friends. Such as they are however, either is at Mr. Finden's service—or perhaps the Artist may be inclined to see them and to select one or the other and judge whether the defects of the later portrait may not be removed. Mr. S. T. C. will be found at home, "The Grove, Highgate" any day after 1 o'clock. His ill health does not permit him to mention an earlier hour. A Friend of S. T. Coleridge's wrote under a portrait of him—"A glow-worm with a pin stuck thro' it, as seen in broad day-light."

CXXIV

TO MRS. ADERS

[1833]

My dear Mrs. Aders,—By my illness or oversight I have occasioned a very sweet vignette to have been made in vain—except for its own beauty. Had I sent you the lines that were to be written on the upright tomb, you and our excellent Miss Denman would have, first, seen the dimension requisite for letters of a distinctly visible and legible size; and secondly, that the homely, plain *Church-yard Christian* verses would not be in keeping with a Muse (though a lovelier I never wooed), nor with a lyre or harp or laurel, or aught else *Parnassian* and allegorical. A rude old yew-tree, or a mountain ash, with a grave or two, or any other characteristic of a village rude church-yard,—such a hint of a landscape was all I meant; but if any figure, rather that of an elderly man

> Thoughtful, with quiet tears upon his cheek.

(Tombless Epitaph. See "Sibylline Leaves.")

But I send the lines, and you and Miss Denman will form your own opinion.

Is one of Wyville's proofs of my face worth Mr. Aders' acceptance? I wrote under the one I sent to Henry Coleridge the line from Ovid, with the translation, thus:

S. T. COLERIDGE, AETAT. SUAE 63.

Not / handsome / was / but / was / eloquent /
"Non formosus erat, sed erat facundus Ulysses."

Translation.

"In truth, he's no beauty!" cry'd Moll, Poll, and Tab;
But they all of them own'd He'd the gift of the Gab.

My best love to Mr. Aders, and believe that as I have
been, so I ever remain your affectionate and trusty friend,

S. T. COLERIDGE.

PS. *I* like the tombstone very much.

The lines when printed would probably have on the
preceding page the advertisement—

EPITAPH ON A POET LITTLE KNOWN, YET BETTER KNOWN BY
THE INITIALS OF HIS NAME THAN BY THE NAME ITSELF

S. T. C.

Stop, Christian Passer-by! Stop, Child of God!
And read with gentle heart. Beneath this sod
A Poet lies: or that, which once seemed He.
O lift one thought in prayer for S. T. C.
That He, who many a year with toilsome breath
Found Death in Life, may here find Life in Death.
Mercy for Praise—*to be forgiven* for Fame
He asked, and hoped thro' Christ. DO THOU the Same.

CXXV

TO JOSEPH HENRY GREEN

Highgate, March 18, 1834

MY DEAREST FRIEND,—This night, Monday, 9 o'clock
Harriet noticed a peculiar red streak or splash, running
from my left eye which had been for many days at morn and

night *weepy* and *weak*, down the cheek along by that old tumor of my left cheek, which I date from the Top of the Brocken, Hartz. Midsummer midnight, 1800, or 1799, I forget which. I have been the whole day unwell, and with old duodenal umbilical uneasiness while I lay in bed, and when I got up sick and wind-strangled— As soon as Harriet noticed the red streak, I immediately felt by the application of my finger a sensible difference of heat between that [and] the corresponding part near the other ear—and sent for Mr. Taylor, who deems it a slight erysipylas, *Erisypelatoid Erythema*—the very thing that carried off my acquaintance-friend Sir George Beaumont, who had likewise the same tumour, in nape of the neck and below the chin, in 5 days from its first very unalarming appearance. Now as I should like to see you before I went, if to go I am, and leave with you the sole Depositorium of my mind and aspirations, which God may suggest to me—therefore if you can, come to me during the week.

S. T. COLERIDGE.

SUPPLEMENT

SUPPLEMENT

LITERARY CRITICISM

CHAPMAN

[HOMER TRANSLATED]

I am so dull, that neither in the original nor in any translation could I ever find any wit or wise purpose in this poem. The whole humour seems to lie in the names. The frogs and mice are not frogs and mice, but men, and yet they do nothing that conveys any satire. In the Greek there is much beauty of language, but the joke is very flat. This is always the way in rude ages;—their serious vein is inimitable,—their comic low and low indeed. The psychological cause is easily stated, and copiously exemplifiable.

BARCLAY

"ARGENIS"

Heaven forbid that this work should not exist in its present form and language! Yet I cannot avoid the wish that it had, during the reign of James I, been moulded into an heroic poem in English octave stanza, or epic blank verse;—which, however, at that time had not been invented, and which, alas! still remains the sole property of the inventor, as if the Muses had given him an unevadible patent for it. Of dramatic blank verse we have many and various specimens;—for example, Shakespeare's as compared with Massinger's, both excellent in their kind:—of lyric, and of what may be called Orphic, or philosophic, blank verse, perfect models may be found in Wordsworth; of colloquial blank verse there are excellent, though not perfect, examples in Cowper;—but of epic blank verse, since Milton, there is not one.

It absolutely distresses me when I reflect that this work, admired as it has been by great men of all ages, and lately, I hear, by the poet Cowper, should be only not unknown to general readers. It has been translated into English two or three times—how, I know not, wretchedly, I doubt not. It affords matter for thought that the last translation (or, rather, in all probability, miserable and faithless abridgment of some former one) was given under another name. What a mournful proof of the incelebrity of this great and amazing work among both the public and the people! For as Words-worth, the greater of the two great men of this age,—(at least, except Davy and him, I have known, read of, heard of, no others)—for as Wordsworth did me the honour of once observing to me, the people and the public are two distinct classes, and, as things go, the former is likely to retain a better taste, the less it is acted on by the latter. Yet Tele-machus is in every mouth, in every school-boy's and school-girl's hand! It is awful to say of a work, like the "Argenis," the style and the Latinity of which, judged (not according to classical pedantry, which pronounces every sentence right which can be found in any book prior to Boetius, however vicious the age, or affected the author, and every sentence wrong, however natural and beautiful, which has been of the author's own combination,—but) according to the universal logic of thought as modified by feeling, is equal to that of Tacitus in energy and genuine conciseness, and is as perspicuous as that of Livy, whilst it is free from the affecta-tions, obscurities, and lust to surprise of the former, and seems a sort of antithesis to the slowness and prolixity of the latter;—(this remark does not, however, impeach even the classicality of the language, which, when the freedom and originality, the easy motion and perfect command of the thoughts, are considered, is truly wonderful):—of such a work it is awful to say, that it would have been well if it had been written in English or Italian verse! Yet the event seems to justify the notion. Alas, it is now too late. What modern work, even of the size of the "Paradise Lost"—much less of the " Faery Queene "—would be read in the present day, or even bought or be likely to be bought, unless it were an instructive work, as the phrase is, like Roscoe's quartos of Leo X, or entertaining like Boswell's three of Dr. Johnson's conversations. It may be fairly objected—what work of surpassing merit has given the proof?—Certainly, none. Yet still there are ominous facts, sufficient, I fear, to afford a certain prophecy of its reception, if such were produced.

1803

SIR THOMAS BROWNE

"RELIGIO MEDICI" II

[They who to salve this would make the deluge particular, proceed upon a principle that I can no way grant, &c.]

But according to the Scripture, the deluge was so gentle as to leave uncrushed the green leaves on the olive tree. If then it was universal, and if (as with the longevity of the antediluvians it must have been) the earth was fully peopled, is it not strange that no buildings remain in the since then uninhabited parts—in America for instance? That no human skeletons are found may be solved from the circumstance of the large proportion of phosphoric acid in human bones. But cities and traces of civilisation? I do not know what to think, unless we might be allowed to consider Noah a *homo repraesentativus*, or the last and nearest of a series taken for the whole.

1808

"RELIGIO MEDICI" III

[And, truely, for the first chapters of *Genesis* I must confesse a great deal of obscurity . . .]

The second chapter of Genesis from v. 4, and the third chapter are to my mind, as evidently symbolical, as the first chapter is literal. The first chapter is manifestly by Moses himself; but the second and third seem to me of far higher antiquity, and have the air of being translated into words from graven stones.

1808

PEPYS

[To church and heard a good sermon of Mr. Gifford's at our Church, upon "seek ye first the Kingdom of Heaven and its righteousness, and all things shall be added to you." A very excellent and persuasive, good and moral sermon. He shewed, like a wise man, that righteousness is a surer moral way of being rich, than sin and villany.]

Highly characteristic. Pepys's only ground of morality was prudence—a shrewd understanding in the service of Self-love, his conscience. He was a *Pollard* man without the *top* (*i.e.*, the Reason as the source—of *Ideas*, or immediate yet not sensuous Truths, having their evidence in themselves; and the Imagination, or idealising Power, of symbols mediating between the Reason and Understanding); but on this account more broadly and luxuriantly branching out from the upper Trunk. For the sobriety and steadfastness of a worldly self-interest substitute inventive Fancy, Will-wantonness (*stat pro ratione voluntas*), and a humourous sense of the emptiness and dream-likeness of human pursuits— and Pepys would have been the *Panurge* of the incomparable Rabelais.

FIELDING

"JONATHAN WILD"

"Jonathan Wild" is assuredly the best of all the fictions in which a villain is throughout the prominent character. But how impossible it is by any force of genius to create a sustained attractive interest for such a groundwork, and how the mind wearies of, and shrinks from, the more than painful interest, the μισητόν of utter depravity,—Fielding himself felt and endeavoured to mitigate and remedy by the (on all other principles) far too large a proportion, and too quick recurrence, of the interposed chapters of moral reflection, like the chorus in the Greek tragedy,—admirable specimens as these chapters are of profound irony and philosophic satire. Chap. vi, Book 2, on Hats,—brief as it is, exceeds any thing even in Swift's "Lilliput," or "Tale of the Tub." How forcibly it applies to the Whigs, Tories, and Radicals of our own time.

Whether the transposition of Fielding's scorching wit (as B. iii, c. xiv) to the mouth of his hero be objectionable on the ground of *incredulus odi*, or is to be admired as answering the author's purpose by unrealizing the story, in order to give a deeper reality to the truths intended,—I must leave doubtful, yet myself inclining to the latter judgment.   27th Feb., 1832

GRAY

"ON A DISTANT PROSPECT OF ETON COLLEGE"

> Say, Father Thames, for thou hast seen
> Full many a sprightly race
> Disporting on thy margent green,
> The paths of pleasure trace;
> Who foremost now delight to cleave,
> With pliant arm, thy glassy wave?
> The captive linnet which enthral?
> What idle progeny succeed
> To chase the rolling circle's speed,
> Or urge the flying ball?
>
> *Gray*

This is the only stanza that appears to me very objectionable in point of diction. This, I must confess, is not only *falsetto* throughout, but is at once harsh and feeble, and very far the worst ten lines in all the works of Mr. Gray, English or Latin, prose or verse.

ROBERT ANDERSON

"LIFE OF PHINEAS FLETCHER"

[Anderson quotes "The Purple Island," Canto XII, stanza 38:
> "A dead man's skull supplied his helmet's place,
> A bone his club, his armour sheets of lead."

Yet the first of these terrific attributes is suggested by Spenser. . .]

Say rather, surgeon's apprentices' tricks!

How natural it is for a common-place mind to be delighted with common-place images, if tricked out in language! and yet not less, tho' differently, struck by the most *outré*. Sympathy with the trivial, wonderment at the monstrous, are the ground springs of a Scotch critic's judgment.   s.t.c.

GEORGE DYER

[That the principal and immediate aim of poetry is, to please, has been opposed by Julius Scaliger, and some other critics. But though I must admit that
omne tulit punctum qui, miscuit utile dulci,
yet will I still abide by Aristotle's and Plutarch's opinion, that the immediate object of poetry is, to please.]

Damned nonsense! But *why* does it please? Because it pleases? O mystery!—If not, some cause out of itself must be found. Mere utility it certainly is not—nor mere goodness—therefore there must be some third power, and that is beauty, i.e., that which *ought* to please. My benevolent friend seems not to have made an obvious distinction, between end and means.—The poet *must* always aim at pleasure as his specific *means;* but surely Milton did; and all ought to aim at something nobler as their end—viz.—to cultivate and predispose the heart of the reader, etc.

CHALMERS

"LIFE OF DANIEL"

[The justice of these remarks cannot be disputed, though some of them are rather too figurative for sober criticism.]

Most genuine! A figurative remark! If this strange writer had any meaning, it must be:—Headly's criticism is just throughout, but conveyed in a style too figurative for prose composition. Chalmers's own remarks are wholly mistaken; —too silly for any criticism, drunk or sober, and in language too flat for any thing. In Daniel's sonnets there is scarcely one good line; while his Hymen's Triumph, of which Chalmers says not one word, exhibits a continued series of first-rate beauties in thought, passion, and imagery, and in language and metre is so faultless, that the style of that poem may without extravagance be declared to be imperishable English. 1820

SIR WALTER SCOTT
"THE HEART OF MIDLOTHIAN"

[Ch. xxxi.

Bunyan was, indeed, a rigid Calvinist.]

Calvinism never put on a less rigid form, never smoothed its brow and softened its voice more winningly than in the "Pilgrim's Progress."

Ch. xlv.

O, if the puir prodigal wad return, sae blythely as the good-man wad kill the fatted calf!—though Brockie's calf will no be fit for killing this three weeks yet!]

This is *wit*, head-work, a falsetto imitation of Shakespeare's Dame Quickly. Half a dozen read-worthy sentences might be written on the difference Sir Walter Scott forgot or never had learnt, that it is the weak memory that is discursive, not the strong feeling. Shakespeare would have made May leave off with "the fatted calf" and given the line following to a second character, Simple, Davy, or Shallow.

"QUENTIN DURWARD"

[Ch. xvi. Quentin's conversation with the Bohemian.]

Characterless or anti-characteristic as Scott's dialogues too commonly are, this is ultra-improbable, superlatively inappropriate.

JOHN GALT
"THE PROVOST"

This work is not for the many; but in the unconscious, perfectly natural irony of self-delusion, in all parts intelligible to the intelligent reader, without the slightest suspicion on the part of the autobiographer, I know of no equal in our literature. The governing trait in the Provost's character is nowhere caricatured. In the character of Betty, John's wife, or the beggar girl, intense selfishness without malignity, as a *nature*, and with all the innocence of a nature, is admirably portrayed. In the Provost a similar *self*ness is united with a *slyness* and a plausibility eminently successful in cheating the man himself into a happy state of constant self-applause. This and "The Entail" would alone suffice to place Galt in the first rank of contemporary novelists—and second only to Sir W. Scott in technique.

BARRY CORNWALL

"DRAMATIC SCENES AND OTHER POEMS"

Barry Cornwall is a poet, *me saltem judice:* and in that sense of the term in which I apply it to Charles Lamb and William Wordsworth. There are poems of great merit, the authors of which I should yet not feel impelled so to designate.

The faults of these poems are no less things of hope than the beauties. Both are just what they ought to be: *i.e.*, NOW.

If B.C. be faithful to his genius, it in due time will warn him that as poetry is the *identity* of all other knowledge, so a poet cannot be a *great* poet but as being likewise and inclusively an historian and naturalist in the light as well as the life of philosophy. All other men's worlds ($\kappa\acute{o}\sigma\mu o\iota$) are *his* chaos.

Hints *obiter* are—Not to permit delicacy and exquisiteness to seduce into effeminacy.

Not to permit beauties by repetition to become mannerism.

To be jealous of *fragmentary* composition—as epicurism of genius, and apple-pie made all of quinces.

Item, that dramatic poetry must be poetry *hid* in thought and passion, not thought or passion disguised in the dress of poetry.

Lastly, to be economic and withholding in similes, figures, &c.—They will all find their place sooner or later, each as the luminary of a sphere of its own. There can be no *galaxy* in poetry, because it is language, *ergo*, successive, *ergo*, every the smallest star must be seen singly.

There are not five metrists in the kingdom, whose works are known by me, to whom I could have held myself allowed to have spoken so plainly. But B.C. is a man of genius, and it depends on himself (competence protecting him from gnawing or distracting cares) to become a rightful *poet—i.e.*, a great man.

O! for such a man worldly prudence is transfigured into the highest spiritual duty. How generous is self-interest in *him*, whose true self is equal to all that is good and hopeful in all ages, as far as the language of Spenser, Shakespeare, and Milton shall become the mother tongue!

A map of the road to Paradise drawn in Purgatory on the confines of Hell by

S.T.C. July 30, 1819

P.S.—The pause after the second syllable in pentameter iambic blank verse is frequent in the poems of Mr. Southey and his imitators. But should it be imitated? Milton uses it, when the weight of the first iambic, trochee, or spondee of the second line requires a pause of preparation at the last foot of the preceding.

TABLE TALK

[FAUST]

C. Have you seen, Mr. F., anything of Lord Byron's poetry?

F. Nothing, Sir, but the Translation of "Faust."

C. And what do you think of that?

F. Being unacquainted, Sir, with the original I cannot speak of its merits as a translation. As a poem I think it meagre, nor do I conceive that the metres are adapted to the subject in English whatever they may be in German.

C. I have been asked why I did not translate the camp scenes in "Wallenstein." The truth is that the labour would have been immense, and besides it would not have been borne in English, to say nothing of the fact that Mrs. Barbould reviewed my translation of the rest of the play and abused it through thick and thin, so that it sold for wastepaper. I remember your uncle telling me that he had picked it up—he approved it, so did Canning to whom he showed it—and so might one or two more, but the edition sold for wastepaper.

F. Had you ever any thought of translating the "Faust"?

C. Yes, Sir, I had, but I was prevented by the consideration that though there are some exquisite passages, the opening chorus, the chapel and the prison scenes for instance, to say nothing of the Brocken scene where he has shown peculiar strength in keeping clear of Shakespeare, he has not taken that wonderful admixture of Witch Fate and Fairy but has kept to the real original witch, and this suits his purpose much better. I say that a great deal of it I do not admire, and some I reprobate. The conception of Wagner is bad: whoever heard of a man who had gained such wonderful proficiency in learning as to call up spirits &c. being discontented?

No, it is not having the power of knowledge that would make a man discontented—neither would such a man have suddenly become a sensualist. The discourses too with the pupil are dull. The Mephistopheles, or whatever the name is, is well executed, but the conception is not original. It was . . . who had before said, "The Devil is the great humourist of the world." There are other parts too which I could not have translated without entering my protests against them in a manner which would hardly have been fair upon the author, for those things are understood in Germany in a spirit very different from what they would infuse here in England. To give you an example, the scene where Mephistopheles is introduced as coming before the Almighty and talking with him would never be borne in English and this whole scene is founded on a mistranslation of a passage in Scripture, the opening of Job. You remember how Satan means properly one who goes his rounds, and hence it came to mean one of those officers whom the king in Eastern countries used to send round to see how his subjects were going on. This power was soon abused and the Satans used to accuse people falsely, and hence the word came to have the meaning now attached to it of a calumniator, a διάβολος, an accuser.

Now in the Book of Job (which is undoubtedly very ancient, before the law for there is no mention of the law in it, undoubtedly the most ancient book in the world) the word Satan meant only this officer, the prime vizier of the Sultan (you remember in the "Arabian Nights" the Caliph and his vizier are very fond of going their rounds for the same purpose). God Almighty is shown to us under the semblance of a mortal king holding his court, and his officer comes, as the book tells us, "from going his rounds on the earth and walking up and down in it," but mind there is nothing like malignity attached to him.

The king asks him concerning Job—the officer answers that he is a perfect man—but (adds he) "He has yet had no temptation; he is prosperous, and he might alter if his circumstances were altered."

The king then commands him to try and to destroy his possessions. (*N.B.*—This is a mistake, *He gives him leave.*)

Again on another day the same things happen and when the officer is asked about Job he says, "He is yet integer but many men will do this. I can say nothing for his integrity as long as his possessions only are touched; but stretch out your hand against his person and see if he will curse Thee then." It is evident that there is no suggestion, no evil in the officer at all—[indeed the belief in Angels and that sort of poultry is nowhere countenanced in the Old Testament and in the New, nowhere else.]

F. Indeed, Sir, I think I know a very strong passage.

C. Well, what is it?

F. Our Saviour tells his disciples when alone with them and apart that a certain kind of Devils goeth not out but by prayer and fasting.

C. Well, and what has that to do with Angels?

F. I beg your pardon, Sir. I thought you included devils in your feathered fowl.

C. There is nothing I say in the New Testament to countenance the belief in Angels. For what are the three first Gospels? Everyone must see that they are mere plain narrations, not of things as they are but of things as they appeared to the ignorant disciples—but when we come to John, Mr. F., there we find the difference. He told things as they were, and therefore you must not believe everything that you read implicitly; and with respect to Devils entering into a man, why it is quite absurd. What do we mean when we say a thing is in another? Why "in" is merely a relative term. [The argument, though I was compelled to assent to it, I am sorry to say was far above my comprehension, and therefore I could not catch it, still less bag it and carry it away,—however it proved that there could be no Devils and still less could there be Devils in a man.] Spirit therefore was not more in a man than it was out of him, the mistake arising from a misconception of the word *in*. As for all notions of men with wings, of course they are absurd in the extreme.

LETTER

TO ROBERT SOUTHEY

Greta Hall, Keswick, July 29, 1802

MY DEAR SOUTHEY,—Nothing has given me half the pleasure, these many, many months, as last week did Edith's heralding to us of a minor Robert; for that it will be a boy, one always takes for granted. From the bottom of my heart I say it, I never knew a man that better deserved to be a father by right of virtues that eminently belonged to him, than yourself; but beside this I have cheering hopes that Edith will be born again, and be a healthy woman. When I said, nothing had given me half the pleasure, I spoke truly, and yet said more than you are perhaps aware of, for, by Lord Lonsdale's death, there are excellent reasons for believing that the Wordsworth's will gain £5,000, the share of which (and no doubt Dorothy will have more than a mere share) will render

William Wordsworth and his sister quite independent. They are now in Yorkshire, and he returns in about a month *one of us* . . . Estliu's sermons, I fear, are mere moral discourses. If so, there is but small chance of their sale. But if he had published a volume of sermons, of the same kind with those which he has published singly, *i.e.*, apologetical and ecclesiastico-historical, *I am almost* confident, they would have a respectable circulation. To publish single sermons is almost always a foolish thing, like single sheet quarto poems. Estliu's sermon on the Sabbath really surprised me. It was well written in style, I mean, and the reasoning throughout is not only sound, but has a cast of novelty in it. A superior sermon altogether it appeared to me. I am myself a little theological, and if any bookseller will take the risque, I shall in a few weeks, possibly, send to the press a small volume under the title of "Letters to the British Critic concerning Granville Sharp's Remarks on the uses of the Definitive article in the Greek Text of the New Testament and the Revd. C. Wordsworth's six letters, to G. Sharp Esqr, in confirmation of the same, together with a Review of the Controversy between Horsley and Priestley respecting the faith of the Primitive Christians." This is no mere dream, like my "Hymns to the Elements," for I have written more than half the work. I purpose afterwards to publish a book containing Tythes and Church Establishment, for I conceit that I can throw great light on the subject. You are not apt to be much surprised at any change in my mind, active as it is, but it will perhaps please you to know that I am become very fond of History, and that I have read much with very great attention. I exceedingly like the job of Amadis de Gaul. I wish you may half as well like the job, in which I shall very shortly appear. Of its sale, I have no doubt; but of its prudence? There's the rub, "Concerning Poetry and the characteristic merits of the Poets, our contemporaries. "One volume Essays, the second Selections.—The essays are on Bloomfield, Burns, Bowles, Cowper, Campbell, Darwin, Hayley, Rogers, C. Smith, Southey, Woolcot, Wordsworth — the Selections from everyone who has written at all, any being above the rank of mere scribblers—Pye and his Dative Case Plural, Pybus, Cottle, etc., etc. The object is not to examine what is good in each writer, but what has *ipso facto* pleased, and to what faculties, or passions, or habits of the mind they may be supposed to have given pleasure. Of course Darwin and Worsdworth having given each a defence of their mode of poetry, and a disquisition on the nature and essence of poetry in general, I shall necessarily be led rather deeper, and these I shall treat of either first or last. But I will apprise you of one thing, that although Wordsworth's Preface is half a child of my own brain, and arose out of conversations so frequent that, with few exceptions, we could scarcely either of us, perhaps, positively say which first started any particular thought (I am speaking of the Preface as it stood in the second volume), yet I am far from going all lengths with Wordsworth. He has written lately a number of poems (thirty-two in all), some of them of considerable length (the longest one hundred and sixty lines), the greater number of these, to my feelings, very excellent compositions, but here and there a daring humbleness of language and versification, and a strict adherence to matter of fact, even to prolixity, that startled me. His alterations, likewise, in "Ruth" perplexed me, and I have thought and thought again, and have not had my doubts solved by Wordsworth. On the contrary, I rather suspect that somewhere or other there is a radical difference in our theoretical opinions respecting poetry; this I shall endeavour to go to the bottom of, and, acting the arbitrator between the old school and the new school, hope to lay down some plain and perspicuous, though not superficial canons of criticism respecting poetry. What an admirable definition Milton gives, quite in an "obiter" way, when he says of poetry, that it is "*simple, sensuous, passionate!*" It truly comprises the whole that can be said on the subject. In the new edition of the L. Ballads there is a valuable appendix, which I am sure you must like, and in the Preface itself considerable additions; one on the dignity and nature of the office and character of a Poet, that is very grand, and of a sort of Verulamian power and majesty, but it is, in parts (and this is the fault, *me judice*, of all the latter half of that Preface), obscure beyond any necessity, and the extreme elaboration and almost constrainedness of the diction contrasted (to my feelings) somewhat harshly with the general style of the Poems, to which the Preface is an introduction. Sara (why, dear Southey! will you write it always Sarah? Sara, methinks, is associated with times that you and I cannot and do not wish ever to forget), Sara said, with some acuteness, that she wished all that part of the Preface to have been in blank verse, and *vice versa*, etc. However, I need not say, that any diversity of opinion on the subject between you and myself, or Wordsworth and myself, can only be small, taken in a *practical* point of view.

I rejoice that your History marches on so victoriously. It is a noble subject, and I have the fullest confidence of your success in it. The influence of the Catholic Religion—the influence of national glory on the individual morals of a people, especially in the downfall of the nobility of Portugal, —the strange fact (which seems to be admitted as with one voice by all travellers) of the vileness of the Portuguese nobles compared with the Spanish, and of the superiority of the Portuguese commonalty to the same class in Spain; and the effects of colonization on a small and not very fruitful country; the effects important, and too often forgotten of absolute accidents, such as the particular character of a race of Princes on a nation—Oh what awful subjects these are! I long to hear you read a few chapters to me. But I conjure you do not let "Madoc" go to sleep. Oh that without words I could cause you to *know* all that I think, all that I feel, all that I hope concerning that Poem! As to myself, all my poetic genius (if ever I really possessed any *genius*, and it was not rather a mere general *aptitude* of talent, and quickness in imitation) is gone, and I have been fool enough to suffer deeply in my mind, regretting the loss, which I attribute to my long and exceedingly severe metaphysical investigations, and these partly to ill-health and partly to private afflictions which rendered any subject, immediately connected with feeling, a source of pain and disquiet to me.

*   *   *

Having written these lines, I rejoice for you as well as for myself, that I am able to inform you, that now for a long time there has been more love and concord in my house than I have known for years before. I had made up my mind to a very awful step, though the struggles of my mind were so violent, that my sleep became the valley of the shadows of Death and my health was in a state truly alarming. It did alarm Mrs. Coleridge. The thought of separation wounded her pride,—she was fully persuaded that deprived of the society of my children and living abroad without any friends I should pine away, and the fears of widowhood came upon her, and though these feelings were wholly selfish, yet they made her *serious* and that was a great point gained. For Mrs. Coleridge's mind has very little that is *bad* in it; it is an innocent mind; but it is light and *unimpressible*, warm in anger, cold in sympathy, and in all disputes uniformly *projects itself forth* to recriminate, insteading of turning itself inward with a silent self-questioning. Our virtues and our vices are exact antitheses. I so attentively watch my own nature that my worst self-delusion is a complete self-knowledge so mixed with intellectual complacency, that my quickness to see and readiness to acknowledge my faults is too often frustrated by the small pain which the sight of them gives me, and the consequent slowness to amend them. Mrs. C. is so stung with the very first thought of being in the wrong, because she never endures to look at her own mind in all its faulty parts, but shelters herself from painful self-enquiry by angry recrimination. Never, I suppose, did the stern, matchmaker bring together two minds so utterly contrariant in their primary and organical constitution. Alas! I have suffered more, I think, from the amiable propensities of my nature than from my worst faults and most erroneous habits, and I have suffered much from both. But, as I said, Mrs. Coleridge was made *serious*, and for the first time since our marriage she felt and acted as beseemed a wife and a mother to a husband and the father of her children. She promised to set about an alteration in her external manners and looks and language, and to fight against her inveterate habits of puny thwarting and unintermitting dyspathy, this immediately, and to do her best endeavours to cherish other feelings. I, on my part, promised to be more attentive to all her feelings of pride, etc., etc., and to try to correct my habits of impetuous censure. We have both kept our promises, and she has found herself so much more happy than she had been for years before, that I have the most confident hopes that this happy revolution in our domestic affairs will be permanent, and that this external conformity will gradually generate a greater inward likeness of thoughts and attachments than has hitherto existed between us. Believe me, if you were here, it would give you a *deep* delight to observe the difference of our minutely conduct towards each other, from that which, I fear, could not but have disturbed your comfort when you were here last. Enough. But I am sure you have not felt it tedious.

NOTES

NOTES

THE following abbreviations have been used:

A.P. for "Anima Poetae," 1895, ed. E. H. Coleridge.

B.L. for "Biographia Literaria," 1907, ed. Shawcross.

"Dykes Campbell" for "Complete Poetical and Dramatic Works," 1893.

L.R. for "Literary Remains," 1836, ed. H. N. Coleridge.

"Letters" for "Letters of Samuel Taylor Coleridge," 1895, ed. E. H. Coleridge.

"Life" for "Life of Samuel Taylor Coleridge," 1893, by J. Dykes Campbell.

"Poems" for "Poetical Works," 1912, ed. E. H. Coleridge.

S.C. for "Shakespearian Criticism," 1930, ed. T. M. Raysor.

T.T. for "Table Talk," 1835, ed. H. N. Coleridge.

U.L. for "Unpublished Letters of Samuel Taylor Coleridge," 1932, ed. E. L. Griggs.

POEMS

The two great modern editions of Coleridge's poems are:

(1) "Complete Poetical and Dramatic Works," 1893. Edited by Dykes Campbell ("Dykes Campbell" in these notes);

(2) "[Complete] Poetical [and Dramatic] Works," 1912. Edited by E. H. Coleridge ("Poems" in these notes).

The first is specially valuable for its explanatory notes, the second for its complete and almost completely accurate collation of all texts and all important MS. variants.

I have followed E. H. Coleridge in basing the text of these poems on Pickering's 1834 edition. Dykes Campbell uses Pickering's edition of 1829—on the grounds that it was "the last upon which Coleridge was able to bestow personal care and attention." E.H.C., on the other hand, had evidence to controvert this statement.

So far as the poems included here are concerned (excepting
"The Devil's Thoughts") the differences between the two texts
are small, and very rarely verbal. Whether a word should or
should not be italicized—divisions into stanzas—hyphenings of
double words: the problems seem to be as minute as that. E. H.
Coleridge made a few alterations in punctuation on his own
authority; most of these I have followed. He also seemed to have
a theory that past participles in "-ed" should be printed either
" 'd," "ed" or "èd," according to how they fitted into the metre.
Coleridge himself was inconsistent in his practice here, so I have
written them in full throughout (except in the case of the earlier
version of the "Ancient Mariner").

The notes to be found at the foot of a few pages of the text are
Coleridge's—those which he retained in 1834. His early practice
was to annotate much more fully.

Of those collections of Coleridge's poems which were published
in his lifetime the ones most frequently referred to in the text are:

"1796": "Poems on Various Subjects."

"1797": Second edition of the above.

"Lyrical Ballads": "Lyrical Ballads, with a few other poems,"
     1798.

"1800": Second edition of the above.

"1802": Third edition of the above.

"1803": Third edition of "Poems on Various Subjects."

"1805": Fourth edition of "Lyrical Ballads."

"Sibylline Leaves": "Sibylline Leaves, a collection of poems,"
     1817.

"1828": "The Poetical Works of S. T. Coleridge, including the
     dramas of Wallenstein, Remorse, and Zapolya."

"1829": Second edition of the above.

"1834": "The Poetical Works of S. T. Coleridge."

"*Sonnet*" (p. 3). First published 1796, where its title is "Effusion
XVIII." Dykes Campbell (p. 538) quotes a letter from Lamb:
"Call [them] sonnets, for heaven's sake, and not 'effusions'."

"*Life*" (p. 3). First published 1834. There are two MSS. of this
poem, on one of which is the note: "Sonnet written just after the
writer left the Country [*i.e.* Devonshire] in Sept. 1789, *aetat* 15".
He was really seventeen, but Coleridge was consistently incorrect
about his age.

p. 3, l. 22: His sister Ann's death followed that of her brother Luke, in 1790.

As a specimen of the kind of changes made by Coleridge when he was correcting from an early MS., the original MS. versions of the words he altered are quoted here:

p. 3, l. 25: barren Steep,
p. 3, l. 27: my ravished eye did sweep.
p. 3, l. 31: Till when death pours at length
p. 3, l. 33: While thought suspended lies in Transport's

"*On Imitation*" (p. 4). First published 1834.

"*Sonnet*" (p. 4). Many of Coleridge's early verses were first published in the "Watchman." Ll. 2-11 appeared in No. V within a longer poem "Recollection," which was made out of four such scraps fitted together. This sonnet was first published as it stands in "Sonnets from Various Authors," 1796.

"*To the Author of 'The Robbers'*" (p. 4). First published ("Effusion XX") in 1796, where Coleridge printed a note: "One night in Winter, on leaving a College-friend's room, with whom I had supped, I carelessly took away with me 'The Robbers' . . .," etc. His feelings are best described in the letter to Southey printed in "Letters," p. 96.

Successive changes made in the first six lines of the text represent efforts to avoid a "bull" (pointed out to him by Charles Lloyd), the sense being nearly "I wish to die, that nothing may stamp me mortal" (*see* "Dykes Campbell," p. 572, where Coleridge's half-serious affirmation that the last six lines of this sonnet are "strong and fiery" is quoted).

p. 4, l. 32: "The Father of Moor in the Play of 'The Robbers'. S.T.C." (Footnote, "1803").

"*To a Young Ass*" (p. 5). First published in the "Morning Chronicle," 30th December, 1794, where the words "in familiar verse" are added to the title.

This poem must be read in the context of the time when Coleridge wrote it, 1794, the year of Pantisocracy. At the end of this year his enthusiasm was already beginning to cool (*see* Index: "Pantisocracy"), and the "Morning Chronicle" version slightly

2 B

toned down the MSS., just as subsequent editions toned down the "Morning Chronicle"; *e.g.* equalitarian variants are:

p. 5, l. 13: MS. and "Chronicle" have "friendly" for the 1796 "gentle," and (l. 14) "scratch thy head" for "pat thy head."

p. 5, l. 19: The earliest MS. only has "Doth thy prophetic soul" for "Do thy prophetic fears".

p. 6, l. 1: In the second MS. (a letter to Southey) and in the "Chronicle" this line ran:

Of high-souled Pantisocracy to dwell,

which in turn is a contraction from seven lines contained in the first MS., the date of which was October, 1794:

Where high-souled Pantisocracy shall dwell!
Where Mirth shall tickle Plenty's ribless side,
And smiles from Beauty's Lip on sunbeams glide,
Where Toil shall wed young Health that charming Lass!
And use his sleek cows for a looking-glass—
Where Rats shall mess with Terriers hand-in-glove
And Mice with Pussy's Whiskers sport in Love.

p. 6, l. 9: MSS. and "Chronicle" have:

The tumult of some scoundrel Monarch's breast.

"Scoundrel Monarch—alter that," wrote Charles Lamb in a letter criticizing the whole poem as too trivial (*ref.* "Dykes Campbell," p. 573).

"*To the Nightingale*" (p. 6). First published 1796.

p. 6, l. 28: *Cf.* "Il Penseroso," l. 62.

p. 6, l. 37: Coleridge was married 4th October, 1795. He did not reprint this poem after 1803.

"*The Eolian Harp*" (p. 7). First published 1796. The present title was added in 1803. In 1796 the titles read as follows: "Effusion XXXV. Composed August 20th, 1795, at Clevedon, Somersetshire." Dykes Campbell suggests that the occasion was a preliminary visit to the honeymoon cottage. Successive textual changes are not very important and are mainly concerned with the elaboration of the thought contained between ll. 23 and 35, p. 7. At the end of 1796 Coleridge considered it his best poem, though he regarded the obviously contemporary "Religious Musings" as his *magnum opus*.

"*Reflections*", etc. (p. 9). First published "Monthly Magazine," October, 1796, where the title is "Reflections on entering into active life. A Poem which affects not to be Poetry." Presumably this refers to the experimental diction. *E.g.* in the "Monthly Magazine" l. 17 is arranged and italicized thus:

And said it was a *blessed little place.*

"*To a Young Friend*" (p. 11). First published in "Poems on the Death of Priscilla Farmer." By her Grandson, 1796. The "Friend" was Charles Lloyd.

"*To the Rev. George Coleridge*" (p. 13). First published 1797, where it forms the Dedication. In a copy of this edition Coleridge wrote: "N.B. If this volume should ever be delivered according to its direction, *i.e.* to Posterity, let it be known that the Reverend George Coleridge was displeased and thought his character endangered by the Dedication."

p. 13, l. 35: "*as the Manchineel,*". Coleridge criticises the over-use of this simile in "Biographia Literaria." (*See* p. 209.)

p. 14, l. 5: "*one Friend,*". (*See* the letter to Poole, p. 525.)

"*This Lime-tree Bower my Prison*" (p. 15). First published in the "Annual Anthology," 1800. At the time this poem was written not only Lamb (without Mary) was a guest but also the Wordsworths, negotiating for their Alfoxden house.

p. 17, *Footnote: Cf.* a MS. note in copy of Gilbert White's "Works," 1802, now in the British Museum (Vol. II, p. 10). Writing of a letter on birds and their different ways of flying, he says: "This letter has disappointed me. I have myself made by collection [?] a better table of characters of Flight and Motion."

"*The Rime of the Ancient Mariner*" (pp. 18, 19 *et seq.*). First printed in the "Lyrical Ballads," 1798. There are three principal accounts of the genesis of this poem, contained in:

(1) "Biographia Literaria," Chapter XIV, where Coleridge describes the original plan of the "Lyrical Ballads." (*See* p. 247 of this volume.)

(2) Dorothy Wordsworth's note, 20th November, 1797:

We have been on another tour: we set out last Monday evening at half-past four. The evening was dark and cloudy;

we went eight miles, William and Coleridge employing themselves in laying the plan of a ballad, to be published with some pieces of William's.

(3) Wordsworth's account, given to the Reverend Alexander Dyce and passed on by him to H. N. Coleridge:

"The Ancient Mariner" was founded on a strange dream, which a friend of Coleridge had, who fancied he saw a skeleton ship, with figures in it. We had both determined to write some poetry for a monthly magazine, the profits of which were to defray the expenses of a little excursion we were to make together. "The Ancient Mariner" was intended for this periodical, but was too long. I had very little share in the composition of it, for I soon found that the style of Coleridge and myself would not assimilate. Besides the lines (in the fourth part)—

> And thou art long, and lank, and brown,
> As is the ribbed sea-sand—

I wrote the stanza (in the first part)—

> He holds him with his glittering eye—
> The Wedding-Guest stood still,
> And listens like a three-years' child:
> The Mariner hath his will.—

and four or five lines more in different parts of the poem, which I could not now point out. The idea of "*shooting an albatross*" *was mine; for I had been reading* "*Shelvocke's Voyages*," *which probably Coleridge never saw.* I also suggested the reanimation of the dead bodies, to work the ship. (*See* "Dykes Campbell," p. 594.)

The above is expanded in a note dictated by Wordsworth to Miss Fenwick, where it is specified that the tour started from Alfoxden. "We set off and proceeded along the Quantock Hills...." ("Dykes Campbell," p. 594). The original intention, apparently, had been for Wordsworth and Coleridge to write alternate cantos, as Southey and Coleridge had written alternate acts of "Robespierre." How quickly they found this impossible is told in the Prefatory Note to "The Wanderings of Cain" ("Poems," p. 286).

It is scarcely necessary to say that the classical essay on "Sources," —"The Road to Xanadu" of Professor Lowes—deals largely with the "Ancient Mariner"; and that it is an essential commentary on the whole poem, and the intricate processes of its creation.

Text: I have printed the poem with the earliest version, of 1798, in italics on the left, and the latest version, of 1834, on the right. The chief interest of the many differences lies in the fact that in the earlier version Coleridge was following more closely and more obviously the literary fashion of the time. The majority of the alterations incorporated in the familiar text are to be found on its second appearance, in 1800, when Coleridge's taste for these ephemeralities seems already to have diminished. It may also have been that his confidence in the poem was shaken by its indifferent reception and by the doubts of Wordsworth, who firmly enumerated "Great Defects" in the poem in his Preface (to the second edition of "L.B.") in 1800. Further and final corrections were made when the poem was printed in "Sibylline Leaves" (where the marginal glosses appeared for the first time).

More than one literary tendency is exemplified in the early text. First the ballad diction, the archaic—sometimes pseudo-archaic—spelling, and with this the "simplicity." The vogue for these things dated officially from the success of Percy's "Reliques"; but major and minor poets, from James Thomson and Shenstone to Chatterton and Gilbert West, had shown similar inclinations since near the beginning of the century. Gray ("Works," Gosse, II, p. 90) spoke of himself and his friends as being "all enraptured and enmarvailed" by West's imitations of Spenser. It was one of the many eighteenth century mannerisms which became "signs of the Romantic revival" in the hands of the new poets. The success of Burns marked the climax of the fashion, and by 1800 it was dying. (*But see* the Letter of 1797 [p. 573] for evidence that "ancientness" was not even by that year generally popular.)

The other *fin de siècle* romanticism which the early version showed, and which Coleridge seemed soon to have regretted, was the graveyard and churchyard gloominess, the charnel-house horror, which was gradually giving way to the more popular and more refined haunted moats of Mrs. Radcliffe (whose books were favourably reviewed by Coleridge in 1794, *see* p. 203). Though this mode was fashionable even after the "Ancient Mariner" was written, Coleridge successfully eliminated in the second edition the few false notes in his poem which seem due to it.

The differences in spelling all through are obvious. Examples of changed words are the "Pheere" of 1798 (part iii, p. 28, l. 27) changed to "mate" in 1800, and "eldritch" (part iv, p. 32, l. 15) changed first to "ghastly" in 1800 and then, in 1817, to "rotting."

In part i, p. 22, l. 9, "The Marineres gave it biscuit-worms," was considered too uncouth by Coleridge in 1800. A modification

of the "horrors" is the omission in that year of the stanza beginning p. 28, l. 28, in the early text. The ballad simplicity of stanzas
like the one beginning "The Marineres all 'gan pull the ropes,"
(p. 40) was thought pedestrian in 1800, and so on.

pp. 18, 19: *Title*. In the "Lyrical Ballads" of 1800 (this includes "Lyrical Ballads" 1802, 1805, the "Ancient Mariner" text
of which does not differ from 1800) the sub-title "A Poet's
Reverie" was added. Probably omitted later because of Lamb's
objections: "It is as bad as Bottom the Weaver's declaration that
he is not a lion, but only the scenical representation of a lion."
(From a letter to Wordsworth, 30th January, 1801. Lamb continues: "For me, I was never so affected with any human Tale.
After first reading it, I was totally possessed with it for many
days," etc. (*v.* "Works," Lucas, VI, 209).

p. 25, l. 18: "*The furrow followed free;*". In 1817 only, this
line is:

The furrow streamed off free;

Coleridge added to it the note:

In former editions the line was,

The furrow followed free:

But I had not been long on board a ship, before I perceived
that this was the image as seen by a spectator from the shore,
or from another vessel. From the ship itself, the *Wake* appears
like a brook flowing off from the stern.

p. 27, l. 9: For the "Jew, Josephus," and the "Michael Psellus"
of the margin *cf.* the list of books ordered by Coleridge in 1796
(p. 567); the first one mentioned in the list contains the "De
Daemonibus" of Psellus, for the use made of whose demonology
in the "Ancient Mariner" *cf.* "Xanadu," pp. 232-4.

p. 31, ll. 15 to 24: "*The Sun's rim dips; the stars rush out:*". These
ten lines are the most important late addition: they first appeared
in "Sibylline Leaves," but the date of composition is unknown.

p. 41, l. 15: "*sky-lark*". It will be seen that the earlier version
has "Lavrock." One of Professor Lowes' most striking comparisons is between this passage and Chaucer's "Romaunt of the
Rose." Professor Lowes ("The Road to Xanadu," p. 334) quotes
a text known to Coleridge:

There mightin men se many flockes
Of Turtels and of Laverockes. . . .
Thei song ther song, as faire and wel

As angels doen espirituell. . . .
Layis of love full wel sowning
Thei songin in ther jargoning.

"Christabel" (p. 58). First published in 1816 (with "Kubla Khan" and "The Pains of Sleep." It was not included in "Sibylline Leaves").

That the genesis of "Christabel" is comparable to that of the "Ancient Mariner" in its connection with Coleridge's miscellaneous reading was shown by E. H. Coleridge in his invaluable privately printed edition of the poem. He gives a list of half a dozen books, all obscure, which Coleridge "probably" had some reminiscence of, including the "De Daemonibus" of the Psellus mentioned in the Marginalia of the "Ancient Mariner." (*But see* Lowes ["Xanadu," p. 4n.] on the obscurity of this question.)

Up to within a few years of his death Coleridge believed that he would be able to finish this poem. He was constantly regretting its incompletion. (*See also* Index: "Christabel".) The most important sentences refer:

(1) To the delay in its publication, in a letter to Humphry Davy, 9th October, 1800:

The "Christabel" was running up to 1300 [*sic*] lines, and was so much admired by Wordsworth that he thought it indelicate to print two volumes with his name in which so much of another man's was included; and, which was of more consequence, the poem was in direct opposition to the very purpose for which the "Lyrical Ballads" was published, *viz.* our experiment to see how far those passions which alone give any value to extraordinary incidents were capable of interesting in and for themselves in the incidents of common life ("Letters," I, p. 337).

(2) To his difficulties with its composition, in a letter to Wedgwood from Keswick, 1st November, 1800:

But immediately on my arrival in this country I undertook to finish a poem which I had begun, entitled "Christabel," for a second volume of the "Lyrical Ballads." I tried to perform my promise; but the deep unutterable Disgust, which I had suffered in the translation of that accursed "Wallenstein," seemed to have stricken me with barrenness—for I tried and tried, and nothing would come of it. I desisted with a deeper dejection than I am willing to remember. The wind from the Skiddaw and Borrowdale was often as loud as wind need be— and many a walk in the clouds on the mountains did I take; but all would not do—till one day I dined out at the house of a neighbouring clergyman, and somehow or other drank so much wine, that I found some effort and dexterity requisite to balance myself on the hither edge of sobriety. The next day, my verse making faculties returned to me, and I proceeded successfully—till my poem grew so long and in Wordsworth's opinion so impressive, that he rejected it from his volume as disproportionate both in size and merit, and as discordant in it's character. In the meantime, I had gotten myself entangled in the old Sorites of the old Sophist, Procrastination— I had suffered my necessary business to accumulate so terribly, that I neglected to write to any one—till the Pain, I suffered from not writing, made me waste as many hours in dreaming about it, as would have sufficed for the letter-writing of half a life ("Unpublished Letters," I, p. 158).

(3) To his annoyance at the antagonistic reviews which appeared on its first publication—especially the notice in the "Edinburgh Review," which he ascribed to Hazlitt. This fills four pages of the last chapter of "Biographia Literaria," where he contrasts public assaults with private praise, attributing the former to personal enmity.

p. 58, l. 4: "*1797*,". Principally by the dates in Dorothy Wordsworth's Journal (*v. post*) E.H.C. proves that the year was really 1798.

p. 58, l. 6: In 1834 Coleridge cancelled the following passage from the Preface. It follows "Cumberland.":

Since the latter date, my poetic powers have been, till very lately, in a state of suspended animation. But as, in my very first conception of the tale, I had the whole present to my mind, with the wholeness, no less than the liveliness of a vision; I trust that I shall be able to embody in verse the three parts yet to come, in the course of the present year.

p. 58, ll. 12, 13: "*charges of plagiarism*". Actually, of course, these were often the other way. The poem was much circulated in manuscript. Byron acknowledged indebtedness in a note to the "Siege of Corinth," 1816, referring to "That wild and singularly original and beautiful poem." (It was his request to Murray that led to the publication of the poem.) But in half a dozen lines of Byron's works phrases are incorporated, sometimes without quotation marks. I have included Coleridge's discussion of the indebtedness of Scott among the Letters, p. 636. Scott had one of the MSS. read or recited to him by a friend in 1802. His "Lay of the Last Minstrel" appeared in 1805, similar in some of its metric and romantic qualities. Two passages, quoted apparently from memory, were used by him later as chapter headings to

"The Black Dwarf" and "The Betrothed." He made no public acknowledgment till 1830 (*see* the "Plagiarism Letter," p. 636).

p. 59, l. 7: "*Tu—whit!——Tu—whoo!*". In Cottle's "Early Recollections" (I, p. 138) a letter is printed from a friend describing Coleridge talking on a Harz Mountain excursion in 1799:

> He would perhaps comment at full length upon such a line as "Tu—whit!——Tu—whoo!" that we might not fall into the mistake of supposing originality to be its sole merit.

Since the rhythm of the opening stanza depends on how this line is spoken, it is worth mentioning that in three of the five MSS. the line is written "Tu—u—whoo! Tu—u—whoo!" Coleridge probably "sang" it.

p. 59, l. 11: "*Hath a toothless mastiff bitch;*". All the printed versions except 1834 print the following Tennysonian variant to this line (made in response to the wishes of an "honoured friend"):

> Hath a toothless mastiff which

A first tentative alteration was:

> Sir Leoline the Baron bold
> Hath a toothless mastiff old;

Charles Lamb suggested:

> Sir Leoline, the baron round,
> Hath a toothless mastiff hound.

p. 59, l. 21: "*It covers but not hides the sky.*". (*Cf.* p. 155.) By referring to the "Gutch Memorandum Book" and to Dorothy Wordsworth's Journals, it is possible to trace the evolution of some of these opening lines. On 25th January, 1798, she wrote:

> The sky spread over with one continuous cloud, whitened by the light of the moon.

On 27th February:

> The sky flat . . . a thin white cloud.

p. 60, l. 19: "*The one red leaf,*". The classic instance of indebtedness to or collaboration with Dorothy Wordsworth. On 7th March she wrote:

> One only leaf upon the top of a tree—the sole remaining leaf—danced round and round like a rag blown by the wind.

p. 63, l. 23: "*And jealous of the listening air*". This line was added in 1828.

p. 64, l. 10: "*My mother made it . . .*"   After this line in four MSS., but no printed versions, are added the lines:

> Nay, drink it up, I pray you do,
> Believe me it will comfort you.

Cf. the rather prosaic MS. version of "And faintly said, ' 'tis over now!' " (p. 64, l. 36):

> And faintly said I'm better now.

p. 65, l. 31: "*Behold! her bosom . . .*"   In MSS.:

> Are lean and old and foul of hue.

follows this line.

p. 65, l. 33: "*O shield her! shield sweet Christabel!*". Coleridge's alteration of the first edition, which read:

> And must she sleep by Christabel.

The alterations in this part of the text were used by the adverse critics as evidence of hidden immoralities, secret theories that Geraldine was really a man, etc. The "Examiner" review (2nd June, 1816, probably also by Hazlitt) said:

> There is something disgusting at the bottom of his subject which is but ill glossed over by a veil of Della Cruscan sentiment and fine writing, like moonbeams playing on a charnel-house, or flowers strewed on a dead body.

p. 70, l. 1: "*Alas! they had been friends in youth;*". The "Edinburgh Review" suggested that the lines beginning here seemed the only passage which could possibly be said to contain poetical merit, "and even these are not very brilliant, nor is the leading thought original——"

"*The Conclusion to Part II*" (p. 76): These lines were originally written in a letter to Southey, 6th May, 1801. E.H.C. tries to show that the passage was not so disconnected with the rest of the poem as appears, but had some kind of significance of contrast or analogy. It may, he thinks, like "Where is the grave of Sir Arthur O'Kellyn?" have been a fragment of the Third Part. In these years following the birth of Hartley, Coleridge's letters and notebooks are full of records of child-habits and psychology.

"*Fire, Famine, and Slaughter*" (p. 77). First published 8th January, 1798, in the "Morning Post," anonymously. In "Sibylline Leaves," in 1828, in 1829 and in 1834, an Apologetic Preface is prefixed. In spite of Coleridge's affection for it, and his belief that it was his "happiest effort in prose composition," it is too long to be included here. The Preface begins by describing a certain dinner party in 1803 at which this anonymous and provocative poem was mentioned in my presence. "I perceived that my illustrious friend [his host, Sotheby] became greatly distressed on my account; but fortunately I was able to preserve fortitude and presence of mind enough to take up the subject without exciting even a suspicion how nearly and painfully it interested me." (De Quincey, "Works," XI, p. 84, gives a different account of the incident, inferring that Coleridge was flustered, that everyone saw the joke except him, that the more put out he became the more the guests "smoked" him.) The Preface then passes, without connecting links, to a comparison between Milton and Jeremy Taylor.

The differences between early and late texts are numerous but unimportant. Small capitals are used for the personifications in the first edition—"printer's-devil's personifications," as Coleridge was to call them later.

"*Frost at Midnight*" (p. 79). First published in 1798 (in a quarto volume with "Fears in Solitude" and "France: an Ode").

p. 79, l. 28: "*Only that film*,". In early editions there is a note:

In all parts of the kingdom these films are called *strangers* and supposed to portend the arrival of some absent friend.

Most of the alterations in the text are compressions. In the first edition the concluding lines were:

Or whether the secret ministery of cold
Shall hang them up in silent icicles,
Quietly shining to the quiet moon,
Like those, my babe! which ere tomorrow's warmth
Have capped their sharp keen points with pendulous drops,
Will catch thine eye, and with their novelty
Suspend thy little soul; then make thee shout,
And stretch and flutter from thy mother's arms
As thou wouldst fly for very eagerness.

"*Lewti*" (p. 81). First published in the "Morning Post," 13th April, 1798, signed "Nicias Erythraeus."

The text underwent many alterations. There are three MS. versions in existence, the first of which starts:

High o'er the silver rocks I roved
To forget the form I loved;
In hopes fond fancy would be kind
And steal my Mary from my mind.

In a later version "Cora" is substituted for "Mary," and this is finally erased for "Lewti." (After the betrothal to Sarah Fricker, many of the female names in the poems were thus altered.)

The mention of "Mary" [Evans] connects the poem with a date at least as early as 1794, and in an interesting note Professor Lowes ("Xanadu," p. 513) points out how long Bartram's "Travels," a book of which 1798 poems show intimate knowledge, had been a favourite with Coleridge. For even in its earliest version "Lewti" contains many reminiscences, including the name "Tamaha" (p. 81, l. 20).

It was originally intended that "Lewti" should be included in the 1798 "Lyrical Ballads," but at the last moment the sheets were withdrawn and "The Nightingale" was substituted.

In the "Morning Post" there are two mediocre additional stanzas which Coleridge cut later.

p. 82, l. 29: "*Hush!*". In "Sibylline Leaves" this was printed "Slush!" but corrected in the Errata ("for *Slush* r. *Hush*").

p. 83, l. 6: "*Voice of the Night! had I the power*". Before "Sibylline Leaves" this line was:

Had I the enviable power.

Lamb had said that "enviable" would damn the finest poem. (*Ref.* "Dykes Campbell".)

"*Fears in Solitude*" (p. 83). First published in 1798 (in the quarto pamphlet, *see* p. 727).

To an autograph MS. Coleridge appended the following note:

N.B. The above is perhaps not Poetry,—but rather a sort of middle thing between Poetry and Oratory—*sermoni propriora.* —Some parts are, I am conscious, too tame even for animated prose.

In this copy, after the sub-title, C. adds: "The Scene the Hill, near Stowey."

The variations in the texts (one text is a long extract quoted in the "Friend," No. II, 8th June, 1809) are extensive but not important.

p. 89, l. 9: "*In such a quiet and surrounded nook,*". Up to "Sibylline Leaves," "nook" was "scene." For his later dislike of this word, *cf.* p. 423.

"The Nightingale" (p. 89). First published 1798. The references in this poem are, of course, to Wordsworth, Dorothy, Hartley and the Stowey country, including the brook of "This Lime-tree Bower My Prison." Dykes Campbell quotes a letter of Wordsworth, written to "Christopher North" (? date):

> What false notions have prevailed from generation to generation of the true character of the Nightingale. As far as my Friend's Poem, in the "Lyrical Ballads," is read, it will contribute greatly to rectify these.

The famous ll. 43 to 47 (p. 91, ll. 2 to 6) describing the nightingale's notes are taken word for word from a fragment in the "Gutch Memorandum Book," and the ll. 102 to 105 (p. 92, ll. 24 to 27) describing Hartley's tears in the moonlight from a rough memorandum a few pages later.

Footnote (p. 90): In 1834 the footnote ended at the words "a line in Milton."

"To ———" (p. 92). First published 1836, in "Literary Remains." From the "Gutch Memorandum Book."

"Kubla Khan" (p. 93). First published 1816 (with "Christabel" and "The Pains of Sleep"). E. H. Coleridge has proved that Coleridge was wrong in his date (1797, *see* Preface) for the composition of this poem. It was really May, 1798.

For the best discussion of the important questions associated with this poem and the manner of its composition, "The Road to Xanadu" must again be cited—for its important discovery that supposed evidence of an earlier version is based on a misreading, its drastic treatment of a Coleridge psycho-analyser who did not verify his references, its full consideration of the effects of drugs on Coleridge's inspiration, and, especially, for its anatomisation of the strange faculty by which he created the images of a poem out of a synthesis of phrases half-remembered from the descriptive prose of travel books. For it was not only the Purchas sentence which Coleridge incorporated. This passage called up others, and Professor Lowes successfully follows the trail through eight or nine authors, including Seneca, Milton and Herodotus.

Preface (p. 93): It was Coleridge's habit to write Prefaces (from the time of the 1796 "Poems" onwards). A well-known letter from Lamb to Wordsworth (26th April, 1816) suggests that Coleridge's motive lay in the fact that he, too, felt his printed poems were diminished for lack of the sound of his own voice reciting them:

> Coleridge is printing "Christabel" by Lord Byron's recommendation to Murray, with what he calls a vision, "Kubla Khan," which said vision he repeats so enchantingly that it irradiates and brings heaven and elysian bowers into my parlour when he sings it or says it; but . . . I fear lest it should be discovered by the lantern of typography and clear reducting to letters no better than nonsense or no sense.

p. 93, l. 15: "*words of the same substance,*". The actual words are:

> In Xamdu did Cublai Can build a stately Palace, encompassing sixteene miles of plaine ground with a wall, wherein are fertile Meddowes, pleasant springs, delightfull Streames, and all sorts of beasts of chase and game, and in the middest thereof a sumptuous house of pleasure, which may be removed from place to place (Purchas, 1617, p. 472).

p. 94. ll. 16, 17: The Greek is from Theocritus, I, 145.

p. 94, l. 18: "*As a contrast to this vision,*". In the first edition "The Pains of Sleep" followed "Kubla Khan."

"*The Homeric Hexameter*" (p. 96).

"*The Ovidian Elegiac Metre*" (p. 96). These were first published in the "Friendship's Offering" for 1834. For Mrs. H. N. Coleridge's defence of Coleridge's unacknowledged indebtedness to Schiller for these lines, and their general connection with the "Plagiarism" question, *see* "Dykes Campbell," p. 616.

"*Lines*" (p. 96). First published "Morning Post," 17th September, 1799. The lines occur in a letter to Mrs. Coleridge, 17th May, 1799.

"*The Devil's Thoughts*" (p. 97). First published "Morning Post," 6th September, 1799. The poem has a complex history. More than half a dozen versions were printed before Coleridge's death, with as many different texts. The poem created a small sensation when it first appeared, and a re-issue of that number of the "Morning Post" was sold. Shelley imitated it in 1812 ("The Devil's Walk"), Byron in 1813 ("The Devil's Drive," which he "took from Porson's 'Devil's Walk'."). Porson died in 1808, but the strange attribution of authorship to the editor of Euripides does not seem to have been publicly denied. For later editions, with illustrations by Cruikshank (1830, "By Professor Porson"), Landseer, etc., *see* "Notes and Queries," 7th ser., VIII, p. 161. (*Ref.* "Dykes Campbell.")

The version here given of 1834 differs completely from those even of 1828 and 1829, being seven stanzas longer. Such major differences between 1828 and 1834 are rare.

p. 100, l. 27: "*General* ——". One MS. fills the space with "Gascoigne," another with "Tarleton."

"*Love*" (p. 101). First published in "Morning Post," 21st December, 1799. The differences between the first version and the practically final version of the 1800 "Lyrical Ballads" are extensive and interesting because they illustrate again Coleridge's connection with contemporary taste:

(1) In the "Morning Post" the title is "Introduction to the Tale of the Dark Ladie" (*i.e.* a fragment first published in 1834).

(2) The whole poem is set within romantic stanzas which were afterwards omitted. The first verses are:

> O leave the Lilly on its stem;
>   O leave the Rose upon the spray;
> O leave the Elder-bloom, fair Maids!
>   And listen to my lay.

> A Cypress and a Myrtle bough,
>   This morn around my harp you twined,
> Because it fashioned mournfully
>   Its murmurs in the wind.

> And now a Tale of Love and Woe,
>   A woeful Tale of Love I sing:
> Hark, gentle Maidens, hark! it sighs
>   And trembles on the string.

> But most, my own dear Genevieve!
>   It sighs and trembles most for thee!
> O come and hear what cruel wrongs
>   Befel the dark Ladie.

The last:

> And now once more a tale of woe,
>   A woeful tale of love I sing;
> For thee, my Genevieve! it sighs
>   And trembles on the string.

When last I sang the cruel scorn
  That crazed this bold and lonely knight,
And how he roamed the mountain woods,
  Nor rested day or night;

I promised thee a sister tale
  Of Man's perfidious Cruelty,
Come, then, and hear what cruel wrong
  Befel the Dark Ladie.

(3) The archaism is defended on anti-modernistic grounds
in a letter to the editor of the "M.P." prefixed to the poem:

SIR,—The following Poem is the Introduction to a somewhat longer one, for which I shall solicit insertion on your next
open day. The use of the Old Ballad word, *Ladie*, for Lady, is
the only piece of obsoleteness in it; and as it is professedly a
tale of ancient times, I trust, that "the affectionate lovers of
venerable antiquity" (as Camden says) will grant me their
pardon, and perhaps may be induced to admit a force and
propriety in it. A heavier objection may be adduced against
the Author, that in these times of fear and expectation, when
novelties *explode* around us in all directions, he should presume
to offer to the public a silly tale of old fashioned love; and,
five years ago, I own, I should have allowed and felt the force
of this objection. But, alas! explosion has succeeded explosion
so rapidly, that novelty itself ceases to appear new; and it is
possible that now, even a simple story, wholly unspired [? un-
inspired] with politics or personality, may find some attention
amid the hubbub of Revolutions, as to those who have resided a
long time by the falls of Niagara, the lowest whispering becomes
distinctly audible.

                                         S. T. COLERIDGE.

In "English Minstrelsy," 1810, the first version of the poem
("these exquisite stanzas") was characteristically given.

For references to facsimile reproductions of MSS. *see* "Poems,"
p. 331.

Coleridge had a high opinion of this poem.

p. 102, l. 12: After "Nor rested day nor night;" the "Morning
Post" has the insertion:

And how he crossed the Woodman's paths
  Tho' briars and swampy mosses beat,
How boughs rebounding scourged his limbs,
  And low stubs gored his feet.

The interest of this stanza lies in a notebook draft of the thought
(*see* "Dykes Campbell," p. 456), in the fact that the image of a
troubled man stubbing his feet recurs elsewhere, and in the record

of Hazlitt: "Coleridge has told me that he himself liked to compose in walking over uneven ground, or breaking through the straggling branches of a copse-wood."

"*Apologia Pro Vita Sua*" (p. 104). First published "Blackwood's," January, 1822.

p. 104, ll. 2 to 5: MS. version:

> The poet's eye in his tipsy hour
> Hath a magnifying power
> Or rather emancipates his eyes
> Of the accidents of size.

"*Ode to Tranquillity*" (p. 104). First published "Morning Post," 4th December, 1801, where two extra stanzas are prefixed, with references to "Statesmen," "the Turk" and "the Consul." These stanzas were never reprinted, and when the poem was included in the "Friend" (No. I) the following sentences preceded it:

> But all intentional allusions to particular persons, all support of, or hostility to, particular parties or factions, I now and for ever utterly disclaim. My Principles command this Abstinence, my Tranquillity requires it.

"*Dejection: An Ode*" (p. 105). First published "Morning Post," 4th October, 1802. The signature is "ΕΣΤΗΣΕ" (*cf.* p. 808). The Ode is included in a letter sent by Coleridge from Keswick to W. Sotheby, 19th July, 1802. Lines from the poem, particularly the stanza containing the line (p. 107, l. 32) "My shaping spirit of Imagination.", were frequently quoted by him in later letters and books in a context which underlines the special meaning and final importance which he gives to the words "Imagination" and "feeling," and his identification of them with "real" life (*see* p. 246 and B.L., II, p. 65). The fact that it was originally addressed to Wordsworth further emphasizes the importance, to Coleridge, of the poem ("I solemnly assure you," he writes to Poole, "that you and Wordsworth are the only men on earth to whom I would have uttered a word on this subject").

The textual changes between the version of the letter, the "Morning Post," and "Sibylline Leaves" have an autobiographical interest. 1802 was a year for Coleridge of renewed intercourse with his friends and of active letter-writing. His friendship with the Wordsworths was at its height. The description of the moon in the first stanza has interconnections with Dorothy's Journal. But after this year the friendship was very gradually to decay (and, for a period, be broken altogether, *see* p. 798). This is reflected in successive editions by the growing vagueness of the personal address to Wordsworth: *e.g.* even from the "Morning Post," as well as from subsequent editions, the following lines of the Letter are omitted after l. 5, p. 106 ("In word, or sigh, or tear—"):

> This, William, well thou know'st
> Is the sore evil which I dread the most
> And oft'nest suffer. In this heartless mood
> To other thoughts by yonder throstle wooed
> That pipes within the larch-tree, not unseen,
> The larch, that pushes out in tassels green
> Its bundled leafits, wooed to mild delights
> By all the tender sounds and gentle sights
> Of this sweet primrose-month and vainly
> O dearest Poet in this heartless mood.

And in the first line of the fourth stanza the "William" of another MS. version became "Wordsworth" in the Letter, "Edmund" in the "Morning Post," and even "Lady" in "Sibylline Leaves."

Also, after l. 20, p. 107 ("All colours a suffusion from that light."), the following passage is omitted from all but the earliest text:

> Calm steadfast Spirit, guided from above,
> O Wordsworth! friend of my devoutest choice,
> Great son of genius! full of light and love
>   Thus, thus dost thou rejoice.
> To thee do all things live from pole to pole,
> Their life the eddying of thy living soul
> Brother and friend of my devoutest choice
> Thus may'st thou ever, evermore rejoice!

Note. It must also be remembered that impersonality in poetry was one of Coleridge's tenets (*cf.* p. 255).

p. 106, l. 17: "*In its own cloudless, starless lake of blue,*". After this is inserted in the Letter the line:

> A boat becalmed! thy own sweet sky-canoe

The reference is to the Prologue of "Peter Bell."

p. 108, Stanza vii: The reference is to "Lucy Gray."

"*Hymn Before Sun-rise*, etc." (p. 109). First published "Morning Post," 11th September, 1802. The idea, many of the images and many of the lines are expanded or translated from a twenty-line German poem addressed to Klopstock by Friederika Brun and called "Chamouni at Sun-rise." Coleridge never spoke of the original, and in spite of the fact that it is De Quincey who, citing this poem, makes the charge, this really seems to be a case of inexplicable plagiarism. For the passage in De Quincey (which originally appeared in "Tait's Magazine," September, 1834) *see* "Works," II, p. 44.

There were many small changes in successive texts. Examples are:

p. 109, l. 31: "*Deep is the air and dark, substantial, black,*"

Before the poem's appearance in the "Friend," the line was:

> Deep is the sky, and black: transpicuous, deep

p. 110, l. 18: "*O struggling with the darkness all the night,*". In a MS. Coleridge wrote:

> I had written a much finer line when Sca'Fell was in my thoughts, *viz.*:—
> O blacker than the darkness all the night

"*An Ode to the Rain*" (p. 112). First published "Morning Post," 7th October, 1802. This poem and the following are representative of a type of verse which fills a fair proportion of the space of "Poetical Works."

"*Answer to a Child's Question*" (p. 114). First published "Morning Post," 16th October, 1802, where the title is "The Language of Birds: Lines spoken extempore, to a little child, in early spring."

The refrain of the last line is taken from Prior's "Song": "One morning very early." (*Ref.* E.H.C.)

"*The Pains of Sleep*" (p. 114). First published (with "Christabel") 1816. The earliest text of the poem is that contained in the letter to Southey, 11th September, 1803 ("Letters," p. 435). For other references to these sufferings, *cf.* pp. 610 and 686. In the letter to Southey there are two interesting variants or additions:

(1) To the second stanza:

> Sense of intolerable wrong,
> And men whom I despised made strong!
> Vain-glorious threats, unmanly vaunting,
> Bad men my boasts and fury taunting:
> Rage, sensual passion, mad'ning Brawl,

(2) To the end of the poem:

> With such let fiends make mockery—
> But I—Oh, wherefore this *on me?*
> Frail is my soul, yea, strengthless wholly,
> Unequal, restless, melancholy.
> But free from Hate and sensual Folly.
> To be beloved is all I need,
> And whom I love, I love indeed.

"*A Beck in Winter*" (p. 116).

"*[Fragments]*" (p. 116). These fragments were first published in 1912, selected by E. H. Coleridge from the MS. notebooks.

"*What is Life?*" (p. 117). First published in "Literary Souvenir," 1829, and not again till "Literary Remains" in 1836.

"*[Fragment]*" (p. 117). First published 1888, in Mrs. Sandford's "Thomas Poole and His Friends."

"*To William Wordsworth*" (p. 117). First published 1817. A version sent in a letter of January, 1807, to Sir George Beaumont ("Coleorton Letters," 1887, I, p. 213) is very different from the later text. For the same reasons that made him alter "Dejection: An Ode" (*see* p. 733) Coleridge removed or made less personal some of his panegyric. *E.g.* in the Letter there is this first line:

> O Friend! O Teacher! God's great gift to me!

and the following long passage which Coleridge never printed. It follows l. 10, p. 119 ("Not learnt, but native, her own natural notes!"):

> Dear shall it be to every human heart,
> To me how more than dearest! me, on whom
> Comfort from thee, and utterance of thy love,
> Came with such heights and depths of harmony,
> Such sense of wings uplifting, that the storm
> Scattered and whirled me, till my thoughts became
> A bodily tumult; and thy faithful hopes,
> Thy hopes of me, dear Friend! by me unfelt!
> Were troublous to me, almost as a voice,
> Familiar once, and more than musical;
> To one cast forth, whose hope had seemed to die
> A wanderer with a worn-out heart
> 'Mid strangers pining with untended wounds.
> O Friend, too well thou know'st, of what sad years
> The long suppression had benumbed my soul,
> That, even as life returns upon the drowned,
> The unusual joy awoke a throng of pains—
> Keen pangs of Love,

At the end of Chapter **X** of the "Biographia Literaria" the ten lines of self-blame (ll. 65 to 75 of the standard text) are quoted as the climax of a long passage in which Coleridge defends himself against the charge of having wasted his talents. The sentences introducing the quotation show Coleridge's changed attitude towards the confessions contained in this poem:

> In this exculpation I hope to be understood as speaking of myself comparatively, and in proportion to the claims which others are entitled to make on my time or my talents. By what I *have* effected am I to be judged by my fellow men; what I *could* have done is a question for my own conscience. On my own account I may perhaps have had sufficient reason to lament my deficiency in self-control, and the neglect of con-centering my powers to the realisation of some permanent work. But to verse rather than to prose, if to either, belongs the voice of mourning for

> Keen pangs of love [&c.].

p. 120, l. 20: "*That happy vision* . . ." In the Letter, between this line and the next is:

> (All whom I deepliest love—in one room all !)

In Coleorton farmhouse in which this was written were staying all the Wordsworth family, including Dorothy, and Sarah Hutchinson. Of Coleridge's own family, Hartley alone.

"*[Fragment]*" (p. 120). First published 1893.

"*A Plaintive Movement*" (p. 121). First published, with twelve other metrical experiments, in "Poems," 1912.

"*Human Life*" (p. 121). First published "Sibylline Leaves."

"*To Nature*" (p. 122). First published 1836 in Allsop's "Letters, Conversations and Recollections."

"*The Knight's Tomb*" (p. 122). First published 1834. The date of composition may be much earlier: the metrical unit which the stanza forms has been thought to relate it to "Christabel." E.H.C. has suggested it may be part of the projected continuation.

"*On Donne's Poetry*" (p. 123). First published 1836 in "Literary Remains."

"*Youth and Age*" (p. 123). First published 1828, in the "Literary Souvenir" (without the last eleven lines). First published complete in 1834. Coleridge printed some of his later verse in magazines of this new "Keepsake" class.

The 1823 date of composition refers to a notebook draft marked with that year. E.H.C. quotes it as follows:

> 10 Sept., 1823. Wednesday Morning, 10 o'clock
>
> On the tenth day of September,
> Eighteen hundred Twenty Three,
> Wednesday morn, and I remember
> Ten on the *Clock* the Hour to be
> [*The Watch and Clock do both agree*]

An *Air* that whizzed διὰ ἐγκεφάλου (right across the diameter of my Brain) exactly like a Hummel Bee, *alias* Dumbeldore, the gentleman with Rappee Spenser [*sic*], with bands of Red, and Orange Plush Breeches, close by my ear, at once sharp and burry, right over the summit of Quantock ⟨item of Skiddaw⟩ at earliest Dawn just between the Nightingale that I stopt to hear in the Copse at the Foot of Quantock, and the first Sky-Lark that was a Song-Fountain, dashing up and sparkling to the Ear's eye, in full column, or ornamented Shaft of sound in the order of Gothic Extravaganza, out of Sight, over the Cornfields on the Descent of the Mountain on the other side —out of sight, tho' twice I beheld its *mute* shoot downward in the sunshine like a falling star of silver:—

ARIA SPONTANEA

Flowers are lovely, Love is flower-like,

[*&c., see* "Poems," p. 1040].

"*Work Without Hope*" (p. 124). First published 1828, in the "Bijou." The date of the sub-title is that of the notebook entry from which the lines are taken. Part of the entry describes this as a "Strain in the manner of George Herbert." (*See* "Dykes Campbell," p. 643.)

p. 124, l. 28: In 1828 there is a misprint: "stags" for "slugs." *Cf.* "Unpublished Letters," II, p. 445:

> By the bye, the Parisian and American Editions have chosen to dignify my "slugs quit their Lair" into "stags" which is really so much grander that I grieve it should be senseless.

"*Song*" (p. 125). First published 1828. Omitted in 1829. Not published again till 1852.

"*Duty Surviving Self-love*" (p. 125). First published 1828. In MS. the poem is preceded by the following note ("Poems," p. 459):

QUESTION, ANSWER, AND SOLILOQUY

And are *you* (said Alia to Constantius, on whose head sickness and sorrow had antedated Winter, ere yet the time of Vintage had passed), Are you the happier for your Philosophy? And the smile of Constantius was as the light from a purple cluster of the vine, gleaming through snowflakes, as he replied, The Boons of Philosophy are of higher worth, than what you, O Alia, mean by Happiness. But I will not seem to evade the question— Am *I* the happier for my Philosophy? The calmer at least and the less unhappy, answered Constantius, for it has enabled me to find that selfless Reason is the best Comforter, and only sure friend of declining Life. At this moment the sounds of a carriage followed by the usual bravura executed on the brazen knocker announced a morning visit: and Alia hastened to receive the party. Meantime the grey-haired philosopher, left to his own musings, continued playing with the thoughts that Alia and Alia's question had excited, till he murmured them to himself in half audible words, which at first casually, and then for the amusement of his ear, he *punctuated* with rhymes, without however conceiting that he had by these means changed them into poetry.

"Cologne" (p. 126). First published in "Friendship's Offering," 1834. Here it is "No. IV" of a series called "Light-heartednesses in Rhyme," and there is a footnote:

As Necessity is the mother of Invention, and extremes beget each other, the facts above recorded may explain how this *ancient* town (which, alas! as sometimes happens with venison, *has been kept too long*), *came to be the birthplace of the most fragrant of spirituous fluids, the* EAU DE COLOGNE.

Coleridge passed through Cologne in July, 1828, on his way back from the Rhine tour.

"The Netherlands" (p. 126). First published 1912.

"Forbearance" (p. 126). First published 1834. The first line is taken from Spenser, "Shepherds Calendar" ("Februarie"):

> Ne ever was to Fortune foeman
> But gently tooke that ungently came.

"Love's Apparition and Evanishment" (p. 127). First published in "Friendship's Offering," 1834, where it is dated "August, 1833." The "Envoy" with which it is now printed was not added till 1852, and its connection with the poem seems conjectural. (*See* "Dykes Campbell," p. 644.) It was taken from a letter to Allsop, 27th April, 1824. (*See* the 1836 "Recollections," II, p. 174.)

DRAMATIC WORKS

"*Fall of Robespierre*" (p. 129). First published 1794, and not again till "Literary Remains," 1836. Coleridge wrote the first, and Southey the last two acts. The song occurs near the end of the act, in a romantic interlude. Though the play was forgotten, the song was liked, and often republished from 1796 onwards (with the title "Domestic Peace"), though not in "Lyrical Ballads" or "Sibylline Leaves."

"*Remorse*" (p. 129). First published 1813, when it was first performed (23rd January). Coleridge began it under the title of "Osorio" in 1797, and sent it to Sheridan at Drury Lane towards the end of that year. But his own doubts were confirmed by Sheridan (as they had been earlier by Bowles), who complained of the obscurity of the last three acts. When, through Byron, the play was eventually accepted under the new title, Coleridge had made considerable alterations and now thought highly of it (*cf.* p. 648). It was a fair popular and a decided financial success. Genest (VIII, p. 354) records that it ran twenty nights (helped by a curtain-raiser towards the end of the run), and describes it as "tolerable . . . some parts of it are beautifully written." (*See also* "Life.")

In this scene, reproduced here in full as a specimen, Alvar, who has escaped the assassination plans of Ordonio, is returned, disguised. Both are the sons of Valdez and both love Teresa.

The last part of the scene is greatly changed from "Osorio." Most of the changes in "Remorse" show a tendency to heighten the "drama" and the dignity. Alvar in "Osorio" (where he is called "Albert") merely places a small picture of the assassination on an altar. A typical minor change is exemplified on p. 130, l. 11:

> Even so!—He had outgrown his infant dress,

which in "Osorio" is

> His infant dress was grown too short for him.

p. 134: "*Act IV, Scene iii*". This speech was not printed till the second edition of the play. For a probable reason why it was not spoken, see p. 321.

p. 135: "*Act V, Scene i*". This is familiar from its appearance in "Lyrical Ballads," 1798 and 1800. The textual differences are very small.

"*Zapolya*" (p. 136). First published 1817. Coleridge wrote this play in 1815 (*see* "Life," p. 218)—not a period of his life when he was likely to make those alterations deemed necessary before it could be acted, which it never was. Yet 2,000 copies sold, and Coleridge included it in 1828, 1829 and 1834.

TRANSLATION

"*The Piccolomini*" (p. 137). First published 1800. The book was a failure, though its merits were recognised later. Carlyle ("Life of Schiller") calls it "the only sufferable translation from the German with which our literature has yet been enriched." Coleridge made it in six weeks, during that period when he was lodging in London working for the "Morning Post." More than one letter speaks of the translator's disgust at his "soul-wearying labour" (*see* Note *ante*, p. 723).

POLITICAL JOURNALISM

"*Conciones ad Populum*" (p. 141). First published 1795. Although this was for Coleridge the year of Pantisocracy, political enthusiasm, and political lectures, nothing (beyond what may have been incorporated in later work) was published except three pamphlets. The first two were printed in November under the title "Conciones ad Populum."

No. 1 (which had appeared earlier in the year under another title) was an Introductory Address, upholding freedom and the French Revolution. No. 2, from which this extract is taken (p. 47), was called "On the Present War." According to the Preface, "the two following addresses were delivered in the month of February, 1795, and were followed by six others in defence of natural and revealed Religion." The text is that of the British Museum copy of this very rare pamphlet. It was republished (together with the rest of the extracts contained in this section, with the exception of the "Prospectus") in the three-volume selection of Coleridge's political journalism published by his daughter in 1850 ("Essays on His Own Times").

p. 142, l. 12: "*Spies and Informers*". *Cf.* B.L. for an account of how later Wordsworth and Coleridge were themselves shadowed because of the political opinions of their friend Thelwall.

On 8th February, 1795, Southey wrote: "Coleridge is writing at the same table; our names are written in the book of destiny, on the same page."

"*The Watchman*" (p. 143). First published 1796. It came to an end after the tenth number (13th May, 1796). For Coleridge's own account of his efforts to make a success of this paper, see p. 236, and Cottle's "Reminiscences," pp. 74 *et seq.*

p. 143, l. 2: "*Prospectus*". For Coleridge's description of his tour of the Midlands with this Prospectus in order to try and collect subscribers for the "Watchman," *cf.* p. 236 of this volume. Only two copies are now known to be in existence, one of which is in the library of Mr. T. J. Wise, who was so kind as to correct this proof-sheet for me. The "Prospectus" was first reprinted at the end of "Life" (now out of print). Cottle's version, printed in his "Recollections," was faked—or at any rate refers to a different Prospectus.

p. 143, l. 5: "Friday, the *5th* Day of February". The date of the first number is 1st March, 1796.

p. 143, ll. 9 to 12: "(*Price four pence*) . . . *every eighth day*,". *Cf.* p. 236.

p. 144, l. 16: "*Arthur Young's Travels*". The title continues: "during the years 1787, 1788 and 1789. Undertaken more particularly with a view of ascertaining the Cultivation, Wealth, Resources, and National Prosperity of the Kingdom of France," 1792-4.

p. 145, ll. 17, 18: "*Lord Grenville's and Mr. Pitt's bills*,". In May, 1794, Grenville moved the first reading of the Habeas Corpus Suspension Bill; in November, 1795, he was concerned with the Treasonable Practices Bill; in December with the Seditious Meetings Bill. Pitt himself was especially connected with the first of these. (At the time this prospectus was being written Pitt was trying to pass measures for the relief of the poor.)

"*Modern Patriotism.*" (p. 146). From No. III, 17th March, 1796.

"*[Abolition.]*" (p. 147). From No. V, 2nd April, 1796.

"*[Mr. Pitt]*" (p. 148). This article ("Morning Post," 19th March, 1800), which has been cited as showing that Coleridge was at this time an unexpectedly proficient journalist, is one of the three S.T.C. contributions to his paper which Stuart admitted were a success. According to Coleridge, he "wasted the prime and manhood of his intellect" on such articles, without proper return. In the previous month Coleridge had made a certain report of a speech of Pitt's which, according to him, "made a great noise." Coleridge had been preaching against Pitt since 1795, and only praised him for his anti-slavery views.

p. 150, footnote: "**To-morrow of Bonaparte.*". "To-morrow" brought no such article. It is impossible to say which of Coleridge's rather impersonal references to the "Consul" at this period could have possibly been the grounds of Bonaparte's threatened "persecution" five years later, though in 1811, *e.g.* in the "Courier," 27th June, there are violent diatribes ("He has dyed every country with blood"): but many of these later "Courier" articles are only conjecturally assigned to Coleridge.

NOTEBOOKS

"*['Gutch Memorandum Book']*" (p. 153). First published in 1896. This very incorrect transcript was made by a German student of Coleridge, Professor Brandl. The original notebook, now in the British Museum, is named after Coleridge's old acquaintance and publisher, J. M. Gutch, who once possessed it. The years covered are 1795-8. Some part of the passages which I have selected have been extensively quoted in "The Road to Xanadu," yet they are so admirably typical and interesting that I have thought it worth while printing them here (*literatim*), if only that they may be seen alone on the page in the right kind of notebook juxtaposition.

Note. Diamond brackets in this excerpt indicate that the word enclosed has been crossed out.

p. 153, l. 5: "*2 Satires*". This extract starts on folio 23 of the notebook. For Coleridge's later habit of drawing up such plans as this for future work *cf.* Note, p. 794. No items on this list materialised.

p. 153, l. 7: "*Poverty*". For Coleridge's poverty at this time *cf.* p. 560.

p. 153, l. 9: "Ωστραλ!" Coleridge is probably using the archaic symbol for στ, though at first sight it looks as if this inexplicable transliteration might stand for *O Israel!* David Hartley was born 19th September, 1796.

p.153, l. 10: "*Tob.*". Coleridge may be thinking of Tobit IV, 3.

p. 153, l. 28: "*8. . . . Halo*". Candlelight specially fascinated Coleridge.

p. 153, l. 32: "*11. Wild Poem*". This strange Greek has been identified (*see* "Xanadu," second edition, p. 604). The first word is the genitive of ἐραστής, a lover. The next two words are transliterations of "hat" (Latin and English respectively). Southey (very intimate with Coleridge at this time) published in 1797 a poem, "Mary, the Maid of the Inn," in which Mary is the *maniac* and the clue to the plot is a *hat*.

p. 154, l. 3: "*16. Hymns to . . . the Elements*". Compare this reference to the hymns with "Xanadu," pp. 74 *et seq*.

p. 154, ll. 14 to 17: "*21. . . . a bold avowal of Berkley's System*". *Cf.* B.L., I, p. 93: "After I had successively studied in the schools of Locke, Berkeley, Leibnitz, and Hartley, and could find in neither of them an abiding place for my reason . . ."

p. 154, l. 18: "*22.*". Fletcher Christian, who headed a famous and popular mutiny against a tyrannical commander in 1789.

p. 154, l. 19: "*23. Military anecdotes*". It was less than two years before this that Coleridge had been bought out of the army.

p. 154, l. 25: "*The Earth feared and was still,*". From Psalm lxxvi. The next two quotations from the Book of Wisdom and Ecclesiasticus respectively.

p.155, l. 4: "*Wisdom, Mother of retired Thought,*". *Cf.* "Destiny of Nations," l. 140.

p. 155, l. 6: "πολυν εσσαμενοι". Brandl gives the reference—from the "Chaldean Oracles." For connections with Psellus and the "Ancient Mariner" *cf.* "Xanadu," p. 235.

p. 155, ll. 22, 23: "*Behind the thin Grey cloud*". *Cf.* "Christabel."

p. 155, l. 27: "*The alligators terrible roar,*". This description is from Bartram's "Travels." For an immense and fascinating note on the discoverers of this fact, on whether alligators were not "good copy at the close of the eighteenth century," etc., *see* "Xanadu," pp. 452 and 453.

p. 156, l. 3: *"Hartley fell down"*. The notebooks, as well as the letters, have from now on frequent records of Hartley, what he said, and thought, and looked like. This description is incorporated in "The Nightingale" (*see* p. 92).

p. 156, l. 7: *"Some wilderness-plot,"*. In "Xanadu," pp. 369 *et seq.*, Professor Lowes connects this phrase with the laudanum letter quoted here on p. 575, with a phrase in Bartram's "Travels," and finally with the "sunny spots of greenery" of "Kubla Khan."

"[Anima Poetae]" (p. 156). The title is E. H. Coleridge's, who published this selection from the notebooks in 1895. Coleridge's contributions to the "Omniana" of 1812 were inserted by himself and are aphorisms more than notes. Isolated notes have on the other hand frequently been published among Coleridgeana, in L.R., in "Allsop," in Gillman's "Life," in "The Road to Xanadu," etc.

E.H.C. diffidently compares his compilation with "Table Talk." But actually it is a book of far greater importance; first because the majority of notes are taken from earlier and more vital periods of Coleridge's life, and secondly because E. H. Coleridge is a better editor than H. N., and unlike him is extremely meticulous in his printing of texts, limiting himself to little more than the revision of stops. Professor Raysor has very kindly allowed me to see his own transcripts of the originals of some of these notes, and in every case E. H. Coleridge, without being pedantic, has limited his alterations to the addition of elucidatory commas and small words. Coleridge often omitted words by mistake, and so regularly that he became interested enough to make observations and try to draw conclusions from this habit. (*See* A.P., p. 181.) The time order of these dates is sometimes conjectural: Mr. Raysor has supplied me with corrected dates for half a dozen entries.

p. 156, l. 28: *"what I call metaphysical poetry"*. Not what Dr. Johnson thus described, though Coleridge was an admirer of Donne. *Cf.* "Letters," p. 372:

You will agree with me that a great poet must be, implicité if not explicité, a profound metaphysician.

p. 157, l. 6: *"Socinianism,"*. A quotation which may be taken as marking the halfway stage in Coleridge's desertion of Unitarianism. (*V.* Index.)

p. 158, l. 4: "*Wolff,*". This must be Christian Wolf, the systematizer of Leibnitz, categorist and common-sense man, mentioned more than once in B.L.

p. 160, ll. 1 to 6: "*Great injury . . . Blackmore,*". Locke's opinion printed in "Works" (1801), IX, pp. 426 and 432, appears to be what Coleridge is thinking of. Locke seems to judge Blackmore to be a good poet on the strength of what he says about hypotheses in medicine in the preface to "King Arthur": "which is an argument to me," says Locke, "that he understands the right method of practising physic."

p. 160, l. 15: "*Intensely hot day; . . .*". For the reminiscence of chill, child and calf-lowing, *cf.* the autobiographical letter on p. 530.

p. 160, l. 29: "*Never to lose*", etc. A favourite thought; *cf.* B.L., I, p. 43; II, p. 94; and S.C., II, p. 122; *and see* the MS. note to the copy of Milton's poems (referred to on p. 772): "We may *outgrow* certain *sorts* of poetry (Young's 'Night-thoughts,' for instance) without arraigning their excellence *proprio genere*. In short, the wise is the genial; and the genial judgement is to distinguish accurately the character and characteristics of each poem, praising them according to . . . their own kind—and to reserve Reprehension for such as have no *character*."

p. 161, l. 6: "*The tree or sea-weed like*". For the "sopha of sods" mentioned in this extract, *cf.* Dorothy Wordsworth's Journal (August, 1800).

p. 163, l. 23: "*What is it that I employ*", etc. *Cf.* the more formal but less effective phrasing of this note where it reappears in the "Friend" in para. 1 of Introductory Essay XV and *cf.* B.L., I, p. 179: "Oh, ye that reverence yourselves, and walk humbly with the divinity in your own hearts, ye are worthy of a better philosophy! Let the dead bury the dead, but do you preserve your human nature, the depth of which was never yet fathomed by a philosophy made up of notions and mere logical entities."

p. 164, l. 37, to p. 165, l. 1: "*I have repeatedly . . . 'Extremes Meet.'*". Coleridge's thought is impregnated with this concept, to support the truth of which he was always collecting evidence. (*See* Miss A. D. Snyder, "The Critical Principle of the Reconciliation of Opposites as Employed by Coleridge," 1918.)

p. 165, ll. 34, 35: "*This evening, . . . Malthus.*". The "Essay on the Principles of Population" was published in 1803. There is a copy in the British Museum annotated by Coleridge.

p. 165, l. 37: "*Because I* ought *not to have done this.*". *Cf.* p. 799.

p. 167, l. 32: "*As I was gazing*". *Cf.* the thought expressed here with page 257.

p. 168, ll. 15, 16: "*Why do we . . . [Stoddart,*". Stoddart (later Sir John) was King's Advocate at Malta, and was his host for a time when Coleridge first went there. Apparently they did not get on in conversation, as both were exponents of monologue. For this guess *see* "Life," p. 145 (*see also* p. 616).

p. 170, ll. 11, 12: "*I have read . . . Reimarus*", *i.e.* "Observations, Moral and Philosophical, on the Instinct of Animals, their Industry, and their Manners." (*Ref.* E.H.C.)

p. 172, ll. 2, 3: "*moral businesses, as mine with Southey or Lloyd*". With Southey, the Pantisocracy quarrel; with Lloyd, at the time when the Coleridges were receiving him as a paying guest (*cf.* p. 11). One of the causes of the quarrel seems to have been the showing by Lloyd to Charles Lamb of a letter from Coleridge, in which Coleridge exemplified the difference between talent and genius in the persons of Charles Lamb and himself.

p. 173, l. 13: " '*shrill-tongued Tapster,*". *Not* in Shakspere.

p. 175, l. 33: "*John Tobin*", with whom (or with whose brother) he had been staying until he sailed for Malta (where this note was written). Allen was a school friend.

p. 176, l. 22: "*Schiller, disgusted with Kotzebuisms,*", etc. This note may be compared with the "Friend" (1818, Sec. II, Essay 1), where the characteristics of France, Germany and England are tabulated and compared.

p. 178, ll. 19, 20: "*Catullus*' . . . 'numine abusum". Carmen, LXXVI, l. 4.

p. 178, ll. 32, 33: "*Pope, . . . perversion, unnatural*". Coleridge was not invariably unappreciative of Pope. *Cf.* the passage near the end of Allsop's "Letters, Conversations," etc., where Allsop quotes letters of Pope which Coleridge enjoyed reading aloud.

p. 181, l. 18: "*Stuart,*". See Note, p. 797.

p. 184, l. 3: "*Lloyd's 'State Worthies'*", *i.e.* "The Statesmen and

Favourites of England since the Reformation; their prudence and policies, successes and miscarriages, advancements and falls, etc.," 1665. The better-known title was prefixed to the title of the second edition.

p. 184, l. 27: "*?1810*". Professor Raysor has given me this new (though queried) date for this paragraph. 1810 is the year of the quarrel with Wordsworth.

p. 187, l. 39; p. 188, l. 1: "'*The Beggar's Petition*'". A recitation piece by T. Moss, Minister of Brierley Hill, Staffordshire, who published "Poems" in 1769.

OMNIANA

First published 1812 ("Omniana, or Horae Otiosiores"). The idea of the book was Southey's, who had been contributing similar fragments to the contemporary "Athenaeum" as early as 1806. Only a small portion of its anonymous contents were by Coleridge. *See* Southey's letter of 5th February, 1811:

> I urged Coleridge to double the intended number of "Omniana" volumes, merely for the sake of making him do something for his family: this requiring, literally, no other trouble than either cutting out of his commonplace books what has for years been accumulating there, or marking the passage off for a transcriber. He promised to add two volumes, and has contributed one sheet, which, I dare say, unless he soon returns to Cumberland, will be all.

Coleridge's "Omniana" contributions were republished, with additions, in "Literary Remains," 1836. In the "Table Talk and Omniana" edited by T. Ashe in 1884, further additions were made from a copy of "Omniana" with MS. notes by Coleridge, now in the British Museum.

p. 195, ll. 13 to 18: "'*Beggar's Opera*' . . . *horror and disgust*". But *cf.* the Letter on p. 598 to his wife (written in 1802) where the play, or Mrs. Billington's performance in it, is "*perfection!*"

At the end of these attacks Coleridge quotes, by way of palliation, Scene iv of Etherege's "Love in a Tub," "for its exquisite, genuine, original humour."

p. 198, l. 7: "*we think of earth, air, water, &c. as dead.*" *Cf.* pp. 467 to 469.

LITERARY CRITICISM

EARLY CRITICISM

"[Mrs. Radcliffe]" (p. 203). First published in the "Critical Review," August, 1794. Republished in "A Wiltshire Parson" [Bowles], 1926, Ed. G. Greever, together with similar criticisms of Mrs. Radcliffe's "Italian" and Lewis's "Monk." For Coleridge's later opinion of the Mrs. Radcliffe school *cf.* p. 721 and for his later opinion of Monk Lewis *cf.* a letter of 1802 ("Unpublished Letters," I, p. 232):

> I have a wife, I have sons, I have an infant Daughter— what excuse could I offer to my conscience if by suffering my own name to be connected with those of Mr. Lewis, or Mr. Moore, I was the *occasion* of their reading the "Monk," or the wanton poems of Thomas Little Esqre? Should I not be an infamous Pander to the Devil in the Seduction of my own offspring? My head turns giddy, my heart sickens, at the very thought of seeing such books in the hands of a child of mine—

p. 203, l. 6: " '*Thine too these golden*' ", etc. From Gray's "Progress of Poesie."

"[Wordsworth]" (p. 205). This note appeared only in the 1796 and 1797 texts of this poem. It was omitted in 1803. "Green radiance" is taken from "An Evening Walk" (1793).

"[Bowles]" (p. 205). From Coleridge's preface to "Sonnets from Various Authors," 1796, a 14 pp. collection containing four of his own sonnets and others by Lamb, Lloyd, Bowles, etc. For Coleridge's inability to resist Prefaces *cf.* "Dykes Campbell," pp. 537 to 559, where they are collected. For Coleridge and Bowles, *see* Note on p. 751.

BIOGRAPHIA LITERARIA

First published 1817. Its genesis dates from the "Lyrica Ballads" and the doctrines which begot them. The various stages of its evolution are summarized in the standard two-volume edition of Shawcross, 1907 (referred to here as B.L.): the relevant quotations from letters are collected in Professor Sampson's selection ("Coleridge: Biographia Literaria, Chapters I-IV, XIV-XXI," etc., 1920).

The part of "Biographia Literaria" which discusses Wordsworth and his views is the direct outcome of the fact that it was Wordsworth who wrote the Prefaces to the later editions of the "Ballads" and not Coleridge, much more qualified for such discussion, and differing widely from its conclusions. Early letters express this disagreement (*cf.* p. 599). But the public answer was long delayed.

The book eventually came to be written almost by accident. In March, 1815, Coleridge was collecting his poems for publication ("Sibylline Leaves"). In May he was writing a Preface. In July he was extending the Preface into an "Autobiographia Literaria," sufficient to fill an introductory volume. This was actually finished by August, but disagreement with his publisher, misunderstandings with the printer, changes of publisher (all of which will be found lamented in "Unpublished Letters"), delayed publication till July, 1817. One hitch was the necessity of issuing "Poems" and "Life" separately, and of enlarging the "Life," accidentally made too long for one volume, into a size sufficient for two. Hence the entirely unnecessary "Critique of Bartram," hence "Satyrane's Letters" (reprinted from the "Friend") and hence the important Chapter XXII on the defects of Wordsworth's poetry.

Text: I have followed Shawcross in keeping the text of 1817. No further editions were issued in Coleridge's lifetime. The second (1847) edition contains "authorized" additions and unauthorized omissions; but the part-editor is the slightly suspect H. N. Coleridge.

Chapter I (p. 206).

p. 206, ll. 25, 26: "*application of the rules, deduced from philosophical principles,*". By this sentence, probably written after the rest of the book was finished, Coleridge meant to bring within the plan of the book his one hundred and thirty-page long philosophical digression.

p. 207, l. 1: "*In 1794,*". Altered in 1847 to "In the spring of 1796," the correct date.

p. 208, ll. 2, 3: "*In the after editions, I pruned the double epithets with no sparing hand,*". But Coleridge did not apply his critical deductions to his own work. *Cf.* the 1796 Sonnet which begins these selections. All five of the double epithets were retained in all editions.

p. 208, ll. 9, 10: "*From that period . . . I have published nothing,*". This was written in 1815. *But see* list of Works.

p. 208, *footnote:* "** The Rev. James Bowyer,*". In De Quincey's list ("Works," XI, p. 92) of Coleridge's "monomaniac likings" (the others are Dr. Andrew Bell, Woolman, and Sir Alexander Ball). *See* T.T., August, 1832, for the account of the "*one* just flogging" Bowyer inflicted.

The description of Bowyer's antipathy to ornate diction shows how eighteenth century taste had already turned. This is of course the Bowyer of Lamb's essay on Christ's Hospital.

p. 209, ll. 1, 2: "*preference . . . of Homer and Theocritus to Virgil,*". In 1824 (*see* p. 483) Coleridge still disliked Virgil, but in 1833 (T.T., 2nd September) he commends his diction.

p. 209, ll. 37, 38: "*Among the similes, . . . the Manchineel fruit,*". *Yet see* the poem on page 13 where the phrase has slipped in.

p. 211, l. 9: "Ne falleretur rotundo . . ." The source of this has not been traced. Is it a bit of Coleridge Latin? He sometimes introduced such Latin or English "quotations" (*v.* Shawcross, B.L., I, p. 206).

p. 211, l. 16: "*Mr. Bowles*". For Coleridge and Bowles *v.* "Life," pp. 17, 18, 77, etc. In "Poems" there are two versions of a sonnet which Coleridge addressed to him ("My heart has thanked thee, Bowles ! for those soft strains"). He was the "god of his idolatry" at least as late as 1796. Disillusion seemed to begin after the personal meeting in 1797. (*See also* Note, B.L., I, p. 207.)

p. 211, l. 33: " '*in whose halls*' ". From Wordsworth's sonnet:

It is not to be thought of that the Flood
Of British freedom, etc.

p. 212, l. 9: "Neque enim debet . . ." Plin., Ep. I, xvi.

p. 212, l. 24: " 'qui laudibus amplis . . .' " Slightly misquoted from Petrarch's "Latin Epistles," No. VII.

For this description of his early days, Lamb's "inspired charity-boy" passage is the classical cross-reference ("Christ's Hospital five-and-thirty years ago").

p. 214, l. 4: "*accidental introduction to an amiable family,*". Mrs. Evans and her daughters (*see* p. 787).

p. 214, ll. 12 to 14: "*have sought a refuge . . . in abstruse researches,*". For "research, the author of self-oblivion," *cf.* p. 107.

p. 214, l. 23: *"Mr.* Crow)". William Crowe, rector of **Alton** Barnes, Wilts. He lectured on poetry at the Royal Institution. His poem, which describes Dorset, was published in 1788. It was admired by Wordsworth and Sam Rogers.

p. 215, l. 11: *"Darwin's* 'Botanic Garden,' ". Erasmus Darwin's poem was published in two parts, in 1789 and 1797. As the contemporary exponent of Pope, he was made an example of by the new poets. His popularity, and the fact that he really seemed to hold that poetry consisted in a metrical and unusually worded paraphrase of prose, makes some study of his poetry necessary for the full understanding of the heat of the poetic diction controversy.

p. 216, ll. 28, 29: *"unfeigned zeal for the honor of a favorite contemporary,"*. For an early opinion of Wordsworth *cf.* p. 205 *ante.*

p. 219, l. 20: *"a copy of verses half ludicrous, half splenetic,"*. This is the "Address to a Young Ass," printed here on p. 5. It was actually the "Reflections on leaving a place of retirement" which had the motto *sermoni propriora.*

p. 220, l. 4: *"Sonnet I"*. These "Sonnets attempted in the manner of contemporary writers" were first published in the "Monthly Magazine," November, 1797.

p. 221, l. 24: *"The following anecdote"*. Coleridge is wrong in his facts here. The epigram was explicitly addressed to a different author altogether. (*V.* Note, B.L., I, p. 212.)

Chapter II (p. 221).

Coleridge has kept to the subject proposed for one complete chapter. Chapter II is a digression on the "supposed irritability of men of Genius" and the injustice of the charge. The calmness of Shakspere, Milton and Spenser—sensitive, but not for personal reasons. Indifference to public opinion has been one of his faults; but his own shortcomings and troubles, he says, are too vast for him to be moved by minor troubles.

p. 222, ll. 16, 17: *"with ostrich carelessness and ostrich oblivion."*. This sentence repeats one of Coleridge's favourite metaphors.

Chapter III (p. 222).

p. 222, l. 28: *"To anonymous critics"*. "The continuous cannonading" of the critics to which Coleridge refers in his opening paragraph is difficult to exemplify. What he had to complain of was lack of notice rather than attacks. Besides, in the "seventeen years" to which he refers he had published so little. Shawcross suggests that Coleridge is referring to insignificant references to his work which cannot now be traced. As in the case of Tennyson, the real attack from the critics came after, not before, the complaint. *But see* "Beauties of the Anti-Jacobin," 1799, p. 306 (quoted by Coleridge in a note at the end of this chapter):

> Since this time he has left his native country, commenced citizen of the world, left his poor children fatherless, and his wife destitute. *Ex his disce* his friends, Lamb and Southey.

It was the fatal prophecy, rather than the calumny, which seemed to disturb Coleridge long after.

p. 222, l. 37: *"the reading public)"*. I have omitted a note on time-wasting.

p. 224, l. 15: *"*Some years ago,"*. This footnote was omitted in the 1847 edition. Jeffrey answered this attack in a note appended to the review of B.L. in the "Edinburgh." He denies some of the criticisms imputed to him, and refers contemptuously to Coleridge's hospitality.

p. 226, l. 39: "I was in habits of intimacy". From his letters it is clear how anxious Coleridge was to disassociate himself from any school of poetry, the Lake School in particular. *Cf.* the extract from Collier's reminiscences, quoted here on p. 475. These third and fourth chapters are written largely to emphasize this point.

p. 227, l. 5: *"with regard to Mr. Southey."*. The Works mentioned in the text are as follows: *"Published with Mr. Lovell,"* "Poems," 1795; *"Joan of Arc,"* 1796; *"two volumes,"* "Poems." 1797.

p. 227, ll. 30, 31: *"Mr. Southey agreed far more with Warton,"*. Joseph Warton's last work, the "Essay on the Writings and Genius of Pope" (vol. I, 1757; vol. II, 1782), dates the beginning of the reaction against the school of Pope. (*But cf.* Dr. Johnson's essay in the "Idler," 9th June, 1759, where Dick Minim, the critic, is inclined to degrade Pope from a poet to a versifier.)

p. 228, ll. 19, 20: *"words of Jeremy Taylor)"*. This quotation has not yet been traced.

Chapter IV (p. 228).

This chapter opens with an account of the reception of the "Lyrical Ballads," and assigns the adverse criticisms to the fact that the Preface focused attention on certain poems, not the best, which were most obviously in accordance with the theories expressed there. Tentative at first, the implied disagreement with Wordsworth becomes more explicit throughout the B.L., and it is impossible not to associate this more critical attitude with the fact that B.L. was the first literary work published since the tragic quarrel of 1810. (*See* p. 798 and the not very pertinent evidence of Crabb Robinson, "Diary," 21st December, 1822: "Of Wordsworth I believe Coleridge judges under personal feelings of unkindness.")

p. 228, ll. 25 to 27: "*During the last year . . . 'Descriptive Sketches*';". Coleridge read this poem in the autumn of 1793, the year of its publication (" 'Descriptive Sketches. In Verse. Taken during a Pedestrian Tour in the Italian, Grison, Swiss and Savoyard Alps.' By W. Wordsworth, B.A., of St. John's, Cambridge"). But "The Evening Walk" had been published earlier in the same year. With this passage compare the 1796 "Footnote" on **p. 205.**

p. 229, ll. 4, 5: "*In the following extract*". Coleridge is quoting ll. 232-47 here from the text of 1815 ("Poems by William Wordsworth"). The less "improved" early version which he had first read began as follows:

> 'Tis storm; and hid in mist from hour to hour,
> All day the floods a deeper murmur pour;
> And mournful sounds, as of a Spirit lost,
> Pipe wild along the hollow-blustering coast,
> Till the sun walking on his western field
> Shakes from behind the clouds his flashing shield.
> Triumphant on the bosom, &c.

p. 229, ll. 34 to 36: "*Psyche . . . an unpublished poem*" did not appear in any of the collected editions during Coleridge's lifetime. It was reprinted in the "Amulet," 1833. Dated (in "Literary Remains") 1808.

p. 230, l. 1: "*my twenty-fourth year*,". Actually there was an earlier, unimportant meeting in 1795, before this one in the autumn of 1796.

p. 230, l. 6: "*the same as those of the 'Female Vagrant,*' ". It *was* the "Female Vagrant," or another part of the longer poem in which those verses were embedded. According to H. N. Coleridge (B.L., 1847) this longer poem "was intituled 'An Adventure on Salisbury Plain.' " The complete poem was first published in 1842 as "Guilt and Sorrow: or Incidents upon Salisbury

Plain." J. P. Collier (v. B.L., I, p. 224) records that Wordsworth did not like the poem, and considered it "was addressed to coarse sympathies." Perhaps this refers to its revolutionary sympathies?

p. 230, l. 10: "*lines 'on re-visiting the Wye*',". "Tintern Abbey."

p. 230, *footnote:* The quotation is from "Descriptive Sketches," ll. 317-24. Coleridge is again quoting from 1815, but the text is unaltered from 1793. On the other hand, by 1845 the whole passage had been considerably altered. Wordsworth, although he was not approving of the B.L., re-wrote most of the lines which Coleridge criticized adversely. The alterations are not considered improvements. (For Wordsworth's opinions *cf.* Crabb Robinson's "Diary," 4th December, 1817: W. tells him that the B.L. "had given him no pleasure. The praise he considered extravagant, and the censure inconsiderate.")

p. 231, ll. 15, 16: " '*To find no contradiction*' ". A passage from the "Friend," No. 5, adapted. An old and recurring thought of Coleridge's. This quotation was omitted from B.L., 1847.

The Burns quotation (from "Tam o' Shanter") is quoted half a dozen times by Coleridge.

p. 232, l. 15: "*fancy and imagination*". For a Note on this distinction *see* B.L., I, xxi *et seq.*

p. 232, l. 20: "*a more opposite translation*". It has been pointed out that "apposite" seems to be the word (B.L. Selections, Sampson).

p. 233, l. 10: " '*Lutes, lobsters, seas of milk,*' ". The line ("Lutes, *laurels*" . . .) is from the fifth act of "Venice Preserved." The Shakspere from "Lear," III, iv.

Coleridge finishes off the chapter by preparing readers for the philosophical section which follows, saying that in pursuing these distinctions he wants to go more to the root of the matter than Wordsworth did in his Prefaces.

Chapter X (p. 234).

p. 234, l. 7: " 'Esemplastic' ". It is Chapter XIII which has the title "On the imagination, or esemplastic power." Shawcross (B.L., I, p. 249) discusses the perhaps unimportant probabilities of Coleridge having borrowed the word from Schelling, constructing it out of a mistaken etymological analysis of the word *Einbildungskraft*, etc.

p. 234, l. 28: "*quant. suff. of thea* . . .". Coleridge had a fatally extensive knowledge of "prescription language."

p. 235, ll. 10, 11: "*Darwin in his Zoonomia;*)". "Zoonomia, or the Laws of Organic Life," 1794-6, his first important prose work.

p. 235, l. 26: "*the word* sensuous;". *V.* N.E.D.:

Apparently invented by Milton, to avoid certain associations of the existing word *sensual*, and from him adopted by Coleridge; evidence of its use in the intervening period is wanting.

Coleridge seems to have been mistaken in saying that it occurs in "many others of our elder writers."

The next quotation in the N.E.D. after C. is from Emerson.

p. 236, ll. 15, 16: "*To establish this distinction was one main object of the FRIEND;*". For Note on the "Friend" *see* p. 773. For Note on "this distinction" (between reason and understanding) *see* p. 776.

p. 236, l. 25: "*I was persuaded*", etc. Questioned by Shawcross.

p. 236, l. 27: "*THE WATCHMAN,*". *See* Note, p. 742. The tour Coleridge here describes took place in January and February, 1796.

p. 236, ll. 33, 34: "*with a flaming prospectus,*". This is reprinted on p. 143.

p. 237, ll. 6, 7: "*a zealous Unitarian in Religion;*". *See* Note on p. 777.

p. 240, l. 34: "'*The sensual and the dark*'". The first fourteen lines of the fifth and last stanza of "France: an Ode," first published "Morning Post," 16th April, 1798.

p. 241, l. 33: " '*In the position, that all reality*", etc. Coleridge first began to read Kant in 1801. In that year the intellect of Kant first took hold of him, he says, "with giant hands." Kant was able to explain on a rational basis the reason: understanding distinctions which Coleridge had hitherto only felt intuitively, and if ever he may be said to have "left" him, it was because, like Spinoza, Kant was not able to give him the personal and governing God he wanted.

p. 242, ll. 28 to 30: "*I become convinced, that religion,* . . . *must have a* moral *origin;*". Shawcross, in a Note on another passage, quotes pertinent sentences. From "1796":

By faith I understand, first, a deduction from experiments

in favour of the existence of something not experienced, and secondly, the motives which attend such a deduction. ("Letters,' p. 202.)

From "1810":

Religious Belief is an act, not of the understanding, but of the will. To become a believer—one must love the doctrines and must resolve with passion to believe. (From Crabb Robinson's "Diary".)

Chapter XII (p. 243).

p. 243, l. 12: "*my own Hierocles,*", *i.e.* my own commentator—Hierocles was a commentator on Pythagoras.

p. 243, ll. 14, 15: "*a treatise of a religious fanatic,*". Shawcross considers Jacob Boehme is intended here. (*See* his Note on Coleridge and Boehme, B.L., I, pp. 242 and 243.)

Chapter XIII (p. 246).

It is to this chapter that the whole philosophic section has been leading, but the point is characteristically reduced to less than a page (the one quoted here).

p. 247, ll. 1, 2: "*the critical essay on the uses of the Supernatural*" is not, of course, found prefixed to the "Ancient Mariner," and in fact was never written.

The taste of Coleridge and his printer for black letter may be noted; it is usually confined to title pages (*e.g.* of "Christabel" and the bastard title page of B.L.).

Chapter XIV (p. 247).

p. 247, l. 34: "*originated the plan of the 'Lyrical Ballads';*". *See* the Note to the "Ancient Mariner," p. 719.

p. 248, ll. 2, 3: "*willing suspension of disbelief*". *Cf.* the lecture-note (S.C., I, p. 100): "Stage presentations are to produce a sort of temporary half-faith, which the Spectator encourages in himself and supports by a voluntary contribution on his own part, because he knows that it is at all times in his power to see the thing as it really is."

p. 248, l. 14: "*preparing . . . 'The Dark Ladie,'*". *See* the Note on "Love," p. 731.

p. 248, ll. 24, 25: "*presented . . . as an* experiment,". The first edition of the "Lyrical Ballads" is preceded by a short "Advertisement":

> The majority of the following poems are to be considered as experiments. They were written chiefly with a view to ascertain how far the language of conversation in the middle and lower classes of society is adapted to the purposes of poetic pleasure. Readers accustomed to the gaudiness and inane phraseology . . .

p. 248, ll. 29, 30: "*To the second edition he added a preface*". The editions of 1800, 1802 and 1805 each had the Preface, each time rewritten by Wordsworth.

p. 248, ll. 35, 36: "*an equivocal expression*) . . . *the language of* real *life*.". How equivocal may be gauged by Wordsworth's contradictory way of putting it, *e.g.:*

(1) "Language of conversation" quoted above.

(2) "A selection of the real language of men in a state of vivid sensation" (1800).

(3) "A selection of language really used by men" (1805).

A fuller list is given in B.L. Selections, Sampson.

p. 249, ll. 25 to 27: "*With many parts of this preface, . . . I never concurred;*". This critical disagreement with Wordsworth was first publicly expressed in the B.L. But there are two important letters showing a very much earlier difference. Both belong to July, 1802. One, to Sotheby, is quoted on p. 598. An extract from the other, to Southey, may be included here:

> But I will apprise you of one thing, that although Wordsworth's Preface is half a child of my own brain, and arose out of conversations so frequent that, with few exceptions, we could scarcely either of us, perhaps, positively say which first started any particular thought . . . yet I am far from going all lengths with Wordsworth. ("Letters," p. 386.)

p. 249, l. 31: "*Mr. Wordsworth in his recent collection*". The "Poems" of 1815. The old "Lyrical Ballads" Preface is here printed at the end, to make room for a new one.

p. 251, l. 17: "*A poem is that species of composition*,", &c. This definition of poetry is repeated in the lectures (*see* p. 313).

p. 252, l. 15: "'Praecipitandus est'". The reference is from Chapter cxviii of the "Satyricon" of Petronius.

p. 253, l. 30: "'*Doubtless this could not be, . . .*'". From "Nosce Teipsum," sec. iv. Coleridge seems as usual to be quoting from memory, as his third stanza is a very rough paraphrase of the original. Most of the extracts in the B.L. have small misquotations. I have not thought it necessary to note these.

Chapter XV (p. 254).

This chapter seems to have been rewritten from notes for the fourth lecture of the 1811-2 series. (*See* the Tomalin report in S.C., II, pp. 87 to 99.)

p. 255, ll. 18, 19: "*choice of subjects very remote*". *Cf.* p. 734.

p. 257, l. 8: " '*Which shoots its being*' ". A version of a line from he last stanza of "France: an Ode."

p. 257, ll. 32, 33: " '*the prophetic soul Of the wide world*' ". *Cf.* Coleridge's early transcription of these lines in a notebook, p. 155, l. 17, 18.

p. 258, l. 33: "Γονίμου μὲν ποιητοῦ——" From Aristophanes, "Frogs," ll. 96 and 97.

p. 260, l. 10: " '*Must* we *be free* . . .' ". This is the sonnet of Wordsworth's which begins

> It is not to be thought of that the Flood.

Chapter XVII (p. 260).

p. 261, ll. 38, 39: "*language taken, . . . from the mouths of men in real life*, ". For Wordsworth's actual words *see* Note, p. 758.

p. 262, ll. 18, 19: "imitation *as distinguished from a mere* copy.". This was one of Coleridge's favourite distinctions. (*Cf.* p. 284.)

p. 262, l. 41: " '*The Mad Mother*,' ". So named in L.B. Later known by the opening words "Her eyes are wild."

p. 265, ll. 2, 3: "*the* persons *of poetry must be clothed with* generic *attributes*,". That this was an old belief of Coleridge's but one which he held with increasing conviction may be seen by studying the textual changes in certain poems noted here on pp. 734 and 736.

p. 265, l. 19: " '*An old man*' ", etc. Coleridge takes this quotation from "Michael" thirty-four lines further.

p. 266, ll. 33, 34: "*the* NURSE *in Shakspere's 'Romeo and Juliet'* ". *Cf.* Coleridge's Notes on the Nurse, p. 369.

p. 267, *footnote:* " * '*I've measured it* . . .'". By 1820 these lines had become:

> Though but of compass small, and bare
> To thirsty winds and parching air.

That the derisive laughter at the "false simplicity" of the "Lyrical Ballads" (in which Coleridge felt himself to be not fairly included) had not yet died down is shown by the tone of an admirer's diffident reference to these lines in 1815:

> On my gently alluding to the lines "three feet long," etc., and confessing that I dared not read them aloud in company, he (W.W.) said "they ought to be liked." (Crabb Robinson, "Diary," 9th May, quoted by Shawcross.)

p. 272, l. 7: "in a state of excitement.". For the actual phrase ("a state of vivid sensation") *see ante*, p. 758.

p. 272, l. 37: *"illustrated by Mr. Wordsworth"*. In the prefatory note to "The Thorn."

Chapter XVIII (p. 273).

p. 273, l. 31: " '*In distant countries*' ". From the poem called "The Last of the Flock."

p. 274, l. 27: "*I am reminded of the sublime prayer*". This poem has not been identified.

p. 274, l. 37: "THE VISION", etc. L. 79 of the "Excursion."

p. 275, l. 3: "*reading ought to differ from talking.*". *Cf.* Lecture vi of 1811-2 (S.C., II, p. 112): "Every man who reads with true sensibility, must read with a tone, since it conveys, with additional effect, the harmony and rhythm of the verse, without in the slightest degree obscuring the meaning."

p. 275, ll. 4, 5: "*Unless therefore the difference denied be that of the mere words,*". Shawcross points out that "mere words" or vocabulary is what Wordsworth *was* referring to.

p. 275, ll. 29, 30: Footnote: "*Joseph Lancaster, . . . Dr. Bell's*". Two rival educationalists. Lancaster stood for the Nonconformists, Bell for the Church of England. Bell was one of (what De Quincey called) Coleridge's monomaniac likings.

p. 278, ll. 4, 5: "*for neither . . . has ever been . . . denied*". Coleridge would not have allowed himself to say this in 1800, the date of the "Preface."

p. 278, ll. 18 to 20: "*metre. . . . to hold in check the workings of passion.*". *Cf.* the letter to Sotheby, p. 599.

p. 280, l. 15: " '*Tell me, thou son*' ", etc. Coleridge's version of Christopher Smart's lines "To the Rev. Mr. Powell, on the Non-Performance of a Promise he made the Author of a Hare."

p. 280, l. 21: "*The reference to the 'Children in the Wood,'* ". In the Preface Wordsworth contrasts a stanza of "The Babes in the Wood" with some nonsense verses and says that the merit of the former lies in the fact not that the words are less like prose, but that they carry more meaning.

p. 282, l. 9: " '*And I have travelled far as Hull, to see*' ", etc. Wordsworth altered these lines in 1820 to:

> And I have travelled weary miles, to see
> If aught which he had owned might still remain for me.

Other lines from these stanzas were altered in 1827.

Chapter XXII (p. 286).

It had been intended to quote this famous chapter complete, but the first two defects enumerated by Coleridge return once again to the already fully represented "prosaic diction" discussion, and the third and fourth are contained in the fifth, with which I have started.

p. 286, l. 39: "*Vol I, p. 320*". The reference is of course to the poem "I wandered lonely as a cloud . . ." Coleridge is still quoting from the "Poems . . . In Two Volumes," 1815.

p. 287, l. 1: "*The second instance*". The poem is called "Gipsies." Coleridge made the same criticism of this poem in 1810. "Had the whole world been standing idle, more powerful arguments to expose the evil could not have been brought forward" (*ref.* Shawcross).

p. 289, l. 33: " '*To whom the grave*' ", etc. Wordsworth later altered these four lines to

> In darkness lost,—the darkness of the grave.

p. 291, l. 6: "*has been already stated:*". At the beginning of Chapter XVI, where Dante is quoted (*De la nobile volgare eloquenza*) on the importance of guarding the purity of the native tongue.

p. 291, l. 24: "*I have ventured to propose*". *See* Chapter I, p. 206.

p. 293, ll. 7-9: "*impulses . . . which . . . a contemporary* poet, *excites in youth*". Coleridge is again referring to Chapter I—the account of his first reading of Bowles.

p. 293, l. 30: " '*Makes audible*' ", etc. *See* p. 119.

p. 293, l. 37: "*page 25, vol 2nd.:*". This page contains stanzas 3 to 6 of "Star Gazers."

p. 293, l. 39: "*'O Reader!'* ", etc. These two stanzas are from "Simon Lee." The italicization of "me" is Coleridge's. The next quotation is from "The Fountain."

p. 295, l. 17: "*'Fit audience find, though few.'* ". "Paradise Lost," VII, l. 31.

p. 295, l. 20: "*Dante . . . Canzoni*—". "Il Convivio," Book II, Chapter i (*Ref.* Sampson.)

p. 296, l. 1: "Πολλά μοι ὑπ' ἀγκῶ-", etc. Pindar. Olymp. II, 149-59. (*Ref.* B.L., 1847.)

p. 296, l. 32: *"description of skating,"*. From "Influences of Natural Objects," etc. In the days when the relationship was still unclouded, Wordsworth had allowed Coleridge to publish the poem in the "Friend" (28th December, 1809).

p. 297, l. 19: *"the description of the blue-cap,"*. The poem is called "The Kitten and the Falling Leaves."

p. 297, l. 24: "*'Three years she grew'* ", etc. The fourth poem of the "Lucy" sequence.

p. 297, l. 39: *"Vol. I, page 134 to 136,"*. The poem begins:

'Tis said, that some have died for love:

p. 298, l. 33: *"In the play of* Fancy,". The fault seems partly to have lain, as Sampson points out, in Wordsworth's habit of classing his poems under such headings as "Poems of the Fancy," "Poems of the Imagination," "Poems Founded on the Affections," etc.

p. 299, l. 1: " '——*add the gleam,*' ". It seems to have been Shawcross who pointed out that the context in which Coleridge has placed these lines has served to perpetuate a common misinterpretation of their meaning, which is not intended to express the insight of "real" vision, or imaginative apprehension, but its opposite, the glamour of a young man's romanticized descriptions. Though he afterwards changed back to the original text, in 1827 Wordsworth altered the lines to:

——add a gleam
Of lustre, never known to sea or land,
But borrowed from the youthful poet's dream.

p. 299, l. 20: *"pinal umbrage"*. Wordsworth wrote "pining umbrage."

p. 299, l. 44: " *'Our birth is but a sleep'* ", &c. Coleridge prints these and succeeding extracts in full.

p. 300, l. 8: *"the poet's last published work,"*. "The White Doe of Rylstone" (1815). I have retained Coleridge's full quotation, since the lines are not so familiar.

p. 301, l. 18: *"Bartram's 'Travels'"*. (1792), p. 36. *Cf.* p. 744.

p. 301, ll. 29, 30: "FIRST GENUINE PHILOSOPHIC POEM." *Cf.* the letters to Sharp and Wordsworth, pp. 610 and 660.

p. 302, l. 3: *"the commander in chief of this unmanly warfare"*. *See* Index, "Jeffrey."

p. 302, l. 33: *"So much for the detractors"*. The apology which follows for "the freedom" with which he has spoken of Wordsworth's defects may be compared with the letter to Allsop, 2nd December, 1818, where he says:

> They knew, too, how long and faithfully I had acted on the maxim, never to admit the *faults* of a work of genius to those who denied or were incapable of feeling and understanding the *beauties;* not from wilful partiality, but as well knowing that in *saying* truth I should, to such critics, convey falsehood. If, in one instance, in my literary life, I have appeared to deviate from this rule, first, it was not till the fame of the writer (which I had been for fourteen years successively toiling like a second Ali to build up) had been established; and, secondly and chiefly, with the purpose and, I may safely add, with the *effect* of rescuing the necessary task from malignant defamers, and in order to set forth the excellences and the trifling proportion which the defects bore to the excellences ("Letters," p. 697).

p. 304, l. 1: " '*When Hope grew round me,*' ", &c. From "Dejection: an Ode," *see* p. 105.

Satyrane's Letters (p. 304).

Coleridge was able to fill forty-eight pages of the second volume of B.L. with these letters, which were rewritten from the correspondence of his first visit to Germany in 1798-9. They had been already published in the "Friend," November-December, 1809, where they were used for the same purpose. The title is explained by the appearance in No. XIV, the "Friend," of a poem (*see* "Poems," p. 413, "A Tombless Epitaph") which begins:

'Tis true, Idoloclastes Satyrane!

In these lines Coleridge describes Satyrane (himself) as the Poet-Philosopher. (The famous Sir Satyrane is of course from the "Faerie Queene," Book I.)

p. 304, l. 28: " '*Their visnomies*' ". A good example of the excellence of Coleridge's misquotings—here more Spenserian than

Spenser. The actual couplet, in No. V of the "Amoretti," begins: "And her faire countenance," etc. Yet "visnomy" is a good Spenserian word (it occurs, for instance, in Sonnet xlv of the same sequence).

p. 306, ll. 15, 16: "*The conversation began on his part*". The subjects of discussion need these notes (*cf.* Shawcross). The "surrender" refers to the second French expedition to Ireland, 1798. Nelson's victory, of Aboukir Bay, 1798. Glover (1712-85) wrote two very long epics, "Leonidas" and the "Athenaid." The "English prose translation from his Messiah" was by Mary and Joseph Collyer, 1763.

Chapter XXIV (p. 309).

p. 309, l. 26: "*With regard to the Unitarians,*". *See* p. 777.

MISCELLANEOUS

The majority of extracts in this sub-section are taken from:

(1) "Literary Remains" (L.R. in the notes), first published in 1836 and edited by H. N. Coleridge. Professor Raysor has been able to show to what an alarming extent H.N.C. must have re-arranged Coleridge MSS., interpolating passages of his own, etc. There are thousands of mistakes, he says, "embodying the most grievous errors." Whenever possible I have taken later editions of the matter contained in "Literary Remains" (in cases of course where the editor has had access to the originals); otherwise I have tried to confine my quotations to the more obviously authentic parts, such as the reports of the lectures of 1818.

(2) "Shaksperian Criticism" (S.C. in the notes), first published in 1930, and edited by T. M. Raysor. These two volumes probably represent the final edition of this division of Coleridge's work. In 1883 appeared "Lectures and Notes on Shakspere," a much enlarged collection of Shakspere criticism edited by T. Ashe. This, besides selections from "Literary Remains," contains hitherto uncollected newspaper reports and shorthand notes of the lectures, notably those unearthed by J. P. Collier, which had been published separately in 1856 ("Seven Lectures on Shakspere and Milton"). S.C. reprints the Shakspere marginalia, the lecture notes and the lecture reports from their

original or best available sources, and includes hitherto un-published reports by Tomalin, etc. As Professor Raysor's edition is absolutely reliable, and as he has been able to use highly inaccessible MSS., I have with permission used his text. The whole book, with its notes and introduction, is invaluable to Coleridge students. I have followed most of its minor conjectural emendations of text.

"[The Agreeable and the Beautiful Distinguished]" (p. 311). From the recapitulation of the third and final essay "On the Principles of Genial Criticism concerning the Fine Arts," etc., first published in "Felix Farley's Bristol Journal," August and September, 1814. These essays were reprinted by Cottle in his "Early Recollections," 1837, and again by T. Ashe in "Coleridge Miscellanies," 1855. They are available now in the Shawcross edition of B.L. They belong to that special Coleridge anthology which could be composed out of the compositions he considered "the best . . . he had ever written." Shawcross (B.L., II, p. 305) points out that in making his distinction Coleridge is refuting the only authoritative aesthetic of his time—Burke's Essay "On the Sublime and Beautiful."

p. 311, ll. 26, 27: *"Mr. Allston's large landscape,".* Coleridge's original motive in writing these essays was to draw attention to the paintings of an unsuccessful friend, which were being exhibited in Bristol at the time.

p. 313, l. 29: *"Poetry is not the proper antithesis to prose,",* etc. This is taken from L.R., II, p. 7, all except for the middle paragraph, which Raysor prints from the notebook original. *Cf.* these definitions with p. 251. Raysor points out that in the "Lyrical Ballads" Preface this antithesis is mentioned by Wordsworth, and he dates the discussion from an anonymous article in the "Monthly Magazine," 1796 (II, p. 453), where the usual antithesis of poetry and prose is criticised.

p. 315, ll. 1 to 5: *"Milton, . . . Speaking of poetry,".* In the essay "Of Education." He is contrasting poetry with rhetoric.

p. 315, ll. 6, 7: *"How awful is the power of words!".* "Our language wants terms of comprehensive generality, implying the kind, not the degree or species, as in that good and necessary word *sensuous,* which we have likewise dropped, opposed to sensual . . ." (A.P., p. 123).

For "sensuous" *cf.* note on p. 756.

p. 316, l. 19: "*It is an art*," &c. Coleridge's usual definition of poetry well epitomised, from Collier's report of the second 1811-2 lecture (S.C., II, p. 66).

"*[False Categories]*" (p. 316). S.C., I, p. 196. From a MS.

"*[The Phenomenon of Prose]*" (p. 317). L.R., II, p. 372.

p. 317, ll. 21, 22: "*Pherecydean origin of prose*". Pherecydes of Scyros seems to have been considered less mythological in Coleridge's time.

"*[Prose Style]*" (p. 317). From the lectures of 1818 (L.R., I, p. 235).

For similar surveys of English prose style *cf.* the manuscript printed on p. 326 and the "Table Talk" discussion on p. 512.

"*[Influence of Public Taste]*" (p. 320). Reprinted from a MS. (S.C., I, p. 208). For the attitude expressed here *cf.* Letter XCVI:

> I loathe parodies of all kinds, and hold even "To wed or not to wed," "To print or not to print," not altogether guiltless, &c.

"*[Meanings of Words]*" (p. 321). A MS. fragment of the lectures of 1808 (S.C., I, p. 181). The anecdote of the Lady at the Cataract of Lodore is often repeated by Coleridge, with different details.

"*[Choice of Words]*" (p. 322). From Collier's report of the 1811-2 lectures (S.C., II, p. 64). These reports of J. P. Collier's are naturally suspect. Raysor has weighed the evidence, and shown good reason to think them authentic.

"*[Languages Compared]*" (p. 323). From Collier's report of 1811-2 (S.C., II, p. 119).

p. 323, l. 23: " '*The learned Greek*',", etc. Collier gives the reference—Act I, Scene i, "Lingua, or the Combat of the Tongue and the Five Senses" (reprinted in Dodsley).

"*[Atrophy of Metaphors]*" (p. 324). From the Tomalin report, 1811-2 (S.C., II, p. 102).

"*[Translators as Critics]*" (p. 324). From Coleridge's Preface to his translation of "The Death of Wallenstein" ("Poems," p. 725). For the "pleasure or disgust" of his own feelings, *cf.* p. 723.

"*[Attitude of Modern Editors]*" (p. 324). From the Tomalin report (S.C., II, p. 99).

"*[Types of Readers]*" (p. 325). From the Collier report (S.C., II, p. 64). This is an adaptation from the Abhoth of the Mishnah, specimens of which Coleridge inserted in the original "Friend," Nos. X and XI. Coleridge's interest in Hebrew led him to make (abortive) arrangements for a collection of "Rabbinical Tales" for Murray in 1817 (*see* "Letters," p. 667).

"*[Reading Aloud]*" (p. 325). Collier's report (S.C., II, p. 112).

"*[Books for Children]*" (p. 326). Tomalin's report (S.C., II, p. 110).

p. 326, l. 21: "*Arabian Nights*". *Cf.* the letter on p. 528.

p. 326, l. 25: "*praise for giving to beggars*,". *Cf.* the lecture on education, 1808; "Such books and such lessons do not teach goodness, but—if I might venture such a word—goodyness" (S.C., II, p. 13).

"*Memoranda*" (p. 326). Reprinted from a hitherto unpublished MS. now in the British Museum (Eg. 2800, f. 53). Whatever its real date (the watermark is 1796), the ideas and phrases connect this scheme with his plan for the 1808 lectures, outlined in a letter to Davy, 11th September, 1807 ("Letters," p. 515):

1. On the genius and writings of Shakspere, relatively to his predecessors and contemporaries. . . .

2. On Spenser, including the metrical romances. . . .

4. Dryden and Pope, including the origin and after history of poetry of witty logic.

p. 326, l. 36: "*Romance on Attila—*". The hexameter romance "Waltharius" of Ekkehart (*fl.* 950).

"*Dante*" (p. 328). From the tenth lecture of 1818 (L.R., I, pp. 153 *et seq.*). Of this lecture, Crabb Robinson records (27th February):

It was on Dante and Milton—one of his very best. He digressed less than usually and really gave information and ideas about the poets he professed to criticise.

To help his friend H. F. Cary, Coleridge in this lecture recommended the translation of Dante. This resulted in the immediate sale of 1,000 copies—a proof of the great influence of this most successful course. (The translation of the "Inferno" in 1805 had been a failure, and Cary had had to publish the complete version at his own expense.)

"*Rabelais*" (p. 330). "Written by Mr. C. in Mr. Gillman's copy of Rabelais" (L.R., I, p. 138).

"*Cervantes*" (p. 331). From the eighth lecture of 1818 (L.R., I, pp. 118 *et seq.*). *See* Crabb Robinson, 20th February:

His subject was Cervantes, but he was more than usually prosing and his tone peculiarly drawling. His digressions on the nature of insanity were carried too far, and his remarks on the book but old and by him often repeated.

"*Chaucer . . . Spenser*" (pp. 332, 333). These two extracts from the third lecture of 1818 (L.R., I, pp. 88 *et seq.*).

"*[His Characteristics]*" (p. 335). In this passage alone I have followed the version in L.R. (II, p. 77) instead of the one in S.C. (I, pp. 225 *et seq.*). H.N.C. has made on this occasion an excellent, and at any rate comprehensible, arrangement of an awkward and distractingly rough MS. He has also usefully interpolated two passages from newspaper reports (of the first Bristol lecture, 1818).

"*[His Conceits]*" (p. 339). This section and the next are from the Collier report of the sixth lecture (S.C., II, pp. 121 *et seq.*).

p. 340, l. 10: "*Had Dr. Johnson lived*", etc. Coleridge's constant repetition of this defence is, of course, partly by way of counterblast to Dr. Johnson's *Preface:*

He [Shakspere] is not long soft and pathetick without some idle conceit, or contemptible equivocation.

"*[First Scenes]*" (p. 340). From a MS. (S.C., I, p. 41).

"*[Shakspere's Advantages]*" (p. 341). Tomalin (S.C., II, p. 84).

"*[Possibilities of the Theatre]*" (p. 342). From a MS. (S.C., I, p. 209).

"*[Shakspere's Critics]*" (p. 344). Collier report (S.C., II, p. 163).

"*[Shakspere's Judgement . . .]*" (p. 345). From a MS. If Professor Raysor is right in dating this note 1808, it is important to those interested in the plagiarism question. In this same year Schlegel was lecturing on Shakspere's judgement in Vienna, using similar terms. Coleridge maintains, and from this note it would seem he rightly maintains, that he did not see these lectures till three years later. *See* Coleridge's Note in B.L., I, p. 22,

Shawcross's comment on the note, and Raysor's summing up (S.C., I, p. 219); and in this volume, the letter on plagiarism, pp. 636 to 642.

"[*Shakspere 'out of time'*]" (p. 346). Collier report, S.C., II, p. 116.

"[*The* I *in Shakspere*]" (p. 347). From the seventh lecture of 1818 —on Beaumont and Fletcher, with whose over-writing Coleridge had been contrasting the restraint of the final words of Othello to Iago.

" '*Love's Labour's Lost*' " (p. 348). From L.R., II, pp. 103 *et seq.*

" '*Romeo and Juliet*' " (p. 351). The Collier report of the seventh lecture of the 1811-2 series. As this is the best report of a good lecture, I have reproduced it complete as a specimen (S.C., II, pp. 128 *et seq.*). Crabb Robinson (9th December, 1811) calls this:

> Coleridge's 7th and incomparably best lecture. C. declaimed with great eloquence on *Love* without wandering from his subject, "Romeo and Juliet." He was spirited; for the greater part intelligible, tho' profound; and he was methodical.

Coleridge's fifth lecture had reached the limit of irrelevance (*cf.* Crabb Robinson, 2nd December):

> An amusing declamation against reviewers, French philosophy, precocity, etc., in the education of children, but unluckily scarcely one observation on Shakspere, Milton, or even on poetry.

p. 354, ll. 25, 26: "*drawn rather from meditation than from observation,*". This distinction is often developed by Coleridge (*cf.* p. 186 and B.L., II, p. 64). *See also* Raysor's interesting note to S.C., II, p. 117, where he deals with its possible origin in Richter or Schelling.

p. 366, l. 25: "*Elwes,*". John Elwes (1714-89), whose "name has become a byword for sordid penury" (D.N.B.).

"[*Notes*]" (p. 367). These notes and those which follow on other plays are taken from the first volume of S.C. Professor Raysor has collected them from two copies of Shakspere, on the fly-leaves, margins, and blank interleaves of which Coleridge wrote his comments. These volumes are now in the British Museum (Theobald's edition, 1773, and the Stockdale edition, 1807).

p. 370, l. 15: "(ἕπομαι, sequor)". Not the derivation of "epic," though the thought seems to have passed through Coleridge's mind that it ought to be. I have retained such interjections to preserve the note character of the extracts.

p. 371, l. 6: "*In this scene*". This paragraph from L.R., II, p. 171.

p. 372, l. 9: "*Theobald adopts the reading 'through'* ". Coleridge is elsewhere impatient of Theobald, identifying him with eighteenth century attempts to "refine" the metre of Shakspere. Coleridge tries to refine the ear of the reader.

p. 373, l. 35: " '*She dreamt last night*,' ", etc. The folios have "statue"; Steevens and Dyce "statua"; the Cambridge text "statuë." The trisyllabic plural occurs in "Richard III," III, vii, l. 25:

> But like dumb statues or breathing stones.

p. 374, l. 27: "'*Hamlet*' *was the play*,", &c. Raysor gives the facts relevant to this paragraph: (1) Coleridge mentioned his analysis of "Hamlet" in a letter to Beaumont, 1st February, 1804 (quoted here on p. 613), but he did not describe it; (2) Coleridge is referring to his lectures of 1808, and seems to have thought that Schlegel's were in 1810; (3) Hazlitt *might* have supported Coleridge, but in his preface to his "Characters of Shakspere's Plays" he pointedly praises Schlegel only (*cf.* Note, p. 768).

p. 375, l. 28: "*We will now pass*", &c. This section of the criticism is taken from the Collier report of the twelfth lecture of 1811-2 (S.C., II, pp. 192 *et seq.*).

p. 379, ll. 27, 28: "*This*, . . . *was merely the excuse Hamlet made to himself*". The gradual evolution in the English eighteenth century of this kind of criticism may be exemplified by the way in which such a comment as this was anticipated independently in (1) William Richardson's "Essays on Shakspere's Dramatic Characters" (1784), and (2) Thomas Robertson's "An Essay on the Character of Hamlet" (1790) (*ref.* Raysor). *See* Professor Nichol Smith's Introduction to "Eighteenth-Century Essays on Shakspere," where it is shown how early "character-study" criticism of Shakspere began to replace neo-classical criticism. (A better-known landmark is Maurice Morgann's "Essay on the Dramatic Character of Falstaff," 1777.)

"*The character of Hamlet*" (p. 384). This passage is from a notebook transcript by E. H. Coleridge.

p. 384, l. 24: " *'Action is transitory,'* ", &c. Wordsworth, "Borderers," III, v (*ref.* Raysor).

" *'Lear'* " (p. 388). As a specimen, the "Lear" marginalia are here reproduced complete (*cf.* S.C., I, pp. 54 *et seq.*).

" *'Macbeth'* " (p. 399). A comment on V, iii, which I have always quoted with admiration, Professor Raysor calls spurious (except for the first line), so I have to debase it to the Notes. It is:

> Now all is *inward*—no more prudential prospective reasonings . . . he puts on despondency, the final heart-armour of the wretched, and would fain think everything shadowy and unsubstantial, as indeed all things are to those who cannot regard them as symbols of goodness.

p. 399, l. 3: " '*Nor heaven peep through*' ", &c. No one has ever been known to support this conjecture of Coleridge's, nor has "het" as a variant for "height" been found.

p. 399, l. 9: "*This low porter soliloquy*". It would not be true to say that Coleridge never accepted the principle of comic relief. He appreciated the dramatic function of the gravediggers. Perhaps he is affected by the coarseness of the porter's second speech.

" *'Tempest'* " (p. 401). From L.R., II, pp. 95 *et seq.*

p. 403, l. 4: "*Before I go further,*". From the Collier report of the ninth lecture of 1811-2. "In making this important distinction between mechanic and organic regularity, Coleridge acknowledged his indebtedness to Schlegel" (Raysor).

"*Donne*" (p. 406). From "Notes on English Divines" (1853), Vol. III, pp. 249 *et seq.* With the second paragraph, *cf.* the note on Milton, p. 414.

"*Ben Jonson*" (p. 406). From L.R., I, pp. 47 *et seq.*

"*Beaumont and Fletcher*" (p. 408). Hitherto unpublished marginalia from a copy of a "complete" Beaumont and Fletcher of 1679 ("Fifty Comedies and Tragedies . . . All in one Volume"). The book is in the British Museum and was once lent to Coleridge by Charles Lamb. It is the original old folio from which Lamb selected his "Specimens," and which he "dragged home late at night, from Barker's in Covent Garden" ("Old China"). The first extract is taken from p. 384 of the second half of the book; the second from p. 578 of the first half.

"*Preface to Seward's Edition:*" (p. 409). From L.R., II, p. 289.

p. 409, ll. 31, 32: *"even now it is but just awaking."*. *Cf.* p. 370.

"Massinger" (p. 410). From L.R., I, p. 108.

"Sir Thomas Browne" (p. 412). From L.R., II, p. 413. It is printed there as a letter, dated 10th March, 1804, and so has been inserted here not quite consistently.

p. 413, l. 20: " '*Treatise on the Quincuncial Plantations*' ". The title is "The Garden of Cyrus. Or the Quincuncial Lozenge, or Network Plantations of the Ancients, Artificially, Naturally, Mystically consider'd."

" '*Religio Medici*' " (p. 414). From L.R., I, p. 241.

"Milton" (p. 414). The first extract is quoted in L.R., I, p. 184, from the "Gutch Memorandum Book." The second is from L.R., I, p. 170—the tenth lecture of 1818. The third, from the same lecture.

Shakspere and Milton were announced in the syllabuses of most of the courses, and were doubtless referred to in all of them. But the records of Milton criticisms are comparatively very scanty. We must wait for Professor Raysor's "Coleridge's Miscellaneous Criticism" for a full collection of these.

" '*Comus*' " (p. 416).

These two notes were written by Coleridge in the margin of a copy of Milton's shorter poems (edited by T. Warton, second edition, 1791). They were printed in an article by Mr. John Drinkwater which appeared in the "London Mercury," September, 1926. The first I have included for its connection with Coleridge's own way of writing poetry.

"Pepys" (p. 417). First published in "Notes, Theologica, Political and Miscellaneous," ed. by Derwent Coleridge, 1853. Coleridge is making a mistake in the text he chooses for his well-justified criticism, because Pepys is referring here to another version of Shakspere's plot—"Sawney the Scot," or the "Taming of the Shrew," by John Lacy. *See* Pepys's reference to it on 19th April, 1667.

"Defoe" (p. 418). From L.R., I, pp. 189 *et seq.* The 1818 lectures.

"Swift" (p. 420). From L.R., I, p. 140. The 1818 lectures.

"Sterne" (p. 420). From L.R., I, p. 139. He is discussed at length, with Swift and Rabelais, in this ninth lecture of 1818, the

subject of which, according to the syllabus, is "the nature and constituents of genuine Humour, and the distinctions of the Humorous from the Witty, the Fanciful, the Droll, and the Odd."

"Junius" (p. 422). From L.R., I, p. 249.

"Charles Tennyson" (p. 423). From a hitherto unpublished note written in the margin of Sonnet XIX of "Sonnets and Fugitive Pieces" by Charles Tennyson [afterwards Turner], 1830. For another criticism *see* the "Table Talk" extract, p. 486.

" *'Remorse'* " (p. 423).

" *'Destiny of Nations'* " (p. 424).

These two MS. notes were first published in 1912. For Coleridge's opinion of "Remorse," *cf. ante*, p. 740.

''THEOLOGICO-METAPHYSICAL''

"[A Sermon]" (p. 437). Printed here for the first time, from a transcript by E. H. Coleridge now in the possession of the Rev. G. H. B. Coleridge.

This is the first of a series of five. The comments of E. H. C. are interesting. He compares this "vision" with the second Lay Sermon, and adds that the course was "delivered at Bristol, on and after Sep. 3rd 1795. 8 o'clock Tuesday evenings. Assembly Coffee House, on the Quay. Six shillings a course."

This sermon is to be compared—perhaps contrasted—with Hazlitt's description of Coleridge preaching, in his essay "My First Acquaintance with the Poets." ("The preacher then launched into his subject, like an eagle dallying with the wind. . . . Poetry and Philosophy had met together. Truth and Genius had embraced, under the eye and with the sanction of Religion.")

"[Priests]" (p. 429). In the successive editions of "Religious Musings" many notes were added or discarded. This one was omitted after 1796.

"The Friend: 1809" (p. 430). The full title begins *"THE FRIEND: a Literary, Moral, and Political Weekly Paper, excluding Personal and Party Politics and Events of the Day. Conducted by S. T. Coleridge of Grasmere, Westmoreland."* The first number appeared 1st June, 1809: the last, 15th March, 1810. Twenty-seven numbers were printed. Coleridge's account

of its publication and failure is to be found in Chapter X of B.L. *See* "Life," pp. 172 *et seq.*, for the extraordinary difficulties Coleridge made for himself in the printing and distribution of the paper.

"*[Erasmus and Voltaire]*" (p. 430, l. 11). From No. VIII, 5th October, 1809. (Part of Essay V, which begins at the fourth paragraph of this issue. Each successive number was simply a separate slice, cut without any reference to the general plan of the work, beginning and ending almost in the middle of a sentence.)

"*[Jacobinism]*" (p. 431, l. 19). From No. XI, 26th October, 1809. *See* "Life," p. 41, where Coleridge's answer (at Cambridge in 1794) to the admonitions of the Master of Jesus is quoted: "I am neither Jacobin nor Democrat, but a Pantisocrat." There is no Jacobinism in the "Watchman." *Cf.* the letter on p. 576.

"*[Taxation]*" (p. 433, l. 35). From No. XII, 9th November, 1809. Coleridge was at this time radical enough to be opposed to the demands for national economy and the agitation against the Poor Laws which came at the end of the war. *See* "Edmund Burke . . . a Study of the Political and Social Thinking of Burke, Wordsworth, Coleridge and Southey," by Alfred Cobban, 1929.

All these extracts were repeated in the 1818 "Friend," with fewer capitals.

"*The Statesman's Manual*" (p. 434, l. 33). The title continues: "Or the Bible the best guide to political skill and foresight. A Lay Sermon addressed to the higher classes of society, with an appendix, containing comments and essays connected with the study of the inspired writings." First published 1816. Sometimes referred to as the "Lay Sermon," or "First Lay Sermon," because it was announced originally as "A Lay Sermon on the Distresses of the Country," &c. *See* "Life," p. 225n., for Hazlitt's review of the pamphlet *from this advertisement*, saying that "one could tell what anything from Coleridge would be as well before as after publication." This review and the letter which followed it (containing the substance of all Hazlitt's later criticism of Coleridge in the "Then" and "Now" vein) started a very open quarrel. *Cf.* p. 670.

"*[The Reading Public]*" (p. 435, l. 14). *Cf.* a similar attack in B.L., Chapter III.

"*The Friend: 1818*" (p. 437, l. 22). Coleridge's *Advertisement* to this second edition ends:

> The present volumes are rather a *rifacciamento* than a new edition. The additions forming so large a proportion of the whole work, and the arrangement being altogether new, I might indeed hesitate in bestowing the title of a republication on a work which can scarcely be said to have been ever published, in the ordinary trade-acceptation of the word.

"*[Danger of Indistinct Conceptions]*" (p. 437, l. 23). These two extracts are from Introductory Essay V and Introductory Essay XIV respectively.

"*[Shakspere and the Science of Method]*" (p. 439, l. 33). From the "second section." A version of this essay first appeared earlier in 1818 as the "General Introduction" to the "Encyclopaedia Metropolitana" (*see* the Letter on p. 671). Coleridge republished it in the "Friend" on the ground that the editors had grossly altered his text ("The proposal of producing *raw materials* for their bookmakers was an insult to which no earthly motive could induce my assent") ("Unpublished Letters," II, p. 226).

Raysor points out that this essay (and the other famous Shaksperian criticism which forms Chapter XV of B.L.) owes nothing to Germany. Coleridge thought highly of the passage. *Cf.* the letter of 1819 (reprinted S.C., II, p. 324):

> Were it in my power, my works should be confined to the second volume of my "Literary Life," the Essays of the third volume of the "Friend," from page 67 to page 265 ["Section II"], with about fifty or sixty pages from the two former volumes, and some half-dozen of my poems.

p. 440, l. 5: "Plato's 2nd Letter". In Coleridge's time this "second epistle" had not been proved a forgery.

"*Aids to Reflection*" (p. 449, l. 1). The title continues: "in the Formation of a Manly Character, on the several grounds of Prudence, Morality and Religion. Illustrated by Select Passages from our Elder Divines, especially from Archbishop Leighton." First published, 1825.

For Coleridge's opinion of Leighton *cf.* p. 196. The book was begun as a selection from the Archbishop's works (*cf.* p. 692). For its reception *cf.* p. 699. The dates of successive editions are, 1825, 1831, 1836, 1837, 1843, 1848, 1854, 1856, &c.

p. 452, *footnote:* In the Introduction, Coleridge has given as the first of his reasons for writing the "Aids," the desire

> to direct the reader's attention to the value of the Science of Words, their use and abuse, and the incalculable advantages attached to the habit of using them appropriately, and with a distinct knowledge of their primary, derivative, and metaphorical senses.

Hence many of the sentences deal with word-meanings.

p. 452, l. 18: *Aphorisms XXVI et seq.* I have omitted some further etymological notes.

I have omitted a long note on the sacramental nature of marriage. As in some other matters, Coleridge writes more concretely of Love in his letters. *Cf.* "Unpublished Letters," II, p. 47 (part of which is quoted, p. 631).

"Bishop Hacket" (p. 455, l. 14). There are over thirty pages of notes on Hacket's sermons in the third volume of L.R.

p. 455, l. 36, to p. 456, l. 1: *"prominent among the characteristics of his . . . generation.".* I have omitted a long note of Coleridgeanly jocose irony at the expense of the "bump of benevolence" and "craniology."

"Of reason and the understanding" (p. 456, ll. 8, 9). For the philosophical connotations of this distinction of Coleridge and its statement by Kant, *see* J. H. Muirhead, "Coleridge as Philosopher," p. 65. The distinction is of course not primarily for him part of any metaphysical framework; it represents a desire to differentiate two modes of experience—"supersensuous," as he calls it in the "Friend," and conceptual. *Cf.* Goethe (quoted by J. M. Murry in this context, "Things to Come," p. 192):

> The Godhead is effective in the living and not in the dead, in the becoming and changing, not in the become and set-fast; and, therefore, similarly, the Reason is concerned only to strive towards the divine through the becoming and the living, and the Understanding only to make use of the become and the set-fast.

He is only at pains to define the distinction and relate it to a philosophy that he may be the better able to use it as a weapon against materialism. *Cf.* the "Friend," 1809, Nos. 5 and 9, and the "Statesman's Manual," Appendix C. It is on "Reason," as conceived by Coleridge, that the possibility of reconciling religion with philosophy depends.

p. 461, l. 26: "*Dr. Magee*". This is William Magee (1766-1831), Archbishop of Dublin, who in 1801 published a work on the doctrine of the Atonement, directed against the Priestleyan Unitarians ("Discourses on the Scriptural Doctrines of Atonement and Sacrifice," 1801. Fifth edition, London, 1832).

"*Confessions of an Inquiring Spirit*" (p. 462, ll. 12, 13). First published 1840, edited by H. N. Coleridge. The seven "letters" which compose it are accessible in Bohn's edition of the "Aids." In the "Harvard Theological Review" for January, 1918, there is an article of interest for students of the history of nineteenth century theology and the Oxford Movement. In his article, "The Place of Coleridge in English Theology," Mr. H. L. Stewart shows how strong was the influence of "Aids" and "Confessions" on that movement.

For the conjectural date 1824, *see* "Life," p. 254n. The beginning of the book mentions Carlyle's translation of "Wilhelm Meister," a copy of which the author gave to Coleridge in June, 1824.

"*[Notes on English Divines]*" (p. 463, l. 5). The title given to a collection, edited by Derwent Coleridge in 1853, of the Notes which form the bulk of Vols. III and IV of L.R. With the exception of forty-two pages in Vol. II the "Notes" are "practically a reprint" of these volumes of L.R. (T. J. Wise, "Bibliography of Coleridge," p. 176).

"*A Vindication*", &c. (p. 465, l. 13). Daniel Waterland, to whom Coleridge refers so frequently in his theological notes, published this book in 1719. It is in part an answer to the "Scripture Doctrine of the Trinity," by Dr. Samuel Clarke (of Arian tendencies).

p. 466, ll. 5, 6: "*during the sixteen months of my aberration from the Catholic Faith,*". In B.L., I, pp. 136 and 137 (Chapter x), Coleridge gives a more familiar account of this period. "I considered the *idea* of the Trinity a fair scholastic inference from the being of God, as a creative intelligence. . . . But seeing in the same no practical or moral bearing, I confined it to the schools of philosophy." *See* "Life," p. 73, for his conversion to Unitarianism at Cambridge in 1793. Shawcross (B.L., I, p. 252) shows the gradations of his conversion back to Trinitarianism. The quotation in this volume from A.P. on p. 157 marks the halfway point. Later he became extremely dogmatic against the "Psilan-thropists" ("presumptuously so-called" Unitarians).

"On the Constitution", &c. (p. 466, ll. 18, 19). First published 1830. This was the only outcome of the plan to add to the "Aids." *See* the letters in U.L. to Edward Coleridge, and the statement that he has determined to form "a compleat system of the Philosophy of Religion, as far as it was possible without such abstruse reasoning as would be intelligible to all but a Few."

p. 466, l. 26: *"Remember that whatever* is, lives.". *Cf.* p. 198.

"Hints towards the Formation", &c. (p. 467, ll. 29 to 31). First published 1848. Edited by Seth B. Watson. There is some controversy as to whether or no Coleridge wrote the essay in conjunction with Gillman.

The passage here quoted is referred to in an article by Joseph Needham in "Science Progress" (April, 1926)—"Coleridge as a Philosophical Biologist," *q.v.* for an interesting comparison of Coleridge's views with those of the German school of *Natur-philosophie*, for his obvious anticipation of the doctrine of Emergent Evolution, etc.

See Muirhead, "Coleridge as Philosopher," pp. 188 *et seq.*, for the relation of this dynamic philosophy of nature with Kant and the biological teachings of Dr. John Hunter (1728-93).

"[Evolution]" (p. 469, l. 21). First published "Modern Language Notes," Vol. XLII, No. 7 (November, 1927), where it is quoted by Miss Snyder in her article "Coleridge on Giordano Bruno." Contrast the following, quoted by Mr. Muirhead from a MS. ("Coleridge as Philosopher," p. 121):

> Wonderful are the efforts of Nature to reconcile chasm with continuity, to vault and nevertheless to glide, though in truth the continuity alone belongs to Nature, the chasms are the effect of a higher principle, limiting the duration and regulating the retention of the products. From the Vermes to the Mammalia, Organic Nature is in every class and everywhere tending to Individuality; but Individuality actually commences in Man. This and many other problems must find their solution in the right "Idea of Nature."

Both these passages are taken from the unpublished notebooks from which Coleridge was hoping to construct his *magnum opus*.

TABLE TALK

"*Crabb Robinson*" (p. 473, l. 3). His records are to be found in the "Diary," first published ("Diary, Reminiscences and Correspondence") 1869. *See* also "Blake, Coleridge, Wordsworth, Lamb, etc." [selections from the remains of C.R.], 1922. Crabb Robinson was known to Coleridge over a long and interesting period (there are notes of his conversation from 1810 onwards), but the method of reproducing the talk is too dry and disjointed to give more than a notebook impression.

p. 473, ll. 28, 29: "*supplying the place of the ancient chorus.*". Raysor (S.C., II, p. 212) points out a parallel from J. P. Richter. But this comment was far from being a commonplace when Coleridge made it.

"*Mr. Justice Coleridge*" (p. 474, l. 17). H. N. Coleridge printed his brother's recollections at the end of his own "Table Talk."

"*J. P. Collier*" (p. 475, l. 2). Already mentioned as the reporter of some of the 1811-2 lectures. He first met Coleridge in July (?), 1811. In the Preface to his published records ("Seven Lectures on Shakspere and Milton," 1856) he prints some interesting fragments from the conversation of Coleridge, Wordsworth, Hazlitt, etc. The style seems authentic (some of the talk he "wrote down very soon after it was delivered"). He describes Coleridge's voice:

> All he says is without effort, but not unfrequently with a sort of musical hum, and a catching of his breath at the end, and sometimes in the middle, of a sentence, enough to make a slight pause, but not so much as to interrupt the flow of his language.

Cf. Carlyle's famous description, in the "Life of Sterling." He seems to have become more mannered as he grew older.

p. 475, l. 5: "*a small volume of verses*". The " 'Poems on various subjects,' . . . *London: Printed for G. G. and J. Robinsons, and J. Cottle, Bookseller, Bristol, 1796*."
Coleridge's poems in the "Lyrical Ballads" were: "The Rime of the Ancyent Marinere"; "The Nightingale"; "The Foster-Mother's Tale"; "The Dungeon."

"*T. Allsop*" (p. 475, l. 29), whose "Letters, Conversations and Recollections of S. T. Coleridge" were published in 1836. He was one of the many young men to whom Coleridge was an inspiration during the Highgate period. He was first attracted by the 1818 lectures: the period of greatest intimacy was 1819-26 (*cf.* p. 805).

Some of these selections may be extracts from letters.

p. 476, l. 27: "*The Malthusian doctrine*". Coleridge attacks Malthus in marginal notes to a copy of the "Essay on Population" now in the British Museum. He attacks industrialism in the "Lay Sermon."

"*J. H. Frere*" (p. 480, l. 21). These remarks on Keats and Shelley were first published in "A Talk with Coleridge," ed. Miss E. M. Green, "Cornhill Magazine," April, 1917. The Keats part I have included instead of the more familiar version of a similar conversation in "Table Talk" (16th August, 1832) because it is fuller and obviously more authentic. As Miss Lowell points out ("John Keats," II, p. 212) no one else ever described Keats as a "loose slack youth" (H. N. Coleridge's version).

Keats met Coleridge and J. H. Green in Millfield Lane. The date of this meeting was the spring of 1819. Keats' accounts of the meeting is to be found in his "Letters." Since it describes the Table Talk more vividly than most of the records, I quote it here:

> Last Sunday I took a walk towards Highgate and in the lane that winds by the side of Lord Mansfield's park I met Mr. Green our Demonstrator at Guy's in conversation with Coleridge—I joined them, after enquiring by a look whether it would be agreeable—I walked with him at his alderman-after-dinner pace for near two miles I suppose. In those two Miles he broached a thousand things—let me see if I can give you a list—Nightingales, Poetry—on Poetical Sensation—Metaphysics—Different genera and species of Dreams—Nightmare—a dream accompanied with a sense of touch—single and double touch—a dream related—First and second consciousness—the difference explained between will and Volition—so many metaphysicians from a want of smoking the second consciousness—Monsters—the Kraken—Mermaids—Southey believes in them—Southey's belief too much diluted—a Ghost story—Good morning—I heard his voice as he came towards me—I heard it as he moved away—I had heard it all the interval—if it may be called so. He was civil enough to ask me to call on him at Highgate. Good night!

Professor A. W. Garrod, in his "Keats," 1926 (pp. 119 *et seq.*), makes an interesting analysis of these subjects, showing how they form a synopsis of much of Coleridge's thinking over twenty years.

For the disparity between Keats' description and that of Coleridge it must be remembered that Coleridge was speaking ten years after the event.

p. 481, ll. 27, 28: *"Shelley was a man of great power"*. Wordsworth's opinion may be illuminatingly contrasted (from Trelawny's "Recollections of the Last Days of Shelley and Byron," 1858):

> I asked him abruptly what he thought of Shelley as a poet. "Nothing," he replied as abruptly.
>
> Seeing my surprise, he added, "A poet who has not produced a good poem before he is twenty-five we may conclude cannot and never will do so."
>
> "The Cenci!" I said eagerly.
>
> "Won't do," he replied, shaking his head.

"H. N. Coleridge" (p. 482, l. 5). His "Specimens of the Table Talk of the late Samuel Taylor Coleridge" was first published in 1835. It is doubtful whether H. N. Coleridge was less fitted for this task of compilation than Green or Gillman would have been. E. H. Coleridge has praised his reliability as an editor. His unreliability has already been discussed (*see* p. 764). In the Preface H.N.C. describes how he overcame the difficulties of comprehension. It is only partly reassuring:

> I can well remember occasions, in which, after listening to Mr. Coleridge for several delightful hours, I have gone away with divers splendid masses of reasoning in my head, the separate beauty and coherency of which I deeply felt; but how they had produced, or how they bore upon, each other, I could not then perceive. In such cases I have mused sometimes even for days afterwards upon the words, till at length, spontaneously as it seemed, "the fire would kindle," and the association, which had escaped my utmost efforts of comprehension before, flash itself all at once upon my mind with the clearness of noon-day light.

p. 483, ll. 11, 12: *" 'letters of yours in the "Courier," ' "*. *Cf.* p. 801.

p. 484, l. 13: *"James Gurney's character"*. The context of the revealing line is in "King John," Act I, Scene i:

> *Bastard:* James Gurney, wilt thou give us leave awhile?
> *Gurney:* Good leave, good Philip.
> *Bastard:*   Philip! Sparrow! James,
>   There's toys abroad: anon I'll tell thee more.
>   [*Exit Gurney.*]

In his note to this extract H.N.C. goes even further:

2 D The very *exit Gurney* is a stroke of James's character.

Coleridge rarely slips into this kind of eulogy—but *cf.* the way he expresses his firm conviction that Shakspere was "a very great actor," in a Note quoted S.C., II, p. 30.

p. 485, l. 4: "*The author of the Athanasian*". Such questions will be found discussed *passim* in "Notes on English Divines."

"*Mr. Tennyson*" (p. 486, l. 8), *i.e.* Charles Tennyson (*v.* p. 773).

"*[Madness:]*", &c. (p. 487, l. 4). Coleridge's fullest analysis of madness is in the eighth lecture of the 1818 series (L.R., I, pp. 113 *et seq.*). He is discussing Don Quixote.

p. 488, ll. 3, 4: "*the 'Diversions of Purley'* ". First published in 1786.

p. 488, ll. 11, 12: "*so divine a subject as language into . . . squibs.*". *Cf.* p. 672.

p. 489 l. 3: " '*grinning for joy,*' ". Who the friend was, and which mountain it really was (*i.e.* Penmaenmawr), are discussed in "The Road to Xanadu," pp. 210 *et seq.* For the walking tour in Wales, see p. 788.

p. 489, l. 11: "*new edition of the 'Pilgrim's Progress'*". Published by Murray in 1830.

p. 489, l. 29: "*Southey's Life of Bunyan*", published in 1830.

p. 491, l. 12: "*The one considers reason a quality,*". *Cf.* "Statesman's Manual," Appendix E (*ref.* H.N.C.):

> Whether ideas are regulative only, according to Aristotle and Kant, or likewise constitutive, and one with the power and life of nature, according to Plato and Plotinus . . . is the highest problem of philosophy, and not part of its nomenclature.

"*[Law of Polarity]*" (p. 497, l. 19). *Cf.* pp. 164 and 746.

p. 497, ll. 26, 27: "*the mechanico-corpuscular philosophy,*". Coleridge's usual term for materialism or for the philosophy "which views all phenomena, material and spiritual, as explicable by the movements of atoms according to mechanical laws." This definition is from the N.E.D., which quotes Coleridge as the earliest user of this term.

p. 500, l. 12: "*I regret . . .* talented,". In the N.E.D. the earliest quotation for this sense of the word is dated 1827.

p. 501, ll. 7, 8: *"have been so achieved by individuals,"*. Coleridge's experience, philosophy and beliefs give, of course, a much deeper meaning to the word individual than can be expressed by its simple sense of independent existence.

"[Don Quixote]" (p. 502, l. 3). *Cf.* p. 331.

p. 502, ll. 27, 28: *"never yet heard more than one preacher"*. Coleridge may be referring to Edward Irving, of whom he was at times a great admirer (*see* Note, p. 784).

p. 505, ll. 10, 11: *"The young men . . . who admire Lord Byron, prefer Goethe"*. That this prophecy with all its implications was to be instantly refuted (*e.g.* by Carlyle) serves as another reminder of the way in which Goethe was consistently misunderstood and under-estimated by Coleridge, perhaps the only Englishman of his generation capable of fully understanding him. Unfortunately Coleridge had been born early enough for Goethe to be associated in his mind with a past enthusiasm, with "Sturm und Drang"— or, worse still, with Wertherism, and abysmal connections with Kotzebue and Klopstock.

p. 506, l. 30: *"Mr. Hayward's version,"*. H. N. C. points out that the date of this comment (16th February, 1833) shows that Coleridge must have read the translation a few weeks before it was first published.

p. 507, ll. 4, 5: *"always on . . . some grand general principle,"*. *Cf.* especially "Conciones ad Populum."

The beginning of this extract has been omitted. Coleridge is preferring this treatment of the problem to (1) treatment by definition of terms, and (2) treatment by the collection of "relevant" facts.

p. 508, l. 35: *"Mr. Tennyson's poems,"*. This is Alfred—Coleridge has already praised Charles (*see ante*). The "1832" poems were published in December of that year. This comment is significantly dated 24th April, 1833—the month in which Lockhart's famous attack on Tennyson appeared in the "Quarterly."

p. 509, ll. 13, 14: *"I can scarcely scan some of his verses."*. Professor Saintsbury, when he read this passage, confessed "that a great awe fell upon him," and that he was almost persuaded "to give up saying anything about prosody at all" ("History of English Prosody," III, p. 186).

p. 514, ll. 22, 23: "*this continuation of 'Faust,'* ". The second part of "Faust" was published in Germany in 1833. The first English translation did not appear till 1839.

"*[Gibbon]*" (p. 515, l. 1). He is criticised by Coleridge here from the point of view of the non-agreement of his historical method with Coleridge's as enunciated on p. 507.

p. 516, l. 11: "*Irving*". Edward Irving (1792-1834), famous rhetorical preacher and founder of the "Holy Catholic Apostolic Church." He enthusiastically dedicated one of his books to Coleridge, whose Thursday evenings he was attending in 1824. Coleridge seems to be sometimes admiring, sometimes patronising (*see* U.L., II, p. 325; and "Letters," p. 723).

And see Lamb, "Letters," 1888, II, p. 126. Writing on 23rd March, 1825, Lamb says:

> . . . have no doubts of IRVING. Let Mr. Mitford drop his disrespect. Irving has prefixed a dedication (of a missionary subject, first part) to Coleridge, the most beautiful, cordial, and sincere. He there acknowledges his obligation to S.T.C. for his knowledge of Gospel truths, the nature of a Christian Church, &c., to the talk of Samuel Taylor Coleridge (at whose Gamaliel feet he sits weekly), rather than to that of all the men living. This from him, the great dandled and petted sectarian—to a religious character so equivocal in the world's eye as that of S.T.C., so foreign to the Kirk's estimate—can this man be a quack?

p. 520, l. 25: "*I am dying*,". This is dated 10th July, fifteen days before Coleridge's death.

LETTERS

Text: The majority of these letters are taken from the two standard collections, namely:

(1) "Letters of Samuel Taylor Coleridge," 1895, edited by E. H. Coleridge (referred to as "Letters" in these notes). These volumes are now out of print.

(2) "Unpublished Letters of Samuel Taylor Coleridge," 1932, edited by E. L. Griggs (referred to as U.L. in these notes).

In "Letters" E. H. Coleridge was making a selection of published and unpublished material; but I have taken his own text of the letters rather than that of the earliest published version because in most cases he seems to have had access to the original MSS.

Some of the earliest letters to be published were notoriously badly treated. The numerous letters to Allsop, published in "Letters, Conversations, Recollections" . . . 1836, seem authentic, though it is sometimes difficult to tell whether a letter, a notebook excerpt, or a conversation is being quoted. But those published in Cottle's "Early Recollections," &c., were wonderfully transformed by their editor, usually with the object of throwing a favourable light on himself.

For a list of other collections and miscellaneous publications of the letters see the "Bibliography" of Mr. T. J. Wise.

In "Unpublished Letters" Professor Griggs has included some items which have already been published but which are either inaccessible or incorrectly reproduced. In every case, however, Professor Griggs has taken his text either from the original holograph pages or from one of E. H. Coleridge's transcripts of that large and important group of letters mysteriously lost in the post between London and Torquay in the eighteen-nineties (v. U.L., I, xii). But Mr. Griggs tells me that he has been able to verify the all but minute correctness of the transcriber.

A difficulty arises from the fact that those letters which depend on E.H.C. for their text will be found to have undergone small modernisations of stops and punctuation. As elsewhere in this volume, I have made no attempt to modernise the rest of the letters for the sake of consistency—if for no other reason, because Coleridge's moods are so often reflected in such details as stops, or their absence.

Letters I to IV: These are not in their chronological position but are placed first in this selection because they describe Coleridge's childhood. The five autobiographical letters to Poole from which they are taken were first printed in the biographical supplement of the 1847 edition of B.L. They are scarcely "letters"—Coleridge wrote them, apparently to please Poole, at Nether Stowey where Poole was his near neighbour. The character of Poole (1765-1837) is described in "Thomas Poole and his Friends," Mrs. Henry Sandford, 1888. There was no one to whom Coleridge wrote more intimately. The friendship was lifelong, though decreasing after 1802. Poole is eulogised in the tenth chapter of "Church and State."

Letter I (p. 525): From "Letters." Of the "Journal of John Woolman" (first published 1774) many editions, selections, &c.,

appeared in the nineteenth century. Of Coleridge's friends, Lamb ("Get the writings of John Woolman by heart"), Crabb Robinson and Edward Irving were special admirers.

Letter II (p. 525): From "Letters." In the British Museum Catalogue the following works by Coleridge's father are included:

(1) "Miscellaneous Dissertations on the Book of Judges," 1768.

(2) "A Critical Latin Grammar: containing clear and distinct rules for boys," &c., 1772.

(3) "A Sermon" preached in 1776.

p. 526, l. 17: *"My eldest brother's"*. In a letter to Poole ("Letters," 305) dated 16th September, 1799, C. is more confidential on the subject of his brothers: "I have three Brothers (that is to say, Relations by Gore)—two are Parsons and one is a Colonel— George and the Colonel good men as times go—very good men; but alas! we have neither Tastes or Feelings in common. This I wisely learnt from their conversation, and did not suffer them to learn it from *mine* . . ." What man pledged to the system of Fraternity, C. asks, could refuse to drink the toast of Church and King in such company? (Capitalizations from the British Museum MS.)

p. 527, l. 29: *"October 20,"*. This is the nearest Coleridge ever got to the correct date of his birth, which was 21st October, 1772.

Letter III (p. 527): From "Letters."

p. 527, l. 35: *"materials for future letters,"*. Much poetry besides "Osorio" was written "from March to October," and there was the visit to the Wordsworths at Racedown.

p. 528, ll. 34, 35: *"Arabian Nights'* ". *Cf.* p. 326.

Letter IV (p. 530): From "Letters." *Cf.* his reminiscence of this incident on p. 160.

Letter V (p. 533): For "George Coleridge" (1764-1828) *see* Letter IV. Letters "home" were for many years letters to George.

Letter VI (p. 534): From U.L. Dr. "Piarce" was the Master of Jesus; Middleton and Le Grice were fellow-students; Sparrow was the headmaster of the school at Hackney where George taught.

p. 534, ll. 30, 31: *"I . . . shall try hard for the Brown's Prize Ode."*. The Greek ode which he wrote for this medal is included in Dykes Campbell, "Poetical Works," p. 476.

Letter VII (p. 535): From U.L. The first mention of drug-taking. *See* Index, "Drugs," for other references. In Gillman's "Life" it is recorded that "half his time from seventeen to eighteen was passed in the sick-ward of Christ's Hospital, afflicted with jaundice and rheumatic fever," as a result of swimming a river in his clothes and letting them dry on his back. The readiness with which doctors at that time prescribed opiates for painful illnesses, and the ease with which they could be bought, help to account for this early use of them.

Letter VIII (p. 536): From "Letters." Coleridge had first met with Mrs. Evans and her three daughters in 1788. *See* "Life," p. 15, and the 1822 letter to Allsop quoted there:

> And oh! from sixteen to nineteen what hours of paradise had Allen and I in escorting the Miss Evanses home on a Saturday, who were then at a milliner's . . . and we used to carry thither, of a summer morning, the pillage of the flower gardens within six miles of town, with sonnet or love-rhyme wrapped round the nosegay.

At the period of the letter quoted in the text Coleridge did not write more to one member of the family than another. *But see post.* I have quoted it complete as an example of the "literary" style to be found in all his letters to the Evanses, unlike his usual manner.

p. 539, l. 7: " '*How long will ye round me be swelling,*' ". The first lines of the "Complaint of Ninathóma," an "imitation of Ossian" first published in 1796.

Letter IX (p. 539): From U.L. It was on 2nd December, 1793, that Coleridge had enlisted in the 15th Light Dragoons under the name Silas Tomkyn Comberbacke. Dykes Campbell suggests that the debt motive may have been less strong than the general unhappiness caused by disappointment in love. But the effect of a debt on Coleridge, though later he was often incurring them, was always extremely painful.

This is the first letter in the manner of extreme humiliation and self-debasement—an attitude of his which some of his friends used later to abhor.

Letter X (p. 542): From "Letters." Coleridge was discharged from the Dragoons on 10th April, 1794.

Letter XI (p. 543): From "Letters." Coleridge had met Southey for the first time a month before this was written, when he was on a visit to Oxford with his friend Allen (*see* "Letters," p. 41). He found Southey with doubts about his own career and with a vague desire to emigrate—all transformed by Coleridge into the definite plan of Pantisocracy.

The best account of Pantisocracy is Poole's, printed in "Thomas Poole and his Friends," I, pp. 97 and 98. The passage begins:

> Twelve gentlemen of good education and liberal principles are to embark with twelve ladies in April next. Previous to their leaving this country they are to have as much intercourse as possible, in order to ascertain each other's dispositions, and firmly to settle every regulation for the government of their future conduct.

It is thought that the suddenness of the engagement to Miss Fricker may be explained by this pantisocratic tenet.

Poole continues:

> The regulations relating to the females strike them as the most difficult; whether the marriage contract shall be dissolved if agreeable to one or both parties, and many other circumstances, are not yet determined.

p. 544, l. 3: " '*The dust flies smothering*,' ", &c. First published "Letters," 1895.

Letter XII (p. 544). From "Letters."

p. 544, l. 16: "*Wrexham,*". A walking tour in Wales followed the visit to Oxford.

p. 544, l. 25: "*Mary Evans,*". *Cf.* Southey's biographical letter to Cottle (quoted "Life," p. 31):

> He made his engagement with Miss Fricker on our return from this journey [to Somerset] at my mother's house in Bath, not a little to my astonishment, because he had talked of being deeply in love with a certain Mary Evans.

Letter XIII (p. 545): From U.L.

Letter XIV (p. 546): From "Letters."

p. 546, l. 22: "*SHAD*". Shadrack, the servant of Southey's aunt.

p. 546, l. 23: "*Make Edith my sister.*". Edith Fricker became Mrs. Southey, Mary Fricker became Mrs. Lovell, so there would have been three and possibly four Fricker sisters to go to America.

p. 546, l. 37: *"I like your sonnets"*. Coleridge quotes from the sonnet beginning "With many a weary step at length I gain." Southey made the first alteration as directed. The "moaning" line eventually became "That eddy in the wild gust moaning by."

p. 547, l. 19: " *'No more my visionary soul'* ", &c. First published (with the title "Pantisocracy") in the "Life and Correspondence of R. Southey," 1849. For discussion of authorship, *see* "Poems," p. 68, and Southey, "Life and Letters," I, p. 224, where in a letter Southey quotes the sonnet as Favell's.

Letter XV (p. 547): From "Letters." The second part of this letter seems to date the first signs of disagreement among the Pantisocrats. But up to October Southey must have been still enthusiastic. On 14th October he wrote to his brother:

> This Pantisocratic scheme has given me new life, new hope, new energy, all the faculties of my mind are dilated; I am weeding out the few lurking prejudices of habit . . .

Letter XVI (p. 550): From "Letters."

Letters XVII, XVIII (pp. 551, 553): From "Letters." This is the period of Coleridge's final term at Cambridge, when Miss Fricker seems to be forgotten. *Cf.* the sonnet "On a Discovery Made Too Late," "Poems," p. 72, and Letter XVIII.

Letter XIX (p. 553): From U.L. George Dyer (1755-1841), author of the "History of the University of Cambridge," &c. But it was his poems which Coleridge and Lamb read and made rather affectionate fun of. Coleridge: He "is really an honest man and I like him."

Letter XX (p. 554): From "Letters." This is the end of Pantisocracy. The letter is too long to quote in full; it continues in the same strain for twelve printed pages: "Curse on all pride ! 'Tis a harlot that buckrams herself up in virtue only that she may fetch a higher price," &c.

Letter XXI (page 556): From U.L. Written while Coleridge was making his Midland tour with the Prospectus of the "Watchman" (*cf.* p. 742).

p. 557, l. 1: *"I preached on Sunday"*. In Chapter x of B.L. he describes his "preaching by the way in most of the great towns."

p. 557, l. 20: "*poor Montgomery*)". Macaulay's Montgomery, imprisoned for libel in 1796.

Letter XXII (p. 558): From "Letters." Cottle (1770-1853) was at this time a bookseller; later, to the amusement of Coleridge and others (*v. post*), he wrote epics. He published the early poems of Coleridge and Southey, and financed the "Watchman." According to "Life," pp. 46 *et seq.*, Coleridge's marriage would not have been possible without Cottle's generosity and advance payments.

Letter XXIII (p. 559): From U.L.

p. 559, l. 36: "*The Essay on Fasting*". No. II of the "Watchman" began with this title and motto:

ESSAY ON FASTS
Wherefore my Bowels shall sound like an Harp
Isaiah xvi, 11

p. 560, l. 33: "*Mrs. Coleridge miscarried—*". But *cf.* the date of he birth of Hartley (p. 562).

p. 561, l. 13: "*The Bishop of Llandaff*". Richard Watson, who had already "answered" Gibbon in "An Apology for Christianity." Coleridge is referring to his "An Apology for the Bible; in a series of letters addressed to T. Paine, author of . . . the Age of Reason," &c., 1796. The pamphlet went through eight editions in three years, and was translated into French, abridged, &c.

p. 561, l. 25: " '*New life and joy*' ", &c. *Cf.* "Poems," p. 96. "The Hour when we shall Meet Again."

Letter XXIV (p. 561): From "Letters." This letter to Thelwall (1764-1834) and the one which follows on p. 565 were written before the two had met. When they did, at Stowey, Thelwall's reputation for republicanism reflected serious suspicion on Coleridge and Wordsworth, in the eyes of the anti-Jacobin authorities (*cf.* B.L., Chapter x).

The criticisms refer to "Religious Musings" (first published 1796). By 1797 there were considerable alterations in the text (including *e.g.* the complete elimination of the "Unshuddered, unaghasted" passage).

"A very dear friend of mine" may be Coleridge's first reference to Wordsworth.

Letter XXV (p. 562): From "Letters." Charles Lloyd was at this time a paying guest of the Coleridges (*cf*. p. 11).

Letter XXVI (p. 563): From "Letters." The tragedy referred to is the death of Lamb's mother, killed by his sister Mary in a fit of madness. Lamb's letter is in "Letters," 1888, I, p. 32:

> Write as religious a letter as possible, but no mention of what is gone and done with. . . . Mention nothing of poetry. I have destroyed every vestige of past vanities of that kind.

Lamb seemed to appreciate Coleridge's reply, but in answer to a third communication written in the same manner, he begins to rebel:

> "Your letters," he says, "especially please us when you talk in a religious strain; not but we are offended occasionally with a certain freedom of expression, a certain air of mysticism. . . . Let us learn to think humbly of ourselves . . ." (*op. cit.*, I, p. 39, &c.).

Letter XXVII (p. 564): From "Letters." E. H. Coleridge quotes a letter of March, 1795, which forms a link with the last opium reference:

> [Amongst other troubles] Mrs. Coleridge dangerously ill. . . . I have been obliged to take laudanum almost every night.

Letter XXVIII (p. 565): From "Letters." There is a collection of references to Coleridge's personal appearance in "The Road to Xanadu," p. 532. The quotation from Southey too easily summarises them:

> Nothing can convey stronger indications of power than his eye, eyebrow, and forehead. Nothing can be more imbecile than all the rest of his face.

p. 566, l. 27: "*Dupuis' twelve octavos*," *i.e.* "Origine de tous les cultes, ou Religion universelle." (*Cf.* L.R., I, p. 289: It is a work written "to prove that Jesus Christ was the Sun, and all Christians worshippers of Mithra.") The 1795 copy in the British Museum has seven volumes octavo. In "The Road to Xanadu" (pp. 231 *et seq.*) Professor Lowes quotes this letter and discusses Dupuis and the authors named in the Postscript with rich details of the ideas and influence Coleridge obtained from them, where they reappear in his poems, &c. The "4674" volume especially is "a *vade mecum* of Neoplatonic daemonology"—Coleridge was filling his mind with the material for the "Ancient Mariner."

Dupuis he was to use in the "Ode to the Departing Year." "Xanadu" is an essential reference for this list. For another catalogue revealing Coleridge's exploration of the unfamiliar, *cf.* A.P., pp. 154-5. The renewed study of these neo-Platonist writers was immediately antecedent to his study and admiration of Plato—"renewed" because Lamb speaks of him (in his "Christ's Hospital" essay) as being deep in the neo-Platonists while still at school.

Letter XXIX (p. 567): From "Letters." After their honeymoon at Clevedon the Coleridges moved temporarily (to be nearer the library) into Bristol. But after the failure of various money-earning plans he conceived an intense desire to move permanently into Stowey. This letter, only part of which is quoted (the rest is full of equally disproportionate feeling), is the third of a series of appeals to Tom Poole, that he should get a house for them in or near Stowey. For some reason Poole was inclined to put difficulties in the way. All the letters are quoted and the extremely Coleridgean situation is discussed in "Thomas Poole and his Friends," Chapters ix and x. Coleridge finally entered the cottage on 31st December.

Letter XXX (p. 569): From "Letters." Southey's "Joan" is "Joan of Arc: an epic poem." Bristol, 1796. For Coleridge's first meeting with Bowles *see* p. 751.

Letter XXXI (p. 570): From U.L.

p. 571, l. 23:"*now for the Penates*". This refers to the "Hymn to the Penates" (*see* "Poetical Works," 1837, II, p. 273, where "Paean" is cut out).

Letter XXXII (p. 572): From U.L. "My Ode" is the "Ode to the Departing Year," first published December, 1796.

Letter XXXIII (p. 573): From "Letters." For the "Monody on the Death of Chatterton" (1790) and the "Songs of the Pixies" (1793) *see* "Poems," pp. 13 and 40.

Letter XXXIV (p. 574): From "Letters." This is the third letter to Josiah Wedgwood, who with his brother Tom was offering help. In December, 1796, when Coleridge was very badly in need of money, he had at first accepted the offer of £100 from Josiah, sent to prevent him from wasting his powers in the work of a Unitarian minister. Later he had refused (5th January, 1798) for reasons set forth at great length. This third letter was the result of a revised offer of a £150 annuity. From now on his letters to the Wedgwoods are coloured by the sense that he ought to be justifying their belief in him.

Letter XXXV (p. 575): From "Letters." The description of the tooth symptoms (before the especially significant reference to laudanum) brings to mind a carefully proved document in "Modern Language Notes," January, 1920, in which the author, Mr. Rea, says that whatever the cause of Coleridge's decay, "it was not spiritual," but was almost certainly due "to osteomyelitis, or impacted teeth."

Letter XXXVI (p. 577): From "Letters." "Estlin (1747-1817) was the Unitarian minister at Bristol. He was a warm supporter of Coleridge during the years 1796-1814" (Griggs). Charles Lloyd had developed symptoms of epilepsy. There is an interesting note by E.H.C., estimating the evidence which connects this letter with Coleridge's visit to a "lonely farm house," the quarrel with Lloyd, Coleridge's first experience of opium, and the composition of "Kubla Khan" (cf. p. 93). In "Poems," p. 295, E.H.C. says that he thinks the reference (in a letter to Estlin of 14th May, 1798) to distress arising from "calumny and ingratitude from men who have been fostered in the bosom of my confidence" must refer to Lloyd.

Letter XXXVII (p. 577): From "Letters." This letter, like others written from Germany, was later "improved" and published ("Friend," 28th December, 1809).

Letter XXXVIII (p. 579): From "Letters." Coleridge left Germany for England on 24th June.

Letters XXXIX, XL (pp. 580, 581): From U.L. Letters to Humphry Davy mark the beginning of Coleridge's interest in science (cf. p. 590). The first letter was written at the time of his greatest journalistic activity, in London. The Coleridges moved into their house at Keswick on 24th July, 1800.

Letters XLI, XLII (pp. 582, 584): From U.L. Coleridge and Godwin had become intimate a year before the date of this letter. There had been an earlier meeting at a time when Coleridge was planning an answer to Godwin's expressed views on morals.

p. 584, ll. 15, 16: "*Miss Bayley's tragedy*". In April, Kemble had produced Joanna Baillie's "De Montfort" at Drury Lane, with Mrs. Siddons in the cast.

Letter XLIII (p. 586): From U.L. Coleridge's bad health became really serious soon after he settled in Keswick. This coincided with a much more serious drug habit, the constant taking of the "Kendal Black Drop"—opium. Long medical descriptions of his symptoms are omitted.

Letter XLIV (p. 586): From "Letters." Calvert is William Calvert, the brother of Raisley (the benefactor of Wordsworth).

Letter XLV (p. 588): From "Letters." That Coleridge's disavowal of the "mechanic philosophy" of Locke and of Hartley (in contemporary letters to Wedgwood) was not primarily due to the influence of Kant is proved according to Shawcross by the date of these letters, written at a time when his study of Kant was only beginning (*see* B.L., I, xxx).

"Christabel" was not published till 1816. Nothing came of the other books—including the one which was "nearly done." Coleridge's letters from this date onwards are increasingly full of references to works which he speaks of as if they were already well in hand, but which in fact were scarcely ever even started. *See* p. 600 for the "Thirst of Spirit" which he had to tell "something honourable" of himself. Even in earlier days Southey had told him that he "spawned plans like a herring."

Letter XLVI (p. 590): From "Letters."

Letter XLVII (p. 590): From "William Godwin: His Friends and Contemporaries."

Letter XLVIII (p. 591): From U.L.

Letter XLIX (p. 593): From U.L. The evidence of this letter makes Coleridge's first expressed dissatisfaction with his marriage earlier than has been supposed (*cf.* "Life," p. 130; U.L., I, p. 182; and "Letters," p. 366).

Letter L (p. 595): From U.L. The reference to Sir James Mackintosh, the philosopher, of whose high reputation Coleridge did not approve, may be compared with another letter to Poole written at the beginning of the year (U.L., I, p. 172):

As to Mackintosh—Lord have pity upon that metaphysics, of which he is a competent judge— I attended five of his lectures—

Letter LI (p. 597): From U.L. The omissions are due to mutilations in the MS.

Letter LII (p. 598): From "Letters." During the December and February of this winter Coleridge was writing for the "Morning Post" and attending Davy's popular lectures at the Royal Institution. In January he visited Stowey.

Letter LIII (p. 598): From "Letters." Sotheby (1757-1833) was in frequent correspondence with the Lake Poets. This letter is quoted as an example of Coleridge's early differentiation, thirteen years before B.L. was published, of his own views from those expressed by Wordsworth in the Preface to L.R. The verses are from Drayton's "Polyolbion." *See* "Letters" for a note on the connection between Bowles's Ogle with the Lieutenant Ogle who was instrumental in procuring Coleridge's discharge from the Army.

Letters LIV to LVI (pp. 600 to 604): From U.L. In November and December of 1802 Coleridge toured South Wales with Tom Wedgwood and Miss Sarah Wedgwood. Coleridge's daughter Sara was born just before he returned home. ("I had never thought of a girl as a possible event; the words child and man-child were perfect synonyms in my feelings. However, I bore the sex with great fortitude." "Letters," p. 416.) With Tom Wedgwood he seems to have definitely "indulged" himself in drugs—the accusation he made against De Quincey (a charge which was warmly reciprocated). *See* U.L., I, p. 252 (a letter dated 17th February, 1803):

Last night I received a four ounce parcel-letter by the Post . . . I *should* have been indignant, if dear Poole's *Squint* of Indignation had not set me a-laughing. On opening it it contained my letter from Gunville, and a parcel, a small one, of *Bang* from Purkis . . . We will have a fair Trial of *Bang*— do bring down some of the Hyoscyamine Pills, and I will give a fair Trial of Opium, Hensbane, and Nepenthe. By the bye, I always considered Homer's account of the *Nepenthe* as a *Banging* Lie.

Letter LVII (p. 605): From "Letters."

Letter LVIII (p. 606): From U.L. Coleridge had written to Southey in the previous month, outlining one of the most enormous of his schemes—a joint production of a "History of British Literature, bibliographical, biographical, and critical." Southey wrote back doubtfully, suggesting something more modest: "to rely upon you for whole quartos ! Dear Coleridge, the smile that comes with that thought is a very melancholy one."

Letter LIX (p. 607): From "Memorials of Coleorton." In these volumes are many good letters from the Lake Poets which have not since been republished. In 1803 (before this letter was written) the artist and his wife stayed at Keswick for some weeks. They had not then met Wordsworth.

p. 607, l. 35: "*Mr. R———*,". (?) Mr. Sam Rogers, author of the "Pleasures of Memory."

Letter LX (p. 608): From U.L. *Cf.* later references to Hazlitt, p. 666.

p. 609, l. 31: "'*To live beloved*'", &c. *See* p. 114, "The Pains of Sleep," and *cf.* this poem with Coleridge's references in this letter and elsewhere to his horrifying nights.

Letter LXI (p. 610): From "Letters." This letter to "Conversation" Sharp explains better than any other Coleridge's feelings when later he believed that Wordsworth had "deserted" him.

Letter LXII (p. 613): From "Memorials of Coleorton."

p. 613, ll. 25, 26: "*just before Shakspere's time*,". Though Coleridge had a fair knowledge of Jacobean drama, he was ignorant of Shakspere's earlier contemporaries.

Letter LXIII (p. 614): From U.L. Coleridge is at Portsmouth waiting for a favourable wind to take him to Malta, where, after a climax of bad health, desperate remedies, and probably of domestic quarrels also, he had decided to go only a few weeks earlier.

Letter LXIV (p. 615): From "Letters." With Dr. Stoddart, in whose house Coleridge at first stayed, Coleridge may have quarrelled; but by 6th July he was an unofficial secretary to Vice-Admiral Sir John Ball (*see* end of letter), the Governor, whose "Life," written in terms of extravagant praise, fills the last pages of the "Friend."

Letter LXV (p. 618): From U.L. Coleridge had been in Rome, but was apparently warned to leave Italy because Napoleon, incensed by articles in the "Morning Post" written about 1800, had ordered his arrest. The evidence seems as if it must be dubious, *but see* "Life," p. 151. Coleridge arrived in England on 11th August. Again, some detailed descriptions of his symptoms have been omitted.

Letter LXVI (p. 619): From "Letters." Hartley had been staying with his father at the Coleorton farmhouse lent to the Wordsworths by Sir George Beaumont. *Cf.* the letter written from that address to Derwent, age six (U.L., I, p. 366).

This letter to Hartley should not be read without looking at Wilkie's portrait, painted in this same year, when Hartley was ten, showing a wistful little boy, young for his age. The portrait is reproduced in "Letters," facing p. 512.

Letter LXVII (p. 622): From U.L. First the Wordsworths, then the Beaumonts, then the Morgans gave Coleridge sympathetic help and an occasional home during this worst period of his career—"the perpetual relays which were laid along Coleridge's path in life." Coleridge was preparing his lectures, living in a room at the top of the "Courier" office in the Strand. He afterwards spent long periods in the Morgans' home.

p. 623, ll. 26, 27: *"what an unthinking man were you,"*. For telling C. that he ought to marry Sarah Fricker?

Letter LXVIII (p. 623): From U.L. De Quincey, *via* Cottle and Poole, had been enabled to meet Coleridge in 1807. For his description of Coleridge, of his talk, of a "frigid" introduction to Mrs. Coleridge and his despondency at seeing "the sad spectacle of powers so majestic already besieged by decay," &c., *see* "Works," II, pp. 38 *et seq.* (with details corrected by "Life," pp. 161 to 163).

Letter LXIX (p. 624): From "Letters." Daniel Stuart, proprietor and editor of the "Morning Post" and "Courier" when Coleridge was writing for those papers. Coleridge was at this time staying with the Wordsworths in their new home at Grasmere.

p. 624, l. 32: *"Wordsworth's pamphlet,"*, on the Convention of Cintra—"Concerning the relations of Great Britain, Spain, and

Portugal, to each other, and to the common enemy, at this crisis, and specially as affected by the Convention of Cintra." 1809. De Quincey attended to the proof reading, &c. For his insistence on a special punctuation cf. "Letters of The Wordsworth Family," ed. Knight, I, p. 449.

Letter LXX (p. 626): From U.L.

Letter LXXI (p. 628): From U.L. Street was the editor of the "Courier." Coleridge is "hard at work" on the "Friend" (see p. 773). It is at this time that he begins to admit openly in his letters that drug-taking is the cause of his distresses.

Letter LXXII (p. 629): From U.L.

Letter LXXIII (p. 629): From "Letters." For Coleridge's defence of his parentheses, cf. p. 631.

Letter LXXIV (p. 631): From U.L.

Letter LXXV (p. 633): From U.L. From November, 1810, till 1816 Coleridge "with few and short interruptions" was residing with the Morgans at 7 Portland Place, Hammersmith (see "Life," pp. 180 et seq.). Rickman, the statistician, he first met before he went to Malta. It was symptomatic of Coleridge's worst periods that he should thus find fault with the weaknesses of his friends. Cf. the letter of 1804 to Mrs. Coleridge:

> I met G. Burnett the day before yesterday in Lincoln's Inn Fields, so nervous, so helpless with such opium-stupidly-wild eyes.
>
> Oh, it made the place one calls the heart feel as it was going to ache ("Letters," p. 467).

Letter LXXVI (p. 634): From U.L. When he was at his lowest Coleridge would attempt to leave the Morgans, only to be brought back by their kindness. The climax of despondency was brought on by his alienation from the Wordsworths—the "festering wound" of this letter. It had been intended in 1810, before Coleridge went to the Morgans, that he should stay with Basil Montagu. But when Montagu had visited Wordsworth, he had apparently been warned against Coleridge's "habits," and been told there was "no hope for him." By a masterpiece of tactlessness Montagu repeated these words, without the probably very ameliorating context, to Coleridge, whose feelings for Wordsworth were profoundly and permanently affected. Whether Montagu exaggerated Wordsworth's criticisms or not it is impossible to say. On 23rd March, 1809, Wordsworth had written to Poole as follows:

> I am sorry to say that nothing appears to me more desirable than that his periodical *Essay* [the *Friend*] should never commence. It is in fact *impossible*—utterly impossible—that he should carry it on. . . . I give it to you as my deliberate opinion, founded upon proofs which have been strengthening for years, that he neither will nor can execute anything of important benefit to himself, his family, or mankind. Neither his talents nor his genius—mighty as they are—nor his vast information will avail him anything . . . he is not capable of acting under any *constraint* of duty or moral obligation ("Letters of the Wordsworth Family," ed. Knight, I, p. 457).

Cf. also Dorothy Wordsworth's letter on this incident in the same volume, p. 541:

> William, for the most benevolent purposes, communicated to a friend a small part of what was known to the whole town of Penrith.

The omission marks in this letter indicate erasures (Griggs).

Letter LXXVII (p. 636): From U.L. The letter is fully discussed and annotated in Raysor, "Shaksperean Criticism," where it is reproduced. The facts relevant to "Christabel" are to be found here on p. 723. In the second part of the letter—the lectures in Flower de Luce Court, Fetter Lane, belonged to the 1811-2 series which Coleridge was then delivering. Lecture Seven (reproduced here, p. 351) is on "Romeo and Juliet." Schlegel's lectures were delivered in 1808, and those which dealt with English drama were published in 1811 (*cf.* p. 770).

Letter LXXVIII (p. 642): From "Letters." Coleridge's last visit to Keswick and the Lakes. E.H.C. dates it between 23rd February and 26th March. Coleridge dramatically did not call on the Wordsworths. *Cf.* the next letter.

Letter LXXIX (p. 643): From U.L. The letter ends as in the text.

Letter LXXX (p. 644): From U.L. The "complaint on the Chest" is interesting in view of the result of the autopsy which was performed after his death:

> The left side of the chest was nearly occupied by the heart, which was immensely enlarged. . . . The right side of the chest was filled with fluid enclosed in a membrane having the appearance of a cyst . . . the lungs on both sides were completely compressed. This will sufficiently account for his bodily sufferings . . . and will explain to you the necessity of subduing these sufferings by narcotics . . . (Lucy E. Watson, "Coleridge at Highgate," 1925, p. 29).

This first attempt to place himself in the hands of a doctor came to nothing.

Letter LXXXI (p. 645): From U.L. Tom Wedgwood had died in 1805, his share of the legacy, £75, being insured by his will. Josiah asked leave to discontinue his own contribution on genuine grounds of poverty. The "play" is "Remorse," which was produced early in 1813.

Letter LXXXII (p. 646): From "Letters." With reference to Coleridge's sensitiveness to criticism it is worth noticing that "The Times" review is by no means so bad as he makes out. *See* E.H.C. ("Letters," p. 603), who also points out that Coleridge was wrong in naming Pasquin. The author who wrote under this pen-name was not in London at the time.

Letter LXXXIII (p. 648): From U.L. *Cf.* Hamlet, p. 380.

Letter LXXXIV (p. 648): From the "Thorny Path of Literature," a pamphlet in which this letter, with explanatory comments, was privately printed by Mr. Axon of Manchester, who reclaimed it from an obscure periodical (whether the "Sunbeam" of 1838 or the "Sylph" of 1839 is not clear from the Introduction: neither is in the British Museum). Mr. Curnick sent his poem (an "Ode on the Victories obtained . . . under . . . Lord Wellington") to Coleridge for criticism. A few lines may be quoted:

> On the auspicious hour that gave thee birth,
> Britannic Mars! rejoicing nature smil'd;
> Cherubic forms declar'd thy future worth,
> And mark'd thee conq'ror in the dreadful field.

Letter LXXXV (p. 650): From U.L. Even at this advanced stage the fact that Coleridge took drugs in dangerous quantities seems to have been unknown to many of his friends. In "Early Recollections" (1837) Cottle published the letters which had passed between Coleridge, Southey and himself over this matter. The premature giving away of confidences, and the extraordinary inaccuracy of Cottle's version of these letters, aroused the anger of friends.

When Cottle together with Coleridge visited Hannah More, "Cottle observed that Coleridge's hand shook so that he spilled wine from a glass he was raising to his lips" ("Life," p. 200). Next day, a friend explained the cause. "It astonished and afflicted me." It should be borne in mind in reading this letter that Coleridge was able later to laugh when Cottle ascribed his downfall to Satanic possession. Though he was indebted to Cottle, C. was inclined to despise him: yet perhaps it was for this very reason that Cottle's moral attitude proved such an effective goad.

The attempt to place himself under Dr. Fox did not materialise, but up to the autumn Coleridge seems to have been at Bristol, nominally under the care of a Dr. Daniel and "a respectable old decayed tradesman," hired to keep him away from the druggist's when he took his walks. But this attempt, like others, was useless.

Postscript: Coleridge delivered a course of lectures at Bristol in April of this year.

Letter LXXXVI (p. 653): From U.L. The omissions in this letter are due to small mutilations of the MS. The next day Coleridge wrote Morgan an equally terrible letter. Almost as desperate are Coleridge's excitedly waggish letters of this period (*e.g.* the one to Morgan quoted in U.L., II, p. 115, where he makes fun of Cottle's epic, the "Messiah").

Letter LXXXVII (p. 654): From "Letters." Wade was one of Coleridge's oldest Bristol friends.

Letter LXXXVIII (p. 655): From "Letters." E.H.C. gives the references to these articles, which are reprinted in "Essays on his own Times." There are eight letters "concerning the Spaniards" (December-January, 1809-10). The character of Pitt is quoted here on p. 148 of this volume. The other articles appeared in the "Morning Post," 1802.

The letter to Beaumont has not been identified.

Letter LXXXIX (p. 659): From "Letters." Kenyon (1784-1856) was a friend of Poole and Southey and was later to be of much help to Mrs. Coleridge. Later still he was the friend of the Brownings.

Letter XC (p. 660): From "Letters." Coleridge had been at Calne, Wiltshire, since November. Hence presumably the mysterious "sweet Calne" instead of Ottery for the "home" of his school friend [Coleridge] mentioned in Lamb's "Christ's Hospital" essay. The first instalment of B.L., to which he is referring at the end of the letter, was sent to the printer on 10th August. I have omitted the opening pages of Coleridge's criticism of the "Excursion" (published 1814).

Letter XCI (p. 662): From U.L. Coleridge had recently written to Byron asking for an introduction and Byron had replied kindly, enquiring about Coleridge's work and suggesting he should write another tragedy (see "Life," p. 216, and U.L., II, p. 146, etc.).

Letter XCII (p. 663): From "Letters." This letter dates the beginning of C.'s partial recovery and the final happier period of his life with the Gillmans in their beautiful house at Highgate (see "Life," p. 219):

Mr. Gillman "had no intention of receiving an inmate," but on April 11 he called at Hatton Garden, when it was arranged that Dr. Adams should drive Coleridge out to High-gate on the following day. Coleridge, however, came alone—he came and talked and conquered, for before the visit was over it was settled that he should begin residence on the next day. "I looked with impatience," writes Gillman, "for the morrow . . ."

And on 26th April Lamb is writing to Wordsworth ("Letters," 1888, I, p. 303):

He is at present under the medical care of a Mr. Gillman (Killman?) a Highgate apothecary, where he plays at leaving off laud—m. I think his essentials not touched; he is very bad; but then he wonderfully picks up another day, and his face, when he repeats his verses, hath its ancient glory; an archangel a little damaged.

Letter XCIII (p. 665): From U.L. Coleridge used the quotation from Dr. Johnson more than once.
This letter was written after the attack on "Christabel" in the

"Edinburgh," which Coleridge believed, probably correctly, to have been written by Hazlitt.

The "Lay Sermon" was the "Statesman's Manual," published later in the year (*cf.* p. 774).

p. 667, l. 6: *"Seven Hymns"*. There are recurrent references to these hymns throughout Coleridge's life. *See* "The Road to Xanadu" *passim*, esp. pp. 74 *et seq.*

p. 667, ll. 15, 16: *"System of Giordano Bruno,"*. For Coleridge's connection with Bruno *see* Miss Snyder's article "Coleridge on Giordano Bruno," "Modern Language Notes," Vol. XLII, No. 7.

p. 667, l. 19: *"an epic poem"*. *Cf.* p. 498.

p. 667, l. 25: " *'God be with thee—'* ", &c. These lines were first published "Morning Post," 15th September, 1801, and were first collected in "Sibylline Leaves," with the title "On Revisiting the Sea-shore, after long absence, under strong medical recommendation not to bathe." It continues:

> Dissuading spake the mild Physician,
> "Those briny waves for thee are Death!"
> But my soul fulfilled her mission,
> And lo! I breathe untroubled breath!

Letter XCIV (p. 668): From U.L. Archdeacon Wrangham was an old Cambridge friend. Southey applied for an injunction to restrain from the publication of his early republican verse drama "Wat Tyler," written in 1794. The suit failed because Lord Eldon held that as it was a mischievous work and contrary to the public welfare, there could not be any property. Therefore it could be published.

The breaks in the middle of the letter are due to illegibility of MS.

Letter XCV (p. 669): From U.L. For the reference to Hazlitt *cf.* p. 774.

p. 671, l. 11: *"Anacreon Moore,"* is Tom Moore. Several parodies or "continuations" of "Christabel" were published. A list is given in E. H. Coleridge's privately printed facsimile edition of the poem. The title of one published in 1816 is:

> *Christabess, by S. T. Colebritche, Esq., a right woeful Poem, translated from the Doggerel by Sir Vinegar Sponge.*

p. 671, l. 32: *"hired myself as a job writer,"*. This refers to the "Encyclopaedia Metropolitana" (*v. ante*).

Letter XCVI (p. 672): From U.L. Coleridge's "*first* poetic effort" was a poem "To Fortune. On buying a Ticket in the Irish Lottery." Mr. Wise, in his "Bibliography of Coleridge," says: "So far as can be ascertained, this poem stands as Coleridge's first appearance in print." It appeared in the "Morning Chronicle" on 7th November, 1793.

Letter XCVII (p. 674): From U.L. Coleridge introduced himself to Cary on the beach at Littlehampton, where Cary was reciting Greek to his son. "Sir," said C., "yours is a face I *should* know. I am Samuel Taylor Coleridge" (*see* D.N.B.: "Cary").

Mr. Geoffrey Keynes has been kind enough to inform me that this copy of "Songs of Innocence and of Experience," which Coleridge borrowed from Tulk, is the one described as copy "I" in his "Bibliography of Blake" (p. 121). "It is a coloured copy belonging to the period *c*. 1800, and now belongs to Lady Rothschild."

Letter XCVIII (p. 674): Coleridge met Tulk the Swedenborgian (1786-1849) in 1817. To Tulk Coleridge wrote twenty-five letters, E.H.C.'s transcripts of which exist. These letters, which are philosophical, "were read at gatherings of the Swedenborgian community" (from "Letters," p. 684n.).

Letter XCIX (p. 676): From "Letters." J. H. Green, whom Coleridge first met in 1817, had been studying philosophy in Germany and was now to become Coleridge's most devoted disciple and stimulating companion. Their regular series of afternoon conversations on philosophy, the germ of the "Thursday evenings," was beginning at this time.

The "Cotton-children Bill" was the "Sir Robert Peel's Bill" on which Coleridge printed two pamphlet letters. It was not till 1833 that part of the Bill, to prevent the employment of children under nine, was passed.

Letter C (p. 677): From "Letters."

Letter CI (p. 679): From U.L. This letter was the result of a visit which Blackwood paid Coleridge in order to ask him for articles. As it was only eighteen months since he had been contemplating a libel action against the paper for having accused him, in reviewing B.L., of deserting his wife and children, Coleridge naturally felt that he must make conditions before he

accepted. These took the form of a letter of advice on how to run
the magazine to the great journalist and editor in whose charge
it lay. The net result of this interchange was the publication of
one sonnet, though a few articles were contributed later. *See*
"Life," pp. 229, 241, 249. There is a good statement of the true
function of a newspaper in "Letters," p. 661.

Letter CII (p. 681): From U.L. Allsop introduced himself to
Wordsworth after one of the 1818 lectures. He was more successful than any of Coleridge's young admirers in gaining his affection
and his confidences. *See* his "Letters, Conversations, and Recollections of S. T. Coleridge," 1836.

Letter CIII (p. 682): From U.L. For the "Hymn" *cf.* p. 667.
The letter ends as in the text.

Letter CIV (p. 683): From U.L.

Letter CV (p. 685): In 1819 Hartley was given a Fellowship at
Oriel. In the "Life," p. 245, Dykes Campbell quotes Derwent
Coleridge:

> At the close of his probationary year he was judged to
> have forfeited his Oriel Fellowship, on the ground, mainly, of
> intemperance. Great efforts were made to reverse the decision.
> He wrote letters to many of the Fellows. His father went to
> Oxford. . . . The sentence might be considered severe, it
> could not be said to be unjust.

For further details and a slightly different point of view, *see*
"Hartley Coleridge: His Life and Work," E. L. Griggs, 1929.

The "Coplestone" of the letter was the provost of Oriel, whom
Coleridge wished to see.

Letter CVI (p. 687): From Allsop's "Letters, Conversations,
and Recollections of S. T. Coleridge," 3rd edn., 1864 (first published 1836). For some of the themes of which this letter is a new
statement, *see* Index: Projected Works.

Letter CVII (p. 688): From "Letters." Hüber's "Treatise on
Ants" is cited again on p. 457.

Letter CVIII (p. 690): From U.L.

Letter CIX (p. 692): From "Letters." For Coleridge's opinion
of Leighton, *cf.* p. 196. A similar admiration is expressed as early

as 1807 (*see* Cottle, "Reminiscences," p. 314). This letter contains the germ of "Aids to Reflection." Murray had been the publisher of "Christabel."

Cf. Letter to Allsop, 30th May, 1822:

> I have at *length*—for I really tore it out of my brain, as it were piecemeal, a bit one day and a bit the day after—finished and sent off a letter of two folio *large* and close-written sheets . . . to Mr. Dawes, the rough copy of which I will show you.

Letter CX (p. 693): From Allsop's "Letters, Conversations," &c. (*op. cit.*).

Letter CXI (p. 695): Cattermole was secretary of the new Royal Society of Literature. Coleridge was to be made one of the ten "Royal Associates," and receive an annuity of 100 guineas. Dykes Campbell suggests that this honour came to him through recent influential friends, Basil Montagu and J. H. Frere. The "Essay" to which Coleridge refers was delivered by him in May, 1825—on the "Prometheus" of Aeschylus. The essay was too long to include here, and the argument is too continuous for extracts.

Letter CXII (p. 696): From U.L. Mr. Griggs (U.L., II, pp. 328 to 330) prints a series of six similar letters to Mr. Dunn, the chemist of Highgate. They prove the problem as to whether or no Coleridge conformed to the Gillman discipline in the matter of drugs. These letters show pathetic evidences of enforced deceit (*see* p. 328, *op. cit.*, where the question is discussed).

Letter CXIII (p. 696): From U.L. Mence was the minister at Highgate (Griggs).

Letter CXIV (p. 698): From U.L. For "Aids" and the quality of its early reputation *cf.* Note, p. 775. Blanco White (1775-1841), whose "Evidences against Catholicism," 1825, Coleridge was reading this month (*see* U.L., II, p. 354), was to become a friend.

p. 698, l. 27: "*Po[o]le's Synopsis*—". Matthew Poole's "Synopsis Criticorum aliorumque S. Scripturae Interpretum," 1699 (*queried ref.*, Griggs).

p. 699, l. 33: "*Addenda*,". There is a long list of Corrections and Amendments to the first edition of "Aids," and Coleridge wrote more comments in the copies he sent to his friends.

Letter CXV (p. 700): From "Letters." It was not till the year before this that the "Thursday evenings" became regular, though they had had their beginnings in the repeated visits of admiring and attentive young men.

Letter CXVI (p. 701): From U.L. "Bruce's remarks on Polygamy" occur in "Travels to Discover the Source of the Nile," by James Bruce, 1790. Coleridge's reference is to the second edition of 1805 (cf. p. 181):

From Suez to the Straits of Babelmandel there exist fully four women to one man, which, I have reason to believe, holds as far as the Line, and 30° beyond it.

Letter CXVII (p. 701): From U.L. These extracts come from a very long letter mainly concerned with Biblical problems.

"Henry's Book" is H. N. Coleridge's "Six Months in the West Indies in 1825," 1826.

Letter CXVIII (p. 703): From U.L. In 1828 appeared "The Poetical Works of S. T. Coleridge, including the Dramas of Wallenstein, Remorse and Zapolya." This letter is mysterious in the light of the fact that when the "300 copies" were exhausted Pickering issued another edition in 1829 with not very extensive revisions; he also had the printing of the 1834 edition. His magazine, the "Bijou" (1828), to which Coleridge refers, printed four poems, including "Work Without Hope" and "Youth and Age." The punctuation reflects C.'s agitation.

Watts was editor of the "Literary Souvenir."

p. 705, ll. 4, 5: "contribution . . . in the 'Amulet': ", i.e. "The Improvisatore" (dialogue and verses preceded by a prose Introduction: "New Thoughts on Old Subjects; or Conversational Dialogues on Interests and Events of Common Life").

Letter CXIX (p. 705): From U.L. The quotation is from "Youth and Age."

Letter CXX (p. 707): From U.L. Cf. Note on the autopsy, p. 800.

Letter CXXI (p. 708): From U.L. Milman, the author of the "History of Latin Christianity," &c. See Griggs, U.L., II, p. 443: "Seven years before, Murray had proposed an edition of Coleridge's poems on the condition that Milman was to select and make such omissions and corrections as should be thought advisable—a proposal indignantly refused by Coleridge."

Letter CXXII (p. 708): From U.L.

Letter CXXIII (p. 709): From U.L. The sketch "by the German artist" (Kayser) is reproduced in "Letters," which also contains the three other most familiar portraits, including the Vandyk pastel now in the National Portrait Gallery.

Letter CXXIV (p. 710): From "Letters." After his visit to the Rhine with Wordsworth in 1828, when for a short time Mrs. Aders received them in her husband's villa at Godesberg, Coleridge and the Aderses became intimate.

Coleridge was preparing the 1834 volume of poems, and wished the epitaph *not* to be written within the outline of a tombstone in a little vignette to be placed at the end of the volume. Apparently he did not approve of Miss Denman's sketch for the vignette, with its Muse (*see* "Poems," p. 491n.).

p. 711, l. 12: "*S. T. C.*". Coleridge disliked the name Samuel and preferred to be known by his initials, which he often used instead of his full signature. He liked to think, also, that 'ΕΣΤΗΣΕ was what he called "Punnic Greek" for "he stands firm" (in correct Greek—ἔστηκε).

p. 711, l. 13: " '*Stop, Christian Passer-by!*' ", &c. First published in 1834. According to E.H.C. there are six MS. versions of this poem, three in letters.

Letter CXXV (p. 711): U.L. It was to J. H. Green that Coleridge had entrusted the systematizing and publication of his religious philosophy. Coleridge died 25th July, 1834.

p. 715: "*Chapman*". T. M. Raysor. *Coleridge's Miscellaneous Criticism* reprinted from L. R.

p. 715: "*Barclay*". *Ibid.*

p. 717: "*Sir Thomas Browne*". *Ibid.*

p. 718: "*Pepys*". *Ibid.*

p. 718: "*Fielding*". T. M. Raysor. L. R. ("Communicated by Mr. Gilman": H.N.C.).

p. 719: "*Gray*". T. M. Raysor. Reprinted from " Notes and Lectures upon Shakespeare, etc".

p. 719: *"Robert Anderson"*. T. M. Raysor. From marginal notes to Anderson's *British Poets*.

p. 720: *"George Dyer"*. T. M. Raysor. Marginal note to Dyer's Poems.

p. 720: *"Chalmers"*. *Ibid.* Reprinted from L. R.

p. 721: *"Sir Walter Scott"*, *Ibid.* Marginal notes to the Waverley Novels.

p. 721: *"Sir Walter Scott"*. *Ibid.*

p. 722: *"John Galt"*. *Ibid.* Marginal notes to *The Provost*.

p. 722: *"Barry Cornwall"*. T. M. Raysor. Written on fly-leaves of Barry Cornwall's *Dramatic Scenes and Other Poems*.

p. 723: *"Table Talk"*. *Faust.* First published *Cornhill Magazine*. See p. 780.

p. 726: *"Letters"*. *To Robert Southey.* From "Letters".

INDEX

INDEX

2 E 2

PRINTED IN GREAT BRITAIN BY ROBERT MACLEHOSE AND CO. LTD.
THE UNIVERSITY PRESS, GLASGOW